LIBERAL WORLDS

Liberal Worlds

JAMES BRYCE
AND THE DEMOCRATIC INTELLECT

H. S. JONES

PRINCETON UNIVERSITY PRESS

PRINCETON & OXFORD

Published by Princeton University Press
41 William Street, Princeton, New Jersey 08540
99 Banbury Road, Oxford OX2 6JX

press.princeton.edu

GPSR Authorized Representative: Easy Access System Europe - Mustamäe tee 50, 10621 Tallinn, Estonia, gpsr.requests@easproject.com

All Rights Reserved

ISBN 978-0-691-18011-3
ISBN (e-book) 978-0-691-27721-9

British Library Cataloging-in-Publication Data is available

Editorial: Ben Tate and Josh Drake
Production Editorial: Jenny Wolkowicki
Jacket design: Chris Ferrante
Production: Danielle Amatucci
Publicity: William Pagdatoon and Charlotte Coyne
Copyeditor: Anita O'Brien

Jacket image: Moore, Ernest, James Bryce, 1st Viscount Bryce, 1907, oil on canvas. © National Portrait Gallery, London

This book has been composed in Arno Pro

Printed in the United States of America

10 9 8 7 6 5 4 3 2 1

MIX
Paper | Supporting responsible forestry
FSC® C008955
www.fsc.org

In memory of Geoffrey Johnson Jones (1928–2020)
and Jose Ferial Harris (1941–2023)

CONTENTS

ILLUSTRATIONS

ACKNOWLEDGMENTS

I OWE A LARGE DEBT of gratitude to the Leverhulme Trust, which awarded me a Major Research Fellowship MRF-2019-062 for the period 2020–2023. A book of this kind would have been unimaginable without such an extended period of concentrated research and writing. I am grateful to the University of Manchester for making it possible for me to take up this fellowship, and for awarding me a further period of Academic Research Leave for the academic year 2023–2024. At an earlier stage, a pilot grant from the John Rylands Research Institute helped me to develop the project, with research assistance from Federica Coluzzi. Liam Stowell also did some valuable work for me on Bryce's correspondence with Gilbert Murray, Arnold Toynbee, and Alfred Zimmern. The School of Arts, Languages and Cultures at the University of Manchester awarded me a grant from its Research Support and Development Fund, which helped to cover the cost of images and associated permissions. The Master and Fellows of St Catherine's College, Oxford, elected me to a Christensen Fellowship for Trinity Term 2021, which enabled me to undertake my first sustained period of work on the Bryce papers in the immediate aftermath of a prolonged period of lockdowns and quasi-lockdowns during the Covid-19 pandemic. I am especially grateful to Professor Kersti Börjars, then Master of the College, for her hospitality during that idyllic term, and to those fellows with whom I interacted through perspex screens at lunch and dinner. Later, the Warden and Fellows of Merton College elected me to a Visiting Research Fellowship for Michaelmas Term 2023, during which I was able to complete a full draft of the book while living in elegant chambers in Postmasters' Hall, in close proximity to the archive. Matthew Grimley was a splendid host at the college.

I have benefited from the help of innumerable librarians and archivists in several countries. It is only right to single out Oliver House and his colleagues in the Special Collections Department of the Bodleian Libraries, where I spent many happy weeks and months working on the Bryce papers and related collections. Among many other archivists who gave me essential help, I should especially mention Clare Hopkins at Trinity College, Oxford, and Rob Petre of Oriel College.

Where manuscript material that may be in copyright has been quoted at length, every reasonable effort has been made to trace the rights holders. For permission to quote from James Bryce's unpublished correspondence and other manuscript material, I am grateful to his two surviving great-great nieces, the presumed rights holders. I thank Lucy McCann of the Bodleian Library for liaising with them. Sarah Prince gave permission to reproduce material from the letters of Meta Gaskell, and the V&A did so in respect of the letters in their ownership in the Wedgwood Collection. I am grateful to Emma Brennan for giving me permission on behalf of Manchester University Press to use in chapter 4 some material that I have already used in work published by that press and cited as appropriate in the text.

Georgios Varouxakis, Duncan Bell, and Colin Kidd wrote letters of support for funding applications. Georgios also read and commented on several chapters, as did Claire Rydell Arcenas, Joshua Bennett, Greg Conti, and Emily Jones. Greg also shared with me material from the Dicey-Bryce correspondence that was invaluable in helping me make a start on the project during the period when the archive was closed. Julia Stapleton pointed me towards the Journals of Hensley Henson, which she has edited, and let me see her transcriptions from parts of the journals that fell chronologically outside the scope of the published journals. I am also very grateful to Princeton University Press's anonymous readers for their helpful and supportive reports on both the original proposal and the draft manuscript.

I take this opportunity to thank many friends, colleagues, and others for assisting my work with insights, nuggets of information, and other kinds of support, many of which they have probably forgotten: here I mention Ian Cawood, Mark Curthoys, Lucy Delap, Heather Ellis, Charlotte Faucher, Louise Fawcett, Peter Ghosh, Chris Godden, Emily Jones, Max Jones, Jo Laycock, Suzanna Maxwell, Frank Mort, Jon Parry, Tamson Pietsch, Eduardo Posada-Carbó, Sam Rutherford, Martina Steber, and Chris Stray.

I have presented aspects of this work at a number of seminars and conferences, and I am grateful in each case to the organizers and participants: the History of Political Ideas seminar at the Institute of Historical Research, London; an AHRC conference on Ethics and the Civil Service: Past, Present and Future at the University of Sussex; the Humboldt University of Berlin; the Institut für Zeitgeschichte, Munich. Gregory Conti invited me to take part in a manuscript workshop at Princeton: since this was based on his monograph on A. V. Dicey, it proved invaluable in clarifying my own thinking about Bryce on democracy and constitutionalism.

Ben Tate must take much of the credit for the early development of this project, and he proved an admirable editor throughout. Hilary Jones's love and support has been constant throughout, as always.

The period when the book was in preparation saw the deaths of two people who in their different ways each had a profound impact on my life and career, and I dedicate it to them.

HSJ
October 2024

ABBREVIATIONS

Bryce's Works

AC   *The American Commonwealth*
HRE   *The Holy Roman Empire*
MD   *Modern Democracies*
SHJ   *Studies in History and Jurisprudence*
UHA   *University and Historical Addresses*

Short-Form References

MS Bryce   Bodleian Library, Oxford: James Bryce papers
ODNB   *Oxford Dictionary of National Biography*

TIMELINE OF BRYCE'S LIFE AND CAREER

1838	Born in Belfast (10 May)
1846	Bryce family move to Glasgow
1846–1853	Glasgow High School
1854	Glasgow University
1857	Scholar of Trinity College, Oxford
1861	Firsts in Greats and in Law and History
1862	Fellow of Oriel College, Oxford
1864	*Holy Roman Empire*
1865–1868	Assistant commissioner for the Schools Inquiry Commission
1867	Called to the bar, Lincoln's Inn
1870	First visit to the United States
1870–1875	Professor of jurisprudence, Owens College, Manchester
1870–1893	Regius Professor of Civil Law, Oxford
1872	Visit to Iceland
1874	Liberal candidate for Wick Burghs (unsuccessful)
1876	Travel in the Caucasus and Armenia; ascent of Ararat
1877	*Transcaucasia and Ararat*
1880–1885	MP (Liberal) for Tower Hamlets
1885–1907	MP (Liberal) for Aberdeen South
1886	Under-secretary for foreign affairs (February to July)
1888	*The American Commonwealth*
1889	Marriage to Marion Ashton (23 July)
1892–1894	Chancellor of the Duchy of Lancaster
1894–1895	President of the Board of Trade
1894–1895	Chairman of Royal Commission on Secondary Education
1897	*Impressions of South Africa*
1905–1907	Chief secretary for Ireland
1907–1913	British ambassador to the United States
1912	*South America: Observations and Impressions*

1913–1917	President of the British Academy
1914	Created Viscount Bryce of Dechmont
1914–1915	Chairman of Inquiry into Alleged German War Outrages in Belgium
1918	Chairman of the Second Chamber Conference
1921	*Modern Democracies*
1922	Death at Sidmouth (22 January)

Introduction

JAMES BRYCE'S DEATH at age eighty-three in January 1922 was reported at length across the globe. The First World War and its aftermath had brought him to the height of his fame. It was understandable that he was mourned in the United States, where he had been an unprecedentedly popular ambassador less than a decade earlier; and likewise among the Armenians, for whose cause he had fought for almost half a century, since he climbed Mount Ararat and fell in love with the land and its people. But a host of other peoples claimed a special bond with Bryce: the Swiss, Bulgarians, Austrians, Czechs, Greeks, and Finns, among many others. For a man who was, at heart, a scholar and a thinker, he was astonishingly well-known.

Today it is indisputable that in the hundred years or so since Bryce's death, his name has fallen from a position of worldwide fame to general obscurity. He is not forgotten in the scholarly world. There is a steady stream of new work on aspects of his thought and career.[1] He crops up in a huge range of different contexts, but there is little sense of him in the round. How did the historian of the Holy Roman Empire connect with the architect of the League of Nations? Or the climber of Ararat with the analyst of American democracy? The apologist for segregation—if such he was—with the humanitarian campaigner? There are many other aspects of Bryce's career that have had minimal scholarly attention: the opponent of women's suffrage, the advocate of Christian unity, the public voice for the humanities when they were first perceived to need a public voice. In reconstructing the life and thinking of an extraordinarily many-sided man, the book aims to give a deep insight into the worldview of British liberalism in the period when liberalism moved from a position of national and international hegemony to the brink of terminal decline.

One could think of others—perhaps Asquith—who offer a similar insight from nearer to the summit of politics; or others—the philosopher Henry

Sidgwick and the jurist Albert Venn Dicey—who had a more clearly delineated intellectual legacy. Lord Acton commanded a greater European renown. What was unique about Bryce was his distinguished activity in so many fields: as a cabinet minister *and* a professor; a campaigner and organizer of public opinion *and* an ambassador; a practitioner of the arts of democratic politics *and* one of the foremost academic students of democratic political systems across the world. The geographical as well as historical reach of his mind was astonishing, too, as was his thirst for discovery, so that in re-creating his life we can trace the encounter between a late Victorian Liberal and the wider world, as well as the imaginative encounter between a late Victorian Liberal and the European past over many centuries.

The literature on Bryce mostly deals with just one aspect of a many-sided figure. That may be inevitable, but it comes at a cost. This book draws attention to some of those costs and sets out to show what a more rounded study can offer. It suggests (in chapter 3) that Bryce's Teutonist sympathies, which were authentic, never dominated his thinking and need to be set against, for instance, his fascination with Rome as a universal city, and his academic specialism in Roman law. It shows (in chapter 6) that his support for Irish Home Rule, in defiance of many of his Ulster Protestant family, is less perplexing when set in the context of a lifelong identification with the cause of small nations. It argues (in chapters 9, 10, and 11) that the questionable position he took on the racial problem in his Romanes lecture in 1902, where he seemed to endorse or at least accept segregation, needs to be seen in the context of a trajectory that eventually led him to embrace a markedly more optimistic sense that racial antagonisms between White and Black were historically contingent, and capable of being overcome with time, education, and an increase in social mixing. Of course there are limitations to a biographical approach, too. But the book has as a core purpose to rescue Bryce from being consigned to a pigeonhole.

A Connected Intellectual

Some years ago I published a study of another Victorian intellectual eminence, Mark Pattison.[2] Pattison and Bryce, though separated in age by twenty-five years, knew each other well and had a high regard for each other. Each had a profoundly historical cast of mind, although both were much else besides historians. They shared a commitment to a number of common causes, from university reform and women's education to the Eastern Question. Each left behind him a number of grand unfinished projects, notably Pattison's projected study of Scaliger and Bryce's of Justinian. But as intellectual types they were polar opposites. Pattison saw the retreat from the world—in the university or the cathedral chapter—as the necessary setting for scholarly originality and regarded business (busy-ness) as the antithesis of the life of the mind. Bryce, by contrast, thrived on activity. His was a life in which scholarly writing (and he published much more than Pattison) was interwoven with public office, incessant campaigning, frequent and lengthy travel, and voluminous correspondence with a huge network of friends and contacts across the world. Furthermore, although with minor exceptions his published work was all single-authored, it was also in a deep sense the fruit of his friendships and networks. His work testified to enduring dialogue with close friends—Dicey and the historian Edward Freeman were particularly important interlocutors, as were Edwin Godkin and Charles Eliot in the United States—while books such as *The American Commonwealth* and *Modern Democracies* drew on his unique facility for 'fact-gathering' conversations, often with wholly new acquaintances. His was a fundamentally relational intellect.

The intellectual relationship between Bryce and Dicey exemplifies the importance of conversation—face-to-face and by letter—in the intellectual development of both men. They first met as undergraduates, fellow members of the Old Mortality Society at Oxford; Dicey was three years older and was elected fellow of Trinity College while Bryce was still an undergraduate at that college, where Dicey taught him for a time. They were travelling companions on the visit to the United States in 1870, a journey that more than any other formed Bryce's public life and intellectual career, and Dicey recalled more than four decades later that 'we accomplished a good deal of thinking in our 8 weeks'. In the same letter Dicey reflected that 'I am certain that conversation has very much improved my own thinking'.[3] Bryce was an important influence on Dicey's magnum opus, the *Lectures Introductory to the Study of Law of the Constitution*, just as Dicey was on Bryce's *American Commonwealth*; and both books could be said to have been germinated during that tour of America in 1870. This was perhaps Bryce's closest relationship outside his family and marriage, but it epitomizes the way in which he developed as a person and as a thinker.[4] There were dozens, even hundreds, of such intellectual relationships—with the Irish American editor Edwin Godkin and the heterodox divine and poet Stopford Brooke, with the Italian historian Ugo Balzani and the feminist mountaineer and philanthropist Emma Winkworth. Bryce's intellectual life cannot be captured without a deep investigation of the networks of acquaintance and friendship in which he operated.[5]

In a Commemoration address at Johns Hopkins University in 1911, on the subject of specialization in university education, he gave a clue as to the way in which he deployed his insatiable curiosity and his ability to extract knowledge and insight from anyone he met: 'The scientific specialist makes interesting company—when I have a chance I always try to get beside him at dinner—because he is able to tell us what we seek to know of the progress of discovery in the growing sciences, and we have only to interrogate him to get at once, without the labour of consulting books, the latest results in the clearest form.'[6] He was a natural synthesizer, but also one who had an extraordinary gift for deriving maximum practical benefit from casual and social encounters, as well as from business meetings. The most vivid account of this aspect of Bryce's personality comes from Henry Morgenthau, the American lawyer and businessman who had recently taken up the role of ambassador to the Ottoman Empire when Bryce met him in Palestine in 1914. They would later become close, as Morgenthau was important in documenting Turkish atrocities against the Armenians in 1915–1916. He recalled:

> On this trip I first had occasion to observe his method of obtaining information, which doubtless accounts for a part of his remarkable equipment as an historian. He was quite the greatest living questioner that I have ever met. He had developed cross examination to a fine art of picking men's brains. Most other men gather their information from books. It was a joy to be permitted to attend his séances with people who possessed information. He first put them completely at ease by ascertaining what subjects they were thoroughly posted on, and then, with a beneficent suavity, he made them willing contributors to his own unlimited store of knowledge. His thirst for facts was unquenchable. Question followed question almost like the report of shots fired from a machine gun. By this process, I have seen him rifle every recess of the minds of men like Schmavonian, who was a storehouse of Turkish history, custom, and tradition, and of Dr Franklin E. Hoskins, who is a profound scholar in Bible history. His method was physically exhausting to his victims, and in the hands of a less delightful personality would have been intolerable. But Lord Bryce was as charming as he was inquisitive, and more than that, he gave out of his vast erudition as freely as he received.[7]

The connected quality of Bryce's intellectual activity has implications for the way in which this book is conceived. Like any intellectual biography, it of course tries to reconstruct the intellectual contexts in which Bryce wrote; but his case cries out for a deeper exploration of the intellectual networks that shaped his thinking. Each chapter aims to home in on one or more important interlocutors, so that we can see Bryce's thinking evolving not in the privacy of the study or the library but amid a life of constant public business, travel, and sociability. The working notes that Bryce left—these are substantial, though not exhaustive by any means—illustrate the way in which his ideas were hammered out in society and amid an active life, with ideas for his next book scribbled on the backs of menus or on parliamentary order papers.

Historiography

Bryce has received a more than respectable amount of scholarly attention, starting with the standard two-volume life produced, at Lady Bryce's invitation, by the historian and cabinet minister H.A.L. Fisher. Fisher was a distinguished man who knew Bryce well, being married to his goddaughter, but the volume is generally regarded as something of a disappointment. Bryce's niece later speculated (having seen the vast mass of papers Bryce left) that Fisher had been given access to only a fragment of the whole.[8] There are two good monographs by the Americanists Edmund Ions and Hugh Tulloch, both of which naturally focus on Bryce's relationship with the United States; a neglected but scholarly study in German by Thomas Kleinknecht; and an agreeable and well-balanced short general life by John T. Seaman.[9] Bryce is, perhaps, a neglected figure in studies of the post-Gladstonian Liberal Party.[10] But he continues to attract attention in the substantially new fields of the history of international thought, the history of humanitarianism, and even the history of walking and mountaineering, as well as in older but resurgent fields such as the history of constitutional thought.[11] He is a central figure in Christopher Harvie's now somewhat forgotten early work, *The Lights of Liberalism*, and also—though less than perhaps he merits—in the classic study of *That Noble Science of Politics* by Stefan Collini, Donald Winch, and John Burrow.[12] There has also been sustained interest from Italian scholars (untranslated and hence largely undigested in the English-language literature), in particular on his constitutional writings and his contributions to the emergent discipline of political science.[13] What we lack, however, is anything like a comprehensive study of Bryce's thought, one that characterizes him in the round.

A word should be said for the rationale for an intellectual *biography*, as distinct from a study of Bryce on constitutionalism, or Bryce on America, or Bryce on democracy, or Bryce on race. All those subjects are well worth studying and are studied here, but they risk losing a sense both of the diversity of Bryce's interests and of their interconnectedness. They thus push out of sight what is surely an insistent set of questions about him: what kind of an intellectual was he? What kind of a public figure? How was the figure of the intellectual harmonized (if indeed it was) with that of the public man? A focus on the man enables us to wrestle with these questions, and to convey a sense of how, in practice, a late Victorian Liberal intellectual thought about questions of constitutionalism, democracy, and public opinion; of gender and the public sphere; of race, empire, and humanitarianism; of war and peace. It enables us to engage not just with well-developed theory but also with *opinion*. What made the vigorous activist for the extension of girls' and women's education at the same time an opponent of women's suffrage—and not just a casual opponent, but one who to the end was among Britain's most tenacious parliamentary critics of women's suffrage? Why was a man who unhesitatingly backed the cause of the North and the Union in the American Civil War—and who had a lifelong revulsion for slavery—also a critic of the extension of the suffrage to former slaves in the wake of that war?

The term *intellectual biography* is in need of some unpacking. In the case of Pattison, this was not a big question: he himself said that he had no history but a mental history, and while that was certainly an overstatement (how could it not be?), it was true that what mattered most about Pattison was the life of his mind. Bryce, by contrast, was a man of many parts who spent most of his adult life in public life of one kind or another: an MP for twenty-seven years, a peer for eight; a cabinet member for about four years under three prime ministers; ambassador for six years; a chair of Royal Commissions and similar inquiries; president of the British Academy; and so on. It would certainly be possible to frame a study of him as a political biography, or a life of the public man. That said, he was a politician of the second rank, who prior to his ambassadorship achieved much less in that domain than his talents suggested he should have; whereas his intellectual eminence was undisputed. It is as an intellectual figure that he really matters.

As an intellectual figure he was a great polymath, a man who was in his element in writing a preface to the 'handy volume' issue of the *Encyclopaedia Britannica* in 1915, and other syntheses of the state of knowledge. But his expertise was concentrated in the study of politics, law, and constitutions, both past and present. His central concerns were of three main kinds. He wrestled with the nature of democratic politics: this was a subject he first wrote about in his contribution to *Essays on Reform* (1867); it was the main theme of his

American Commonwealth (1888); and it was also his central concern in his old age, when he finally published his *Modern Democracies* (1921). Democratic *institutions* certainly interested him, but Collini, Winch, and Burrow do him an injustice by depicting him as a pioneer of the 'how-many-chambers-had-Lady-Macbeth' school of comparative government.[14] The recurrent theme in his writing on democracy was the importance of what we now call political culture, and in particular the role of public opinion: he was one of the first academic writers on politics to give due weight to political parties, the press, and other organs of public opinion. Second, he was concerned with the problem of peace. He is recognized as a leading 'pro-Boer', that is, a critic of the second South African War; and as the presiding grandee in the wartime Bryce Group, which nurtured the vision of a new world order organized by a 'league of nations'. But the peaceful organization of the world was an enduring concern of his, starting with *The Holy Roman Empire* (1864), the book that established his intellectual reputation. That book's focus was on the theory and practice of the medieval empire as a world order, and in a sense that set the agenda for a lifetime's preoccupation with the problem of international governance in a world of nation-states and colonial empires—an interest that paralleled his lifelong preoccupation with nationalism and national identity.[15] His third principal concern straddled the first two: a fascination with the causes of the cohesion or decomposition of states—what he termed 'centripetal' and 'centrifugal' forces—and how they could be managed constitutionally. The nationality question was fundamental here, and we find in Bryce some intriguing tension between his visceral sympathy for small nations struggling to be free (a sympathy that grew stronger with time) and the liberal conviction that the proliferation of small states would prove inimical to both economic progress and cultural vitality. Importantly, the problem of the cohesion and decomposition of states also drew him into the emerging field of race relations. He hoped and believed that the encounter and intermarriage of different racial groups would soften their difference and facilitate peaceful relations. But he agonized about what would happen if, as seemed to be the case in the United States and southern Africa, the antipathy between Whites and Blacks was such as to block any hope of progress through intermarriage.

This brief account of Bryce's distinctive intellectual interests suggests a way in which an intellectual biography can at the same time engage with the public man. He understood democratic politics not just as an academic student of the subject and as an avid traveller, but also as an active politician, one who, though he barely (in Max Weber's terms) 'lived off' politics, was nevertheless a professional.[16] At the same time as he was working on *The American Commonwealth* in the mid-1880s, he was sitting in the Commons and writing commentaries on British politics for the New York weekly, *The Nation*. He analysed the workings of public opinion in the United States and other democratic polities, but he was also fully engaged in trying to shape public opinion through the numerous pressure groups in which he took a leading role, on causes ranging from the defence of the subject nationalities of the Ottoman Empire, above all the Armenians, to the campaign for preservation of common spaces open to the public. He wrote extensively on the politics of federal and unitary states, of multinational empires and settler colonies, but he was also active in wrestling with the Irish Question as a Gladstonian Home Ruler, and also in trying to shape the international order, as a diplomat, a peace campaigner, and an advocate for the incipient League of Nations. So in this book Bryce's thinking about the grand challenges of democratic politics, international organization for peace, and nationality and race will be traced not only through his writings but also through his career as an activist and statesman. His career in high politics will be very much part of the picture, but high politics is viewed primarily as an arena for his intellectual engagement with these grand challenges.

But an 'intellectual biography' of Bryce must also do justice to the relational character of his intellect. What that means is that it must capture the extent and importance of the networks to which he belonged and that helped frame his thinking. It must be thickly contextualized. My contention is that none of the existing studies do justice to this fundamental characteristic of Bryce. To take one important example: none of the existing biographical studies devote more than cursory attention to the importance of women in Bryce's life. They pass fleetingly over his relations with his mother and his sisters Mary and Katharine. Yet Mary lived with him, ran his household, and acted as a kind of political and personal secretary and political hostess for more than a decade before his marriage. We also have no significant analysis of the strikingly close partnership he formed with his wife, Marion, who assumed the roles that Mary Bryce had previously performed, accompanied him on almost all his travels and was undoubtedly a powerful influence on his career, as well as steward of his posthumous reputation.[17] The book also draws attention to a number of close friendships with women—always women of intellectual interests and standing—that clearly meant a lot to Bryce throughout his adult life. They included Alice Stopford Green (1847–1929), historian, Irish nationalist, and widow of Bryce's friend the historian John Richard Green; Emma Winkworth,

née Thomasson, Bolton Unitarian, London hostess, mountaineer, and campaigner for the causes of women's education and women's suffrage; and Anne
Thackeray Ritchie (1837–1919), novelist and novelist's daughter. Bryce was an
early, staunch, and consistent supporter of the cause of girls' and women's education, but he was also a strong and consistent opponent of women's suffrage,
to the end of his life. These are positions that had an intellectual logic that can
be unfolded, but they were also embedded in this network of personal relationships, some of which were damaged by his opposition to the suffrage,
though others were reinforced by it. So this is precisely the kind of issue that
can best be analysed by means of an intellectual biography that places its subject's thinking into a thick context of personal relationships and intellectual
networks. Equally, while Bryce's family background has certainly been covered
in existing studies, the importance of the family in shaping his thinking has
never been written about in any depth. But this was crucial in several important respects. First, while his religious beliefs evolved toward a nondogmatic
but morally serious liberal Protestantism, he remained staunchly attached to
the family's religious heritage that was steeped in the Presbyterianism of the
seventeenth-century Covenanters and the eighteenth-century Seceders. He
remained a firm opponent of ecclesiastical establishments and a consistent
advocate of nondenominational education. Second, the absence of any kind
of break with his parents and their religious heritage tells us something important about Bryce's psychology: in his intellectual evolution he added new
layers—new friendships, allegiances, enthusiasms, interests—but he rarely
shed the old ones, so there are no obvious narrative discontinuities in his life.
There is a suggestion that a less harmonious private life might have nurtured
a greater originality, as it certainly did with Pattison.[18] Third, while relations
with his parents were remarkably harmonious, there were tensions with the
wider family, not least with his Uncle John (Dr Reuben John Bryce) on university tests and especially on Home Rule, so that private lives and public
service interacted in fascinating ways.

The temporal continuity of Bryce's life and career has implications for the
way in which the book is organized. Of course there were some important
turning points around which a narrative can be structured. His entry into Parliament in 1880 was an obvious one; so too was 1888–1889, when within a period of eight months or so he published *The American Commonwealth* and got
married at the age of fifty-one. The appointment as ambassador to the United
States in 1907 was a third. But while entry into Parliament gave him a new
sphere of activity, he did not abandon academia: he retained his Oxford chair

for the first half of his twenty-seven-year stint in Parliament. Even when he resigned his chair, he continued to be active in helping to build the structures of academic life: as a founding fellow of the British Academy, and one of its early presidents, and as a participant in the international academic congresses that started to become an entrenched presence in academic life at the beginning of the twentieth century, including the famous St Louis Congress of 1904. *The American Commonwealth* built on the foundations of his first visit to the United States way back in 1870, and that was itself the fruit of the enthusiasm for American institutions (and the cause of the Union) among the Oxford academic liberals of the 1860s. As ambassador between 1907 and 1913, he played a distinctive and innovative role as a practitioner of what we might now call public or cultural diplomacy, seeking (with a striking degree of success) to make an impact on American public opinion; but this role was possible because of the reputation that *The American Commonwealth* had made for him both as a friend of America and as a sympathetic authority on its institutions.

Moreover, at least three of Bryce's major works had long lives that make them hard to pigeonhole temporally. What I mean by that is not simply that they continued to be read for many years, although that is true. Both *The Holy Roman Empire* and *The American Commonwealth* went through many new editions in Bryce's lifetime, often with substantive revisions, stretching to new chapters as well as revisions of points of interpretation. That means that they belong to several phases of Bryce's career. That is why *The American Commonwealth* is considered briefly in chapter 5 and in detail in chapters 7, 9, and 10. *Modern Democracies*, by contrast, went through only one edition in his lifetime, since it was published in his final year. But it had been conceived as long ago as 1904, and he worked on it, when time allowed, not only up to his entry into the cabinet in December 1905, but also throughout his ambassadorship and throughout his very busy First World War. So while it is analysed in depth in chapter 12, it is anticipated in chapter 10, which shows how some of his thinking on democracy was shaped by his renewed encounter with the American public during his time in Washington.

The question of *temporality* is for that reason a methodologically tricky one to handle in writing about Bryce. He did not abandon causes or friendships, though he acquired new ones, and an important thing to understand about his way of operating as a politician and public intellectual was that he deployed networks formed for one purpose in helping to advance other causes. Thus the American academic and political contacts he built up when writing *The*

American Commonwealth were also deployed to act on American public opinion on behalf of the Armenian people, and later in support of American entry into the First World War. He did not compartmentalize his life, so that at the height of the Home Rule crisis we find him in dialogue with Gladstone about the interpretation of Dante, and as ambassador he used to entertain President Roosevelt with his recitations from Icelandic sagas. His enthusiasm for Dante and for primitive Iceland were motifs or tropes that recurred in unexpected contexts throughout Bryce's career. Something similar could be said about the concept of public opinion. This was central to his analysis of democratic political systems both in *The American Commonwealth* and in *Modern Democracies*. But he had been thinking seriously about the workings of public opinion ever since he worked for the Schools Inquiry Commission back in the 1860s, and as we shall see, public opinion was a recurrent motif in his political activity as well as in his political science. So while the book is organized both chronologically and thematically, there is necessarily frequent use of retrospectives and indeed prospectives; and if Irish Home Rule and *The American Commonwealth* are dealt with in separate chapters, we also have to take the opportunity to peer across these artificial walls to acknowledge that Bryce was working on the two simultaneously. Indeed, less than six weeks separated the completion of *The American Commonwealth* from *Two Centuries of Irish History*, the volume he edited at Gladstone's instigation as part of a concerted effort to make the intellectual case for Home Rule.

A Democratic Intellect?

The book's subtitle recalls George Davie's famous work in which he characterized the idea of the democratic intellect as the distinguishing feature of the Scottish educational tradition.[19] As chapter 1 shows, Bryce was shaped by that tradition, both because he spent three formative years at Glasgow University before he proceeded to Oxford, but also because his family was steeped in the Scottish university tradition as practised at Glasgow in particular. Bryce's famed polymathy bore the recognizable marks of his formation in the Scottish university tradition before its anglicization.

To call Bryce's intellect a 'democratic' one is not to imply that he was a democrat in an absolute sense. He belonged to the democratic wing of the Liberal Party in the 1860s and 1870s, but by the end of his life he looked back nostalgically on the time when he could view the coming of democracy optimistically. The book shows in chapter 7 and elsewhere that he was attached to both the archetypal nineteenth-century Liberal doctrine of *capacity* and the republican belief that any viable free political order must depend on the nurturing of civic virtue. He was consistently opposed to the idea of an abstract *right* to vote. But the theory and practice of democracy stood at the heart of his intellectual concerns, from his contribution to *Essays on Reform* in 1867 to his *Modern Democracies* in 1921, and that is a second reason for the title.

The third and most important reason is that what most distinguished Bryce as a type of public moralist was his sustained preoccupation with public opinion. This was the pivotal concept in his analysis of American democracy in *The American Commonwealth*, and later the pivotal concept in his comparative analysis of democratic systems in *Modern Democracies*. Just as important, what was most distinctive about his political career was his engagement with public opinion: as a single-issue campaigner for access to open spaces at home or for the rights of oppressed peoples overseas; as a democratic ambassador who forged a new kind of relationship with the American people; and finally as one of those who, in the First World War and after, identified the formation of an international public opinion as the only sure route to peace. But for Bryce public opinion was never just a datum with which politicians had to reckon. It had to be led, and the leadership of public opinion was central to the vocation of the intellectual-in-politics. Above all else he was in public life to educate and to shape public opinion, in Britain and abroad.

1

The Formation
of a Democratic Intellect

BELFAST-GLASGOW-OXFORD

A Scots-Ulster Inheritance: The Bryces and the Youngs

James Bryce was born in Belfast in May 1838 and lived his early years there, before the family settled in Glasgow when he was eight. His parents, James and Margaret Bryce, had both been born and raised in Ulster. Thereafter his boyhood holidays were spent in rural Ulster, and at the age of fifteen he returned to Belfast to stay with his uncle for a time and attend classes at the Belfast Academy. But Bryce in later life never called himself or thought of himself as an Ulsterman or an Irishman. He recalled that in his boyhood in Ulster many local farmers in Down and Antrim spoke broad Scotch of the kind that might have been heard in Ayrshire or Galloway: they considered themselves to be fully Scottish, their commercial relations were with Scotland rather than with Dublin, and they dismissively referred to the Catholic populations of the Glens of Antrim and the Mourne Mountains as 'thae Eerish'.[1] If their sons wished to train for the Presbyterian ministry or for another learned profession, they would be sent to Glasgow University, as Bryce's father and several of his uncles were.[2] Bryce might sometimes call himself a Scotchman, for the Bryces were Lowlanders, from Lanarkshire, and his grandfather had taken refuge across the Irish Sea only in 1805. More often he spoke of himself as an Englishman: the Lowlanders were after all (according to the familiar racial typologies of the time) of Teutonic stock, closer to the English than to the Celts of the Highlands and most of Ireland.[3] Still, the Scots-Ulster upbringing shaped him in innumerable ways.

Bryce's family will feature a good deal in this book; not just in the more biographical sections, but even in the analysis of Bryce's thinking about education and about democracy, about Home Rule and about women's suffrage.[4] That reflects the strikingly important place the family occupied in his life. He grew up in a close-knit family with a powerful set of family legends. He remained remarkably close to his parents, brother, and sisters long into adult life. His sister Mary shared and ran his household (and, latterly, his brother's) in London for many years before both brothers married within a year of each other, a combination that devastated the two sisters. Mary's death in 1927 was reported in *The Times*, which recalled that 'from 1875 to Bryce's marriage in 1889 their house was a centre of hospitality where politicians and lawyers, artists, and men of letters met other friends from all over the world.'[5] During this time she managed much of his political diary and correspondence, especially during his lengthy overseas travels, and continued to provide some support of this kind even after his marriage, especially when the Bryces were on foreign holidays, which were long and frequent. The younger sister, Katharine—and Mary too from 1889—kept house for their widowed and invalid mother in London (Campden Hill Square) from 1877 until Margaret Bryce's death in 1903. Mrs Bryce was well-known to all Bryce's closest friends, and to many of his wider circle of acquaintances.

The family made decisions collectively, to quite a striking degree. Bryce was five years older than his brother Annan, and nine and twelve years older than his sisters Mary and Katharine.[6] He took a quasi-parental interest in their upbringing, and especially in their education. In letters to his parents he would often refer to his sisters as 'the children', and even long into their adulthood he would address them 'Dear Children' when he wrote to both of them.[7] He frequently offered them educational advice, sometimes a little gratingly: 'It will be a good thing for you to write often, as it is very good practice in Grammar and many other kinds of knowledge. Besides there is nothing nicer in a lady than that she shd be able to write good letters.'[8] This would include guidance on study: 'remember that the really useful and improving plan is to learn one thing perfectly and understanding everything about it so far as you go in it. To explain what I mean—it is far better to be able to do one fable in Phaedrus without a mistake—translation, parsing and all, than to blunder through two or three making many mistakes.'[9] He told Mary, aged thirteen, that once she had finished Caesar she should move on to Ovid rather than to Virgil, since the latter 'is very difficult to understand, though not so hard just to translate into English.'[10]

FIGURE 1.1. James Bryce, LLD (1806–1877), 'a firm Presbyterian and a sincere Voluntary'.

We know a good deal about the Bryce family background. Bryce himself
wrote biographical notices, published anonymously, on both his father and his
grandfather for the *Dictionary of National Biography*, at the invitation of its
founding editor, his close friend and climbing companion, Leslie Stephen.[11]
With his uncle, Dr Reuben John Bryce, he wrote an obituary of his father for
the *United Presbyterian Magazine*. Bryce's papers also contain a substantial box
of genealogical material, which includes a short notice that Bryce wrote on the
death of his mother. There is other material solicited by H.A.L. Fisher when
he was engaged in writing the two-volume life of Bryce that appeared in 1927.

Bryce's father and grandfather were both also named James, which creates
some danger of confusion. Here 'Bryce' is used to refer to the subject of the

FIGURE 1.2. Margaret Bryce, née Young (1813–1903): 'Her
mind was singularly open to the last.'

book. His father will usually be referred to as Dr Bryce: a title he used, when
acquired rather late in life, whereas his son, though he was a doctor of civil law
(DCL), was never, or almost never, called Dr Bryce.[12] Dr Bryce's father will
be referred to either as the Revd James Bryce or as Bryce of Killaig; Killaig
being the village near Coleraine in County Londonderry where he served as
minister of an Anti-Burgher congregation for many years.[13] Bryce of Killaig
was descended, on both his mother's and his father's side, from Lanarkshire
landowners who had backed the Covenanters in the seventeenth century and
(on his mother's side) lost much of their land as a result.[14] He studied at

FIGURE 1.3. Annan Bryce (1843–1923), Bryce's younger brother.

Glasgow University, although he did not graduate, and at the Anti-Burghers' Divinity Hall; shortly after his ordination he married Catherine Annan, a Fifeshire woman whom he had first met when she was a nine year-old pupil at the school in Auchtermuchty where he taught before ordination.[15] Suspended from his ministry in Wick after being accused of latitudinarianism by the Synod, he accepted an invitation to Ireland and finally settled at Killaig.

Bryce of Killaig loomed large in the mythology of the Bryce family, who cherished the religious patrimony he passed on. This was recounted as the story of the sacrifice of material interest for the sake of principle. The Anti-Burghers among whom he grew up were the most hard-line of Scots Presbyterians in matters of ecclesiology, or church organization considered as a part of theology. They were a branch of the Secession Church: their ancestors had seceded from the Kirk in the 1730s on the question of lay patronage, which they felt infringed on the right of congregations to choose their own minister. The Anti-Burghers split with the remainder of the Secession in 1747 over

FIGURE 1.4. Mary Bryce (1847–1927) and Katharine Bryce
(1850–1917), Bryce's sisters.

whether to approve the religious clause in the Burgess Oath, in which town
burgesses, on taking office, declared their full-hearted allegiance to 'the true
religion presently professed within this realm and authorized by the laws
thereof', and renounced 'the Roman religion called Papistry'. For the Anti-
Burghers, it was sinful to take this oath, which amounted to an endorsement
of state religion, whereas the Burghers thought it simply a statement of Protestantism and a denunciation of Roman Catholicism.

  At Wick the Revd James Bryce was a controversial figure because of his
strong, not to say idiosyncratic, views on relations of church and state: on his

arrival at the church he took the view that the celebration of marriages was a civil and not a religious function, which should therefore not be undertaken by ministers of religion.[16] As the episode was recounted by his grandson, he was accused before the Antiburgher Synod of latitudinarianism 'because he had minimised the difference between his own and other denominations of Christians, had condemned the extreme assumption of power by the clergy, and had argued that the dogmatic creeds of the church received too much respect as compared with the scriptures'. He was suspended for two years, and when restored to his functions he was indignant at the religious intolerance prevalent in Scotland, and settled in Ireland as minister of the Anti-Burgher congregation of Killaig. There he split again, on the question of the *regium donum*. This was an annual payment, finally abolished in 1869, made by the Crown through the Lord Lieutenant to the Presbyterian ministers. Formerly it was treated as a free gift and paid without conditions; now it was significantly increased in value but subject to the requirement that the recipient should take the oath of allegiance; the Lord-Lieutenant was also given a veto on its bestowal. The Anti-Burgher ministers protested at these terms, but Bryce of Killaig was alone in standing firm and refusing to take it. In his grandson's words, he held 'that the requirements were dishonouring to Christ as the supreme head of the church, and tended to enslave a minister of religion and to degrade his office'.[17] He continued to minister to his congregation in conditions of some penury, and as he gradually attracted allies he founded the Associate Presbytery of Ireland (1811). Shortly after his death this body, which consisted of no more than half a dozen ministers and no more than eight congregations, joined the United Presbyterian Church, which had been formed in 1847 by the union of the United Secession Church and the Relief Church.[18] In the time of Bryce's boyhood the United Presbyterians (with whom the Bryces worshipped when they moved to Glasgow) were a strong and wealthy body, especially in the Glasgow area, where they were probably the largest denomination; and they took an active part in missionary work overseas.[19] At the merger the ministers of the Associate Presbytery were allowed to persist in their refusal of the Regium Donum, which was in any case abolished in 1869; but they had to renounce their adherence to the old Anti-Burgher practice of excluding from their worship all hymns and paraphrases (that is, any compositions not using the words of scripture).[20]

In short, the Secession churches had seceded from the Kirk on questions of ecclesiology. They took a hard line against lay patronage, which they deemed a form of Erastianism.[21] Among the Secessionists, the Anti-Burghers took a notably intransigent line, in that they interpreted the Burgess Oath as a form of submission to state religion. Among the Anti-Burghers, Bryce of Killaig was almost uniquely hard-line, in that he refused the Regium Donum. Voluntaryism was thus at the core of the family's religious identity. On the other hand, they were by no means extreme on questions of doctrine. The problems Bryce of Killaig had encountered at Wick arose from the perception that he was doctrinally lax. And the United Presbyterian tradition to which the Bryces adhered latterly was increasingly liberal in questions of doctrine, in particular in its interpretation of the Westminster Confession. When the United Presbyterians finally united with the Free Church in 1900, it was the perceived doctrinal relaxation that union entailed that precipitated the secession of the 'Wee Free' minority within the Free Church. So it would not be right to suppose that Bryce was raised among the 'cave-dwellers of Puritanism'.[22]

The Bryces of Killaig brought up their large family often in conditions of acute poverty; but the children were talented and were taught Greek by their mother, and the sons proceeded to successful professional careers.[23] The eldest, the Revd Dr Reuben John Bryce (always known in the family as John, but known in other circles as Reuben), was head of the Belfast Academy, and pastor of a small Secession Church in Belfast; 'Uncle John', who was unmarried, was an important presence in his nephew's life, in boyhood and well beyond, and was an important interlocutor, always passionate and sometimes querulous too.[24] The second son, Robert, was a doctor in Belfast, and the sixth, William, a doctor in Edinburgh. The fourth son, Thomas Annan, taught mathematics at Belfast Academy and later in Toronto. David, the fifth son, became an accountant in Belfast, while the youngest, Archibald, taught classics at the Royal High School, Edinburgh, and later served as rector of the Edinburgh Collegiate School; he was a more than competent classical scholar. The third son, James—Bryce's father—taught mathematics and geography first at the Belfast Academy, where his older brother was head, and then at the Glasgow High School. He was evidently a gifted teacher. One of his Belfast pupils was his future brother-in-law, the distinguished architect Robert Young. Young recalled his mathematics classes as the best teaching he received at the academy. His teacher made a deep impression, for his classes in botany, mineralogy, and geology as well as mathematics: 'I remember how he accompanied his pupils to places of geological interest, such as Colin Glen, Woodburn, Whitehead and the Cavehill quarries, where with hammer and chisel he would show how that the very rocks were full of wonders and sermons in stone.'[25]

James Bryce the second married Robert Young's older sister, Margaret, the eldest daughter of James Young (1773–1846), a leading wholesale woollen merchant in Belfast and Abbeyville, County Antrim. She had been her future husband's pupil at the Belfast Academy.[26] What information we have on the Young family comes from the autobiographical fragments left by her brother Robert.[27] Back in the seventeenth century the Youngs had settled on the estate of the absentee Marquis of Hertford, near Lough Neagh in County Antrim. James Young was the son of a tenant farmer at Dundrod, on the Hertford estate. He served his apprenticeship with his uncle, a weaver in Glenavy, and set up his own business as a warehouseman in Belfast in 1795. He was remembered as 'well educated and much respected both in public & private life, but silent & reserved by nature, & not of a very sociable disposition'. His wife 'had a vein of Celtic blood' and 'was of a much more easy & vivacious temperament, but was not a woman of special intellectual power'.[28] James Young was an elder and treasurer of Rosemary Street Presbyterian Church in Belfast, whose pastor was Dr Samuel Hanna.[29] Dr Hanna was a notable figure in Ulster Presbyterianism: he had served as moderator of the General Synod (that is, not the Secession Synod) shortly before Margaret Young's birth, and served as professor of divinity and church history at the Belfast Academical Institution from its foundation. He was a strong Calvinist but not an extreme one, belonging rather to the moderate wing of 'Old Light' evangelicalism.[30] We cannot infer too much about the Young family's religion from their pastor's theology, but this at least gives us a flavour of the kind of religious upbringing Bryce's mother would have had.

Margaret Bryce was, according to many accounts, a remarkable woman who had a particularly strong bond with her elder son. She was well read from an early age thanks to her father's library and 'had a mind of much force & grasp'. As a girl and as a young woman, she had 'a good deal of vivacity, a great love of argument, & considerable power of repartee, & would often amuse her family with her witty sallies'.[31] Something of an invalid from middle age due to a heart condition, she nevertheless remained intellectually active into extreme old age. Practically all Bryce's close friends got to know her well, especially during the long years of her widowhood. When she was in her final year Dicey told Bryce that 'I have very rarely seen anyone approaching her age so full of animation & of interest in every thing that is going on.'[32] 'She was ninety years of age', Bryce wrote to Charles W. Eliot on her death, 'and had preserved not only all her mental powers but all her interests in an extraordinary degree'.[33] Her mind was 'wonderfully clear and strong' to the end, he told another friend, and (this is particularly striking) 'she was the centre of all her relatives, on my father's side as well as her own, by her fresh interest in the present'.[34] 'Her mind was singularly open to the last', he recalled some years later.[35] She was evidently a gifted conversationalist, like her son, and friends' letters to Bryce about her after her death often commented on how much the friends would miss 'those delightful long talks with her'.[36] For Emma Winkworth, who leaned to scepticism, it was her religious faith that made a particular impression: 'I felt it was a privilege to love your mother, & to sit at her feet & feel her own strong faith & goodness kindle mine anew.'[37]

If Bryce had a special bond with his mother, his relationship with his father was no less close. It was certainly from his father that he acquired his love of outdoor pursuits, and especially of the outdoor scientific pursuits of geology and botany, and they spent many hours together in these activities, especially during holidays. Dr Bryce was mathematical master of Glasgow High School from 1846 until 1874, where he was evidently popular with the students, as he had been in Belfast. He was the author of a *Treatise on Algebra* (1837) but best known as a geologist, in which capacity he published some notable papers in learned journals. He died in a rock fall while undertaking geological fieldwork on the shores of Loch Ness in 1877: this was the one big trauma of Bryce's life. Shortly afterwards he acknowledged that it was to his father that he owed 'whatever taste he possesses for geographical observation and for the beauties of nature'.[38] A graduate of Glasgow University, Dr Bryce was an active campaigner for the reform of the Scottish universities, and in particular for a greater role for the graduates in their governance. It was this work that primarily won him a doctorate of laws from the university in 1858. University reform was another interest that he passed on to his elder son.

The fullest source on Dr Bryce's religion is the memoir written by his son, with input from Uncle John: the best-informed authorities, though perhaps not the most objective. They record his religious beliefs and practice as follows:

> Sprung from an old Covenanting stock, brought up in a pious home, and by his own matured convictions a firm Presbyterian and a sincere Voluntary, Dr Bryce was throughout his life an active and earnest member in Ireland of the Church founded by his father, and, after he came to Scotland, of the United Presbyterian Church. While in Glasgow, he was for many years an elder in the Shamrock Street Church, of which he had been one of the founders; and in Edinburgh he was again elected to the eldership in the

church at Morningside, of which Dr Mair is pastor. No one could be more zealous or faithful in the discharge of his presbyterial duties. In Glasgow, fatigued as he was by the labours of the week, he undertook the management of the Shamrock Street Church Sabbath school, organized it from the first, and taught in it two hours every Sabbath, even when his family, who feared the effect on his health, endeavoured to persuade him to leave the work to younger men. The supposed difficulties of reconciling the conclusions of science with the truths of Christianity cast no shadow upon his pure and truthful spirit. Although a thorough man of science, accepting everything which geology has proved, and never hesitating to defend it when assailed, he was none the less a simple and pious Christian. Nature and revelation were to him only two different modes in which the wisdom and goodness of the Most High were set forth to men, and he never admitted that there could be any contradiction between them. Indeed, his love of nature and delight in her study were intensified by the clearness with which he saw God manifested in the beauty of the world and the skill of its workmanship.[39]

The brother and the son may not have been the most neutral sources on Dr Bryce's religion, but there is no reason to doubt the authenticity of this portrait, allowing for the natural tendency of an obituary notice to present its subject's best side. Just as significantly, however, their account tells us something not just about the subject but also about the authors and their own sense of what was important about the family's religious identity. It is noteworthy that they emphasize that Dr Bryce was not just 'a firm Presbyterian' but 'a sincere Voluntary', in upper case: further affirmation that voluntaryism was at the heart of the Bryces' religious identity.

Biographical notes on Bryce in his widow's hand shed more light on his father's—and indeed his mother's—religious stance. It seems very likely that this is Bryce himself speaking here, although it could be that it is Marion Bryce's attempt to construct a biographical sketch after his death on the basis of her own many conversations with him, his mother, and his sisters. 'The family belonged to [the] United Presbyterian Church of Scotland', the notes record, '& some of the older members were rigid & austere in their creed according to the fashion of the time; but his parents, though firm adherents, were not of this type, & in spite of the strict observance of certain rules & customs during childhood his mind was never forced into narrow channels & he developed on his own lines.'[40]

Among the more 'rigid & austere' members of the older generation was Uncle John. He was much more opinionated on religious (and other) matters than either his brother or his nephew. In personality he seems to have been the family member who most resembled Bryce of Killaig in terms of cussed pursuit of *idées fixes*. His commitment to voluntaryism was tenacious. We shall get a flavour of this when we consider his involvement in discussions around Bryce's candidature for Oxford college fellowships in 1861–1862. Voluntaryism was a cause he championed on the United Presbyterian Church's Synod, notably when the question of union with the Free Church first came up in 1863. Formally, he spoke in favour of exploring the possible terms of a union but pleaded for 'full time' to be 'given for the consideration of the matter'. He warned of the danger of a sacrifice of fundamental principle: 'there was also the honour of our Lord Jesus Christ, which ought to be the main foundation of their [the United Presbyterians'] Voluntaryism.' Compulsory support of religion was both unjust to fellow men and 'an affront to the Saviour'.[41] There is evidence that he tried to invoke the authority of his own father, Bryce of Killaig, in resisting any watering down of voluntaryist principles.[42] This is a subject on which his younger brother may well have taken a different, more liberal, line. 'What probability is there of this Free & Un. Presb. union being carried out?', Bryce asked his father in 1863. 'You I suppose are in favour.'[43]

It is impossible to define Bryce's religious heritage without some reference to the single most important event in nineteenth-century Scottish history, the 'Great Disruption' of 1843 that split the Kirk. The impact on the Bryce family was indirect, since they had broken with the Kirk some generations previously; and they were committed opponents of the very idea of an ecclesiastical establishment, whereas what was at stake in 1843 was the correct interpretation of what the principle of establishment implied. But the split happened when Bryce was five: it had obvious ramifications for Presbyterian Ulster, and in any case it was still very much a current event when the family moved to Glasgow three years later. Certainly Bryce had a profound awareness that religion, and religious divisions, had a centrality in Scottish life that far exceeded the importance of religion in English life, great though that was in his lifetime. As he wrote to Dicey in 1916, 'the history of Scotland from John Knox to Robertson Smith is an ecclesiastical history, just as the internal history of the Roman Empire from Athanasius to Heraclius—three centuries—is ecclesiastical & not political.'[44]

The Bryces' voluntaryist stance made them naturally sympathetic to Thomas Chalmers and the other leaders of the Disruption in that the key principle of the Free Church was 'non-intrusionism': no minister should be imposed on a parish against the will of the congregation. Dr Chalmers, whom Bryce later called (in connection with poor law reform) one of the 'best men of the older generation', evidently had an important influence on the Bryce family, and on Uncle John in particular, even though they disagreed about the legitimacy of a church establishment.[45]

Marion Bryce's biographical notes on her husband shrewdly draw attention to a remarkable feature of his upbringing which he may well have discussed with her: 'it is evident, in tracing the gradual development of the boy through his childhood & boyhood, that both parents treated him as an individual to be taken seriously, talked to, & even consulted, at an age when most boys would have been considered either too young to understand, or too young to be burdened with such responsibility.' She thought this probably owed something to his unusual maturity as a boy but also contributed to that maturity in a way that might have been counterproductive: 'though it attached him to both of them with singularly deep & passionate affection it was too great a strain upon his spiritual & emotional nature, of which he felt the effects all his life.' The weight of worldly decisions gave him 'a strain of melancholy' and detracted from the carefreeness of boyhood.

Marion's reflections on how Bryce coped with episodes of depression, if such they were, are equally interesting, and they cast light on his passion for long foreign holidays in later life:

> What helped him most to put away these burdens was to escape into the mountains, & follow up the burns, & hunt for rare plants. From quite a child he would be his father's companion in these rambles among the Irish & Scottish hills. His father was an ardent lover of nature—not only taking intense pleasure in natural beauty, but as an expert in botany & geology, astronomy & meteorology; & James Bryce learnt to care for all these things & acquire some knowledge of them almost unconsciously. During school days his life had to be lived in towns, but all the holidays were spent in some beautiful spot by the sea & the mountains, & the lakes of Ireland & Scotland, & there was hardly a place in either that he did not connect with early memories.[46]

Long foreign holidays—especially walking and climbing holidays—were a regular and important feature of his adult life, and these reflections help to explain why.[47]

A Scottish Education

Bryce was educated at Glasgow High School, where his father taught. He was evidently bored by school by the age of fifteen, probably having exhausted what it had to offer him by way of intellectual challenge, and was keen to go on to university then, but his father and uncle preferred him to wait, and he spent the academic year 1853–1854 in Belfast, living and studying with his Uncle John. He matriculated at Glasgow University at sixteen, which was by no means exceptional at the time.[48] At Glasgow he was a beneficiary of the broad-based common curriculum of the Scottish universities, based on the classics, philosophy, mathematics, and the experimental sciences. In retrospect he thought he had been well taught. In an autobiographical fragment reproduced in Fisher's biography, Bryce recalled his studies in some detail.[49] In his first year he took Latin (the senior class), Greek (the middle), and logic. The professor of Latin ('Humanity') was William Ramsay: Bryce remembered him as 'a man then of about sixty', but in fact he was not yet fifty. When Bryce went on to Trinity College, Oxford, one of the other scholars was Ramsay's nephew, George Gilbert Ramsay, who would go on to succeed his uncle in the chair of Humanity in 1863. Bryce had a notable regard for the elder Ramsay: 'an admirable teacher, stimulating and vivacious, a complete master of his subject, and author of one of the best Classical textbooks extant'. He taught twice a day: the morning class was catechetical (instruction based on question and answer), while the afternoon lecture would expound an author, in this case Catullus. His Greek counterpart was Edmund Lushington, who was the brother-in-law of the poet Tennyson: 'more learned and a scholar of finer quality than Ramsay, but not so stimulating a teacher'. Bryce got to know Lushington quite well in later life, in spite of political differences (Lushington being a Whig who opposed Gladstone on Home Rule and much else), and had a great affection for him: 'a perfect example of the finished scholar who led the philosophic life, seeming to desire nothing beyond what he had, and finding his happiness in the enjoyment of intellectual pleasures'. Finally the professor of logic, 'Logic Bob', was Robert Buchanan, an ordained Church of Scotland minister who taught in the tradition of the Scottish 'common sense' school of his eighteenth-century predecessor, Thomas Reid. Bryce recalled the lectures— two hours, the first exposition, the second testing the class's knowledge and understanding—as fresh and skilful. They were perhaps somewhat dated— there was no Kant or Hegel, Fichte or Schelling—but 'in their simple treatment of the fundamentals of psychology and logic they were highly appreciated by the students and very profitable'. Buchanan was, Bryce thought, a far better teacher than his Edinburgh counterpart, the much more learned and eminent Sir William Hamilton.

In his second year he took senior Greek, with Lushington again, the subject being the Agamemnon: translation and commentary on the language taking precedence over a fine appreciation of the poetry. There were also some exercises in translation from English into Homeric hexameters: this was 'the only kind of classical verse composition I ever enjoyed or attained any facility in', for he liked Homer more than any other ancient poet he had by then encountered. The other subject was mathematics, taught by Professor Hugh Blackburn, 'an excellent mathematician, but a poor teacher'. Bryce, who thought he had 'only a mediocre capacity' in mathematics, was voted third prize for this class: it was, he thought, a reflection of the poor quality of the teaching that the awards did not reflect ability at all accurately.

He recalled keen competition among the undergraduates, who, according to the custom of the Scottish universities, decided the award of class prizes by democratic vote. His most notable achievement was to win Lord Jeffrey's Gold Medal for Greek, which was one of the two awarded by the professors. This gave particular pleasure to his father, who had won the same prize.[50] He later reflected on the Scottish universities, in comparison with Oxford and Cambridge: 'there are no residential colleges like those of England, so the undergraduates live in lodgings, where they please, and thus there is less of social student life. But the instruction is stimulating; and the undergraduates, being mostly poor men, and coming of a diligent and aspiring stock, are more generally studious and hard-working and self-reliant than are those of Oxford and Cambridge.'[51]

The strength of the bond that connected the Bryce family and Glasgow University calls for some reflections on the importance of the Scottish educational tradition in Bryce's formation. The classic study of the intellectual context of the Scottish universities in the nineteenth century is Davie's *Democratic Intellect*. First published in 1961, it was a lament for the loss of the indigenous tradition of university education that was largely extinguished by the Anglicization process of the second half of the nineteenth century and after. For Davie, the universities were central to Scottish national identity, and what was distinctive about the education they offered was that there was a broad common curriculum followed by all undergraduates, before they embarked on their professional training. The Scottish curriculum embraced classics, philosophy (logic, including the philosophy of knowledge, and ethics), English literature, the experimental sciences, and mathematics.[52] Davie also suggests that this broad-based curriculum was taught in such a way as to foster cross-fertilization between the disciplines, and that each discipline was taught so as to balance its specialist aspects with a sense of its place in the wider map of knowledge.[53]

Plenty of flaws have been noted in Davie's account. He played down the importance of religion in Scottish identity, not least because it did not altogether fit his agenda of depicting the Scottish intellect as outward-looking and cosmopolitan whereas the English was cramped and provincial. While philosophy did indeed stand at the heart of the Scottish curriculum, this ceased to be a point of contrast with the English universities in the course of the nineteenth century, for at Oxford philosophy stood at the heart of Greats (ancient history and ancient and modern philosophy) in its heyday, as it also later stood at the heart of philosophy, politics, and economics (PPE) as originally conceived. Anyone familiar with early Victorian Oxford will raise an eyebrow at the suggestion that the education it offered was 'specialist': in Bryce's time all undergraduates had to read Classical Moderations followed by Greats, and to graduate they had to follow Greats with a second school (Mathematics, Natural Sciences, Theology, or Law and History). Bryce himself sat Greats, Mathematics (as a pass school), and then Law and History.

That said, long after his glittering success at Oxford, Bryce continued to defend the distinctive merits of the Scottish system. He told his uncle in 1868 that the Glasgow course was 'much better' than the Oxford one, though English scholarship was better than Scottish.[54] Half a century later he told Gilbert Murray that he 'considered the old Scottish University course, with its seven compulsory subjects—Latin, Greek, Mathematics, Moral Philosophy, Natural Philosophy, Logic, and English—seven sound subjects and no nonsense—was the best educational training in the kingdom'.[55] In fact English was added after Bryce's time; in his autobiographical fragment he noted that as a gap, along with history, which the Scottish universities were curiously slow to take up. It seems likely that Bryce's characteristic historical-mindedness started to form at Oxford, not Glasgow. Nevertheless, when we reflect on Bryce's remarkable gift for deeply informed encyclopaedic surveys of the state of knowledge, it is hard to resist the conclusion that the Scottish academic tradition shaped him profoundly.[56]

A Sincere Voluntary at Oxford

Much as Bryce professed his attachment to the Scottish educational tradition as exemplified by Glasgow, he was keen to go on to Oxford, in spite of the obstacles that lay in his way, and even though it meant leaving Glasgow without taking his degree. That he made this choice tells us a lot about his ambition. As will become clear, he never thereafter contemplated returning to Scotland to pursue his career there.

The obstacles that stood between him and Oxford were clear. First, there was the expense. At Glasgow, fees were low and he could live at home, three miles away. Student lifestyle was economical, since most of the students were poor, some of them supporting themselves by paid work for the six months or so when there were no classes. Oxford, by contrast, was expensive, not just because of the academic fees, but because residence in college was mandatory, and college rooms and the associated lifestyle came at a price. So he would need a scholarship.

Then there was the religious question. Historically, admission to the university had been restricted to those who were willing to subscribe to the Thirty-Nine Articles of the Church of England. The test was applied both at matriculation and at graduation, whereas at Cambridge it was applied only at graduation. The Oxford University Act of 1854 had, among much else, abolished religious tests at matriculation and at graduation for the BA degree, and for other bachelors' degrees, such as the bachelor of civil law (BCL), which were second degrees. Tests remained in place, however, for higher degrees: that is, the MA and the three higher doctorates in divinity, medicine, and civil law. That was essentially because these degrees gave access to positions of authority within the university. Tests also remained in place, under the terms of the Act of Uniformity of 1662, for college fellowships and other college and university offices.

So in principle Oxford's undergraduate education was open to a non-Anglican such as Bryce, although the 1854 act did not unleash a large influx of dissenting undergraduates. While the act stipulated that 'it shall not be necessary' to take an oath or make any declaration on matriculating or on graduating, it did not explicitly require colleges to admit undergraduates without regard to confessional allegiance, and some colleges, or some heads, continued to try to exclude dissenters. There would have been no difficulty had Bryce been able to apply to Balliol, as was his preference: Balliol was academically the most distinguished college and was, moreover, the Scottish college, a connection sustained by the Snell Exhibitions for students of Glasgow University who wished to proceed to Oxford. It was also theologically liberal. But Bryce discovered, to his consternation, that candidates for the Snell Exhibitions must have been born in Scotland: he was born in Belfast and so was excluded, even though the Bryces had unimpeachably strong connections with Glasgow University.[57] Bryce absolutely needed the financial support of a scholarship or exhibition, and, aged nineteen when he had done three years at Glasgow, he felt he could not delay his entry to Oxford to try his hand at other Balliol scholarships.[58] Different colleges, however, held scholarship examinations at different times of the year. Bryce's ambitions now lighted on Trinity College, which (he was informed) then stood next to Balliol in academic seriousness.

The story of what happened next is well enough known, since it was told by Fisher, quoting extensively from Bryce's letters to his parents, written from the lodgings he had taken in Oxford while sitting the scholarship examinations. But it merits a fresh telling because it is so fundamental to Bryce's career, and an important prelude to his later struggle with religious tests at Oriel. The college had been headed since 1850 by the elderly High Churchman John Wilson (1790–1873). Having seen Bryce's baptism certificate (a requirement for all candidates) and asked about his presbyterianism, the president tried to insist on Bryce's signing a declaration of conformity and adherence to the articles and liturgy of the Church of England; but Bryce held firm and came top in the scholarship examination, and the fellows overruled the president and elected him. It was, wrote Lewis Campbell, fellow of Queen's, 'the triumph of liberalism in Oxford'.[59] But what matters here are the principles that Bryce and his family asserted.

Bryce's letters to his father are illuminating. They set out the issues: would he be required in a particular college to subscribe to the Thirty-Nine Articles? Would he be required to attend chapel? And would he be expected to receive the sacrament? Nothing of individual colleges' requirements was set out in black and white, and he had to go about gathering intelligence, or at least hearsay, on the practice of different colleges. Thus George Luke of Balliol, a Scottish Presbyterian, told him that he believed (wrongly, as it happens) that at Trinity every commoner, and even more so every scholar, must sign the articles.[60] This Bryce would not do.[61] This was not because of conscientious dissent from the articles themselves, most of which caused fewer problems for a Scottish Presbyterian than for a Tractarian. The issue was one of the *appearance* of conformity. That was a point Bryce reiterated.[62] A requirement to receive the sacrament (there was, in fact, no indication that any college had such a requirement) would probably also be a sticking point; simple attendance at chapel less so. This was because attendance at chapel was understood as 'a part of College business, like lectures or meals, in fact its principal use is as a sort of roll-call to see what men are at College'.[63] If he refused the sacrament there would be even less ground to suspect him of conforming to the Established

Church; and if he were to refuse a Trinity scholarship because of a requirement to subscribe, this would free him to take a scholarship elsewhere with no risk at all that the suspicion of conformity would fall on him.

What is striking here is the focus on perception: it was not the intrinsic meaning of an act such as attending chapel that carried weight, but its social meaning. How would his attendance at college chapel be understood, in college, in the wider university, and beyond? If its social meaning was that he was taking a full part in the life of the college, that was no problem at all, whereas if its social meaning was that of an act of conformity, that would rule it out.

Why was he concerned about the perception of conformity? Here family is crucial. He was certainly concerned about family opinion, both on this occasion and again four years later when he was weighing options for fellowship competitions.[64] But family members had no real way of knowing what the social meaning of the acceptance of a scholarship would be in Oxford. Rather, Bryce's foremost concern seems to have been with the collective honour of the family. Their religious identity was critical in shaping their family identity: 'I think it likely that if asked to sign at Trinity I shall be told it is merely a form, but to me that would not make it less wrong to do it. From the moment I heard of it, I determined not for a thousand times the honour and the money to do it. Yet surely we are eccentric, for I feel certain there is no one else in Oxford or Cambridge, & very very few in Scotland who feel as we do on this point.'[65] That he wrote in the first person plural, about how 'we' feel, is typical and very revealing. So too is the hint of reservations about the family tradition, alongside a determination to adhere to it.

Trinity College

Bryce entered Trinity the year that its new ordinances came into effect. Among other things, these removed the clerical restrictions from five of the fellowships and freed all fellowships from restrictions attached to place of birth or upbringing. It was hardly a moment of revolution. The president, John Wilson, was a high churchman who was both active in promoting the improvement of academic standards and keen to do what he could do exert his authority to defend the interests of the church as understood by the High Church party. But his authority—like that of other college heads—was clipped by the ordinances, which removed his veto over decisions of the governing body. Still, the clerical element among the fellowship remained large: larger, indeed, than in many other colleges.

Trinity had the reputation of being a college of learned high churchmen, and this was the tradition that Wilson sought to uphold. Bryce later recalled that when he arrived at the college there was not a single high churchman among the scholars, which was no doubt evidence of a generational shift among Oxford undergraduates in the decade or so after Newman's defection; but even so the church ethos at Trinity evidently remained strong.[66] In his diary for January 1858 he records 'Long and fierce discussions about K[ing] Charles the Martyr', noting that 'Almost everyone seems disposed to believe in him'. Observance of 30 January as the anniversary of the execution of Charles I had been prescribed in the Book of Common Prayer since the Restoration of 1660, though it was to be removed in 1859; it was encouraged, in particular, by the Tractarians. Bryce spoke to the dean to excuse himself from chapel on that day and arranged for a portrait of Cromwell to be sent from Glasgow so that he could hang it in his rooms. 'It is really a marvel how the English church adheres to Charles, & persists in abusing England's greatest hero. It seems to have become to them in some manner identified with their church spirit, which is certainly prodigiously strong, and seems to be abating very slowly. Even these Broad Churchmen, who hold there is no real difference between one sect and church and another, manifest it strongly. He recorded having 'had to sustain constant arguments on the character of Oliver Cromwell, whom I of course entirely admire and love'.[67] The Victorian cult of Cromwell was still in its early days, having been galvanized by Thomas Carlyle in the 1840s. It had a particular appeal to nonconformists.[68]

The career patterns of his contemporaries tend to confirm that Trinity remained more than usually churchy, as well as academically able. Of the twelve scholars in residence at the start of 1858, no fewer than eight were to become fellows of colleges: three at Trinity, two at Oriel, and one each at Brasenose, Queen's, and University College. One was Bryce; the other seven all took holy orders. Three of these became schoolmasters: one of these died young, but the other two became headmasters. The other four fellows were appointed to livings under the patronage of their college. Of the four who did not win fellowships, one was ordained and became successively a professor, an archdeacon, and a college principal; another become headmaster of a preparatory school and editor of classical texts for use in schools; another was appointed as professor of humanity (i.e., Latin) at the University of Glasgow just two years after graduation. The eighth, the younger son of a baronet, was commissioned in the Cape Mounted Riflemen and subsequently entered commerce before being declared bankrupt. This man—Hamilton Sabine

Pasley—was the only one of the scholars who did not become either a don or a schoolmaster.

There is no evidence of Bryce encountering any religious difficulties once he was at Trinity. The chapel was integral to college life: regulations made in Bryce's first term specified that divine service (mattins and evensong) would be celebrated every morning and evening in term, and for some part of each vacation. Sermons were to be preached at least twice a term; and Holy Communion was to be celebrated at least twice a term, by the president or, in his place, by the vice-president, the dean, or the senior tutor.[69] The fact that Bryce sought permission to absent himself on the Feast of Charles King and Martyr indicates that he otherwise complied with the expectation that he would attend chapel regularly; equally, however, he did not receive the sacrament, and he certainly continued to regard this as a sticking point. So much will be clear when we come to his election as fellow of Oriel.

We know more of Bryce's religious practice as an undergraduate than we do of any subsequent part of his life. In addition to college chapel, on Sundays he would often accompany a friend to church either in the city or, more commonly, in a neighbouring village: Cumnor, Eynsham, and Iffley on successive Sundays in February 1859. He thus made no special effort to avoid Anglican worship or to seek out free church alternatives, which existed, though they were sparse. On Sunday evenings he would sometimes attend Evensong in one of the colleges with a choral tradition, New College or Magdalen in particular: 'the chanting and music is splendid', he told his mother, regretting that Trinity did not have music.[70] He would often attend university sermons in the University Church of St Mary the Virgin, and he certainly went to hear the Bampton Lectures, an important annual series of theological lectures given from the pulpit of St Mary's in place of the University Sermon. In 1858 he attended the notable series of Bampton Lectures in which H. L. Mansel, the future dean of St Paul's, ingeniously constructed a defence of doctrinal orthodoxy on the foundations of Kantian metaphysics: the following year Bryce looked back on Mansel's 'magnificent displays of ability'.[71] In general, the young Bryce was forthright in his appraisal of preachers: Dr Hook, the newly appointed dean of Chichester, was 'a fine honest man'; a college sermon by Wayte was 'rather good, but deficient in closeness and force', while another by Wayte's colleague Meyrick was 'not very powerful'.[72] A. S. Farrar of Queen's preached an able university sermon on 'the beneficent distribution of pain'. Farrar had been brought up as a Wesleyan Methodist, but the Scots Presbyterian thought the sermon 'rather optimist and Kingsleian—and perhaps too rhetorical'.[73]

FIGURE 1.5. The chapel of Trinity College, Oxford. Photograph by one of Bryce's undergraduate contemporaries, Henry E. Hulton.

Bryce occupied the same rooms throughout his years at Trinity, from Michaelmas 1857 to Hilary 1862: a sitting room with a view of the Garden Quad, and a bedroom looking onto Durham quad.[74] The Garden Quad was designed by Wren, and the gardens themselves were and remain among the glories of Oxford, so Bryce's attachment to his college is understandable. A sense of his undergraduate life, and the social and intellectual networks he was starting to construct within the university, can be re-created thanks to the one diary that exists for these years, covering sparsely the Hilary Term (January–March 1858) but in much more detail the Hilary Term of the following year. His immediate social circle was within college, and more specifically among the scholars of Trinity: all those who went on to college fellowships and some of the other scholars are mentioned, but almost no other Trinity undergraduates, which reflects the social division that separated the 'reading men'—those aspiring to high honours—from those who saw the college more as a finishing school. Bryce would go for long walks, almost every day, with one of the Trinity scholars: so in one week we find him walking with Charles Eddy on Sunday, James Marshall on Monday, Edward Boyle on Tuesday, William Collett on

Wednesday, Marshall again on Thursday, Eddy on Friday—and then Dicey (Scholar of Balliol) on Saturday.[75] He would often breakfast with friends—usually though not always college friends—and often took lunch with Eddy and Marshall.

Relations with his college tutors were good. Of eleven or at most twelve fellows, three held office as tutor: Samuel Wayte, Frederick Meyrick, and North Pinder. Two others (Robert Bartlett and Robinson Ellis) were lecturers. By the standards of the time this suggests a college that took its educational work seriously. All the tutors and lecturers were in orders, except for Ellis, who would remain a layman. Wayte, who succeeded to the presidency in 1866, was an influential figure the College and, as we shall see later, in Bryce's own career, but Bryce was not intimate with him. Bryce was closest to North Pinder and Robinson Ellis, both of them young men, Pinder aged 30 and Ellis 24 in 1858. Each would occasionally join Bryce on walks; Bryce and Pinder would sometimes breakfast together; and Ellis and Bartlett would sometimes come to scholars' breakfasts.[76] The practice of inviting guests to breakfast remained with Bryce for the remainder of his life.[77]

The closest of Bryce's Trinity friends was James McCall Marshall, who went on to a fellowship at Brasenose and a career as a schoolmaster, culminating in the headmastership of Durham School and parish ministry in the Ripon diocese. Bryce would often visit him at Dulwich, where he taught as second master from 1869 to 1884.[78] Bryce kept in touch with several of the other Trinity scholars of his time. In 1873 and 1875, years for which we have reasonably complete engagement diaries, we find him lecturing at Lampeter at the invitation of his Trinity contemporary the Revd Charles Gresford Edmonds, now professor of Latin at St David's College; staying in the Leicestershire parish of Newbold Verdon as the guest of the Revd William Gordon Cole (fellow of Trinity 1859–1870), rector of this college living since 1868; and visiting the Chiltern parish of Rotherfield Greys, another Trinity living, where his former tutor North Pinder was now rector.[79]

Important as Trinity was to Bryce, some of his most enduring Oxford friendships were made beyond the college. He had a circle of close friends at Corpus Christi, including Reginald Bosworth Smith, Kenelm Digby, Henry Nettleship, and Edward Donner, but the most important friendship of all was with Dicey of Balliol. He already knew Dicey well even before Dicey was elected fellow of Trinity in 1860, and they remained lifelong friends. Dicey was a regular walking companion, and they discussed issues of contemporary politics: 'the Italian question and Bright's agitation' (5 February 1859). Dicey and

Bryce both belonged to two notable intercollegiate intellectual discussion groups: the Essay Society and Old Mortality. The former was founded back in 1853 by Charles Pearson of Exeter and others; the latter, modelled on it in some ways, was founded by a group of Balliol undergraduates (Dicey included) in 1857, and Bryce was elected a member in November 1857, his first term.[80] Bryce records a 'clear and practical essay' on 'Capital Punishment' by Dicey in February 1858, and another by T. H. Green on 'Political Idealism' the previous term. Among the dons, an important influence on this group of undergraduates was John Conington, Corpus Professor of Latin, who was a member of the Essay Society and would entertain selected members to breakfast, as in February 1859, when Bryce was invited along with T. H. Green, William Harcourt, John Addington Symonds, the chemist Augustus Vernon Harcourt, and the Regius Professor of Ecclesiastical History, A. P. Stanley, who read a paper on 'Marriage' in March 1859. Two young fellows of Balliol who were associated with this circle were the ancient historian and philosopher W. L. Newman and the future judge Charles Bowen. Bryce recorded being impressed by Conington, Newman, and Bowen: 'It was rather a fine thing then to see three such able men discussing great questions, and think of the probable future of two of them.'[81] He later remembered Conington as 'a singularly gifted and singularly amiable man.'[82] The easiness of the social relations between dons and undergraduates—in particular, between younger college fellows and scholars—was patent and was a distinctive characteristic of this period. Both Freeman and Goldwin Smith noticed, on returning to Oxford in the 1880s, that something important of the old Oxford had been weakened with the advent of married dons in significant numbers. 'The old college life is all but destroyed', wrote Freeman; in Smith's words, what was lost was an 'old, close, corporate feeling, the old intimate comradeship of men and boys.'[83]

It has to be said in this context that this was one of Oxford's homoerotic moments.[84] Among the more or less openly homosexual men in Bryce's circle were John Addington Symonds, who took an active part in the Essay Society, A. C. Swinburne, a founding member of Old Mortality, and Walter Pater, who joined Old Mortality rather later. Like Bryce, Pater and Symonds would both later join the Century Club, where many of the university men of this generation socialized once they had left Oxford. It is clear enough from Conington's relations with Symonds that he was homosexual by inclination: 'Conington was scrupulously moral and cautious', recalled Symonds. 'Yet he sympathized with romantic attachments for boys.'[85] Others of this generation who should be mentioned in this context include Arthur Sidgwick and Oscar Browning:

FIGURE 1.6. Members of the Old Mortality Society, Oxford, in 1860: Bryce, standing second from right; T. H. Green, centre; A. V. Dicey, seated second from right; Aeneas Mackay, standing on right; A. C. Swinburne, seated second from left; and T. E. Holland, seated on right.

both Cambridge men who made careers as schoolmasters before returning to college fellowships (Sidgwick's, unusually for the time, was at Oxford), and both well-known to Bryce through the Ad Eundem dining club, which Sidgwick cofounded with his two brothers. Homophilia was closely aligned with Hellenism: as Samuel Rutherford has written, 'Men such as Browning, Walter Pater, and John Addington Symonds, all very close in age to Sidgwick, couched academic and autobiographical writing about homoerotic desire squarely within a classical tradition, favoring models of same-sex desire that were age-unequal, had some pedagogic content, and emphasized distant appreciation of beauty over sexual contact.'[86] Bryce, who lacked a public school training, was not remotely homosexual, as far as we can tell; and while the men mentioned were very much part of his circle, he was not notably close to any of them.[87] Though a prize-winning Greek scholar at both Glasgow and Oxford, he was much more of a Latinist and a Romanist than a Hellenist by intellectual taste.[88] His social life as an undergraduate was necessarily homosocial: this was before the era of women's colleges, or indeed of married dons with families. But the social life he lived once he had left Oxford was strongly heterosocial, featuring frequent attendance at dance parties in London. If he married late, at fifty-one, this was not for the sake of trying earlier.

How, then, did Bryce and his contemporaries 'perform' masculinity? Bryce's undergraduate days preceded the cult of athleticism, which really gained pace from the 1870s, when sport became a principal site for the 'performance' of masculinity at Oxford and Cambridge, as indeed in the public schools.[89] He seems to have shown little interest in team games, and indeed he would later be a persistent critic of the cult of athleticism.[90] Rowing was already in vogue, and Bryce followed the fortunes of the college boat, but mostly as a spectator rather than as a participant.[91] He certainly attended to his physical prowess, joining a gym in Oxford, and reporting his 'various exercises which develop one's muscles superbly'.[92] He would later become a keen and accomplished mountaineer: this was a quintessentially manly pursuit, but of the individualistic kind, and in fact Bryce was notably encouraging to women mountaineers.[93] In the 1890s he was an early adopter of the new cult of cycling, but he almost always cycled in mixed parties, usually with Marion, his wife.

In his undergraduate days, the main outlet for his competitive instincts was the quest for university prizes and scholarships, and in this he was spectacularly successful, winning the Gaisford Prize for Greek Prose in 1860, the Gaisford Prize for Greek Verse in 1861, a Vinerian Scholarship in 1861, a Craven Scholarship in 1862, the Chancellor's Latin Essay Prize in 1862, and the Arnold Prize in History in 1863. These were in addition to his Trinity scholarship (1857) and his Oriel fellowship (1862), and firsts in Honour Moderations (1859), Greats (1861), and Law and Modern History (also 1861, the following term). This was an exceptional performance even in this most competitive of eras at Oxford. It made the pursuit of a college fellowship the obvious next step.

2

Religious Tests
and Secular Vocations

University Tests and the Voluntaryist Conscience

The extraordinary success of Bryce's undergraduate career was crowned with his election as a fellow of Oriel College in April 1862. His record of three firsts and a string of university prizes made a college fellowship a natural aspiration. Prior to the University Commissioners' reforms, fellowships carried with them one significant obligation that was a deterrent to some, even many, potential candidates: in the overwhelming majority of cases, they required their holders to proceed to holy orders within a stipulated period. Now a substantial proportion (probably a majority) of fellowships were secularized, and for Bryce's cohort a nonclerical fellowship seemed to offer benefits without any corresponding drawbacks. A fellow was not required to teach, or even to reside in Oxford beyond the first year. The only obligation was not to marry. As long as he remained single, he received a stipend of around £200 to £250, which would, in effect, give him the financial security to launch himself on a professional career: perhaps in education or the church, but alternatively at the bar or in the 'higher journalism'. The customary stipend was set at a level that was minimally sufficient for a bachelor to live a comfortable middle-class lifestyle in London.[1] This was the golden age of the 'prize fellowship', a category that now survives only at All Souls.

For Bryce, however, there was one difficulty: even lay fellowships remained subject to religious tests. The story of how he wrestled with this difficulty is even more revealing, though much less well-known, than the story of how he came to be elected Scholar of Trinity. Legal and statutory restrictions remained in place that debarred non-Anglicans from fellowships. There were no nonconformist college fellows at all, at either Oxford or Cambridge.[2] At

Cambridge, where the senior wrangler (winner of the top first in the mathematical tripos) was by custom elected fellow of his college, nonconformist senior wranglers in both 1860 and 1861 had been denied the usual progression to a fellowship.[3] Election to a fellowship might therefore reasonably be assumed to imply conformity to the Church of England, as in law it did. Fisher treats the matter cursorily, associating the difficulty merely with the provost of Oriel's stubborn attachment to ecclesiastical orthodoxy. But legally Provost Hawkins had a case. The letters Bryce wrote to his parents (none in the other direction survive for this period) are quite extraordinary, yet they do not feature in Fisher or in any other biographical study. Between 27 April 1861 (when he was preparing to sit Greats) and 21 April 1862 (the day the Oriel fellowship examination began), he wrote his father no fewer than eighteen letters dealing with the question, and his mother five. Sometimes these letters simply reported on developments, but mostly they pleaded for his father's opinion: 'I greatly wish we had come to some sort even of an approximate conclusion about fellowships' (27 April 1861); 'I am every day questioned or advised by someone or other about the matter . . . pray tell me at once what you think' (25 October 1861); 'Am I to consider that you quite give up the idea of Lincoln—owing to M.A. & the 39? You have never distinctly said so' (28 November 1861).[4]

It was not that Bryce lacked self-reliance or decisiveness. On other matters, such as the upbringing and education of his brother and sisters, he offered advice that other parents might consider verging on impertinent.[5] Rather, he had a strong sense that these were collective family decisions, in which his parents were entitled to a say. That was in part because they were decisions about his career, which would affect the extent of his financial dependence on his parents and indeed his ability to contribute (as he later would) to the family's resources.[6] But, even more important, because of the confessional significance of an Oxford college fellowship, they potentially affected the family's sense of its own religious integrity.

What was at stake? The Act of 1854, which opened the university to non-Anglican undergraduates, left untouched the religious tests attached to fellowships and other offices, and also to the higher degrees. These tests took two forms. First, the Act of Uniformity (1662) required fellows to make a declaration of conformity to the liturgy of the Church of England. Second, fellows of almost all colleges were required to proceed within a specified period to a higher degree, sometimes the MA, sometimes either the MA or a higher doctorate; and those higher degrees required the graduand to subscribe to the Thirty-Nine Articles of the Church of England.

FIGURE 2.1. James Bryce, around the time of his election as
fellow of Oriel (1862).

The questions that confronted Bryce and his family were therefore these:
first, what did the declaration of conformity imply? The difficulty in answering
this question lay in the fact that the Act of Uniformity rested on the premise
that fellows of colleges were in (or preparing for) holy orders: it was an attempt
to impose the authority of the prayer book on clergy. What did it mean for
laymen? If it meant simply a willingness to attend college chapel, that was no
more than Bryce had already been doing as an undergraduate. Or did it mean
receiving the sacrament? Did it also imply regular attendance at Anglican

places of worship when not in Oxford—something that Bryce would certainly have regarded as an imposition at this time?

Second, what did subscription to the Thirty-Nine Articles imply? Bryce, and his father, had few objections on doctrinal grounds to the content of the articles, which were, after all, primarily directed against Roman Catholicism. Still, the very fact that Tractarians who privately (or even publicly) dissented from much of the doctrinal content of the articles were happy enough to subscribe pointed to the problem. The question of subscription was not, in essence, about doctrine but about church membership. For Bryce to subscribe might be taken to imply that he was a member of the Church of England and not a Presbyterian, and that he was loathe to do. There was the additional point—although this was rarely articulated in the correspondence on this question: the very use of credal formulae as tests, especially as tests imposed by secular authority, was alien to the Bryces' religious tradition.

Third, these two questions of principle were tied up with questions of tactics and questions of career aims. That was because, whereas all colleges were in the same position as regards the obligations imposed by the Act of Uniformity, they had different rules as to the obligation for a fellow to proceed to the MA and/or a higher doctorate. Four colleges were in the frame, as due to elect to nonclerical fellowships either in Michaelmas 1861 or in the calendar year 1862. These were, in chronological order, Lincoln, Queen's, Oriel, and Balliol. Unfortunately for Bryce, the one that came first, Lincoln, also had the worst conditions as far as he was concerned, since it would require him to take his MA within two or three years, or else to resign. Ultimately he came to the conclusion that to hold a fellowship for two or three years only would be to squander much of the benefit of being elected fellow. The college that came last, Balliol, was the most desirable from Bryce's point of view: not only was it the most liberal college, and the most academically distinguished, but, crucially, it did not require fellows to proceed to a higher degree, and hence he might hold a fellowship for life, as long as he did not marry (the possibility of marriage is, curiously enough, not mentioned at all in any of this correspondence). But Bryce well knew that to sit out three fellowship competitions in order to wait for Balliol would be a big gamble. The competition at Balliol would be the stiffest of all: as he well knew, such was Balliol's domination of the class lists that a large proportion of the candidates who were considered electable in fellowship competitions were Balliol men, who would certainly compete for a fellowship at their own college and might be expected to have some advantage. A near miss at Balliol might leave him stranded, and by that time he would be well into his twenty-fifth year.

Implicit here were assumptions about career aims. Rationally, waiting for Balliol might make sense if he were set on an academic career: the work he would undertake while preparing for the fellowship examination—coaching, competing for prizes, writing—would not be wasted, and if he were successful he would have the benefit of a fellowship potentially tenable for life. Indisputably the academic life held considerable attractions for Bryce: many more than a legal career, about which he rarely spoke with any great affection. But precisely because an academic career appealed to him, he spelt out his reasons for not pursuing it with great clarity in a letter to his father in March 1862: tutorial teaching was a young man's work which would pall with time; his position as a religious outsider would be a barrier between him and his pupils; and the progression from a tutorship to schoolmastering (a common career trajectory at the time) offered limited prospects for laymen, especially non-Anglican ones. As yet the civic colleges (the nascent civic universities) did not cross his mind as options: not surprisingly, for there was really only Owens College, Manchester, which was just starting to grow after a faltering start; and of course there was University College, London. It is more striking, however, that the Scottish universities did not enter into his deliberations. So a London career it was, probably at the bar; and for that course he needed a fellowship sooner rather than later. Hence he focused on Queen's and Oriel, where he might hold a fellowship for about eight years, rather longer than the average tenure of a fellowship. The greater prestige of an Oriel fellowship clinched the decision.

What evidently complicated the decision—or, if not the ultimate decision, at least the diplomacy surrounding it—was the extreme stance, fitfully expressed, taken by Uncle John. We have hundreds of his letters to Bryce, and Bryce's to him, but none that touch on this question at this time. There certainly were some letters between the two of them dealing with the matter that have not survived, but on the whole the conversation seems to have been a triangular one, in which Uncle John would bend his brother's ear on the question, and Dr Bryce would then have to communicate these conversations to his son. Uncle John took the view that the declaration of conformity would itself constitute a betrayal of the Bryces' religious patrimony. This was never a view that would appeal to Bryce, who in his heart was determined on a fellowship; and his parents seem to have shared his view that, in the end, the declaration would do no more than describe what was in any case Bryce's practice at Trinity.

The flavour of Uncle John's interventions can best be tasted if we read Dr Bryce's letters to him on the fellowship question in August 1861. These letters sum up in great detail the way in which Bryce and his parents were thinking.

First of all, Dr Bryce firmly told his elder brother: 'you are mistaken about the state of matters in Oxford—neither James nor I would even think of his going in for a fellowship to sell our principles. He will go in as a presbyterian; the Electors knowing him to be such.'[7] He drove the message home in a fuller letter the following week. Uncle John objected to the substance of the Thirty-Nine Articles, and in particular Article 37, the article 'Of the civil magistrate', which asserted the principle of royal supremacy. Uncle John thought this lapsed into Erastianism, or the subjection of the church to the secular power, this being, to most Scottish Presbyterians (not just Voluntaryists and Secessionists), the besetting sin of the Church of England. Dr Bryce disagreed: he thought the article ambiguous rather than 'a clear assertion of Erastianism'. This was not, however, the immediate bone of contention: 'the question of signing the articles would only come up when (and if) the taking of the MA is required—at which point JB might resign his fellowship.' The Act of Uniformity was more immediately relevant:

It provides that every elected fellow shall 'conform to the Liturgy' of the E[nglish] Ch[urch]. It is not always enforced, but of course might be. The question is What does this declaration amount to? It does not imply membership, or joining in their communion, nor any approval of the doctrine or discipline of the Ch. of Eng. This I had already heard from a Fellow of Oxford, to whom I wrote for information prior to the receipt of your first letter.[8] I see it confirmed by a statement in a Patriot you sent me—that the Cambridge Univ Com[issione]rs have enacted that in future everyone elected to a fellowship shall besides signing the Act of Unif[ormity] declare himself a "bonâ fide" member of the Ch. of Eng, implying of course that the declaration of the Act of Unif does not amount to membership.[9] No such additional restriction exists in Oxford. James has examined the Act and tells me that its other clauses show that it meant originally to apply to Ministers, & to have included Fellows of Colleges, as being then almost always clergymen. This, however, is not to the purpose. Actually, I am told, this conformity promised means attendance, at least occasionally, on the services of the Ch in [meaning of?] England. This is what I meant by saying that James would have no more to do than he had been doing. To what extent the attendance is promised I can hardly say. Legally it may originally have meant habitual attendance, practically now it would not . . . prevent him from attending a Presb. place of worship in London—for as I will explain presently, we always have proposed that Jas shall intimate as much if elected—indeed I before mentioned this to you. In Oxford Jas prefers attending the Eng. ch. to the Indep[endents] or Bapt[ist]s, feeling more sympathy with the former. You ascribe very high views indeed to the latter—far higher than they put forth—they are political voluntaries—as you very well know many of our own U.P.s are.[10] The very fathers of the Secession held the Estab principle—while for years the Eng. High Ch. party have been claiming total independence of the State for their Church. But you surely know all this. To the Eng. service Jas has no objection; tho' of course neither he or I wd express approval of the system. The Act of Unif gives no such approval. As to his connection with the state—he wishes me to let you know exactly his own feeling on this point. He thinks the principle of an Estab^t wrong, but not a vital point nor one to affect attendance at the service of an Estab^t. Nor did he ever think so, though his view of the church of Eng generally may be somewhat modified by knowing more of it, he says his hesitation, when first he went to Oxford was of exactly the same nature as it is now:—it is, and then was, as to the point of honour involved. He does not feel it religiously wrong to promise conformity seeing no difference between the ch. of Eng & ourselves such as shd prevent it.—This, then, is the only rule applying in every college. The law accordingly is not what you supposed, nor apparently the same as at Cambridge. Of course Stirling's case is nothing to us—yet even in his it seems the Cambridge rules are different, and that it was to the Art[icle]s. he objected, not to the Act of Unif, which he must have known of, in any case. You mention Stirling's case in the way of a protest.[11] Such a point one wd understand were it likely to be of any use. Here it wd not—1st because anyone can say that Jas wd not have got a fellowship—a fellowship <u>necessarily follows</u> a Wranglership at Cambridge.[12] Many Oxford <u>firsts</u> never get fellowships tho' they try. 2nd because the change must come from Parl. not from Oxford, and no interest is felt in the question on the part of the country. You refer to your own case—but you know how disappointed you were years ago that no one ever took it up—it was never mentioned.

As I have told you we think that James can let it be known he is a Presbyterian—and tho' he wd conform wd not engage to give regular attendance away from Oxford, or become a <u>bonâ fide</u> member. This is a course wh in some colleges wd make his chance of election less, no matter what the result of the examination; and of course it wd be foolish to try it, in any college where there was not a prospect that the Electors would judge fairly by examination and not let his views be any obstacle. We are not quite sure how far conformity is understood to mean anything wh. such avowal would be needed to guard against; but in many ways it seems to us an open and fair course to pursue, and would leave James free, as to any claims the college might think it had on him. To us it seems that to obtain a fellowship so wd be a more useful course than to leave it untried—useful, as tending to open and liberalize the colleges, many of which are willing to do what they can. That Dissenters do not go in is because they have not the chance, they have not come to Oxford at all—and you quite mistake if you think that the question of a State church is one on which either they or the Scotch Voluntaries would make a religious stand.

That, Dr Bryce concluded, dealt with 'all the important points on which you have spoken in your letter; and I hope you will be satisfied'. He insisted that 'I am very far either from spurning your advice or wishing you not to interfere'.[13] But the tone and the substance both make it clear that there had been a serious disagreement.

Bryce opted not to stand for election either at Lincoln in December 1861 or at Queen's in January 1862, but instead to wait for the Oriel election. In both these cases, close friends of his were elected: at Lincoln, Henry Nettleship, and at Queen's, Bryce's Trinity contemporary Charles Eddy. Instead he waited on Oriel: it had greater prestige than either Lincoln or Queen's, although in truth Oriel had lost much of its academic standing; and it offered greater security for Bryce than Lincoln in particular. But whereas Lincoln had recently elected to its headship the increasingly freethinking Mark Pattison, Oriel's provost was one of the leading defenders of Anglican preeminence in the university. Edward Hawkins, born before the French Revolution, had been elected provost in preference to John Keble as long ago as 1828, ten years before Bryce was born. Hawkins had been closely associated with the theologically advanced Noetics in the 1820s, but during his prolonged headship he proved an autocratic and increasingly conservative force.[14] It is clear both from Bryce's family correspondence and from Hawkins's notes on college meetings that the provost did his utmost to prevent Bryce's election.[15]

The heart of the matter was this. Bryce was advised by Samuel Wayte, fellow and future president of Trinity, that nothing in Oriel's statutes could justify Hawkins in refusing to admit a non-Anglican as fellow: indeed, 'the phrase "member of the Ch. of England" was studiously avoided throughout the new ordinances of the Commissioners'.[16] Hawkins knew this, and he took his stand on the matter of liturgical conformity, and what it implied in terms of receiving the sacrament. Bryce told his father on 21 April that the provost, though allowing him to sit the examination, had shown him a passage in the college statutes which, he alleged, said that a fellow who did not take the sacrament could be ejected. 'This I don't believe—nor does Wayte.'[17] The provost's notes record that the College Meeting of 9 April had agreed 'that Mr Bryce (Presbyterian) might be admitted as a Candidate conforming—upon the strength of Sir J. W. Awdry's opinion'.[18] They proceed: '[and Provost then shewed him §40 of the Ordinance and told him that we had an Opinion to the effect that <u>Conformity</u> required participating in the <u>Communion</u> according to the last Rubric but one of the Communion office & that our Statutes required a present intention on the part of the Candidate to communicate, but the Provost did not require him to declare his intention upon the subject at present.]'[19]

§40 read: 'In case the Provost or any Fellow of the College shall contumaciously cease to conform to the Liturgy of the United Church of England and Ireland as by law established, such contumacious ceasing to conform shall be a cause for depriving the Provost of his Provostship, and any such Fellow of his Fellowship.'[20]

On 25 April the provost recorded Bryce's election and added the following notes:

Shall we refer the questions respecting the meaning of 'Conformity' & 'contrarian nonconformity' in the new ordinance 39.40 to the Chancellor under para 48? No.[21] Or shall an opinion of Council be taken upon them? Now agreed by the majority.

Or shall we defer the question till October?

Whose opinion? Sir J. D. Harding & Selwyn agreed.[22]

The words 'contrarian nonconformity' were Hawkins's. They do not appear in the Ordinance itself, and he might have unconsciously substituted them for 'contumacious ceasing to conform'.

We appear to have no evidence of the opinion offered by the two barristers consulted: one of them, Sir John Dorney Harding, the Queen's advocate general, suffered a breakdown in the summer of 1862 and probably never gave an opinion to his old college.[23] But the final episode occurred a year later, on the expiry of Bryce's period of probation. The provost minuted on 6 April 1863: '<u>James Bryce admitted actual Fellow</u>—(with the usual oaths & Declaration). J^s B had never partaken of the Lord's Supper at Oriel during his Probationary Year, having been advised to the contrary—"cd not receive it here at present"—This after repeated remonstrances from Provost.' He asked himself: 'Now will he take it here by & by?'[24]

The election attracted some public attention, since religious tests were a matter of public controversy. *The Spectator*—then a liberal paper—congratulated 'the College of Arnold and Whately' in vindicating 'its old reputation for freedom of thought', but it considered the election 'of unprecedented importance'. It correctly noted that Bryce was 'professedly a Presbyterian, although he has no objection to attend the services of the Church of England'. But it went on to mangle the story: 'As, unfortunately, the enactments of the University are less liberal in tone than the Provost and Fellows of Oriel, it may become a question some years hence how far Mr Bryce will be able to comply with the requirements of the Act of Uniformity.'[25] Hawkins was anything but liberal in his handling of the case, and it was primarily the college statutes rather than the 'enactments of the University' that he invoked. The Act of Uniformity, though relevant, was of less concern to Bryce than the requirement to proceed to the MA or higher doctorate and what that might imply.

Both Hawkins and Bryce were to be important contributors to the controversy about clerical and university tests as it heightened in the course of the 1860s. Hawkins addressed the subject of university tests in a pamphlet of 1866. There he noted that 'many or most of the Fellows do not comply with the law, but neglect to make the Declaration of Conformity, relying upon an annual Indemnity Act'. Hawkins suggested that it would be better if the Declaration of Conformity were required to be made at the time of admission to a fellowship, and before the person (normally the college head) admitting to the fellowship. But the following argument was still more relevant:

> But whether it be actually made or not, the intention of an Indemnity Act, if I understand it aright, is not to supersede the Law itself, but to exempt persons under certain circumstances from its penalties. A Fellow of a College as a man of honour, knowing that he has been admitted to his Fellowship under the condition of Conformity, will consider himself under the same obligation, whether he has or has not actually made the required Declaration to that effect.

Without giving the source, he directly quoted the words of the Oriel ordinance:

> But religion in this place is that of the Church of England. Divine Service in our Colleges is to be performed under the same ordinances, 'according to the Liturgy of the United Church of England and Ireland'. Contumaciously ceasing to conform to that Liturgy is to be 'a cause for depriving a Fellow of his Fellowship'.[26]

Not surprisingly, Bryce only really started to be attached to Oriel when Hawkins, at the end of 1874, went into effective retirement at Rochester Cathedral, where he held a canonry that was attached to his provostship.

Hawkins was not alone in continuing to gnaw away at the issues involved in the Oriel election. So did Uncle John. Not all the correspondence with his nephew in the mid-1860s survives, but we have enough to reconstruct some important exchanges. When Bryce took his BCL at the appointed time in 1865, he casually mentioned that he was in Oxford to take a degree. Was he deliberately winding his uncle up? If so, he succeeded: 'Was it M.A.? If so, how did you manage with them about subscription?'[27] At around the same time, Bryce published (anonymously, as was the custom) an article in the (nonconformist) *North British Review* on the question of religious tests in the English universities.[28] Uncle John gave his opinion:

> The only hesitation I have about advising the reprinting is my high opinion of the ability with which it is written. You know that I disapprove very strongly of the morality of one part of it; & therefore, the abler it is as a whole, the more mischief will flow from the prestige which its intellectual power in the other parts displayed, will give it. If you wd rectify that to me most painful passage, I wd recommend its separate publication with all my heart.[29]

What was the morality of which Uncle John very strongly disapproved? He is not explicit, but if we read Bryce's article in conjunction with the correspondence among the Bryce family about the fellowship question it is easy enough to identify the section of the article he must have had in mind. An important element in Bryce's argument was that tests were self-defeating. While the tests did indeed keep some people away from the university altogether, or deter them from competing for fellowships, in a greater number of cases the effect was simply to make the test into a meaningless formality. Nobody could be blamed, Bryce suggested, for subscribing in order to be eligible for emoluments for which they were morally entitled to compete. 'To call such men dishonest or unscrupulous because they subscribe, would be eminently unjust. They act for what they believe to be the best, and choose of two evils that which seems the lesser.'[30]

Uncle John certainly regarded that as a piece of casuistry, and he also thought it accurately described the position Bryce was in as a dissenter who held a college fellowship. Never one to hold back from saying what he thought, he told his nephew: 'every man who refuses to be a martyr is a traitor, but it is very hard to say so or think so of a good-natured, warm-hearted, genial fellow whose conversation over a glass of wine or a cup of coffee one enjoys immensely, and who, in every other act of his life seems an honourable and high-principled man.'[31]

Curiously, Bryce declares in the article, as if stating a straightforward fact, that 'the Nonconformists, the great majority of whom might sign the Articles as honestly as an Anglican, are unable to declare their conformity to the Liturgy, since that would be tantamount to forsaking the religious community in which they have been brought up. Practically, many of them probably would conform, but when it is thus put to them it becomes a point of honour to refuse.'[32] This echoes the kind of language Bryce used in his letters to his parents, and indeed the arguments he was thinking out loud: except that he concluded that conformity to the liturgy was not, for him, a stumbling-block.[33]

Considered as a whole, however, the article was squarely in line with voluntaryist principles. In particular, Bryce drew a sharp distinction between the sphere of the university and that of the church:

The object for which the Church exists is to preserve and teach religious truth; and if that truth takes a dogmatic form, creeds and formularies of doctrine may be a necessary part of the ecclesiastical system, since it is by them that her teaching is shaped. But the objects for which the University exists are education and learning, the training of the human mind, and the advancement of human knowledge: objects quite distinct from the enforcement of dogmatic truth, distinct even from the formation of a moral and religious character. It may indeed be said that the great aim of all education is to make men better, and that for this religious teaching and even religious dogma are indispensable. True, but it does not therefore follow that the training of the intellect and the moulding of the heart are indissolubly connected, and should be done by the same persons in the same way. As a matter of fact, we see that they are quite distinct. They appeal to different parts of our nature. The capacity for receiving the one is frequently out of all proportion to that for the other: so also is the capacity for teaching them. Strictly speaking, religion cannot be taught at all; and so far as it can be, should be taught first at home, and afterwards by the Church, whose peculiar function it is do so. Intellectual education not only can, but must be and is pursued quite apart from theology, in a religious spirit, no doubt, but without reference to doctrine. To mix up the teaching of religious dogma with the teaching of Latin and Greek, of the natural sciences, of jurisprudence and logic, even of history and metaphysics, would pervert and impede all these studies, while it made religion itself ridiculous.[34]

This is a really interesting and important passage. This conception of the relationship between education and religion was by no means generally shared in Victorian Britain, even among those who shared Bryce's politics. Gladstone took the Tractarian view that the primary aim of education must be religious.[35] The Whig-Liberals and the Liberal Anglicans (overlapping but not identical categories), who differed with Gladstone on most religious matters, agreed with him that religion and education were interconnected and that education should cultivate true religion.[36] They differed from Gladstone in that they tended to conflate true religion with morality, whereas he tended to conflate it with right doctrine—a quite fundamental difference, as Jonathan Parry has demonstrated.[37] Many leading nonconformists were voluntaryists on education, which meant that they opposed state aid to elementary schools on the basis that existing schools were denominational and mostly Anglican. But the idea that the objects of religion and education were radically distinct—or, to put it differently, that religious education could be wholly separated from secular education—was a position that the United Presbyterians made distinctively their own. 'It is not within the province of Civil Government to provide for the *religious* instruction of the subject, and . . . this Department of the Education of the young belongs exclusively to the Parent and the Church.' So declaimed the United Presbyterian Church at its founding in 1847, and so it reiterated half a century later in opposing the Voluntary Schools (England) Bill, 1897.[38] A radical opposition to state support for religion implied a radical separation of secular from religious education, and hence a 'low' conception of the objects of secular education: low not in the sense that secular education was unimportant, but rather in the sense that it could not be expected to fulfil religious purposes.

Oriel in Bryce's Time

The college into whose fellowship Bryce was elected in 1862 was a compact one, though by no means small by the standards of the time. The governing body consisted of a provost and fifteen fellows, and there were around seventy undergraduates. It was presided over by Dr Edward Hawkins, who had occupied the provostship since 1827. Astonishingly enough, Hawkins would remain in office until his death a full two decades after Bryce's election. The fellowship in many ways embodied an Oxford in transition. Four of Bryce's colleagues would retain their fellowships until death; another, David Monro, would be elected to the provostship in 1882 and remain there until his death. But only five fellows were in holy orders (the minimum allowed by the ordinance of 1857), which made the common room more secular than most: strikingly so, for a college famed as the birthplace of Tractarianism. At neighbouring Corpus Christi, ten fellows out of twenty were ordained; across the High Street, seven out of ten fellows at Lincoln and all twelve at Brasenose.[39]

At the beginning of the nineteenth century, during the headships of John Eveleigh and Edward Copleston, Oriel had ascended to academic primacy in the university, and in the era of the theologically liberal Noetics in the 1820s an Oriel fellowship was prized almost above any other distinction in Oxford.[40] That was no longer the case, but it was still a common room of some eminence, not least because the college retained a preference for competitive election, which meant that almost all the fellows were elected from other colleges, though not from outside Oxford. They included Charles Neate, the senior fellow, elected from Lincoln College the year after Hawkins succeeded to the provostship: a layman and (of course) unmarried, he died in 1879 after over half a century as a fellow. When Bryce arrived, Neate had just completed a five-year stint as Drummond Professor of Political Economy; a year later, he would be elected Liberal MP for the borough of Oxford. Other notable colleagues included J. W. Burgon, future dean of Chichester, a traditionalist High Churchman whose Newdigate Prize poem portrayed Petra in Jordan as 'A rose-red city half as old as time'. Charles Henry Pearson, a fellow since 1854, was an ambitious historian, professor at King's College, London; but from 1864 he held his fellowship in plurality with a farm in South Australia which he cultivated industriously. He contributed a defence of Australian institutions to *Essays on Reform*, the 1867 manifesto of the academic liberals, to which Bryce was another notable contributor. Pearson married in South Australia in 1872, so vacating his fellowship. A. G. Butler, brother-in-law of Josephine Butler, was the first and notably successful headmaster of Haileybury, before returning to Oriel, where he was mentor to the young Cecil Rhodes.[41] He was in Anglican orders, as most public school headmasters of the time were, and this seems to have counted against him in the provostship election of 1882, for after their experience with Hawkins, the fellows were keen to exercise their newly acquired right to elect a layman. The successful candidate on that occasion, David Monro, was the closest to Bryce and probably the nearest thing to an academic of the modern type. A Homer scholar, he was, with Bryce, one of the original fellows of the British Academy at its foundation in 1902.[42]

All held their fellowships on condition of celibacy, a requirement that had been reasserted by the ordinance of 1857. There were occasional ways around that: Drummond Chase, fellow since 1842, was appointed principal of St Mary Hall in 1857, under an agreement that upon his death the hall, which had historically close connections with Oriel, would become its property. He, like other heads, was permitted to marry, and the college reelected him to his fellowship. Similarly, it had been established by the commissioners giving effect to the University of Oxford Act of 1854 that the Regius Professorship of Modern History would be held in conjunction with a professor-fellowship (initially the only one) at Oriel; since professors were free to marry, it was held that a professor-fellowship was not subject to the celibacy requirement. William Stubbs, who was married, was duly elected by the college on appointment to the chair in 1866.

Since 1857 no fellowship had been subject to clerical restrictions, as long as the threshold of five clerical fellows was achieved. That made it possible for Bryce, a layman, to be elected. But the celibacy requirement meant that a fellowship was not straightforwardly a route into an academic career, and Bryce himself seems to have ruled out this option at an early stage. He lived in college in his probationary year, as he was required to do; but once that year was over he never lived in Oxford again.[43] He moved briefly to Heidelberg, where he studied with the great Roman lawyer Vangerow and worked on his book on the Holy Roman Empire, and then settled in London, where he read for the bar as a member of Lincoln's Inn. But he retained his fellowship until July 1890, the first anniversary of his marriage, and on his resignation he was elected professor-fellow by virtue of his tenure of the Regius Professorship of Civil Law, which he had held for twenty years. When he finally resigned that chair in 1893 and his fellowship therefore lapsed, the college elected him honorary fellow. So the relationship with the college continued uninterrupted for almost sixty years.

Early in his Oriel years Bryce was sharply critical of the college in much of his private correspondence. Shortly after his election he told his father that 'the fellows of Oriel in residence are not at all a remarkable set of men—the fame of the body rests much more on its non-residents—and more I think on previous ones than on the present generation.'[44] Writing to his father again in 1867, when his brother Annan expressed a desire to go to Oxford, Bryce remarked that 'he does not seem to know that there is all the difference in the world between a good college and a bad one. In Oriel, for instance, which belongs to the latter class, he would have had no society worth having, and not much tuition of a high order.'[45] No doubt these remarks reflected something of the tensions that harmed the college while Hawkins remained in office;

when he retreated to Rochester in 1874, Bryce's opinion of the college improved, and his later relations with his colleagues and with the college as an institution were warm. Three successive provosts—Munro, Shadwell, and Phelps—were good friends of his.

University Liberalism

There was, in fact, a curious dénouement to the story of Bryce's election at Oriel. Inevitably, it was not straightforward. Bryce had explained to his parents that at Oriel he could keep his fellowship for eight years before having to take a higher degree (MA or DCL) and to subscribe to the Thirty-Nine Articles. In fact that was an abridgement of a complex set of rules. Had he wished to proceed to Master of Arts and not to a higher doctorate, he would have had to do so by the thirty-third term from his matriculation, that is, by the summer of 1865. That would have given him only three years or so in his fellowship. But to take the Doctorate of Civil Law he would first have to take the BCL degree, also by the summer of 1865, and then to proceed to the doctorate within six years of the date of conferment of the BCL. It was only the DCL and not the BCL that required subscription to the articles, so this was a preferable course for Bryce. He took the BCL (as we have seen) in February 1865, which meant that he was *eligible* to take the DCL from February 1870 and *required* to take it by February 1871.[46]

Quite what Bryce proposed to do once the period had elapsed is unclear. But the rules were by no means pellucid, and it was certainly not unknown for a college fellow, through oversight, to fail to meet the statutory requirement to proceed to a higher degree. The Oriel ordinances wisely gave the provost the power to grant an additional year. Probably Bryce intended to sit tight and wait for the college to move against him: the provost would no doubt have wanted to do this, though he might have struggled to get the support of the fellows. But in the event this was not necessary. In April 1870—eight years to the month from his election at Oriel—Bryce was appointed by Gladstone to the Regius Professorship of Civil Law.[47] It was striking, at a time when university and college offices were still subject to the Act of Uniformity, that the Crown should offer an appointment of such prestige to Oxford's most prominent free churchman, but what were the implications for Bryce's dilemma?[48] The professorship did not then, as it did after Bryce, carry a college fellowship with it as a matter of course, so in that sense it did not resolve the matter; nor (as we shall see) was the salary sufficient to dispense with the need for the fellowship stipend. But it did raise the possibility—a legally contestable one—that, should Bryce's fellowship be held to have been forfeited, it might be possible for the college to elect him to a professor fellowship.[49] But that too was not necessary. For in the wake of his appointment to the Regius Professorship, the degree of Doctor of Civil Law was conferred on him by decree of Convocation. This was the standard way in which an Oxford degree (usually MA) was conferred on (for example) a newly elected professor who was not an Oxford graduate, nor able to 'incorporate' a degree from Cambridge or Dublin.[50] Probably this was the result of some behind-the-scenes negotiation, and it was clearly expedient, for one of his duties as Regius Professor would be to examine any candidates for the DCL. We have to assume that Bryce was not asked to subscribe to the Thirty-Nine Articles, for otherwise he could have had the degree conferred in Congregation in the usual way. He never did proceed to the MA, even though the Universities Tests Act abolished the subscription requirement the following year.[51]

This act was the product of a political struggle that was Bryce's first real involvement in a political campaign. By family tradition Bryce was firmly Liberal; and Scottish burgh politics was overwhelmingly Liberal during the time he was growing up in Glasgow.[52] There was never any question of his own political identity, but his Liberal, indeed Radical, sympathies were surely cemented by his struggles with the confessional university in 1857 and 1862. Conflicts over the relations between church and state stood at the heart of the political battles of the time, and Bryce's generation was one in which political liberalism was in the ascendancy at Oxford and Cambridge.[53] He certainly emerged from the Oriel experience not just as a convinced Liberal but as a politically active one.

It happened that Bryce's election at Oriel coincided with the moment when academic conservatives at Oxford, led by Dr Pusey, were becoming better organized, and, as a consequence, liberals were losing confidence in their ability to open up the university through purely internal reform. Further legislative intervention would be necessary, not least because one of the surviving tests, the Act of Uniformity, by definition could not be removed by the university alone. So Oxford liberals looked to parliamentary Liberals as their saviours; but at the same time they knew that the parliamentary struggle would be a difficult one and could probably be won only with extra-parliamentary backing.

Bryce was active in this campaign, both in drafting bills and in helping to organize the extra-parliamentary agitation. He was also, intriguingly, the subject of debate. Nobody mentioned him by name, but his case was certainly referred to in the Commons. In June 1865, leading the debate on his Tests Abolition (Oxford) Bill, George Goschen noted that while for most Oxford graduates the acquisition of the letters 'MA' were of little consequence, beyond conferring the parliamentary franchise, the case was different for those seeking an academic career (he did not quite use those words):

> But to remain permanently at Oxford, and to take part in that Oxford life which begins, strictly speaking, after the career of the undergraduate is past, it is necessary either to proceed to the higher academical degree, or to incur that odium of nonconformity or eccentricity so often fatal to later prospects no less than to present comfort. I know a case in point at this moment. A Scotch Presbyterian, highly distinguished in Oxford examinations, who as a Bachelor of Arts has been most useful to his college, must, by the rules of that college, proceed to the higher degree of Master of Arts. He holds a fellowship now, but this fellowship must be vacated, and his position in the University be abandoned, if he does not sign the Thirty-nine Articles and the 36th Canon, now, after being a fellow of his college for several years. I ask the House, is this a grievance, or is it not? And is it a grievance to that individual only, and not rather to that important section of the country to which he belongs?[54]

What was worse was that an opponent of the bill, Joseph Henley, a Tory MP for Oxfordshire, picked up on this reference and asked, pointedly, about 'the case of the unfortunate Presbyterian gentleman' who would be forced to give up his 'educational course' once the time to take the MA arrived. 'How was it that the Act of Uniformity did not keep that gentleman out of College altogether?'[55]

Bryce told his father that he could not be sure that he was the case in point, but surely he must have known, since he certainly knew of all the junior fellows who were of an age to proceed to the MA and must have been perfectly aware that there were no other Scottish Presbyterians among them.[56] If we ask how his case had become sufficiently well-known to be raised in Parliament, the clue may be found elsewhere in the same debate. Goschen was himself an Oriel man, and, more important, another speaker in favour of the bill was the recently elected Liberal member for the City of Oxford, none other than Charles Neate, fellow of Oriel. If Neate was indeed Goschen's informant, it is interesting that he seems not to have been aware, as Bryce must have been by now, that he could at least defer the parting of the ways by taking the BCL now and the DCL in five or six years.

The Faith of an Academic Liberal

What do we know of Bryce's mature religious thought? He was always reticent on the subject, and his biographers from Fisher onward have mimicked that reticence. But the subject matters, for Christian morality was fundamental to his politics; increasingly so as he saw that morality eroded in the early twentieth century. His widow wrote that 'He had a strong Puritan inheritance in his blood which remained with him throughout life, but it took the form of moral tests & standards, & not creeds or theology'.[57] That interpretation was echoed in the tribute at Bryce's memorial service by Ernest Barnes, canon of Westminster Abbey, and later bishop of Birmingham. Barnes noted that religion held 'a foremost place' among Bryce's 'varied enthusiasms'. He remained a faithful Presbyterian, though he often attended Anglican services, especially at the Abbey, and, as 'a typical Scotsman', he enjoyed a good sermon.[58] Certainly he could write with critical acumen about sermons and preachers: the Anglican Bishop Wilberforce and Dr Candlish of the Free Church of Scotland; the evangelical Charles Spurgeon and the Puseyite Henry Liddon; and, among Americans, the Congregationalist Henry Ward Beecher and (a particular favourite) Dr Phillips Brooks of the Episcopal Church.[59] Bryce was, said Barnes, 'a modern Evangelical' in his theological outlook: modern, because he was acutely aware of the impact that modern science and critical scholarship must have on religion; but evangelical, because he saw the absurdity in the Catholic claim to doctrinal infallibility, and also because there was in him 'a certain moral austerity'. While he appreciated that there could be no institutional Christianity without dogma, he never confused dogma with true religion.[60] He was most drawn to those churchmen, such as Phillips Brooks, who stood above denominational and doctrinal divisions. Brooks's sermons dwelt on a passage of scripture as 'an expression of ethical truth', and as a preacher he seemed 'to belong equally to all the churches, or rather to that Catholic congregation of Christian men dispersed throughout the world which is above them all'.[61]

Family correspondence sheds some more light on Bryce's mature religious position. First, it seems that on Bryce's twenty-first birthday, in May 1859, his father wrote to him concerning his 'adopting a decided course of religious profession'. The letter itself does not survive: we know about it only because Dr Bryce alluded to it in a letter to his brother. His son's reply does not touch this topic. This leaves us somewhat in the dark as to what Dr Bryce may have meant by this expression.[62] Conceivably it indicates a family wish that Bryce might follow his grandfather and uncle into the ordained ministry: if so, it is striking that the subject appears not to have been mentioned again. In May 1869 we find Bryce responding to a letter from his mother (again, a letter that does not survive) in which she had regretted that there was such divergence between their religious views. It pained him to think that this was his mother's impression, and he set out to reassure her, but in a way that gives us a sense of why Mrs Bryce thought her son heterodox:

> Some divergence there is, I fear, but (as I once said nearly three years ago) it is more in expression than in substance. It would be impossible to explain in a letter how this is; nor indeed, unhappily, am I quite sure what I do think: things seem so difficult & perplexed. But you will believe that I have earnestly wished and striven to cling to the beliefs I was brought up in; and even if I find the form of some of them unsuited to the conceptions one must form of the Divinity and his relations to his creatures, I do trust nevertheless to have preserved faith in the infinite importance of Christ the Son of God's life and death. How far I am from realizing all that that ought to mean, or living in the sense of it, and succeeding in carrying out even the smallest of his precepts, I am painfully conscious: it is only at rare moments that one seems to catch a glimpse of the effect these truths ought to have upon one's duty to others and on purity and elevation in the life of the soul. But you will believe that, however vaguely I can express what I mean, I am at heart really in unison with you and all those others whom I love best, Papa & Uncle John & Uncle William and Aunt Lizzie, whose example as well as whose teachings have been so precious to me, the greatest blessing any one can receive from God in this life. And you know it is at least not any love for this world & its pleasures (wh have long seemed to me empty and miserable) that keeps me back; it would be the intensest relief to feel more sure of what wd make a dreary present more tolerable.[63]

The only other glimpse we get of tensions between parents and son on religious questions comes from an episode in 1874, when Dr and Mrs Bryce were upset to read that their son subscribed to a monument to Spinoza, to be erected in The Hague. Again, Mrs Bryce's letter does not survive, but her son's does, along with one to his father. Bryce wrote to defend his position, arguing that the monument acknowledged Spinoza's philosophical eminence and did not in the least imply acceptance of his religious opinions, which were in any case those of one raised in the Jewish faith:

Why in the world shd it be supposed that subscribing to the monument to a great man of the past implies any approval of his religious opinions? Spinoza was one of the greatest philosophers who ever lived, and certainly deserves a monument. He never was a Christian, but a Jew; and so far as I know, he never attacked Xty in any way. It is not of his religious opinions that we think when he is mentioned, but of his metaphysical genius. . . . I do not at all complain of your writing to me about it, but am heartily and deeply sorry for the way Papa seems from what you say to have taken it. If I cd have dreamt he wd have so taken it, I wd have declined to join, but cannot see that it was possible for one to imagine that any such meaning wd be attached to it. As for a constituency, I don't care at all: if a man is to live under the fear of having innocent acts turned against him, better keep out of public life altogether. For your annoyance I care a great deal, but must continue to think that it has no real ground, and believe you will think so too when you understand what my view of the matter (and as I believe the view of the world in general so far as it attends to the matter) is.[64]

This was on the eve of the dissolution of Parliament (26 January), and Dr Bryce was evidently concerned that a hint of religious heterodoxy would hamper his son's chance of selection. Bryce told his father (who by this time had calmed down a little) that Spinoza's name did not have the significance he (Dr Bryce) attributed to it. 'That he was an atheist, in the proper sense of the term, I should not have thought—but I have not read him sufficiently to judge. Certainly however he is not, now, chiefly known & thought of as an advocate of any anti-theistic views—but simply as a great metaphysician.' In any case, the published list of subscribers to the memorial expressly declared that subscription should not be taken to imply any expression of opinion as to Spinoza's philosophical views.[65]

Spinoza had, in fact, usually been regarded as the personification of atheism in the eighteenth century: this was what William Warburton in 1738 called 'the impious phantasm of *Spinozism*'. By end of the century he was starting to be reappraised: the German poet Novalis called him a 'God-intoxicated man', and Goethe endorsed this rediscovery. In nineteenth-century Britain there was a major revival of interest in and indeed enthusiasm for the Dutch philosopher: in the first place among the *Westminster Review* circle, George Henry Lewes and George Eliot in the lead. But other protagonists in the Spinoza cult included Coleridge and the Unitarian divine James Martineau, so his appeal was eclectic. What seems clear is that Dr Bryce, enlightened as he was in many ways, was articulating a rather outdated and stereotyped view of Spinoza, whereas Bryce, whether or not he took part in the Spinoza cult, was inclined to regard him historically. The disagreement at least points to an important generational divide, as well as to Bryce's antipathy for dogmatic constraints on freedom of inquiry.

We know that he appreciated liturgical music, and that as an Oxford undergraduate and later he often went to evensong at New College or sometimes Magdalen—two chapels with strong musical traditions: 'the chanting and music is splendid. I wish very much we had music in our own chapel.'[66] The quality of the music was something he often noted when visiting churches overseas: in Cologne Cathedral, for instance.[67] But when he went to Pontifical High Mass for Christmas at St Peter's, Rome, we find the Protestant speaking:

> As a spectacle nothing could be more perfect; the building, the gorgeous robes, superbly various, the rites, the music, the incense rising in odorous clouds, all was the result of the most perfect taste and skill excited for many centuries in choosing from and embellishing the ancient customs of the church; and all equally fitted to impress the senses. But it was very little more than a spectacle. The choir sang splendidly, but the people did not join: they all, save here and there a German or English Protestant knelt when the host was elevated by the pope, but there was no rational and intelligent participation in the worship, plenty indeed of devotional feeling, but a devotion which is rather of the senses than the intellect, and seems to have little or no influence on their conduct.[68]

Still more striking than his critique of the Roman liturgy for its lack of 'rational and intelligent participation', however, was his critique of the temporal power of the papacy, 'this gaudy ostentation of being secular princes', 'the great slur upon Catholicism here'. This was a recurrent theme in his notes and letters from his visit to Rome. 'Everything in Rome and the papal provinces generally witnesses to the debasing and enslaving character of ecclesiastical rule. The city is horribly dirty and ill drained, there are no manufactures, agriculture languishes, the police are powerless except for the annoyance of travellers; the people detest their government.' Still more important, the intermingling of spiritual and temporal powers did nothing for religion, except superficially. 'Everything wears the guise of religion, but it is a religion which has little or nothing to do with morality and is rejected or accepted in a very modified sense by all the more intelligent.'[69] The identification of true religion with morality is important here; combined with the dismissal of religion that could not appeal to the intelligence, it confirms Ernest Barnes's depiction of him as a modern Evangelical. Curiously, he told his father that in advance of the visit to Rome he thought it might turn him Catholic. But in fact his verdict was withering:

> The worship of modern Italy, so far as one can judge from the outside, is paganism, and a paganism unredeemed by the virtues of the ancients, a paganism which is superstition without faith, and sceptical without philosophy. That an Anglican however should be made a Catholic by coming to Rome one can well understand, seeing indeed that no man can logically be an Anglican at all, but must either trust himself far more boldly to the conclusions of human reason, as Protestantism in its genuine forms does, or else fling himself with eyes tight shut, into the bosom of an infallible church. Indeed the wonder is that more Anglicans don't take the latter alternative. Speaking generally, one could say that Rome, if it impressed men's religion at all, would make of the strong sceptics, and Catholics only of the weak.[70]

That was a stance to which Bryce continued to adhere into old age. 'You know that there is no one who dislikes the political action of the Roman Church and in a sense even fears it more than I do', he wrote to Dicey in 1913.[71]

There is an important glimpse into Bryce's religious thinking in a letter from his publisher, Alexander Macmillan, in 1866. Macmillan was writing to Bryce about the second edition of *The Holy Roman Empire*, which appeared later that year. Bryce had clearly mentioned the subject of *Ecce Homo*, the life of Jesus published by Macmillan late in 1865. This anonymous book caused a huge religious controversy, since in foregrounding Christ's humanity it seemed to play down his divinity. It was, said the Evangelical Lord Shaftesbury, 'the most pestilential book ever vomited from the jaws of Hell'.[72] But it was also widely admired in Bryce's circle, not least by his mentors, Goldwin Smith and A. P. Stanley.[73] The violence of the response encouraged fevered speculation as to its authorship. Bryce clearly joined in this speculation, putting to Macmillan the widely canvassed view that Goldwin Smith must be the author.[74] Macmillan replied: 'Goldwin Smith is certainly not the author of "Ecce Homo."' Shall I tell you. When it came to me anonymously—as it did at first, and I had read it throughly I guessed to be yours. I don't think I could have guessed G.S.'

Frustratingly, although the Macmillan archive in the British Library contains a huge cache of letters from Bryce, the crucial ones he wrote on this subject are missing. So we do not know how he responded to the notion that Macmillan had thought he might be the author. But he was evidently an admirer: 'I am glad you like "Ecce Homo"', Macmillan wrote in his next letter. 'Can't you review it in the <u>Times</u>—or somewhere else—say a Glasgow or Edinburgh paper.' As far as we know, Bryce did not do so, but not out of want of inclination: 'I should like very much to write something about it, that is—in six weeks' time, for now I have not a moment. I have not the entrée of the Times—or that would be best. The Glasgow papers are all wretched—as to Edinburgh I may enquire. There are one or two things I should particularly like to say about Ecce Homo. The Saturday objects to theology or I would try there.'[75]

The author was not Bryce, of course, but John Robert Seeley, then a little-known young Cambridge graduate who had recently taken up the Chair of Latin at University College, London, though he would achieve fame as a modern historian, author of *The Expansion of England*, and Regius Professor at Cambridge. But it tells us something about Bryce that he admired the book, and also that Macmillan thought he might be the author. Because he did not in the event write the review he discussed with Macmillan, there is little direct evidence of Bryce's opinion of the book. His Oxford friend Henry Nettleship, a fellow of Lincoln, wrote in February that the chief excitement in common room had been about *Ecce Homo*—'very cleverly written, & the man has a hold of ethics'. But Nettleship evidently did not think of Bryce as a possible author: 'The man I should think is a rather refined Millite, who sometimes nearly rises into spirituality.'[76] One can hardly speculate without evidence as to what the 'one or two things' Bryce would have liked to say about the book were; but, still, the message of the book was straightforward enough, and it aligned with one of his central convictions. Seeley argued that Christ taught a system of positive morality, and that this was the essence of Christianity. There was a 'Christian moral reformation' in which the 'feeling of humanity' was transformed from 'a feeble restraining power' into 'an inspiring passion'.[77] That constitutes a fine summary of Bryce's mature faith.

3

The Making of the Historian

THE HOLY ROMAN EMPIRE AND AFTER

IN 1850 THE UNIVERSITY OF OXFORD received half the proceeds of a subscription in memory of the late Dr Thomas Arnold, Regius Professor of Modern History at Oxford and headmaster of Rugby School. It used the funds to endow the Arnold Historical Essay Prize, to be awarded annually, alternately in ancient and modern history. The subject was to be decided by the judges, the Regius Professor of Modern History, the Regius Professor of Ecclesiastical History, and the Camden Professor of Ancient History. In the Hilary term 1862—some months before Bryce's election at Oriel—the judges announced the subject of the following year's competition: the Holy Roman Empire. As an accomplished university prize-winner, and one of four first classes on the most recent class list published by the examiners in law and modern history, Bryce must have known that he stood a good chance of winning the prize, worth £42. Robert Wright—elected fellow of Oriel a year before Bryce—was the prize-winner in 1862. Two years before that, the winner was Dicey.

Bryce was duly awarded the prize a year later, and he read from it in June at Encaenia, the university's annual commemoration. The Chancellor's English Essay read on the same occasion was John Addington Symonds's on 'The Renaissance', so this must count as one of the more notable of prize-lists, judged in terms of its literary fruits.[1] It was a requirement that the winning essay should appear in print, and Bryce published a revised and extended version with Macmillan, in conjunction with the Oxford publisher, Thomas Shrimpton, in October 1864, thus launching his enduring relationship with Macmillan, who published practically all his books.[2] *The Holy Roman Empire* very quickly established Bryce's academic and literary reputation. He produced a substantially revised and extended edition in 1866, and thereafter the book remained in print throughout his lifetime and for decades afterwards, with new editions in 1871, 1873, 1875, 1876, 1884, 1887, 1904, and 1913, many of them incorporating substantive changes or additions. Thus the fourth edition (1873) included a new supplementary chapter on 'The New German Empire', appearing *after* the conclusion; while the 1904 edition included a new chapter on the eastern empire.[3] It was well-known in continental Europe, thanks to translations into German (Arthur Winckler, 1873), Italian (Count Ugo Balzani, 1886), French (Emile Domergue, 1890, with a preface by Ernest Lavisse), Russian (Dmity Petrushevskii, 1891), and Hungarian (Armin Balogh, 1903). It rapidly came to be regarded as a classic, and many thought it the best of Bryce's books. The greatest of students of historiography, Arnaldo Momigliano, called it 'one of the seminal books of the historiography of the nineteenth century'.[4] Yet it has received practically no sustained attention in modern scholarship.[5]

What was it about Bryce's book that made it a classic? A cussed reviewer in the *Spectator* thought it 'over full of facts and dates', but in reality it differs from most of Bryce's other books in that it was not intended to convey 'facts'.[6] Instead it was driven by one big idea, the idea that for medieval Europe the Roman Empire still existed and endured because it was indestructible. As Bryce saw it, the Holy Roman Empire, finally extinguished by Napoleon in 1806, was an institution—literally 'the oldest political institution in the world'—which linked the first century with the nineteenth. The chronological span was so vast that there was patently no possibility of tracing its course at all closely. Instead, Bryce opted to dwell 'on the inner nature of the Empire'.[7] He analysed this in terms of political theory, or what we might call conceptual history—what did 'empire' mean to people in the past? He also analysed it in terms of its heritage, and in particular its fusion of Roman and Teutonic elements.

Bryce wrote the book because he had won the Arnold Prize, and he entered the prize because it was the natural course for a junior fellow in his position, especially one who was starting to identify himself as an historian. And the subject of the essay was set for him. To that extent, Bryce's agency was limited. But the Holy Roman Empire suited him perfectly. The subject had grandeur, for a start. As he reflected on submitting the essay, 'Of course one felt excessively disgusted at having to put on paper and send in anything so trivial and mean on so immense and noble a subject; except that its very grandeur was a sort of consolation, since one could never have hoped to have been adequate in any case.'[8]

Bryce, Freeman, and the Holy Roman Empire

Bryce's most important interlocutor on the subject of the Holy Roman Empire was Edward Augustus Freeman, the medieval historian. Like Bryce, Freeman was a Trinity man, having been a scholar and a fellow in the 1840s, when he fell deeply under Tractarian influence, from which he subsequently retreated. He spent most of his career as an independent scholar living near Wells in Somerset, thanks to a private income supplemented by income from journalism and authorship.[9] He was proud to call himself a 'Zummerzet freeholder'. It was only in 1884 that he finally received academic preferment and returned to Oxford as Regius Professor, a role that came to him too late, and in which he was largely ineffective. When Bryce met him he was known chiefly for his famously robust reviewing for the *Saturday Review*, which specialized in the genre; the work that would establish his reputation, the *History of the Norman Conquest*, was published in six volumes between 1867 and 1879. Politically he was an idiosyncratic English radical, an advocate of the liberties of the ancient constitution: he supported Gladstone and backed him on Irish disestablishment and later on Home Rule. 'Essentially Teutonic in his whole personality', according to his biographer, he was also a Teutonist in his interpretation of history: one who believed in the continuity of English history from the Germanic settlements to his own day.[10] In the literature Bryce is conventionally twinned with Freeman as an exponent of Teutonist history and much else. The extent to which Bryce in fact shared Freeman's outlook is a question that will recur at a number of points in this book; what is clear is that Freeman was one of Bryce's most important interlocutors, and a huge quantity of their correspondence (Bryce's as well as Freeman's) survives.

Bryce's closeness to Freeman is well-known, but the nature of the relationship is curiously often misstated. Freeman was not Bryce's teacher, in any formal sense: he was not resident in Oxford at all while Bryce was.[11] He examined in the Law and History School immediately before Bryce's time (1857 and 1858) and immediately after (1863 and 1864) but was not examining when Bryce sat that examination in 1861, and in fact it seems that they did not meet until Bryce had completed his undergraduate studies. Their first encounter was in December 1861, when both were guests of North Pinder, Bryce's former tutor, in the South Oxfordshire parish of Rotherfield Greys, where Pinder had accepted a college living. It was during that stay that Bryce received news of his First in the Law and History School, as well of his success in winning the lucrative Vinerian Scholarship. His description of Freeman in a letter to his

FIGURE 3.1. Edward Augustus Freeman (1823–1892),
'a queer sort of character, an historical student and writer
in the Saturday; as well as author of some books'.

father did not indicate any prior knowledge of Freeman's work, nor, indeed, did it seem to promise a close friendship: 'a queer sort of character, an historical student and writer in the Saturday; as well as author of some books'.[12]

The correspondence with Freeman gives some indication of Bryce's reading for the essay. In August 1862, during a holiday in Dresden, he read the multivolume *Geschichte der deutschen Kaiserzeit*, by Ranke's pupil Wilhelm von Giesebrecht, who had just succeeded Sybel as professor of history at Munich.[13] From there he moved onto 'the big Pertz': the *Monumenta Germaniae Historica*, a multivolume compilation of primary sources for German history, edited by Georg Heinrich Pertz.[14] Back in Oxford, amid the burdens of his tutorial work, he was reading in the Bodleian, though 'in a rather scattered and indeterminate way: reading anywhere or anyhow what seemed likely to work into any part of so vast a subject.[15] Later researchers will sympathize.

When he won the prize, Bryce acknowledged Freeman's contribution: 'it is chiefly to you that I owe it, to your encouragement sympathy and advice.'[16] But we have some meaty correspondence between the two men from the period when Bryce was working on the essay, and there is little evidence that Freeman was providing him with substantive guidance on his reading. Bryce wrote:

> Some very funny old books I have encountered. Have you ever seen Radolfus de Columna[17] or Petrus de Andlo?[18] Or Alciatus.[19] Liudprand[20] is interesting: & I am going to attack Otto Frisingensis, & look carefully through the <u>Leges</u> in Pertz. Couringius & Boeclerus, jurists apparently about 1600, seem capital fellows, though with their Protestant bias against the religious pretensions of the Kaiser, & hence against universal dominion. Dante is the boldest & finest in that line. Is Pfeffel, whom I went carefully through, supposed to be a good authority? Do you know anything of Waitz—Deutsche Verfassungsgeschichte? The last book I have come across is a history of Germany from the death of Fred. II of Prussia till 1815 by a certain Ludwig Haüsser [sic], Professor at Heidelberg, & a great authority there.[21] I was puzzled a long time to find when <u>sacrum imperium</u> began, not being able to get it before Friedrich I; I find now Boeclerus says it began then: do you know of any earlier date.[22]

Bryce certainly used Freeman as a sounding board for testing out ideas about how he might approach writing an essay on so vast a topic: 'Scarce yet do I see any reasonable way of treating it, unless by commenting on the different periods and trying to sketch the chief results of the thing as a whole to Germany & to the world.' He added: 'I despair most of any decent knowledge of the constitution of the more recent Empire—since Kaiser Max I, & of the complications among which it went to pieces.' He was also conscious that 'one ought to be able to say something about the problems of modern Germany: the Bund: the eager pursuit of the Idea of Unity: of the means they seem to have as yet no notion.'[23] But there is little to indicate that Freeman gave any detailed advice.

Freeman read a proof copy prior to publication but made no substantive input at that stage. The Holy Roman Empire was not in any sense written under Freeman's shadow. Rather, he was important in two respects. First, he reviewed it both for the Saturday Review and for the North British Review, and his enthusiastic endorsement was instrumental in winning public attention for Bryce's book. Second, the period when Bryce was working on the Holy Roman Empire—the prize essay, the first edition of the book, and also the second edition—coincided with the period when Freeman was completing the first volume of his *History of Federal Government* (1863) and then embarking on the second volume, which remained incomplete, and indeed barely started, though he did write a chapter on the federations of ancient and medieval Italy, and a fragment on the German Confederation of 1815.[24] Bryce's expertise as the authority on the Holy Roman Empire was something Freeman planned to draw on in embarking on the second volume, and Bryce, when in Heidelberg, was extraordinarily industrious in hunting down German sources for Freeman's proposed study of quasi-federal structures in medieval Germany.[25] Freeman wrote in January 1865:

> I am still reading, but only reading, at both Swiss and German matters—I mean for Fed. Gov. as I am also reading again your H.R.E. with renewed and increased admiration, which I hope to give out in the North British. I trust you will come here as soon as you can possibly do after you come back. There are so many things which we have to talk to one another about, touching our respective works, which can be done in no place so conveniently as in my Library. So let this be a fixed thing. I want your guidance very much for the German part. For the Swiss part my scheme is pretty well drawn out in my head, tho' it will take some time to carry it into effect but for the German I am still at sea, hardly knowing what to read and what not. Yet I mean it to be quite a short Chapter.[26]

In writing a history of the Holy Roman Empire at this time, Bryce was entering a historiographical field where the stakes were high. It is well established that in the era of European nationalism, the history of the early Middle Ages was politically charged, since the study of the barbarian tribes that overran the empire, and of the relationship between the western empire and its successor states, were perceived to have clear implications for the understanding of modern nations.[27] The history of the Holy Roman Empire in particular had clear implications for the struggle for national unification in nineteenth-century Germany. Bryce's letters from Heidelberg in 1863 show him keenly interested in the political situation. 'Heidelberg is quite a metropolis of the philo-Prussian, or as their enemies call it, Kleindeutsch party in S. Germany; Hausser [*sic*] and Bluntschli are leaders among them.' He continued: 'He [Häusser] and the liberals generally of the Prussian school have taken up a position of antagonism to the imperial system; whether however they carry this back to the mediaeval Reich I know not, believing rather that it mainly is a part of anti-Hapsburgism.'[28]

The Roman and the Teuton

The essay Bryce submitted for the Arnold Prize in 1863 does not survive, it seems. We know that he revised it substantially for publication in 1864, but that first edition still takes the form of an essay, not formally divided into chapters, although there is a table of contents. The reader navigates the text by means of subheadings in the margins, rather than by means of the chapter breaks that first appeared in the 1866 edition. It is therefore reasonable to surmise that structurally the book published in 1864 was similar to the essay submitted the previous year, even if the text had been substantially amplified in the meantime. In any case, it was the 1864 book that first established Bryce's reputation, and it makes sense to analyse it in some depth.[29]

The reader who comes to *The Holy Roman Empire* with a prior knowledge of some of Bryce's later works will be struck by the difference in style. The later Bryce had a preference for a simple, unadorned style, befitting one who sought to come before his readers as one presenting them with 'the facts'. *The Holy Roman Empire*, by contrast, has more than an echo of Gibbon's *Decline and Fall*, not least in its opening passages: 'That ostentation of humility, which the subtle policy of Augustus had conceived, and the jealous hypocrisy of Tiberius maintained, was gradually dropped by their successors till despotism became at last recognized in principle as the government of the Roman Empire.'[30] Here the subject (the later Roman Empire) is Gibbonian; so is the theme, the demise of civic virtue and the triumph of despotism; and so too is the style, in which agency is attributed not to the person of the emperor but to his attributes, to Augustus's 'subtle policy' and to Tiberius's 'jealous hypocrisy'. Gibbon's influence on Bryce has never really been discussed, but the connections were several. Bryce's first paper to the Old Mortality Society, following his election in November 1857, was on Gibbon on the origins of monasticism and asceticism; Gibbon's civic republicanism was certainly to his taste; and we know that he read Gibbon when revising his Arnold Prize essay for publication.[31] He later came to the view that Gibbon was 'not much of a researcher' and was intellectually below Macaulay, but the debt was still significant.[32]

The central theme in the book was historical continuity, or the 'unity of history', to use a term much invoked in Victorian debates, notably by Goldwin

Smith and Freeman, if not by Thomas Arnold, to whom the concept should be traced. This is how Bryce introduced his subject:

> Strictly speaking, it is from the year 800 A.D., when a King of the Franks was crowned Emperor of the Romans by Pope Leo III, that the beginning of the Holy Roman Empire must be dated. But in history there is nothing isolated, and just as to explain a modern Act of Parliament or a modern conveyance of lands we must go back to the feudal customs of the thirteenth century, so among the institutions of the Middle Ages there is scarcely one which can be understood until it is traced up either to classical or to primitive Teutonic antiquity.[33]

Bryce also introduced here the principal interpretative tool that he used to analyse the long history of the Holy Roman Empire: the interplay of classical/ Roman and Teutonic. His account of Charlemagne's coronation by Pope Leo III on Christmas Day AD 800 was particularly striking. This was 'not only the central event of the Middle Ages' but also 'one of those very few events of which, taking them singly, it may be said that if they had not happened, the history of the world would have been different'.[34] What exactly was so important about it? Describing the coronation shout, when Charles was proclaimed Emperor, Bryce writes: 'In that shout, echoed by the Franks without, was pronounced the union, so long in preparation, so mighty in its consequences, of the Roman and the Teuton, of the memories and the civilization of the South with the fresh energy of the North, and from that moment modern history begins.'[35]

Bryce is commonly discussed in the literature as a Teutonist, one who celebrated the distinctive contribution of the Teutonic race to European history. The broadly Germanophile position he adopted in the politics of the 1860s was echoed at points in his history. He was, in particular, dismissive of attempts by French historians to claim Charlemagne as a forerunner of the French monarchy:

> No claim can be more groundless than that which the modern French, the sons of the Latinized Kelt, set up to the Teutonic Charles. At Rome he might assume the chlamys and the sandals, but at the head of his Frankish host he strictly adhered to the customs of his country, and was beloved by his people as the very ideal of their own character and habits. Of strength and stature almost super-human; in swimming and hunting unsurpassed; steadfast and terrible in fight, to his friends gentle and condescending, he was a Roman, much less a Gaul, in nothing but his culture and his width of

view, otherwise a thorough Teuton. The centre of his realm was the Rhine; his capitals Aachen and Engilenheim; his army German; his sympathies shown in the collecting of the old hero-lays, the composition of a German grammar, the ordinance against confining prayer to the three languages, were all for the race from which he sprang, and whose advance, represented by the victory of Austrasia over Neustria and Aquitaine, spread a second Germanic wave over the conquered countries.[36]

Bryce's disdain for French historians' attempts to claim Charlemagne has been invoked to locate him as a Teutonist historian: even by Steinberg, whose treatment of the subject is generally judicious. Steinberg implies that Bryce maintained that a Teutonic racial inheritance enabled ideas of freedom and equality to survive rather more successfully in modern German states than in France, whereas the reality is that Bryce says any such inheritance made little if any difference in the modern world:

> The tendency of the Teuton was and is to the independence of the individual life, to the mutual repulsion, if the phrase may be permitted, of the social atoms, as contrasted with Keltic and so-called Romanic peoples, among which the unit is more completely absorbed in the mass, who live possessed by a common idea which they are driven to realize in the concrete. Teutonic states have been little more successful than their neighbours in the establishment of free constitutions. Their assemblies meet, and vote, and are dissolved, and nothing comes of it: their citizens endure without greatly resenting outrages that would raise the more excitable French and Italians in revolt.[37]

But in fact, as Steinberg himself recognizes, Bryce's claim was not that Charlemagne's empire was Teutonic; it was that it was a blend of the Roman with the Teutonic. This was fundamental:

> There were in his Empire, as in his own mind, two elements; those two from the union and mutual action and reaction of which modern civilization has arisen. These vast domains, reaching from the Ebro to the Carpathian mountains, from the Eyder to the Liris, were all the conquests of the Frankish sword, and were still governed almost exclusively by viceroys and officers of Frankish blood. But the conception of the Empire, that which made it a State and not a mere mass of subject tribes like those great Eastern dominions which rise and perish in a lifetime, the realms of Sesostris, or Attila, or Timur, was inherited from an older and a grander system, was not

Teutonic but Roman—Roman in its ordered rule, in its uniformity and precision, in its endeavour to subject the individual to the system—Roman in its effort to realize a certain limited and human perfection, whose very completeness shall exclude the hope of further progress. And the bond, too, by which the Empire was held together was Roman in its origin, although Roman in a sense which would have surprised Trajan or Severus, could it have been foretold them. The ecclesiastical body was already organized and centralized, and it was in his rule over the ecclesiastical body that the secret of Charles's power lay. Every Christian—Frank, Gaul, or Italian—owed loyalty to the head and defender of his religion: the unity of the Empire was a reflection of the unity of the Church.[38]

It was the blending of the opposite qualities of Teuton and Roman that Bryce saw as fundamental to the medieval empire. Was it a racial interpretation of medieval history, of a kind that abounded in the eighteenth and nineteenth centuries? The Teutonic is clearly a racial or ethnographic category, at least in origin, but the Roman is institutional rather than racial, and in this text Bryce is much more concerned with institutional forms as embodiments of the spirit of particular peoples than he is with questions of racial stock or miscegenation.[39]

There is a broader point here concerning Bryce's intellectual identity, and his place in nineteenth-century historiography. There is no question that Bryce was indebted to the Teutonic myth: in particular, to the idea that free institutions were, as Montesquieu put it, 'found in the [Germanic] forests'.[40] He studied in Germany and was immersed in the German historical tradition. Later, he achieved greater fame as the leading Victorian interpreter of the United States and as a promoter of Anglo-American understanding, and he was a firm partisan of the view that the origins of American history were to be found in England, and especially in the traditions of the English common law. But he was trained in *Roman* law: this was the subject he had primarily studied at Heidelberg, and this was the subject in which he held his Oxford chair.[41] He had not, indeed, published on civil law when appointed to profess the subject, but his claim to authority in this field derived in large measure from his *Holy Roman Empire*, where he pointed out the importance of Roman law as an agent of institutional continuity across the centuries: 'The Church excepted, no agent did so much to keep alive the memory of Roman institutions.'[42] One of his central preoccupations as Regius Professor was with the relationship between Roman and English law.[43] It is curious that the many accounts of Bryce as a Teutonist pass over his academic profile as a Roman lawyer.[44] To understand Bryce better, we have to focus not on the Teutonic in isolation, but on the interplay of the Teutonic and the Roman. This was of a piece with his wider interest in the tension between centralizing and decentralizing principles, or between centripetal and centrifugal forces, in law and politics and history.[45]

Bryce travelled widely across Europe, and of course far beyond; and while he loved Switzerland and was fascinated by Iceland—both countries in which he thought that free institutions could be traced to Teutonic origins—he was as likely to spend holidays in southern France or the Italian Alps. His closest friend among continental European academics and intellectuals was not a German but an Italian, the historian Count Ugo Balzani; and while Bryce was certainly an enthusiast for German unification in the 1860s, it was the Italian cause that really excited his enthusiasm, along with many of his Oxford contemporaries.[46] While he undoubtedly thought that the Teutonic peoples had made an important and distinctive contribution to European history and to the development of political institutions, it would be quite wrong to suppose that he thought them superior or that he cared only or primarily for them. Equally, it would be wrong to imagine that he saw any purely Teutonic peoples—Iceland excepted—in the Europe of his time. He explicitly said that he did not.[47]

Above all, the city of Rome occupied a vital place in Bryce's imagination. He first visited in December 1864, after the publication of his *Holy Roman Empire*, but before the publication of the second edition (1866), which included a new chapter on the City of Rome in the Middle Ages. He evidently conceived this during this visit, when he met Ferdinand Gregorovius, whose multivolume history of the city of Rome in the Middle Ages was one of his principal sources in this new chapter.[48] He was repelled by what he saw of Catholicism in Italy: 'paganism, and a paganism unredeemed by the virtues of the ancients'; but more curious, perhaps, is that he told his father that he had thought in advance that he 'might turn Catholic here'. This was surely highly unlikely, but the significance of the remark is that it suggests that he knew that Rome would capture his imagination. He wrote to his mother that Rome 'has a character unlike not only our own but any and every other capital in Europe, just because it remains still the capital not of a nation but of Christendom. No where else has one the same feeling of cosmopolitanism.'[49]

That same letter went on to give a very full characterization of his impressions of the city, alongside what he had expected:

You remember how Clough's hero expresses his disappointment with Rome. That is not the word for the feeling of the place; though it is meaner, dirtier, more prosaic, more wholly modern than any traveller expects. It is not disappointing, for it is real, and expresses in its form and dress all his [*sic*] character and history. But it is perfectly unlike what fancy had pictured it. The ruins are not below one's ideas of them, for they point to a splendour and wealth and grandeur of conception and execution in the times of the later republic and empire such as no modern city makes the feeblest approach to. But all is so changed that one gives up in despair the notion of reconstructing the ancient city, and contrary to all my expectation, that which has most interested me, has seemed most suggestive and capable of giving really definite and valuable results, has been the monuments of primitive Christianity: the old churches with their singular mosaics, the catacombs with their paintings, the sarcophagi with their emblematic devices. Especially interesting was the visit to the catacombs with Rossi, who knows and explains them better than anyone else, having devoted his life to their exploration.[50]

The pivotal chapter of *The Holy Roman Empire*, and more or less the longest, was the one on the 'Theory of the Mediaeval Empire'. It was one of the earliest Victorian forays into the study of the history of political thought, and more than anything else stands out as marking the book as one that was well ahead of its time, at least in Britain. 'To most persons', wrote Benjamin Jowett in 1866, 'the very notion that ideas have a history is a new one.'[51] But even before Jowett wrote this it seems to have come easily to Bryce. He wrote at the outset that he was concerned with the empire 'not as a State but as an Institution, an institution created by and embodying a wonderful system of ideas'.[52] In his chapter on the 'Theory of the Mediaeval Empire', he explored that theory as the legacy of 'the two great ideas which expiring antiquity bequeathed to the ages that followed', namely, 'those of a World-Monarchy and a World-Religion'.[53] What Rome stood for was, above all else, the idea of a political union that transcended the barriers of race; and this idea was mirrored in the emergence of a world religion in which just as God was one, so was humanity.[54]

This account of the relationship between Roman imperial rule and the Christian religion, and of their fusion in the idea of the Holy Empire, is striking. Just as Roman dominion brought a common language and a common law to peoples formerly thought to be irretrievably divided by ineradicable racial differences, so Christianity 'banished ... from the soul' the idea of natural differences 'by substituting for the variety of local pantheons the belief in one God, before whom all men are equal'.[55] Bryce's first edition appeared in the same year as a much more enduringly famous work, Fustel de Coulanges's

La Cité antique. Bryce cannot have known Fustel's work when he wrote, though he knew and admired it later; but the two men gave very similar appraisals of the revolutionary impact of Christianity as a religion that was, in Fustel's words, 'not the domestic religion of any family, the national religion of any city, or of any race'.[56] Or in Bryce's words: 'Because divinity was divided, humanity had been divided likewise; the doctrine of the unity of God now enforced the unity of man, who had been created in His image'.[57] We have here a clear sense of how in the historian of the Holy Roman Empire was prefigured the later campaigner for both humanitarian and ecumenical causes. Appalled as he was by the Roman Catholicism of his own time, and by the temporal power of the papacy, he nevertheless had a powerful sense of the grandeur of the idea of the unity of the church and the unity of humanity.[58] His Presbyterian anti-Catholicism was much tempered by his historical-mindedness and quest for the brotherhood of humanity.[59]

Federalism and Constitutionalism

How does Bryce's first book relate to his constitutional thinking? The Holy Roman Empire has sometimes been treated as a federal structure of sorts, and not without some plausibility.[60] That conception of the empire can be traced back at least as far as Montesquieu, who labelled the Holy Roman Empire 'the federative republic of Germany'.[61] The American founding fathers—in particular, Benjamin Franklin and James Madison—were influenced by this conception of the empire as a federal or rather confederal structure, but they were also acutely conscious of its inadequacy. In Bryce's own immediate circle, Freeman held the idea of federalism to be antithetical to that of empire (and hence was dismissive of projects for imperial federation in the British Empire) and therefore took the view that 'with the Holy Roman Empire, distinctly as an Empire, the historian of Federal Government has no concern'. But, he went on, 'indirectly, the position of the Empire has had no small share in producing a state of things which the Federal historian cannot leave unnoticed'. He observed that the Germany of his time—he was writing in 1863—was bound by a federal tie, that of the German Confederation of 1815, a *Staatenbund* (confederation) rather than a *Bundesstaat* (federal state), but with federal laws and a federal Diet (*Bundestag*). And that structure was 'largely influenced by the history of the defunct Holy Roman Empire'.[62]

It is unclear exactly how Bryce saw the connection between *The Holy Roman Empire* and his writings on federalism. It is highly likely that he saw some link: the prize essay was first written, and the book first published, during the American Civil War, a war of secession which was widely understood in Britain to turn on the issue of state rights in a federal structure.[63] But if Bryce did see a connection, it was rather implicit than explicit in his terminology. His principal interest was in the medieval idea of a universal empire; but also in the tension between the dual role of the emperor: both (notionally) world emperor and German king. He traced the process whereby, in order to secure election, a putative candidate would effectively relinquish some of his sovereign rights, so that by the time of the Renaissance, the German Empire had been transformed from a state into 'a sort of confederation or body of states, united indeed for some of the purposes of government, but separate and independent for others more important'.[64] Following the Peace of Westphalia of 1648, the empire's bounds were reduced and the relics of its 'Roman' character were effectively shed; it was now 'in everything but title purely and solely a German Empire': indeed, barely even an empire properly speaking, 'but a Confederation, and that of the loosest sort'. It had 'no common treasury, no efficient common tribunals, no means of coercing a refractory member', and the different states were administered separately without regard to each other.[65] Bryce was scathing about the condition of the post-Westphalian confederal empire, with 'three hundred petty principalities between the Alps and the Baltic, each with its own laws, its own courts, in which the ceremonious pomp of Versailles was faintly reproduced, its little armies, its separate coinage, its tolls and custom houses on the frontier, its crowd of meddlesome and pedantic officials, presided over by a prime minister who was generally the unworthy favourite of his prince, and the pensioner of some foreign court'. It was a 'vicious system, which paralyzed the trade, the literature, and the political thought of Germany', brought fully into being by the Peace of Westphalia, which, 'by emancipating the princes from imperial control, had made them despots in their own territories'.[66]

That passage was a classic exposition of mid-nineteenth-century liberalism's antagonism towards small-state particularism, which liberals identified as the enemy both of social and economic progress and of civil and political liberties. 'The impoverishment of the inferior nobility and the decline of the commercial cities caused by a war that had lasted a whole generation, removed every counterpoise to the power of the electors and princes, and made absolutism supreme just where absolutism wants all its justification, in states too small to have any public opinion, states in which everything depends on the monarch, and the monarch depends on his favourites.'[67] The idea that there were 'states too small to have any public opinion' is a particularly fertile notion here. That public opinion was the ultimate governing power in a liberal society was a fundamental conviction of Bryce's, and it did a lot of work in both his writings (notably in *The American Commonwealth*) and his political practice. But what were its pre-conditions? This isolated remark dating from 1864 is too laconic to enable us to draw any firm conclusions, but Bryce's insight here seems to have been that public opinion depended on the existence of a thriving civil society, and that depended on the existence of political units that surpassed a minimum size.[68]

Especially revealing was Bryce's analysis of the relationship between feudal-ism and modern state-formation in France, England, and Germany. In France, the king as feudal head absorbed all the powers of the state to himself, and the aristocracy was left with a residue of politically worthless privileges. In England, by contrast, the aristocracy allied with the commons to curtail the powers of the crown, so creating a bridge between feudalism and constitu-tional monarchy. So far, this echoed Tocqueville's account in *L'Ancien Régime et la Révolution* (1856). But Bryce extended the comparison:

> In Germany, everything was taken from the sovereign, and nothing given to the people; the representatives of those who had been fief-holders of the first and second rank before the Great Interregnum were now independent potentates; and what had once been a monarchy was now an aristocratic federation. The Diet, originally an assembly of magnates meeting from time to time like our early English Parliaments, became in A.D. 1654 a permanent body, at which the electors, princes, and cities were represented by their envoys. In other words, it was now not a national council, but an interna-tional congress of diplomatists.[69]

For Bryce, then, the history of the slow decline of the Holy Roman Empire was also a history of the stifling of German nationhood: 'the sacrifice of impe-rial, or rather federal, rights to state rights'.[70] This formulation, present from the first edition onward, must in the first instance have been intended to bring the American Civil War to his readers' minds. But it was not simply the tri-umph of what he would later call centrifugal forces within a federal structure: it was, at the same time, the appropriation of public powers and sovereign prerogatives by the descendants of feudal vassals. Hence, as Bryce saw it, the enfeeblement of any kind of public purpose in Germany:

> It would be hard to find, from the Peace of Westphalia to the French Revo-lution, a single grand character or a single noble enterprise; a single sacrifice made to great public interests, a single instance in which the welfare of

nations was preferred to the selfish passions of their princes. The military history of those times will always be read with interest; but free and progressive countries have a history of peace not less rich and varied than that of war; and when we ask for an account of the political life of Germany in the eighteenth century, we hear nothing but the scandals of buzzing courts, and the wrangling of diplomatists at never-ending congresses.[71]

The course of German history was marked out as something distinct from 'the general movement towards aggregation' which had dominated European and world history since the thirteenth century.[72]

What Bryce most deplored, however, was not decentralization, but the enfeeblement of public purpose. In *The Holy Roman Empire*, then, Bryce did not attempt an analysis of German federalism. But he certainly painted a picture of that federalism, or rather confederalism, as it existed in the last century and a half of the empire's existence; and that picture was a relentlessly negative one. The reason, it would seem, was simply that in the context of a history of German nationhood, the federalism of this period represented a regression in which the forces that held Germany together were enfeebled and those that tended to fragment it were strengthened. This was very much a perspective from the 1860s, a period when for British Liberals German nationalism was a progressive movement to be wholeheartedly welcomed. Bryce fully recognized—or came to recognize—that in some circumstances—those, for instance, of the United States when the Continental Congress met—a federal constitution could serve as engine of the greatest possible degree of centralization, since the centrifugal forces would not tolerate any further accrual of power by the centre.[73] He always warned against drawing absolute inferences about political forms from the experience of one time or one place. But he could not find in the confederalism of the later Holy Roman Empire anything but decay.

This analysis of the argument of the *Holy Roman Empire* suggests that its greatness lay in the encounter between a precocious historical intelligence and a grand and noble theme that engaged Bryce's passion as well as his intellect. But how far does a study of its reception—both immediate and subsequent—confirm this inference?

Inevitably, reviewers differed in their opinions. The Roman Catholic weekly, *The Tablet*, thought that 'the main idea pervading the book' was 'a misconception of history on the part of the author'. Its objection was that Bryce treated the Roman Catholic Church not as a divinely ordained institution but as the product of the Roman Empire. Bryce's judgment that 'without

the Roman Empire there could not be a Roman, nor by a necessary consequence a Catholic and Apostolic Church' was, the reviewer thought, a 'soph-
ism', though one 'pardonable enough in a Protestant, whose mind cannot
conceive a Church separated from and independent of the State'. Perhaps the
reviewer, knowing Bryce to be a fellow of Oriel, assumed him to be a conforming member of the Church of England; still, Bryce must have smiled a little at
this radical misconstrual of his ecclesiological standpoint. He also riled this
reviewer by his treatment of the papacy as a temporal power whose chief object was territorial gain. 'Mr Bryce must feel ashamed that the eyes of the infidel Gibbon were less blinded by prejudice than his own.'[74]

The *Pall Mall Gazette*, reviewing the fourth edition (1873), focused on the
relevance of Bryce's history to the politics of Germany in the nineteenth century;
not surprisingly, since the main new feature of that edition was the inclusion of
a supplementary chapter on the new German Empire. The reviewer saw it as
'a fair, temperate—indeed, cautious—review of the history of Germany during
the present century' but also detected 'a decided sympathy not only with the
German and Italian peoples, but especially with "those very 'sentimental' or
'romantic' politicians" who were persecuted—as Mazzini by Piedmont—by the
very Governments which were at last to enter into their labours.'[75]

Bryce was certainly helped by his friends, and not just Freeman. Dicey reviewed the book for *Macmillan's Magazine* and was unstinting in his praise:
'Mr Bryce has laid before the public, in a marvellously short space, and in a
masterly manner, a history, not so much of the Holy Roman Empire itself, as
of the ideas which the Empire embodied, and of the changing opinions and
theories by which an institution which in later days seemed, and, indeed, was,
a mere mass of anomalies, was kept alive.'[76] Dicey located Bryce's work
squarely within a then barely emergent field of the history of ideas: 'It is to the
history of ideas and of institutions—which are, in fact, one thing from two
points of view—that we must look for the solution of at least half the moral
and political problems of the day.'[77] Dicey is not usually identified as thinker
with the temperament of the intellectual historian, but this may be to do him
an injustice. In any case, he wrote here not just as a friend of Bryce, but also as
a pupil of Pattison as well as Jowett.[78] He developed the point further:

> The great merit of [Bryce's] work, and that which gives it importance for
> our present purpose, lies in the skill and originality with which he traces
> out what may be termed the ideal history of the Empire. Ideas and institu-
> tions are, as we have before said, often almost the same thing from two

different aspects. This is true of all institutions. The actual power of an English law court consists, to a great extent, in the power attributed to it through the popular ideas of the respect due to law. But what is true, in some degree, of all institutions, was true, in an infinitely greater degree, of the Holy Roman Empire. . . . In the height of its strength, as in the time of its weakness, the strength of the Holy Roman Empire lay in the awe with which it impressed the world. What then was the source of this awe? Mr Bryce finds it to have depended on certain mediaeval doctrines and theories which have now almost ceased to exert influence.

Specifically, it derived from 'the notion that the universality and the unity of the Church were bound up with the universality and the unity of the Empire; or, as Mr Bryce again and again puts it, a universal Church and a universal Empire were but two aspects of the conception of the necessary unity of the whole society of Christians'.[79]

There was nothing about Teutonism in Dicey's review. His conclusion was that Bryce was 'a writer who knows what it is to write history in a philosophic spirit'.[80] Indeed, this, the first of Bryce's many works, was the most philosophic of all.

Dicey's review set the standard for incisive commentary on Bryce's work. Continental European reviewers largely endorsed his reading. In France, the Nancy historian Christian Pfister, an emerging authority on the history of Alsace and Lorraine, was impressed by the French edition that appeared in 1890, and identified Bryce's purpose more acutely than did most English reviewers: 'He has investigated what ideas this word "empire" awoke in men's minds in the different great epochs of history.' This was a manifestly important theme: 'In truth, it constitutes a complete philosophy of the history of Germany, Italy, and the countries of western Europe.' He went on to take Bryce to task for a number of factual slips and mistranscriptions. More fundamentally, he thought that Bryce's Protestant convictions came through rather more than was appropriate: like the reviewer in the *Tablet*, he found that 'he is not always impartial in regard to the pope, whom he continually reproaches for being concerned to extend his temporal domain.' Not surprisingly for a reviewer from Nancy, he found Bryce too warm in his enthusiasm for the German Empire of 1871, the chapter on which was 'without doubt the weakest in the book'. There was not a word of commiseration for the people of Alsace-Lorraine. Nonetheless, Pfister thought it one of the most profound books he had read for a long time.[81]

The Historical Aspect of Democracy

Bryce built on his authority as the historian of the Holy Roman Empire in his contribution to *Essays on Reform* in 1867, the work that publicly identified him with the advanced Liberals of Oxford and Cambridge, who favoured a more democratic political system.

The Parliament that passed the Reform Act of that year had no intention of making Britain a democracy; indeed, few at the outset wanted household suffrage in boroughs, which was what in the event was enshrined in the 1867 act.[82] Most MPs on both sides were loyal to the ideal of a mixed constitution in which no class exercised a majority.[83] Popular radicals who backed household suffrage did so by appealing to the prescriptive authority of the ancient constitution rather than to abstract democratic principles. So much is well-known.[84] But the act's passage nevertheless precipitated a renewed debate on democracy as a political ideal, largely because its most lucid critics—Robert Lowe on the Liberal side, Viscount Cranborne (later Lord Salisbury) on the Conservative—framed it as an act that would lead inexorably to democracy.[85] The advanced Liberals—mostly young fellows of Oxford and Cambridge colleges—who collaborated in producing the *Essays on Reform* did not set out to make the positive case for democracy, but they did aim to refute the central arguments propounded on the antidemocratic side. George Brodrick offered an extended critique of Lowe's utilitarian argument that the 1832 settlement had the effect of producing a House of Commons to which the most competent men in the country could and did get elected, and that democratic reform would make it harder for the ablest men to achieve office. Dicey attacked the 'balance of classes' theory, according to which the aim of parliamentary representation should be to 'mirror' the country by ensuring that the equilibrium of different classes and interests was duly reflected in the Commons. The experience of Australia and the United States—much invoked by opponents of reform—were studied by Charles Pearson and Goldwin Smith, who both set out to demonstrate that those experiences did not tell at all decisively against the cause of democracy.[86] For his part, Bryce was assigned the task of refuting the 'lessons' that Lowe and other critics tried to derive from the historical experience of democratic institutions.

Bryce here drew on his authority as the historian of the Holy Roman Empire. He spoke for the younger generation of historians, reared on the new conception of history as a science. Implicitly he suggested that Lowe and other parliamentary critics of democracy were hamstrung by a jejune understanding of history, which encouraged them to pillage the past at random for 'lessons' about democracy without regard for the historical context of these democratic experiments. For Bryce, the study of history was no longer confined to a record of 'public events, wars and treaties, intrigues and seditions'; instead, the scientific historian was concerned 'to investigate, and strike so far as he may to reproduce, in its entirety that portion of the past whereof he treats'.[87] This point, which might surprise anyone used to the cliché that Victorian historiography was about high politics and the constitution, was one that Bryce would reiterate elsewhere.[88] History had become more of a science, 'more delicate, more complex, more minutely analytic', and had 'abolished those broad and sweeping generalizations which it was formerly the fashion to draw from a few facts taken at random'. Facile lessons about particular political institutions could no longer be drawn, since they now had to be understood in their intellectual, social, and religious contexts.[89] What lessons about the workings of 'democracy' in the modern world could be derived from ancient Greece, where states were small, representative government unknown, social structures simple, and citizens' militias rather than standing armies the normal way of waging war? In any case, the ancient republics were not really democracies at all, but 'oligarchies of masters among a multitude of slaves'.[90] 'Democracy in its true sense' depended on the Christian principle of the spiritual equality of all men before God.[91]

Bryce made much use of the distinction between social structure and political institutions. This would have been familiar to him from the thinkers of the Scottish Enlightenment, such as Adam Smith, Adam Ferguson, and (perhaps most important for Bryce) the historian William Robertson; but it had been made still better known by Guizot and the other liberal historians of the French Restoration.[92] They used it explicitly to refute the counterrevolutionary case.[93] Tocqueville, in this respect a disciple of Guizot's, applied it both in his Democracy in America (1835–1840) and in his study of The Old Régime and the Revolution (1856). In particular, Bryce followed the analysis Tocqueville developed in the latter work: in terms of social structure, France was already democratizing before the revolution, and the revolution was due to the failure of political institutions to adapt to changing social conditions. It was not the experiment with democratic institutions in the French Revolution that had led to more than half a century of political instability, but rather the lack of long experience of free institutions and self-government.[94]

The kind of historicist argument Bryce advanced here was quite familiar in nineteenth-century France: it has echoes of Guizot and Tocqueville certainly, but also of Constant and Fustel de Coulanges.[95] But in Victorian Britain, where (even more than on the continent) the classics enjoyed great cultural prestige and dominated elite education, it was much rarer to find such an explicit statement of the structural gulf that separated the ancient world from the modern.[96] What was most characteristic of Bryce was the way in which he framed the historicist argument. To the historian, he thought, no form of government could be absolutely the best, for 'every proposal of political change is a question to be discussed not on abstract grounds, but with reference to the particular States and nations in question; not because abstract principles are untrue or unimportant, but because they are applicable under such a variety of restrictions and modifications that their establishment carries us but a very little way towards the solution of any practical problem'.[97] Empirical knowledge matters profoundly, therefore, in the resolution of political issues; and that was a conviction which strengthened in Bryce's mind as he got older. It was the foundation of what he tried to do in *Modern Democracies*. That said, he maintained that the course of history did provide grounds for a belief in 'a certain progress of the race in political matters': some political systems could be shown by history to belong to the past, others to the future. This belief in the empirical fact of progress was another that endured.[98]

Two further points about this essay deserve emphasis, since they point to lasting truths about Bryce's attitude to democracy. The first is that his account of the qualities of democracy was strongly republican.[99] He defined democracy as 'the participation of the whole nation in the direction of its own affairs'. That might look uncontroversial, but Bryce also pointed to the moral effects of democratic participation. Democracy, he thought, has 'a stimulating power such as belongs to no other form of government'. In particular: 'by giving the sense of a common interest and purpose it gives unity and strength to the whole State; it rouses the rich and powerful by obliging them to retain their influence not by privilege so much as by energy and intellectual eminence; it elevates the humbler classes by enlarging their scope of vision and their sense of responsibility.' Where the poor were corrupt, as sometimes happened in democratic systems, it was a consequence of their lack of a 'direct interest in politics': the solution was not to deprive them of political rights, but to ensure that they were conscious of their 'share in the government of the country' and developed a high conception of their own responsibilities.[100] Bryce's republican sympathies are something we shall return to in a later chapter. But it is important to notice that these sympathies were present from the very beginning of his political career. As we shall also see, he did not think that this position implied universal suffrage; and, historically, the republican position rarely had.

Next, Bryce warned against the dangers of class government, and thought that it was most likely to arise in a plutocracy, that is, a regime in which political rights were dependent on wealth. No plutocracy has ever governed for the public good, he maintained; and every plutocracy was brought to an end 'either by its own luxury and corruption, or by the hatred of its subjects'. One particular danger to which plutocracies were liable was the rise of the demagogue: the figure who poses as the advocate of the poor against the rich has space to operate in a system in which the rich govern in their own interest rather than for the public good.[101] In other words, the salient virtue of democratic institutions was that they obliged elites to seek to govern in the public interest. But for Bryce it was the public interest, not the popular will, that was the ultimate test of political legitimacy. He was a republican first, and a democrat second.

There was one final theme, the most Brycean of all. He commended the Swiss Confederation as 'not only the sole true and pure democracy of modern Europe', but also 'a signal example of the value of democratic institutions among a people capable of using them'.[102] Switzerland attracted widespread admiration in Victorian Britain, especially from radicals and republicans.[103] In Bryce it was especially enduring. He told the diplomat Esme Howard in 1914 that Switzerland was 'the only country where Democracy inspires—or sustains—hopes'; and Dicey in 1918 that it was 'the only country which knows how to work democracy'.[104] In *Modern Democracies* he tried to explain this phenomenon by devoting six chapters to the practice of democracy in Switzerland

There was nothing in this essay that Bryce would have repudiated later in life. The position he took in 1867 was that Britain would be better governed with a wider, *more* democratic franchise; and by 'better governed' he meant governed in such a way as to promote the public good, as opposed to serving sectional or class interests. 'We advocated democracy sixty years ago', he reminded Dicey in 1920, 'in the belief that government by the whole people <u>would be</u> for the benefit of the whole people. Whether it has so turned out is another affair. They are not the same thing.'[105] Even so, their 'advocacy' of democracy never went as far as an unqualified demand for universal manhood suffrage. Dicey's contribution to *Essays on Reform* was 'the most unflinchingly democratic' piece in the book, according to John Morley; but he later wrote that he wished that the Liberals had backed Bright's proposals for household suffrage in 1859: a more restrictive franchise than those finally adopted in 1867. We lack Bryce's reply, but this was something like his own position.[106] In

Modern Democracies he wrote—in connection with women's suffrage, which he thought a violation of this principle—that in Britain it had been generally accepted at the time of the Second Reform Act that 'fitness for the exercise of the suffrage should be a pre-condition to the grant of it'.[107]

The Historian at Large

Astonishing as it may seem after *The Holy Roman Empire*, Bryce never again wrote a book on history. In 1883 he consoled himself for the likelihood of being passed over for government office by reflecting that it would be better 'to do something substantial in history, and write this book about Justinian and the Goths. It is absurd never to have done anything in that line but the Holy Roman Empire at 23 years of age'.[108] Yet he never did. It was not that he deserted history for law: apart from a short work on the Trade Marks Registration Acts of 1875 and 1876, he wrote no books on law.[109] He was known to the public as an historian, in spite of the lack of a substantial historical *oeuvre*, and that characterization was right for several reasons.

First, Bryce was very active in the organization of the historical profession. He was closely involved from the 1860s onward in plans for the establishment of a learned journal in the subject, and when the *English Historical Review* finally came into being in 1886, under the editorship of Mandell Creighton, it was Bryce, on the eve of taking office in Gladstone's third ministry, who wrote the anonymous 'Prefatory Note', a kind of prospectus or manifesto for the new journal.[110] He also published an important article on Justinian in the journal's eighth issue.[111] When the British Academy was established in 1902, Bryce was one of the founding fellows and joined the History section.[112] When the first International Congress of the Historical Sciences was held in Rome in 1903, Bryce served as one of the vice-presidents, representing the British Academy. When the third Congress was held in London ten years later, Bryce was appointed president, although the delay in completion of his ambassadorial duties in Washington meant that he was not able to attend, and his presidential address was read on his behalf by Adolphus Ward.

Second, although Bryce did not write another historical book after *The Holy Roman Empire*, many if not most of his works were inflected by a historical way of thinking: the 'historical method', to use a term that was much in vogue in Bryce's lifetime. That could mean many different things, but in relation to Bryce it is best understood as a propensity to understand a phenomenon in terms of its origins, and often very remote origins.

This was the 'unity of history' at work. As we have seen in considering his essay on 'The Historical Aspect of Democracy', Bryce deployed a kind of historicism to resist simplistic attempts to derive 'lessons' from history for the present. At the same time, like Freeman, he felt the past to be a living thing, and deep historical comparisons came easily to him; increasingly so as his career progressed. 'Things look dark in Serbia', he wrote to Herbert Fisher toward the end of 1915: 'yet they were worse at Kossovo in 1387. Absit omen.'[113]

4

Manchester and Educational Reform

Bryce's Manchester

In April 1865 Lord Taunton wrote to Bryce to appoint him, as an assistant commissioner, to investigate the schools of Lancashire for the Schools Inquiry Commission which Taunton had been asked to chair.[1] Whether Lancashire was Bryce's choice is uncertain. He evidently expressed interest in reporting on continental Europe, but Matthew Arnold had already been lined up for that task.[2] Certainly the commission's secretary, the Cambridge classicist Henry Roby, invited him to express a preference, and Bryce knew that he was to investigate Lancashire before he received Taunton's letter.[3] It would have been a politically astute choice, for the campaign for the abolition of university tests, having met apparently unmoveable resistance from conservatives within the universities, was now moving beyond Oxford and Cambridge to attempt to form an alliance with the nonconformist liberalism of the provinces. If anywhere was the heartland of nonconformist liberalism, it was Manchester and the mill towns that surrounded it. Bryce soon came to look to the possibility of selection as Liberal candidate for a constituency in the region, although in the end those aspirations were frustrated.[4] But if it was not Bryce's choice it was a fortuitous slice of luck, for the encounter with Lancashire—and Manchester in particular—was to have a lasting influence on his life and career, in a number of different ways.

Oxford's place in Bryce's life is obvious; Manchester's is much less so.[5] He never lived in the North West of England. But the city and its region had a decisive influence on his intellectual, political, and indeed personal development. First, his work for the Taunton Commission gave him access to the educational networks of the region, and to its social and cultural elites, at an important time in its history, and his report brought him some renown in Lancashire. Second, he taught at Owens College, the forerunner of the University of Manchester: he was a part-time lecturer there between 1867 and 1870 and then served as professor of law (still part-time) from 1870 to 1875. He was also responsible for drafting the constitution for the remodelled Owens College of 1870. He later served as an examiner in history for the federal Victoria University (c. 1881–1885), and as governor of Owens College (1882–1891), of the federal Victoria University (from 1895 until its dissolution in 1903), and then of the Victoria University of Manchester (1903–1908 and 1913–1922).[6] His links with the university endured practically to the end of his life, for he was chosen to open the new Arts Building in 1919.[7] Third, as a barrister in Sir John Holker's chambers, he practised on the northern circuit. Bryce's diaries from 1873 and 1875 (few others survive) show him frequently on train journeys north, to both Manchester and Liverpool. Fourth, his younger brother Annan—later a Liberal MP—lived there briefly in the 1870s, between his graduation from Balliol (1872) and his departure for India on behalf of the East India merchants, Wallace Brothers. Much later, in 1889, Bryce married Marion Ashton, daughter of the Hyde mill-owner Thomas Ashton. The latter, whom Bryce first got to know through his Schools Inquiry work, was an influential figure in the lay governance of Owens College, and of the Manchester Grammar School and the Hulme Trust, and a prominent figure in the Manchester business community. He was a man whom Bryce came to admire hugely: 'I cannot think of any one I have ever known who combined such extraordinary clearness of vision and force of will with so austere a devotion to duty and so entire a forgetfulness of his own interests or his own fame in the world.'[8] Finally, his first cabinet position, in 1892–1894, was the post of chancellor of the Duchy of Lancaster, a post which, he told correspondents, was not onerous, but 'odd work it is, what there is of it, chiefly appointing magistrates and presenting clergymen to livings in the Church of England, to which I do not belong'.[9] It was, of course, focused on the County of Lancashire, and Bryce spent a good deal of time corresponding with Manchester Liberals on the appointment of magistrates, who he was determined should be more representative of Liberal and nonconformist opinion than they had been hitherto.

The period when Bryce was visiting Manchester regularly—from 1865 to 1875 or thereabouts—was a remarkably important one in the city's history, and especially in the shaping of its cultural and educational institutions.[10] The new Town Hall was built in the period 1868–1877, and the new Royal Exchange

opened in 1874. In 1872 C. P. Scott began his fifty-seven-year tenure as editor
of the *Manchester Guardian*, in the course of which he would transform it into
the leading organ of advanced Liberal opinion. Frederick Walker was in the
ascendancy as a reforming high master of Manchester Grammar School, and
Bryce reported for the Taunton Commission on his notable success in the face
of initial scepticism from local opinion. The Manchester High School for Girls
was founded in 1874, an important landmark for girls' education in the north
of England, and an initiative that owed more than a little to the impact made
by Bryce's report for the Taunton Commission. The reshaping, or 'extension',
of Owens College, which entailed its relocation to the premises still occupied
by the university on what was then the southernmost edge of the city, was
really a second foundation and launched the college toward its quest for full
university status. In 1870 James Fraser became bishop of Manchester: he was
the second occupant of that see, and his sixteen-year episcopate was distinguished by its profound impact on the Manchester public, across denominations and indeed faiths. Fraser, as it happens, was Bryce's predecessor at Oriel
and one of his fellow assistant commissioners for the Taunton Commission.[11]
Fraser's educational expertise helped to secure him the appointment. In the
letter offering him the see, Gladstone called Manchester 'the centre of the
modern life of the country'.[12]

The diaries enable us to reconstruct Bryce's north-west networks much
more effectively than his correspondence does, since he records the people he
met, stayed with, and dined with. They show him to have been very well connected in educated professional and business circles in both Manchester and
Liverpool: academic colleagues at Owens College, but also and more particularly those involved in the lay government of the college, and in the promotion
of initiatives in girls' and women's education. Strikingly, he moved in predominantly Unitarian circles. A close contact was Robert Dukinfield Darbishire, a
Manchester solicitor who often instructed Bryce but who was also a personal
friend and political ally with whom he stayed.[13] The Darbishires were a prominent Unitarian family, members of Cross Street Chapel, the famous stronghold of Manchester Unitarianism, and were close friends of the Gaskells, who
probably introduced them to Bryce.[14] They were also leading members of the
Manchester Literary and Philosophical Society.[15] Robert, who became a
trustee of the chapel (1864–1877), was educated at Manchester New College
while it was still in Manchester: this notable dissenting academy, predominantly Unitarian in character, was the descendant of Manchester Academy
and, more remotely, of Warrington Academy, and the ancestor of what is now

Harris Manchester College, Oxford.[16] There he was taught there by F. W. Newman, the brother of the future saint, and graduated with a University of London BA (1st Division); he later served as co-secretary to the college for thirty-seven years, covering almost the entire period when the college was located in London as well as its early years in Oxford.[17] He was an influential proponent (against James Martineau) of the move to Oxford, and he edited a set of essays, characteristically entitled *Theology and Piety: Alike Free*, to mark the college's relocation.[18] Darbishire was an advanced Liberal in politics, though firmly opposed both to socialism and to trade unionism.[19] He was also theologically serious—the proprietor, with James Martineau, of the *National Review*, the journal edited by Walter Bagehot and Richard Holt Hutton.[20] He has good claim to be regarded as the most important Unitarian layman of his time, but since he eschewed any kind of memorial, he has eluded historians' attention. If he is remembered at all now, it is for his philanthropic work, from his own resources but also, more importantly, as one of the trustees of Sir Joseph Whitworth's estate. It was Darbishire who was responsible for the creation of Whitworth Park and the Whitworth Art Gallery. An active amateur geologist, archaeologist, and collector, he was a driving figure behind the creation of the Manchester Museum.[21] He was President of the Manchester Literary and Philosophical Society (1886), a Hibbert Trustee for three decades (1874–1903), and much else besides.[22]

Darbishire was prominent in the campaign for the abolition of religious tests at Oxford and Cambridge, which first brought him and Bryce together.[23] It was he and Bryce who organized the meeting in support of tests abolition at the Free Trade Hall in Manchester in April 1866, at which the principal speaker was Dr Frederick Temple, headmaster of Rugby and future Archbishop of Canterbury. This was a major attempt to construct the alliance of Oxford and Manchester that Goldwin Smith advocated as the means to secure the abolition of the tests. Temple was a leading member—according to some accounts (including Bryce's), *the* leading member—of the Taunton Commission, through which Bryce knew him well; and it was Bryce who took advantage of that connection to invite Temple to speak.[24] Bryce also unsuccessfully invited the Balliol philosopher T. H. Green, an Old Mortality contemporary and a fellow assistant commissioner on the Taunton Commission, but instead George Brodrick of Merton agreed to come and speak.[25] He told the meeting that he thought it 'a happy and auspicious circumstance' that the movement that had begun in Oxford should be taken up in Manchester, for Manchester 'above all other places was capable of supplying that motive power without which no movement in this country could be successful' and was in addition 'the centre of those very classes of England the promoters of this movement were anxious to attract to Oxford'.[26] Temple in particular evidently made an impression on Darbishire, who sent his son Godfrey to Rugby the following year. This represented a significant softening in the attitude of Manchester Unitarianism toward the Anglican public schools: Thomas Ashton sent his eldest son to Rugby in 1868.[27] Temple looms large in the Darbishire family correspondence of the period, and Robert Darbishire invited him to stay with them in 1869 when Temple visited Manchester to address a temperance meeting.

The other cause that brought Bryce and Darbishire together was the promotion of girls' and women's education. The Darbishires were closely involved with the founding of the Manchester High School for Girls in 1874.[28] With Bryce, Robert Darbishire drew up a scheme for the incorporation of the High School under the Companies Act in 1877.[29] He was the leading advocate of the admission of women to Owens College and resigned from the College Council when he was defeated in 1875; much later he cofounded the first women's hall at Owens, Ashburne Hall, in 1900.[30] His wife Harriet belonged to the Cobb family, notable Unitarians in Banbury.[31] She was equally close to Bryce and had strong intellectual tastes: she devoured *The American Commonwealth*, whereas her husband evidently found it harder going.[32] She was honorary secretary of the Manchester Association for the Education of Women, served on the Council of the Manchester and Salford College for Women, and was a devoted friend to the High School, where she was a governor for a quarter of a century.[33]

Like the Darbishire family, Bryce was also close to the Gaskells. Elizabeth Gaskell died of heart failure in November 1865, shortly after Bryce started work for the Taunton Commission, so he knew her only briefly.[34] But he was a frequent visitor to the Gaskell family's house in Plymouth Grove, Manchester, where the widowed William Gaskell (minister of Cross Street Chapel) lived with his unmarried daughters, Margaret (Meta) and Julia.[35] As we shall see in the next chapter, Bryce became especially close to Meta, and the two were on the brink of getting engaged in 1872. Like the Darbishires, Meta Gaskell was one of the founders of the Manchester High School for Girls and became a governor.

Bryce was well connected with Unitarians in Liverpool too, in particular with the Rathbones. He was already close to William Rathbone VI, merchant and philanthropist (and father of Eleanor Rathbone), but as MP for South-West Lancashire, Rathbone based himself in London for most of the year. In Liverpool Bryce would dine or stay with other members of the Rathbone family, in particular William's brother Philip. The Rathbones had historically been Quakers, but William Rathbone's father (also William) had broken with the Friends and identified with Unitarianism, marrying a member of the Unitarian Greg family of Quarry Bank in Cheshire. The younger William Rathbone was closely associated with the Unitarian community in Liverpool, under the influence both of his mother and of his brother-in-law, John Hamilton Thom, minister of the famous Renshaw Street Chapel, Liverpool's counterpart of Cross Street. William Rathbone VI sat as a Liberal MP more or less throughout the period of Gladstone's ascendancy, and Bryce spent several continental holidays with the Rathbones: a tour of central Greece in 1885, for instance, and a stay at the Rathbones' villa in Alassio on the Italian riviera the following year.[36] Rathbone was strongly committed to an ethic of the public responsibilities attached to great wealth, an ethic celebrated in Eleanor Rathbone's memoir of her father. She depicted a man who cared 'a great deal for the ethical and spiritual side of religious teaching and very little for questions of doctrine': a perspective that Bryce certainly shared.[37]

Importantly for Bryce, William Rathbone's closest friend was Thomas Ashton of Hyde, Bryce's future father-in-law. Rathbone and Ashton studied together in Heidelberg (where Bryce himself studied, much later), and they became brothers-in-law when both married daughters of Rathbone's former business partner, Samuel Gair. One of Rathbone's sons would be given the forenames Thomas Ashton. The Ashtons were themselves notable Unitarians, associated with Manchester New College, which Thomas Ashton served as treasurer, as well as some of Bryce's favourite educational causes, such as Owens College and the Manchester High School for Girls.[38] He fully endorsed Rathbone's values, and was as notable in building civic institutions in Manchester as Rathbone was in Liverpool. Thomas Ashton was, in fact, a singularly important force in reshaping Manchester's educational landscape, as the leading figure both in the extension of Owens College and in the reform of the Hulme Trust. He was, in his son-in-law's words, a man 'whose energy and solid judgment made everyone feel that no enterprise he undertook could fail to be carried through'.[39]

The other important connection in the North West was with the Winkworths of Bolton.[40] Emma Winkworth was the daughter of Thomas Thomasson, the Bolton cotton manufacturer, Cobdenite, and democrat; her husband, Stephen, another cotton master, was the younger brother of the translators and hymn-writers Susanna and Catherine Winkworth.[41] Thomasson was raised as a Quaker but married outside the Society and thereafter moved in Unitarian

FIGURE 4.1. Thomas Ashton (1818–1898), cotton manufacturer, Manchester Unitarian, and father of Marion Bryce.

circles. The Winkworth family were Anglican by upbringing, but Susanna and
Catherine were very close to the Gaskells, whom they had known since the
late 1840s, when they attended William Gaskell's classes at Manchester New
College, and they were strongly attracted to the Unitarianism of the Gaskell
circle in Manchester.[42] It was, indeed, Elizabeth Gaskell who introduced Bryce
to Stephen Winkworth when he was starting his Schools Inquiry work in
May 1865.[43] Catherine Winkworth recalled that 'the Unitarians in Manchester
were, as a body, faraway superior to any other in intellect, culture and refine-
ment of manners'.[44] The Winkworths were also close to the Darbishire family.
Stephen and Emma Winkworth were mountaineers and devoted supporters
of girls' and women's education: Emma was one of the original subscribers to
the Manchester High School for Girls, and her brother, John Pennington

Thomasson MP, also lent the committee £10,000 at a low mortgage rate to enable it to acquire its premises.[45] Emma also gave generously to both Girton and Newnham.[46] She served on the College Council at Newnham for nearly half a century, from 1880 to 1925. It seems likely that Bryce was introduced to the Winkworths by Goldwin Smith, who knew them well, probably in the first instance through Cobden.[47] In any case, he became intimate friends with both, Emma in particular, and stayed with them frequently in the 1870s. On what seems to have been the first occasion, in February 1871, he told his sister Kate: 'Mrs W is an interesting character, of quite an uncommon type, brought up by a Unitarian manufacturer of immense wealth in the most stringent radicalism. She is a lively bright creature of strong will and great vigour, having climbed the Jungfrau, and I know not what other peaks.'[48] Her husband died in his fifties in 1886, and in later years Emma lived mostly in London, where her house, Holly Lodge on Campden Hill (once the home of Macaulay), was famous for her summer garden parties.[49] On her death Bryce wrote to Dicey: 'She was one of the truest friends & one of the purest finest souls we have known.'[50] On Bryce's death in 1922, the Winkworths' son, Stephen, told Marion that 'I think he was Mamma & Papa's most beloved and admired friend.'[51]

Whether these connections indicated that Bryce himself was drawn to Unitarianism is unclear. He had a lifelong Christian commitment, apparently unquestioned, but of an undoctrinaire and nonsectarian kind. He was firm in refusing any temptation to conform to the Establishment, but he would happily worship in Anglican churches when appropriate: at New College chapel when in Oxford, at Manchester Cathedral, and sometimes, with his Anglican friends, at their parish church. His Manchester friends included a number of Anglicans, in particular two of his Oxford contemporaries or near-contemporaries, the poet and schools inspector Erasmus Henry Brodie and the Liberal politician and shipping magnate Edward (later Sir Edward) Donner. Incidentally, Manchester had two United Presbyterian congregations, but there is no evidence that Bryce sought them out or had any dealings with them.[52]

It is unlikely that Bryce was drawn to Unitarianism by doctrinal doubt about Trinitarianism. Indeed, he sometimes expressed some antipathy toward 'those more extreme views' that had sprung out of Unitarianism.[53] In spite of his associations with the Darbishires and the Rathbones, he apparently did not frequent the great Unitarian churches of the region, such as Cross Street Chapel in Manchester or Renshaw Street Chapel in Liverpool. Instead he probably simply found Unitarian circles culturally sympathetic, not least because the central principle of Unitarianism was a devotion to free inquiry in matters of religion, and a staunch opposition to doctrinal creeds of all kinds. In addition, the Unitarians were fiercely attached to the cause of girls' and women's education.[54] A striking number of his Manchester friends—men and women—were associated with the founding of the Manchester High School for Girls, either as subscribers or as governors, or both. They included the Anglicans Brodie and Donner as well as Unitarians such as the Ashtons, the Darbishires, and the Gaskells. Bryce himself had no formal connection with the High School, but its foundation was a cause close to his heart, since as an assistant commissioner for the Taunton Commission he had drawn attention to the urgent need for the provision of girls' secondary education in the North West and had pressed the case for the redeployment of surplus endowments for this purpose. The history of the High School by its second headmistress, Sara Burstall, is clear about the extent of Bryce's involvement in the school's establishment, noting that in the years up to 1874 he was 'constantly in Manchester, and meeting the group of men and women who were interested in this question.'[55]

The Schools Inquiry Commission

When Bryce was offered the Schools Inquiry appointment, his former tutor North Pinder counselled him to turn it down: 'Don't let them divert you from the main line.'[56] It was indeed a distraction from his embryonic legal career. But the benefits were significant: the pay was good (£50 a month for eight months—later extended—plus 15 shillings per day for expenses), and, as his father put it to him, he would make contacts who could certainly be useful to him afterwards; a prediction that certainly proved true, but perhaps in ways he did not foresee.[57] It was by no means an unusual career step for a young college fellow: among the other assistant commissioners were several college fellows, including T. H. Green of Balliol and Bryce's Oriel colleague, the future judge Robert Wright. A legal background was thought useful preparation for the investigative work to be undertaken by the assistant commissioners, not least because the problem of the disposition of endowments threw up notoriously difficult legal challenges.

For Bryce there was no doubt an additional attraction. He was a natural educator and, indeed, a natural examiner. In reading his family correspondence, it is intriguing to see how much interest he took in his sisters' education. 'All that you want to write well is practice—without which few or none can express themselves readily', he told his twenty-year-old sister, Katharine, in

1871. 'You have plenty of good ideas—or at least the power of mastering them if your knowledge was wider—but expression is a matter of training.'[58] Well into their adulthood, he prescribed them courses of reading. Two years later he recommended that Mary, then twenty-five, should read Dugald Stewart, to 'give you an idea of abstract studies', the historians Freeman, Gibbon, Macaulay, and Milman, the English poets, Wilhelm von Humboldt, and (a particular favourite of his) the Norse sagas, the Heimskringla and the Njáls.[59] He came from a family of schoolteachers, and both his father and his Uncle John had strong views on the questions the Taunton Commission dealt with. His father offered advice on how his son should set about his role as assistant commissioner and spoke as one who had undergone a visitation by 'Mr Commissioner Harvey' for the Argyll Commission, the Scottish counterpart to the Taunton Commission.[60]

Uncle John even gave evidence to the commission, perhaps taking advantage of his son's access to the commissioners to secure this opportunity. The evidence he gave was typical of the man: opinionated, idiosyncratic, perhaps crotchety, and betraying a somewhat inflated sense of his own importance. None of these characteristics was shared by his nephew. But the content of Dr Bryce's evidence was nevertheless fascinating: he expounded a philosophy of education derived, he said, immediately from Dugald Stewart and ultimately from Condillac, according to which there was 'a scientific art of education, which should bear the same relation to mental philosophy that the science and art of medicine bears to anatomy and physiology'. Because the educational art had scientific foundations as solid as the medical art has, it followed, he argued, that teachers needed a training as rigorous as that afforded to medical doctors. He therefore proposed that each university should establish a Professorship of Pedeutics (his term), or the art of educating. Student teachers should be required to attend professorial courses and to demonstrate their ability to implement the principles taught, whereupon they would become certified teachers, eligible for appointment in 'all schools of public foundation, including schools founded by private benevolence.'[61]

Dr Bryce had been propounding these ideas for four decades, beginning with a pamphlet in 1828 in which he sketched a 'system of national education' for Ireland.[62] This rested on a vision of making

teaching into a fourth learned profession, by establishing a Professor of the Art [of Education] in every University,—by requiring from those who study under him a good previous education, and, in particular, an acquaintance with the science of mind,—and by making a certificate of attendance on his instructions an indispensable for every public charge connected with the education of youth, from the presidencies of our richest and most illustrious colleges, to the masterships of our humblest village schools.[63]

He contested the assumption that 'a man who understands a subject must be qualified to teach it': even the profoundest scholar also 'has to learn how to communicate his knowledge, and how to train the young mind to think for itself'. He advocated a system of national education for Ireland modelled on the Scottish system of burgh and parochial schools, together with several universities distributed across the country; with the proviso that, in Scotland and in Ireland, the masterships in the national schools should be freed from any restriction to members of the established church. 'Imitate Scotland when she is right, supply what she has omitted, and avoid her footsteps where she is wrong.'[64]

Three other key principles that Dr Bryce helped instil in his nephew were adumbrated in his *Sketch of a Plan for a System of National Education*. One was a defence of the principle of public provision of education: here he drew closely but not uncritically on Thomas Chalmers's case for the endowment of education. A second was a decided preference for the 'rational and manly principle' of the management of schools 'by persons on the spot': somewhat counterintuitively, he thought that this principle would be secured by public provision, since 'private societies are apt to claim and exercise a power over the schools which is injurious'.[65] The third was the principle that national education should be capable of comprehending religious pluralism. In the 1850s Dr Bryce developed his critique of the denominational restrictions that, in practice, prevented the schools and universities of Scotland from being properly national institutions, as they were intended to be.[66] And in the last years of his life in the 1880s, he became fixated on campaigning against the Roman Catholics' establishment of denominational training colleges, which he thought would destroy 'the original non-sectarian character of the National Schools'.[67] We find echoes of many of these themes—not least, a fierce insistence on nonsectarianism in education—in Bryce's own career.[68]

The central problem with which Bryce wrestled in his Schools Inquiry work was the need to remodel centuries-old endowments to meet modern challenges: the movement of population, the demand for a 'modern' curriculum encompassing the sciences and modern languages, and the need to provide an academic education for girls. The education of girls was a notably important point for Bryce, whose report was instrumental in ensuring that the commission gave this issue due centrality in its recommendations.[69] The remodelling of endowments was a problem that far transcended schools. It was a nationwide issue, but it was especially acute in Manchester, for two reasons in particular: first, the city was the home of three notable educational charities, managed by the feoffees of Chetham's Hospital, the feoffees (later, trustees and then governors) of the Manchester Grammar School, and the trustees of William Hulme's charity. In the first half of the nineteenth century, all three bodies were dominated by the Anglican gentry of the surrounding area, such as the Egertons of Tatton, near Knutsford. Second, Manchester had a politically conscious professional and mercantile middle class with strong links to religious nonconformity. They resented the dominance of a social elite, overwhelmingly Anglican and Tory, who mostly lived at some distance from the city.[70] The control of charitable trusts, especially educational trusts, was therefore politically charged, and there were prolonged contests over the control and reform of these three trusts.[71] Significantly, when Henry Roscoe first approached his fellow Unitarian Thomas Ashton for assistance with the reform—or 'extension'—of Owens College, Ashton objected 'that the Governors of the private Trust were strong Churchmen and mainly Tories, with whom he had little sympathy'. He was wrong, in fact, about the trustees of Owens College, as he would go on to discover; but the fact that he had this perception was certainly due to the scars he bore from the fights over the Hulme and Manchester Grammar School trusts.[72]

One of Bryce's distinctive concerns in his report was with the composition of the governing bodies of educational trusts. He found that 'governing bodies are now too narrow, and would be improved by the infusion of a representative element'.[73] Later he reiterated the point in recommending 'the reconstitution of governing bodies so as to introduce everywhere a representative element, and to give the townspeople a more direct and lively interest in the welfare of the school'.[74] This was a particular concern of Bryce's, although Joshua Fitch in his parallel report on Yorkshire schools also held that 'the constitution of governing bodies' was one reason for the decline in the endowed grammar schools he investigated in Yorkshire.[75] Fitch was especially interesting on this point, observing that members of governing bodies needed two qualities which were rarely combined: 'specific knowledge of the neighbourhood and its wants', and 'a general knowledge of education, and on the principles on which it should be given'. The former would be most likely to be found in 'reputable and intelligent inhabitants of the place'; the latter, by 'men of higher education at a distance, who are free from local prejudices, and who are capable of taking what Comte calls *vues d'ensemble*'. Governing bodies should be so constituted as to allow for an appropriate number of both.[76] But it was Bryce who formulated the concept of the *representative* governance of a trust, a concept which was introduced into English public discourse by the Schools Inquiry Commission and its aftermath.

Bryce was clear that an active governing body aware of its public responsibilities was essential to the effective operation of an endowed school. We can get a sense of his concerns from his reports on schools which he thought particularly defective in this regard. Blackburn Free Grammar School could trace its origins to a pre-Reformation grammar school taught by a chantry priest and was reestablished under Elizabeth I with a permanent income out of the extinguished chantry endowment. Bryce evidently regarded it as inadequate: it had fewer than a hundred pupils on its roll, whereas he judged that the population of Blackburn and surrounding towns was sufficient to sustain a grammar school of three hundred boys or more. It did not send boys on to Oxford or Cambridge. Some of the reasons for its failure were common to much of Lancashire, such as parents' lack of interest in any kind of liberal education, whether classical or modern. But the specific reasons were much more to do with the inadequacy of the governance. There were no fewer than fifty governors, of whom it was rarely possible to get as many as five or six at a meeting; and they were a self-electing body who excluded non-Anglicans, with the result that nonconformists in the town regarded the school as an alien institution to which they would not subscribe, for instance for new buildings. Apart from new and larger buildings, the single most important change needed was 'the reconstitution of the governing body, diminishing its numbers, infusing into it a representative element, and placing it in communication with some central authority which may stimulate and guide its action in raising the character of the school'.[77]

Middleton Grammar School, north of Manchester, presented the interesting (but by no means unique) case of a school governed by an Oxford college. Brasenose College had received property held in trust for the school from an Elizabethan Principal of the college, Alexander Nowell, the dean of St Paul's. It continued to pay only the annual amount stipulated by Nowell, even though the property had multiplied in value; and fellows of the college rarely visited the school.[78] This was an egregious instance of neglect by a distant governing body, which effectively considered its role as that of patron, appointing the headmaster but then leaving the running of the school entirely in his hands.

The school had only thirty-seven boys and girls on its roll and did not send pupils to university, in spite of the availability of a closed scholarship at Brasenose. Bryce's recommendations were, first, the building of a new school house and, second, 'the establishment of a local governing body who are likely to interest themselves in its welfare'.[79]

At Bolton Free Grammar School, where the foundation was reformed by Act of Parliament in 1788, the trustees were a body of twelve, which Bryce thought an appropriate size, and they were required to be freeholders in the parish. But they also were required to be Anglicans, and it was a self-electing body. In practice it was difficult to get a quorum of seven, and decisions were effectively delegated to an Education Committee with a quorum of three. The school, Bryce found, had 'no air of prosperity about it'. He recommended that 'a representative element ought to be infused into the trust, so as to stimulate the action of the board of trustees, and give to the town more interest in the school'.[80]

What did Bryce mean by a representative element? He had a particular admiration for the Lancaster Free Grammar School, whose fifteenth-century founder entrusted it, along with an endowment, to the care of the mayor and corporation. The success of the school, which had 158 pupils, exemplified 'the advantage of making the management of a school really public': it ensured that the local inhabitants took pride in the school because they regarded it as theirs. He noted that the effective management of Lancaster Grammar School did not prove that other town councils would be equally judicious if entrusted with control over schools, but he at least inferred that 'cases like Lancaster show the desirability of infusing a representative element into those boards of trustees, which are at present, like those of so many Lancashire schools, stagnant, exclusive, devoid of public spirit'.[81] In other words, Bryce did not equate a representative trust with control by elected councillors. He primarily meant a body of trustees who were broadly accountable to local and in some cases national public opinion.

The largest and best-endowed school inspected by Bryce was Manchester Grammar School: it was one of those endowments of sufficient national importance that the commissioners themselves made formal recommendations in their report.[82] The composition of the body of twelve trustees ('feoffees') had been much contested but substantially reformed in 1849, and when Bryce visited he found them to be 'persons of influence in the city, [who] appear to enjoy its confidence, and although the cares of business do not permit them to give much continuous attention to the school affairs, they seem to take a lively interest in its welfare'. They did not yet include Thomas Ashton, who was appointed governor in 1868, but Bryce probably first met his future father-in-law on one of his Schools Inquiry visits.[83] Bryce was, however, critical of the fragmentation of responsibility embodied in the school's constitution, which he found 'somewhat complicated'.[84] The head ('high master') and the usher were appointed not by the feoffees but by the president of Corpus Christi College, Oxford, who otherwise had no role in the school; while the dean of Manchester was ex officio visitor, and in conjunction with the high master he had the responsibility of appointing the other teaching staff. The commission thought that it was inadvisable to have 'more than two seats of authority' in a school, namely, more than the Governing Body and the head, and recommended that the separate powers of the president of Corpus Christi and the dean of Manchester should be abolished, though they might be ex officio governors. This recommendation was implemented in the scheme drawn up by the Charity Commission in 1875 and implemented in amended form in 1877. The president of Corpus Christi and the dean of Manchester became ex officio governors, along with the mayors of Manchester and Salford; six representative governors were appointed by the Corporations of Manchester and Salford, by the justices of the peace for Manchester and Salford, the Manchester and Salford School Boards, and the Universities of Oxford and Cambridge. These twelve would be balanced by 'co-optative' governors: initially the twelve existing trustees, who were entitled to serve for life, and gradually falling to nine.[85]

As we shall see shortly, the transformation that the Taunton Commission wrought in the governance of endowed schools—in particular, the movement away from close trusts to more properly public governing bodies with a strong 'representative' element—was mirrored remarkably closely in the reorganization of Owens College, Manchester, at the same time. Bryce was intimately involved here, too, and the constitution that he helped shape subsequently provided the model for the governance of English civic universities.

Remaking Owens College

Bryce investigated Owens College as part of his work for the Taunton Commission: partly because it was an educational endowment, though a very recent one, but mainly because he thought that the existence of a college providing university-level education was an important stimulus to secondary schooling, as well as having an ennobling influence on the cultural life of a city. Among the industrial towns and cities, Manchester was unique in having such a college. Founded in 1851, it struggled in its early years but started to expand

FIGURE 4.2. Owens College, Quay Street, Manchester, as it was when Bryce first visited in the spring of 1866: 'I found people in Manchester who did not so much as know of its existence.'

in the early 1860s and was already acquiring some recognition for the distinction of its professors. Nevertheless, when Bryce investigated it, the college had around 130 day students, and he thought it ought to have three or four times as many.

Bryce thought the explanation lay primarily in parental attitudes and those of the business community, but he also thought the college was handicapped by its location and premises:

> Then the buildings of the college are in every way unsuited to its need, they stand in one of the most obscure parts of the city, and consist of small rooms in a private house, roughly adapted to their present purpose. Lying thus out of sight, the college has in a manner been out of mind also. I found people in Manchester who did not so much as know of its existence, while in some quarters its very newness and its unsectarian character seem to have created against it an unworthy and groundless prejudice.[86]

It is very likely that his connection with the college developed out of his interview with its principal, Joseph Greenwood, for the Schools Inquiry Commission.[87] He interviewed Greenwood in the spring of 1866 and the following year was appointed as lecturer to assist the professor of jurisprudence, Richard Christie. He continued on that basis until he was appointed to succeed

Christie in the chair of Jurisprudence and Law, which he held from 1870 until his resignation in 1875. This was not designed as a full-time appointment: the salary was £75 a year (increased to £120 in 1871), whereas a full-time professor might command a salary of £300–400; but in addition he was entitled to two-thirds of the fees.[88] Christie, his predecessor, had also been professor of ancient and modern history and of political economy and had a growing practice at the chancery bar. The requirement was to give at least eighteen lectures, but it allowed Bryce to employ an approved deputy for some of them. His practice was initially to give two courses of six or seven lectures each (later reduced to one), at 4.30 or 5 p.m., usually in the autumn and sometimes in the spring; and he preferred to fulfil his duties in concentrated form, in two or three weeks.[89] He could therefore hold the chair concurrently with the Regius Professorship at Oxford (itself a nonresident chair, with a miserly salary of £140, later raised by £300), as well as his practice on the Northern Circuit.[90] He also remained a fellow of Oriel, with a stipend in the region of £250.

Bryce was at Owens at a pivotal point in the college's history. Even though he thought student numbers much lower than they should be, they were starting to run up against the capacity of the premises. The overcrowded building in Quay Street (Richard Cobden's old house in the city centre) was manifestly inadequate, and a scheme was conceived for the radical reconstruction of the college as an institution and its relocation to more spacious premises in the parish of Chorlton-on-Medlock, to the south of the city. This entailed the creation of a new institution, the 'extension college', funded by an appeal for subscriptions from the business community of the city: once instituted, the college would then merge with the existing institution to create a new corporate entity, one freed from the shackles of John Owens's will.[91] This project was the work of three men in particular: Henry Roscoe, the distinguished professor of chemistry, whose brainchild it was; Joseph Greenwood, the principal, a man of organizational genius; and the mill-owner and Heidelberg graduate Thomas Ashton, Bryce's future father-in-law. These were the three men singled out for tribute in Bryce's reflections half a century later.[92]

The Extension College's constitution committee commissioned Bryce to draft a constitution for the college in June 1869.[93] That they appointed him to this role—a year before he took on the Chair of Law—is striking and needs some explanation. As a practising lawyer, he was far less experienced than two members of the committee, Darbishire and Christie; and he had published nothing on the law. There is little evidence bearing on how he came to be appointed. But we do have the instructions issued to Bryce by the constitutional committee. We also have the draft that Bryce produced, and the amendments made first by the constitution committee and then by the Owens trustees, and of course the agreed text, which varied but slightly from Bryce's draft.[94] The central feature of that text is the tripartite division in the governance of the college, with power distributed among three distinct bodies: the Court of Governors, which was the supreme governing body; the Council, which was responsible for day-to-day operations, financial management, and the preparation of business for the Court; and the Senate, which was responsible for the strictly academic or educational side of the college's work. These powers were not formally separate, for the members of the Council were elected by the other two bodies, eight by the Court, two by the Senate, the other two being ex officio members; Senate consisted of the professors, who were appointed by Council; while Senate and Council had (limited) representation on the Court. Importantly, lay governors predominated, and, equally, lay members elected by the Court from among its own lay members greatly outnumbered the academic members on Council. One other feature deserves notice: there was representation on the Court for former students of the college (designated 'associates', not 'graduates', for the college did not award degrees in its own right). This was a status that had come into being in 1858, with strict criteria for admission; but now for the first time the associates had a formal role in governance.

This scheme of governance was adopted by the federal Victoria University on its foundation in 1880, and because that university, when it was dissolved in 1903, gave birth to three independent universities (Manchester, Liverpool, and Leeds), it thereafter became the standard governance model for English universities, with the inevitable exceptions of Oxford and Cambridge. It institutionalized the role of laymen (meaning, in this context, nonacademics) in university governance, while at the same time planting the seeds of academic self-government in the civic universities. Where did Bryce derive the idea of the tripartite division, or how did he conceive it, if, indeed, it was his conception? What problems was it designed to address?

Bryce was of course familiar with other kinds of academic organization, in particular the Gothic federalism of Oxford and Cambridge: a delicate equilibrium of quite another kind. A more obvious model for Owens College was University College, London, which, like Owens, repudiated any kind of religious tests.[95] The Owens Extension Committee certainly studied its scheme of governance.[96] It had a Council and an Academic Senate. It was, however, a proprietorial institution until 1869, when private legislation put an end to proprietorial rights but transformed shareholders into governors with a right to nominate their successors, alongside life governors appointed by Council.[97] Senate was defined in the bylaws rather than in the college's constitution and was formally advisory, with no clearly demarcated area of responsibility for (e.g.) the college's studies and discipline; nor was there professorial representation on Council. There was no structured relationship with public authorities, civic or national. In this sense its governance model, though suggestive, was much less advanced than that forged by Owens in 1870.

Bryce was even more familiar with the Scottish universities. These were themselves in a position of flux in this period. The Act of 1858 imposed a large degree of homogeneity on institutions that had previously been very different. It put an end, for instance, to Edinburgh University's subjection to the town council. Henceforth they were governed according to a tripartite institutional structure. In their case (as, in fact, in Bryce's initial draft for Owens), the Court was the small executive body—seven members, of whom one (the rector, elected by the student body) by tradition did not attend. The Senate (or *senatus academicus*) consisted of the professors and had a similar role to its counterpart at Manchester; while the General Council consisted of the graduates of the university. This system of governance gave no influence to the city, or to the professional or business communities of the region, except insofar as they could incidentally speak through the graduates in Council. Indeed, in the case of Edinburgh, the Act of 1858 liberated the university from its subordination to municipal opinion.

What was distinctive and new about the Owens College scheme was the institutionalization of the dominant role of lay members in the structures of authority. Here Bryce's scheme had a clear purpose. For under the terms of John Owens's will, the college had since its foundation been ruled by a body of trustees, somewhat in the manner of an American private college. The trustees were appointed in the first instance by Owens himself, mostly from among his friends in the Manchester business community: his business partner, George Faulkner, was the first chairman of the trustees; Faulkner's successor was Alderman William Neild, a calico printer and latterly banker, and on his death in 1864, Neild was succeeded by his son Alfred. Pragmatically, it was necessary to the success of the extension movement that it should have the backing of the existing trustees, who had in any case proved, for the most part, both committed to the interests of the college and careful not to step on the toes of the principal and professors. The extension committee too, being chiefly focused on raising subscriptions from the Manchester business community, was dominated by laymen with commercial or professional backgrounds, such

FIGURE 4.3. Owens College Senate in academic year 1872–1873. Bryce is third from the right; Adolphus Ward is speaking; Henry Roscoe is seated at the front on Ward's left; and the principal, Joseph Greenwood, is in the chair on the far right.

as Thomas Ashton and Robert Darbishire. So the explanation for the preponderance of laymen in the governance of the incorporated college lay on the one hand in path dependency, and on the other in the power of money. The Council appointed in 1870 drew substantially on the outgoing trustees: Robert Darbishire, Murray Gladstone (the prime minister's cousin), and W. H. Houldsworth were members of both bodies, and Alfred Neild, the last chairman and treasurer of the Trustees, was the first chairman of the Council and treasurer of the college. Some of these—Darbishire above all—had been closely involved in the extension movement, and they were joined on the Council by the leading figures of that movement: Thomas Ashton, Richard Christie, and (as a representative of Senate) Henry Roscoe.

It was Ashton who expounded the thinking behind the new constitution in his address to a subscribers' meeting in December 1869. The aim was to have a governing body that was small enough to ensure that each member felt a sense of individual responsibility, but also large enough to ensure stability, no one member being crucial to the college's management. It was also important to ensure accountability to public opinion, through nominated members, including those nominated by central and local government. Above all the constitution committee had sought to design a safeguards against 'what seemed to be the natural tendency of all institutions to permit the growth of abuses amongst them'.[98] Or, as the Owens College Extension Act of 1870 would put it, there was a need to place higher education in Manchester and its neighbourhood 'under the management of a public body rather than of trustees of private nomination'.[99]

The constitution committee was clearly echoing key passages in Bryce's report on Lancashire schools for the Schools Inquiry Commission, published in 1868.[100] In the first place, Bryce explicitly discussed the question of the optimal size of a governing body. He noted that in Lancashire schools, this varied between six and fifty: 'The advantages both of the greater and of the lesser number are sufficiently plain. Where there are many there is less likely to be corruption; there is a greater accessibility to public opinion, and a better chance of having all sorts of interests, feelings, and parties fairly represented. On the other hand, a small board is more efficient and practical, meets at shorter notice, and cares more about its functions.' A governing body as large as twenty, he thought—let alone fifty—'must form an unwieldy and cumbersome body', since 'what is everybody's business becomes nobody's; the sense of responsibility upon each is so small that it practically disappears'. The consensus among people Bryce consulted was that a body of ten or twelve was roughly the right size to administer the school well and at the same time to be broadly representative of the public.[101]

Ashton's summary of the thinking that lay behind the proposed constitution for Owens College picked up on Bryce's key points. There was a balance to be struck between the advantages of compactness (efficiency, individual responsibility) and those of scale: for Ashton, the argument for scale was chiefly to do with permanence and stability, whereas for Bryce it was to do with responsiveness to public opinion; but Ashton picked up on the latter point too in noting the role of nominated members of Court in the Owens constitution. Bryce stipulated that the ideal governing body should have ten to twelve members, and his draft constitution provided for a Council of twelve (plus the president): eight elected by the Court from among its own (non-Senatorial) members; two professors elected by the Senate; and the principal and the treasurer ex officio.

Bryce was centrally concerned to affirm the *public* character of endowed schools and the *public* responsibility of their trustees. He and Fitch pointed to the tendency of close foundations to become corrupt and inward-looking, as had happened to some notorious *causes célèbres* such as the north-west educational charity, the Hulme Trust. They urged the importance of publicity—notably, the publication of the trust's accounts—as a remedy for the danger of corruption. 'Publicity acts as a constant check on negligence and waste', wrote Fitch; 'it increases the interest of the inhabitants in the charity and their knowledge of its affairs.'[102] Bryce argued that their publicity was one of the strengths of endowed schools: it gave them and their masters a social status which proprietorial schools could not match; it made them more independent of parents and, at the same time, more accountable to public opinion. Whereas in France and Germany these objects were achieved by the direct subjection of schools to the state, in England the same goals were pursued 'in a manner more conformable to the genius of English institutions', by committing these powers to local bodies considered as representative of the local community. But, crucially:

> The success of such a system must evidently depend upon the extent in which this idea—the idea of trusteeship as a delegated authority, which is to be exercised for the good of and in accordance with the wishes of the people—is recognized and acted upon. A trustee is surely bound in honour, not only to do his best for the school funds and the school teaching, but also to endeavour to interest the inhabitants in the welfare of their school, to make no unnecessary secret of its management, to admit the most deserving of his fellow townsmen, whether or not they are his personal friends, to a share in the government, and in this way to let the Board of Trustees be as nearly as possible a fair and equal representation of the probity, intelligence, and public spirit of the neighbourhood. In other words, the existing oligarchical system can be defended and justified only on the hypothesis that it attains all the benefits of a democratic one without its accompanying evils.
>
> Trustees, however, although they do not repudiate this view when it is proposed to them, sometimes forget it in practice, and look upon their office as a private and personal affair, carrying with it some little honour and power which they are entitled to use as they think fit, so long as they turn it to no sordid end. . . . They even begin to fancy it the hereditary possession of their family or their connexion; and nephews, brothers-in-law, or friends are placed, when occasion offers, upon the trust, to the exclusion of men more earnest and more competent.[103]

In the light of these remarks, we can see very clearly what the Owens College trustees had in mind when they commissioned Bryce to draft a constitution for the incorporated college. Owens, they told him, had become a public service and should therefore become a public institution, as distinct from a private trust with private trustees. The choice of governors should reflect this new standing as a public institution: they should include representatives of government, local dignitaries, office-holders such as the bishop of Manchester, men of distinction in the community, local and national, representatives of the professoriate, representatives of the former students of the college.[104] They would certainly have read Bryce's report on Lancashire schools, and it is easy to see why they thought of him when faced with the task of framing a scheme of governance for such a college. Indeed, since Bryce's report for the Taunton Commission rode roughshod over the modern distinction—not fully assimilated until three decades later—between 'secondary' and 'higher' education—he had himself made the case for something like the 'extension' of the college, including 'the subscriptions and sympathy of Lancashire people', better relations with the mercantile and manufacturing classes of the region, 'more imposing and commodious buildings', and 'a more assured public position and reputation'.[105]

In his alertness to the significance of the distinction between a private trust and a public institution, Bryce was an important figure, but one who stood close to the mainstream of advanced Liberal thinking in the Gladstonian era.[106] But in considering the problem of the relationship between the professoriate and laymen in the governance of Owens College, Bryce added something distinctive to the mix. His vision was of a college in which laymen were numerically preponderant both on the Court of Governors and on Council, so as to guard against the danger that academics would run the college in their own group interest rather than serving the wider public interest. But at the same time, these laymen would acknowledge that the college could prosper only if it could recruit, develop, and retain distinguished scholars and scientists, and to do that it must give them free rein in purely academic matters. There could be institutional safeguards, notably in allowing the Senate full authority over the curriculum, but since control of the purse-strings in the end affected all activities in the college, it also required qualities of wisdom, prudence, and moderation among the lay governors. Where did this vision come from? It is impossible to demonstrate the point, but there is a striking affinity with the ecclesiastical polity of the Presbyterian churches, with which Bryce was of course thoroughly familiar.[107] In particular, the distinction between

ruling elders (laymen) and teaching elders (clergy) was fundamental, as was
the imperative that the ruling elders, though supreme in their own domain,
should not encroach on the prerogatives of the clergy. That is the most likely
source for Bryce's understanding of the proper relationship between lay governors and academics in a well-ordered modern university, and it underpinned
the constitution he prepared for Owens College.

Educational Endowments

This whole episode was of real importance in Victorian politics, as well as
leaving an enduring mark on Bryce's outlook. Gladstone's first ministry set
about implementing the central recommendations of the Taunton Commission by establishing the Endowed Schools Commission, with extensive powers to restructure endowments and to produce revised schemes of governance
for the schools within its remit. It was the commissioners who were primarily
responsible for entrenching the notion of representative government of educational charities that Bryce had articulated. But the Taunton Commission
had concluded by recognizing that 'the whole field which we have traversed is
beset with questions which have been made matter of eager controversy', and
that its recommendations would inevitably arouse 'animadversion and dissent'.[108] So it proved, and it was the Endowed Schools Commissioners who
received most of the abuse, in particular when they set about dismantling Anglican monopolies on governing bodies. The ability of the Conservatives to
mobilize middle-class opinion in London on this issue has been invoked to as
an important factor in explaining Disraeli's election victory of 1874—the first
clear-cut Conservative majority for over thirty years.[109]

One of the leading members of the Taunton Commission, Lord Lyttelton,
was appointed as one of the three Endowed Schools Commissioners in 1869.
The Taunton Commission's secretary, Henry Roby, was appointed as the secretary of the new commission, and succeeded as a commissioner in his own
right in 1872. Meanwhile, of the assistant commissioners, Bryce and Fitch were
notably vocal in defence of the commission's work and of the principles of the
public control of educational endowments, and the right of government-
appointed commissioners to override the wishes of a testator a few centuries
previously.[110] That meant taking issue with the Conservative defence of what
Disraeli in 1873 called 'the sacredness of Endowments'. But the controversy
also pitted Bryce against his fellow Liberal Robert Lowe, by now (1868–1873)
chancellor of the exchequer: 'the most eminent—and almost the last—of our

strict economists of the good old school'.[111] Lowe took something of a market-fundamentalist line, which Bryce deemed harsh, narrow, and rigid: Endowments, he thought, acted as bounties, unfairly subsidizing inefficient suppliers and hence distorting the market.[112] Bryce's retort was not to defend the system of endowments in itself, but to argue that education was by its very nature a public good which could not be left to the market. Hence, 'it is not so much endowed schools that are needed as public schools, an organized system of places of instruction of different grades, established all over the country wherever the population is large enough to need them, placed under some sort of authorized control and supervision, and receiving from their publicity a guarantee of efficiency which both private and endowed schools at present want'.[113] Endowments, then, were one form of public provision of education, appropriate for secondary and higher education as direct public funding through the rates was for elementary schooling. Whereas Lowe thought that their history showed endowed foundations to be by their nature always pernicious, Bryce thought them 'pernicious only when left to themselves', and the important principle was 'to treat them as so much public money, to be disposed of as public wisdom thinks best'.[114]

———

Bryce concluded by noting that in addition to the mass of grammar school endowments and the like investigated by the Taunton Commission, there was also 'a multitude of foundations for other charitable purposes, usually administered by small bodies of negligent trustees, under the provisions of wills or deeds of gift made two or three centuries ago'. These were especially numerous, and especially valuable, in the City of London, where he estimated their aggregate revenue to run into the tens of thousands of pounds annually.[115] Many of them were 'positively noxious', and the great majority 'utterly useless'; and Bryce urged the new government to consider whether they might be brought under public control, and in some cases channelled to support the public schools.[116]

It was in fact the Disraeli government which eventually tried to kill the issue by setting up a Royal Commission under the aged Duke of Northumberland in 1878. It produced its report—somewhat insipid for the taste of London radicals—in 1880. By now Bryce was himself sitting in the Commons as the representative of a notably populous London constituency, Tower Hamlets, and Lancashire had been instrumental in drawing Bryce's attention to the importance of the question of misused or unproductive endowments: the City of London was, as the historian David Owen puts it, 'an incomparable museum' for the 'connoisseur of obsolete charities'.[117] Much of Bryce's first parliamentary term was taken up in piloting through parliament a piece of legislation that went significantly beyond the recommendations of the Northumberland Commission. The Parochial Charities Act of 1883 was, perhaps, the greatest legislative achievement of his parliamentary career, not least because he had to outmanœuvre the proponents of a rival, more moderate, bill, promoted by the City churchwardens in defence of their own vested interest in the charitable property they managed. The act empowered the Charity Commissioners to review all City charities and classify each as either 'ecclesiastical' or 'general', and to produce a scheme for the more productive use for public benefit of the general charities. The scheme eventually proposed by the commissioners strongly favoured the interests of technical education, especially in the form of the nascent London polytechnics; indeed Bryce thought it rather overinvested in this cause, which he believed to be of such recognized importance that it could secure ample funds from other sources.[118]

In these debates Bryce was a resolute proponent of the principle that the endowments of charities constituted public property, and that a trustee of such a charity had no 'vested right and interest' in the property but was rightly considered a 'public officer'.[119] He and many of his fellow reformers believed that the needs of secondary education—and higher education too—could be adequately met by an appropriate mix of tuition fees and endowments, provided that existing educational endowments, together with obsolete parochial charities, could be reorganized to serve the public interest. At a time when total endowment income across England and Wales considerably exceeded total central and local government expenditure on education, science, and art, poor relief, and hospitals, this was not an absurd belief. But when, almost three decades after the Taunton Commission sat, Bryce chaired the next major Royal Commission on what was by then known as secondary education, he found himself persuaded that endowments, however efficiently organized, could no longer suffice.[120]

5

A Liberal Ascent

PEAKS AND TROUGHS IN THE 1870S

"On the Whole a Failure"

In March 1873, as he approached his thirty-fifth birthday, Bryce wrote a fascinating letter to his mother. In it he mulled over his career prospects. His ambition to enter parliament was clear: he had unsuccessfully sought selection to contest the Wick by-election the previous year. But he was unsure whether a seat in the Commons would be compatible with his legal practice and his Oxford chair. He contemplated the prospect of giving up politics to concentrate on the law, but the latter had not hitherto been encouraging. Alternatively he could make politics his main object, relying on his chair and his savings to live on. In any case, he had a strong sense that he was reaching a juncture in his life and would need to make choices of paths to take and not to take.[1]

Bryce had a meteoric rise with the stunning success of his *Holy Roman Empire*, the crucial work he did especially for female education through the Schools Inquiry Commission, and his appointment as Regius Professor at the age of only thirty-two. But as the 1870s progressed he and others came to feel that his career had stalled. Academic law gave plenty of scope for him to pursue his intellectual interests, but he found his work at the bar stultifying and not very lucrative. In his diary, where he does not give much vent to emotion, we sense his frustration at time wasted at court hoping for briefs or waiting for cases to be heard: 'wait about for case in vain'; 'to Court: nought there'; 'Allen v Edwards keeps me till late then postponed'.[2] At the same time he was enormously busy, juggling his diverse commitments. These included work at the bar in London, Manchester, and Liverpool; professorial duties in Oxford and Manchester, and, after he had resigned from Owens College, at the Council of

Legal Education; examining at London University; his political career (he stood unsuccessfully as one of two Liberal candidates for Wick in the 1874 election); and a demanding social life in London, Manchester, Liverpool, Oxford, and beyond. He continued to write for the periodical press but cannot have had much time for fundamental intellectual work. Almost a quarter of a century elapsed between *The Holy Roman Empire* (1864) and his next work of enduring significance, *The American Commonwealth* (1888). The novelist Henry James, a good friend, wrote of him in 1879:

> He is a distinctly able fellow, but he gives one the impression of being on the whole a failure. He has had three conflicting dispositions—to literature (History)—to the law—& to politics—& he has not made a complete thing of any of them. He is now however trying to throw himself into politics—to stand for the Tower Hamlets. I am afraid he won't succeed—he belongs to the class of young doctrinaire ~~Liberals~~ Radicals (they are all growing old in it) who don't take the "popular heart" & seem booked to remain out of affairs. They are all tainted with priggishness—though Bryce less so than some of the others.[3]

In the same year, the American historian (and member of the Adams political dynasty) Henry Adams called him 'poor Bryce, who should have been now the best historian in England'.[4]

In the next ten years Bryce established himself as an MP, held ministerial office, and published his greatest work. But at the time, the judgment did not seem wholly unreasonable. In truth it was probably Bryce's own assessment.[5] A letter in 1878 from his good friend, the schools inspector Erasmus Brodie, confirms as much.[6] Brodie was 'grieved to hear' that Bryce was not currently doing law work but assured him that 'even without success at the bar . . . when I compare the achievements of my friends, I know hardly any who has done what you have done'. Brodie counselled Bryce that 'unless you see som[ewha]t clearly that this success [at the bar] will come', he should abandon the bar entirely to concentrate on politics and literature. The implication was that dissipation of effort had been an obstacle to professional success. But 'I don't urge you to abandon politics, because I don't think you could live without them'.[7]

We lack Bryce's side of the correspondence with Brodie, but his letters to his family amply confirm his dissatisfaction with his bar work, which 'hitherto has not been encouraging'.[8] He would travel to Oxford to lecture twice a week, in the afternoon, sometimes returning on the last train, sometimes (especially on Saturdays) staying the night.[9] It was a young man's lifestyle, and Bryce was starting to feel middle-aged:

> The sense of the importance of deciding on one's course in life has suddenly flashed on me, as it were, with the fact that I am nearly 35, half way to the three score & ten, wh[ich] I don't expect or particularly desire to reach. How odd it is, the way in wh[ich] one's life may be really quite different while its external conditions are the same. The last 3 months seem to me altogether unlike the corresponding three of 1872: one's ideas & run of thought wholly changed: one seemed young then & middle aged now; & things that might be postponed then appear to call for decision now.[10]

Brodie was not alone among Bryce's friends in cautioning him against dissipation of his activities in too many directions. The Manchester banker Edward Donner—an Oxford contemporary, and someone Bryce often stayed with in Manchester—wrote a highly illuminating letter in 1873 in which he reported on what people in Manchester (solicitors in particular) said of Bryce, and urged him to take a more businesslike attitude to his career at the bar:

> We were dining at the Sales last night, & old Sale asked me where you were, & said he should really like to know whether you meant to stick to your profession or not. He also said that he would be in London before long, & meant to see you & ask you this question himself, as he had a good deal of work which wanted doing. The fact is that the impression is all the time gaining ground here that you are always setting off somewhere to lecture, or to attend meetings or to do something or other, & that you don't intend to follow up the bar. I also believe that the sort of rumours which are from time to time repeated in the papers to the effect that 'Dr Bryce is mentioned as a probable candidate for a northern constituency' & c do you harm with attorneys. I have twice been told that when you were wanted for work in London you were absent.

Donner acknowledged that these reports might be exaggerated, but he felt that 'if you are depending upon the bar for your career you must take some steps to cut off the lecturing, & throw the energy which you now expend on outside things into getting & keeping business. No attorney will employ a man whom he thinks to be merely a bird of passage.' Donner, who was a firm Liberal but not of the democratic wing of the party, was also sceptical of the wisdom of entering Parliament: 'I don't want to see you a delegate.'[11]

There is a good deal of family correspondence in which Bryce deliberates on career options. One repeated temptation was the possibility of service in

India as Legal Member of the Viceroy's Council—a position held by a number of luminaries in Victorian intellectual and political life, including Sir Henry Maine, Sir James Fitzjames Stephen, Lord Hobhouse, and Sir Courtenay Il- bert. He first speculated about this option in 1872, when in the event the posi- tion was offered to Hobhouse in succession to Stephen.[12] It was tempting to Bryce because the salary, a very ample £8,000 a year, would (he calculated) allow him to return after five years' service with savings of some £30,000: enough to give him the financial security needed for a political career.[13] But being unable to see his family for five years was a major deterrent. Bryce may have been offered the position five years later, in succession to Hobhouse, and definitely was in 1881, when he turned it down.[14]

It is obvious from his correspondence on the Indian appointment that un- derstanding Bryce's career choices in the 1870s requires a sense of his financial position.[15] This was far from straightforward. In the year 1872 he earned in the region of £120 from his chair at Owens College: this included fees as well as salary and allows for the deduction of more than £177 to pay fees to Thomp- son, Dicey, and Holland, his assistant lecturers. They each gave one course of lectures; Bryce himself gave two. In addition, his lectures for the Liverpool Law Society commanded a salary of £100, paid via Owens College. From Ox- ford he drew his fellowship stipend at Oriel: £200, sometimes rather more; and his salary as Regius Professor, which after tax was worth a little over £130, paid partly by the University Chest but mostly by the Church Commissioners, in respect of the canonry that had once been attached to the chair. Oxford examining and similar duties (notably, as presenter of degrees) were worth rather more than £70, and his duties as examiner for the University of London rather less than £100. That meant that his academic work brought him more than £700. He gave up the Owens College chair in 1875, but his appointment to a professorship at the Council of Legal Education from 1877 proved more lucrative: £525 a year, for eighteen lectures, which would have boosted his aca- demic income to over £1000. By then his salary as Regius Professor had been increased by £300.[16] His literary work—writing for the *American Law Review*, the *Saturday Review*, *Macmillan's Magazine*, the *Pall Mall Gazette*, and the *Cornhill* together earned rather more than £50. His earnings at the bar were unpredictable and certainly not his main income: over £130 in 1872, but appar- ently only around £43 the following year; and there were significant profes- sional costs to be set against those earnings at the bar.[17] Overall his expendi- ture was around £400 a year, but that was on the basis of living in bachelor chambers in 12 Hereford Gardens on the Grosvenor Estate in Mayfair; if he were to run a home, he reckoned that his expenditure would rise to at least £700.[18] When he took a house in 1875, it was at a rent of £160 a year: and that was a home he and Mary shared briefly with a fellow barrister, Frederick Verney, and his wife Maude.[19]

This pattern of income calls for some interpretation. Bryce was certainly pursuing a portfolio career *avant la lettre*. Even if we confine ourselves to his academic work, which was his main source of earnings, he held not one professorial chair but two, with examining duties at a third university, and his college fellowship too. He paid assistant lecturers out of his own salary. His practice at the bar was more important as a source of social status and a reinforcement of his credentials as an academic lawyer than for the income alone. He was building up a diverse range of literary connections which would stand him in good stead in later years, but at this stage it fell far short of providing an income he could live on. In total he was probably able to save about half of his annual earnings of £800 or more, which was important as he sought to build up a private income capable of sustaining a parliamentary career.

One option he certainly considered as a way of enhancing his literary income was a journal editorship. His friend Leslie Stephen was on a salary of £500 a year as editor of the *Cornhill Magazine* and was paid in addition for his own contributions. That was much less than Stephen's late father-in-law, W. M. Thackeray, had been paid, but it conferred substantial financial security to support a literary career.[20] Among Bryce's political contemporaries, this was the route taken, most conspicuously, by John Morley, who served as editor of the *Fortnightly Review* from 1867 until 1882, at a salary of around £800; he also edited the *Pall Mall Gazette* (1880–1883, at £2000 a year) and *Macmillan's Magazine* from 1883 to 1885. Bryce was certainly offered the editorship of the Cobdenite *Morning Star* in the 1860s, probably in 1865 or thereabouts: quite why he declined is uncertain, but the offer coincided with his work for the Schools Inquiry Commission, so perhaps the timing was just wrong.[21] Bryce later said that he was not sufficiently methodical for the role of journal editor, and this probably showed an astute sense of his own strengths and weaknesses.[22] That said, Morley's political career certainly benefited from the public voice and of course the patronage his editorships gave him.

Conversely, Bryce's work for the Schools Inquiry Commission, as well as his intellectual standing, brought offers of political roles too. George Goschen, who was president of the Poor Law Board in Gladstone's first government, invited Bryce to become his private secretary in the spring of 1869. Bryce was certainly tempted by this invitation but turned it down to focus on the bar. As he told his father, 'this is the fourth good offer within three months—so 'tis burning one's ships with a vengeance'.[23]

It is unclear what the others were, unless the offer from the *Morning Star* came at this time. But we do know that Bryce had been expecting Sir Travers Twiss to resign the Regius Professorship of Civil Law for some time, and that he certainly regarded himself as a strong claimant to the chair. This might well have been the reason why he declined other appointments at this time. As Dicey wrote when congratulating him on his appointment to the chair a year later, 'I am the more pleased at this event as it completely justifies our view of Göschen's offer.'[24] If this represents Dicey's and Bryce's shared view of the matter, it indicates that academic preferment still mattered to Bryce, and his family correspondence confirms how much he wanted the Regius Professorship. If he were to contemplate a political career, he needed a substantial degree of financial security. That was not simply in order to live once elected, since MPs were not paid a salary until shortly after Bryce stood down from Parliament in 1907. It was also a matter of being able to support the cost of a campaign, especially in a hard-fought constituency. So he told his father in 1875: 'Caird has been urging me on the Glasgow people: & it seems there is some chance of my being run: but they say it will cost £1000.[25] I said I did not think I cd afford to spend more than £300 or £400. This is all in confidence: but if you hear anything further esp about the expense, I shd be glad to know. I agree that there is slight chance of success.'[26]

Miss Gaskell and the Theory of Friendship

One important unknown as Bryce contemplated his prospects was marriage. In the 1860s it was not on his agenda: without an independent income, he had to make his way in a career first. But by the early 1870s he was starting to regard marriage as a viable prospect, even if he was sometimes inclined to be despondent about his chances. His social life of the period shows him clearly seeking the company of women. So on one Wednesday in February 1873, we find him working on an article at home in the morning, then taking a train to Oxford to lecture in the afternoon, dining with the president of Trinity, and then taking a late train back to London to go to a dance hosted by George Murray Smith, the publisher. Why was he so keen to rush back? The clue is in the end of the entry: 'to dance at G. M. Smith's, where S. Kensington Circle'. This was the Onslow Garden ménage of Leslie and Minny Stephen and Minny's sister, Anne Thackeray (later Lady Ritchie), probably with some of their friends.

Anne Thackeray had been at the centre of Bryce's social life since around 1866, both in London and at Freshwater Bay on the Isle of Wight, where he spent a number of springtime holidays with them.[27] Her circle included her cousins, the Ritchies: Indeed she married one of them, Richmond Ritchie, who was seventeen years her junior, and Bryce was dismayed. The Ritchies were prominent in Bryce's social circles in the 1860s and 1870s: Richmond's older brother, William ('a shy mathematical youth of twenty-two') frustrated Bryce by marrying Magdalene Brookfield, a famous beauty of the Freshwater set; while their sister, Augusta, married the mountaineer Douglas Freshfield. From Bryce's point of view, this was all a major disappointment.[28]

The closest he came to marriage was with Margaret (Meta) Gaskell, the second daughter of Elizabeth Gaskell and her husband William. This relationship has not, curiously, been noticed either in the literature on Bryce or in the larger literature on the Gaskell family, yet it is hiding in plain sight in the archive.[29] The surviving correspondence is intriguing and remarkable. As we have seen in a previous chapter, Elizabeth Gaskell was an early point of contact for Bryce when he visited Manchester on his Schools Inquiry work in 1865. She died suddenly six months later, but he was a frequent visitor to the surviving Gaskell household, which consisted of William and his two unmarried daughters, Meta and Julia.[30] The Gaskells' house, a mile from the centre of Manchester in Plymouth Grove on the eastern edge of the affluent and gated Victoria Park, was a notable social salon, even after the novelist's death. Meta had been engaged many years before, in 1857, when she was nineteen, to an Indian army officer named Charles Hill, but had broken off the engagement the following year when information from his sisters made her doubt his character.[31] The first evidence of the relationship between her and Bryce comes from 1871 and early 1872, when he recurs in Meta's letters to her friend Effie Wedgwood, the daughter of Hensleigh Wedgwood and niece by marriage of Charles Darwin.[32] Meta kept asserting her confidence that she and Bryce were committed to each other, but Effie responded by sowing doubts. When Effie said she was anxious for Meta, Meta asked (anxiously) what she had heard. Had Miss Stephen (Leslie Stephen's sister, Milly) told her he had been flirting with other women? No, replied Effie: not Milly Stephen, but Julia Tollemache.[33]

Meta was undeterred, at least on the surface:

You did more than right to tell me openly about Miss Tollemache. I cannot say how I value such frankness, nor what a sense of security 'knowing the worst' always gives me. I am not in the least ostrich-like. As long as there is anything left untold, I have always horrible misconceptions of the possible extent and danger. In this case, spite of my being infected with some of your mistrust of men, & spite of the V. L. experience, I cannot—simply cannot—have the slightest doubt or uncertainty.[34] I hope that I am not copying Miss Tollemache in just telling you briefly the last grounds for this security: that Mr. Bryce last Sunday week loaded his conversation, before Julia, with the broadest doubles entendres—(I hate the word, but know no other)—saying that his real object in coming to Manchester was to see me—etc. & openly that if I was going to Mrs. Leister's ball on the following Tuesday, he wd. go—if I wasn't, he wd.n't—And he went, tho' feeling very unwell. And did everything that was possible in the great crowd, where every word was over-heard—&—(to repeat this is very Miss Tollemache-y!)—told me by a clever double entendre that I was 'perfect'—& then wrote on leaving Manchester to say that 'on leaving it, he felt as if he had hardly been here at all, having had so few chances of seeing friends', & that there were 'ever so many things about which he had hoped to speak to me'—And went off very unwell.

Of course I may be mistaken—tho' Julia says that it is impossible. And death & illness & estrangement following on misrepresentation, are always possibilities; and I find uncertainty (of the future only) very, very trying. But otherwise . . .[35]

What was clear from this sequence of letters in 1871–1872 was, first, that Bryce and Meta both thought that there was a genuine bond existing between them; second, that Bryce did not yet think he was secure enough in his profession to commit to marriage; and third, that he had other young women friends, mostly in London rather than Manchester.[36] This fed Meta's insecurity, which was not made easier by Bryce's tendency to disappear for extended periods: 'You can't think how trying this "total eclipse" sometimes becomes—even tho' I don't, or rather oughtn't to, distrust him for a moment.'[37] Finally, much of Meta's information about Bryce's feelings and his intentions came from Harriet Darbishire, whom Bryce evidently used as a confidante: probably (for he was all his life sensitive to these matters) he confided in her in the knowledge that she was close to Meta.

The correspondence between Meta and Effie ends in February 1872, but it would be wrong to suppose that this was because the relationship between Meta and Bryce fizzled out at this point. The letter of 6 February 1872 is in fact the last surviving letter between Meta and Effie on any subject, quite possibly because Effie got married the following year to the Permanent Secretary of the

Board of Trade, T. H. Farrer. The marriage no doubt weakened the intimacy between the two friends, but it probably also meant that Effie's practices in retaining or destroying correspondence changed. In fact in the last letter we have, Meta reports that Bryce has suggested that they should start to write to each other, something that Meta agreed to, even though she conceded that it was something of a defiance to social convention, given that they were neither married nor engaged.[38]

The relationship endured for several years more. The letters we have between Meta and Bryce are not numerous, and they may very well not represent the entirety of the correspondence, but they indicate an authentic intimacy, even tenderness:

> I keep reproaching myself for not having offered you some luncheon today—instead of forcing you to drink that weak, cold coffee. You looked so dreadfully tired that I can't help fearing that you have been going through great anxiety about your father. You are always so kind when we are in anxiety about our father that I must tell you once more how much I feel for you about it all. But I do trust that full power may be restored. It would be too sad if the happy 'walks over the hills' were really over for ever.[39]

Yet when Bryce was 'wretchedly unwell' in the run-up to Christmas 1876, the Gaskells only heard indirectly.[40]

Bryce resigned his chair at Owens College in 1875, and thereafter he was in the North West much less often: Meta had to wait for the arrival of the Chancery Court.[41] The decreasing frequency of his visits probably exacerbated her anxiety, and her susceptibility to the rumours she heard. The issues came to a head in the late spring and early summer of 1877 or 1878. We have a sequence of letters written in the space of a few weeks. Was it 1877 or 1878? The latter is much the more likely, because Meta expresses the hope that his work on behalf of the Armenian people might bear fruit; and it was really in 1878 that Bryce became publicly identified with the Armenian cause. Indeed, the British campaign on behalf of the Armenians was launched at a meeting at Bryce's house in March, Bryce himself being appointed secretary of the committee that was formed.[42] The meeting had been preceded by an important letter in *The Times* in which Bryce set out the Armenian case in advance of the Congress of Berlin. When Meta concluded her letter of 9 July, 'How earnestly I hope that all your efforts on behalf of Armenia will be rewarded,' she was surely picking up on his letter in *The Times* three days before; a letter which had been followed up by a fellow Armenophile, Lord Carnarvon, the day before Meta wrote.[43] Just a week before, *The Times* and other newspapers had carried reports on the meeting held at Westminster Abbey on behalf of the Anglo-Armenian Committee: Bryce was the prime mover.[44]

Bryce wrote on or around 31 May to ask if he had offended Meta in some way. Quite what prompted him to ask is unclear. Meta responded that she admired those who had the courage to ask in these circumstances, and that she was touched that he had done so. Still, she was concerned that a true explanation, the only kind she could in conscience give, would wound him. She was not offended at all and hoped she had not given that impression:

> I have, however, I admit, rather withdrawn from unnecessary intercourse with you, and this has been in consequence of a change in the perfect confidence that I used to feel in you.
>
> I have been told, by different people, of your having ... (one must use the regular argot, however hateful) ... of your having 'paid attentions' to several women without 'meaning anything':—in fact of your having tried to make them care for you without there being any serious feeling on your part towards them.

Meta at first defended Bryce from these charges and refused to believe them. But:

> Soon after this, I was told by a woman herself that she had been fully led to believe in your attachment to her.—I need hardly say that the confidence was completely unsought by me.—Even here, I tried to believe you quite innocent, and to attribute the mistake and the suffering to an imaginative temperament on the woman's part. Since that, however, I have been led to believe that there are other instances; and a friend on whose judgment I have great reliance has persuaded me that it is not right to continue a friendship under changed conditions of respect and confidence.
>
> If you were not a very clever, quick-sighted man, I could more easily acquit you. A stupid or absent-minded man would probably, through inability to recognize <u>how</u> he had erred in the first case, have not known how to avoid giving the same pain to others in the future. Any woman naturally undergoes a change of feeling towards a man who (she is repeatedly assured) has shown disregard of the happiness and dignity of other women.
>
> At the same time, I have <u>never once</u> allowed myself to condemn you without remembering the old, wise words, 'Audi alteram partem'; nor have I either repeated these things or allowed them to be said in my hearing

without protecting that you ought not to be condemned unheard in your own defence. Have I written 'hardly', or unkindly? If so, I have indeed misrepresented my feeling in the matter.

I must earnestly entreat you to believe how very painful if has been for me to write all this. I cannot bear to seem to 'judge' you. I am deeply convinced how very little one person can appreciate the temptations to which another is exposed, and God knows how unfit I think myself to take up the position of superiority that I appear to assume.

Also, I can see that the whole thing may be one of those unfortunate 'situations', where appearances are curiously against some one who yet is perfectly innocent. I can also imagine that circumstances may prevent your ever offering any defence or explanation, even if you are absolutely blameless. One's relations with people are so complex, and involve so many delicate duties and scruples.

This seems a most ungrateful return to make for all the kindness and 'loyalty' of your letter—for which I thank you from my heart.[45]

In this instance—unusually—we have an indication of the nature of Bryce's reply in the form of his draft letter, partly in note form. That he drafted a response before writing a fair copy is an indication that he wanted to get the wording just right. He was clear that for one accused of such offences, no denial could be of any use. Nevertheless he was explicit that 'I d[o] n[ot] k[now] & can hardly even guess, wh[ich] cases you refer to'. His conscience was clear, but the circulation of the stories made him 'fear lest I may have been blind where sight wd have been useful', and the episode had convinced him 'that I have been unwise in trusting to a theory of friendship betw[een] m[en] & w[omen] wh[ich] seems impract[ical] now in England, perh[aps] anywhere.'[46]

This is obviously a fascinating response. It is clear from what we know of Bryce's social life both from his diary and from his correspondence that whatever understanding he had with Meta Gaskell did not in his view require him to avoid the company of other unmarried women of his age or younger. His defence was that he genuinely believed that a single man and a single woman could be friends without suspicion of any romantic attachment or prospect of marriage. He was pushing at the limits of social conventions and found them more resistant than he had supposed.

Diplomatically this was probably the best defence Bryce could offer, but it is also authentic. He certainly did value the company of intelligent women even (perhaps especially) when marriage was not a prospect, which may account for the close friendship he enjoyed with married women such as Emma Winkworth. But the idea of a 'theory' of friendship between men and women also provides a suggestion of why Bryce spent so much time in predominantly Unitarian company in Manchester and Liverpool. These were the social circles in which he hoped that freer relations between men and women were becoming possible.[47] It is certainly striking that the two women with whom marriage was a serious prospect—Meta Gaskell and then Marion Ashton—were both Manchester Unitarians. So too were the two married women in whom he confided, Harriet Darbishire and (if we stretch Manchester as far as Bolton) Emma Winkworth.

However Bryce eventually phrased the letter he sent, it was not a conspicuous success. Meta replied that his letter had 'hurt me terribly', and that he would not have written in that way had he 'realized how much I have already suffered in this affair'. Still, she 'fully and perfectly' acquitted him of the charges that she had heard: full, precise, and detailed though they were. She thought that if he had heard the full details as they had reached her, he would only have wondered how she had managed to take his side for so long. She concluded, emolliently:

> I have often longed intensely for such a denial as you now give: but <u>could</u> I have asked for it?
>
> Won't you forgive me, when I assure you, solemnly, that I have only tried to do what was right?[48]

Bryce replied again on 7 June. This time we have no evidence of the content, beyond Meta's reply. This came a month later: She explained that at first she thought he probably would prefer no response, and then, when she came to feel that her silence might be construed as ingratitude, she was taken ill. This time she tried to say that she regarded the issue as over:

> Instead of ingratitude, I felt real gratitude for your very great kindness in replying so fully and so patiently to each point in my previous letter—a letter which I bear by no means deserved such kindness. I thought your letter of June 7th very fine and magnanimous in several ways: if you will forgive me for saying so.
>
> One more word. If next time that I am in London, anything in my conduct should unfortunately give you the impression of there still being any lingering mistrust in my mind, will you <u>promise</u> me to believe that it is not that, but some awkward conjunction of circumstances to which such

conduct must be attributed? (I can't be less enigmatical!) But you will trust me to be still loyal in my trust of you—won't you?—whatever happens.

It is the final sentence that helps us to place the letter chronologically: 'How earnestly I hope that all your efforts on behalf of Armenia will be rewarded!'[49]

That was not quite the end of the correspondence. There was a letter from Meta in October 1878 to invite Bryce to dinner if he would be in Manchester for the Chancery Court. This was a warm and friendly letter, asking about Bryce's mother, a year or so into her widowhood. But it could not be described as intimate. She appeared to be indicating (and perhaps this was Bryce's wish too, now) that she wanted them to be on friendly terms, but nothing more. There is a curious absence of further correspondence. Did Meta write either to Bryce or to Marion to offer congratulations on their engagement in 1889? It would seem not.

A rather astounding letter from Emma Winkworth in 1874 casts more light on the marriage question. Mrs Winkworth had been reading *Middlemarch*, published a couple of years previously. Bryce had spoken to her of his hopes of marriage, but also (obliquely, it seems) of some of his fears. Reading *Middlemarch* seems to have helped her to understand his meaning:

> I heard from Mr Dicey how busy you are and I am very glad, if it means you are fast making the wherewithal to have the 'canny wee house' and the 'canny wee fire' for the 'canny wee wifie' we must all some day hope to 'praise & admire'! I found out later in Middlemarch from Mr Casaubon not having it, to understand more fully than I did when you spoke it, your fear of not being able to be all she might crave,—to someone!—I find myself very often fully realizing what friends mean when they are gone—St[ephen] often tells me I am too full of my own ideas to have room to take in other people's—and so it often is. To balance this, I also taste the flavour when I chew the cud![50]

We are unlikely ever to get any further glimpses of whatever concerns Bryce may have had about his sexual potency or his libido. If we read the unhappy saga of the failed relationship with Meta Gaskell as evidence of Bryce's failure to commit, it is entirely possible that sexual anxieties as well as financial concerns contributed to this. But equally there were other reasons why he might have hesitated about marrying her. Perhaps he feared that she was too attached to Manchester, whereas Bryce was evidently committed to a career based in London.

The Vacations of the Scholar

The 1870s were the decade in which Bryce made a name for himself as an adventurous and intrepid traveller. This did not help his quest for a marriage partner: Meta was clearly frustrated by his periodic 'total eclipse', when he would disappear from view for weeks or even months. He had developed a taste for travel in the 1860s, notably in his climbing tour of Transylvania with Leslie Stephen in 1866, but before 1870 his journeys were in continental Europe and the British Isles. In the 1870s he made three remarkable journeys further afield, all of which he wrote about and all of which made a lifelong impression on him and shaped his destiny in important ways. The first was his tour of the eastern seaboard of the United States in the company of Dicey (Stephen's cousin) in the late summer and autumn of 1870. Since this gave rise, many years later, to *The American Commonwealth*, it is very well-known and obviously a formative event in his literary and political career. It laid the foundation for Bryce's reputation as an authority on the United States, which would be a central component of his public profile. He also formed lasting friendships, notably with Edwin Godkin of *The Nation* and Charles Eliot of Harvard, which would be of profound importance to his intellectual life. The second was his visit to Iceland in the autumn of 1872 in the company of Courtenay Ilbert and Æneas Mackay. Alone of the three journeys, this produced no book, but it could count three or even four articles among its fruits, including Bryce's first proper travel-writing.[51] While he did not fall in love with contemporary Iceland, he was certainly fascinated with it; and he did fall in love both with Norse mythology and with a picture he formed for himself of primitive Iceland. Iceland, contemporary and primitive, was an astonishingly frequent motif in Bryce's writings. Finally, there was his Transcaucasian tour of 1876, during which he climbed Mount Ararat. He was not, as was sometimes claimed in jest, the first man since Noah to stand on the peak of Ararat.[52] The first modern ascent was by the German-born naturalist Friedrich Parrot about half a century earlier, and there were three other recorded ascents before Bryce, including one by a British army officer, Major Robert Stuart.[53] Nevertheless it was a notable feat that established him in the public mind as a mountaineer as well as a traveller, not least because Bryce made the final ascent alone. Bishop Fraser of Manchester thought the feat 'makes you take rank with quite the first class of mountaineers'.[54] More importantly, the visit fixed his passionate commitment to the Christians of Armenia. In the course of his career he worked for many humanitarian causes, but that of the Armenians was the one that was

FIGURE 5.1. 'Great and Little Ararat from the North-East', from Bryce's *Transcaucasia and Ararat.*

closest to his heart and the one that won him most acclaim. He wrote a notable account of this visit, *Transcaucasia and Ararat*, which was published in the autumn of 1877, not long after the death of his father, 'one whose companion he had been in mountain expeditions from childhood, and to whom he owes whatever taste he possesses for geographical observation and for the beauties of nature'.[55]

All we know of what drew Bryce, Ilbert, and Mackay to Iceland in 1872 is that Ilbert recalled that their intention had been to visit Norway, but that Mackay, who was living in Edinburgh and practising at the Scottish bar, heard of a trading steamer that was due to sail from Leith to the east coast of Iceland and to return three weeks later. It was Mackay who planned the three-week holiday, riding from Seyðisfjörður on the east coast up round the north coast and down the west coast as far as Reykjavik, from where they would sail back. But when they were at Akureyri, around the centre of the north coast, they heard the news that the return sailing was cancelled, and they had to make a valiant journey across the vast and largely uninhabited deserted centre of the island to try to catch the next mail steamer. There were four possible routes, and they—'a party of seventeen horses, three guides, and three Englishmen'— chose one that had not been attempted for fifteen years or so. In the event the steamer they were hoping to catch did not arrive. The result was a protracted stay of over a month in Reykjavik and a total stay in Iceland that was some three times as long as they had planned, causing Bryce to reschedule his Manchester lectures; but at the same time they had a much more vivid picture of the whole of the island, and at a time when Iceland was starting to capture the enthusiasm of Victorian travellers and intellectuals (including Richard Burton and William Morris), Bryce's articles offered a fresh and distinctive perspective.[56]

Bryce was undoubtedly captivated by the physicality of the island: not its beauty, for even at its most spectacular it lacked, he thought, the harmonious perfection of the kind of landscape he had encountered in the Lake District and in the Swiss Alps; but certainly its raw bleakness:

> Everywhere is silence, desolation, monotony; one is awed by the presence of the most tremendous forces of nature—fire which has reared these peaks and poured out these lava torrents; frost which rends the rocks and soil and frowns down on you from the interminable ice ridges. One knows oneself surrounded by a tempestuous ocean, far removed from even those outposts of civilization, Norway and the Shetland isles; in a land wholly out of relation to the rest of the world, and unaffected by its fortunes; a land where nothing has happened for many centuries; a land which seems not designed for man at all, but left waste for nature to toss wildly about the materials she did not need elsewhere, and disport her in sudden displays of her own terrible powers.[57]

But equally his historical imagination was captured by the Icelandic sagas: by being able to place them in their own environment, but also by the thought of what a gulf separated the men he had read about in the sagas from the Icelanders he met on his stay in the island. During his enforced sojourn in Reykjavik, he took lessons and acquired a competent reading knowledge of the Icelandic language; but he could not converse, and few of the islanders spoke any English, fewer still German or French; sometimes he got by speaking dog Latin with a Lutheran priest.[58] So this was not like a visit to the United States, where he gathered information through constant conversation. In Iceland he was reliant on the evidence of his eyes, reinforced by snippets from the occasional interlocutor with whom he could have an authentic conversation, but also fired by an imagination that feasted on the sagas.

Yet on this foundation rested a lifetime's store of lessons for the modern world. We shall see this in more depth when we come to examine in the next chapter how Bryce thought that Iceland had something to teach British statesmen grappling with the Irish Question; and not only them, but all who engaged with the place of small nations in modern Europe. Iceland was a constant to which Bryce returned in his writings and his public pronouncements to the end of his life. Even in *Modern Democracies*—published well-nigh half a century after Bryce visited Iceland—he drew comparisons between tenth-century Iceland and the modern-day Tahitians and Basutos: all these peoples found a way of balancing the government of a strong man with control by public opinion.[59]

Iceland even made an appearance, and a particularly fascinating one, in the introduction to *The American Commonwealth*. There Bryce aptly invoked his Icelandic experience to illustrate the gulf between what the traveller sees and what the people to whom he recounts his adventures take in. The passage is so revealing that it deserves to be quoted at length:

> Sixteen years ago I travelled in Iceland with two friends. We crossed the great Desert by a seldom trodden track, encountering, during two months of late autumn, rains, tempests, snow-storms, and other hardships too numerous to recount. But the scenery was so grand and solemn, the life so novel, the character of the people so attractive, the historic and poetic traditions so inspiring, that we returned full of delight with the marvellous isle. When we expressed this enchantment to our English friends, we were questioned about the conditions of travel, and forced to admit that we had been frozen and starved, that we had sought sleep in swamps or on rocks, that the Icelanders lived in huts scattered through a wilderness, with none of the luxuries and few even of the comforts of life. Our friends passed over the record of impressions to dwell on the record of physical experiences, and conceived a notion of the island totally different from that which we had meant to convey. We perceived too late how much easier it is to state tangible facts than to communicate impressions.

It was the same for the European visitor to the United States. The states and their people 'make on the visitor an impression so strong, so deep, so fascinating, so inwoven with a hundred threads of imagination and emotion, that he cannot hope to reproduce it in words, and to pass it on undiluted to other minds'. By contrast, the 'broad facts of politics' were easier to convey, but the latter without the former were utterly misleading:

> The European reader grasps these tangible facts, and, judging them as though they existed under European conditions, draws from them

conclusions disparaging to the country and the people. What he probably fails to do, because this is what the writer is most likely to fail in enabling him to do, is to realize the existence in the American people of a reserve of force and patriotism more than sufficient to sweep away all the evils which are now tolerated, and to make the politics of the country worthy of its material grandeur and of the private virtues of its inhabitants. America excites an admiration which must be felt upon the spot to be understood.[60]

Here we have Bryce constructing a claim to authority derived not from academic learning, though of course he had that abundantly, but from the direct observation of the traveller. But not just any traveller: it was vital that the faculty of observation should be *trained*, as his faculty of observation of the natural world had been trained from a young age by his father.[61]

The encounter with Armenia in 1876 was even more pivotal to Bryce's career than his visit to Iceland, because it did much to shape Bryce's political identity in two ways. First, the myth of the conqueror of Ararat and the second Noah, even the man who found a relic of the Ark, tells us something about celebrity in Victorian Britain. Second, and more importantly, the campaign on behalf of the Armenians was the first and most enduring of the great humanitarian causes into which Bryce threw himself. The timing was fortuitous. The Eastern Question had burst back onto the political agenda in the spring of 1876—just months before Bryce's tour—with the Bulgarian insurrection against Ottoman rule and its violent and indiscriminate suppression by irregular Ottoman troops. Gladstone's famous pamphlet, *The Bulgarian Horrors and the Question of the East*, was published on the very day that Bryce set off from Tiflis (Tbilisi, the modern-day capital of Georgia, and then the seat of Imperial Russia's Viceroyalty of the Caucasus) to Erivan (Yerevan, the modern-day capital of Armenia), and just a week before his ascent of Ararat. At this stage, Transcaucasia was not at the centre of the political contest, but it became so the following year when Russia declared war on the Ottoman Empire and occupied large parts of its eastern provinces, including much of the territory inhabited by Armenians. Fundamental to Russia's stance was its claim to act as the protector of the oppressed Christian population of the region, and under the terms of the Treaty of San Stefano, which also established an autonomous principality of Bulgaria, some Armenian territories were ceded to Russia, and others would be occupied until such time as reforms to protect the Armenians were implemented. The Disraeli government was at the forefront of the Great Power reaction which forced a renegotiation of the treaty at the Congress of Berlin. This significantly reduced Russia's territorial gains and restored Armenian lands to the Ottoman regime, which was bound to put into effect 'the ameliorations and reforms demanded by local requirements in the regions inhabited by the Armenians.'[62]

How far did Bryce set out to weave the myth of the man who climbed Ararat? He certainly took the trouble to ensure that his father inserted a notice in *The Times* to report the ascent. He did not make inflated claims for himself, but simply recorded that this was 'believed to be either the third or fourth ascent', after Parrot and Abich, and (he had some reservations about adding this) that 'the last 4,000 ft had to be climbed alone, the Cossack escort refusing to go further'. Perhaps the final sentence is the most interesting: 'The Armenians of the neighbourhood believe the mountain to be inaccessible, and insist that Noah's ark still exists upon the summit.'[63] How far the Armenians believed this is impossible to ascertain, but Bryce told his sister Mary that the abbot of the monastery of Etchmiadzin refused to believe that he could have climbed Ararat, and he told Katharine that 'the people here believe that no one, since Noah, has ever been to the top.'[64]

On his return, Bryce engaged in a vigorous programme of dissemination that embraced both accounts of his travels and political reflections on the Eastern Question. Into the first category fell an article on Transcaucasia for the *Cornhill Magazine* in May 1877, one on the ascent of Mount Ararat in the *Alpine Journal*, and a paper 'On Armenia and Mount Ararat' in the *Proceedings of the Geographical Society*; into the second, an article on 'Russia and Turkey' in the *Fortnightly Review*, one on 'Constantinople' in *Macmillan's Magazine*, and one on 'The Future of Asiatic Turkey' in the *Fortnightly Review*. Many of these built on public lectures: for example, at the Royal Institution (March 1877) and the Royal Geographical Society (February 1878). And to cap them all was his famous book, *Transcaucasia and Ararat*, published by Macmillan in the autumn of 1877.

In 'Russia and Turkey' he set out his argument that 'the mistake of England has been in leaving Russia all these years, and more especially since the insurrection broke out in Herzegovina, the sole championship (whether real or apparent) of good government and the welfare of the Christian population in Turkey.'[65] But it was in the piece on 'The Future of Asiatic Turkey' that he made for the first time the case for British intervention on behalf of the Armenian people. 'The sufferings of the Armenians have been greater than those of Bulgarians or Bosnians,' and 'It is impossible to conceive a stronger case for the benevolent intervention of the European Powers, and especially of England, than the circumstances of Armenia make out.' He argued that the

FIGURE 5.2. *Vanity Fair* caricature of Bryce, 1893: 'He was the first man after Noah to climb Mount Ararat.'

best way of checking Russian advance in Asia would be to nurture the development of the Armenian nationality. He did not explicitly refer to his visit, but in making the case for Armenian nationhood, he clearly wrote as someone with firsthand knowledge: The Armenian nation 'combines with a strong individuality and corporate spirit great flexibility of mind, and a power of adapting itself to varying conditions of life'.[66]

Bryce's critics would maintain that his wholehearted enthusiasm for the Armenian cause was a mere 'crotchet', a fanatical obsession with a particular cause at the expense of the wider picture. There are grounds for thinking that his attachment to the cause was, later in his career, a barrier to his appointment to the foreign secretaryship, for which on the basis of knowledge of the issues he was better qualified than any of his contemporaries. It is interesting to find him in this article already anticipating and trying to rebut this line of criticism:

> To many persons any belief in moral forces seems visionary. Italian unity was a dream of poets and conspirators, German unity the crotchet of doctrinaire professors. One must not be afraid of terms of this kind. I do not deny that the interest which those who advocate the cause of the Armenian nation feel, is partly a sentimental interest. They think that its glorious history, its intellectual achievements, the tenacity with which it has clung to its faith and its national memories, infinitely strengthen the claim which its sufferings raise to the consideration of Europe.

But he also maintained that because Armenian nationhood had an authentic basis it had the potential to civilize Asiatic Turkey, and moreover that it was the best barrier to Russian expansion in the region.[67] To use later terminology, Bryce did not accept the binary between 'idealism' and 'realism' in the study of international politics. The sentiment of nationality was an empirical fact.

He certainly felt strongly the sensation of having left Europe and hence being far from home, and he stressed that this sensation was far more marked than when he visited America:

> One is half way to India here, only Persia, on whose bare red mountains I am looking, & Beloochistan [sic: Balochistan] between; & I am tempted to go on, see Annan & come back by Bombay. A long long way off does England seem, further than when I was on the Mississipi [sic] in 1870. Dear child, how I hope to see you all again, and feel as if I could scarcely bear to come so far away again, out of hearing of you for so long.[68]

It is curious that the sense of remoteness was much more vivid in Armenia than it had been in Iceland, which, though half the distance, was by most measures also much less accessible.

There is another intriguing dimension of Bryce's thinking about the Armenian question that calls for comment. He was conscious that the great difficulty in making the case for the *political* nationhood of the Armenians was that they were dispersed. The immediate vicinity of Ararat was populated mostly by Armenians, but the territory was not large enough, nor the inhabitants numerous enough, to form a viable nation, even in the context of some kind of federal solution to the nationalities question in the Ottoman Empire, and more generally in Asia Minor and southeastern Europe. There was, however, a sizeable Armenian diaspora across the territory of the Ottoman Empire, and of course in Europe too. Much of 'Armenia' was underpopulated, and its economic potential unexploited. Bryce therefore speculated about the possibility of settlement or inward migration as a solution, since 'what the Armenians need is a centre, a land which they may call their own, and which they may in time, as its wealth and numerical strength increases, build up into a State'.[69]

This prompts the speculation that Bryce envisaged a solution to the Armenian question analogous to the Zionist solution to the Jewish Question that was first formulated as a response to the pogroms unleashed shortly afterwards in the Russian Empire in the wake of the assassination of Tsar Alexander II in 1881. Bryce was not especially closely engaged with the Jewish Question, but he evidently had some philo-Semitic sympathies and speculated on the possibilities of a return of the Jewish people to Palestine even before Zionism took shape as a political movement. In January 1881, before the assassination of Alexander II, we find him, as the newly elected MP for Tower Hamlets, giving a lecture at the Jewish Working Men's Club and Institute in Houndsditch, in his constituency. His subject was 'Asia Minor, Its Past and Its Future'. The richly fertile land of the region had decayed under the rule of the Turks, 'a nation without art, without science, and without literature'. Once fertile lands had become sterile deserts, and the only remedy was the overthrow of the Sultan. Bryce (as reported in the press) concluded with what looks like a proto-Zionist declaration:

> It was the wish of all men that Palestine should come back into the hands of its ancient rulers, the Jews, and to this end the first emigrants must be agriculturists, whose ranks could be recruited from the persecuted Jews of Roumania, Poland, and, he was sorry to say, Germany. The fertile slopes of Palestine would thus be again clad with vines, her now sterile deserts would become golden corn-fields. The world would look forward to the time when the Jewish race would again possess their ancient home.[70]

He later gave nuanced support to the Zionist cause, not least as part of his efforts to facilitate American entry into the First World War.[71] Whether it is right to suggest that he looked at these questions—the Armenian and the Palestinian—through settler colonialist spectacles is questionable, however, unless all kinds of organized resettlement are defined as settler colonialism. In the Armenian case, unlike the Palestinian, he thought primarily in terms of internal migration from other Ottoman lands. He was animated above all by detestation of Turkish rule and a sense of the challenges in the way of post-Ottoman reconstruction of these regions.

Transcaucasia and Ararat was important in cementing Bryce's literary reputation. Evidence of this is supplied by his election as a member of the Athenaeum in February 1878, under its Rule II, which allowed the club's committee to elect each year up to nine men who were judged 'of distinguished eminence in Science, Literature, or the Arts, or for Public Service'. Aged a little under forty at the time of his election, Bryce was in the youngest decile of Rule II members at the time of their election. He was already an habitué of clubland, as a member of the New University Club, the Savile, and the Century, but the Athenaeum had a social cachet that the others could not match, and membership cemented his place in what Leslie Stephen called 'the higher intellectual stratum of London society'. His election at a young age under Rule II was a significant mark of distinction and somewhat belied Henry James's judgment.[72] The most meritocratic of the high-status clubs, the Athenaeum came to play an important role in his social and intellectual life: he served on its committee in the 1890s and was much canvassed by aspiring members.

Politics as a Vocation

Bryce's entry into the literary world in the 1860s had been so striking a success that one has to wonder why he did not concentrate his efforts on becoming, in Henry Adams's words, 'the best historian in England'. Why, in particular, did he seek a parliamentary seat? This, after all, was a major distraction in the 1870s. Once he had a seat—in particular, once he moved from Tower Hamlets to Aberdeen South in 1885—he had the stability and security that enabled him to travel and to write, at least at moments of political quietness. Aberdeen was a safe seat, and he was normally able to limit his visits to two stays a year.[73] But in the 1870s he had to spend time cultivating prospective constituency organizations, in London, in Lancashire, in Newcastle, and in the northeast of Scotland. Wick, the most northerly borough represented at Westminster, consumed his time in fruitless inter-Liberal contests: first in 1872, when he failed to gain selection for the by-election, and again in 1874, when he stood and lost as the Radical candidate against the moderate Liberal, the telegraph entrepreneur John Pender. In the course of the 1874 campaign, he met a constituent who had been baptized by Bryce's grandfather, almost eighty years before.[74] During the 1874 Parliament he was mentioned whenever by-elections occurred in Scotland: in Kirkcaldy, where there was a by election in April 1875 following the death of the Liberal MP Robert Reid; in the Glasgow and Aberdeen Universities seat, where the Conservatives held the seat in a by-election in November 1876, and Perth and Leith, in both of which he declined to be considered for selection for by-elections in January 1878.[75] In the case of the Universities seat, he might have hoped to have some prospect of at least standing, given his father's prominence as a leading figure in the Glasgow graduates' campaign for a share in the government of the university. He wrote to his father thus:

> Stirling tells me that the Aberdeen committee did not vote for me, because they considered that the Glasgow people had determined otherwise, so there was no use, but they stated clearly before accepting Kirkwood, that they wd have preferred me. It seems to me that the money difficulty is part of the objection to me, but that it is mainly
>
> α/ The prophet in his own country feeling
>
> β/ The idea that I am not one of them, but produced under other influences & likely to be in some points out of sympathy with them
>
> γ/ An ignorance of the sort of position wh. I think I may claim in England
>
> Δ/ The notion that I am the friend of those in the College whom they least like—Caird and Nichol.
>
> Anyhow it is much better. I could not have afforded to throw away even £300; but am a little disgusted at having no platform at present to say anything from.[76]

In the later 1870s he was an industrious Radical organizer within the Liberal ranks, and his prominence on the advanced wing of the party certainly helped secure him an opening. Tower Hamlets was among the most populous seats in the country, a slum constituency with large Jewish and Irish populations, and a significant population of German workers too, whom Bryce (according to legend) impressed by addressing in their own language. As was not uncommon in the days of two-member constituencies, intraparty contests were as important as interparty ones: in 1868, two Liberals were elected, against one Conservative, one other Liberal, and a Lib-Lab candidate; in 1874, the Conservative future Chancellor Charles Ritchie was elected at the head of the poll along with the Liberal Joseph Samuda, and three Liberals were unsuccessful.

Bryce's fight in 1880 was less with Ritchie than with Samuda, who had backed Disraeli's foreign policy and was regarded in the Liberal press as no more than a nominal Liberal, 'as much a Beaconsfieldian as his Conservative colleague, Mr Ritchie'.[77] In any event, Bryce headed the poll, unexpectedly beating Ritchie as well as Samuda in a hard-fought race. His friends attributed his success to his hard work in *educating* the constituency in the twelve months since his selection.[78] The remark is significant: It probably reflected the way Bryce understood and talked about his own role in shaping public opinion.

If we judge from his correspondence, political life did not bring him fulfilment. Even on the eve of the election campaign that took him to the Commons for the first time, he wrote to a friend that 'it is much pleasanter to think about Morocco or Norway [holiday destinations] than about these things nearer home'.[79] Once in Parliament he would complain incessantly of 'the petty distractions of parliamentary life' which kept him from writing.[80] So he wrote to Oliver Wendell Holmes Jr in 1892:

> Though politics have absorbed so much of my times these twelve years, I do not find myself growing fonder of them, or even more excited about them. On the contrary, one is rather struck by their touching only the upper surface of things: they are winds ruffling it, while the ocean current sweeps along independent of them. The atmosphere of strife with antagonists and of rivalry, sometimes sinking into selfish elbowings and jealousies among members of the same party, is repellent: one knew before of its existence, but did not realize how disagreeable to take part in it. The opportunities for studying human nature and for comprehending history, are abundant, but one is mostly too much occupied with present trivialities, urgent trivialities of a question to be got up or a speech to be made, to have time to muse upon them.[81]

In 1877 he counselled Freeman against parliamentary ambitions, telling him that he would find the Commons uncongenial, and that his vocation was with the pen.[82] But many observers would say much the same of Bryce himself. He may have reached the same conclusion: when he finally achieved cabinet rank in 1892, he thought it no very great achievement. It might be 'an opportunity for trying to exercise influence in the right direction', but he feared that 'my métier does not lie in this kind of personal influence, perhaps from want of insistence, perhaps from seeing or wishing to see both sides too much'.[83] Donner, on the other hand, thought that Bryce could not live without politics. What, then, drew him to public life?

The answer may be simply that he had a republican sense that the political life was the highest form of existence. He had certainly picked up from Bagehot in particular a noble vision of the House of Commons as the educator of the nation, and when he finally entered Parliament in 1880 it was a disappointment to find that the picture painted by Bagehot was rapidly becoming out of date. Although he seems never to have questioned his Liberal allegiance, and intellectually believed in the worth of the two-party system, he was not by nature a partisan.

The dimension of political life that particularly attracted Bryce was the single-issue campaign. In the 1860s he cut his teeth on the campaign for the abolition of university tests, and after his return from Armenia in 1876 he threw himself into the campaign for humanitarian intervention on behalf of the Armenians and the other oppressed nationalities of the Ottoman Empire. This latter cause was an enthusiasm for the rest of his life. Other causes to which he was devoted were those for open spaces, including access to mountains, for which he was the leading parliamentary spokesman. He later became publicly identified with the campaign against the Boer War and, latterly, the movement for what became the League of Nations. These causes were of different kinds: some were questions of high politics where Bryce spoke for a large segment of Liberal opinion, whereas others were akin to personal obsessions. But all were causes that involved working to move and to shape public opinion. All involved extra-parliamentary organization, and public meetings and letters to the press were their typical modus operandi.

A sense of Bryce's priorities at the outset of his parliamentary career is conveyed by a letter he wrote to Mary in the autumn of 1880 from Constantinople, where he was staying at the British Embassy as the guest of the Goschens: George Goschen, Liberal MP for Ripon, was serving temporarily as special ambassador to the Ottoman Empire in order to oversee the implementation of the territorial arrangements prescribed by the Congress of Berlin in 1880. Bryce wrote: 'If in reading your D[aily] News daily you see anything of importance relating to the 'Amlets or to any subject I go in for, e.g. City Charities, Armenians, Disestablishment in Scotland, House of Lords, please cut it out & keep it for me, since I don't always get papers read.'[84] The City Charities issue was to be Bryce's major legislative concern in the 1880–1885 Parliament, and as a jurist with a particular interest in endowments and sitting for a London constituency he played a leading role in guiding the Parochial Charities Bill through the Commons. The three other issues mentioned were to be abiding concerns for the rest of his career.

He might well have added open spaces, for that campaign was important in shaping Bryce's public and political persona. It drew on the passions for nature and the outdoors that he had imbibed from his father; but it also, quite specifically, enabled him to derive some political capital from his reputation as a mountaineer after the conquest of Ararat. The Commons Preservation Society had been founded in 1865 by George Shaw Lefevre (later Lord Eversley), who remained the guiding figure in the society for decades. Bryce was active from its early days and was chairman from 1880 to 1884, in his first term in Parliament. Like the National Trust, in which Bryce would also be an important figure at its foundation in 1895, the society attracted cross-party support, but with rather more from Liberals and Radicals than Conservatives: John Stuart Mill, Sir Charles Dilke, Henry Fawcett, and William Morris were all keen supporters. It had a particular focus in its early years on the urban commons, especially in London, but Fawcett was instrumental in encouraging the society to give as much attention to the rural commons. This was a cause that Bryce championed, tabling the first 'right to roam' bill in the form of the Access to Mountains (Scotland) Bill of 1884: thereafter he or a parliamentary colleague made an annual attempt to introduce a similar bill, known as the 'Bryce bill', and the project was eventually realized in the Access to Mountains Act of 1939. Another key parliamentary struggle was to ensure that the question of commons preservation was fully taken into account in railway construction schemes. Bryce was, for instance, instrumental in amending what became the Light Railways Act of 1896 to insert a clause imposing on the Board of Agriculture a duty to ensure that any proposed light railway should cause no more injury to the commons than was absolutely necessary, and that an equivalent area should be added to the commons.[85]

Bryce's political career was in two respects characteristic of his time. It drew on the nineteenth-century obsession with the political 'question': the Irish Question, the Eastern Question, the Social Question, the Jewish Question, the Negro Question, and so on.[86] But more specifically, his parliamentary career coincided with the dominance of the public meeting as a mode of political activity. Tom Crewe has tracked the number of extra-parliamentary speeches made by political leaders in the late nineteenth century and finds a big leap from the 1880s onward.[87] This was a symptom of the kind of political shift that Bryce would trace in his articles for the New York Nation in the 1880s. Still, Bryce did far more than reflect the political characteristics of his age. He was terrier-like in his pursuit of his favourite causes. Public opinion was to be a central concept in his analysis of democratic systems, but at the same time his political career was fundamentally devoted to the shaping of public opinion.

Bryce entered Parliament, then, because he wanted to be able to shape public opinion, and he began with a Bagehotian sense that the best place to shape opinion was on the floor of the House of Commons. Even though Parliament proved a disappointment to him (and he proved a disappointment, at least on the floor of the House), it remained true that a seat in the Commons gave him a public status that was indispensable in securing him platforms for his campaigning. Moreover, while parliamentary and electoral business was certainly a distraction from his literary work, the public status of a Member of Parliament and government minister also enhanced the kind of authority his writings could command. It was not an irrational move, though it was certainly one about which he felt some ambivalence.

6

Home Rule and Small-Nation Nationalism

IRELAND AND ICELAND

BRYCE WAS BORN IN BELFAST and lived there until the age of eight. Both his parents were born in Ulster and had lived their lives there (apart from a period as a student in Glasgow in his father's case) until the family moved to Glasgow in 1846. His mother's side of the family had roots in Ulster going back to the seventeenth century. Although he is sometimes called an Ulsterman, or even an Irishman, Bryce never thought of himself in that way.[1] Still, Ireland mattered to him and played an important part in his life and career. In his boyhood, after he and his family had left Belfast, they spent many holidays in Ireland, and he acquired a profound knowledge of its topography and love for its scenery that never left him. In public life, he was from 1886 onwards one of the foremost proponents of the Gladstonian case for Home Rule, and he wrote widely on the Irish Question for the British and for the American public.[2] His last cabinet position was as chief secretary for Ireland, and to the end of his life he remained deeply engaged with the prospects of a resolution. His last parliamentary speech, the month before he died, was on the Anglo-Irish Treaty, which would bring the Irish Free State into being.[3]

Conversion Narratives: How Bryce Became a Home Ruler

Bryce was accused by Unionist contemporaries, and has been subsequently accused by historians, of performing a *volte face* on the Home Rule question, and of doing so in a way that ran counter to the logic of his constitutional theory, and hence could only be explained as an unprincipled adaptation to the demands of party politics. His Uncle John, Dr R. J. Bryce, accused him of 'yielding to witchery which Gladstone exercises over so many minds.'[4] Joseph Chamberlain, with whom Bryce would cross swords on a number of occasions, called him 'just a snivelling professor, who turned Home Ruler because he found that Aberdeen would have it so, and that there was a chance of office.'[5] The historian Christopher Harvie, who wrote illuminatingly on Bryce in the 1970s, thought that Bryce's case for Home Rule was 'constitutionally illogical' and his conversion was sudden, since as late as September 1885 he was making an 'essentially unionist argument—not at all dissimilar to Dicey's' in one of his articles in *The Nation*.[6]

More recently Jordan Rudinsky has made the case for the importance, and logical cogency, of Bryce's 'innovative imperial constitutionalism.'[7] Essentially, Rudinsky takes seriously the distinction Bryce drew between de jure and de facto sovereignty—seeing it really as a reworking of Dicey's distinction between legal and political sovereignty—and makes the case for the coherence of Bryce's argument that, under Home Rule, the Westminster Parliament would retain its de jure sovereignty over Ireland, whereas it would of course be morally constrained to be true to its commitment that it would not amend the terms of the Home Rule settlement without the consent of the members of the Irish Parliament. Moral constraints of this kind were by no means new in British constitutional practice. The same kind of constraint underpinned the relationship between Westminster and the parliaments of the self-governing colonies. Suffice to say that there is at least a credible case for the consistency of Bryce's broadly Diceyan account of parliamentary sovereignty and his support for Home Rule, in which case Bryce's critics need to make a stronger case than they have yet done for convicting him of an opportunist volte-face. In fact, as we shall now see, there are very good grounds for thinking that Bryce had been coming round to the Home Rule cause for three or four years before his public conversion.

Bryce answered his critics at some length in his conversion narrative, 'How We Became Home Rulers', published in 1887 both in the *Contemporary Review* and in the *Handbook of Home Rule* that he edited at Gladstone's behest. There he set out to rebut the allegation of 'sudden, and therefore, it would seem, dishonest change of view' that was commonly levelled at the Gladstonian Liberals. Bryce's answer took the form of a year-by-year account, based on his own personal recollections, 'of the phases of opinion and feeling through which I myself, and the friends whom I knew most intimately in the House of Commons, passed during the Parliament which sat from 1880 till 1885.'[8] It is an interesting and important text. Although the essay obviously had a political purpose, as a piece of apologetics, Bryce wrote as an historian who saw that 'the causes which underlie changes of opinion are among the most obscure phenomena in history, because those who undergo these changes are often only half conscious of them, and do not think of recording that which is imperceptible in its growth, and whose importance is not realized till it already belongs to the past.' He therefore hoped that his narrative, 'if executed with proper fairness and truth', 'may, as a study in contemporary history, be of some little interest to those who in future will attempt to understand our present conflict.'[9]

The essay offered a session-by-session account of the 1880 Parliament, and of the insensible steps by which Bryce and his fellow Liberals began to look more favourably on the possibility of Irish self-government. The year 1882 was pivotal: not only did the evident futility of coercion make many Liberals reluctant to support Forster's Prevention of Crimes Bill, but the obstructionist tactics of the Home Rule MPs were so successful as to make it quite clear that they would prevent the Liberal government enacting the programme on which it was elected:

> Nothing was done to reorganize local government, to reform the liquor laws, to improve secondary education, to deal with the housing of the poor, or a dozen other urgent questions, because we were busy with Ireland; and yet how little more loyal or contented did Ireland seem to be for all we had done. We began to ask whether Home Rule might not be as much an English and Scotch question as an Irish question. It was, at any rate, clear that to allow Ireland to manage her own affairs would open a prospect for England and Scotland to obtain time to attend to theirs.[10]

England's (and Scotland's) case for Irish Home Rule rested on the perception that parliamentary government at Westminster was being rendered impossible by the existence of a large Irish party whose principal tactic was obstruction. As Gladstone would put it when defending his second Home Rule Bill, 'the Irish Question is the curse of this House. It is the great and standing impediment to the effective performance of its duties.'[11]

Whether or not Bryce's critics were persuaded, his account is broadly supported by the archival record, which seems to indicate a distinct openness to Home Rule by 1882. In June of that year Edwin Godkin wrote to him that 'I find myself slowly and steadily becoming at the age of fifty a Home Ruler.'[12] Bryce replied, discussing Godkin's 'American View of Ireland', which he was helping to place with the editor of the *Nineteenth Century*: 'It was curious to me to notice that you stated several of the reasons by which I have been half uncon-sciously, and altogether unwittingly, been [sic] drifting in the direction of Home Rule, Repeal, whatever one is to call it.'[13] Godkin's article emphasized the mutual antipathy of the Irish and the British—and in particular the hatred of the British for the Irish—as a key reason for the inevitability of Home Rule.[14] He also, less controversially, argued that the Irish sense of nationality (which he did not share) was a fact of political life which meant that representative government accountable to a unitary Imperial Parliament at Westminster would never satisfy the Irish, who would always see themselves as a permanent minority doomed to be oppressed by an alien majority.[15] 'The truth is', he concluded, '—and it is the truth as to the new Repression Bill as well as of the old Coercion Bill—that these measures for pacifying Ireland must fail as long as they are English measures which are sent across the Channel as the devices of Englishmen and Scotchmen, who in the opinion of the Irish hate and despise the Irish.'[16]

Bryce's letter endorsing Godkin's article is by no means the sole evidence that Bryce's views on Ireland were shifting in the direction of Home Rule as early as 1882. There is an intriguing letter from Dicey in April 1887 in which Dicey says that he and Bryce had both known for the last three years that when the Irish issue came to be fought, they would find each other on different sides. That does not take one as back as far as 1882, but it does take us back to 1884, well before Gladstone's conversion to Home Rule and well before Bryce left Tower Hamlets for Aberdeen. In any case, Chamberlain's assertion that Bryce's conversion to Home Rule was due to pressure from his Aberdeen constituents is perverse to the point of ignorance. Bryce was happy to leave Tower Hamlets (which was in any case split into seven single-member constituencies in 1885) because the workload was enormous: it was among the ten most populous constituencies, and one of the poorest. It also had a sizeable Irish population which agitated for the Home Rule cause, and Bryce found that an irritant because he was resistant to anything that savoured of the imperative mandate. His retrospective account certainly recorded that Liberals sitting for 'large working-class constituencies' found their constituents naturally sympathetic to the Irish cause.[17] There is no evidence that he felt pressure either way from his Aberdeen constituents. His constituency was a very safe one, and only in the 'khaki' election of 1900 was his reelection in any doubt.

Jonathan Parry has noted that those Liberals who were most repulsed by the idea of Home Rule 'tended to be those most defensive of the rule of law, most strenuously attached to church establishments, most respectful of the power of mind, and most concerned about the maintenance of a

FIGURE 6.1. Edwin Lawrence Godkin (1831–1902),
New York public moralist and editor of *The Nation*.

"disinterested" economic policy'.[18] All except the second of these four predic-
tors might have led observers to expect to find Bryce in the Unionist camp.
But, as we shall see, his attachment to what Parry calls the myth of 'national
and imperial integration under the rule of law' was much more nuanced than,
for instance, Dicey's or Goldwin Smith's. In particular, his wide comparative
perspective on the management of centralizing and decentralizing forces in
modern states made him appreciate the risks that an unyielding defence of the
unitary principle could prove self-defeating.

Family Politics

Public and private were enmeshed in Bryce's engagement with the Irish Question. His conversion to the cause of Home Rule caused a rift within his Scots-
Ulster Presbyterian family. Many family members supported him, not least his

mother, brother, and sisters; but others were fiercely on the other side. One uncle, Archibald Hamilton Bryce (1824–1904), the classical scholar and head-master of the Edinburgh Collegiate School, was especially vociferous on the Unionist side, and the correspondence between him and his nephew was barely temperate. In March 1887 he accused Bryce of writing 'with <u>undue heat</u>', and protested that 'I certainly did not <u>mean</u> to say anything wantonly to insult you or hurt your feelings in any way'. He said he 'knew that <u>you</u> had a semi-Irish feel-ing long before Gladstone had it, as shown in the interest you took about Davitt some years ago': further evidence that Bryce's conversion was not driven by political expediency. He continued in such a way as to indicate that what made him so passionate was the sense that he *knew* conditions in Ireland whereas many Home Rule Liberals, including Gladstone himself, simply did not:

> I feel however so acutely in this Irish business, having known for 25 years the <u>class</u> of people who <u>alone</u> take part in the agitation, that I cannot speak with patience about the conduct of those who wheeled so suddenly round—for what reason soever it may have been. Did you know Ireland & the Irish as I do, I am quite sure you wd think differently on the Irish ques-tion. I had better for the future avoid politics in my letters, & run no risk of estranging friends.[19]

If he strove thereafter to patch up relations, he did not do a good job. He went on to write a pamphlet supporting the Unionist cause.[20] This originated in the form of a series of letters published in the *Aberdeen Journal* from October to December 1888, and to write in this vein for a newspaper in his nephew's con-stituency was tactless at best. He later got into an acrimonious correspondence with Bryce when he apparently colluded with the Conservative MP for Down East, James Rentoul, who asserted in the Commons in 1893 that Bryce (by now chancellor of the Duchy of Lancaster) was opposed by his whole family on the Home Rule question.[21] Bryce took particular umbrage at the suggestion that his father and grandfather would have disapproved of his political stance.[22]

The break with Uncle John was even more traumatic, because the relation-ship was a closer one. Dr R. J. Bryce had an intriguing perspective on the Irish Question, a subtler one than his younger brother Archibald's, and one that seems to have left an enduring imprint on Bryce's own view of the world. He thought that England had risen to greatness through the amalgamation of races: a policy that 'had fused Britons, Saxons, Danes, and Normans into one mighty, free, and prosperous nation'. His nephew certainly shared the principle that progress and peace depended on the commingling of different races. For

Uncle John the problem with British policy in Ireland over seven centuries was that it had set up obstacles to prevent the fusion of races. 'Laws of the most atrocious kind were enacted, forbidding the English in Ireland from intermarrying with the Irish; and those English who had done so were branded as "degenerate English."' This prohibition of intermarriage predated the Reformation, from which Dr Bryce concluded that the essence of the Irish Question was racial rather than religious.[23]

He put this view at some length to his nephew, not long before the latter was elected to Parliament for the first time:

> Events are every day making it clearer that my view about Ireland is right:—viz that our statesmen of both parties have been totally wrong in regarding difference of religion as a factor of any great importance in producing our disorders. You know I have all along held that the fons et origo mali is the difference of race; & that it is only as a badge of race that religion has any significance. The Celtic Race have all along held that the land is theirs; & their clergy have all along held that the church property was theirs; & there has been an alliance offensive & defensive between them. The clergy did not encourage "Home" Rule or Repeal till after Mr Gladstone's unfortunate "Disestablishment" measure placed them in such a position that they had the strongest motives to join in it openly, or encourage it in a quieter way. Nothing could be more certain than that the Irish Church Act has intensified sevenfold the long cherished desire of the aboriginal race for a total separation from England.[24]

It was a very long letter—Dr Bryce's letters almost always were—but his nephew noted that it was a 'most interesting letter with whose views about Ireland I almost wholly (if it is not presumptuous in me to say so) agree'.[25] The practical upshot was this: since the religious question was merely superstructural, concessions to the Catholic hierarchy were pointless. The Catholic laity could only be won over by serious land reform; and once they were so won over, they would no longer be under the thumbs of the bishops.

Uncle and nephew did indeed agree about many aspects of the Irish Question. Both deplored 'the mischievous policy of the Government in thinking that they can govern Ireland through the Hierarchy and in throwing education into their hands'. Bryce (nephew) shared his uncle's view that the role of religious divisions in the Irish problem had been exaggerated.[26] Both were fiercely attached to 'the principle of undenominational education', which, Bryce thought, had been 'abandoned first by the Tories & then by the misguided Forster'.[27]

They regretted the replacement of the Queen's University with the Royal University of Ireland in 1880, partly because the establishment of the latter provided an indirect subsidy to sectarian colleges, notably the 'Catholic University' (University College, Dublin, as it became in 1882).[28] They also both deplored the partisanship of the Orangemen: 'they are as bad as the nationalists'.[29]

On one aspect of the subject they had a long-standing disagreement, however. Uncle John was a persistent critic of Gladstone, whom he deemed 'overrated in all respects except as a financier': 'an excellent Chancellor of the Exchequer, but he has been a failure as a prime minister in nearly every thing he has done'. As a speaker he was inferior to Bright and Cairns (the latter a former pupil of Dr Bryce's at the Belfast Academy), he 'lacked that large grasp of mind which is essential to a philosophic statesman', and he was too much driven by the whims of public opinion.[30] He had never understood the Irish Question: in particular, he was mistaken in regarding the Catholic laity as 'priest-ridden creatures', and mistaken therefore in believing that disestablishment—actually only a 'pretended disestablishment'—would pacify Ireland.[31]

The sense that Home Rule had permanently injured the closeness of the bond between uncle and nephew leaps out from their correspondence. The language on Uncle John's side was impassioned even by his standards. He was 'deeply grieved'. He felt that he was sticking to the policy that Bryce himself had long advocated: the 'hold on' policy:

> You are scarcely correct in saying that I had nothing to propose anent Home Rule.[32] I said your own idea of a "hold on policy" working out reforms by wise administration & taking practical measures for amalgamating the two nations by impartial treatment & what I pointed out was the rational way, not by heaping law upon law in the statute book, but by using the influence of the govt to discourage divisions & promote unity—keep the two naughty children in order—the Orangemen & the R.C. Bishops. Mr Gladstone pampered the ones & the Tories the others.[33]

Dr Bryce had nothing of the Protestant bigot about him: 'I wd <u>stamp upon</u> Orange magistrates & R Cath priests by a stern impartiality in resisting the arrogance of both.'[34] Why then did he regard the prospect of Home Rule with such horror? The answer seems to be that he thought it would inevitably entrench rather than ameliorate the division between the 'two nations', precisely because it would make this 'stern impartiality' impossible. It would be 'followed by all the horrors of civil war, embittered by religious hatred'.[35] This position had a certain logic to it: in effect, the argument was that the division between the two communities was so deep that self-government was impossible; the only solution was enlightened administration ('stern impartiality') by imperial statesmen with the aim of bringing the two communities together in the long term. It was the perspective of an Enlightenment Whig and was shared by many Liberal Union-ists, including Dicey and Sidgwick. The flaw was that it did not grasp the power of the sentiment of nationality, nor (curiously) did it adequately measure the extent of anti-English feeling in both communities, and especially the Catholic.

Bryce undoubtedly shared his uncle's antagonism to Home Rule at the time of his election to Parliament in 1880. He was under pressure from the large Irish community in Tower Hamlets to say what he would do for Ireland, and he wrote to Uncle John: 'I wish you could tell me what can be done, in the way of legislation, for Ireland that wd help to soothe the Home Rulers, for whose crotchet I of course can't vote: whether there is really anything we can do to meet them about the land.'[36] The dismissal of Home Rule as a 'crotchet'—a favourite piece of vocabulary in Victorian politics to dismiss the nostrums of (usually) radical reformers—was quite characteristic: the unspoken question was, what practical benefits would result from Home Rule? And the unspoken answer was, none at all. 'I refused Home Rule two months ago', he wrote exactly two months later, at the start of the election campaign.[37] Face-to-face encounter with 'the tiresome folly of Parnell's party' in the Commons can hardly have helped attract him to the Home Rule cause; but, he told Uncle John, 'It needs my recollection of all that you impressed so forcibly upon me regarding the wrongs of the past to make me resolved not to impute to the people the mistakes of their representatives but still feel them to be after all the injured party.'[38]

It is clear that Bryce's position on the Home Rule question was softening in the course of 1882. We know this from his correspondence with Godkin, who followed a similar trajectory, but even in his letters to a trenchant oppo-nent of Home Rule such as Uncle John the evolution in his thinking is evident. The most telling letter was written in June 1882:

The North of Ireland seems, if I may judge from what the Ulster members tell me, as well as from their votes, to be in favour of this Prevention of Crime Bill; & to be growing quite fierce at the idea of any concession to the Parnel-lites in the direction of Home Rule. If we once could get the Land Act fairly into working order, we may try whether the discontent abates. If it doesn't, if the Irish members remain as obstructive here, & the Fenian conspirators as active in Ireland, then some change will have to be made. A democratic country such as England is becoming cannot permanently maintain a

system of severe repression in Ireland, nor a country governed by a representative assembly permanently tolerate such a section as the Irish
members—the Parnellite 35, soon to become 70, have shewn themselves.

The longer one looks at the matter, the more difficult does the problem
seem with what is & must be the <u>English</u> parliament—for the vast English
majority gives it its character—governing Ireland. Yet all the schemes of
Home Rule yet suggested are quite as unpromising.[39]

This was an effective digest of the nub of Godkin's argument. Bryce clearly had
no great confidence in the practicalities of Home Rule at this stage: in truth,
he never did. But he had already reached the conclusions which really made
Home Rule inescapable from his perspective. A policy of coercion cannot be
long sustained in a democratic state, and, equally, democratic government was
being made impossible by the obstructionist tactics of the Home Rulers, who
were destined to double in number once the franchise was extended. Hence
Bryce's conclusion that if the Land Act did not seriously ameliorate Irish discontent, 'then some change will have to be made'. It is unclear whether his
uncle was able to read between the lines here; it would seem not. But Bryce's
meaning is unmistakable.

In 1886 Bryce was happy to concede that his position on Home Rule had
changed, and that his uncle could at least claim consistency: 'I am more surprised to find myself for it than to find you against it'. But his fundamental
argument was the inevitability of self-government for Ireland, and the absence
of a credible alternative policy:

The last six sessions in Parliament, and my observation of the behaviour of
English parties have made me feel certain that Home Rule must come:
if so, the sooner it comes the better; rather more peaceably than after more
embittered struggles. The late Bill was very imperfect: and <u>between ourselves</u>,
the way the question has been handled since last August very unwise and
calculated to provoke anger and suspicion on the part of cautious Liberals.
I see & admit all—or nearly all—the objections. But then I see no other
course possible, nor does any opponent indicate one.

Having denied that he was under the sway of Gladstone's authority, he went on:
'It is my conviction that we must give up trying to govern the Irish like children,
& must just let them make their bed & lie in it, that determines my vote.'[40]

Bryce, unlike his uncle, was a long-standing admirer of Gladstone. 'There is
a wonderful grace and fineness about both his thoughts and his manner', he
wrote to his mother after hearing him speak in the Commons on the University

Tests Abolition Bill, an issue on which Gladstone and Bryce took rather different positions.[41] Bryce's mother and his sisters in particular shared his Gladstonian sympathies, which were much strengthened by the stance Gladstone took on the Bulgarian atrocities in 1876.[42] In any case there is no doubt that Bryce did work very closely with Gladstone on the Irish Question. In July 1886 Gladstone—still (just) in office, though the Government of Ireland Bill had been defeated in the Commons the previous month, asked Bryce to 'take in hand the manipulation of the Irish subject, or the superintendence of that manipulation, in the aspects which belong 1 (& mainly) to history 2. to an outlook beyond these shores'. He evidently respected Bryce's expertise on overseas politics and constitutions as well as his credentials as an historian. The prime minister went on, 'the whole iniquities of the Union, and the subsequent English history which is shameful though less profoundly & unmixedly shameful, must be laid bare & become common property', and added: 'remember that Corn Law Repeal was neither (generally) cared about nor understood till Cobden illuminated it with his admirable intellect, Bright putting in the passion.'[43] In Bryce's circles the campaign against the corn laws was widely recognized as the model for how to shape public opinion in a liberal (and Liberal) direction, and Gladstone evidently looked to Bryce and his collaborators to do for Home Rule what Cobden did for free trade. This was just two weeks after Uncle John had accused Bryce of yielding to Gladstone's 'witchery'. Bryce replied to Gladstone that 'any wish you may express will always have the greatest authority for me'.[44] Two volumes, in the end, came out of his 'literary campaign'.[45] In 1887 Bryce edited, and contributed two pieces to, the *Handbook of Home Rule*, an important collection of essays published in periodicals over the previous year, together with three new articles; it included a piece by Gladstone written at very short notice.[46] The following year a volume on *Two Centuries of Irish History* appeared under the editorship of Barry O'Brien, the Parnellite journalist: Bryce, who had put in a lot of work towards the assemblage of the contributors, wrote the introduction.[47] Indeed, Bryce noted that it was a book 'which I have taken no small pains to bring before the world'.[48]

Large Nations, Small Nations, and the Liberal Case for Home Rule

One of the central issues in the Home Rule controversy, and the one that mattered to constitutional theorists, was whether the (re)establishment of an Irish Parliament with devolved legislative powers was compatible with the principle of parliamentary sovereignty—that is, the absolute legal sovereignty of the Crown in Parliament—as enunciated by Dicey in his *Law of the Constitution*. Dicey himself was the leading polemicist for the view that it was not compatible. Gladstone read the *Law of the Constitution* at Bryce's suggestion and admired and cited it (naturally enough, he did not see it as constituting an argument against Home Rule). Bryce's own speech on the 2nd Reading of the Home Rule Bill was the most sophisticated constitutional defence of the compatibility of the bill with parliamentary sovereignty.

Equally, the Home Rule controversy brought questions of federalism to the fore in British politics, and really for the first time. Freeman was writing on federalism in history, and Bryce was writing about the modern world's first great federal system. There is much more to be said about this 'federal moment', not least because federal solutions were on the agenda in European politics too—especially in Switzerland and in Germany—and indeed in the British Empire, with the establishment of the Confederation of Canada (1867), the growth of the federal movement in Australia from the 1880s, and the formation of the Imperial Federation movement.[49] 'Our own age has been a federal age', wrote Charles Dilke in 1890.[50] The federal reconstruction of the UK— 'Home Rule All Round', as it was called—went much further than Gladstone's government wanted to go in 1886, not least because it would entail the abandonment of what Bryce termed Britain's 'flexible' constitution, and Bryce himself never supported it.[51] But Bryce had a profound interest in federal systems, and more generally in unions of states and other complex political organisms of that kind. He had, after all, made his scholarly reputation with a brilliant analytical history of the Holy Roman Empire.

Bryce conceptualized federalism as just one answer to the broader problem of the constitutional management of the tensions between centripetal and centrifugal political forces in the age of nationalism. This was the subject of an important piece he wrote on the eve of the Home Rule crisis—an essay first given as a public lecture in Oxford, and much later published as 'The Action of Centripetal and Centrifugal Forces on Political Constitutions', in his two-volume collection, *Studies in History and Jurisprudence* (1901). The dating of this lecture is of some importance. In *Studies in History and Jurisprudence*, Bryce says that it 'was composed in the early part of 1885'. When it was later republished in a single-volume collection, he recalled that it was 'sketched out in the days before Mr Gladstone had given his approval to that demand'.[52] The 'early part of 1885' does not quite correspond to 'the days before' Gladstone's 'Hawarden Kite', when, in December 1885, he was first reported as having come round to support for Home Rule. In fact we know that the lecture was delivered in the hall of Oriel College in February 1886—actually about a week after Bryce's appointment as under-secretary at the Foreign Office in Gladstone's short-lived third ministry. According to the *Oxford Magazine*, this 'singularly interesting' lecture was 'well attended—especially by the Professors and teachers of the Law Faculty', and 'was of a more popular nature than might have been predicted from the title'—which suggests something of its political bite.[53] It is a fascinating and rather neglected piece that has some claim to be Bryce's most elaborate exposition of his political theory. It certainly provides his fullest discussion of nationality, prior to his wartime 'The Principle of Nationality and Its Applications' of 1918.[54]

He was not the first to transfer the concepts of centripetal and centrifugal forces from Newtonian astronomy to the study of political institutions—we can find the terms used figuratively in Madison and Hamilton, and sporadically in American political discourse of the Antebellum. In Britain, Gladstone wrote in 1870 of the 'centripetal and centrifugal forces . . . engaged in mortal tug' in the Habsburg Dual Monarchy.[55] The terminology is also a recurrent feature of the published writings and correspondence of Lord Acton: the first I have discovered, referring to 'the centrifugal or State-rights principle', dates from the year of the outbreak of the American Civil War.[56] It was also used occasionally with reference to the government of India.[57] Bryce did not use the terms in the *Holy Roman Empire* in its earliest editions, but the term 'centrifugal' appeared in the new supplemental chapter on 'The New German Empire' in 1873 and subsequent editions. They were a recurrent feature of the analysis presented in the *American Commonwealth* from its first edition: ten usages in all across the three volumes, in each case the two terms being used in antithesis.

Although he was not the inventor of the centrifugal/centripetal binary as applied to politics, Bryce was the first to give these concepts close attention as analytical tools in the study of politics and constitutions. His fundamental questions were these: what are the forces that hold political communities together, and what are the forces that tend to their disaggregation? And what implications do these forces have for constitutional organization? In addressing these questions, Bryce was probably influenced by John Stuart Mill's chapter on nationality in his *Considerations on Representative Government*, but there are still stronger echoes of the French orientalist Ernest Renan's famous lecture, 'What Is a Nation?', delivered less than four years before Bryce gave his lecture.[58] Renan's lecture was published separately in 1882, but there is no evidence that Bryce encountered it, and since it attracted scant attention in

Britain at the time, there is no reason why he should have.[59] Like Renan, Bryce wrestled with the significance of the different factors that made for political cohesion: on the one hand, material interest; on the other, influences of emotion or sentiment flowing from community of race or language or a shared cultural heritage.[60] All mattered, but, like Renan, Bryce eschewed determinism. So, for instance, 'Mere identity of origin does not count for much, as witness the ardent Hungarian patriotism of most of the Germans and Jews settled in Hungary, with perhaps no drop of Magyar blood in their veins.'[61] Bryce adhered thereafter to this account of race and nation: his last work, published a few weeks after his death, contained a strikingly similar statement of the various 'bonds of union' that made a nation: racial sentiment and religious sentiment, certainly, but also 'that sense of community which is created by the use of a common language, the possession of a common literature, the recollection of common achievements or sufferings in the past, the existence of common customs and habits of thought, common ideals and aspirations.'[62]

Bryce was not, however, engaged in trying to define the nation and did not venture a voluntaristic definition along the lines of Renan's famous 'daily plebiscite'. He said much more than Renan did about the obstacles that racial difference placed in the way of political cohesion. But when we read the lecture alongside a set of letters he wrote to *The Times* in 1887 in the course of a controversy with the Liberal Unionist MP and anthropologist Sir John Lubbock, the affinity with Renan becomes clearer still.[63] Lubbock seized on Gladstone's remark that there were no fewer than 'four real nationalities' in the United Kingdom. Lubbock took it for granted that 'real nationalities' must mean 'races', and set out to show at some length that in terms of racial stock there was no clear distinction between the English and the Welsh, the Scots and the Irish. Bryce responded tersely: Lubbock's 'interesting letter . . . entirely misses the bearing of Mr Gladstone's remark by confusing races with nationalities.' He went on to explain: 'A nationality may be made up of any number of races, because race is only one of several elements which go to create a nationality.' The point of Gladstone's observation was, in Bryce's explanation, that in a question such as the Irish Question that clearly turned on national sentiment, it was important to attend to 'the opinion of each of the nationalities surviving in our islands'. The point was not to suppress Irish nationality, for it had not been necessary to suppress Scottish nationality in order to ensure that Scotland could be governed peaceably as an integral part of the United Kingdom. The point was to acknowledge Irish nationality—meaning the subjective sense of nationhood—and to seek ways of harmonizing it with an 'imperial'

patriotism.[64] It is intriguing to find that the other participants in this controversy (all of them opposing Bryce's position) struggled to understand a subjective
conception of nationality. Bryce's conception was not exclusively subjective,
any more than Renan's was, but the dispute shows clearly how close Bryce was
to Renan on this point: there could be no nationality without a subjective
sense of belonging. This mattered in the context of the Home Rule controversy, because the reality of Ireland's political nationhood was something that
Gladstonians asserted and Unionists typically denied.[65]

What is perhaps most important about the lecture on 'centripetal and centrifugal forces' is that it shows Bryce conceptualizing questions he would write
about in more depth in the *American Commonwealth*—and shows him wrestling with the implications of these questions for Home Rule. He was intrigued
by the Janus-faced quality of nationality: a force for cohesion in some cases,
for dissolution in others. 'The patriotism which makes a Magyar desire that
Hungary should absorb Croatia, and that which makes a Croat desire to sever
his country from Hungary, are essentially the same sentiment, though, as regards the monarchy of the Hungarian Crown, the sentiment operates with the
Magyar as an attractive, with the Croat as a repulsive force.' But he was also
fascinated by instances—historical and contemporary—where 'local' and
'imperial' patriotism had coexisted: in Bavaria, for instance, and still more in
Scotland.[66] While material progress tended to break down local particularism
and so to make for unity, or identification with the larger group, the march of
civilization also tended to re-ignite 'historical memories' and 'resentment at
old injuries': hence the phenomenon of substate nationalism.

This all raised the question of how states should handle the problem of
particularism or substate nationalism in such a way as to contain it, and prevent separation—for Bryce certainly shared the dominant assumption of
European liberals of his time that the future lay with fewer and larger political
entities, and that this was on the whole a good thing. The liberal programme
could not be enacted in 'states too small to have any public opinion', to use the
expression he deployed in his analysis of the post-Westphalian Holy Roman
Empire.[67] He deplored the slow decline of the Holy Roman Empire, which he
read as a history of the stifling of German nationhood: 'the sacrifice of imperial, or rather federal, rights to state rights', a formulation (present from the
first edition onwards) that must have been intended to bring the American
Civil War to his readers' minds.[68] But it did not follow that uncompromising
centralism was the best way of suppressing separatism. Bryce thought that
history proved otherwise:

Everybody can now see [he may have overestimated his readers here] that Rome ought to have admitted the Italian allies to the franchise long before the Social War, that Catholic Emancipation ought to have been enacted by the Irish Parliament in 1786 or by the British Parliament immediately after the Union of 1800, that Denmark ought not to have waited till 1874, before she conceded a qualified autonomy to Iceland, that the same country might probably have retained Schleswig-Holstein if she had yielded long before the war of 1864 some of the demands made by the German inhabitants of those duchies.[69]

The implications for Ireland were unspoken but were crystal-clear. Indeed, when reprinting this piece in the 1905 volume, *Constitutions*, Bryce wrote that the lecture was stimulated 'partly by the recent history of Iceland, partly by the Irish demand for Home Rule'.[70]

Iceland

Bryce was indeed fascinated by small nations, as the reference to Iceland makes clear: if Ireland was small in population, Iceland was tiny, its population about one-eightieth that of Ireland and not much more than that of the Isle of Man. But we may wonder what the experience of Iceland, and other small European states, had to do with the relations between Great Britain and Ireland.

Bryce repeatedly brought before Gladstone—partly at his instigation—evidence and parallels from other countries where forms of legislative devolution had been attempted. His letters to Gladstone are full of snippets such as: (from the Isle of Man) 'I am endeavouring to make out how their system of self government works both locally and in its relation to the Government of Great Britain'; and 'I have just returned from a visit to Croatia, where I have been enquiring into the working of the "Home Rule system" as one may call it, which unites that Kingdom to Hungary: and as to the South Slavonic problem generally' (this on his honeymoon, in fact).[71] Again, in 1892—on the eve of the general election—'in Norway and Sweden I hope to learn something definite and trustworthy regarding the relations of the two Governments and peoples, a subject which will again have a practical interest after the general election. I rejoice to think that the judgment of the country in favour of your policy seems to be more and more clear and decisive as time goes on.'[72] Gladstone's parliamentary speeches on Home Rule, both in 1886 and in 1893, depended very substantially on these parallels: he invoked the relations of

Sweden and Norway, which had legislatures independent of each other, and the dualism of Austria-Hungary; and he maintained that these expedients— especially in the first case—had made 'the union of the two countries, which at one time seemed hopeless and impossible . . . close, and . . . growing closer from day to day'.[73] He picked up on the observation of Joseph Cowen, the Liberal backbencher, that 'the separation of Legislatures is often the union of countries, and the union of Legislatures is often the severance of countries'. The latter point, Gladstone thought, was illustrated by the cases of American independence from Britain and that of Belgium from the Netherlands; and in support of the former point he (somewhat boldly) invoked the examples of Crete, the Lebanon, and Samos in relation to the Ottoman Empire, as well as Norway in relation to Sweden, Iceland in relation to Denmark, and Hungary in relation to Austria. He also maintained that the relative autonomy the Austrians allowed to Galicia made for smoother relations with its Polish population than were possible between either Russia or Prussia and their Polish territories. Finally, he invoked the example of Canada, where formidable differences with Britain 'were completely cured and healed by the establishment of a responsible Government with a free Executive'.[74]

Gladstone reiterated these arguments in 1893, again citing Austro-Hungarian dualism, the separation of Belgium from the Netherlands, and the failure of the union of Russia with its Polish territories. He also now noted the case of federal Germany, where he thought the federal solution had been attended with 'complete success'.[75] Successful 'incorporating Unions'—he meant unitary states, such as those of France, Italy, and Spain—were those 'favoured by incidents of history, geography, language, race', and not reliant on force deployed against unwilling regions.[76]

Bryce himself made one important intervention in the Commons on the Home Rule question in 1886: a lengthy speech on the Second Reading on 17 May. He was usually considered to have been a rather ineffective Commons performer, although he was a practised and accomplished public speaker in other settings; but this speech was one that won him real plaudits, even from his opponents. It was given some three months after his Oxford lecture, and he echoed one of the central points of that lecture: 'In one way or other this problem of reconciling unity of government with local autonomy and national diversities has confronted nearly all the States of modern Europe.' He cited Austro-Hungarian dualism: 'how much more stable [is] its fabric than in the days before 1867, when the rights of Hungary were ignored and the semblance of unity maintained by the disciples of Metternich.' He invoked the federalism of the German Empire: Bavaria is very unlike Prussia in many respects, not just religion; and yet since 1870 the two states had worked harmoniously together. With moderate conciliation and recognition of a measure of autonomy, Holland might have retained Belgium, and Denmark might have kept Schleswig-Hollstein.[77]

Next he cited the instance that was most distinctively his own. 'It is an instance on a small scale, because the population of the Island is small; but it relates to a country which ought to be interesting to us, not only from the ties of blood which unite us to its people, but from the splendour, unrivalled in the modern world, of its early literature—I mean the case of Iceland.' The cries of 'Oh!' betrayed the scepticism of his audience about what Iceland could have to tell the United Kingdom. Bryce's riposte was illuminating: 'Hon. Members opposite seem curiously anxious to have no information upon this subject. I suppose they would rather I should tread again the weary round of hackneyed arguments which we have listened to from those Benches, than that I should endeavour to throw light upon the subject by means of some new illustration.' Perhaps naively, Bryce expected knowledge and information to carry weight on the floor of the House. Lord Randolph Churchill asked the distance between Iceland and Denmark—over a thousand miles—with the implication that the government of a territory so remote from the mainland could have no lessons for Britain and Ireland, though Bryce maintained that it made 'no substantial difference' to his argument. He went on to argue—citing 'an eminent Icelander'—that 'relations between the two countries are now incomparably more peaceful than they were before 1874, owing to the recognition by the Constitution of the Icelanders as a people capable of taking care of themselves.'[78]

Bryce's fascination with the Icelandic case is intriguing. He had in fact been discussing foreign analogues to Irish Home Rule with Freeman, who himself wrote prolifically on the question; and they agreed that from a constitutional point of view, the Icelandic case was the best one. But there is also an important back story here, for Bryce (as we have seen) had visited Iceland with Ilbert and Mackay back in 1872, and that was just two years before large legislative powers were devolved on the Althing in 1874. The fact that Bryce had visited Iceland is important, because it tells us something about the sources of Bryce's expertise in questions of foreign politics. His extensive travels gave him a certain authority, not least on Iceland, on which he had published a number of articles, including one in the *Saturday Review* on Icelandic politics. But he also consulted others. In the Icelandic case, his main authority was Eiríkr Magnússon, the Icelandic patriot, scholar, and lexicographer who was on the staff of the Cambridge University Library: he and Bryce had an extended correspondence, and he was the 'eminent Icelander' whom Bryce cited in the Commons in May 1886. Through Freeman he also consulted Gudbrand Vigfússon, who had been based in Oxford for two decades and was now Reader in Scandinavian. Whereas Magnússon was impressively well informed, Vigfússon was 'not much interested in modern things', according to Freeman.[79] At the same time he was taking soundings about other instances of 'home rule': on Finland he consulted the Foreign Office Librarian, Sir Edward Hertslet, who supplied a memorandum on Finland. This memorandum began with the *Encyclopaedia Britannica*'s article on Finland both under Swedish rule and under Russian rule following its cession in 1809—an illustration of the lack of reliable and accessible literature on the subject—but he also drew on despatches written by British diplomats, such as Horace Rumbold from St Petersburg in 1869. Hertslet noted that Alexander I had pledged, as had his successors, to preserve the religion, laws, and liberties of the country, and that Finland was 'the freest and best governed part of the Russian Empire'. In 1861 Russia granted Finland a political constitution, and Hertslet referred to a report written by Lord Napier, British ambassador in St Petersburg.

Bryce added:

What is most remarkable in the recent history of Finland is the extraordinary development of national Finnish feeling as opposed not merely to Russian influence but to those Swedish influences which formerly dominated the country. The Finnish tongue has become the main organ even of the higher literature, though Swedish alone was used by the upper classes even forty or fifty years ago, while Russian seems to make no way at all. Yet along with this strong national sentiment there was not in 1876 when I visited Finland, and I fancy there is not now, any political discontent. The sentimental side of nationality, finding its legitimate satisfaction in self government and in the sphere of literary and scientific culture, causes no trouble to the Russian Government in the field of politics. Nihilism, for instance, seems to have struck no root in Finland, nor has Russia found it necessary to extend thither to repressive measures used in the rest of her European dominions.[80]

The reference to his own visit was quite characteristic: personal experience through travel was always critical to Bryce's ability to speak with *authority* about matters for foreign politics.

Bryce was not, in fact, the first to deploy the Icelandic case in support of the argument for Home Rule. Two Irish MPs, one a Liberal, the other now a

Home Ruler, invoked it in 1874 (the year of Icelandic legislative devolution), though Disraeli mocked them for introducing 'that happy exemplar of Iceland ... in so grave a manner.'[81] Mockery was, indeed, a common response to the invocation of Iceland. Bryce's friend and Liberal colleague G. O. Trevelyan told the Commons: 'I was tempted by the example of my hon. Friend the Under Secretary of State for Foreign Affairs (Mr. Bryce), who went 1,100 miles across the sea to Iceland. He had to go all that distance in order to find a country that would bear out his argument; and the day after he made that speech the Parliament of Iceland behaved in such a turbulent manner towards the country with which it was connected that it had to be suspended.'[82] It turned out that this was a wholly inaccurate account, and that the dissolution of the Icelandic Parliament had been a perfectly regular one. But, in the face of such ridicule, why was Bryce so attached to the Icelandic parallel?

Partly it was an expression of his romantic attachment to the rights, but even more the virtues, of small nations, especially (importantly) small *historic* nations. As he wrote in 1914, 'The small States, whose absorption is now threatened, have been potent and useful—perhaps the most potent and useful—factors in the advance of civilization.'[83] He had a notable admiration for the Swiss—for their constitution, and even more so for their political traditions, especially the tradition of self-government. Some three decades later he told his friend, the diplomat Esme Howard, that Switzerland had 'the best working system of government in the world', adding that 'there have been in modern times only two successful democracies—that of Switzerland and the Orange Free State.'[84] The admiration for Switzerland, if not of the Orange Free State, is understandable and was quite widely shared among Victorian Liberals, not least by Freeman. Iceland was more unusual.

Iceland had attracted British visitors for some time before Bryce and his party went. Notable visitors in the 1860s had included the Oxford clerical don and Scandinavian scholar Frederick Metcalfe, Sabine Baring-Gould, who would achieve fame as a hymn-writer and author of *Onward Christian Soldiers*, and, most importantly, the saga-translator George Dasent. William Morris, who would become possibly the most famous Victorian friend of Iceland, visited both in 1871 and in 1873; Trollope—another intrepid traveller—in 1878. Bryce and his party were in Iceland at the same time as the explorer (Sir) Richard Burton, the aficionado of Oriental erotica; and as (Sir) Courtenay Ilbert, one of Bryce's party, recalled elliptically, 'No two great travellers ever differed from each other more profoundly, in sympathies, antipathies, and points of view, than Bryce and Burton.'[85] But none of these really had much to say about

Iceland as a political community. Norway was quite a point of reference in Victorian political, social, and economic thought, notably in the work of Samuel Laing, who admired its sturdy peasant proprietors; and Erskine May, in a somewhat Teutonist manner, portrayed the Scandinavian countries as 'renowned for their free, and even democratic, institutions'.[86] But no one seems to have thought of Iceland in this light before Bryce.[87]

Bryce wrote quite extensively about Iceland. There were two articles in the *Saturday Review* in 1872–1873, one on Icelandic travel, the other on Iceland's politics.[88] There were articles in Leslie Stephen's *Cornhill Review* and in the *Alpine Journal*, and the very first of more than three hundred pieces in Godkin's *Nation* was a review of Cleasby and Vigfusson's *Icelandic Dictionary*, where, inter alia, he lamented that the great Icelandic law book, *Grágás*, had to be read either in Icelandic or in Latin, 'and then in very unsatisfactory editions'.[89] But the piece in which he broke new ground was the lecture he gave on 'Primitive Iceland' at Oxford in May 1873; many years later this was published in his *Studies in History and Jurisprudence*.[90] Here he identified primitive Iceland as a site of legal and constitutional innovation.[91]

He seems to have come to see Iceland in this light during the 1872 visit, when he had already started to explore Icelandic law. He wrote from Reykjavik to his friend, the historian J. R. Green, and recorded that he had engaged a professor to teach him some Icelandic, 'enough [he hoped] to be able to read the Sagas and Grey Goose—their famous 12th century law book'.[92] The following month, back in England, he picked up the same subject in a letter to Freeman. He had evidently returned from Iceland keen to tell Freeman and others all about the country; but more than that, he was absorbed in its early legal history. 'I have lost all interest in public matters, and care more about Olaf Tryggvason and Úlfljótr [he writes Úlfljót] & Skapti Þóroddsson than about Gladstone or even Bismarck'.[93] He urged Freeman to 'work up Icelandic law' when writing the final volume of his Norman Conquest, and he pointed to the law books on which he should concentrate: 'read thro' Grágás at least if not also through Jarusida and Jónsbók'. He went on, still more importantly: 'And when you come to Vol III of Fed Govt there must be a chapter on the Icelandic Republic, wh. was in an irregular fashion federal: if you like I'll give a sketch of it wh. you can deal with as you please.'[94] Freeman did not follow Bryce's advice on either point: Volume 5 of the *Norman Conquest* made no reference to Icelandic law, and his *History of Federal Government* never reached a second, let alone a third volume; but this was not for any lack of interest in Icelandic history and politics.

Some of Bryce's arguments drew on the common tropes of Teutonist historiography, in particular the focus on two institutions that the Norse settlers of the ninth and tenth centuries brought to Iceland, namely, the practice of joint worship in the temple, and the assembly ('the Thing') of all freemen to determine lawsuits and to handle matters of common interest. These were, Bryce writes, 'part of the common heritage of the Teutonic race'.[95] But the subsequent analysis contains much that is new and interesting. He stresses the antiquity of the Althing (or Alþing), which first met in 930:

> one of the oldest national assemblies in the civilized world, and one of the very few which did not, like the English Parliament and the Diet of the Romano-Germanic Empire, grow up imperceptibly and, so to speak, naturally, from small beginnings, but was formally and of set purpose established, by what would have been called, had paper existed, a paper constitution, that is to say by the deliberate agreement of independent groups of men, seeking to attain the common ends of order and justice.[96]

But it was a law-court, and a legislature only insofar as it *declared* the law: it was not part of a state apparatus, for there was no executive, and the Alþing was not just the centre of the political life of the Republic, but it was, indeed, the only way in which the Republic acted as a collective whole. There was no public expenditure, nor were any taxes levied. 'The Icelandic Republic was in fact a government developed only upon its judicial and (to a much smaller extent) upon its legislative side, omitting altogether the executive and international sides, which were in the Greek and Roman world, and have again in the modern world, become so important.'[97]

Bryce pointed out that this system was 'full of interest and suggestion' (a very Brycean expression), 'as well to the student of legal theory as to the constitutional historian'. Specifically, he thought it told against the Austinian conception of law, according to which law could only be understood as the command of a sovereign, and in fact Bryce would repeatedly cross swords with Austin's ghost.

> Some modern theorists derive law from the State, and cannot think of law as existing without a State. A few among them have in England gone so far as to deny that Customary Law is law at all, and to define all Law as a Command issued by the State power. But here in Iceland we find Law, and indeed (as will appear presently) a complex and highly developed legal system, existing without the institutions which make a State; for a community

such as has been described, though for convenience it may perhaps be called a Republic, is clearly not a State in the usual sense of the word. Of Iceland, indeed, one may say that so far from the State creating the Law, the Law created the State—that is to say, such State organization as existed came into being for the sake of deciding lawsuits. There it ended. When the decision had been given, the action of the Republic stopped. . . . Law in fact existed without any public responsibility for enforcing it, the sanction, on which modern jurists so often dwell as being vital to the conception of law, being found partly in public opinion, partly in the greater insecurity which attached to the life of the person who disregarded a judgement.[98]

Iceland resembled other European polities of the early Middle Ages in that in them too law predated the executive power: that is, it could be traced back to customs that were recognized and obeyed before there was any power to enforce them. 'But Iceland is unique as the example of a community which had a great deal of law and no central Executive, a great many Courts and no authority to carry out their judgements.'[99]

The historical possession of a distinctive set of public institutions was one thing that made nineteenth-century Iceland an authentic nationality, in spite of her tiny and dispersed population and the absence of anything resembling the normal components of civil society. The other key factor was something Bryce dwelt on in his 'Impressions of Iceland': a national memory preserved above all through familiarity with the Sagas. 'It is this knowledge of the Sagas that has more than anything else given a measure of elevation as well as culture to his [the average Icelander's] mind. It has stimulated his imagination, and added to his people and country a sort of historical dignity which their position in the modern world could never entitle them to.' He noted that, although there were no schools in Iceland apart from the Schola Latina at Reykjavik, literacy was near universal, and almost every house had a library: indeed, 'twice, in spots of rather exceptional wretchedness, I found exceptionally good ones—one chiefly of legal and historical treatises, the other an excellent collection of Sagas and poetry.'[100]

Bryce's Icelandic interests embraced current politics as well as the Middle Ages. In the same year that he gave his lecture on Iceland, he published two articles on Iceland in the *Saturday Review*, one of them giving the traveller's perspective, the other addressing politics. The latter described the very limited autonomy at that time enjoyed by Iceland (before the reforms of 1874): a consultative Althing which met for a month every two years, and a governor, based in Reykjavík, who was always a Dane and whose administrative powers were limited, since matters of consequence were referred to the ministry in Copenhagen. He then went on to outline the drive for constitutional reform, and the aims of the Icelandic national movement: the Danes were willing to concede legislative initiative to the Althing but were not willing to allow the creation of an Icelandic ministry responsible to that body. Iceland felt no affinity with Denmark, and the national movement—which on the whole recognized that Iceland was too poor and sparsely populated to be fully independent—was more attracted to union with Norway or even with Britain. While Bryce did not indicate his sources, it is clear that he must have engaged in extended political discussions while in Reykjavík, in spite of language barriers.

Bryce came across as broadly sympathetic to the Icelandic national movement, and that was confirmed the following year, when *The Times* published a piece by its Danish correspondent on the significance of the legislative autonomy conceded to Iceland in the year of its millennial celebrations.[101] The correspondent saw the new constitution as a far-sighted and generous measure, 'conceived in a very liberal spirit, having in most of its articles been closely moulded upon the Danish Charter of 1849, one of the freest in Europe'. And, while he acknowledged that it had been uncertain how it would be received by Icelandic opinion, he enthusiastically reported the positive response that the Althing had recorded. In consequence, a royal visit was planned. It was Bryce who wrote to contradict this account.[102] He acknowledged that *The Times*'s correspondent had faithfully represented Copenhagen's impression of Iceland's response but pointed out the 'the Danes are proverbially blind to the true feelings of their dependencies'. 'Communications lately received'— presumably private correspondence to Bryce—'give an account very different from your correspondent's of the attitude of the Icelandic people.' No one much was satisfied with the constitutional settlement: some rejected it altogether, while others—more numerous—saw it simply as a first stage to an ampler measure of Home Rule. Bryce was in no doubt that when the Althing next met—the following summer—it would reiterate the demands it had consistently urged for some years.

Although Bryce published nothing substantial on Iceland after the essay on 'Primitive Iceland', his fascination with the country remained. Writing a fifty-page 'Introduction to the History of the World' for Arthur Mee's *Harmsworth History of the World* in 1907, he devoted a striking paragraph to Iceland as an instance of one of the small nations which had 'counted for more than the larger nations to whose annals a larger space is routinely allotted'. He thought

Iceland in this respect the counterpart in the modern world of Israel in the ancient.[103] He told George Prothero in 1910 that he would rather live in the United States than anywhere else in the world, 'except perhaps in Hawaii—or in Iceland'.[104] In a preface for a book on the Nordic countries in 1916, he reiterated the central thesis of 'Primitive Iceland', that Iceland had been for nearly four centuries the only independent republic, and one uniquely constituted, 'for the government was nothing but a system of law courts, administering a most elaborate system of laws'. And he restated the argument about Home Rule too: since legislative devolution had been conceded, relations between Denmark and Iceland had much improved, 'and furnished another argument to those who hold that peace and progress are best secured by the application of the principles of liberty and self-government'. The history of all the Northern countries, he concluded, 'well deserves far more attention from Englishmen than it has hitherto received'.[105] The following year he concluded his distinguished four-year term as President of the British Academy with a magisterial survey of the whole range of the humanities and the social sciences, looking forward to their likely progress over the next thirty years. Here he noted the need for 'a history of Iceland, a subject on which little has been written, except in Danish, since the days of Konrad Maurer'.[106] And finally, his last book, *International Relations*, published a month after his death in 1922, was the text of eight lectures delivered at Williams College in Massachusetts the previous summer, almost half a century after his sole visit to Iceland. Here, intriguingly, he invoked the instance of medieval Iceland in support of his conception of international law as law properly so called, because it had the sanction of international public opinion. 'In Iceland there was no State, but a number of virtually independent communities, and these communities had a great number of rules which they all recognized as having the authority of settled custom.'[107]

———

Bryce's fascination with Iceland is important because it illuminates two things in particular: It helps us to understand better the position he occupied in the small nation/large nation debate, and it helps us to appreciate more fully the stance he took on Irish Home Rule.

Bryce was by no mean immune to the widespread conviction among the Liberals (British and European) of his time that large nation-states were (other things being equal) preferable to smaller ones. In his *Holy Roman Empire* he gave vent to the Liberal animus against small-state particularism, which frustrated both commerce and free communication across a large territory. This sense of the advantage of a strong central state protecting minorities and promoting economic and cultural development through the impartial administration of law was reinforced by the lessons of the American Civil War, on which Bryce and the university liberals of his time sided with the federal cause against 'state rights' as well as slavery. Alongside imperial pride, this kind of case for the political benefits of scale was one of the mainsprings of the flight of late Victorian intellectuals away from the Liberal Party in the wake of Gladstone's championship of Home Rule. He also saw value in the imperial bond, where it held together settler colonies and the mother country which shared a common set of traditions and values. But Bryce also recognized—as many of his friends and acquaintances who became Liberal Unionists were reluctant to recognize—that other things very often were not equal. While Dicey thought that the only public opinion that mattered in relation to the Irish Question was the public opinion of the *United Kingdom* electoral body, Bryce saw that this was to beg the question. Once the Irish had demonstrated, and demonstrated consistently, not only a settled sense of political nationhood but also an indifference to imperial patriotism, it was self-defeating to try to coerce them into being good imperial citizens.

That Bryce's embrace of Home Rule is so often treated as an anomaly and an inconsistency is itself a curiosity. If there was a consistent theme in Bryce's career in international politics, it was his consistent identification with the cause of small nations struggling in the face of injustice. He championed the Icelander against the Dane, and the Armenian, the Greek, and the Bulgarian against the Turk; the Boer against the British, and the Tyrolese against the Italian. Viewed in this perspective, it made perfect sense to sympathize with the cause of Home Rule.

7

Democracy, European
and American

DEMOCRACY WAS A CENTRAL THREAD in Bryce's intellectual concerns, as well as the framework for his political career. In his twenties, he was assigned the task of writing on 'The Historical Aspect of Democracy' for *Essays on Reform*, that fascinating manifesto of university liberalism in the age of the Second Reform Act; and in the last year of life, he finally published his two large volumes on *Modern Democracies*, a work that had been his major literary project for almost twenty years.[1] In the meantime, he had made his worldwide reputation as the author of the preeminent study of the leading democratic experiment in the modern world, *The American Commonwealth*.

Bryce was, of course, not just a student of democracy but a practitioner too, and it is important to grasp the nature of his vocation; in particular, the rival pulls of 'science' and politics as vocations, to use Max Weber's terminology. As a young man, Bryce had certainly been tempted by the prospect of a university career, even though the academic career structure was only just coming into being at the time. But he rejected this option, as he recalled, because he thought that a university was 'not the best place in which to keep up energy or to be abreast of the general movements of the world'.[2] He was not turning against an intellectual or a scholarly vocation, however: he simply held that one could not properly understand the contemporary world as a mere observer. Conversely, having entered politics, he was frustrated by 'the petty distractions of parliamentary life' which prevented him completing big books: in this case, *The American Commonwealth*.[3] 'I am getting more & more to feel', he told Daniel Coit Gilman in 1891, 'that literary or historical people ought to quit politics as soon as they have seen enough to give them a sense of what the concrete facts of that rather repulsive pursuit are'.[4] Here Bryce disclosed something very revealing about what he thought he was doing in public life: he wanted to understand the political world of his time, and he thought that a spell as a practitioner was instrumentally necessary; he also knew that if he was to play his part in shaping public opinion (something he certainly regarded as part of the intellectual's vocation), Parliament offered an unrivalled platform; but parliamentary life brought him little fulfilment, and he considered himself something of an outsider.

His attitudes toward democracy followed a curious trajectory, though not a unique one. He thought himself a democrat when that was the stance of a radical minority; but in his later years, when to be a democrat was mainstream, he was a critic, though a nuanced one. His essay in 1867 defended democracy against those of its detractors who thought that historical experience—whether of the Athenians or of the French Revolution—was sufficient to refute its proponents. This was at a time when British opinion was overwhelmingly opposed to democracy. By the 1880s he had become convinced—as had many of his contemporaries—not only that the triumph of democracy was inevitable, but that in substance Britain had already become a democracy. Whether or not it was desirable, it was an irreversible movement. When he wrote *Modern Democracies*, the democratic principle was close to being the touchstone of political legitimacy in Britain, the United States, and elsewhere. Yet Bryce was more of a critic of democracy than ever: not so much in the pages of *Modern Democracies*, where he hoped to come before his readers as an even-handed presenter of 'the facts' of the working of democratic systems; but certainly in his correspondence with close friends such as Dicey. 'It was a better world when it was still possible to believe in Democracy', he wrote in 1920, recalling their tour of the United States fifty years before.[5]

The Advent of Pure Democracy?

The period when Bryce was developing his constitutional ideas, and writing *The American Commonwealth*, was a period of political and constitutional ferment in Britain, when Gladstone's second and third ministries were wrestling on the one hand with a stand-off with the House of Lords over the extension of the county franchise, and on the other with the government of Ireland in the face of the upsurge of nationalist agitation and terrorist atrocities. We can track Bryce's engagement with these issues through his regular reports for the New York *Nation*—he was, in effect, its UK parliamentary correspondent in these years. The very titles of his articles are enough to convey the atmosphere:

'The Parliamentary Crisis', 'More Irish Troubles', 'The Irish Trouble in a New Shape', 'The Approach of Another Crisis', 'More Parliamentary Troubles', 'The Party Game and the Constitutional Crisis', 'Surrender, or Compromise?', 'England: a Political Crisis', 'England: the Ministerial Crisis'. 'England has been in perpetual unrest, throbbing and quivering with effort and passion, ever since 1876', Bryce wrote with a touch of melodrama in February 1885.[6]

The 1880s were a time of social transformation in Britain. This was a formative moment, notably, in the emergence of class as a dominant social category.[7] It was also a time of political upheaval, as Irish nationalism threatened to make the United Kingdom ungovernable, and Gladstone's response—Home Rule— split the Whig-Liberal-Radical coalition and inaugurated two decades of Conservative-Unionist dominance. The confrontation between Lords and Commons—or, better, between the Lords and an elected government with a Commons majority—came to a head for the first time. Even before the Home Rule crisis, Bryce thought that Britain was undergoing a fundamental political transformation, one that made her definitively a democracy.[8] It is well established by historians that in the period 1885–1918 British political commentators took it for granted that they were living in a democracy, even though only about 60 percent of adult men—and no women—were entitled to vote in national elections.[9] But we lack a clear sense of how and when that self-understanding emerged, and what, precisely, was held to make Britain a democracy. To get clearer answers to these questions, we need to pay closer attention to Bryce, and to his dialogues with Dicey in particular, in the 1880s. Bryce's articles for *The Nation*—and Dicey's too—are fundamental here but have never been studied at all systematically.

There were four fundamental points in Bryce's analysis of democratic politics in these articles. The first was the erosion of the authority of Parliament and hence of the representative principle as it had traditionally been understood, notably by Burke in his famous speech to the electors of Bristol in 1774. For Burke the Member of Parliament owed his constituents his independent judgment, rather than obedience to their opinions on particular issues. By the 1880s, according to Bryce, the people, rather than their representatives, came to be seen as 'the direct arbiters of a great political issue'.[10] Bryce saw this as undermining the authority of Parliament and so disturbing the constitution: the expression of 'the new principle of the sovereignty of the majority of the people as opposed to old usage of the sovereignty of the majority of the House of Commons'.[11] In February 1885 he declared England 'now a pure democracy in theory', except insofar as the House of Lords was able to act as a restraining power; and he thought little remained even of that countervailing power.[12]

Second, for Bryce a key mechanism in the transformation of a representative democracy into a pure democracy was the growth of party machines. These operated both to control a mass electorate and to give the populace, or at least party members, a decisive voice in the selection of candidates. This phenomenon, which had its roots in the United States, is conventionally traced in the United Kingdom to the new political methods deployed by the Birmingham Liberal Association to secure its electoral triumphs in 1868. The classic account of the 'Birmingham caucus'—and indeed of party organization both in Britain and in the United States—was to be found in the work of the Paris-based Russian émigré Moisei Ostrogorski, in his *Democracy and the Organization of Political Parties* (1902). Ostrogorski's book was translated from French, but the English edition in fact preceded the French, and it appeared with a preface by Bryce. It was indeed Bryce—with whom Ostrogorski had entered into correspondence about American political parties—who suggested that he should extend his project to include Britain.[13] Bryce's preface—written at the suggestion of the publisher, Alexander Macmillan, who felt it was needed to ensure a readership in Britain—praised the author as 'a singularly painstaking and intelligent student' who was 'both scientific in method and philosophical in spirit', but he also thought he 'exaggerates the power and the poison of what he calls the Caucus in England'.[14] Bryce was nothing if not polite, and already by 1902 he was a practised writer of prefaces, so it was striking that he used his preface not just to praise Ostrogorski (which he did), but also to point out that an important part of his analysis was wrong.

Bryce wrote in February 1885 that Britain was at the same stage the United States had been at sixty years before, when the machinery of primaries and conventions was created to deal with the enlarged electorate. The British counterpart was the Liberal Party's establishment of local associations in every constituency. But—anticipating what he would later write in his preface to Ostrogorski—Bryce eschewed a pessimistic acceptance that Britain must inevitably follow in America's wake, and this was why he did not want to take Ostrogorski's conclusions on board. He fully realized that the tendency of local party organizations would be to turn the MP from a representative into a mere delegate, but the deference of the poor would act as a counterweight, so that if MPs did turn into delegates, 'it will be rather because candidates may wish to grovel than because electors wish to trample'.[15]

The third point was that if constituency party associations were the instruments of democratic transformation at the local level, their national counterpart was the emergence of the party programme as the platform on which a prospective government hoped to be elected—and as the basis of the government's legitimacy once elected. On the 1885 election campaign Bryce wrote:

> It is to Mr Gladstone that the right of speaking for all belongs, and his manifesto, issued on Sept 19 in the form of an address to the electors of the county of Edinburgh, is now the official platform of the Opposition, almost as if it had been adopted, as in America, by a national party convention.
>
> Such a platform is a comparatively new thing in our politics, and it is another mark of the extent to which statesmen address their reasonings directly to the electors, instead of, as formerly, simply standing on their general merits and party character, and reserving arguments for the House of Commons.[16]

That Gladstone's personal manifesto to his constituents became at the same time his party's platform pointed to the fourth element in Bryce's analysis: the importance of the plebiscitary leader with a direct connection to the people.[17] To an extent, this analysis had already been anticipated by Bagehot, who wrote presciently of Gladstone's Greenwich speech of 1871 that it marked 'the coming of the time when it will be one of the most important qualifications of a prime minister to exert a direct control over the masses . . . to reach them, not as his views may be filtered through an intermediate class of political teachers and writers, but *directly* by the vitality of his own mind'.[18] In the literature on the emergence of plebiscitary leadership in democracies, Gladstone is often taken as the exemplar, as Max Weber used him in his analysis of charismatic leadership: 'a Caesarist plebiscitary element, the dictator of the electoral battlefield, entered the political arena'.[19] Bryce's account of the American caucus was certainly an important influence on Weber (who, unusually, fully approved of the triumph of the party machine), and in Weber's analysis the caucus underpinned Gladstone's charismatic authority. It was in the articles for *The Nation*—rather than his biographical essay on Gladstone—that Bryce came closest to anticipating Weber's later account of the charismatic leader.[20] But in these articles it was Joseph Chamberlain who is repeatedly singled out not only as the coming man, but as the man who more than any other personified the new politics.[21]

It is interesting that in Bryce's presentation of his argument, the idea that the individual leader's importance grows with the growth of democracy is seen

FIGURE 7.1. William Ewart Gladstone (1809–1898)
as brooding Byronic hero.

as true but *counter-intuitive*. It runs counter, he thought, to the intuition that democracy takes power away from the individual leader and places it in the hands of the masses. In a discussion of Gladstone (now in opposition) in August 1885, he wrote that 'in our new democracies, the individual man seems *still* to count for as much as in the oligarchies of earlier days'.[22] 'Still' articulates the commonsensical intuition that the individual leader ought to have a diminished role in a democracy. But Bryce was on the point of developing the significantly new insight that the advent of popular rule could potentially reinforce the power of the leader.[23] 'The advance of the popular power does not in England, or perhaps in any country, eliminate the personal element from politics, although it obliges the leader to adopt himself more and more to the wishes and emotions of his followers.'[24] This was an insight he would build on

in his analysis of the American presidency. The presidency was initially conceived as a monarchical mechanism, a restraint on popular power, and that
perception of the institution had persisted; but Bryce expected that it would
increasingly become a vehicle for the popular will. He stressed that the American president was strong because he derived his authority from the people: he
was deemed to represent the people no less than the members of Congress
did. So: 'Public opinion governs by and through him no less than them, and
makes him powerful even against a popularly elected Congress. This is a fact
to be remembered by those Europeans who seek in the strengthening of the
hereditary principle a cure for the faults of government by assemblies. And it
also suggests the risk that attaches to power vested in the hands of a leader
directly chosen by the people.'[25] When Bryce first wrote these words, in 1888,
France was in the midst of the Boulangist crisis, when General Boulanger
threatened to overturn the institutions of the Republic by means of a populist
'appel au peuple'. This was a key moment in the crisis of parliamentary liberalism in Europe. 'Why doesn't some one go to France & give us a real philosophical study of Boulangism? It is as instructive as a Greek city revolution',
wrote Bryce to Henry Sidgwick in April 1888, thanking him for criticisms of
some draft chapters of *The American Commonwealth*.[26] Bryce was not simply
engaged in an Anglo-American dialogue: continental European politics always
enthralled him.

Bryce developed his point about the growing power of the party leaders at
some length in connection with the Gladstone-Salisbury compact to resolve
the question of the redistribution of seats so as to end the stand-off between
Lords and Commons over the Franchise Bill of 1884. He was struck by the fact
that the backbenchers fell into line and thought that this 'habit of obedience
to a chief who commands the country' might well survive. 'It is another symptom of the diminished respect for Parliament which the nation feels, of the
growing power of party organizations, of the tendency of the masses to deliver
themselves up into the hands of a single man. In this present instance the man
is gifted with unrivalled experience; but the democratic leaders of the future
may obtain the same authority with less title to it, and a weaker sense of responsibility for its temperate use than Gladstone feels.'[27] Not everyone commended Gladstone for his temperate qualities.

Bryce's musings on the erosion of the authority of Parliament and the growing tendency of political leaders to behave as though the people were the arbiters of major political issues are suggestive of Dicey's crucial distinction
between legal and political sovereignty—a distinction formulated for the first

time in Dicey's *Law of the Constitution* in 1885. For Dicey, the sovereignty of Parliament—or, strictly, the Crown-in-Parliament—was a fundamental principle of English constitutional law. But to assert the legal sovereignty of Parliament was not at all to deny the political fact that the ultimate source of authority was 'the nation' or, more precisely, 'the majority of the electors'.[28] That was the locus of political sovereignty, and it was enforced by a series of constitutional conventions that determined, for example, the circumstances in which the unelected House must defer to the elected House and those in which the monarch might dismiss a ministry which possessed the confidence of the Commons and dissolve Parliament.

That, however, had been the case at least since the late eighteenth century, as Dicey's analysis made clear: it was not an analysis of the rise of democracy. Dicey acknowledged this: he used his distinction to analyse the significance of George III's dissolution of Parliament in 1784, but at this time the electorate 'represented little else than the land-owners and the traders of the country, and was quite unlike the huge body of householders who today control the destinies of England'.[29] Bryce, by contrast, was making a point about the transformation in the nature of political sovereignty wrought by the advent of what he termed pure democracy in the 1880s.

American Democracy

Bryce engaged most fully with the problems attending the advent of a democratic political system in his *American Commonwealth*, a book which was shaped by a dialogue with Dicey that had been proceeding intermittently ever since the two men visited the United States for the first time in 1870. Of all Bryce's works, this is the one that has received most attention in the literature: indeed, it is the only one that has received monographic treatment.[30] Even so, it has never really been satisfactorily placed in the context of Victorian political thought. It is a work that really deserves repositioning in the Victorian literature on the 'science of politics' and on constitutionalism: it belongs with Dicey's *Law of the Constitution*, Sidgwick's *Elements of Politics*, and Maine's *Popular Government*, to cite but three. It has some claim to be the single most important and influential Victorian foray into the field of comparative politics.

That this is the proper context for reading the *American Commonwealth* is clear enough from reading Bryce's introduction, a brief but quite remarkably illuminating prospectus for the work as a whole. Bryce began by setting out a basic rationale for the book: although the American system was recognized as highly distinctive, indeed unique, and although Americans were patently proud of their institutions, even so no one, American or European, had ever attempted to give a comprehensive account of the United States 'both as a Government and as a Nation'. His aim, he explained, was to be comprehensive but not exhaustive: he would attempt to cover everything of importance but would give particular attention to subjects where he had real value to add: subjects on which he had particular knowledge or expertise, or which had not been covered by others. Thus the American common-school system had been much written about and needed no extensive treatment, whereas European observers had generally neglected American universities.[31] This last point was undoubtedly a good call: Bryce first visited the United States just at the start of a period which saw a remarkable transformation in American higher education in the wake of the Civil War. Charles W. Eliot, who would become a close friend of Bryce's for half a century, had been appointed to the presidency of Harvard the year before, and the first wave of land-grant universities were coming into being. By the time Bryce published his first edition in 1888, the vitality of American universities was such that it really needed proper treatment by a European observer.

Among European observers of American democracy, Tocqueville was the obvious point of comparison, and Bryce distinguished his own approach shrewdly from that of his predecessor. Tocqueville had been principally concerned to analyse the nature of democracy as a political and social system and was interested in America as an exemplar of generic democracy. Against Tocqueville, Bryce announced that he did not regard the unique features of the United States as, *ipso facto*, evidence of the distinctive characteristics of democracy. They could equally well be treated as the fruits of 'the history and traditions of the race', its 'fundamental ideas', and 'its material environment'.[32] This might look like quite a trite late Victorian observation that societies are profoundly shaped by geography and by the deep past. Bryce certainly believed that, but the more interesting point is that he uses this observation to urge a more sophisticated approach to comparative politics than was usual at the time. He implicitly compared what he was doing here with what he had done with comparative history in his essay on 'The Historical Aspect of Democracy' in the *Essays on Reform*. The 'chief practical use of history' was 'to deliver us from plausible historical analogies', he wrote, which was just the point of his 1867 essay. In much the same way, the value of a real understanding of the institutions of other countries was 'to expose sometimes the ill-grounded hopes, sometimes the empty fears, which loose reports about those nations generate'. His political science would aim to qualify and indeed to undermine straightforward inferences from the experience of other countries: 'Direct inferences from the success or failure of a particular constitutional arrangement or political usage in another country are rarely sound, because the conditions differ in so many respects that there can be no certainty that what flourishes or languishes under other skies and in another soil will likewise flourish or languish in our own.'[33]

It is important to recognize that this was Bryce's objective. Just as in his contribution to *Essays on Reform* he had set out to show that the historical 'evidence' often adduced was not capable of bearing the weight generally heaped on it by opponents of democracy in the middle of the nineteenth century, so *The American Commonwealth* was intended to show that much the same point could be made about invocations of contemporary experiments with democracy. This helps explain something that many readers of the book have often found surprising or perplexing. Knowing that Bryce wrote as a friend of American democracy, readers have often been confused to find him echoing much of what European critics of democracy said about the United States. Even Dicey shared something of this confusion about where his friend stood: while giving lurid descriptions of corruption and political immorality, Bryce was nevertheless convinced that public opinion was 'on the whole wholesome and upright'.[34] In no sense did he gloss over the weaknesses. He was very candid indeed in his account of the spoils system, for instance, and British antidemocrats were at a loss to understand why Bryce had not drawn their antidemocratic inferences.[35] Equally, when he wrote the preface to Ostrogorski's *Democracy and the Organisation of Political Parties*—a decade and a half after the first publication of *The American Commonwealth*—he was critical of Ostrogorski for grossly exaggerating the progress that the caucus had made in Britain. Ostrogorski thought that the caucus was an inherent vice of the party system in a democracy and hence tried to find alternatives to parties as institutions for the organization of opinion in democratic systems; Bryce agreed that the system was an abuse but thought it a consequence of distinctive features of the American system and had little intrinsically to do with party democracy as such.

Bryce then went on to spell out the structure of the book, which was published initially as three volumes, though subsequently as two. The organization was pellucid for a book of such complexity of detail. It proceeded, as it were, from top to bottom: first, federal government; next, the state governments, next the political parties, and then public opinion. The book was then completed with, fifth, some historical illustrations, and sixth a consideration of nonpolitical institutions. It embraced civil society and high politics, informal as well as formal political organization, but whereas Tocqueville's purpose had been to analyse a new type of society, Bryce's was to understand how the American polity worked. Tocqueville stripped away all that was peculiar about America to reveal the essential characteristics of modern democracy beneath, whereas Bryce wanted to understand those peculiarities so as better to inform European discussion of democratic institutions. There was much that was new here. He gave far more attention to state governments and state constitutions than previous writers had done, and he was the first scholarly student of American politics, or indeed of any political system, to give adequate recognition to the role of political parties.

But the most significant innovation, and the one that was really fundamental to Bryce's intellectual outlook, was the importance he attached to public opinion, 'the mind and conscience of the whole nation', and indeed 'the central point of the whole American polity'.[36] From the outset public opinion is depicted as a largely benign force, one capable of taming some of the wilder manifestations of party spirit. Parties of course participated in public opinion and helped to shape it; but they did not make it. Rather, 'it stands above the parties, being cooler and larger minded than they are; it awes party leaders and holds in check party organizations'.[37] It was in *The American Commonwealth* that Bryce first offered a developed analysis of a concept that came to be central to his political thought and, indeed, to his political activity.

If Bryce set out to understand what was peculiar about the United States, how then could his book contribute to wider debates about democracy? One answer to this question is that he tried to disarm those who made illegitimate use of comparisons with American institutions. A case in point was the American Supreme Court. British observers typically thought that it showed what happened when judges were placed above the elected legislature: most thought this a bad thing, and incompatible with parliamentary sovereignty, though others, such as Sir Henry Maine, saw potential merits in an institution that could be a brake on the supremacy of the legislature. For Maine, the Supreme Court was 'a virtually unique creation', an experiment whose success had blinded people to its novelty.[38] Bryce's argument was that it was quite wrong to see the courts in general as being 'above' legislators, any more than they were in the British system. In fact, he insisted, perhaps counter-intuitively, that the role of the courts in the American system was deeply rooted in English common law practice: 'the natural outgrowth of common law doctrines', and 'but a part of that priceless heritage of the English Common Law which the colonists carried with them across the sea, and which they have preserved and developed in a manner worthy of its free spirit and lofty traditions'.[39] What was different about the United States was that it had a rigid constitution that defined the role of Congress.[40] That constitution was the supreme law, whereas in Britain an act of Parliament was supreme; and the 'supremacy' of the American Supreme Court derived from the supremacy of the constitution which it was responsible for interpreting. Bryce saw that if England were to adopt a rigid constitution a supreme court would not be necessary, and without such a constitution a supreme court would have no effect. In the Home Rule debates in 1886—before *The American Commonwealth* was published or, indeed, written—Bryce anticipated this argument in taking to task the Liberal Unionist Sir Henry James, who had maintained that the Home Rule Bill would subordinate Parliament to the Privy Council, much as Congress was subordinate to the Supreme Court. This was, Bryce thought, a misinterpretation of American institutions: 'The Supreme Court is out of the reach of Congress, not because it is a Law Court, but because it is the authorized interpreter, or, as one may say, the living voice of a document superior in authority to the will of Congress.'[41]

Bryce was here deploying a form of comparative politics, though one inflected with a deep sense not so much (here) of the importance of political culture as of the complexity of a system of institutions, which meant that each institution had to be understood in terms of its place in that wider system. His most extended piece of comparative analysis came in his very illuminating chapter entitled 'Comparison of the American and European Systems'. This was, essentially, a comparison between presidential government, in which the executive is not responsible to parliament, and cabinet government, in which the executive is (in Bagehot's words) 'a committee of the legislative body'.[42] Bryce certainly thought cabinet government a preferable system, because it permitted greater 'executive vigour', and because the party holding the majority in the lower house was clearly responsible for the exercise of power and could be held accountable for it. The American presidential system was characterized by 'want of unity' which was 'painfully felt in a crisis'. But the main thrust of his argument was that either system could work effectively when sustained by supportive habits and traditions and would work badly without those supports. The English system (like Bagehot, he wrote 'English') was admired as 'a masterpiece of delicate equipoises and complicated mechanism', but applied elsewhere it would be (and was) 'full of difficulties and dangers'.

Likewise it was thanks to the political gifts of the American people that an imperfect set of institutions could be made to work:

> So the American people have a practical aptitude for politics, a clearness of vision and capacity for self-control never equalled by any other nation. In 1861 they brushed aside their darling legalities, allowed the executive to exert novel powers, passed lightly laws whose constitutionality remains doubtful, raised an enormous army, and contracted a prodigious debt. Romans could not have been more energetic in their sense of civic duty, nor more trustful to their magistrates.... Such a people can work any Constitution.[43]

Bryce's *American Commonwealth* is often, perhaps usually, treated as a product of the Teutonist intellectual tradition, and Bryce is supposed to have imputed Americans' adeptness in the operation of free institutions to their 'Anglo-Saxon' roots.[44] But a note of scepticism would be in order. Bryce avoided the term 'Anglo-Saxon', contrary to the impression often given. In the whole text the term appears just twice, once in a quotation from Goschen, and once in a footnote tracing the etymology of the English word 'Town'.[45] He certainly thought that the institutions of the American republic (especially the state constitutions) were powerfully shaped by colonial-era institutions, which were themselves, of course, indebted to English or British institutional forms. But the main thrust of his interpretation was that while the institutional continuities were real and important, those institutions worked very differently in the context of a radically different society and a radically different constitutional system, and he certainly set out to show his readers how *different* American political practices were from British practices. When Freeman made a lecture tour of the United States in 1881, he surprised his hosts by objecting to being introduced as a 'foreign' visitor: he and his hosts shared a common Englishness, he firmly believed.[46] Bryce, much as he might work to promote Anglo-American friendship, took a different position: in *The American Commonwealth* he explicitly wrote as a '*European* traveller' revealing the United States to a *European* readership.[47] The adjective 'English' was overwhelmingly used to designate institutions: 'the English constitution' 'the English common law', and so forth.

Universal Suffrage

Bryce never accepted that democracy necessarily implied universal suffrage, and he resisted arguments for suffrage extension based on abstract right. He was a consistent opponent of women's suffrage to the end of his life, even after it had been conceded (not yet universally) in 1918. He also opposed the extension of the suffrage to all men in that same Act of 1918. He followed American Mugwumps such as Godkin in thinking the immediate enfranchisement of ex-slaves in the Reconstruction era had been a mistake.[48] To understand Bryce's position, it is important to see the interconnections between these issues. He was not primarily concerned to exclude women, or Black Americans, or the English poor, from the vote; he wanted to suggest that there had to be a positive case for their inclusion. For him the relevant criteria were republican ones: what would the new voters bring to enhance the political community? Were there sound guarantees that (given their lack of experience) they would not prove to be sources of corruption?

Bryce's most common objection to the enfranchisement of women was that most women did not want it. That became a harder argument to make the more active the suffrage movement grew, but it is worth thinking further about the reasons why Bryce attached so much importance to this consideration. After all, the argument could be pressed, and indeed was pressed by John Stuart Mill and some of his followers, that political life was itself a school of citizenship: one could hardly expect new voters to be richly endowed with civic virtue before their first exercise of the right to vote, but the fact of having the vote would help engage them with the issues at stake and in time nurture the qualities required of the active citizen.[49] Bryce was far from oblivious to the educative qualities of political activity: indeed, it was an important theme in his own thinking.[50] But he was much more alive to the dangers of enfranchising large numbers of new voters without evidence of an aptitude for political life. Politically disengaged electors were vulnerable to influence—from family members and employers—and, still worse, were easy prey for demagogues. It was not just that they added little to the political community: they would detract from it if they proved susceptible to ill-informed populist campaigns. So the extension of democratic rights could work counter to free government, and the latter was more important to him than the former. In that sense we see Bryce deploying a republican case against universal suffrage especially if conceived as a matter of rights.

We can see this point most clearly by considering Bryce's analysis of the effects of the mass enfranchisement of ex-slaves in the American South in the wake of the Civil War. This large-scale enfranchisement of voters who lacked any kind of political education opened the door, he argued, to wholesale corruption, as the new voters were 'organized' and manipulated by Republicans from the North: 'those white adventurers whose scanty stock of portable property won for them the name of "carpet-baggers". Bryce gave an unusually vivid and one-sided account of the outcome: 'Such a Saturnalia of robbery and jobbery has seldom been seen in any civilized country, and certainly never before under the forms of free self-government. The coloured voters could hardly be blamed for blindly following the guides who represented to them the party to which they owed their liberty; and as they had little property, taxation did not press upon them nor the increase of debt alarm them.' Legislatures became 'reckless and corrupt', the judiciary subservient, the administration wasteful, and there was widespread jobbery of public contracts.[51] All this Bryce attributed to the premature enfranchisement of the entire (adult male) Black population. He gave an illuminating account of how differently this mass enfranchisement looked to European and to American eyes: 'To nearly all Europeans such a step seemed and still seems monstrous. No people could be imagined more hopelessly unfit for political power than this host of slaves; and their unfitness became all the more dangerous because the classes among whom the new voters ought to have found guidance were partly disfranchised and partly forced into hostility.' Americans thought differently. To them, there was no true citizenship without the suffrage. The Civil War, Bryce noted, had given a stimulus to 'the abstract theory of human rights', by which he meant 'the doctrine of absolute democratic equality and the rights of man as man'.[52]

Bryce here articulated an account of the perversion of American democracy in the era of Reconstruction that owed much to his Mugwump friends such as Godkin. This kind of critique of the Reconstruction era subsequently came to dominate the historiography of the period under the influence of the Columbia historians and political scientists John Burgess and William A. Dunning, and it was anticipated in the historical writings of Bryce's close friend James Ford Rhodes. It was not fully dislodged until the 1960s.[53] Needless to say, it is now discredited. The racial dimension of Bryce's interpretation will be picked up in chapter 9. The point to be highlighted here is the remarkable way in which Bryce's critique of the workings of the Black franchise in the United States aligned with the case he made against women's suffrage. Just as in the American case, he emphasized the radical increase in the size of the electorate, which more than doubled in some southern states, so in the case of women's suffrage in Britain the point he kept returning to was the question whether it was remotely sensible to contemplate doubling the size of the electorate in one go.[54] 'Why should we make such an experiment, which can have no other effect than to double our constituencies?' So he asked in the Commons in 1892. The bill in question on that occasion was a relatively modest measure, admitting only about a million women voters, but that did not satisfy Bryce: 'We know perfectly well the matter cannot stop there.'[55] It was an argument that continued to matter to him. 'Can anybody really suppose that to double the electorate by adding millions of women who know and care nothing about public affairs will improve our Government?', he asked Dicey (who agreed with him) in 1913.[56]

Likewise, just as in the American case the acceptance of the wholesale enfranchisement of politically inexperienced and mostly uneducated ex-slaves was attributable, in Bryce's eyes, to 'the abstract theory of human rights', so in the case of the enfranchisement of women in Britain he objected that proponents had recourse to that same theory. 'We want something more than abstract argument to justify our acceptance of the principle which it embodies', he told the Commons in 1884, opposing an attempt to amend the Representation of the People Bill so as to give the vote to women. But abstract theory was 'a dangerous guide in politics'.[57] He made the same point in 1892: 'We are asked to make this great change on pure abstract theory', and yet 'there is nothing more pernicious in politics than abstract doctrine, and no worse habit can a country contract than that of yielding to abstract doctrine'.[58] It had never been the English practice to legislate on the basis of abstract natural rights, he told the Lords in December 1917, in his last parliamentary attempt to resist what he surely by then knew was inevitable; and to reinforce the point he suggested that anyone who wanted to know where the implementation of the abstract doctrine of natural rights would lead should look at Russia.[59] He equally surely knew that Marxism did not appeal to natural rights, abstract or not; but what he fundamentally objected to was the politics of revolution.

In both cases he thought that outcomes were what mattered: actual outcomes in the case of the enfranchisement of American Black men, and probable outcomes in the case of the enfranchisement of British women. The mass enfranchisement of a population with no political experience and (Bryce believed) little interest in politics led to 'a Saturnalia of robbery and jobbery' and the erosion of standards of good government. So in approaching the question of the enfranchisement of women, Bryce asked whether it would tend to improve or to depress the quality of public discourse and decision-making. Would it elevate, or would it depress, the 'tone of public life' (a favourite Brycean term)? Would it produce 'a better Parliament', one able more effectively to 'reflect the opinion of the majority of the constituencies'? Bryce was convinced that it would not, and the reason he kept coming back to was that women showed little interest in politics: 'They know little and care less about political questions.'[60] They were comparable in this respect to the Black population of the American South, which (as he would put it in his Romanes lecture at Oxford in 1902) was 'really unfit to exercise political power, whether from ignorance, or from an indifference that would dispose it to sell its votes, or from a propensity to sudden and unreasoning impulses'.[61] Ignorance, corruptibility, and impulsiveness were all attributes that undermined the quality of public life. Mass enfranchisement of women, another largely dependent section of the population, would have as deleterious an outcome as had the enfranchisement of ex-slaves in the American South.

Republicanism

The logic of Bryce's position was that he prized republican values above democracy per se.[62] His was a moderate republicanism, Roman rather than Athenian in inspiration, and concerned with the creation and maintenance of the institutional forms and cultural norms that sustain government under law and the supremacy of the public good. It was a republican sensibility, rather than a republican doctrine, and had nothing intrinsically to do with conceptions of popular sovereignty and direct democracy that belong to the tradition recently recovered under the label 'radical republicanism'.[63] But it was nevertheless authentically republican, and Bryce would not have rejected the term.

The republican tradition in political thought is really a construction of political theorists and historians of political thought writing since the 1970s, and so 'republicanism' did not have the same connotations in Bryce's time.[64] In much of the pioneering research, republicanism has been depicted conceptually antithetical to liberalism and, historically, extinguished by it in the nineteenth century.[65] But the importance of republican strains in a number of varieties of Victorian political thought is now well established.[66] Among these Victorian Liberal sympathizers with a republican ethos, Bryce does not normally feature, though close friends and allies of his such as T. H. Green, J. R. Green, and Freeman all do.[67] Bryce himself was very conscious of the importance of this sensibility. Consider his characterization of the politics of one of his own historical and political mentors, Goldwin Smith:

> Regarded as a politician Goldwin Smith belonged to a type rare in his own generation and now practically extinct, a type whose nearest affinities were to be found in the republicans of Rome or, still better, such English statesmen of the seventeenth century as Pym, or Sir Henry Vane the younger or

Algernon Sidney. He was an austere moralist, with more of the ancient Stoic than of the Christian in his view of life, and his politics were built on the foundation of his ethics. Theoretically a republican, and practically, as he would have deemed himself, a democrat, there was nothing Jeffersonian in his view of the people. He felt for the sufferings of the poor as a Christian ought to do, and he valued human equality as a philosopher ought to do. He disliked courts and all distinctions of rank, and above all the power of wealth. But he had no great faith in the multitude. His Radicalism in British politics expressed itself not so much in wishing to deliver power to the masses as in wishing to take it away from the classes that were, as he thought, abusing it for their selfish purposes.[68]

Pym, Vane, and Sidney all feature in the modern literature on republican political thought, from Pocock's *Machiavellian Moment* onward. Vane and Sidney were invoked (with Marvell and Harrington) in one of the most powerful nineteenth-century lamentations for the demise of republican values, Wordsworth's *England, 1802*: 'these moralists', Wordsworth called them; men who 'call'd Milton friend'.[69] Not only did Bryce explicitly class Smith with the seventeenth-century moralists who are now routinely classed as republican or 'neo-Roman', but he also used the word: Smith was 'theoretically a republican'.

Bryce was not Goldwin Smith, and his ethics were much more those of the Christian than those of the Stoic. But he was formed intellectually by Smith's professorial lectures, and still more by his leadership of Oxford Liberalism in the era of the struggle against religious tests. And many of Smith's consistent intellectual and political positions were Bryce's too: the philo-Americanism, the trenchant opposition to slavery, and the equally trenchant support for the Union in the Civil War, the opposition to women's suffrage, the belief that democratic institutions required a foundation of cultural homogeneity.[70] In characterizing Smith's position, Bryce also spoke for himself when he wrote of a radicalism that was less concerned to confer power upon the masses than to remove it from 'the classes', itself a distinctively Gladstonian expression. Democracy was good when conceived in a hard-headed way as a means of imposing constraints on the exercise of unaccountable power by the privileged. But when it became a faith—so that the more democratic an institution was, the better and more legitimate it was, whatever the consequences—the outcome was the establishment of a new form of unaccountable power.

As a young man, in the 1850s and 1860s, Bryce had a strong republican sensibility formed by the Commonwealth tradition as well as by the emancipatory nationalism of Europe in 1848.[71] This manifested itself in his keenness to display his portrait of Cromwell in his rooms at Trinity, in self-conscious resistance to the cult of 'Charles King and Martyr' that prevailed among his fellow undergraduates. Equally he was an enthusiastic supporter of the cause of Italian unification, and he even wanted to volunteer to fight in Garibaldi's army until (a characteristic touch that this was the sticking point) it was pointed out to him that this would mean forfeiting his college scholarship. Even as a ten-year-old he had taken a keen interest in the 1848 revolutions, and the men of 1848—Mazzini, Garibaldi, Kossuth—remained important reference points for him, as they were to many Victorian Liberals and Radicals who found in the European nationalisms of midcentury uplifting visions of brotherhood and public duty.[72] As a schoolboy he heard Kossuth speak in Edinburgh, and when on his honeymoon in 1889 he made a point of visiting the great Hungarian leader in Turin.[73] Like other Oxford undergraduates of his generation, he was taught Italian by Mazzini's ally, Aurelio Saffi, and he called to pay homage to his former tutor during a holiday in the Romagna in October 1882.[74] He retained to the end of his life a veneration for 'the generation of pure-souled revolutionaries, like Mazzini, Kossuth and D. Manin and Aurelio Saffi'.[75] Before he got to know Queen Victoria well as a cabinet minister in the 1890s, he had a strong suspicion of monarchy. 'What a blessing it is to get into a republican country', he wrote to his father from Switzerland in 1866, 'whether [sic] the free air of Equality blows around you, and no insolent privilege treads down a subject class! France is republican in one sense and England in another, Switzerland in both.'[76] In 1872 he was appalled by the national thanksgiving for the recovery of the Prince of Wales from typhoid: 'London is turned upside down by this ridiculous procession—'tis eno' to make a man a republican to see such a fuss about the recovery from illness of a worthless youth—as if the future of the country depended on him, & there is something almost blasphemous in rendering solemn thanks to Heaven with such pomp for a thing we know that we none of us care two straws about.'[77]

Bryce made copious use of the vocabulary of republicanism: most obviously, 'virtue' and 'public spirit' were the qualities that typified healthy political communities; they were sapped by the insidious forces of 'corruption' and 'demagoguery'.[78] The word 'corruption' and its cognates ('corrupt', 'corrupted', 'corrupting') pervaded The American Commonwealth (126 uses), as well as Bryce's later works.[79] In a strikingly large number of cases, reference to corruption occurs in close proximity to discussion of civic virtue or its antithesis, civic apathy. In his chapter on New York politics under Tammany, he blamed the degeneration of city government on, among other things, the apathy of the wealthy and educated classes.[80]

A few examples of the many collocations of this kind will reinforce this point. Imagining what he calls an 'Ideal Democracy', Bryce wrote that it would have citizens who give 'close and constant attention to public affairs'. With citizens as electors, 'the legislature will be composed of upright and capable men, single-minded in their wish to serve the nation. Bribery in constituencies, corruption among public servants, will have disappeared.'[81] In Switzerland—the nearest thing, in Bryce's experience, to an ideal democracy—he noted the absence of titles, decorations, ribbons, medals and similar, which in France and England have been 'instruments of a sort of corruption'; conversely, he found 'the constant teaching in the schools of civic duty'.[82] In an interesting variant, he wrote that American politicians spoke not in the spirit of 'disinterested virtue' but in 'the hard commercial spirit which pervades the meetings of a joint-stock company': so here civic virtue stood in antithesis to the mentality of the commercial world, a familiar antithesis in the literature on the republican tradition. This occurred in a discussion of 'the tone of public life', a favourite locution by which Bryce typically meant the presence or absence of forms of corruption broadly understood.[83]

Bryce's fear of the demagogue as the antithesis of civic virtue and the instrument of the downfall of republics should also be noticed here. This appeared in the analysis both in *The American Commonwealth* and in *Modern Democracies*, but Bryce gave himself free rein in his correspondence, especially with Godkin and Dicey. He told Dicey in 1915 that Britain since 1880 had produced 'three formidable demagogues'. He took it for granted that Dicey would know who he meant. They obviously did not include Disraeli, who left office in 1880. Bryce certainly regarded him as verging on a demagogue, though he had a certain admiration for him: he later told Dicey that he wanted to undertake a comparison between him and 'three subsequent demagogues, all of them much inferior to him: one a Tory, one a Liberal, one both'.[84] The last was clearly Chamberlain, who was, Bryce told the German editor and Left Liberal politician Theodor Barth, 'by far the best specimen of the demagogue England has yet produced'.[85] The first, the Tory, was equally certainly Lord Randolph Churchill, who, like Chamberlain, was a prominent figure in Bryce's pieces in *The Nation* in the 1880s. He told Godkin in 1886 that Churchill was 'as finished a demagogue as any republic could produce': a formulation that makes clear the connection that existed in Bryce's mind between a republic and demagogues.[86] We must surmise that the Liberal was Lloyd George, although textual evidence for this is harder to supply. Elsewhere, it was the American Republican James G. Blaine—the candidate Grover Cleveland defeated, with the help of Godkin and the Mugwumps in 1884—whom Bryce classed as the archetypal demagogue, as well as the epitome of corruption.[87] Some of Bryce's friends—certainly Goldwin Smith, and probably Dicey, and probably Uncle John too—would have classed Gladstone as a demagogue, and indeed many of the accusations that Bryce made against Churchill and Chamberlain and Lloyd George were echoed in the criticisms that Liberal Unionists in particular made of Gladstone.[88] But for Bryce it was a matter of fundamental conviction that Gladstone was no demagogue. As he later put it in some manuscript notes for *Modern Democracies*: 'Chapter on Demagogues: who is. WEG not.'[89]

What was demagogic about Blaine and Chamberlain, Churchill and Lloyd George? In *The American Commonwealth* Bryce described demagogues as 'adventurers' who deceived the people with 'fallacious reasoning and specious persuasions'; though he added that oligarchies as well as democracies were vulnerable to demagoguery, since an 'aristocratic mob' could be played just as much as a democratic mob could.[90] In *Modern Democracies* he offered a similar definition: the demagogue was 'one who tries to lure the people by captivating speech, playing upon their passions, or promising to secure for them some benefit.' Germany, Italy, and Britain had proved more susceptible to demagoguery than America or France, Bryce thought: France, in particular, was 'intensely critical' and so hard to take in with eloquent rhetoric.[91]

Bryce's republican sympathies, and his antipathy to the a priori case for universal suffrage, both owed a lot to his distinctive kind of Presbyterian background. His sympathy for the Cromwellian cause in the English Civil War was surely rooted in his Scots-Ulster Presbyterianism, and the 'strong Puritan inheritance in his blood', which, according to his wife, 'remained with him throughout life'.[92] Addressing the Scotch-Irish Society of Pennsylvania in 1909, he reflected on the role of the Scots-Irish settlers in shaping American politics:

> It is, moreover, an interesting historical fact that the system of Presbyterian church government which these settlers brought with them had much to do with the formation of a republican spirit in this country and with the growth of those habits which enabled your ancestors to work republican institutions. The machinery of that system is eminently republican, for it consists of representative councils, leading up to a supreme representative body, the General Assembly.

He noted that one of the men who signed the Declaration of Independence was the president of Princeton, the Scots Presbyterian minister, John Witherspoon.[93]

Beyond that Bryce's family—his Uncle John in particular—instructed him as a boy in a clear set of political principles. When he entered Parliament in 1880 and was almost immediately confronted with the prospect of a collision between Lords and Commons, he found himself thinking 'of the instruction you gave me in the principles of the British Constitution on the outside car going down the Shore Road [in Belfast] when I did not expect to have to know them to such practical account.'[94] What principles exactly? His uncle recalled later in the year that he and Bryce's father had been 'educated in advanced Whig principles', including a 'firm belief in the justice & wisdom of Catholic emancipation.'[95] That was in the context of a discussion of the Irish Question, on which Dr Bryce certainly had strong views. But he also had strong views about the suffrage:

> If I were thirty or even twenty years younger, I wd get up an agitation for a law making disfranchisement a punishment—or rather part of the punishment—for certain offences, & for an educational test for political power in all its grades—from the electorate to the peerage. But if I remember aright I bored you [with?] on this some months ago, & so I won't follow up on the matter now. My view, if carried out wd go far to check both plutocracy & ochlocracy between which as Sallust says 'respublica quae media est??' [The correct quote seems to be 'res publica, quae media fuerat, dilacerata.'][96]

The limitation of the franchise was, in fact, something of an *idée fixe* for Uncle John. In 1871 he responded to an article of Bryce's on poor relief in the United States by picking up on the suggestion that disorder in New York arises from 'the application of universal suffrage to a set of conditions for which it is quite unfit'. 'I shd like to know what these are', he retorted, 'as distinct from the "conditions" elsewhere, wh. make universal suffrage safe. In my opinion universal suffrage, à la lettre, is never safe: it is suicidal in a community to enfranchise ignorance & vice, municipally or nationally.'[97] He went into print with these views, in a letter published in the Belfast daily newspapers, *The Northern Whig* and *The Belfast Newsletter*, in 1884. Dr Bryce argued for moral and educational qualifications for the franchise: on the one hand, positive qualifications—'that a man be proved possessed of a certain amount of education and intelligence before he can be placed on the register'; and on the other, the institution of disqualifications for 'moral' offences such as serial convictions for being drunk and disorderly, or for aggravated assault, or for failure to get one's children educated. These proposals would, he concluded, 'gradually weed out of the constituencies the clans of voters most liable to corrupting influences and most unfit, intellectually and morally, to judge of public questions and of the fitness of candidates'.[98]

We lack Bryce's direct response to this argument, which was made in the context of parliamentary deliberation on what became the Third Reform Act. But a few weeks later he wrote: 'I am not sanguine of getting any educational qualification introduced into the Franchise Bill—tho' fully agreeing with you in desiring it. Samuel Smith the new member for Liverpool, a noble fellow & the best of our Scottish Presbyterians here, has been discussing it with me, & we are trying to collect opinions. But the Government want to avoid all amendments so as to push the Bill quicker through.'[99] Whether he made any kind of effort is unclear. He knew well how to manage his uncle's crotchety obsessions with idiosyncratic causes. Uncle John made some noise in Belfast in agitating for what he called his 'Anti-blackguards franchise' movement, and an amendment along these lines was indeed moved unsuccessfully as the Franchise Bill progressed through the Commons, both at the committee stage and at the report stage. Bryce reported in November that 'there was really no possibility of doing anything here [HoC] about your Blackguard Franchise'.[100] But the kind of political outlook with which Bryce was familiar from boyhood is very clear: political life was a sphere for the exercise of the moral virtues, and known personal immorality—as well as illiteracy or lack of education—should be a disqualification. Bryce was fully aware of the obstacles to the implementation of such restrictions, but equally he thought them right in principle. In particular, he had an enduring sense of the threat to a healthy political order from the existence of a section of the electorate who were 'most liable to corrupting influences'.

In November 1884 he offered his uncle a summing up of his position on the Third Reform Act: that is, the Franchise Act of 1884 and the Redistribution Act of 1885:

The two Bills together amount to a revolution, but whether a good or bad one, who can say? There is much to discourage hopes, something also to quicken them. My belief is that we shall have in the coming age better laws but worse law makers—not as much a paradox as it seems. Conditions will probably be more equal and laws less oppressive, but the machinery of politics & character of politicians will probably decline; decline below what it was between 1830 & 70 but not down the level of 1730–70.[101]

'Better laws but worse law makers' is a revealing phrase. The advent of something close to 'pure democracy' would make Members of Parliament more subservient, even servile, towards their electorate and thus tend to depress the quality of parliamentary debate. But the fact that the electorate had become much more inclusive in composition would tend to ensure laws that better reflected the public interest.

Dr Bryce's opinions were not necessarily those of his nephew: 'You are much more of a democrat than I am', he wrote back in 1865.[102] The older man deplored 'Disraeli's most absurd "illiterate" franchise', whereas his nephew sided with the democrats, at least in public, in 1867.[103] But a suspicion of universal suffrage, at least when introduced for frivolous reasons of opportunism or when advocated on a priori grounds, was an enduring theme in Bryce's intellectual and political career; not least, as we have seen, in his trenchant opposition to women's suffrage. 'As no evidence has been given, or can be given, for the existence of this or any other abstract natural right, the question furnishes no common ground for argument', he pronounced in opposing women's suffrage in the Lords in 1917, 'and we in England have happily never legislated upon the basis of abstract natural rights.'[104]

Bryce's cussed refusal of suffrage claims grounded in abstract rights might suggest that his republicanism owed something to the ancient constitutionalist tradition, which accorded prescriptive authority to history (and, typically, deep history) in determining constitutional legitimacy. That tradition, though clearly distinct from civic republicanism, had some crossovers with it and was an important source of Victorian republican values.[105] The period covered by Bryce's career was one that, in Jose Harris's analysis, saw the British polity transformed from one still rooted in the idea of an ancient constitution to one captured (in Graham Wallas's words) by the notion of the 'great society'.[106] Among his friends, Freeman (aptly named) was certainly an ancient constitutionalist. Bryce endorsed the notion of the 'unity of history' propounded by Freeman and drew copiously on insights from history, ancient and modern. But he was as likely to invoke global history as national history or even the history of 'Greater Britain', and in fact he explicitly rejected the prescriptive authority of the past. His essay on 'The Historical Aspect of Democracy' in 1867 was resoundingly modernist in conception: the historical process was progressive rather than cyclical, and hence the 'lessons' of history were to be applied with the utmost caution.

Critics of Democracy

European intellectual life in Bryce's time did not lack trenchant critics of democracy. In France, Hippolyte Taine and Gustave Le Bon, pioneers of crowd psychology, portrayed mass politics as the sphere not of rational deliberation but of wilful passions. In Italy, Vilfredo Pareto and Gaetano Mosca set out to demonstrate that all political systems were oligarchies, and democratic elections were simply a different means of selecting the rulers. In Britain, where there was less of an impulse to frame a critique of democracy in terms of social theory, a host of prominent intellectuals offered pessimistic accounts of the spectre of democracy. Among these were Maine's *Popular Government* (1885) and W. E. H. Lecky's *Democracy and Liberty* (1896).[107]

Whatever his reservations about democratic practice as he observed it, Bryce is emphatically not to be classed with these writers. Indeed, though he knew both Maine and Lecky well, professed to like them, and admired much of their work, he was persistently critical of these two books. The principal reason was that he thought they drew simplistic conclusions from the American experience, failing to understand the national and local contexts, and seeking in particular to draw general conclusions about democracy. For Bryce the question was not at all whether democracy was good or bad: everything depended on the context in which it operated. The key thing was to understand the circumstances that enabled it to operate so as to sustain civic virtue rather than to erode it.

That was why Lecky was confused by Bryce's discussion of the spoils system, thinking it self-contradictory.[108] Lecky made copious use of Bryce's account of the spoils system and the working of corruption in the American system but found his chapter on corruption 'somewhat curious', in that Bryce seemed to want to minimize its significance.[109] The difference is clear. Lecky was sure to insist that his readers should see that the spoils system 'is very distinctly a product of democracy', and, indeed, that in general 'many of the causes of the vices of American government are inherent in democracy'.[110] The two 'aggravating causes' that he mentioned were relatively trivial ones: the rule that a member of Congress must be resident in the state he represented and the generous salaries they were paid both worked against attracting the right kind of people to legislative office. Bryce's point, by contrast, was that 'every feature of the machine is the result of patent causes'. Lecky quoted that remark but did not fully grasp the point it was intended to make. The causes were local ones, and the system of spoils was functional in the American system. It was not at all embedded in the nature of democratic politics.

Bryce and Maine were for some years professorial colleagues at Oxford, but this did not stop Bryce from being quite cutting, and repeatedly so, about *Popular Government* and indeed its author.[111] 'For some time past his [Maine's] reputation as a close thinker has been declining', he told Godkin; even *Ancient Law*—unquestionably Maine's masterpiece—was in Bryce's opinion 'full of flimsy theories and inaccuracies'. But Maine wrote exceptionally readably, and this ensured a readership for *Popular Government* in spite of his inadequate knowledge of America and its constitution.[112] As Bryce told Sidgwick in 1887, 'He doesn't seem to me to come near understanding America: does not even quite understand the U.S. Constitution; and his charges against democracy generally are as self-contradictory as his historical instances are one-sided and flimsy.' There was, he added, a stronger case to be made against democracy than the one Maine offered, though he did not tell Sidgwick what it was.[113] Lecky's *Democracy and Liberty* was no better: it was 'a very thin, rather confused, and indeed superficial book, without serious grappling with the real problems', and Lecky 'does not seem to me to understand America in the least'. These views were shared, he thought, by 'most people here who have examined his book carefully with knowledge of the topics'.[114]

Bryce had a low opinion of both books because both tried to draw superficial inferences from the American experience. It was not simply that they were negative: Maine, in fact, thought that Britain could usefully borrow from American institutions that served as brakes on the popular will, such as the Supreme Court and the Senate. But indiscriminate borrowing of institutions—expecting similar outcomes in radically different contexts—was just as shallow as using foreign experiences to discredit entire systems of government. Maine was in error in using the Swiss experience to demonstrate that the referendum was a conservative institution, for 'the circumstances of that little country, so largely one of peasant proprietors, differ altogether from those of the U.K. To me it is very doubtful whether a Referendum would not with us bear radical, not conservative, fruit.'[115] But Maine was equally wrong to think that the South American experience was sufficient to discredit democracy: 'Whenever he seeks to supply a link or point an epigram in his long indictment of democracy, [Maine] constantly refers to the South American republics as instances of its failure in this or that respect.'[116] Although Bryce was an early practitioner of the comparative study of political institutions—a practice that dominated Anglo-American political science for most of the twentieth century—he repeatedly warned against exaggerating the effectiveness of institutions ('mechanical contrivances') in politics, favouring instead a recognition of the importance of cultural factors in determining the outcomes of particular institutional arrangements: 'The true value of a political contrivance resides not in its ingenuity but in its adaptation to the temper and circumstances of the people for whom it is designed, in its power of using, fostering, and giving a legal form to those forces of sentiment and interest which it finds in being.'[117]

Bryce was by no means averse to drawing on the experience of other countries to inform British political debate. This was, as we saw in chapter 6, his most distinctive contribution to the Home Rule controversy. But he had little interest in being known as someone who was adept at invoking other states for clever debating points. He wanted to be recognized as someone who could speak with authority, on the basis of historical and jurisprudential knowledge of course, but even more so by virtue of having visited the countries in question and studied them at first hand. After all, he had made three extended tours of the United States by the time he wrote *The American Commonwealth*; Maine, by contrast, did not visit at all.

8

Intimate Politics at Home

DOMESTICITY, GENDER, AND RELIGION

Sisters and Brothers

Historians are becoming more alive to the private and domestic foundations of public careers: the careers of politicians, but also those of public intellectuals.[1] In Bryce's case this is inescapable. His birth family was intimately involved in his adult life in ways that clearly traversed any distinction we might try to draw between the public and the domestic. When he was seeking selection for Scottish constituencies, he relied heavily on his father to liaise with local Liberal notables on his behalf to keep his name in the frame.[2] His sister Mary kept house for him in Great Cumberland Place, then in Norfolk Square, and then in Bryanston Square between 1875 and his marriage in 1889; for the last few years, his brother Annan shared the household, and Annan and his family lived in the Bryanston Square house until Annan's death in 1923. Mary was a central figure in Bryce's life as he made his literary and political career. Henry James, who dined with them in 1878, recalled that 'his pretty Scotch sister, who keeps his house . . . has the prettiest Scotch brogue'.[3] Mary did not simply look after the management of the household, important though that was: she helped Bryce to entertain; she managed his diary and his correspondence, especially during his long absences on foreign travel; and she acted as his first sounding-board for his thinking both about political questions and his literary career. The relationship was much like a marriage: 'Aunt Bessie is mistaken', he told her: 'you are "better to me than ten" wives.' 'Meditate, my sweetest, on this tiresome question [a possible house move]: your prudence I have learnt to respect & trust, but I fear the cares of housekeeping for you.'[4]

Mary was devastated when she learnt in March 1889 that Bryce was to get married, just months after his younger brother. Her letters give vent to her feelings: she felt much like a wife cast aside. 'Perhaps I am wrong', she wrote in December that year, five months after the marriage, 'but I do think that you should be the last person in the world to reproach me. Surely after those 13 years of perfect love & <u>trust</u> you can still <u>trust</u> me & believe that I do what I do for good reasons—partly no doubt I shrink from additional pain to myself but also for other & better reasons which I feel it would perhaps be impossible for you to understand; but which my judgment tells me are right & safe.'[5] She certainly felt that she had made sacrifices for her brother—both brothers—and that they had both married when she was too old to have any prospects. The following August she continued:

> The 94th Psalm last night seemed rather appropriate to one's condition.
> Certainly life has lost for me much that made it not only sweeter but better for one's moral nature.
> And it is worse now than if it had come earlier when one had years to look forward to—a future in which the past could in some measure have been forgotten.[6]

'O Lord God, to whom vengeance belongeth; O God, to whom vengeance belongeth, shew thyself.' Was it the psalmist's opening verse that Mary called to mind?

These letters, incidentally, give the merest glimpse of Mary's sense of betrayal. So much is clear from a letter from Bryce's niece and executor, Margery Bryce, to her brother almost sixty years later, when, the Second World War over, she was sorting through her uncle's papers some years after Marion's death. 'Very many family letters from Aunt Minnie to Uncle James were found of a most painful nature—& all of which I destroyed, and none of which should ever have been kept by Uncle James.' The letters we have are the ones that fortuitously escaped her notice.[7]

The younger sister, Katharine, was a confidante too. When their mother, physically something of an invalid from middle age, moved to London on being widowed in 1877, Katharine moved in with her to keep house and look after her in Streatham and then in Campden Hill Square. Mrs Bryce and Katharine, almost as much as Mary and (latterly) Annan, were very much part of Bryce's social life, and his friends knew them well. He did not draw boundaries between his family and other segments of his social circle; nor between his private and public lives.

The Family Life of an Antisuffragist

Bryce married Marion Ashton on Tuesday, 23 July 1889, at Gee Cross Unitarian Chapel in the Cheshire mill town of Hyde. They were married by a doughty Unitarian divine, Henry Enfield Dowson, who ministered at Gee Cross (where generations of Ashtons had worshipped) from 1867 to 1925. At the time of the marriage Bryce was fifty-one, and well-established in his political, academic, and literary careers; Marion was thirty-five, the second daughter of Thomas Ashton, whose career of public service had encompassed the offices of high sheriff of Lancashire and mayor of Hyde. It was universally agreed by those close to them that the Bryces' marriage was a remarkably happy one, founded on a perfect match of tastes and interests: 'Never was there a more perfect married life', wrote Jessie Ilbert.[8] One crucial bond was a shared enthusiasm for travel and for America in particular. Marion's mother, formerly Elizabeth Gair, was born and raised in Liverpool, where her father was a partner in Baring Brothers, but she came from a well-established Bostonian family who had once been Baptists but were latterly Unitarians.[9] Elizabeth's older sister, Lucretia, born before the move to Liverpool, had been baptized by the celebrated Unitarian theologian and preacher, William Ellery Channing. Marion and her brothers and sisters knew America well.[10] Their aunt Lucretia Gair married William Rathbone, and two of her younger sisters married into the Greg family, so the family was well connected in Unitarian circles on both sides of the Atlantic. Marion was a cultured woman, educated at home to a high standard: she knew several languages, ancient and modern, relished travel, and was committed to both Liberal politics and dissenting faith.[11] Before her marriage she was president of the Hyde Women's Liberal Association; later she was chair of the Women's National Liberal Association in 1900, and later still vice-president of the Women's Liberal Federation. 'No man or woman in the party laboured for it more steadfastly—in its troubled times no less than in the heyday of prosperity', wrote an obituarist.[12] Curiously, however, Marion's place in Bryce's life has been treated sketchily in existing biographical studies, and that is a major omission.[13]

Bryce had known Thomas Ashton for over twenty years by the time of the marriage. Contrary to an account later given by Shena Simon, he did not meet Marion at this time.[14] Quite when and how the relationship blossomed is unclear: Bryce was not much in Manchester after 1875, and certainly not after his election to Parliament in 1880, so it is likely that they met, or met again, in London, where the Ashtons had a house in Belgravia. Marion was certainly in Belgravia when the engagement was announced in March 1889: she wrote from there to Blanche Rathbone, the wife of her cousin William Gair Rathbone, telling her: 'It has been in both our minds for some time, but we only settled matters last Wednesday.'[15] What 'some time' meant here is unclear, for Bryce had only got back from India the previous month. We have no letters between them during his Indian tour, and neither did any of Bryce's letters to his mother or his sisters mention Marion. She herself said that she had fallen in love when reading his work, which is no doubt a comfort to authors everywhere: certainly Marion's American background would have made her well-disposed to a study of *The American Commonwealth*. A letter she wrote to Bryce on the eve of their wedding suggests that they had been growing closer over the last two years: 'When I look back through the last two years, & see how many thoughts of you are crowded into them, & trace the gradual growth of feeling for you from the first curious sense of attraction to the deep & earnest & unfaltering love that possesses me now, I feel that on Tuesday I shall reap the harvest indeed, & gain what to me is more than life or any other thing.'[16] Other correspondence makes it clear that when Marion had visited Oxford the previous summer (not to meet Bryce), he was in her mind, but the possibility of an engagement was not.[17] It is curious that none of Bryce's letters to his mother and sisters from his Indian tour mentioned Marion at all: an indication, perhaps, that they were not yet aware of the developing relationship and that Bryce knew that Mary would take it badly. It is intriguing to discover, however, from one of his letters to Katharine, that while in Coonoor in the Nilgiri hills he met Marion's brother Tom (the former MP for Hyde) and his wife Eva, who were on their way to Ceylon: 'She is lively & bright & I liked her much better than the night she dined with us in B[ryanston] Square.'[18]

Certainly friends who met him during his Indian tour were astonished to be told of his engagement just a few weeks after his return. Henry Roby, the secretary of the Taunton Commission of the 1860s, had spent time with Bryce on the return journey. He had made his career in business in Manchester and knew Marion well from the Manchester High School for Girls, where Marion was a governor, as was Roby's wife Matilda. On hearing of the engagement he wrote to Bryce:

I am astounded at your coolness on the eve of a great event. Judging from your philosophic manner on board the Peshawar and in Italy I disbelieved the news of your engagement when I first heard it. Not that I saw anything unlikely in the thing per se. I believe you have each made an excellent choice. Miss Ashton is a favourite of mine, and if you make as pleasant a companion in the journey of life as you made from Brindisi to Naples, she will have no ground for complaint.[19]

Photographs of Marion taken on her engagement depict a young(ish) woman of independence, determination, and steadiness of purpose.[20] She exuded competence.[21] She was good-looking, with piercing blue eyes and fine bone structure.[22] Godkin, who met her a month before the wedding, remarked on her 'very attractive face, fine eyes, a vivacious but sweet manner, a delightful voice'.[23] The Ashton sisters had been educated at home, but to a high standard: Marion learned three modern European languages and Latin and then turned to Greek at the age of eighteen.[24] On their engagement she was flattered at Bryce's suggestion that they should read Greek and Latin together: 'Perhaps if I work hard now until we are married I may rub up enough of my former knowledge to make it worth while trying'.[25]

At the age of thirty-five, Marion had had a long spinsterhood and was well aware of the fact. She wrote revealingly about how she felt that she had for long had to suppress her emotional and intimate side:

> I may tell you now that one of the things that gave me the deepest pain in my struggle for duty was this load of self-repression & the consciousness that in the course I was taking I must make up my mind to shut off one half of my nature—& that the deeper side. I knew, too, that there would be a great temptation to become cynical, & hard & self contained under this effort, & I prayed with all my might for strength to keep a kindly & tender human sympathy through it all & be able to turn the power of feeling I knew I possessed into other channels of good & usefulness. I was not very successful, but at least I tried.[26]

We lack Bryce's side of this correspondence, but Marion indicates that these self-revelatory confessions of hers were stimulated by his observation that a change was being worked in the textures of their being, which seems to imply that his own feelings were not dissimilar. The following January he wrote from Oxford:

> Oxford begins now to seem strange without you—yet here more than any other where I have the strange mixed feeling of the old life and the new, like a new M.S. written on a half effaced palimpsest, here however the new writing being far more precious than the old. But why did we let life run on so long without knowing one another? Yet let me rather be thankful that there came at last what might never have come at all and is far better than I had hoped.[27]

FIGURE 8.1. Photographic portrait of Marion Ashton
(1854–1939), taken on her engagement to Bryce in March 1889.

It was certainly a good marriage from Bryce's point of view, for Thomas
Ashton was a man of great wealth, one of the very few Manchester cotton
masters who became a half-millionaire, and was able to provide well for his
numerous children.[28] That said, marriage did not immediately transform
Bryce's financial circumstances. In 1889 he still held three important sources

of academic income: his fellowship at Oriel (worth around £250 a year), the Regius professorship (by now worth around £440 a year gross), and his professorship at the Council of Legal Education, which brought him £500 a year. So his official academic income was in the region of £1200. But the Oriel fellowship was conditional on celibacy and had to be vacated on the first anniversary of the marriage.[29] The Council of Legal Education terminated his appointment in 1889, which he certainly felt as an ill-timed financial blow.[30] Finally, the Regius professorship probably became less attractive once he was married, since it required frequent visits to Oxford; and in any case (though the chair was ill-paid and explicitly intended to be nonresident) the tensions between his professorial responsibilities and his parliamentary career had long attracted comment.[31] His appointment to the cabinet in 1892 precipitated his resignation at the end of the 1892–1893 academic year. So his financial circumstances were changing: official income diminished and then vanished, except of course for those periods when he was in government. On the other hand, the success of *The American Commonwealth* was a major boost to his literary earnings, not least because frequent reprints and new editions ensured that royalty income remained substantial throughout the remainder of his life. It was probably not by chance that marriage followed so soon after the book's appearance.

Marion's papers contain a number of useful sets of household accounts which shed light on their financial circumstances at particular moments. There is a good set from 1897, a year when Bryce had no income from public office. It also (importantly) predated the death of Thomas Ashton. In that year the Bryces had a combined income for the year of rather more than £3000: that was a very good middle-class income but did not make them rich. Of this, over a quarter was Marion's: income of £555 from a trust fund, and the remainder in investment income, mostly from Ashton Brothers shares. Bryce's literary income stood just short of £500, and his investment income at around £1800, of which around £200 came from Ashton Brothers shares given to him by his father-in-law.[32] Their expenditure came to less than £2000, so they were very comfortably in surplus, as they needed to be, for this was around the time they were building their country home, Hindleap Lodge, near Forest Row in Sussex.[33] Marion's father, who died in January 1898, bequeathed her an additional trust fund of £14,000, which would probably have added some £600–700 to her annual income. She inherited a further £2,500 on her mother's death in 1914.[34]

Marion had five sisters, of whom four were already married. Two, Harriet and Katharine, married Arthur and Charles Lupton, brothers from an old mercantile and gentry family in Leeds. The Luptons were active in Leeds Unitarian circles, notably at the famous Mill Hill Chapel, which rivalled Cross Street in Manchester and Renshaw Street in Liverpool. The youngest sisters both married wealthy Manchester businessmen: Grace married the shipping merchant Philip Kessler, and Charlotte married Edward Tootal Broadhurst, cotton manufacturer. Whereas the Luptons were firm Liberals, Broadhurst was an active Conservative, though he was denounced as a Mugwump by his party when his commitment to free trade led him to back the Liberal candidate for Manchester North-West, Winston Churchill, both in the general election of 1906 and in the 1908 by election, which Churchill lost.[35]

One sister remained unmarried, and she was arguably the most notable of the five. She is certainly the one whose name lives on. After her father's death, Margaret Ashton was active in local politics, first as a Liberal and latterly (when the Liberals dragged their heels on women's suffrage) as an Independent and then in the Labour Party. She was the first woman to be elected to the Manchester City Council, as an Independent in 1908, and was notably active on its Public Health Committee. She was a vocal though nonmilitant suffragist, and in the First World War adopted an unpopular pacifist stance. C. P. Scott of the *Manchester Guardian* commissioned a portrait of her in 1925 and offered it to the City Council, which refused it, citing her antiwar stance.

Margaret was certainly unhappy at Marion's marriage: she said so, to Bryce himself, in a quite remarkably ungracious letter. 'I cannot say that you will be to me a very welcome visitor', she wrote, 'but I do hope you will be able to come on Friday that I may begin to get used to the situation, and you to me— both of which will need time no doubt.'[36] There is some indication that the marriage might have taken place sooner had it not been for her resistance: Margaret said as much in the same letter. Those scholars who have commented on the matter infer that she was horrified that her sister should be marrying a leading opponent of women's suffrage.[37] This seems unlikely. Bryce's position was certainly known, for he had spoken against the enfranchisement of women in the Commons in 1884, but his stance was not yet notorious, nor was it unusual enough to attract attention at the time. Margaret was only just becoming active in public life at the time of the Bryces' marriage, initially as cofounder of the Manchester Women's Guardian Association, and she was not yet an active suffrage campaigner. In fact Shena Simon, who knew her well, says quite explicitly that Margaret only became interested in women's suffrage much later.[38] In any case, Margaret explained herself in her letter to Bryce: 'In the mean time, if you think this a curt and unkind letter (and I must own—it isn't as nice as it might be) you will have to ask Marion for my sentiments in general on prospective brothers in law which will make you think well of this effort.'[39] She resented her sister's marriage, but not her choice of husband.

In fact, Bryce seems to have had a cordial relationship with Margaret, in spite of the political differences that developed. She congratulated him warmly, and banteringly, on his appointment to the cabinet in 1892.[40] Margaret would occasionally accompany the Bryces on holiday, for instance on a cycling holiday in Germany in 1898, when he found her 'a brisk & vivacious companion who, tho' not strong, has lots of spirit for fatigue'.[41] The Bryces would stay with her when visiting Manchester once Thomas Ashton had died and his widow moved to London.[42] The women's suffrage question seems to have impinged on the relationship (but not to damage it) only in the 1900s. Something of the sensitivity of the issue, but also the flavour of the relationship between brother-in-law and sister-in-law, comes out in a series of letters Marion wrote to him in the autumn of 1906, when going to and fro between England and Dublin:

> That energetic spirit [Margaret] has gone off to a committee at Preston this morning, & is to return this afternoon in time to take a drive with Mother after tea. She talked about the Suffrage Congress in Copenhagen & the people she met there quite freely & quietly & I asked her about various things in connection with it, but I avoided all discussion of its merits.[43] She realises that these extreme people do harm, but she is not surprised that some people should pursue violent methods under the circumstances. The notorious Mrs Montefiore was there, & Mgt learns privately that she is a thorough "undesirable"—indeed, not respectable. One wonders that a person in a glass house should advertise herself so prominently.[44]

And then, a few months later:

> I am thinking of using some of my lonely time in putting together some of my reasons & objections to Women's Suffrage—reasons not necessarily barring it out, but which make one feel that a good deal has yet to be thought out, & which these noisy advocates & ignorant followers have never considered. But don't tell Mgt this, & please don't teaze her or argue with her on the subject. She is quite unreasonable & it will do no good, & may only cause sore feeling. I don't think she will speak to you about it at all, & it is better to leave her alone. Only if she asks you why these heroines should have severer sentences than men you may tell her that she is mistaken & the men would have got more under similar circumstances.[45]

FIGURE 8.2. Gladstone visiting the Ashton family at Ford Bank, Didsbury, December 1889. Bryce is at front left; Marion is at back left, next to Margaret Ashton. In the centre front are Catherine and William Gladstone and Thomas Ashton; Elizabeth Ashton is behind her husband, and behind her is probably her daughter Katharine Lupton; at front right is probably Katharine's husband, Charles Lupton.

This is a revealing letter. The impression it gives is that Bryce, who certainly had a strongly developed sense of humour and playfulness, rather enjoyed the opportunity to tease Margaret on the subject.[46]

Mary and Katharine—the former in particular—certainly felt displaced by Marion, but they continued to play an important role in Bryce's public as well as private life, not least in managing his diary and correspondence during the Bryces' lengthy overseas tours. During the American visit in the late summer and autumn of 1890, this even included finding out such fundamental details as the date when Parliament would reconvene following the summer recess. 'As to Parliament—we think it meets about the middle of November, but we don't think they fixed <u>any day</u>—however I shall write Mr Ilbert—& he may know the exact day—& I shall send you work next mail.'[47] Following the Bryces' return from South Africa in December 1895, Mary reported to her brother about the business that needed his attention; and on other occasions she would send abstracts of letters she had opened in his absence.[48]

Mary had an especially deep interest in politics, both the issues and the personalities. She had strong views on questions of foreign and imperial policy in particular and was often forthright in offering political advice, even on the Venezuela boundary dispute in January 1896.[49] In April 1897 Bryce had Mary and Katharine to lunch in Marion's absence, and he reported to her that 'I had a severe lecture for my low moral tone in the matter of Rhodes, Jameson & the Raid'.[50] Both sisters shared their brother's visceral sympathies and antipathies. The most important of all their allegiances, apart from to the Liberal Party itself, was to Gladstone. On his death Bryce wrote to Katharine:

> I knew you would feel deeply the departure of the noble old hero who has made the country greater by his presence since ever you can remember. How well I remember the first time I ever saw him, when I was still an undergraduate here, and he delivered a speech in the Museum at Oxford, in 1860, I think it was, & Mr Boyle & I were taken by dear old Sammy Wayte who knew him well.[51] Since then, what a rich and varied life, associated with nearly everything that has passed in the world as well as in England.

He added:

> One can't help wishing that many of those who now join in this acclamation of departed greatness had restrained their party rancour during his life, and treated with due respect a character whose purity and elevation they might have felt, and would have felt had they cared to have insight and justice.[52]

They were not always uncritical of Gladstone. When she heard him speak at the Newcastle conference of the National Liberal Federation in October 1891 Mary thought it 'a wonderful sight' and considered the speech good, but added 'there did not seem much that was new in it', and a few years later she thought him 'too moderate' on Armenia.[53] His High Church sympathies and sacramentalism were alien to Bryce and to Marion (more, in fact, than to Mary and Katharine).[54] But loyalty to Gladstone was a fundamental commitment shared by the two sisters and their two brothers, and by their mother too.

The antihero was, not surprisingly, Joseph Chamberlain: 'One hates this ascendancy of Chamberlain quite becoming a Dictator', wrote Mary early in

1896.[55] Some years earlier Bryce had been in the United States at the same time as Chamberlain, who was 'much bored with his two months in the U.S.'. To be bored by the United States was, for Bryce, the indication of a man without breadth of interests or hinterland: he had 'no interest in the country or people, & no small talk—in fact appearing to have no particular interest in life save English politics. Not like our G.O.M.'[56] The antipathy to Chamberlain reached its crescendo with the Boer War and, thereafter, his tariff reform campaign. He personified militarism and protectionism, both of which were anathema to the Bryces. Still worse, he was a defector from the Liberal Party, and from Gladstone.

Women's Suffrage

Bryce was a staunch opponent of the enfranchisement of women. That is well-known and discussed, though briefly, by biographers from Fisher to Seaman, as well as by historians of antisuffragism such as Brian Harrison.[57] This was an enduring commitment: Bryce spoke against women's suffrage consistently in both Houses over a period of thirty-four years, stretching from the Reform Bill of 1884 to that of 1918.[58] He was also a key agitator for the organized mobilization of antisuffragist opinion—though he did not, it seems, make many (or, perhaps, any) extra-parliamentary speeches on the subject.[59] In *Modern Democracies*—published in the last year of his life—he remained unreconciled to women's suffrage.[60]

Conversely, he worked tirelessly on behalf of many women's causes, not least that of girls' and women's education, starting with his work on the Schools Inquiry Commission. In his report he noted caustically that 'although the world has now existed for several thousand years, the notion that women have minds as cultivable and as well worth cultivating as men' was regarded as a shocking paradox.[61] He made the case for public bodies to do as much for the education of girls as of boys, since women constitute half the population, and 'not the less important half, when we consider how much depends upon mothers'.[62] He argued, indeed, that the 'elevation of the English commercial class to a higher level of knowledge, taste, and culture' depended more than anything on the improvement in the education of girls.[63] In the wake of the commission he was an active member of the North of England Council for the Higher Education of Women, the Women's Education Union (he served on its Central Committee), and a member of the council of the Girls' Public Day School Company (later Trust).[64] Josephine Butler, who worked closely with him on the North of England Council, wrote in support of his candidature at Wick in the 1874 General Election, commending him as a Scotchman with the right views on women.[65] He was closely involved with Girton College from its origins, though not without some disagreements with Emily Davies on matters of policy. It was he who suggested its incorporation as a joint-stock company under the Companies Acts of 1862 and 1867, and under the governance arrangements instituted by the articles of association he became a 'member' of the college—a position analogous to serving on the Court of Governors of a civic college or university—and remained in this position for fifty years. He also served on its Executive Committee in its early days.[66] Equally, through the North of England Council and the university extension movement with which it was entwined he was also closely involved with the creation of Newnham.[67] He was on the management committee of Bedford College and a governor of Royal Holloway College, so his involvement in women's university education was hard to rival.[68] Emily Penrose, who was successively principal of Bedford, Royal Holloway, and Somerville, spoke warmly both of his role in advancing her career and of his influence on the cause of women's and girls' education.[69] In the Commons, he sponsored the Infant Custody Bill of 1884, taking up a key feminist cause, though the bill was seriously watered down in its passage through Parliament, and the Act of 1886 was a disappointment to its feminist backers.[70] When he spoke against women's suffrage in Parliament, he more than once prefaced or concluded his remarks with an emphatic assertion of his credentials as an active proponent of women's claim to 'the fullest social equality'.[71] His commitment to the advancement of women's educational and professional opportunities was just as authentic as his opposition to their enfranchisement. As far as can be established, he regarded women as collaborators rather than as the passive beneficiaries of the reforming efforts of men: he worked *with* women activists and not just on their behalf. The Royal Commission on Secondary Education (1895), which he chaired, was the first Royal Commission to include women members: three of them, Lucy Cavendish (Lady Frederick Cavendish), Sophie Bryant, the headmistress of North London Collegiate School, and Eleanor Sidgwick, the principal of Newnham College. He seems not to have been involved in their appointment, although all were prior friends or associates of his; but he was already on record as a supporter of the appointment of women to Royal Commissions.[72]

Furthermore, Bryce knew, and in many cases knew very well, many of the leading feminists of the time, including those who were active in the campaign for the suffrage. His social circles included Emily Davies, Barbara Bodichon,

Helen Taylor, the Pankhurst family, Elizabeth Garrett Anderson, John and Alice Westlake, Emma Winkworth, and many others.[73] Winkworth was an especially intimate friend, and their closeness was unimpeded by their difference on the suffrage question.[74] Bryce thought her 'a beautiful soul' and wrote that 'I have never known a warmer heart than hers or a purer and more truthful nature'.[75] Given his immersion in these circles, it can hardly be claimed that he was unaware of the force of the case for women's enfranchisement.

It was by no means rare to combine active support for the promotion of the education of girls and women with opposition to women's suffrage.[76] The leading voice in the women's antisuffrage campaign, Mary Ward (the novelist Mrs Humphry Ward), had been one of the founders of Somerville College. Ward was heterodox in religious doctrine, but the founders of the women's colleges in Oxford also included a number from High Church backgrounds who were motivated by a vision of the contribution of higher education to the nurturing of Christian womanhood and certainly did not want women's education to mimic that of men. They included Elizabeth Wordsworth, the first principal of Lady Margaret Hall, daughter and niece of High Church bishops, and a tacit backer of the antisuffragist cause.[77] At Girton, by contrast, Emily Davies championed the cause of equality and insisted that this must be pursued by a course of education identical to that provided for men, and culminating in the same examinations. Bryce did not really share either Davies's perspective or Wordsworth's. Like his friend Henry Sidgwick, he saw an opportunity for innovation in the fact that women were not necessarily aiming to compete in the same labour market as men and did not necessarily aspire to emerge from college with qualifications. That meant there was the possibility of escaping from the tyranny of the examination system, and indeed from the backwardness of the established university curriculum.[78] For Bryce and Sidgwick, like Pattison before them, women could and should be educated differently not because the curriculum for men was unsuited to them but because something better could be offered.[79]

That said, Bryce's allies in fighting for women's education sometimes found his tenacious resistance to their arguments for the suffrage surprising and immensely disappointing, and some of them attacked him all the more bitterly for that reason. Elizabeth Wolstenholme Elmy, the Manchester feminist campaigner who worked with him on the North of England Council and on the Infant Custody Bill of 1884, could scarcely hide a personal animus when she wrote to the *Manchester Guardian* in 1898, following a speech by Bryce at the Manchester Reform Club: 'His hostility to the enfranchisement of women is painfully notorious.' She went on: 'Obviously for him woman is not yet, in his opinion, a part of humanity'—a remark that must have wounded a celebrated campaigner for humanitarian causes; and although a mere woman, 'one whom the law holds to be lower than the felon, the lunatic, or the infant', she contended that the case for women's suffrage rested on 'the broad principle of justice, which Mr Bryce seems to have quite forgotten, and which yet was the source of the whole vitality of the Liberal party in the days when it really did a great work'. She asked whether Bryce was content, like Gladstone, to be known as 'the enemy of justice to the mother half of humanity', and she concluded with a stirring declaration that in the end the cause of justice would 'defeat all lovers of expediency and half-hearted humanitarians'.[80] In other writings, Wolstenholme Elmy accused Bryce of involvement in a successful filibuster to prevent discussion of the Women's Enfranchisement Bill in May 1905, and a little later she identified him as one of the three most determined opponent of women's suffrage in the Campbell-Bannerman cabinet.[81]

When reading these remarks, it is impossible not to be acutely conscious of the rifts that the question of women's suffrage created in the Liberal Party. These rifts were replicated to the full in the wider Bryce family, for whereas Bryce, his wife, his sisters, and his brother Annan were all antisuffragists, Marion's sister Margaret and Annan's wife Violet were both enthusiastic backers of enfranchisement, as were Annan and Violet's four children. Violet Bryce caused a stir in the press by staying away from her husband's Inverness constituency during the campaign for the January 1910 election by prolonging a visit to the United States, where she had been staying with her brother-in-law: 'It must not be inferred', noted one American newspaper, 'that her brother-in-law, the British Ambassador, is [a suffragist], for Mr James Bryce enjoys the diplomatic privilege of not having opinions.'[82] Bryce was anything but a dogmatist by nature, and his mind was rarely closed, but he was stalwart in resisting women's suffrage to the end. Some of his friends—Goldwin Smith and Dicey—came to antisuffragism after initially looking sympathetically on the cause, but Bryce was never in favour.[83] So what underpinned his stance?

Unusually for him, he wrote little on the subject, other than an important chapter in *The American Commonwealth* and some of his political commentary pieces for *The Nation* (New York). These were not works of advocacy. But his parliamentary speeches were meaty and distinguished carefully between the antisuffragist arguments that carried weight for him and those he dismissed as spurious. Juxtaposing these texts with Dicey's important statement of the antisuffragist case in *Letters to a Friend on Votes for Women* (1909) is revealing.

There were a number of common antisuffragist arguments which Bryce explicitly or implicitly rejected. For a start, there was the 'physical force' argument, which became increasingly influential in an atmosphere of intensified militarism and imperialism at the start of the twentieth century. This argument weighed heavily with Dicey, who put it as follows: 'The basis of all government is force, which means in the last resort physical strength. But predominant force lies in the hands of men.'[84] If universal suffrage were conceded, women would outnumber men, and in principle a law could be passed which had the support of women but not of men. There could be no confidence that it could be enforced. This argument, absurd though it now looks, was taken seriously by Henry Sidgwick, who felt it necessary to explain in scrupulous detail why he rejected it.[85] Reasonably enough, Bryce gave this argument short shrift: does anyone really believe that such a case would arise? Neither did he, either publicly or privately, invoke arguments about women's conservatism: if the case for the justice of enfranchisement were sound, it should be enacted whatever the electoral effects.[86]

The staple argument against women's suffrage rested on the idea that nature, or God, had ordained 'separate spheres' for men and women. Brian Harrison and others in his wake have emphasized that beliefs about separate spheres were central to the antisuffragist mind-set.[87] Bryce's friend and first biographer H.A.L. Fisher thought it 'repugnant to his [Bryce's] chivalrous conception of the other sex that they should be involved in the hard clash and sordid struggles of the political arena'.[88] That may indeed be so, and Fisher's wife (a prominent suffragist) was Bryce's goddaughter, and both knew him well, so the testimony is important. Marion took the view that the suffrage would compromise women's distinctive contribution to social life: 'I do not want women to be "like men". I have a very deep appreciation of the dignity of the power & the personality of my sex, & I want to see women develop women's powers and character & influence in the highest sense.'[89] But separate spheres arguments were not to the fore in Bryce's speeches and writings.[90] On the contrary, he conceded that he had no objection in principle the idea of the woman voter: 'If we could admit the few women who do take an interest in political questions, without admitting those who do not, I should see no objection; for I do not argue that sex, as sex, ought to disqualify. It is not because women are women, but because the conditions of their lives have not qualified them for the exercise of political power, that they are unfitted to exercise the franchise.'[91]

Instead, Bryce insisted that the question should be addressed 'rather more from the political than from the social point of view. It is the political interests of the country that we have to study.'[92] The spectre of social disorder resulting from the confusion of gender roles did not alarm him. For Bryce, the question did not turn on conceptions of gender so much as on the likely impact of franchise extension on the workings of the political system. Like Dicey, Bryce approached the question from a consequentialist perspective. Would the enfranchisement of women tend to improve or to depress the quality of public discourse and decision-making? Would it elevate, or would it depress, the 'tone of public life'? Would it produce 'a better Parliament', one able more effectively to 'reflect the opinion of the majority of the constituencies'? Bryce was convinced that it would not, and the reason he kept coming back to was that women showed little interest in politics: 'they know little and care less about political questions.'[93] Perhaps that was another way of putting Annan Bryce's objection, as summarized by his wife Violet: 'women are natural born Conservatives, and to give them the suffrage would put the Conservatives in power for an indefinite period.'[94]

The insistence that women were uninterested in politics and did not want the vote no doubt irritated the suffrage campaigners, especially as the campaign gained momentum in the Edwardian period.[95] Bryce was well-connected among women antisuffragists such as Mary Ward and Ethel Harrison (the wife of his friend Frederic Harrison) and clearly persuaded himself that they spoke for commonsensical public opinion; the suffragist and (still more) suffragette campaigners were (in today's tendentious parlance) an 'activist' minority. One of Bryce's weaknesses was a tendency to have too much confidence in his 'flair' as a trained observer of public opinion. As we have seen, while Bryce was alive to the Tocqueville-Mill argument that political participation could have an educative quality, he attached more weight to the dangers in the sudden enfranchisement of a large number of new voters. There were always new voters in any electoral body, if only those who had just reached twenty-one; they did not intrinsically pose a danger, because they were a small minority. The scale of the increase in the electorate that women's enfranchisement would entail was the point he dwelt on. Was the doubling in the size of the electorate really a sensible move?[96] Uninformed or uninterested voters were vulnerable to influence—from family members and employers—and, still worse, were easy prey for demagogues. It was not just that they added little to the political community: they would detract from it if susceptible to ill-informed populist campaigns. So the extension of democratic rights could work counter to free government, and the latter was more important to him than the former. In that sense we see Bryce deploying a republican case against universal suffrage especially if conceived as a matter of rights.

FIGURE 8.3. Margery Bryce (daughter of Annan and Violet Bryce and niece of James Bryce) as Joan of Arc at a suffragette pageant in June 1911.

Bryce was in Washington when the campaign for women's suffrage attained the height of its militancy, both in Britain and in the United States. He may well have been relieved that his obligation of political neutrality enabled him to escape the acrimony that would no doubt have come his way as a leading cabinet opponent of women's suffrage. There was a hint in the American press that it was a topic not to be broached at the embassy.[97] Certainly Violet Bryce caused him something of an embarrassment when visiting the United States, and staying for part of the time at the embassy, for while in America she spoke at suffrage meetings and gave interviews in the American press about her position, and why she was declining to return to Britain to campaign for her husband in Inverness.[98] Violet's four children all shared her commitment to women's suffrage, she emphasized; and indeed in June 1911, when the suffragettes organized a mass procession and historically themed pageant in London a few days before George V's coronation, her daughter Margery attracted a good deal of publicity by appearing on horseback dressed as Joan of Arc in silver armour. Her photograph as Joan of Arc was widely published in the national newspapers.[99] There is some indication that her mother might have had a hand in managing her public relations, in that preprocession photographs of

Margery in the role were published in the press some days in advance. The photograph was attributed to Val l'Estrange, a professional photographer and probably a relative of Violet's.[100] Margery had already acquired some celebrity as a pioneer of women riding astride a horse, and several of the press reports pointedly recorded that she 'rode astride a white charger'.[101] Boadicea, by contrast, rode side-saddle.

Married Life

On her engagement in March 1889, Marion wrote to her fiancé in terms that inevitably remind the reader of Dorothea Brooke in George Eliot's *Middlemarch*, a novel with which she was certainly familiar. She professed herself 'more than ever determined to be a better woman than I have been, in order that I might help you the more' and continued: 'It has always been my ideal of happiness in the highest sense in this life to help others to push forward to something better & purer & higher, & the thought that you have chosen me to help you in your life is a happiness so intense that sometimes it is almost pain. I know you understand what I mean.'[102] She also made it clear that she had no wish to change his lifestyle or to cut him off from his friends, but that she wanted to be part of that life.

Marion was well educated, by governesses rather than at school, and knew ancient as well as modern languages. Following their engagement, Bryce suggested they should read Latin and Greek together. Perhaps this was not everyone's idea of marital happiness, but Marion's only fear was that she would reveal herself a 'poor scholar' in such company. She resolved to work hard on her languages so that by the time they were married she might have recovered 'enough of my former knowledge to make it worth while trying'.[103] In any case, she was evidently a woman of learned taste: Jowett's *Dialogues of Plato* was a particular favourite.[104] She and Bryce often read Dante together.[105]

The bond between husband and wife was unusually close, and Marion was henceforth a fundamental part of Bryce's public as well as private life. When they spent time among 'our constituents' (Marion's locution) in Aberdeen, as they did, typically, twice a year, there was a clear division of labour. As Marion wrote to an American friend during one such visit, 'James is busy here with all sorts of work, giving addresses on various subjects, seeing people, receiving deputations, etc, while I do the social part.'[106] On these visits they usually stayed with Dr Angus Fraser, a medical practitioner and leading figure in the Aberdeen

Liberal Association; another of their close friends was Sir John Forbes Clark, second baronet and retired diplomat, who lived on the Tillypronie Estate in the house built for his father, who had been Queen Victoria's physician.[107]

She certainly regarded her role as being to support her husband's public career rather than to develop one of her own, but Marion was by no means a reticent wife. She remained politically active and was regarded as an excellent public speaker, 'enthusiastic and definite in her opinions'.[108] The surviving notes for her speeches—and they are (mostly) notes rather than full texts— confirm a woman of trenchant opinions rooted in Manchester Liberalism.[109] These surviving speeches mostly date from the later years of the long period of Tory hegemony brought to an end by the 1906 general election, and we find repeated invocation of a simple narrative of nineteenth-century Britain. This began with the era of Liberal dominance characterized by economic, social, and political progress between 1832 and 1874: its chief accomplishments being the extension of the franchise, the abolition of slavery, the abolition of the corn laws, the establishment of state education, and the abolition of religious tests. This golden age was followed by a period of political indifference, Jingoism, corruption, Chamberlainism, and Tory reaction that set in with Disraeli's victory in 1874 and accelerated after 1886.[110] The Chamberlainite programme of imperial expansion and protectionism was the culmination of this narrative of decline. As a child, Marion met Cobden as a visitor to the Ashton family home, and her speeches were infused with a Cobdenite vision in which free trade induced peaceful relations among nations.[111] When a Women's Free Trade Union was set up in 1903, she threw herself into its activities with verve, serving on its committee, addressing meetings, and drafting a leaflet on its behalf.[112] Press reports on her speeches show that she was not afraid to tackle controversial subjects, such as the Boer War (Didsbury Liberal Club, November 1900), and indeed she joined the South African Conciliation Committee earlier that same year, 'for the dissemination of accurate information on the whole dispute in South Africa, and for the consideration as soon as a proper opportunity arises of some peaceable settlement of the great conflict between this country and the Boer Republics'.[113] Usually she echoed her husband's public positions: In 1903 she took the Tory government to task for its 'costly foreign policy' and its 'unsound and wasteful economic administration'.[114] There are no identifiable cases of their taking different positions, in public or in private, on any political issue. But there were certain causes she made her own, in particular that of careers for educated women. She was a very active

FIGURE 8.4. Hindleap, the house built by the Bryces in Forest Row, Sussex, in the late 1890s. 'The more the progress of man disappoints, the more does one seem to fall back upon the tranquil sweetness of nature.'

supporter of the Central Employment Bureau for Women and Students' Careers Association and served as its president in the 1930s.[115]

Hindleap, the country retreat they built in the High Weald, adjacent to Ashdown Forest, meant a great deal to both Bryce and Marion and was a focal point for their married life.[116] Marion lived there in widowhood until her death at the end of 1939. They both valued the solace it offered away from the busy-ness of London life. Bryce told his American friend, the artist Sarah Wyman Whitman, that the Sussex scenery had 'a breezy amplitude which is inspiriting, with wide prospects over great reaches of wooded country to distant downs, behind which, scarce visible, lies the sea'. The Sussex forests lacked the majesty of their American counterparts, but he appreciated their 'variety and tenderness' and regretted that 'this sylvan and hill scenery of Southern England has never had a poet to express its sentiment as Wordsworth did for Cumbria'.[117] The Bryces were early adopters of the vogue for cycling, which began in the 1890s. This offered them fresh opportunities to explore the Weald and Downs countryside and also became a favourite holiday pursuit in France in springtime.[118]

The Free Churchman in Politics

Bryce's marriage to a member of a prominent northern Unitarian family certainly cemented his identity as a nonconformist or (as he preferred to say) a free churchman in public life.[119] What evidence there is suggests that he and

Marion were much of the same mind in religious as in political matters. Bryce was never active in church politics, unlike some other parliamentarians of his time. His denominational identity diminished with age, not least because the United Presbyterians had little presence in England. He certainly never sought out its churches.[120] If he had a regular place of worship either in London or in Sussex, there is little in the archival record to show it. His diaries from the 1870s occasionally record church attendance in Oxford or Manchester, but Marion's diaries from the 1900s never do, and his correspondence rarely mentions church services except when (during holidays) he attended as much for purposes of anthropological observation as for worship. He told Marion that Sir George Bruce had asked him to join the English Presbyterian Church in St John's Wood, although there is no evidence that he did join.[121] But he was well-known for supporting nonconformist causes, and when a prominent public man was needed, he was one of the first choices. That pattern began early. When a Nonconformist Union was established in Oxford in the early 1880s, by Robert F. Horton, the Congregationalist fellow of New College, Bryce was named its president, and he attended its meetings when he could.[122] He remained president when it was later superseded by a Society for the Promotion of Religious Equality.[123] Long thereafter Bryce remained the most prominent Oxonian free churchman. In 1911 the Church of Scotland, the United Free Church of Scotland, and the Presbyterian Church of England set up a joint chaplaincy in Oxford, on the site in Alfred Street of the former stables of the Bear Inn.[124] Bryce, as a notable Presbyterian, laid the foundation stone on 6 June 1914. He declared that there was no intention of making the new chapel a sectarian institution, working for sectarian aims: Presbyterian students need not be withdrawn from their college chapels, but Presbyterians felt that 'the Presbyterian Church theory should be represented in the University, where every branch of Christian life and thought ought to be represented'.[125]

Bryce's central interest in religious questions lay at the interface of church and academy. He was an influential proponent of a learned church and of a nonsectarian academy. This was the unfinished business that remained in the wake of the Universities Tests Act of 1871. That act had removed religious tests for university offices, except for professorships of divinity, and for the higher degrees, except in divinity; it had also abolished tests for college offices and emoluments in the 'old foundations': that is, colleges and halls founded prior to 1870. But the divinity faculties remained in Anglican hands, and 'new foundations' were untouched by the act. Most of the act's keenest proponents, such as Bryce, favoured mixed education in nondenominational colleges. But while the act swept away most religious tests associated with existing endowments, it left open the possibility of the creation of new denominational colleges. Gladstone favoured that solution, which is one reason why he acquiesced in a measure about which he had long-standing reservations. He urged the nonconformists to establish themselves at Oxford and Cambridge by creating denominational colleges of their own. In fact it was Anglicans who took advantage of this provision in the Act: Keble College (Oxford, 1870—it counted as a new foundation, though it narrowly preceded the act), Hertford College (Oxford, 1874), and Selwyn College (Cambridge, 1882) were all strongly Anglican foundations. The first women's college in Oxford was also conceived as an Anglican foundation: this proved to be a divisive proposition, and the solution was the creation of two colleges, the Anglican Lady Margaret Hall and the nondenominational Somerville Hall (both 1879).[126] Nonconformists began the move to Oxford in the 1880s with the migration of Mansfield College (1886) and Manchester College (1889), in both cases (like the women's colleges) outside the formal structures of the university.

Bryce had a very clear position in these debates about the place of denominational restrictions in universities. He was against them. In 1884 he contributed a piece on 'The Free Churches and a Theological Faculty' to the heavyweight nonconformist periodical, the *British Quarterly Review*: Bryce's article was paired with one by Andrew Fairbairn, who would shortly be appointed the first principal of Mansfield College.[127] Bryce's piece was driven by the belief that it would be desirable if more candidates for the ministry in the nonconformist denominations were to be educated at Oxford and Cambridge, alongside their Anglican counterparts. He deprecated denominational colleges and deplored 'the establishment of sectarian foundations such as Keble and Selwyn', on the ground that 'the value of University life largely consists in the free intermingling of young men of different persuasions'. Nonconformist students at Oxford and Cambridge could be admitted to any of the old foundations, which were all now nondenominational in terms of their admissions and elections to scholarships and fellowships; or they could, if they wish, register as noncollegiate students. What was needed was a free theological faculty, a rival to the existing Faculty of Divinity, which remained firmly in Anglican hands.[128]

Considered in a context in which both Mansfield (Spring Hill College) and Manchester College were contemplating a move to Oxford, the point of Bryce's article, and Fairbairn's too, was clear: it was to make the case for these moves. Bryce did not think of them as dissenting counterparts to Keble and Hertford, but as free theological faculties, needed for just as long as the official

Faculty of Divinity remained an Anglican monopoly. Bryce had in fact already raised his voice in support of the case for moving one or more of the nonconformist colleges to Oxford, when in April 1883 he spoke at the laying of the foundation stone of Lyndhurst Road Congregational Church in Hampstead, where Robert Horton was to minister. He noted that it was the first time in English history that a fellow and tutor of an Oxford or Cambridge college had also been pastor to a nonconformist congregation. He thought that the establishment of a nonconformist training college in Oxford or Cambridge would provide a further stimulus to the arrival of more nonconformists into the old universities.[129]

The bitterest denominational struggles in politics in Bryce's lifetime were on educational questions, and especially on the problem of denominational religious teaching in schools supported by the ratepayer. This was a problem on which Bryce had a clear and consistent stance. He strongly endorsed the principle enshrined in the Cowper-Temple clause in the 1870 Education Act. This stipulated that religious teaching in Board Schools (elementary schools run by elected School Boards) should be nondenominational in character. He thought that what was important about religious instruction in elementary schools was its communication of scriptural knowledge and Christian moral teaching: points on which the great majority of Christians agreed. But Bryce agreed with those critics of the 1870 Act who criticized it for not imposing the duty to provide religious teaching of a nonsectarian character. While his resistance to Anglican dogma on the rates is well-known, not least because he took the lead in the Liberal opposition to Balfour's Education Act of 1902, he attached just as much importance to the provision of instruction in the basics of Christianity. In his last two decades he came to place increasing emphasis on the importance of Christian teaching as the foundation of a common morality, at least in the West, and hence as the basis for civics too.

Bryce gave a trenchant, though laconic, statement of his position in a letter to the Manchester social reformer and Ruskinian philanthropist Thomas Coglan Horsfall in 1898:

As regards Denominational Schools & the whole religious difficulty, which you discuss in a very suggestive way, it is hard to state one's views briefly, but I should be disposed to hold

1. That it is undesirable to sever children into groups on sectarian lines.
2. That the present system is unjust & oppressive to dissenting parents in many country places, rarely in towns.

3. That the value of religious instruction, though great, does not lie in the points on which Christians (i.e. 99/100 of Protestant Christians) differ.

4. That it does not lie at all in the use of sectarian formularies.

5. Hence—That the undenominational instruction given in the better Board Schools contains all that a school needs to give—or rather, qua school, can give in the way of such instruction as tends to make young people good members of Church & commonwealth.

6. That no denominational management—involving strict denominationalism in choice of teachers—can be justified in schools supported by State funds.

7. That arrangements might well be made for enabling such parents as desire distinctive sectarian instruction for their children to have it. It is only a mere handful who wish to have anything more specific than the better Board Schools give.

Accordingly the best solution seems to me to be Universal Board Schools, plus arrangements which shall secure good religious instruction everywhere, and permit those who desire specifically sectarian instruction to have it; and also plus the freedom, which one is told School Boards think they do not possess, to choose a teacher with some regard to his religious tone and influence.[130]

The suggestion that Board Schools should be required to give religious instruction was opposed, not so much by secularists as by those—in some cases 'extreme Nonconformists', in others members of 'the Voluntary school party' (Roman Catholics and Anglicans)—who held that religious teaching, to have any value, *must* be doctrinally clear.[131]

The interface of education and religion continued to dominate Bryce's public life in his last cabinet role, the chief secretaryship for Ireland, which he held for just over a year from December 1905. The development of an adequate system of university education in Ireland had defied several governments from the 1830s onward: in particular, the failure of Gladstone's scheme in 1873 precipitated the fall of his first government. If Bryce's tenure of the Irish office was generally regarded as less than a success, the main reason may have been that he got enmeshed in the pursuit of a university reorganization modelled on the 1873 scheme: one based on the conversion of the University of Dublin (hitherto coterminous with its sole college, Trinity) into a single national university—a teaching university, not just an examining one—and the creation of a new college in Dublin which, while formally nondenominational in character, would in practice be predominantly Catholic. Trinity's opposition made this scheme unattainable, and when Bryce left for Washington, his successor, Augustine Birrell, unceremoniously consigned it to the bin and replaced it with an alternative plan that left Trinity untouched.[132] But the episode tells us a good deal about Bryce. It reveals the importance he attached to the university question as a matter of public policy: he looked forward to the creation in Ireland of a university that, on the model of the Scottish universities, engaged the interest and allegiance of the bulk of the population (Catholic as well as Protestant) and educated a substantial proportion of the elementary schoolteachers. But it was also important that the constituent colleges should not be narrowly denominational: a university education 'ought to be free and not controlled nor hampered by any external authority, civil or ecclesiastical; it ought not to be such as to narrow the mind; it ought to be given in common to men of different classes and different creeds in order that it might unite instead of dividing; and it should dispel instead of fostering prejudice and misconceptions.'[133] Birrell, though a nonconformist by background, was an acknowledged agnostic who was less hampered by the pursuit of high principle and avoided the unwinnable war with Trinity College.

Educational questions of this kind were certainly capable of arousing Bryce's ancestral religious identity, precisely because they bore on the relationship between state and church. But he was not at ease in sectarian denominational politics and was well-connected with liberal-minded clerics across denominational boundaries.[134] His religious enthusiasms increasingly focused on the prospects of interdenominational cooperation, and indeed the cause of Christian Reunion, in the loosest sense. One early anticipation of that movement in Britain was the so-called Christian Conference, set up in 1881 by the future dean of Ripon, W. H. Fremantle, who at that time was rector of St Mary's, Bryanston Square (Bryce was then living nearby, in Norfolk Square). The aim was to hold biannual meetings to 'promote mutual knowledge and sympathy between men of various denominations', with the goal of 'making the life of English people generally more Christian'. Members of the conference included a number of Bryce's close friends: his teacher and mentor Dean Stanley, Stopford Brooke, and Canon Samuel Barnett.[135] Barnett, previously Fremantle's curate, was now vicar of St Jude's Whitechapel and the founder of Toynbee Hall, both of them located in Bryce's Tower Hamlets constituency. Bryce was called on to chair meetings from time to time: notably the first open conference, held at Sion College in June 1896. He chaired the morning session, on 'The Progress of the Movement Towards Union Among Christians': the speakers were the Revd Hugh Price Hughes, president of the Free Church Congress; Lord Radstock; and the Revd Dr Brooke Herford. In his address Bryce pointed out that work among the poor at home and missionary work abroad offered fields for interdenominational cooperation without any need for 'union of organizations'.[136] That was a characteristic theme in Bryce's pronouncements on this subject: 'Unity will not be won by Uniform running all minds into one mould', he wrote in some notes for another speech on the Unity of Christendom: The achievement of unity was less important than finding arenas for interdenominational cooperation, where the *desire* for unity could find practical expression.[137] As we shall see, the commitment to working for practical Christian unity, especially in missionary work, was a particularly important theme in Bryce's public addresses during his ambassadorship in Washington.

We can reconstruct something of the texture of Bryce's faith from his friendships and, equally, from what he wrote of those he admired. That is not to conflate his opinions with theirs: it is, however, to suggest that we can learn much from the qualities that he invoked as admirable in others. In 1911 he wrote to his doctor and good friend Sir Thomas Barlow of the death of the Congregationalist divine, Dr John Paton, a Scotsman of a religious heritage not unlike Bryce's, though they did not know each other well. For Bryce 'his goodness, his simplicity genuineness, loving spirit & earnestness impressed me so much that I had formed a great admiration for him'. He added, importantly: 'What you say as to the comparative rarity now of the old type of a Liberal who was a Liberal because he so read his Christianity is true, and sometimes depresses me.'[138] Bryce saw himself as such a Liberal.

The same letter mentioned the Liberal MP John Edward Ellis, also recently deceased, as an instance of a similar kind of Christian in (Liberal) politics. Ellis was a Quaker, and in his preface to a life of Ellis published in 1914, Bryce wrote of some of the distinctive qualities of the Quaker in public life.[139] This was a type exemplified, he thought, by Ellis among parliamentarians and by Bryce's friend Robert Spence Watson outside Parliament: 'Among the notable features of that type was an unswerving loyalty to duty. Duty presented itself in the form of a body of certain definite principles of absolute obligation. The principles were definite and absolute because they were not taken from the concrete nor based upon the general practice of mankind, but were directly drawn from the Divine law as laid down in Scripture.' These principles included the doctrine of human equality. Quakers were not levellers, but they 'were no

respecters of persons'. They treated all human beings alike, 'without distinctions of race or rank or colour'. Hence they were among the first to denounce
Black slavery, and later 'they took up the cause of those backward races which
had come under the power of Britain and were always ready to work for their
protection against injustice'. Likewise they drew from the New Testament their
opposition to war: for some Quakers, this was construed in absolute terms,
and nonresistance regarded as a duty; whereas others, like John Bright, equally
clear in their antimilitarism, strongly endorsed the cause of the North in the
American Civil War, regarding this as an instance of a war 'waged for high aims
vital to human progress'.[140]

These were qualities he thought Ellis exemplified to the full. Like Bright,
'he applied to all questions a moral standard, conceiving the standard to be
the same for peoples and for individuals'. He held that military aggression and
cruelty toward subject peoples could not be justified by British interests, and
that 'the same justice was due to the weak as to the strong, to the backward
and coloured races as to white men'. The terminology is Bryce's rather than
Ellis's: it obviously reveals an acceptance of the existence of a racial hierarchy,
in the sense that some races were conceived as further up the ladder of civilization than others; equally, it expresses a rejection of the idea that civilizational
differences implied differences of moral worth.[141] But the central point for
now is that Bryce applauded in Ellis and his fellow Quakers the belief that
moral principles grounded in the divine law were as imperative for nations as
for individuals, in public life as in private life.

Bryce had many friends in many walks of life, but a number of his closest
friends were divines of various denominations, starting with A. P. Stanley, who
as Regius Professor of Ecclesiastical History had been a notable influence on
Bryce as an Oxford undergraduate.[142] Most of them were characterized by a
mixture of theological liberalism and moral austerity: especially a moral austerity that bore fruit in public duty rather than in merely private virtue. Perhaps the closest of these friends was the Free Church minister, Orientalist, and
Old Testament scholar William Robertson Smith, who was at the centre of a
notorious ecclesiastical controversy in the 1870s, when he was arraigned on
charges of heresy before the Free Church General Assembly and eventually
driven from his chair at the Free Church College of Divinity at Aberdeen.
There was much to draw Bryce and Robertson Smith together, not least shared
polymathic tastes: Robertson Smith was editor-in-chief of the ninth edition
of the *Encyclopaedia Britannica*.[143] But what Bryce admired in him above all
was the single-minded commitment to truth as disclosed by free inquiry, a

commitment maintained even in opposition to his own career interest.[144] He was 'one of the most remarkable men of his time'.[145]

Another long-standing friend was Stopford Brooke, and in him too Bryce admired the honest searcher after truth, the personification of free inquiry in matters of religion. Brooke was an Anglican priest in the tradition of F. D. Maurice and was a famously brilliant preacher in the 1860s and 1870s, based for the most part in proprietary chapels. His sermons were much admired by Queen Victoria, who wanted to make him Canon of Westminster. But in 1880 he broke with the Church of England and gravitated towards Unitarianism, and his religious stance bore more than a trace of pantheism. There was much that Bryce found attractive in Brooke: certainly the charm of his conversation, and certainly too his diverse passions that included nature and poetry, for Brooke wrote prolifically on poetry, and not least on the English Romantic poets. He also had a commitment to social reform at home and humanitarianism abroad. Brooke's learned and original sermons free of fixed dogma certainly appealed. That is not so say that they were at one on questions of religion and morality. When Bryce gave some lectures at Berkeley on New Testament ethics, Brooke asked if he had kept the text, for he would like to read them: 'though it was not ethics that Christ preached', he added; a point at which Bryce would surely have demurred.[146]

Among the Anglican hierarchy, Bryce had a number of close friends, including Archbishop Randall Davidson, a Trinity man and a Scotsman of Presbyterian heritage.[147] But the closest of these prelatical friends may well have been Hensley Henson, vicar of St Margaret's, Westminster, dean of Durham, and bishop successively of Hereford and Durham.[148] Temperamentally the judicious Bryce was very different from Henson, a pugnacious controversialist. But they shared a historical-mindedness as well as, in Henson's maturity, a commitment to Christian unity and a belief in the priority of the moral teachings of the Gospel. Henson most fully developed the latter point in his Gifford lectures on *Christian Morality*, given many years after Bryce's death but citing him a number of times. In those lectures Henson argued, in the tradition of Bishop Butler, for Christian morality as an articulation of a kind of natural religion: 'The morality which Christ's religion properly requires is precisely that which the conscience and reason of modernly [*sic*] civilized men approve.'[149]

Bryce was increasingly committed to a nondenominational Christian unity founded on a shared heritage of biblical teaching and Christian morality, and he was convinced that that morality was binding as much in public life as in private. At the core of Christian morality stood the principle of the moral equality of all human beings as children of one Creator. What he did not derive from that principle was a belief in equality of *political rights*. He opposed women's suffrage, even though he was keenly committed to girls' and women's education as a logical inference from the Christian principle of human equality. Race was another area in which the moral equality of human beings came into conflict with the old republican belief in citizenship conceived less as a set of rights than as a bundle of duties tied to the possession of capacity. This was such a central problem in Bryce's politics and writing in the 1890s and beyond that it needs a chapter to itself.

9

Race Relations

Advanced and Backward Races

On 7 June 1902, Bryce delivered the Romanes lecture in the Sheldonian Theatre at Oxford. The series, which rapidly established itself as Oxford's flagship
annual public lecture, had been endowed in 1891 by the evolutionary biologist
George Romanes, who stipulated that the selection of lectures should be
'determined with reference either (a) to general eminence in art, literature or
science, or (b) to special claims for discussing any particular subject of high
interest at the time'.[1] The first lecturer was Gladstone, shortly after he became
prime minister for the fourth and last time. He presented 'An Academic
Sketch', a grand survey of the relations between religion and learning since
the fall of Rome; a subject that (we may speculate) few of his successors as
prime minister would have handled with any adroitness. Speakers in the in-
tervening decade had included T. H. Huxley, whose 'Evolution and Ethics'
possibly ranks as the most influential of all the Romanes lectures; Holman
Hunt, who reflected optimistically on 'The Obligations of Universities
Towards Art'; and Mandell Creighton, bishop of Peterborough, on 'The
English National Character'. The year before Bryce spoke, illness had prevented Lord Acton from delivering his planned lecture on 'The German
School of History', although many of his notes survive, which it has to be said
rather epitomizes Acton's intellectual career. The list of later lectures provides
a checklist of the British (and, occasionally, overseas) intellectual establishment. The first woman to speak was Violet Bonham Carter as late as 1963: She
spoke on 'The Impact of Personality in Politics', a subject that would no
doubt have resonated with her father, H. H. Asquith, when he gave the lecture in 1918. The first nonwhite lecturer was the economist Amartya Sen on
'Reason and Identity' in 1998.

The Romanes lecture would always attract a large attendance, but the Sheldonian was more than usually crowded for Bryce's lecture; and an American correspondent noted a significant number of Americans, including professors and college presidents, which was no doubt a tribute to Bryce's standing in the United States even some years before he became ambassador.[2] He chose to speak on 'The Relations of the Advanced and the Backward Races of Mankind'. This was a question that had obvious contemporary relevance in 1902, and as we shall see, Bryce had 'special claims' to speak on it, quite apart from the 'general eminence' he certainly commanded in literature and science. 'Nothing he [Bryce] has written or spoken is, whether one agrees with his views or not, likely to produce so much effect as the address delivered at Oxford on the 7th of June.' So wrote Dicey in a rather dissentient review in *The Nation*. The lecture 'raises in a clear form the most perplexing question of the time'.[3] That question was how the vastly increased scale of contact between different races could be managed so as to avert race conflict. For Bryce one of the most striking achievements of the nineteenth century had been the exploration of the globe, so much so that whereas knowledge of the physical sciences could be expected to go on increasing, 'the exploration of this earth is now all but finished'. At the same time, conquest and/or settlement meant that the great majority of the 'backward' races had been subjected, economically or politically, by 'advanced' races. Bryce set out to analyse 'the phenomena that attend the contact of the civilized and uncivilized races, whether by way of conquest, or of trade, or of settlement on the same ground'.[4]

Bryce considered the various ways in which contact between races of very different strengths could be resolved. The weaker race could be erased, or absorbed, or the two could intermarry and thus be effectively fused into a new and different race, or the two could live alongside each other without interbreeding. He thought that the first two were more likely to occur where the two races were very far apart in strength, whereas the challenges in the future would tend to concern races more closely matched in strength, so that 'neither yields to and sinks beneath the other'. When two such races come into contact, there are two possible outcomes, Bryce suggested: mixture by intermarriage, or remaining separate, in which case they will necessarily influence each other but will not mingle their blood.[5]

Bryce was in no illusion about racial purity. He noted that the 'commingling' of races was a very common phenomenon that had produced 'all the great peoples of the world'. In France, Gauls, Iberians, and Teutons had been blended into one nation; in Germany, Teutons, Slavs, and Celts; in Russia,

Slavs, Finns, and Turks or Mongols. Likewise in India and in Eastern Asia. But he also noted cases where intermarriage did not occur. Why did it not? 'Nothing really arrests intermarriage except physical repulsion, and physical repulsion exists only where there is a marked difference in physical aspect, and especially in colour. Roughly speaking . . . we may say that while all the races of the same, or a similar, colour intermarry freely, those of one colour intermarry very little with those of another.'[6] This repulsion was, he thought, 'most marked as between the white and the black races'; and, specifically, it was strongest among whites of Teutonic origin, such as the English.

This trope was so common in Bryce's writings that we have to ask where it came from.[7] Was he normalizing a repulsion that he himself felt? Was it the result of travel, his observations being (of course) heavily mediated by informants and interlocutors who were numerous but not randomly chosen? It seems likely, in fact, to have come from some of his mentors: Goldwin Smith in particular. Smith wrote to Charles Eliot Norton in April 1865: 'The negro question will, I fear, be a great difficulty. You cannot have a pariah caste without fatally derogating from the essential principles of your Republic. On the other hand from the difference of color and the physical repugnance, amalgamation seems unlikely.'[8] Later in the year Smith told Norton that he thought there could be no real political equality without social fusion, and the latter could not occur in the face of 'the difference of color and the physical antipathy'. He looked to 'Negro emigration on a large scale' as the answer.[9] We have already seen that Smith was important in reinforcing Bryce's republican values. He believed, as Bryce did too, that a republican political order rested on the foundation of a certain cultural homogeneity; and without intermarriage, racial difference posed a potentially fatal barrier to a self-governing community.

Bryce thought that in general fusion by intermarriage was desirable, since it eroded racial differences and the possibility of racial conflict. As a rule he thought that this was the route to peace and moral and social progress. But what of those instances where physical repulsion was such that intermarriage was unlikely to occur to a sufficient extent? He was thinking, certainly, of the United States, but also of South Africa, which was much in his mind and the minds of his audience: he was speaking just a week after the end of the Second South African War (Boer War). In cases such as these, racial antagonisms would be sure to appear, except where (as in Algeria) the races were geographically separate, the one largely rural and the other largely urban. But elsewhere antagonism was hard to avoid:

It arises from Inequality, because as one of the races is stronger in intelligence and will, its average members treat members of the weaker race scornfully or roughly, when they can do so with impunity. It arises from Dissimilarity of character, because neither race understands the other's way of thinking and feeling, so that each gives offence even without meaning it. It arises from Distrust, because the sense of not comprehending one another makes each suspect the other of faithlessness or guile.[10]

These causes of antagonism were exacerbated by political causes, more serious the more democratic the political order. If the 'inferior' race were excluded from an otherwise democratic suffrage, they would be susceptible to oppression and would be likely to resent the contrast between equality of civil and human rights and inequality of political rights. If they were included on equal terms, the likelihood would be that parties would organize on racial lines and two nations would crystallize, so making the country ungovernable. Bryce reiterated his belief that it had been a mistake to enfranchise all the Black men in the postbellum American South: it would have been better 'to postpone the bestowal of this dangerous boon.'[11] This was, he thought, 'the general opinion of dispassionate men'; men who, as it happened, tended to be white. He recognized, however, that there was no easy course, for 'rocks and shoals were set thick round every course.'[12]

If blending of the races by intermarriage was highly unlikely in these cases, was separation a solution? Bryce took this notion seriously, with the result that his argument is sometimes depicted as an apology for apartheid *avant la lettre*, or at least for the kind of racial policies pursued by Jan Smuts in interwar South Africa.[13] Dicey, in the review already cited, took this to be the cornerstone of 'Mr Bryce's policy'. He challenged it in a very Diceyesque way. Separation would stereotype the divisions and make them rigid. Bryce's suffrage proposals were 'in themselves wise', but Dicey warned that 'constitutional devices which are ingenious and beneficial are, after all, merely devices for tiding over a period of transition'. In practice, Dicey argued, social separation would tend to undermine the security of civil equality; and, finally, 'a system of caste, whatever its merits, is inconsistent with the democratic spirit'.[14] This was an argument that echoed the case made by Dicey in *Essays on Reform*, where he maintained that the proponents of a suffrage designed to ensure the 'balance of classes' were effectively introducing the representation of orders.[15]

These were cogent arguments on Dicey's part, but it may still be doubted whether they accurately represented the case made in the Romanes lecture.

Did that lecture really set out a 'policy' of separation of the races? Did that policy really urge the discouragement, if not the outright prohibition, of inter-marriage between Whites and Blacks?[16] Bryce certainly maintained that the data—he admitted that they were imperfect, but did not say which data he had in mind—suggested that the mixture of very dissimilar races (such as White Europeans with Blacks) tended to diminish rather than improve the racial 'stock' of the more advanced race. He was also arguing against a policy of pro-moting miscegenation, but then his starting point was that physical repulsion meant that miscegenation was not likely to happen. He did not believe in the power of law to effect a change in moral attitudes such that two races which did not intermarry could nevertheless live together harmoniously. In the text he simply noted that 'the wisest men among the coloured people of the South-ern States of America' did not desire intermarriage with the Whites, but pre-ferred that the Black race should develop 'as a separate people, on its own lines'. He declined to elaborate on what that might mean in practice.[17] We might speculate who these 'wisest men' were. Were they, in fact, Booker T. Washing-ton, the ex-slave who was a vocal and active proponent of professional and practical education as the sure route to social advancement for the Black com-munity of America? And if so, was Washington really telling Bryce what Bryce wanted to hear, not what Washington wanted to say?[18]

In the United States, the lecture was not widely reviewed or reported on, except in *The Nation*, which carried a full report by the American classicist and Oxford resident Louis Dyer, as well as Dicey's comment.[19] Its literary editor, Wendell Phillips Garrison—a friend and regular correspondent of Bryce's—disapproved: 'I fear you will comfort both our Imperialists & our lynchers, for the latter have caste for their stronghold, and it seems to me you justify caste.'[20] This letter has been frequently quoted.[21] What is not usually acknowledged is that Garrison had not in fact read the lecture at this time, and he was presum-ably therefore dependent on Dyer's report and the first part of Dicey's com-ment (he had not yet received the rest); as well as on the impressions he had formed from the third edition of *The American Commonwealth*.[22] Dyer's report made no mention of statutory restrictions on marriage at all. It must, therefore, have been Dicey's comment that shaped Garrison's understanding of Bryce's argument. On this basis he certainly took Bryce to be an advocate of statutory restrictions on intermarriage:

Frederic Bancroft of Washington, one of our younger historical writers, author of a Life of Seward, lately made a study of ante-bellum conditions in the South, in a visit to the spot. I suggested to him that he ascertain, if he could, how far the penalties for intermarriage had availed to check illicit intercourse between the two races. He did not reach a very positive conclusion, but thought he saw that amalgamation was still going on, in opposition to the efforts working to raise the chastity of the blacks. There can be no law in India against Eur-Asian commingling, and why should you look with sympathy on such statutes here? Why not leave the whole thing to nature? I know what the Southern whites will reply, but what should you & I hold on that subject?[23]

It would be fascinating to have Bryce's response, but alas it has apparently not survived. We can, however, be sure that Bryce did reply, and Garrison's next letter enables us to make a tentative reconstruction of the nature of that reply. Having said that he had not yet read the lecture, Garrison continued:

Having never conversed with Booker Washington on the Southern situation generally, I do not know his attitude towards what used to be called 'miscegenation'. I can well believe that he is no advocate of a striving on the part of the blacks to inter-marry with the whites; but that he should object to a natural legal sexual commingling, I cannot conceive; much less that he should praise the existing legislation which makes such union a penal offence, for this is based on the old slavery idea of the sub-human character of the negro. I understand his general policy to be to put all other considerations to one side—questions of suffrage, of co-education, of hotel and railroad treatment, &c—in favour of a determined effort to build up the freedmen by education into beings who must command the respect of the whites, & shame them by comparison with the most degraded of their own color. This is wise, and it can be accomplished only by his keeping his mouth shut about his inner convictions on the general subject of 'liberty, equality & fraternity'.[24]

Bryce had evidently invoked Booker Washington in support of his position on racial intermarriage; and he equally evidently had not sought to correct Garrison's impression that the Romanes lecture had defended statutory regulation, or at least acquiesced in it.[25]

At the very least we can say that the reception of the lecture indicates some ambiguity in what Bryce was saying about the statutory regulation of intermarriage. That in itself deserves comment. From the time that he started to interest himself seriously in racial questions, which (as we shall see) was during his visit to India in 1888–1889, Bryce consistently maintained that the blending of different races through intermarriage was intrinsically a good thing, since it softened racial differences and potential racial antagonisms and thus offered a path to peaceful social relations. Race relations came to be a problem only in those instances where two races cohabiting in the same territory were resistant to intermarriage. This tended to happen where there was physical repulsion on at least one side, and he thought that was generally the result of a stark difference of skin colour; though he also recognized that some European races (the Teutonic, in particular) were more susceptible to this kind of physical repulsion than were others (southern Europeans, notably). Even if this kind of physical repulsion was not quite a fact of nature, he did regard it as a kind of social fact which politicians and political thinkers had to work with. But fundamentally it was also a problem: indeed, *the* problem without which 'race relations' as a subject of investigation need hardly exist. Yet here in the Romanes lecture there is a suggestion of a very different perspective: miscegenation might threaten the quality of the racial stock. He recognized that the data on this subject were scanty, as well he might; but if this spectre of racial decline were well-founded, he implied, the physical repulsion that Teutonic European Whites felt for Blacks could be regarded as socially functional.[26]

In grappling with the question of where the Romanes lecture sits in Bryce's intellectual and political trajectory, we need to locate it in its precise context. We have already noticed that the lecture was given in the (very) immediate aftermath of the Boer War. Bryce was deeply engaged in the politics of that war, as a leading pro-Boer and one who had written an important book on South Africa just two years before the war's outbreak.[27] The British imperial army's long struggle to overcome the forces of the two small Boer Republics (the Transvaal and the Orange Free State) gave rise to a moral panic at home about the 'physical deterioration of the race' manifested in the poor physical quality of army recruits, which was supposed to have been caused by the living conditions of the urban poor in industrial Britain. This panic led to the appointment, a year after Bryce gave the Romanes lecture, of the Inter-Departmental Committee on Physical Deterioration, under the chairmanship of Sir Almeric Fitzroy, clerk of the Privy Council. Fitzroy's committee came to the conclusion that there was no evidence for the notion of racial degeneration. Thereafter the moral panic subsided. Bryce was not directly engaged with questions about physical deterioration, but in confronting questions of the impact of intermarriage on the racial stock he was handling ideas that were very much part of the currency of public argument in the

Edwardian period. The notion of a 'stock' was derived from nineteenth-century linguistics, but the concept of a 'racial stock' really took off right at the beginning of the twentieth century, before peaking (not altogether surprisingly) around 1937–1941.[28] So in the Romanes lecture he was invoking a newly fashionable idea.

Another aspect of Bryce's response to the politics of the Boer War is relevant here. He was appalled at the way in which public opinion was suborned by a combination of demagogic politics (Chamberlain), the press barons, and crude jingoism. The Khaki election of 1900 in particular made him despair of the future of democracy, and it was in this context that he conceived the idea for what became, many years later, *Modern Democracies*. Jingoistic imperialism seemed to be in the ascendant in the United States, too, in the era of McKinley (1897–1901). Bryce thought that the vices of demagoguery and jingoism were most likely to be resisted by an electorate that was, in large majority, politically interested and engaged. As we shall see, he certainly thought that the enfranchisement of politically disengaged groups—Blacks in the United States, women (potentially) everywhere—made the electorate more susceptible to corruption and degradation.

Contrary to what has sometimes been implied, Bryce was not much upbraided by his contemporaries, apart from Dicey and Garrison, for the line of argument he advanced in the Romanes lecture, disturbing as it looks in retrospect.[29] An important exception to this was the Jamaican-born British medical practitioner and forerunner of Pan-Africanism, Theophilus Scholes, who in 1908 denounced Bryce for the casual way in which he assumed the existence of 'superior' and 'inferior' races. Scholes quoted at length the passage in the Romanes lecture in which Bryce discussed the 'data' on the effect of intermarriage on the average quality of the racial 'stock'. Bryce, he thought, had 'arrived at conclusions that are unfavourable to intermarriages between the black and white races'. This was significant because Bryce was a man of importance, 'a philosophical historian and an eminent statesman', someone whose opinions would certainly attract attention in the United States, where the 'race question' was 'the question of all questions'. Yet these opinions were formed on the basis of data that, on Bryce's own admission, were 'imperfect'. This was dangerous: the race question was of such importance that 'where there are no reliable data available, such a subject enjoins the observance of silence until reliable data should be procured'. Bryce may indeed have drawn his conclusions tentatively, but they were propositions that tended to confirm the bias of the average reader, who would therefore tend to skim over the qualifications and alight on the conclusions themselves. The 'great weight' of his authority would thus serve to 'support and stimulate the excesses of an irrational, an ungoverned, and an ignoble prejudice'.[30]

Bryce was far from alone in being picked out as a target by Scholes: John Morley was another, discussed with Bryce as a pair. Indeed, Scholes's target was what he saw as a wider hardening of racial attitudes that had been going on in Britain since the 1880s: He also cited the *Spectator*'s protest against Theodore Roosevelt's entertaining of Booker Washington in the White House. But if Scholes was right to criticize Bryce for the casual way in which he gave credence to the racial prejudice of American whites, Scholes's own explanation was perhaps all too casual in itself. He argued that cosying up to the racial prejudices of the white 'Anglo-Saxon' population of the United States, the British Establishment was influenced by its pursuit of a policy of Anglo-American friendship. That meant sacrificing the weaker of the two sections of the American population. How that squared with the British press's attack on President Roosevelt for being too close to a (very moderate) Black leader is not at all clear.[31] Moreover, as it happens, the period when Bryce was most active in nurturing Anglo-American rapprochement—from 1907 to 1917, the period stretching from his appointment as ambassador to American entry into the First World War—was also the period when his views on racial questions softened markedly, so that (as we shall see) he ended his career as a trenchant critic of racial speculations and racial explanations.

How Did Bryce Discover the 'Race Problem'?

Race relations were not at all prominent, however, in the first edition of *The American Commonwealth*.[32] It was in the 1894 edition that Bryce included the chapters on 'The South since the War' and 'The Present and Future of the Negro'. In the preface he wrote that these additional chapters 'belonged to the original plan of the book, but . . . it was found impossible to insert [them] in the first edition'. Even if this is indeed true—and the evidence in fact suggests the contrary—it is nevertheless worth asking why Bryce seems to have attached so much more importance to the race problem in 1894 than in 1888. What was the significance of his visit to India, between October 1888 and February 1889? In the interval between the first and third editions of the *American Commonwealth*, he had also made a further visit to the United States, this time in Marion's company, in the late summer and early autumn of 1890. During that trip he wrote a long and intriguing letter to his mother from

Richmond, Virginia, in which he discussed 'the "Race Problem", as they call it'. He considered this

> a dismal legacy of slavery, because there is not the slightest prospect of any amalgamation of the races, yet the negro is a good sort of creature, less intoxicated by liberty & equality than anyone would have foretold. He works pretty fairly, does not drink very badly, nor do they quarrel among themselves. Insanity has begun to increase rapidly among them & there is a good deal of petty theft. The southerners say that all would be well if he had not a vote, because designing politicians seek to use him. But if he had no vote, he might perhaps be illtreated: for the whites would have no motive for conciliating him. The best solution would probably be to enfranchise only the better educated better-off negroes: but the objection is that an educational test would exclude many whites also. The whole position is so full of interest that one would like to spend 6 months investigating it in various Southern States. It is complicated with Federal politics, because the Republicans are trying to make the Federal Government interfere to protect the negro in his voting. On the whole while my judgment on the moral & social condition of the country remains substantially the same, I find the politics slightly worse than I have described them in the book—especially as regards electoral corruption—& half fear that the shadows ought in another edition to be deepened.[33]

This sets out several of Bryce's enduring convictions about the race question in the South. First, there was no prospect of intermarriage on anything like the scale needed for 'amalgamation' of the races to occur. Second, mass enfranchisement of the southern Blacks in the wake of emancipation had probably been a mistake, but one that was understandable, and could not easily now be remedied, because a race-based franchise was unthinkable, and it was equally difficult to retreat from universal manhood suffrage for Whites. Third, there was a recognition that the enfranchisement of the Blacks was an effective safeguard at least against the grossest forms of oppression. The letter also suggests that Bryce had arrived at a level of insight into the race question that he had not previously attained, which was why he was now reporting on it to his mother and telling her how useful it would be to be able to spend six months studying the race problems of the South.

It was indeed in the immediate aftermath of that visit to the United States in August–October 1890 that Bryce began—for the first time—to start addressing the question of race, both in the American context and in a broader historical-geographical context. This is something that is obscured in the literature: Lake and Reynolds, for instance, suggest, quite mistakenly, that Bryce had been building up a file of notes on 'The negro problem' since 1885, whereas it is demonstrable that his substantial notes on the question date from 1891–1892 or thereabouts.[34] He published his 'Thoughts on the Negro Problem' in the *North American Review* in December 1891 and next turned his attention to 'The Migrations of the Races of Men' in the *Contemporary Review* and the *Scottish Geographical Magazine* in July and August 1892. There followed the new edition of *The American Commonwealth* in 1894 and *Impressions of South Africa* in 1897, the outcome of a visit in the later months of 1895. Viewed thus, we can see the Romanes lecture as the fruit of a growing fascination—even obsession—with the race question in the 1890s, an obsession that receded somewhat thereafter.

India

If the fourth visit to the United States was important in triggering Bryce's fascination with race relations, the ground was prepared by his visit to India in the winter of 1888–1889, just as *The American Commonwealth* went to press. This is a point of some importance: his racial anxieties were instigated by travel—to India, to the American South, to South Africa—and only later pacified by travel to South America and further visits to the American South.[35] The significance of the Indian visit can be explored with the aid of Bryce's very substantial correspondence from the subcontinent: in particular, his letters to his mother and his sisters. Race is not, in fact, a central preoccupation in that correspondence, whereas a world-historical perspective certainly is. As he wrote to his mother from the Gulf of Suez, on the outward journey:

> The Canal also marked the beginning of the new part of the journey to me—as I had never before been S[outh] of Ismailia—and the departure from the world of Greek Civilization and the Roman Empire. I have oddly enough formed the habit of always asking whether one is inside or outside of the Roman Empire. One doesn't think of asking this when voyaging to America, because one starts from Britain, which was so little Romanized, and because the ancients knew of nothing at all beyond the Atlantic. But in passing from the world of Greek letters and Roman arms and laws in the Mediterranean into those undiscovered and mysterious regions in which they placed all sorts of wonders, natural & human from the time of Homer & Herodotus down to those of Procop, one feels the transition directly.[36]

When he reached India, the comparisons with the Roman Empire recurred. The Bengali people—especially the Hindus—were, he thought, 'quicker, more apt & willing to learn, and altogether more plausible than the men of Upper India, much like the Greeks under the Roman Empire.'[37] The houses occupied by Anglo-Indians were 'large, cool, airy, each in a large plot of ground, often with lawn tennis', and had 'multitudes of servants, just like slaves in ancient Rome'. 'One would soon get lazy & demoralized. I wonder our men retain so much energy.'[38] On his return, he summed up his visit in a letter to Sidgwick: 'India infinitely more instructive historically than I had expected: it explains many ancient & mediaeval matters.'[39]

On the question of race relations, the most interesting letter was one he wrote to his mother from the Hooghly River on 30 November (and completed in Madras on 5 December). He regretted the low quality of the Indian Civil Service: they were hard-working and motivated by a desire to promote the welfare of the Indian people, but 'rather wanting in imagination and sympathy, less inspired by the extraordinary and unprecedented phenomena of the country than might have been expected'. He went on: 'Since the unhappy so-called Ilbert Bill there has been a marked change in the attitude of Europeans to natives, especially in Bengal; and the natives complain bitterly that the civilians as well as the military & the planters, treat them with arrogance & make them feel their social inferiority as well as political subordination.'[40] He continued by saying that all he had seen made him certain that he had made the right decision in not pursuing a career in the Indian Civil Service.[41] An I.C.S. career would certainly have made him better off 'in a worldly point of view': by now he could have earned a pension of £1,000 a year and saved £20,000 or so. 'And on the whole, intensely interesting as the work of governing India would be, and still more the opportunity of studying India, I do not regret not having taken—even apart altogether from the reason wh. was then decisive, and from the mortifications I would have had over what wd have been the Bryce Bill—the post which Hartington offered in 1881.' When he met, by invitation, 'twenty leading natives' in Calcutta and had a long conversation with them, he noted that they complained not only of the expense of the government and their lack of influence on it, but also of 'the hauteur with which Anglo Indians treat them'. This, he thought, was 'the real difficulty'. He rather sympathized with the views of two young Oxford-educated High Church missionaries who deplored Anglo-Indian attitudes and saw these, rather than the unrest of the indigenous population, as the root of the problem. Interestingly, Bryce thought British rule in India firmly established, in spite of the evidence of racial tensions he found: 'One doesn't see why, if frontier wars can be averted with Russia and France, we should not reign for another century.'[42]

A year after Bryce's return from India, one of the Myers brothers—probably the poet Ernest Myers—told Marion that Bryce was 'peculiarly fitted to criticise and set forth the political & social systems of other countries' and urged him to write something on India comparable to *The American Commonwealth*.[43] This would indeed have been a fascinating undertaking, but in fact Bryce limited himself to an essay comparing the Roman Empire with the British Empire in India, and a parallel one comparing the diffusion of English law throughout the world with the diffusion of Roman law.[44] The first of these texts, however, is important for understanding the evolution of Bryce's thinking about race.

The essay does present a difficulty, in that we do not know when it was first composed. It was first published in 1901 and republished with only superficial changes in 1914. But it is uncertain whether Bryce composed it for the first time when preparing it for publication in *Studies in History and Jurisprudence*. In the preface to *Studies* he notes that some of the essays published in those volumes originated as public lectures during his tenure of the Regius Professorship at Oxford, which he relinquished in 1893.[45] In some cases he indicates in footnotes which essays were first delivered in this form, but we can also be certain that many of the other essays had also been delivered first as Oxford lectures: the piece on 'Primitive Iceland' was given as a lecture in May 1873, that on 'The Nature of Sovereignty' in May 1891, that on 'The Law of Nature' in April 1892, and that on 'Obedience' in November 1892.[46] Hence, from the fact that Bryce's footnotes do not indicate the prior form of the piece on Rome and British rule in India, we cannot infer that it was not delivered as a lecture. We do, in fact, have in Bryce's hand the text of a lecture on 'Roman Administration and Law Illustrated from [the] British Empire in India'.[47] This is not close enough to 'The Roman Empire and the British Empire in India' to be regarded as the basis of the latter, but it covers much of the same ground. Since Bryce relinquished his Oxford chair four years or so after his return from India, the most likely scenario is that this lecture was given in Oxford in the aftermath of that visit. There is no indication that he returned to this manuscript text when preparing the essay, and it therefore seems likely that the latter was written specially for *Studies in History and Jurisprudence*, but that it drew on a comparison that Bryce had been thinking about ever since 1888.

If that supposition is right, what implications does it have for a narrative of how and when Bryce's racial preoccupations took shape?

Already in the lecture, Bryce identified the racial question as something that marked out the British Empire in India as different from Roman imperial rule. The provincial subjects of the Roman Empire—Gauls and Greeks and so forth—belonged to ethnological groups not very remote from those of their conquerors from central Italy. And even the inhabitants of Spain, Pannonia, Syria, and Armenia 'were not so marked off from the Romans that one might not be mistaken for the other: there was certainly nothing to excite any sense of remoteness or repulsion'.[48] By contrast:

> The Englishman in India is a fair skinned man among a multitude of races, differing widely among themselves but alike in being dark skinned, and so sharply marked off from himself. The only exception is the Parsi, whose white tint is but faintly suffused with yellow; while among the descendants of Arabs and of the immigrants from Central Asia and more rarely among the very high cast Brahmins we find faces which are rather brown than black. Still taken broadly the population of India is black; and this face which distinguishes the English from all the other conquerors, and especially from the Afghans and Moguls, has an immense influence in preventing assimilation and intermarriage, and in keeping up in a conspicuous and unmistakeable way, the sense of unlikeness and even of repulsion between the ruler and the subject. A member of Council in Calcutta would find it far harder to treat a native Indian preacher as an equal than a Roman Senator found it to treat St Paul; while the humbler sort of Roman could not on the score of his colour look down on wealthy provincials as the humblest Anglo-Indian now does upon rich Hindus of a lineage which reaches back to ten or fifteen centuries.[49]

Moreover, the superiority of the Romans over their subjects was essentially confined to the military sphere: the Greeks were superior in literature, art, and science', and Athens remained the 'intellectual capital of the world' long after Rome had become its political capital. Throughout the empire the Roman officer or administrator typically found himself amid a population just as intelligent and cultivated as he was familiar with at home. In India, by contrast:

> The superiority of the conquering race is not more marked in the military than it is in the pacific elements of civilization. We have learnt practically nothing from India except a taste for certain kinds of carpets . . . and the whole of modern Indian education—as well literary as scientific—is based upon Western ideas and methods; so much so that it is now chiefly by

European scholars that the ancient lore of India is treasured and sustained, and the investigation into the philo[lo]gy as well of the Dravidian and Kolarian as of the Aryan tongues prosecuted. In point of acuteness and acquisitive powers some of the Indian races or castes stand very high: but even those that stand highest are inferior in constructive gifts and in intellectual persistence to the European who has received an equivalent training.[50]

We find here the concept of racial repulsion based not on racial difference per se, but specifically on difference of skin colour; and in particular the difference between White and Black. That was a concept that was absent from the first edition of *The American Commonwealth*, which went to press just as Bryce was about to leave for India. So if this lecture was indeed given in the aftermath of his return from India, we have clear grounds for believing that the tour of India was indeed responsible for something of a transformation in Bryce's racial thinking. We also find the idea of the typical Indian skin colour as 'black': that was by no means the norm among the racial classifications prevalent in Bryce's time, although some ethnographers would have classed the Dravidian population of southern India as dark brown or black in complexion.[51] But in classifying the Indians—most of them—as 'black', Bryce tends to conflate the racial question in India with its analogue in the United States. Rhetorically that is a very striking move.

If Bryce's visit to India was pivotal in launching the intense interest in race relations that permeated his writings in the 1890s and the early years of the following decade, the timing of the visit was surely crucial. Bryce was evidently conscious of the deterioration of race relations as a result of the Ilbert Bill controversy of 1883–1884. The Ilbert Bill—drafted by Bryce's friend Courtenay Ilbert, the legal member of the Viceroy's Council—proposed to amend the provision in the Indian Criminal Procedure Act of 1861 that stipulated that, outside the three presidency towns of Madras, Bombay, and Calcutta, 'European British subjects' could not be tried by courts presided over by an Indian magistrate. Ilbert's proposal—backed by the Viceroy, Lord Ripon— was grounded in the Liberal vision of imperial rule in India as a preparation for ultimate self-government. It provoked a backlash from the Anglo-Indian community, for whom the attempt to erode separate status founded on race was a step too far. As Ilbert told Bryce, 'The opposition is really directed not against the Bill itself, which is a very small measure, but against the policy of which it is the necessary development, the policy, namely, of admitting natives to the civil service.'[52] Ripon was eventually forced to adopt a compromise proposal. But the essential point is that this was one of those key moments in the history of British rule in India—the suppression of the 'mutiny' of 1857 was obviously another—which, small though the original issue was, had an enduring and harmful impact on relations between the Anglo-Indians and the indigenous population. Its repercussions were certainly still being felt at the time of Bryce's visit, and no doubt sharpened his sense of the haughtiness of the Anglo-Indians, of whom he generally formed a negative opinion. Indeed, in his assessments of race relations in many parts of the world Bryce was more often inclined to cast the blame—if blame were due—on the whites rather than on the subject or indigenous population. That did not mean, however, that he saw the solution in perfect equality, at least for the foreseeable future. On the contrary: 'Every one admits in his heart that it is impossible to ignore the differences which make one group of races unfit for the institutions which have given energy and contentment to another more favourably placed.'[53]

The American South

Bryce's first significant analysis of the racial problems of the American South was his article 'Thoughts on the Negro Problem', published in December 1891.[54] In that piece he struck from the outset a somewhat optimistic note. The social progress made by the Black population of the American South in the quarter of a century or so since Emancipation was strikingly good. It has to be added that that judgment should be set in the context of Bryce's underlying assumption that progress was necessarily both slow and fragile, since it had to overcome the heavy weight of deep historical forces: 'History and science tell us that social and moral advancement is an extremely slow process, because it issues from a change in the physical as well as mental nature of a race.'[55] So he came to the question in the expectation that significant progress would take several generations, not one. Against that background he was heartened to find the southern Blacks displaying promising signs of the classic Victorian virtues of self-help and self-improvement:

> The best proof of progress is that fact that the negroes have begun to help themselves; that they are supporting their own churches and schools more liberally, organizing charitable societies for their own benefit, showing an increased desire for education, and profiting by it. . . . Freedom has done for them in twenty-six years more than any one who knew how slavery left them had a right to expect.[56]

But there was a stark limit to assimilation into (white) American society: social intercourse between White and Black was restricted to business relations
and domestic service, and the informal mixing of the races that occurred in
the era of slavery had been eliminated. Blacks and Whites lived largely segre-
gated lives. Most importantly, intermarriage was forbidden either by law or by
social norms.

Bryce was clear that he saw segregation as part of the problem, not part of
the solution: 'the sharp and harsh social separation which now exists is fraught
with trouble, and may become dangerous when the weaker race has grown in
intelligence and courage'.[57] His central concern in this piece, however, was not
with segregation or with intermarriage but with the suffrage question. He outlined the argument he would develop further in the two new chapters he
added to *The American Commonwealth* two years later. He was sharply critical
of the outcome of the Fifteenth Amendment, which prohibited the denial of
the right to vote on the basis of race. This was an 'extreme' application of 'the
favorite democratic dogma that the gift of a right carries with it the capacity
to exercise that right', and its effect was to enfranchise 'a mass of people not
merely ignorant, but destitute of the very rudiments of political aptitude'.
'Children of ten would have been fitter for such an experiment.' In western
Europe, among 'peoples naturally far more gifted, as their primitive literatures
prove', large sections of the population are 'scarcely fit for electoral rights'. How
much more much that be the case, he asked, for the southern Blacks in the
United States: 'It is little more than a century . . . since the negro of west Africa
came in contact with civilized man; only a quarter of a century since he was
made a legal person capable of holding even private civil rights.'[58]

Bryce coupled this statement of the doctrine of capacity with a first adum-
bration of the critique of the politics of the era of Reconstruction that would
come to be such an influential part of *The American Commonwealth*. At the
heart of his argument was the postulate that the enfranchisement of 'unfit'
voters brings corruption in its train: 'The unfitness of the negro was demonstrated on a colossal scale and with ruinous results in the reconstruction period, when his vote, manipulated by the so-called white carpet-baggers, ruled
the States that had seceded, placed unscrupulous adventurers in the highest
posts, wasted the public revenues, piled up stupendous fabrics of State debt.'
So 'dismal' was the misgovernment of the South that Bryce sympathized with
the reaction of the southern Whites, who determined that their self-
preservation required that they should ensure 'that power shall never again
pass into the hands which so misused it'.[59]

He fully accepted that there was no possibility of overturning the Fifteenth Amendment, and even if it had been possible it would not have been desirable to give legal force to discrimination on the basis of race. That would exacerbate race relations rather than improving them. It was, however, both legal and justifiable to restrict the franchise according to educational criteria, which would have a much bigger impact on the Black than the White electorate.[60]

There were three key elements to Bryce's conviction that the Black population of the American South was predominantly unfit for the franchise. One was his own observation of the condition of Blacks in the South during his visits of 1881 and 1883, and again in 1890; a second was the experience of the Black vote in the Reconstruction era. But the third was effectively an a priori doctrine that *a population* could not within a generation advance from a condition of slavery to the kind of moral and intellectual condition necessary for active citizenship. There is something puzzling about this argument. It is one thing to say that the generation of 1865—Blacks who had been brought up in slavery—were not 'fit' for the vote when they were granted it. According to the lights of the liberal doctrine of capacity, that was undoubtedly true: a condition of slavery could never be a training in citizenship. But why should we assume a priori that the same would be true of those reaching adulthood in 1891, or indeed a decade or more earlier? They had lived their whole lives in a state of freedom. Maybe Bryce meant simply that Black children had far fewer educational opportunities because they were sent to different (and worse) schools. Or perhaps he was emphasizing that only so much can be done by a school, that parents necessarily have a leading role in the education of the child, and that this is the means by which radical inequalities are transmitted through the generations. Both are possible explanations for Bryce's position, but we might have expected him, in that case, to have been more attentive to empirical evidence about the schooling and parenting of Black American children.

The other possibility is that Bryce's entrenched assumption that the legacy of slavery on the mental and moral condition of the ex-slave population would take more than a generation to overcome in fact disclosed hidden Social Lamarckian assumptions, according to which moral and intellectual habits instilled by slavery were transmitted to children and grandchildren born in freedom. At one level it is surprising to find Bryce drawing on an implicit Lamarckism. He was (unlike his father) a convinced Darwinian, and he had, moreover, a low opinion of Herbert Spencer, who was the most important propagator of Social Lamarckism in the Victorian period.[61] But the point about Social Lamarckism in the nineteenth century is that it was rarely stated theoretically: it appealed to a sort of common sense intuition that the weight of history was heavy, and it acted through the inheritance of habits and customs.

In his new chapters for the 1894 edition of *The American Commonwealth*, Bryce expanded the argument he had outlined in 'Thoughts on the Negro Problem'. In the chapter on 'The South Since the War', he wrestled with the 'peculiar and menacing problem' facing the South: 'The presence of a mass of negroes much larger than was the whole population of the Union in A.D. 1800, persons who, though they are legally and industrially members of the nation, are still virtually an alien element, unabsorbed and unabsorbable'.[62] That statement of the problem drew on the standard assumptions about the basis for self-government that he had absorbed from Goldwin Smith and, indeed, from John Stuart Mill's *Considerations on Representative Government*. It was also, of course, written from the point of view of the White majority: faced with two populations that effectively lived apart, he defined the Whites as the nation and the Blacks as the 'alien' population that was resistant to absorption. If pushed on that, he would no doubt have retorted that it was the White settlers of 'English' origin who had 'made a nation' capable of self-government.

He went on to develop his famous account of the horrors of corruption in the Reconstruction period. The enforced enfranchisement of Black men who, having been living in slavery until recently, were 'wholly unfit for citizenship', and who, owning little property, 'had no interest, as taxpayers, in good government', opened the door to wholesale corruption. The new voters were 'organized' and manipulated by 'those white adventurers whose scanty stock of portable property won for them the name of "carpet-baggers"'.[63]

Bryce was entirely frank when he said that the Black voters were not to blame. The blame lay with the Republican carpet-baggers and, of course, with the Republican federal legislators who had enfranchised the ex-slave population.[64] But, blameless or not, the Black voters were the problem, as he saw it, and the solution was either to disenfranchise them or to suppress the effective size of the Black electorate. In fact in *The American Commonwealth*, Bryce was too discreet to come before his readers as an advocate of de jure or de facto disenfranchisement. In a particularly interesting passage, he noted that Americans and Europeans had notably different perspectives on the right to vote, and that Europeans, unlike Americans, thought recently emancipated slaves obviously and hopelessly unfit to exercise the vote. That was a view that rested on the conception of the vote as a trust whose exercise should be confined to

those with the capacity to use it well. That was alien to the American perspective: 'American eyes, however, see the matter in a different light. To them it is
an axiom that without the suffrage there is no true citizenship, and the negro
would have appeared to be scarcely free had he received only the private and
passive, and not also the public and active rights of a citizen.' Some northern
states had historically had race-based exclusions from the franchise. But the
abolitionist movement and the Civil War had given 'an immense stimulus to
the abstract theory of human rights, and had made the negro so much an
object of sympathy to the Northern people, that these restrictions were vanis-
hing before the doctrine of absolute democratic equality and the rights of
man as man'.[65]

Bryce's own views on these questions were clear, not least from his parliamentary speeches on women's suffrage: he was a resolute opponent of 'the
abstract theory of human rights' as a way of determining suffrage laws. Just a
few months after he wrote 'Thoughts on the Negro Problem', he gave a lengthy
speech in the Commons opposing women's suffrage, complaining that 'we are
asked to make this great change on pure abstract theory', whereas hitherto all
franchise reforms had been introduced as practical remedies to specific defects.[66] But in *The American Commonwealth* he strove for even-handedness,
recognizing, in particular, that the existence of Black suffrage was a guarantee
that the interests of the Black population would not be neglected and a barrier
to the reintroduction of race distinctions into law.[67]

South Africa

Next to the United States, the most important setting in which Bryce wrestled
with racial conflict was South Africa, where he made an extended visit, in
Marion's company, in the autumn of 1895 that formed the basis for the book
he published two years later. His closest friend and correspondent in South
Africa was John Xavier Merriman, the Liberal and anti-imperialist parliamen-
tarian who would serve as the last prime minister of Cape Colony from 1908
to 1910. Merriman first made contact following the publication of Bryce's
'Thoughts on the Negro Problem'. Merriman, who was in London at the time,
stressed how much Cape Colony had to learn from the experience of the
American South. In particular, he was keen to learn more about options for
restricting the franchise on the basis of property or education so as to ensure
that white voters were not 'swamped' by Blacks. He tended to favour Bryce's
suggestion of an educational test.[68] A few days later—having arranged to meet

Bryce to discuss the franchise question—he warned Bryce that it was a mistake to think that the South African problem resolved itself into 'a sort of faction-fight between English and Dutch'. Rather, its essence was 'the silent struggle that is going on between black and white along the whole line'.[69]

This sounds like an anticipation of the approach to race relations in South Africa championed by Milner's 'Kindergarten' and later by Jan Smuts, prime minister from 1919 to 1924: a union of White races to maintain the subjection of the Black population.[70] But Merriman's position was more complex: he was a resolute defender of the 'Cape Qualified Franchise', which (unlike the franchise laws in the Boer republics) rejected disqualifications on the basis of race. When the Union of South Africa came into being in 1910, it was Merriman, as the outgoing prime minister of Cape Province, who negotiated an exemption which allowed it to retain the Black suffrage while introducing property- and education-based qualifications applying to Blacks and Whites alike.

Bryce was close to Merriman and was later close to Smuts, but it would be a mistake to conflate his approach to race relations with either of theirs. Relations between Blacks and Whites by no means dominated Bryce's account of South Africa. In fact, for all Merriman's warning, the 'race conflict' that Bryce highlighted, notably in the preface to the third edition in 1899, was the conflict between the Boer republics and the British colonies. He did, however, include a substantial chapter entitled 'Blacks and Whites'. This chapter drew attention to some salient facts about race relations in South Africa. The first was the numerical preponderance of Blacks over Whites, everywhere except Cape Town and the Witwatersrand; a preponderance that was tending to increase rather than to diminish. A second was that this made the British colonies of South Africa—Cape Colony and Natal—anomalous in the British Empire. As he pointed out, the general rule in British imperial government was that colonies settled by a predominantly European population were granted self-government, whereas those inhabited chiefly by a Black or 'coloured' population were governed as Crown Colonies by executive officials appointed from Whitehall. The Crown Colonies were overwhelmingly located in the tropics, while the self-governing colonies were located in the temperate zone, where white Europeans found it easier to settle. The two South African colonies were anomalous because self-government was granted because of the large European settler population, even though Blacks were in the majority. It therefore raised the question of whether it was possible to restrict the franchise, and on what basis. As Bryce wrote:

The general difficulty of adjusting the relations of a higher and a lower race, serious under every kind of government, here presents itself in the special form of the construction of a political system which, while democratic as regards one of the races, cannot safely be made democratic as regards the other. This difficulty, though new in the British empire, is not new in the Southern States of America, which have been struggling with it for years; and it is instructive to compare the experience of South Africa with that through which the Southern States have passed since the War of Secession.[71]

He noted that no 'colour line' was drawn when representative government was established in Cape Colony in 1853, and it was only in 1892 that the franchise was restricted on the basis of a combination of educational and property-based qualifications.[72]

Third, Bryce highlighted the fact—'the capital feature of South African life'—that all unskilled work was done by Black people. The climate was not such as to make manual labour impossible for white Europeans; rather, this division was a legacy of the colonization of South Africa in the seventeenth century, when Black slaves were available to be imported from other parts of Africa to provide cheap labour.

When he visited South Africa, Bryce was struck by 'the strong feeling of dislike and contempt—one might almost say of hostility—which the bulk of the whites show to their black neighbours'. This was clearly not due to political resentment, as in the American South. He attributed it in part to the legacy of slavery, in part to physical aversion, and in part to 'an incompatibility of character and temper, which makes the faults of the coloured man more offensive to the white than the (perhaps morally as grave) faults of his own white stock'. He went on to offer some reflections on the psychological roots of racial antagonism:

> Whoever has travelled among people of a race greatly weaker than his own must have sometimes been conscious of an impatience or irritation which arises when the native either fails to understand or neglects to obey the command given. The sense of his superior intelligence and energy of will produces in the European a sort of tyrannous spirit, which will not conde-scend to argue with the native, but overbears him by sheer force, and is prone to resort to physical coercion. Even just men, who have the deepest theoretical respect for human rights, are apt to be carried away by the con-sciousness of superior strength, and to become despotic, if not harsh. To escape this fault, a man must be either a saint or a sluggard. And the

tendency to race enmity lies very deep in human nature. Perhaps it is a survival from the times when each race could maintain itself only by slaughtering its rivals.[73]

It is hardly a surprise to find that Bryce was firmly in support of the restricted franchise in the two British colonies: it would be looked on favourably, he thought, by 'any one who has seen the evils which in America has followed the grant of the suffrage to persons unfit for it'. He recognized that it would be 'impolitic' to frame exclusions explicitly in terms of race; and he also thought that, since there were educated Kafirs (*sic*) and Indians who were just as capable of exercising the vote responsibly as the average white voter, it sent the right signals to the white population—who were inclined to despise all nonwhites—that such members of the 'coloured' population should be part of the electorate. Over time they would constitute a growing part.

> But to toss the gift of political power into the lap of a multitude of persons who are not only ignorant, but in mind children rather than men, is not to confer a boon, but to inflict an injury. So far as I could judge, this is the view of the most sensible natives in Cape Colony itself, and of the missionaries also, who have been the steadiest friends of their race. What is especially desirable is to safeguard the private rights of the native, and to secure for him his due share of the land, by retaining which he will retain a measure of independence. The less he is thrown into the whirlpool of party politics the better.[74]

It was clear that Bryce had the American South continually in mind when visiting and writing about South Africa. Indeed, he drew an extended comparison between the Black populations of the two countries. There were obviously structural differences: Blacks were a small minority in the United States, and even in the South they were in the majority only in a few states; in South Africa, they were in the majority by a big distance. Though he believed—on what evidence, it is hard to know—that the Bantu races were at least equal to the American Blacks, he thought them distinctly inferior in terms of education and 'habits of industry': the American Blacks having had the doubtful benefit of 'the industrial training of nearly two centuries of plantation life or domestic service', as well as having extensive contact with white workers, something that their South African counterparts lacked.[75] He also argued—significantly—that the exercise of the vote since emancipation had had a stimulating effect on the Black population of the American South: something that he appears not to have conceded in his writings on the United States. But he thought the similarities between the two cases outweighed the differences: 'In both countries one race rules over the other. The stronger despises and dislikes the weaker; the weaker submits patiently to the stronger. But the weaker makes in education and in property a progress which will some day bring it much nearer to the stronger than it is now.'[76] As in the American South, so in South Africa: intermarriage was rare and was (Bryce thought) unlikely to increase significantly; it had declined in South Africa since the abolition of slavery, as it had in the American South. White opinion universally condemned intermarriage: 'and rightly', interpolated Bryce, anticipating his Romanes lecture; 'for as things are now the white race would lose more by the admixture than the coloured race would gain'.[77]

This left Bryce anxious, even fearful, when he speculated about the future. Because intermarriage would remain rare, the Blacks would remain sharply marked off from the white population. But they would become better educated, would compete with whites in commercial and even professional life, would acquire property, and would constitute a growing proportion of the electorate. They could be expected to lose much of their subservience and acquire political consciousness. All that would create 'a grave or even a perilous' situation for both races, 'if the feeling and behaviour of the whites continue to be what they are now'. All that could save the situation would be 'some great change in human thought and feeling, or some undreamt-of discovery in the physical world, that can be imagined as likely to affect the progress of the natives and the attitude of the whites toward them'.[78]

He also speculated about when this perilous turning-point might be reached. Not for a long time, he thought. 'Many thousands of years', perhaps, as Lake and Reynolds have him say? No: a century, or possibly two, for 'fast as the world moves in our time, it must take several generations to develop a race so backward as the Kafirs'.[79]

It is natural to dwell on the language Bryce uses to depict the Black population: always emphasizing its relative backwardness, its deficiency in the kind of 'intelligence' that comes from education and the discipline of modern economic life, and also in the moral or psychological qualities—self-control, temperance, foresight—instilled by that same discipline. He was not antagonistic, but his sympathy was of a condescending kind. Blacks were typically depicted as akin to children. But it is only right to balance this with his opinions of the white population. He was rarely at all positive about settler populations or colonial castes. They displayed a hostility towards the Blacks which was not reciprocated, but might well be in future. So:

> The main thing to be done seems to be to soften the feelings of the average white and to mend his manners. At present he considers the native to exist solely for his own benefit. He is harsh or gentle according to his own temper; but whether harsh or gentle, he is apt to think of the black man much as he thinks of an ox, and to ignore a native's rights when they are inconvenient to himself.
>
> Could he be got to feel more kindly toward the native, and to treat him, if not as an equal, which he is not, yet as a child, the social aspect of the problem—and it is not the least serious aspect—would be completely altered.[80]

Bryce's racial writings are conventionally cited as forming a kind of apologia for British imperialism. But when Bryce wrote about the practice of imperial rule, it was generally in negative terms, and negative not least because imperial conquest and colonial settlement produced interracial contact of a kind that gave rise to apparently insoluble problems. Its moral effects on both 'backward' and 'advanced' races were predominantly harmful. Bryce did not advocate the dismantling of empire, and he thought the continued union of the self-governing white settler colonies with the United Kingdom was a beneficent force in world politics; but he was rarely a proponent of imperial expansion.

The Turn to Racial Optimism: South America

Never was Bryce as pessimistic about the future of race relations as in his Romanes lecture, and never again did he flirt with separate-race spaces as a solution. We can trace the emergence of a new note of racial optimism in his book on South America, published in 1912 following an extended visit while on leave from his embassy in the autumn of 1910: this was an important book which, though lacking in fundamental originality, was very well-received in Europe, the United States, and especially South America itself.[81] Bryce had long been aware of the different pattern of race relations that had developed in South America: in his Romanes lecture he had maintained that it was among the Teutons that racial repulsion for Blacks was strongest and noted that intermarriage between Whites and Blacks was common in South America, and also in Cuba, which he had visited in 1901.[82] But personal encounter with the countries of South America during his visit in 1910 undoubtedly made an impression on him that counted for much more than the abstract knowledge that relations between the races were very different from the southern states of the United States.

The book was structured by country or region, tracing the route the Bryces took, starting from the isthmus of Panama and proceeding down the Peruvian coast, moving inland across Bolivia, then through Chile and across the Andes to the strait of Magellan, before a northward sweep through Argentina, Uruguay, and Brazil. These chapters were mostly focused on the kind of *Landeskunde* for which Bryce had a lifelong talent. He aimed 'to individualize, so to speak, the chief countries of South America, so as to bring out the chief characteristics, natural and human, of each of them'. The natural was at least as important as the human: measured in pages, significantly more so. By contrast, 'Of the political history of these republics very little is said in this book, and of their current politics nothing at all.'[83] That was something of an exaggeration. The book finished with five analytical chapters: one on nation-building, another on race relations, a third comparing South America with North America and with Europe, and also exploring their reciprocal relations; then a fourth on 'The Conditions of Political Life in Spanish-American Republics', which somewhat belied Bryce's declaration that he did not touch on current politics, and finally 'Some Reflections and Forecasts'.

The chapter on 'The Relations of Races in South America' echoes, in its title, the theme of the Romanes lecture and raises the same questions: 'Does the blending of one race with another tend to weaken or to improve the breed, and how far are any marked qualities of one parent stock transmissible by blood to a mixed progeny which is placed in and powerfully affected by a different environment?' For the study of these questions, Bryce observed, Spanish America offered 'a large and varied field' and one that had been little examined.[84] But if the questions posed were similar to those Bryce addressed in the Romanes lecture, his answers were different in tone and, in important respects, different in substance too.

This was apparent, for instance, in his discussion of Brazil, where the Black population did not experience 'that repulsion which marks the attitude of the whites to the negroes in North America and South Africa', and where intermarriage was frequent.[85] What were the outcomes? 'Brazil is the one country in the world, besides the Portuguese colonies on the east and west coasts of Africa, in which a fusion of the European and African races is proceeding unchecked by law or custom. The doctrines of human equality and human solidarity have here their perfect work. The result is so far satisfactory that there is little or no class friction.'

Whereas in the Romanes lecture Bryce was somewhat pessimistic (while acknowledging the lack of data) about the impact of miscegenation on the quality of the 'racial stock', now, at least as far as Brazil was concerned, he was an agnostic leaning definitely in the direction of optimism. His optimism seemed to rely excessively (as his pessimism had) on anecdotal instances. But his key message was this: 'Assumptions and preconceptions must be eschewed, however plausible they may seem.' Among those assumptions and preconceptions were, it would seem, those that had infused his approach in the Romanes lecture about the spectre of racial decline resulting from intermarriage.[86]

He drew three conclusions about race relations from the South American evidence. The first picked up on the last point: the fusion of two races did not necessarily produce a race with qualities intermediate between the 'stronger' and the 'weaker' of the parent races. The Peruvian mestizo was, Bryce thought, equal in intellect to the Spanish colonial; conversely, the Mexican mestizo was by no means superior to the indigenous Tarascan or Zapotee. In his Romanes lecture and his inaugural address to the Sociological Society, Bryce lamented the lack of data on these questions, and it is unclear whether the rather firm conclusions he drew about South America were grounded in anything more than the impressions of the admittedly experienced and observant traveller. Still, the firmness of the conclusion was striking.

The second conclusion was a trenchant assessment of the impact of conquest and colonization on subject races: The effect was 'depressing and almost ruinous'. Inca civilization had reached a stage which, though below that of the ancient Egyptians and Babylonians, was notably high in view of the isolation of the Incas from other 'progressive peoples'. This was effectively wiped out: 'The impact of Spanish invasion not only shattered their own rudimentary civilization to pieces, but so took all the heart and spirit out of them that they have made practically no advances during four centuries, and have profited hardly at all by the western civilization of their masters.'[87] Needless to add, these were not the words of an apologist for the unmixed blessings of European colonialism.

Third, the ease of intermarriage by the Spaniards and Portuguese with native 'Indians' and with Black ex-slaves demonstrated that 'race repugnance' was 'no such constant and permanent factor in human affairs as members of the Teutonic peoples are apt to assume'. There was little race repulsion either in the ancient world or among Muslims or Chinese in the modern world. What was Bryce's conclusion? Not that race repugnance was intrinsic to the Teutons, nor that it had an evolutionary advantage for them; rather, he speculated that 'since the phenomenon is not of the essence of human nature, it may not be always as strong among the Teutonic peoples as it is to-day'.[88] In suggesting that 'race repugnance' might be a Teutonic abnormality, Bryce anticipated what was to become a commonplace among African American thinkers and others in the first half of the twentieth century, W.E.B. Du Bois among them.

Speculating about the future, Bryce thought it certain—or at least 'as certain as anything in human affairs can be'—that aboriginal, European, and African races in South America would ultimately be fused. The quality of the resulting mixed race was less predictable. He worried that 'the Portuguese of tropical Brazil may suffer from the further infusion of an element the moral fibre of which is conspicuously weak' but noted that 'there are those who argue that the blood of the superior race must ultimately transmute the whole'. Moreover, he was now much more sceptical about the rush to attribute the present-day character of a racial group such as the American Indians to 'inherent defects' rather than to 'their melancholy history'. 'There may be in the Indian stock a reserve of strength, dormant but not extinct, ready to respond to a new stimulus and to shoot upwards under more inspiriting conditions.'[89]

———

This chapter has questioned an increasingly widespread reading of Bryce's Romanes lecture, and his writings on the American South and on South Africa of the 1890s, as the works of a hard-line white supremacist.[90] Questions of race relations were essentially absent from his published work before 1891, and while he certainly showed signs of being obsessed with these questions between 1891 and 1902, this was the obsession of someone who was grappling for solutions to a problem he regarded at the time as an insoluble one. The position he took in the Romanes lecture was by no means the trenchant stance depicted in the literature. It was tentative and anxious. Moreover, this was one phase in Bryce's development as a race relations thinker. During his ambassadorship, and especially after his visit to South America in 1910, he gradually shifted to a much more optimistic perspective on the prospects of racial harmony. He may well, in fact, have been wrong in his somewhat complacent interpretation of racial relations in South America, but the conclusion he drew was that racial repugnance of Whites for Blacks was by no means natural or universal, even among Teutonic Whites, but a contingent historical phenomenon.

Bryce was an important figure in the emergence of race relations as an academic field. The invention and definition of that field is usually ascribed to Robert E. Park, the founder of the 'Chicago school' of race relations, and Bryce was a significant point of reference for Park, something that (as far as I am aware) has not previously been noticed. Park's *Introduction to the Science of Sociology*, co-authored with his Chicago colleague Ernest W. Burgess in 1921, cited the Romanes lecture (the first item listed in the bibliography under 'Race Relations in General'). Park and Burgess also cited Bryce's *Race Sentiment as a Factor in History* (1915), his *American Commonwealth*, his *Impressions of South Africa*, his *Studies in History and Jurisprudence*, his 'Migrations of the Races of Men Considered Historically', and several ephemeral pieces from American journals. They also included an extract from his wartime address on 'War and Human Progress'. A generation later, Bryce was again a frequent point of reference for the Swedish Social Democratic economist and sociologist Gunnar Myrdal in his study of the American 'negro problem', commissioned by the Carnegie Corporation. Myrdal made extensive use both of the Romanes lecture and, inevitably, of *The American Commonwealth*. Bryce would have wholeheartedly endorsed Myrdal's analysis of the Reconstruction period:

> Successful democracy has never been established anywhere in the world except by considerable exertions of the masses themselves, masses who have been fairly well educated and who are public spirited from the start, and who, in addition, during the struggle for representation and power, have acquired political experience and built up organized civic movements of their own. What happened in Reconstruction was, on the contrary, that without their asking for it, almost a million Negro men, most of whom had not only been kept in total ignorance, but who in the protected slave existence had lacked any opportunity to live a self-directed life, were suddenly enfranchised.[91]

Myrdal's work was praised by Du Bois for his critique of racial inequality and was cited by the United States Supreme Court in its landmark ruling in the case of *Brown v. Board of Education* (1954). These facts give a salutary warning against a Manichaean reading of the genealogy of ideas about race and race relations.[92]

10

Bryce and the American People

PUBLIC MORALIST, CULTURAL DIPLOMAT

The Go-between

Bryce received the offer of the ambassadorship to the United States in December 1906. He told friends that he accepted after some hesitation, citing his lack of diplomatic experience and his reluctance to leave the work he was engaged in in Ireland after only a year.[1] He was in fact generally thought to have been less than successful in the chief secretaryship: partly, perhaps, because he pursued his *idées fixes* on the Irish university question, with apparently little regard to the likelihood of a positive outcome. It is sometimes suggested that Campbell Bannerman may have seized on the vacant ambassadorship as an opportunity to enable Bryce to leave the cabinet with good grace, but in fact it was Sir Edward Grey in particular who pressed for the appointment.[2] It proved to be an inspired one, though not without its controversies, especially on Canadian tariffs. Bryce's lasting legacy was a closer bond between the British and American governments, and especially between the British and American peoples. 'A great amount of the good feeling of the U.S.A. towards England must be directly due to you', Gilbert Murray told him in 1914. 'It would have been vastly different eight or nine years ago.'[3]

Whereas in the first half of twentieth century it became quite common to appoint politicians to Washington—of the next eight after Bryce, three were former or future foreign secretaries—this had not been the case in the nineteenth century, and there is some indication that career diplomats resented the appointment.[4] So it was certainly an unusual one. Bryce declined a peerage, judging (after consulting American friends) that American opinion would think more highly of an untitled ambassador.[5] This was a shrewd move. Bryce

253

FIGURE 10.1. The British Embassy in Washington, DC, around the time of Bryce's ambassadorship.

was perceived as a different kind of ambassador, and in fact, not since Richard Pakenham (an earl's nephew) in the 1840s had there been an untitled British ambassador in Washington.

On arrival, Bryce was better known to the American people than any new ambassador; probably than any established ambassador too. That was almost wholly due to the success of *The American Commonwealth*. Not only did that book go through many editions in New York as well as in London, but it also appeared in an abridged edition for college students prepared by Bryce himself with the assistance of the Iowa political scientist Jesse Macy.[6] Extracts from the book or exercises based on it were much used in high school classes in 'civics', a neologism coined in the 1880s, just before Bryce's first edition was published.[7] The most notable illustration of this use was a book entitled *Outlines of Civics*, by a San Francisco history teacher, Frederick H. Clark. This bore the subtitle *Being a Supplement to Bryce's "American Commonwealth", Abridged Edition*. The book set a series of exercises for students to attempt based on Bryce's abridged edition. In the preface, the distinguished Stanford sociologist George Elliott Howard commended the publishers' 'happy thought' in preparing the abridged edition for use in high schools, for the book was well suited for use as a textbook. Indeed, 'to the American citizen it has become emphatically an "epoch-making" book, for it has become a centre of influence for good in our political life. We have instinctively deferred to the judgments of the wise observer who has looked at us from the outside, and in them the reformer and the honest thinker have found encouragement and support.'[8] Many other civics textbooks made copious reference to Bryce.[9] He was useful for the purpose, because not only did he provide a comprehensive and apparently objective account of the workings of the American political system, but it was also an account which was imbued with civic values. After all, Bryce had himself written about 'The Teaching of Civic Duty', for both American and British readerships, and regretted that the English language lacked an equivalent to the French word *civisme*.[10] These American civics textbooks tended to go through numerous editions. Many, probably the majority of, American undergraduates during Bryce's ambassadorship would have previously encountered his work in school civics, which helps account for the frequent invitations he received to speak at universities, at student societies as well as grand institutional events.

If Bryce arrived endowed with a large cultural capital, he made the most of it in the course of his lengthy stay as ambassador. During his ambassadorship he was in great demand as a public speaker at a wide variety of events. 'The number of invitations he is receiving to visit various places & give addresses is bewildering', Marion told her mother in March 1907, soon after their arrival, '& if there were 20 of him instead of one it would not suffice.'[11] Declining invitations was hard: if he tried to do so, he often came under pressure to change his mind and make an exception.[12] Henry Adams wrote that Bryce 'has three speeches a day to make till his chariot tips him out'.[13] Adams thought Bryce loved it, which was why Marion was unable to stop him accepting so many invitations. Important though his strictly diplomatic work was, especially for relations between the United States and Canada, his tenure of the office was notable above all as a pioneering exercise in *public* and *cultural* diplomacy, practices that are usually thought to have been shaped after the First World War rather than before it.[14] 'I feel that I have come out largely for the sake of talking to Universities', he remarked to his friend Charles Eliot, the president of Harvard.[15] It was more than universities, however. 'It is laborious making these long journeys and being run "on schedule" as they say', he told Lady Ilbert in 1908. But 'here public sentiment is more important as compared with the attitude of the Government than anywhere else in the world'.[16] This was an unusually explicit statement of what he thought the point of his ambassadorship was. On his return in 1913 he told a Pilgrims Society dinner in London that 'there is a friendship of Governments and a friendship of peoples', the former being shifting and unstable, but the latter much durable if it was founded on 'community of language, of literature, of institutions, of traditions, of ideals'.[17] His role as ambassador had been to remind the American people of what they had in common with the British, in spite of political rifts.

By no means was everything to his taste. On arrival he foresaw 'an awful time here with what are called "social functions" which things my soul hateth'. But he recognized that it was 'all in the day's work'.[18] He used the profile he already enjoyed in America due to the success of *The American Commonwealth* to ensure that he was able to act on American public opinion. No ambassador had ever travelled as widely within the United States. Marion's letters home (possibly not a neutral source) reported the exuberant reception he received: 'He is of course being made much of here & everyone seems delighted that he has come. The warmth & appreciation with which he is welcomed are really very striking, & the President declares that there has been nothing like it since Lafayette came over.'[19] Bryce's letters also constantly referred to the effusiveness of his reception, although he attributed this in part to the exuberance of the American character.[20]

He was probably disappointed, overall, with the outcomes of his 'high' diplomatic work, active though he was in this respect. He put in a lot of work on US-Canadian relations in particular, where he was able to take advantage of a long-standing friendship with Governor-General Albert Grey, the fourth Earl Grey, who had formerly been a Liberal parliamentary colleague. His first official act as ambassador was to visit Canada, and as the Canadian prime minister, Sir Wilfred Laurier, put it, 'Mr Bryce . . . has done something new in connection with British diplomacy in America. He has visited Canada.'[21] There were protracted negotiations over tariffs and fisheries, but the main fruit of these negotiations was to have been the Reciprocity Treaty. That was a sensitive issue not just in North America, where the Canadians had long felt that they were being sacrificed for the benefit of Anglo-American relations, but also in Britain, where the Unionists were committed to tariff reform and Imperial Preference. The Canadian Liberals under Sir Wilfred Laurier signed up to the treaty, but their Conservative opponents, encouraged by their British counterparts, made it an electoral issue in the general election of 1911, which they won, having ignited anti-American sentiment, and the treaty was dead. One Canadian newspaper of Conservative sympathies commented: 'The London Post points out that the action of the people of Canada places Ambassador Bryce in a delicate position. Certainly the British ambassador seems to have taken a leading part in the attempt to kidnap Canada and present it to his American flatterers.'[22] In this sense, Bryce's political career might not have been an advantage, especially at a time of intense partisanship in British domestic politics, especially on the tariff question.

A similar fate awaited the Taft Arbitration Treaties of 1911, in which Bryce was closely involved. One newspaper called these treaties 'the greatest step ever taken toward world-wide peace'; but they were never ratified by the Senate.[23] They were opposed, notably, by Theodore Roosevelt, who argued that questions of 'national honor' should be excepted. In a retrospective on his time as ambassador, Bryce singled this out as a notable disappointment and observed that it 'could have been carried had those chiefly concerned taken more pains': he thought that the Taft administration had been negligent in failing to square opinion in the Senate at an early stage.[24]

Bryce was able to draw on a degree of intimacy with members of the American political elite. Roosevelt, who was president for the first two years, was a long-standing friend: 'You remember his dining with us in Bryanston Square', Bryce wrote to his sisters, evidently referring to a dinner party in the 1880s, almost certainly before he published *The American Commonwealth*.[25] They had shared interests in nature and rugged walks: 'Three days ago I had a very funny walk, or rather scramble, with the President. He led me along the steep rocky banks of a stream, choosing the roughest places to go up or down, and getting the maximum of violent exercise out of our 5 or 6 miles ramble, & talking all the while. We heard & saw many wild birds: he knows & loves them.' Still, he was happiest in the company of university men and their wives. The jurist Oliver Wendell Holmes was a few years into a thirty-year term as a justice of the Supreme Court. 'The Holmeses are on the whole the best company we have here, & the most familiar', Bryce told his sisters. 'He has most about him of that University type, lawyer or scholar, which habit has made most congenial.'[26]

American opinion overwhelmingly lauded Bryce for his 'democratic' persona.[27] He was 'the scholarly, democratic Englishman who knows more about Americans and the American commonwealth than do many native Americans'.[28] When rumours circulated at the end of 1909 that he was to be recalled to make room 'for some lord or knight or baronet', and these rumours were authoritatively denied, the American press rejoiced: 'Diplomacy in Europe is considered a preserve of the aristocracy, but James Bryce is representative of that middle class in Britain, whom we Americans understand and appreciate because, like ourselves, it believes in work, brains, education and character, and has small respect for birth as birth.' Aristocratic diplomats had usually

failed to understand the Americans, whereas 'plain Mr Bryce without a handle
to his name has proved a success here as much as some of our genial and eloquent representatives at St James have proved successes there'.[29] When a further rumour of his imminent retirement or recall circulated in the spring of
1910, one newspaper commented: 'Of course Ambassador Bryce would not
quit his post. He is scheduled to deliver six commencement orations, three
laymens [sic] missionary addresses and respond to eleven banquet toasts all
in the next month.'[30]

Marion is largely ignored in existing accounts of Bryce's ambassadorship,
and yet it is surely recognized that wives mattered even more in diplomacy
than in other kinds of public work.[31] Bryce knew that well: 'The duties we have
to discharge at Washington will fall on my wife fully as much as on me,' he told
Sir Thomas Barlow on the eve of their departure for the United States.[32] Her
public image was less sharply defined than that of her husband, but nevertheless she was much in the press. Her predecessor, Lady Durand, was remembered for her elaborate receptions, and there is a hint that Marion was less
active as a hostess: 'The Bryces have the respect and good will of all, though
the butterfly element would be happier if Mrs Bryce would use more of the
ten thousand a year allowed for incidental social expenses for their benefit.'[33]
Bostonians, however, greeted her as one of their own, who was 'related to over
a score of Boston's oldest and wealthiest families'.[34]

The Sun of New York described Marion in 1911 as 'the most capable woman
in the diplomatic circle' (that is, among the various ambassadors' wives in
Washington): 'She is typically a woman of affairs and conducts a ceremonious
routine of dinners, teas and luncheons. The embassy is the scene of many formal dinners, and some of the customs that were omitted during the régime of
Lord [sic] and Lady Durand have been revived. Visitors mark the restoration
of the original walnut woodwork and heavy crimson hangings that give an air
of solidity to the surroundings.'[35] Marion was well known in Washington for
her skill as a salad-maker, in which she displayed 'an inventiveness that amounts
to genius', according to the Washington Post.[36] She also seems to have taken up
vegetarianism and was, for a time, an advocate of the cause who won converts
in the fashionable summer resort of Bar Harbor in Maine.[37] An article on fashion, again in the Washington Post, in February 1912 singled her out as 'one of
those rare women quite untrammeled by the tyranny of fashion, who wears her
clothes with great self-satisfaction and a wholesome dignity that might profit-
ably be imitated by scores of her American sisters. Mrs Bryce, as her Washington friends well know, is fond of color, being a handsome woman with the

FIGURE 10.2. Photographic portrait of Marion Bryce, taken in Dublin shortly before the Bryces' departure for Washington, around 1906.

complexion of a girl, she can well indulge in the pinks, the blues, and the yellows which constitute her most becoming evening gowns and demitoilets.'[38]

Bryce was certainly a success as ambassador, and the role (as he redefined it) suited his qualities well, but whether he was entirely happy in the office may be questioned. His remoteness from Britain, and from British politics in particular, was something he mentioned frequently. 'I have only the faintest means here of following events', he complained to John Morley in 1908, 'for American newspapers tell one nothing about the other hemisphere, and I can seldom find leisure to read the Times, itself needing to be often discounted.'[39]

The Public Moralist in America

Bryce spoke on many subjects. He was regularly in demand to give commencement addresses or to speak at Phi Beta Kappa Societies and the like at universities across the United States, and at an early stage he had to seek advice on how best to manage these requests, which far exceeded his capacity to meet them.[40] Charles Eliot was firm enough in his advice, though he was by no means neutral in the matter: 'It is not to be thought of that you speak at any other American institution of learning before speaking at Harvard.'[41] In the space of six weeks in May–June 1907 he spoke at seven public events away from Washington, five of them at universities: yet 'I reject five for every one I accept'. He addressed the students of Bryn Mawr on 'Special Vocations for American Women', the University of Chicago on 'The Influence of Scientific and Literary Studies Respectively on the Happiness of Life', the University of Illinois on 'The Value of History for Politics' and 'What a University May Do for a New Country', and Phi Beta Kappa at Harvard on 'What Do We Mean by Progress'. A sample of university addresses in subsequent years included commencement addresses at the University of Wisconsin in June 1908 and (as Chancellor) at Union College, Schenectady, New York, in June 1911, and three addresses at Amherst in 1909.[42] This last was an endowed series of Henry Ward Beecher lectures shared by the departments of history, modern government, and political economy, and Bryce spoke on 'True Conceptions of Liberty' under the auspices of the modern government department. He was often called on to speak at events marking anniversaries: commemorating Thomas Jefferson and the founding of the University of Virginia (Charlottesville, in April 1908), and the centenary of Lincoln's birth with an address at Springfield, Illinois, in February 1909.[43] The year 1909 was one for centenaries, and on 29 December Bryce gave the Gladstone commemoration address at Carnegie Hall in New York, in which he stressed Gladstone's contribution to Anglo-American friendship through his consent to arbitration in the Alabama case. 'Everybody now recognizes that this was an act of the highest wisdom, for it removed a cause of quarrel between Britain and Canada on the one side and the United States on the other, and laid the foundation of that friendship which now happily exists and which he so much rejoiced to see growing during his later years.'[44]

This was a huge speaking burden. Bryce's usual habit was to speak from a brief set of notes, often pencil notes on one sheet of paper. But he changed his practice during his ambassadorship, out of a distrust of the competence of

American press reporters: 'The badness of reporting here obliges me to write out the addresses beforehand, else the press will make nonsense of them.'[45] Because he disliked being tied down to a script, what he did most of the time was to write an extensive summary for the press, but to speak more freely to that text.[46] Needless to say, this change of practice reflected at the same time the importance Bryce, as ambassador, attached to ensuring that his words were accurately reported in the press.

Something of the manner in which Bryce addressed American audiences can be gleaned from the advice he offered other British visitors who came out to do lecture series or similar events in the United States. One such was the Catholic writer Wilfrid Ward, whom Bryce knew through the Synthetic Society and other places. Ward gave the Lowell lectures at Harvard in 1914 and was evidently using the opportunity to address a range of other audiences at the same time. Bryce made three suggestions: Ward should make an effort to speak slowly and enunciate more clearly than he would in England, since 'they don't always catch our way of pronouncing words'. He should avoid allusions: those which were obvious to British audiences might not be to Americans. Finally, Ward should not be deterred by the absence of applause, or even heckling, along the way. This did not indicate lack of appreciation, but rather that the audience was paying attention. Applause, usually very genuine, would come at the end.[47]

Ever since his first visit to the United States in 1870, Bryce had been an important intermediary between the British and American academic worlds. That first visit took place at a time of flux and extraordinary vitality in the American universities.[48] The first wave of land-grant colleges—many of them the seeds of state universities—had come into being in the wake of the Civil War. Cornell University, itself a land-grant institution, though a privately endowed one, was opened in 1868, with Andrew Dickson White as its first president. Harvard entered a new era with Eliot's appointment as president in 1869: in his forty-year period in office, he drove a process of institutional transformation that encompassed the establishment of professional schools, an ambitious broadening of the curriculum through the system of electives, and a commitment to research as a core purpose of the university. A few years later (1876), Johns Hopkins University was founded in Baltimore, and its first president, Daniel Coit Gilman, pressed forward with a bold plan to create a new kind of university focused on research and graduate education. Bryce met White, Eliot, and Gilman on his visit in 1870, and all became good friends of his.[49] They were all important interlocutors as Bryce wrote the chapter on universities (in later editions, two chapters) for *The American Commonwealth*.[50] In successive editions of that book, Bryce was one of the first to spell out to a European readership (and indeed to an American) the originality of the American higher education system and the importance of the transformations taking place.

Specifically, this is how Bryce concluded his chapter:

> But if I may venture to state the impression which the American universities have made upon me, I will say that while of all the institutions of the country they are those of which the Americans speak most modestly, and indeed deprecatingly, they are those which seem to be at this moment making the swiftest progress, and to have the brightest promise for the future. They are supplying exactly those things which European critics have hitherto found lacking to America: and they are contributing to her political as well as to her contemplative life elements of inestimable worth.[51]

One reason was certainly that the best American universities were on the cusp of drawing on a par with (if not overtaking) 'the ancient universities of Europe', not least because their resources would soon far exceed those the German universities had to pursue the same goals. Even more important than material resources, however, they already had 'an ardour and industry among the teachers which equals that displayed fifty years ago in Germany by the foremost men of the generation which raised the German schools to their glorious pre-eminence'.[52] If Bryce did not quite say it in so many words, the message was clear: what German universities had been to the nineteenth century, American elite universities would be to the twentieth. In that he was surely right, and he was among the first to see it.

But Bryce did not simply focus on the East Coast elite universities. He was equally interested in the proliferation of small colleges, especially in the Mississippi states and the Pacific states. He was well aware that many of these were providing an education far below what European universities might regard as a degree-level university education, and he noted that American educational reformers complained that higher education was weakened by the dissipation of resources across too many institutions. But against that consideration he stressed the benefits that small colleges conferred in rural and small-town America through their ability to act on the public:

> They get hold of a multitude of poor men, who might never resort to a distant place of education. They set learning in a visible form, plain, indeed,

and humble, but dignified even in her humility, before the eyes of a rustic people, in whom the love of knowledge, naturally strong, might never break from the bud into the flower but for the care of some zealous gardener. They give the chance of rising in some intellectual walk of life to many a strong and earnest nature who might otherwise have remained an artisan or store-keeper, and perhaps failed in those avocations. They light up in many a country town what is at first only a farthing rushlight, but which, when the town swells to a city, or when endowments flow in, or when some able teacher is placed in charge, becomes a lamp of growing flame, which may finally throw its rays over the whole State in which it stands.[53]

Just as Bryce was prescient in foreseeing that the East Coast research universities would come to lead the world, so he was insightful in identifying the democracy of the intellect as an equally important characteristic of the American system.[54] This helps explain why he put in so much time and effort into delivering addresses at sundry colleges, great and small, across the United States.

As ambassador, Bryce was obliged to maintain a certain restraint, but one of his favourite causes which he did feel free to promote was the protection of the environment. Speaking at Burlington, Vermont, on the tercentenary of the discovery of Lake Champlain (July 1909), he urged New England 'to spare the woods wherever they are an element of beauty, to prevent unsightly buildings from destroying some exquisite prospect, to keep open the mountains and allow no one to debar pedestrians from climbing to their tops and wandering along their slopes'.[55] In 1912 he addressed the American Civic Association on 'National Parks—the Need of the Future'. Invoking his own role in the Commons Preservation Society and the National Trust, he dwelt on 'our duty to the future' and on 'the benefits which the preservation of places of natural beauty may confer on the community'.[56] He was prescient in seeing the incursion that the motor car was likely to make on such places as the Yosemite Valley in California:

> May a word be permitted on that subject? If Adam had known what harm the serpent was going to work, he would have tried to prevent him from finding lodgment in Eden; and if you stop to realize what the result of the automobile will be in that wonderful, that incomparable valley, you will keep it out. . . .
>
> It will of course be said that the automobile might be allowed to come up to the principal hotels and go no further. If it is allowed to go so far as that, it will soon be allowed to go wherever there is a road to bear it. Do not

let the serpent enter Eden at all. Our friends who possess automobiles are numerous, wealthy, and powerful, but as all the rest of the North American Continent is open to them they are not gravely injured when one valley, besides parts of Mount Desert Island, is reserved for those who walk or ride.[57]

If he started with the Fall, he ended by invoking a theology of Creation:

Let us think of the future. We are trustees for the future. We are not here for ourselves alone. All these gifts were not given to us to be used by one generation, or with the thought of one generation only before our minds. We are the heirs of those who have gone before, and charged with the duty we owe to those who come after, and there is no duty which seems more clearly incumbent on us than that of handing on to them undiminished opportunities and facilities for the enjoyment of some of the best gifts that the Creator has bestowed upon his children.[58]

A particularly striking (and previously unnoticed) feature of Bryce's public engagements as ambassador is just how many addresses were to religious associations and conferences of one kind or another.[59] They are not included in the volume of *University and Historical Addresses* that he published shortly after leaving the ambassadorship, and they are hard to reassemble, since the published texts or press reports are generally buried in obscure places. He addressed the Laymen's Missionary Convention in Chattanooga in April 1908.[60] He spoke to the Pennsylvania Bible Society in Philadelphia, the Chicago Conference on Religious Education (February 1909), the Pacific School of Religion at Berkeley, and the Presbyterian Conference in Baltimore, among many others, not to mention the host of similar invitations he had to decline.[61] That tells us something about the profile he enjoyed as a public figure who was at ease engaging with religious questions. It helped that these were questions of public importance but not ones perceived as political, and hence there was no problem with an ambassador addressing them. That did not mean they were bland: either the questions he addressed, or the content of his speeches. He was clear that there were things he *wanted* to say on these questions. When he gave an address on religious and moral education to the Religious Education Association in Chicago in 1909, he told his sisters: 'It was a difficult topic, but I have been feeling bound to take some opportunity of delivering my testimony on the matter.'[62]

What did he have to say? He summarized his objects succinctly to his sisters: 'I dwell on the tendencies adverse to religious life in our time & the need for stemming them by increased efforts to familiarize young people with the Bible and to base practical morality upon religious belief.' A press report quoted him as saying:

> While fully recognizing the increased activity of the churches and of such organizations as the Young Men's Christian Association and the Christian Endeavor Society, the tendencies in large sections of a rapidly growing population toward indifference in religion and toward a diminished reverence for the sanctions which religion provides is conspicuous enough to make it necessary for them to put forth all their exertion to vindicate for religion its place in the training of the young throughout the whole course of life.[63]

Two distinctive elements in Bryce's religious outlook are present here: first, the centrality of the Bible, in particular as an instrument for teaching the Christian religion; and second the relationship between religion and morality. Even if the latter could in principle exist without the former, the fact was that in Western societies the Christian religion was the foundation of 'practical morality', and the decline of the former would tend to lead to the erosion of the latter.[64]

Bryce thought that society had become more materialistic, and that the growth of the 'passion for pleasure' had eroded 'notions of duty and self control'. In particular, 'the claim of the individual to indulge his will, or it may be his caprice, in some matters of serious import to society such as, for instance, the marriage relation, has become more avowed and more aggressive'.[65] Marion's remark that Bryce had 'a strong Puritan inheritance in his blood' comes to mind: indeed, he noted that some sections of the community—in particular, 'those who are of native American stock' (by this phrase, he meant of English or British descent) were fortunate to inherit 'the old New England traditions of moral earnestness and religious practice', and the resilience of these traditions meant that 'a form of Puritanism, much broadened and softened, has not wholly vanished'. But large-scale immigration had undermined the salience of the Puritan inheritance in American society.[66]

The same anxiety about the growth of hedonism and the enfeeblement of notions of duty was foregrounded in the lectures Bryce gave at Berkeley on the subject of 'Religion and Ethics in Modern Life'. As he told his sisters, the lectures were 'practically an exposition of the moral teachings of the Gospels and an attempt to apply them to certain modern social problems, economic & political'. He dilated on what had driven him to address these issues: it was a confrontation with the realities of American society in the twentieth century.

'My "spirit was stirred within me when I saw the city wholly given to idolatry",
idolatry of material progress, of pleasure, & of themselves as Californians &
U.S. citizens. So I took up my parable & tried to shew them, as far as I could "a
more excellent way."'[67] He may have thought that California was in particular
need of such a sermon, though it was (he said elsewhere) his favourite state.[68]
It amused him that an old man with an Ulster accent came up to him afterwards, congratulated him, and said he was reminded of Bryce's Uncle John
preaching in the York Street Church in Belfast.

One of Bryce's concerns was that the erosion of religious practice brought
in its train a deterioration in levels of basic religious knowledge among the
public, and this undermined the cultural foundations for a shared morality.
This was a particular problem for the United States, he thought, because the
principle of the state's neutrality in matters of religion had been understood to
imply that religious education should have no place in the public school. Bryce
remained faithful to the principle of universal nondenominational religious
instruction. He highlighted the problem with the American approach, which
resembled that proposed in the 1870s by the hardline nonconformist zealots
of the National Education League, who preferred to dispense with religious
instruction rather than to strip it of doctrinal content: 'in thus escaping the
clash of denominational pretensions, you are left facing the difficulty of how
the children of the nation are to receive any instruction at all in religious
matters, which many of us, and certainly you of this Association, deem to be
of the highest significance for the nation's life and welfare.'[69]

Bryce's reflections on missionary work are highly relevant in this context.
The address he gave to the Laymen's Missionary Convention of the South in
1908 was a Brycean tour de force, which traced the history of missions from
the beginnings of the conception of religious mission in early Christianity,
right up to the entanglement of missionary work with western imperial expansion in the present. He echoed his long-standing belief that missionary work
was a field that had much to gain from the advent of 'a fraternal spirit which
seeks to make all the religious bodies work together, aiming not at uniformity
in organization, but at friendly coöperation in a common cause'. But his particular focus was on the relationship between Christian mission and the many
other influences 'now exercised, more powerfully than ever before, by the civilized upon the uncivilized or savage peoples'.[70] He depicted European conquest in terms that were by no means complacent or triumphalist. 'In half a
century or less that which we call European civilization will have overspread
the earth and extinguished the organizations and customs of the savage and

semi-civilized tribes or nations. The native tribes will have been broken up, native kingdoms will have vanished, native customs will have gone; everywhere the white man will have established his influence and destroyed the old native ways of life.' This was a tale of destruction and *extinction* that caused someone with a profound historical sensibility like Bryce to tremble. 'Things which have endured from the Stone Age until now are at last coming to a perpetual end, and will be no more. They will vanish from the face of the earth. This is something that has never happened before and can never happen again.'[71] He had no wish to whitewash the motives that underpinned western expansion:

> It was at the prompting of our own interests that we of the white races disturbed their ancient ways of life, for we went among them, some few doubtless with a desire to do good, but the great majority from a desire to make money and to exploit the world's resources for profit of the white man. Under the ægis of his government, he is taking the agricultural wealth from the soil, the forests from the hills, and the minerals out of the rocks, all for his own benefit. Of all this wealth nothing, except perhaps a meagre wage for manual labour, goes to the native.[72]

The ascendancy of Western material civilization over 'savage' and 'semi-civilized' peoples brought in its wake the destruction of these peoples' ancient customs and beliefs, and hence also of ancient morality. 'If you destroy these, their morality falls to the ground and is gone, and they are left with nothing, adrift upon a wide and shoreless sea.'[73] Christian missions to the peoples whose ancient customs had been swept aside were thus, for Bryce, a functional necessity to fill the void left by the destruction of primitive culture: 'Unless they receive some new moral basis of life, some beliefs and motives and precepts which can appeal to their hearts and rule their conduct, can restrain bad impulses, and instil worthy conceptions of life and duty and worship, their last state may be worse than the first.'[74]

Bryce's religious convictions did not change radically in the course of his adult life, but his religious persona did. While he was certainly still capable of taking the leadership in fighting for some of the great nonconformist causes, notably in the struggle against the 1902 Education Act, he increasingly positioned himself in interdenominational terms. His friends were as likely to be Anglican prelates (Randall Davidson, Hensley Henson, Phillips Brooks) as scholarly nonconformist divines (Andrew Fairbairn, Joseph Estlin Carpenter). The softening of confessional rivalries in the wake of the First World War is a familiar historiographical narrative, but in Bryce's case it preceded the war and was hastened by his long stay in the United States.[75] He had long been committed to the cause of Christian Reunion, which he envisaged taking the form of closer interdenominational working, especially in missionary activities, rather than of formal institutional unity, which he feared would be a needlessly complicated distraction.[76]

In spite of his ecumenical persona, sacramentalism continued to baffle him, the doctrine of the Real Presence in particular: this was a point he kept returning to in his correspondence with his sisters, whenever he was obliged (as he was from time to time as ambassador) to attend a Roman Catholic mass. One instance was the High Mass at St Patrick's Church, Washington, to mark the sixtieth anniversary of the coronation of the Emperor Francis Joseph:

> All the diplom. Corps, in full toggery of gold lace &c. together with the President & Vice Prest of the U.S. attended High Mass in honour of this occasion, Cardinal Gibbons, head of the R.C. Church in the U.S. was there with a herd of priests & a bishop; there was a highly trained Choir performing elaborate music in a fluid way. And the priest made out of a wafer the Body and Blood of Christ, while we Protestants looked on, with a Buddhist, Takahira, beside us, and a Muslim, Mirza Mohammad Khan, behind us, & a Jew (Strauss) to the left of us, and sundry others who were not Christians or anything at all, in the offing.[77] Such is this world, and all this has come to such a strange development out of that chapter (XI) in First Corinthians.[78] No one seemed to think there was anything strange about it all, so quickly is the meaning & substance of things forgotten.[79]

Conversely, when he visited Japan in 1913 and attended a Buddhist temple in Tokyo, he was struck by the resemblance to the Roman Catholic or Anglo-Catholic mass, to the advantage of neither:

> We stopped at a small Buddhist temple to watch the service. A heavy looking priest was burning incense and making genuflections towards a sort of altar, just like a Roman priest. Monks seated beside him were intoning a sort of hymn. An acolyte was ringing a little bell and at intervals striking a gong. Two or three worshippers were looking on, taking no part in the service. The whole performance was so similar to the Roman that one wished to have had a Ritualist friend there and asked him what he thought of it all. The only difference from the Mass, viz. the offering up of the victim God in the form of a wafer is not to the credit of our religion as against even

this debased form of Buddhism. I had felt like saying "How can this sort of thing last now that the Japanese are exposed to Western influences?" when the thought of the Mass in Spain—and indeed elsewhere—suddenly struck and silenced me.[80]

Someone with a Comtean mind-set might have observed the curiously similar practices in radically different religious traditions and concluded that there was something universal about the human need for ritual and ceremony. Bryce found this perspective alien: he was convinced that ritual was a source of disunity rather than a force for unity. Christian ecumenism must be founded on the common denominator of biblical morality.

Curiously, we know more about Bryce's religious practice, or at least his church-going practice, during his ambassadorship than we do for any other period since his undergraduate days at Trinity. For most of his life there is no record of where he went to church. He hardly ever mentioned Sunday services in his correspondence. That was to a large extent because from the mid-1870s until 1907 he was mostly living in London and his sisters and (from 1877) his mother were there too; so was his brother, for large tracts of that time. So he had no reason to write them the kinds of letters that would involve recording that kind of detail. From 1907 to 1913 things were different, and while it was not something he recorded punctiliously, there is enough detail to build up a picture of his pattern of worship. He records a visit, soon after his arrival in Washington, to the chief Presbyterian church in the capital, the Church of the Covenant, sometimes called the National Presbyterian Church. He was also known to frequent the New York Avenue Presbyterian Church, where he would be shown to the pew that President Lincoln had customarily occupied.[81] When the embassy relocated to Intervale in New Hampshire for the (long) summer, Bryce notes that he and Marion usually went to the Congregational Church, though sometimes to the Episcopal.[82]

In parallel with his Christian moralism, and perhaps in tension with it, we also find Bryce's republican moralism much in evidence: indeed, as with his Christian moralism, he seemed to feel much freer to give voice to it in the United States than in Britain. That was partly because he was even more aware of the urgent need for the inculcation of an ethic of citizenship in the United States, not least because large-scale immigration from Ireland, continental Europe, and latterly China and Japan threatened to erode the shared political and ethical heritage that held the nation together. But he also knew that this was a way in which he could address large public issues without breaching the obligation of political neutrality; in addition, he knew that American audiences (more than their British counterparts) lapped up the sermon-like public speech.

Bryce's fullest statement on civic virtue was not to a popular audience, however, but to an academic one. In October 1908 he gave the Yale Lectures on the Responsibilities of Citizenship: a series of four. His lectures were published in book form by Yale University Press and Oxford University Press under the title *The Hindrances to Good Citizenship*. He said at the outset that when he first received the invitation he wondered whether the subject was not one that should better be addressed by an American; but he came to the conclusion that 'the fundamental problems of citizenship are the same in all free countries', and that there were advantages in addressing an American audience from a European point of view.[83] This is a striking way of putting it, given that the literature on Bryce overwhelmingly emphasizes his Anglo-Saxonism or Teutonism. Yet as in *The American Commonwealth*, in *The Hindrances to Good Citizenship* Bryce presented himself not as an Anglo-Saxon cousin but as a European.

Bryce went on to posit that the theory of popular government assumed both 'intellectual capacity' and 'moral zeal' on the part of the citizens. A democracy which lacked civic zeal would not be a democracy but 'a government of the many by the view', while a democracy in which intellectual capacity was lacking would have bad laws.[84]

On the surface, a large gulf separated *The Hindrances to Good Citizenship* in genre and subject-matter from *Modern Democracies*. The former was an ethical statement on civics; the latter an empirical study of political institutions: one fact after another, some critics have implied. Yet the former in fact anticipated many of the themes Bryce would develop at greater length in the latter. In particular, the context he set out in the introduction was one of disillusionment with the reality of free government, which had severely disappointed the hopes invested in it in the middle of the nineteenth century. The fundamental reason was straightforward:

> The citizens have failed to respond to the demand for active virtue and intelligent public spirit which free government makes and must make. Everywhere there is the same contrast between that which the theory of democracy requires and that which the practice of democracy reveals. . . . Thus the deficiencies which free governments show reduce themselves to the failure of the citizens to reach the needed standard of civic excellence.[85]

One point he emphasized in his second lecture in particular, and which would come to feature prominently in *Modern Democracies*, not least in his chapters on Australia, was the impact of the expansion of the scope of state action on the nature of the polity. As the state—whether central government or local authorities—took more and more duties upon itself, and as it became itself an employer on a large scale, so too there grew the danger that private interests might come to dominate public business. There was something almost Rousseauesque about Bryce's analysis of the intermingling of public and private interests:

> The more any public authority, be it a county or city, or a State of this Union, or any national government, either itself undertakes, or interferes with the conduct by private persons of, any matter in which money can be either made or spent, the more grounds does it supply to private persons for trying to influence its action in the direction which will benefit such persons. So much the more, therefore, will those persons have a private interest different from the interest of the community, so much the more will they be tempted to raise their voices and give their votes with a view, not to the common good, but to their own pockets.[86]

When we see the extent to which *The Hindrances to Good Citizenship* set out the agenda for Bryce's great *summa*, we can see that these lectures, neglected as they have been, were really at the heart of Bryce's thinking. Equally, we might want to think of *Modern Democracies* as an attempt to grapple again with how far, and how, modern democracies had succeeded in removing or working round the hindrances to good citizenship. The relationship between ethics and the polity was very much at its heart. In the final chapter of *Hindrances*, on 'How to Overcome the Obstacles', Bryce distinguishes between two kinds of remedies that might be sought to improve the workings of systems of government: the mechanical and the ethical. Mechanical remedies were concerned with laws and political institutions, whereas the ethical were 'those which affect the character and spirit of the people'. National character was a central concern of ethics, to Bryce's mind, and he thought that fundamental progress in politics could best be achieved by 'raising the intelligence and virtue of the citizens', although he well understood the difficulties that stood in the way.[87]

Bryce's lectures were organized around the three failings that together accounted for the weaknesses of the body of citizens: indolence, private self-interest, and party spirit. Indolence led citizens to prefer private pleasures to political participation, and led them to put aside hard thinking in favour of the consumption of one-sided news coverage that comforted their prejudices. Private self-interest led them to see politics as a way of maximizing personal gains and minimizing personal losses. And party spirit, though it sprang from an authentic interest in the public good, nevertheless made that good less likely to prevail, because it hindered the formation of a consensual public opinion.

Again, this anticipates *Modern Democracies*. A decade later, when he was in the final throes of the research for that work, he asked a Canadian correspondent, the economist James Mavor, these three questions:

1) To what extent are the Provincial Legislatures tainted by corruption and jobbery?
2) Has the level and tone of politics generally risen or declined (in Provinces & in the Dominions) within the last twenty years?
3) Does the power of party organizations increase? I believe they are not very powerful, only much what we have in England.[88]

The second broadly corresponds to the danger of indolence; the first closely corresponds to the danger of private self-interest; and the third even more closely corresponds to the danger of party spirit.

Bryce's analysis of party spirit deserves some attention, if only because it suggests a comparison with the work of his protégé Ostrogorski, who was centrally concerned to explore mechanisms that might overturn the stranglehold of party organizations on modern democratic systems. Bryce's perspective was not the same as that of the Russian émigré: whereas Ostrogorski wanted democracy without parties, Bryce knew that to be impossible. Parties were, he thought, 'a practical necessity'; and indeed he thought that a party system—specifically, a two-party system—was a prerequisite for an effective system of parliamentary government.[89] The party spirit had this advantage, in comparison with indolence, that 'it does at any rate stimulate the interest of the citizen'; and unlike private self-interest, it was not sordid. Its fault lay in excess: the excess of 'a feeling in itself natural and wholesome'.[90]

It is a historiographical curiosity that amid the upsurge of interest in the discourses of citizenship, public spirit, and civic virtue in late Victorian and Edwardian social, political, and moral thought, Bryce has been essentially absent.[91] Yet Bryce was nothing if not a public moralist, and one whose discourse was saturated with the language of civic duty and virtue. He was one of the earliest to seize on the importance of civic education.

Christian Humanitarianism

The sphere in which Bryce most hoped to see Christian morality put to work was that of relations between peoples and nations. This was possibly Bryce's central preoccupation in the last decade or so of his life, as he wrestled with the challenge posed to the nineteenth-century liberal outlook by the rise of Anglo-German antagonism and then the First World War itself. In May 1909 he spoke on the subject of 'Allegiance to Humanity' at the Lake Mohonk Conference on International Arbitration. There he made the case for a conception of patriotism that was consistent with, not hostile to, a love of humanity: 'Our country is not the only thing to which we owe our allegiance. It is owed also to justice and to humanity. Patriotism consists not in waving a flag but in striving that our country shall be righteous as well as strong. A state is not the less strong for being resolved to use its strength in a temperate and pacific spirit.'[92]

One of his last public addresses—and possibly the last he ever gave in the United States—was the Stafford Little lecture that he delivered at Princeton on 28 September 1921. As the *Daily Princetonian* reported the lecture, Bryce outlined the history of the relations of state, church, and public opinion. 'The ideal democracy', he thought, 'is one in which the forces of intellect and emotion are most completely sovereign in the state' and 'in which the state as a civil and physical power is most subordinated to intellect and morality. The church is one of these forces: each individual who possesses an opinion is one; and the university is one which oftentimes proves to be the most powerful.'[93]

Black America

Bryce periodically felt free to address the American people on the problem of race. Racial questions were evidently not deemed too sensitive or 'political' for a diplomat to tackle. Invited to give the principal address at the farmers' national congress in Raleigh, North Carolina, in November 1909, he urged southern farmers to cooperate with the work of colleges such as Booker T. Washington's Tuskegee Institute in Alabama and Hampton Normal and Industrial Institute in Virginia, which were providing agricultural as well as industrial training for Blacks.

He need hardly say [as the press reported the speech] that the habit of settled industry was not natural to all races. It was in the white races the result of many centuries spent under natural conditions of climate and soil which had

compelled men to work. The colored race had lacked this training and was
still behind. But they were advancing, and he believed that such institutions
as Hampton and Tuskegee were doing immense good by sending out men
who knew something of agriculture as an industry in which skill was useful
and who had acquired the habit of steady and assiduous work.[94]

It was during his ambassadorship that Bryce prepared his last fully revised
edition of *The American Commonwealth*, published in 1910. This included, notably, a new chapter entitled 'Further reflections on the negro problem'. This carefully balanced the optimistic perspective, which emphasized the extent of the
social and economic progress of the Black population, with the more pessimistic
point of view, which instead emphasized the spectre of intensified racial conflict
as the material condition of Blacks improved; but on the whole, Bryce seemed
to lean toward optimism. He still wrote from the white point of view: when he
referred to 'the Southern view of the negro', the Black population was evidently
regarded as the 'other', not an integral part of the community. Equally, the 'optimistic' indicators included the fact that the ratio of Blacks to Whites in the
population was declining rather than growing, and this was due in large measure
to 'the still high rate of negro mortality'.[95] But he was also able to cite objective
data on economic and social progress: the increase in property-ownership, professional employment, and educational attainment among Blacks.

Bryce's ambassadorship came at a critically important period in the intellectual and political history of race relations internationally, and in the development of Black politics in the United States. Internationally, a landmark was the
Universal Races Congress held in London in 1911. This was the brainchild of two
central figures in the international ethical movement, both of them Jews: the
Hungarian Gustav Spiller, who was secretary of the International Union of Ethical Societies, and the German-born Felix Adler, professor of political and social
ethics at Columbia University. It was at the first International Moral Education
Congress in London in 1908 that they announced their plan.[96] Bryce had numerous connections with the ethical movement in its broadest sense, not least as
the original chair of what became a major international inquiry into moral instruction in schools under Michael Sadler.[97] It is interesting to speculate what
kind of involvement he might have had in the Universal Races Congress had his
ambassadorship not prevented his involvement. The connection between the
study of race relations and the moral education movement is an intriguing one
which (as we shall see) gives a clue as to Bryce's own evolving standpoint. It also
helps us to understand why the subject of race relations was one on which Bryce

had so much to say, not least during his ambassadorship. It was in integral part of his preoccupation with civics.

In the United States, Black politics of the time were dominated by 'an epic ideological struggle' between two titanic figures in the black community: Booker T. Washington and W.E.B. Du Bois.[98] They stood for two rival strategies for Black advancement. Washington advocated an evolutionary and accommodationist strategy, focusing on communal self-help to achieve social, economic, and educational gains, while deferring political emancipation to some way in the future. Du Bois, by contrast, prioritized the political struggle and considered that any social and economic gains would be nugatory without political equality. Washington's base was the Tuskegee Institute, a Black teacher-training college and industrial institute, which he headed from its founding in 1881. Du Bois was professor of history and economics at Atlanta University, Georgia, a 'negro university': the first university, in fact, to award degrees to African Americans. He took a low view of the kind of vocational and industrial education provided at Tuskegee and instead prioritized higher education as the route to develop Black leadership. He was a leading figure in Pan-Africanism and cofounded the National Association for the Advancement of Colored People in 1909—at just the moment when Bryce was working on his revisions of *The American Commonwealth*. Washington had twice offered Du Bois employment at Tuskegee—the first time (1890) to teach mathematics, and the second time (1902–1903) to act as director of public relations.[99] But the rift between the two Black leaders came into the open in 1903, when Du Bois in *The Souls of Black Folk* criticized the limitations of Washington's programme of industrial progress. What drove Du Bois's public opposition to Washington seems, on his own account, to have been not fundamental disagreement on matters of substance so much as resentment at what he called 'the ascendancy of Mr Booker T. Washington', indeed 'Mr Washington's cult': the fact that white elites regarded him as the sole spokesman for the Black community.[100] This served as a barrier to 'that peculiarly valuable education which a group receives when by search and criticism it finds and commissions its own leaders'.[101]

Bryce was certainly aware of, and indeed discussed, these two tendencies, though he saw no epic ideological struggle. He gave a balanced summary of the two positions: possibly there was a hint of greater sympathy with Washington's position, which he depicted as one grounded in realism and the long view. Du Bois and his allies, by contrast, 'find it hard to practise this patience', and some were starting 'to organize themselves in a more aggressive spirit for common help and protection'. But above all Bryce stressed what the two

FIGURE 10.3. Booker T. Washington (centre front), Andrew Carnegie (seated next to Washington), and the faculty of the Tuskegee Institute in 1906.

positions had in common: a novel kind of 'race solidarity' or 'race-consciousness', a feeling that the Blacks could not advance themselves by 'seeking favours from the Whites' but must instead progress by their own efforts. That did not mean individualistic self-help alone. It meant communal solidarity: mutualism certainly, and a commitment to using their consumer power to benefit Black businesses rather than white. This was a strategy that Dicey would certainly have disapproved of: in other contexts he denounced the boycott (as a form of collective action by consumers) as manifestly an assault on freedom.[102] Bryce, however, appears to have been favourably disposed.[103]

Bryce certainly knew Washington well, and he visited him at Tuskegee in November 1908. Washington commented on Bryce's new chapter in draft, and the chapter should be read in that light.[104] Bryce is generally considered, not without reason, to have echoed Washington's accommodationism. Hugh Tulloch, who takes this position, adds that he did not give serious consideration to Du Bois's position.[105] Du Bois, however, does not appear to have regarded Bryce as an antagonist. He cited Bryce's work without a hint of criticism, even the Romanes lecture on the subject of racial amalgamation.[106] Bryce was consulted at an early stage about Du Bois's proposed *Encyclopedia of the Negro Race* and responded sympathetically.[107] Du Bois then tried quite hard (though in the end unsuccessfully) to get Bryce to address the Annual Negro Conference at Atlanta University in 1909, when the subject was 'Efforts for Social Betterment Among Negro Americans'.[108] He again cited Bryce in his book *The Negro* in 1915: on the Basuto National Assembly, on primitive religion among the Kaffirs, on intermarriage in South America, and especially on the fusion of races in Brazil.[109] The nature of their intellectual relationship is intriguing, for Du Bois was an early critic of the negative interpretation of Reconstruction associated with the 'Dunning School' and anticipated by Bryce in *The American Commonwealth*.[110] Micol Seigel has suggested that Du Bois was being tactically selective: drawing on Bryce's authority, but using evidence he supplied to counter the main thrust of his argument.[111] Clearly considerations of rhetorical and political tactics were at work, but there is a risk of exaggerating Du Bois's instrumentalism here. If Du Bois really regarded Bryce as an antagonist who could nevertheless be made to serve the cause of Black emancipation against his will, it is understandable that he might have invited Bryce to speak at the Annual Negro Conference, but harder to appreciate why his advice on the *Encyclopedia of the Negro Race* should have been sought.

We need to take seriously the possibility that Du Bois, though fully aware of his differences with Bryce, did not regard him as a hard-line antagonist, but as an influential authority whose position was malleable in important respects. If that was Du Bois's opinion, he was surely correct. Bryce's pessimism about race relations in the United States diminished markedly during his ambassadorship, and the shift in his attitudes was accelerated by his tour of South America towards the end of 1910. One of the lessons he derived from that tour was that the physical repulsion that he regarded as a barrier to intermarriage of Blacks and Whites in the United States, South Africa, and elsewhere was anything but a natural and universal phenomenon. If it was stronger among the Teutonic than among other white races, that might be a cultural rather than a physical fact, and hence might be capable of change.

South America was, indeed, an important point of reference in Bryce's new chapter. For the most part it served as a contrast to the United States: in part, certainly, to highlight the contingency of the North American position. For instance, people of 'mixed blood' were reckoned as White in South America but as Black in the North: 'In Latin America whoever is not black is white: in Teutonic America whoever is not white is black.' Intermarriage was, he pointed out, illegal in all the southern states of the United States, and in eleven of the northern and western states; but miscegenation was evidently still common, since he reckoned (with perhaps undue precision) 'not quite one-third' of the Black population were in fact of mixed race. Marriage bars evidently had the effect of reinforcing the solidarity of non-Whites: 'that racial consciousness to which I have already referred has been drawing all sections of the African race together, disposing the lighter coloured, since they can get no nearer to the whites, to identify themselves with the mass of those who belong to their own stock.'[112] The marriage bars were, according to Garrison and Dicey, what Bryce had advocated, or at least supported, in his Romanes lecture eight years before. He cannot be said to have written about them with any enthusiasm in 1910. On the contrary: his keynote, though mixed with stereotypes about racial character, was one of sympathy with oppressed Blacks, especially the more highly edu-cated ones and those of mixed race who were physically barely distinguishable from whites, since they might be expected to resent segregation all the more:

> Among these light-coloured people, it is on those who, knowing their white relatives by sight, and forced to feel that persons by nature their cousins— perhaps even their brothers or sisters—are placed above them on a level to which they cannot climb, that the sense of social inequality presses most cruelly. But it presses on every educated negro. He may have studied at a Northern university, may have associated there in a friendly if not intimate way with white students, may have passed his examinations with equal credit. In face and figure he may be scarcely distinguishable from them. But in after life an impassable barrier will stand between him and them. That under such conditions there should be bitterness can excite no surprise. The wonder rather is that not more bitterness finds expression; and this may be ascribed partly to the simple faith and religious resignation which lie deep in the negro character, partly also to the fact that the coloured people have from childhood grown up accustomed to it, so that the contrast becomes keenly painful only to a few. It is fortunate that the African race is not naturally sullen or vindictive, and that its gaiety of temper finds many alleviations for the trials of life.[113]

Bryce ended his new chapter on the 'negro problem' with a very characteristic passage, in which he combined the persona of the authority on race relations with the persona of the Christian moralist:

> The question whether the races can live peaceably together is at bottom a moral question, a question of good feeling, of humanity, of the application

of the principles of the Gospel. Race antagonism is no doubt a strong sentiment. Many a time it has shown its formidable power. Yet it may decline under the influence of reason and good feeling. In 1810 slavery existed over nearly the whole of the American continent and its islands. Those whom it shocked were few, and fewer still contemplated its abolition. Even so late as 1860 it was defended on principle and defended out of the Bible. When the sentiment of a common humanity has so grown and improved within a century as to destroy slavery everywhere, may it not be that a like sentiment will soften the bitterness of race friction also? It is at any rate in that direction that the stream of change is running.[114]

This might look like hoping for the best in defiance of the facts: an accusation that was certainly levelled at Bryce in different contexts. But he was writing towards the start of a century that did indeed witness a dramatic change in moral sensibilities on questions of racial antagonism. In Bryce's lifetime notions of racial hierarchy were deeply ingrained in the mental worlds of most white Westerners, and not only them. Understandings of the world in terms of racial difference were regarded as intellectually advanced (capable of generating radically new insights in the historical and social sciences) and ethically neutral. The twentieth century saw the politics of race at work in Nazi Germany, apartheid South Africa, and many other regimes across the world; but it also saw a shift in sensibilities in the course of which these ideas came to be intellectually discredited and morally anathematized, though of course not eradicated. That shift probably began in the early decades of the century. Bryce could hardly be said to have foreseen this transformation in all its fullness, but he seems at least to have had a glimpse of its possibilities.

———

The Bryces left Washington with some regret in 1913. 'It is a sad wrench to both of us to leave this country where we have been received everywhere with such unceasing kindness', Bryce wrote to his good friend (and fellow Scot) Andrew Carnegie, with whom he had corresponded regularly about problems of peacemaking in the face of the threats of jingoism and militarism, as well as about racial problems in the American South. But he knew the time was right: 'It seemed to us that duty rather called us home, and there are two big books, begun long ago, which I desire if possible to finish while some strength remains, & which could not be finished here.'[115] They were the biography of Justinian—destined to remain unfinished—and, the immediate priority, the big book on democracy, on which he had already been collecting material for a decade. But world events would get in the way of that too.

'No British Ambassador within living memory has been so widely popular in the United States of America, or has exercised so healthy and beneficent an influence on behalf of his country.' So pronounced Lord Curzon, once a political opponent, soon after Bryce's return to Britain.[116] Lawrence Lowell, the president of Harvard, went even further: 'There is no British subject who has the influence over the people of the United States that you have.'[117] That was in January 1917, when Lowell was urging Bryce to come to the United States to speak in favour of the League to Enforce Peace, the American counterpart of the League of Nations Society, founded in Britain later that year. If his vigorous programme of speech-making during his ambassadorship had enabled Bryce to build up a huge cultural capital in the United States, it was a capital on which he had to draw abundantly in wartime, as the leading go-between seeking to act on American opinion to facilitate the entry of the United States into the war on the Allied side. This is a central theme of the next chapter.

11

The War of Words

FOR SOMEONE who was in his seventy-seventh year in August 1914, Bryce was exceptionally busy during the First World War.[1] He chaired an official UK committee of inquiry into German war atrocities in Belgium; he undertook a formally unofficial inquiry, with Arnold Toynbee, into Ottoman atrocities in Armenia; at Lloyd George's invitation he chaired a conference on the reform of the Second Chamber; and he presided over the Bryce Group, which had a formative role in developing the idea of an international organization for the avoidance of war that came to fruition in the League of Nations. Along with other historians and jurists, he was vocal in articulating the war aims of the Entente powers, with a view especially to influencing public opinion in the neutral nations, and not least in the United States.[2] He was active in public, or behind the scenes, in a host of wartime campaigns—for charitable aid for Belgium, Armenia, and Syria and Palestine; against retaliatory bombing; against concessions to Ulster in resolving the Irish question; and so on.[3] These activities are well known, and much debated, but they are only half the story. He was also astonishingly busy in the world of learned societies: as president of the British Academy from 1913 to 1917; the Classical Association in 1916–1917; the newly formed Council of Humanistic Studies; and the (also newly formed) Council for the Study of International Relations. He was much in demand—even more than ever—as a public voice for history, writing for, presiding at, and addressing anniversary commemorations for Jan Hus (quincentenary, 1915), Magna Carta (septcentenary, 1915), Anglo-American Peace (centenary, 1915), Walter Raleigh (tercentenary, 1918), and later Dante (sexcentenary, 1921).[4] Throughout his career, Bryce moved back and forth between the worlds of politics and of scholarship, but probably at no other point was he so productively amphibious.

International Ethics and the Mobilization of Minds

Bryce's approach to questions of international politics was always infused with a strong dose of ethics. The Gladstonian fight against 'Beaconsfieldism' in the 1870s was a formative moment in his political career; the more so because it coincided with Bryce's own discovery of Armenia in 1876. 'It seems as if we had forsaken Christian principles altogether in our foreign policy, and had no thought but of the rights of the strongest', he wrote to Elizabeth Spence Watson in 1879, anticipating what he would say about Germany in the Great War.[5] The second major formative moment was the campaign against the Boer War. Chamberlainism, like Beaconsfieldism, was not simply a betrayal of ethical principles in foreign policy: he thought it tended to corrupt the body politic at home too. In 1901 he told another leading pro-Boer, W. T. Stead, that the country needed 'nothing less than a spiritual revival' to reverse 'the loss of all the old moral feelings'. He feared that 'moral declension is the harbinger of other evils also'.[6] In both instances Bryce tended to personalize the evil. Disraeli lowered British public life, though not as much as Chamberlain, who 'has done more than anyone to degrade our politics'.[7]

In the summer of 1914 Bryce was minded to oppose Britain's entry into the war until Germany's violation of Belgium's neutrality settled the matter for him. Thereafter he quickly became one of the foremost scholar-propagandists making the moral case for the Allied cause. The case for war was unimpeachable, he thought, because it turned on the protection of 'the faith of treaties and the safety of small nations'.[8] As he told Dicey in 1915: 'If we don't win, international morality will have received from the conduct of the German Govt a frightful setback; and treaty obligations will no longer count for anything.'[9] For Bryce what was at stake in the war was respect for international law and indeed for international morality: these were challenged by a German government which held (with the backing of German public opinion) 'that the State stands above all morality and all human feeling'.[10] This construction of the war was placed at the centre of his pamphlet on 'Neutral Nations and the War', published in the autumn of 1914 and much disseminated in English and in translation in the neutral countries. This is how the pamphlet opened:

> The present war has had some unexpected consequences. It has called the attention of the world outside Germany to certain amazing doctrines proclaimed there, which strike at the root of all international morality, as well as of all international law, and which threaten a return to the primitive savagery when every tribe was wont to plunder and massacre its neighbours.[11]

Bryce seized on General von Bernhardi's book, *Germany and the Next War* (1911), which, so he maintained, invoked Treitschke and other German authors in support of the doctrine that the state stood above all moral values: that the state was, indeed, the source of morality. In the face of this doctrine, which seemed to authorize the wholesale absorption of smaller by larger states, Bryce gave voice to his most articulate defence of the world-historical importance of small nations: 'History declares that no nation, however great, is entitled to try to impose its type of civilization on others. No race, not even the Teutonic or the Anglo-Saxon, is entitled to claim the leadership of humanity. Each people has in its time contributed something that was distinctively its own, and the world is far richer thereby than if any one race, however gifted, had established a permanent ascendancy.'[12] Some readers might have baulked at the declaration that 'We of the English-speaking race do not claim for ourselves, any more than we admit in others, any right to dominate by force or to impose our own type of civilization on less powerful races.'[13] But Bryce's point was not so much about practice as about doctrine. He acknowledged that many states had been guilty periodically of trampling on the rights of their smaller neighbours (more distant ones were not mentioned). What had changed, he thought, was that Germany's new ideologues declared this to be the highest form of statehood.

The point he especially objected to in the doctrines of 'the Bernhardi school' was the idea that war was a principal driver of human progress. Bryce understood the nobility of the idea of giving one's life for one's country, but he resisted any broader notion that war was morally uplifting.[14] He was far too much of a Cobdenite at heart to see war as a historically progressive force: 'The world advances not . . . only or even mainly by Fighting. It advances mainly by Thinking and by a process of reciprocal teaching and learning, by a continuous and unconscious co-operation of all its strongest and finest minds.'[15] That implied the fusion of races and nations, not the triumph and domination of one over another: 'Each race—Hellenic and Italic, Celtic and Teutonic, Iberian and Slavonic—has something to give, each something to learn; and when their blood is blent the mixed stock may combine the gifts of both.'[16]

From an early stage, the Great War was seen as a war that would require the mobilization of minds as well as of bodies: what the French historian Elie Halévy later called 'the organization of enthusiasm'.[17] For H. G. Wells, writing presciently in the early days of the war, 'the ultimate purpose of this war is propaganda, the destruction of certain beliefs and the creation of others'.[18] Academics on both sides threw themselves into this effort more zealously than they might have been happy with in retrospect.

Some of Bryce's activities have been extensively studied. The report on German war atrocities, in particular, is the subject of a huge literature.[19] Bryce himself is always treated as the dominant figure, although the membership of his committee was distinguished. The standard critique holds that the Bryce committee, under pressure from the government, had limited itself to a study of the written record of the depositions of Belgian refugees in Britain, and of French and British soldiers, and to the evidence of documents such as diaries taken from German soldiers who had been killed or taken prisoner. The committee failed to undertake a systematic investigation of the truth of even a sample of these depositions, and, while conceding that some of them certainly contained exaggerations or fabrications, the overall weight of the testimony was enough to convince them of the broad veracity of the allegations of German atrocities. Bryce himself seems to have been responsible for resisting pressure from the one dissenting member of his committee, the Cobdenite and former Liberal MP Harold Cox, to examine witnesses directly. All this was in spite of the fact that Bryce's initial response to the allegations of German outrages against the civilian population of Belgium was one of scepticism; and in spite of the fact that, though persuaded of the necessity of British entry into the war following the invasion of Belgium, he never yielded to jingoism.[20]

Probably it was a mistake on Bryce's part to accept the chairmanship of the inquiry, since neither government nor the public was in a mood to be content with a nuanced report. It has tended to damage his posthumous reputation. One scholar has called it 'one of Britain's most shameful propaganda endeavours at any time in the war'.[21] That is hyperbole. Recent historical work, while not exonerating the Bryce committee from criticisms of its methods, has tended to confirm the broad thrust of the allegations of German war crimes.[22] It was true that the Germans summarily executed civilian hostages, or used them as human shields; true that property, including cultural property was deliberately destroyed; true that women and girls were raped.[23] While the depositions were cited somewhat indiscriminately—on the unsatisfactory basis that some might have been false, but they could not all be—there was sufficient diary evidence to vindicate the broad picture.[24] When the French philologist Joseph Bédier studied German soldiers' diaries in the possession of the French General Staff, he came to broadly similar conclusions.[25] The committee was at fault—under pressure of time—in not being scrupulous enough in following procedures that would have stood up in a court of law, but it does not follow that the report was a piece of misinformation, as has been claimed. It did align Bryce too closely with the official mind, however, whereas in fact he was to show himself both a tireless advocate of the Allied cause, especially among the neutral nations, and at the same time a critic of government policy, in particular when there was any suspicion of retaliatory action directed at civilian populations.[26] He saw clearly that nuance and balance were victims of total war. Whether he appreciated this in his own conduct is doubtful.

If Bryce is sometimes depicted as a dupe in the matter of the German atrocities, this can hardly be said of the report on the Ottoman atrocities in Armenia. Exposing the Turkish oppression of Armenia had been a central activity of his for four decades, and especially since 1894–1896, when massacres in eastern Anatolia killed a hundred thousand Armenians or more.[27] But though Bryce was absolutely not a tool of the British government here, there was of course a propagandist context: the Entente powers were reeling at the impact, especially on the opinion of American Jews, of the evidence of atrocities committed in the Jewish Pale by retreating Russian troops. Evidence of Turkish atrocities in Armenia would be a powerful counterweight as far as the British government was concerned.[28] Hence Bryce's report, though prepared at the request of the foreign secretary, was presented as if it had been conducted on his own initiative. The report consisted essentially of an assemblage of documentary evidence, collated by Arnold Toynbee. It carried only the briefest of prefaces by Bryce himself, together with supporting statements from Herbert Fisher, Gilbert Murray, and the former president of the American Bar Association, Moorfield Storey. The conclusion to the preface was authentically Brycean, with a twin invocation of facts and public opinion:

> It is evidently desirable not only that ascertained facts should be put on record for the sake of future historians, while the events are still fresh in living memory, but also that the public opinion of the belligerent nations— and, I may add, of neutral peoples also—should be enabled by a knowledge of what has happened in Asia Minor and Armenia to exercise its judgment on the course proper to be followed when, at the end of the present war, a political re-settlement of the Nearer East has to be undertaken.[29]

The British government patently wanted to act on public opinion, especially in the United States. But Bryce also had a lifelong interest both in studying and in shaping public opinion; and in fact it was on the Armenian question that he had probably had most success in creating a favourable and informed international public opinion; even though any tangible benefits for the Armenian people themselves were not felt in his lifetime. He was successful primarily because he had been able, since the mid-1890s at least, to bring his American networks into play.[30] And in the early weeks of the war—long before he embarked on the report on the atrocities in Belgium, let alone the Armenian war—he had emerged as a key figure in presenting Britain's war aims to the neutral powers, and not just the United States. Needless to say, the report remains hugely contested in Turkey today, since the fact of the genocide itself is contested there.[31] The essential veracity of the account it presented is not questioned in mainstream historiography.

Armenia remained central to Bryce's concerns in international politics. He spoke on the Armenian question in the Lords on 28 July 1915, 6 October 1915, 3 November 1918, and 20 February 1919. The wartime minute book of the British Armenia Committee shows him figuring repeatedly, though he was not a member of the committee. At the end of the war he lobbied Lord Robert Cecil (Foreign Office under-secretary of state) on behalf of the committee, putting the Armenians' claims for proper consideration in a peace settlement. In February 1919 he pressed on Curzon the case for taking into account the wishes of the Armenians when assigning the mandate for Armenia; and for the British Armenia Committee that meant giving the mandate to the United States. In September 1919 the committee discussed the possibility of sending a delegation to the United States to urge America to accept the mandate. Bryce would be consulted on this.[32]

Another issue that surged up the international political agenda as the Ottoman Empire crumbled was the Palestinian question, and in particular the Zionist project of encouraging Jewish settlements with a view to (re-)establishing a Jewish homeland. The Armenian and the Jewish questions were intertwined in quite complex ways. As Toynbee recognized with hindsight, his report on the Armenian genocide was useful to the Allies at a time when they were seeking to coax the United States to enter the war; equally, the Balfour Declaration, which built on negotiations that preceded American entry into the war, was evidently intended to raise the reputation of the Allies in the eyes of Jewish opinion in the United States.[33]

Bryce had long-standing sympathies for the Zionist cause, dating back as far as the early 1880s, when he represented a constituency with a notably large Jewish population. In his case these sympathies were nourished by the kind of philo-Semitism that was by no means unusual among British nonconformists. This is another instance where it is important not to be misled by conflating Bryce's views with those of Freeman, who often gave vent to crude anti-Semitic prejudice, especially in denouncing Disraeli. Bryce's position was very different. In a preface to a book on *The Jew in London* in 1900, he speculated about 'the permanence of Jewish nationality in the future'. There were, it seemed, two possible futures for Anglo-Jewry in Bryce's mind. One was the continued erosion of religious orthodoxy, in which case, with the demise of the externalities of religious identity, barriers to intermarriage would disappear; and intermarriage was 'by far the most potent solvent of racial distinctions'. But Bryce seemed to have a sense that something important would be lost by the erosion of Jewish nationhood, for 'if the race remains distinctive and cohesive, it will probably be a potent force in Europe for generations to come, not only by its undoubted talents and energy, but in virtue of its remarkable cohesion, which so greatly increases the force its individual men of wealth and ability can put forth'. But the distinctiveness of the Jewish race depended fundamentally on the distinctiveness of the Jewish religion: 'the religion of Israel is the ark of Jewish nationality.'[34] It can readily be seen how the second of these possible futures for Anglo-Jewry, and indeed Euro-Jewry, could issue in Zionism.

The Bryces visited Palestine in the spring of 1914, on the eve of the European crisis that precipitated war. This was, Bryce told Esme Howard, 'a pilgrimage which has long been on my mind', and while his account of that visit has little to say of the politics of the country, the visit certainly rekindled his interest in another land suffering (as he saw it) poverty and degradation due to the iniquities of Ottoman rule.[35] Under an honest government, he thought, Palestine might become 'a prosperous and even populous country', even taking its place in 'the civilisation of the moment'. The Muslim population were 'a strong and often handsome race, naturally equal to the races of southern Europe'. Bryce observed that there were substantial Jewish settlements and a Jewish quarter in Jerusalem; but he also lamented that it was 'a land of the past, a land of memories—memories of religion, but chiefly of religious war'.[36]

That was the background to Bryce's engagement with the Zionist cause in the context of Turkish wartime atrocities against Jewish and Christian populations in Palestine. These aroused renewed interest in the colonization of the country: the Geographical Society heard a paper on the subject by the medical missionary E. W. G. Masterman (brother of the Liberal cabinet minister Charles Masterman) in March 1917, and Bryce led the discussion, invoking his own 'scanty knowledge' of Palestine, deploring the negligence and latterly the destructiveness of Turkish rule, and concluding that any protectorate to be exercised over the country could best be held by a Protestant power.[37] In May 1917 it was reported that the *New York Jewish Morning Journal* had received a cable from Bryce, recording 'much sympathetic interest taken here in re-establishment of Jews in Palestine', but also pointing out that substantial investment was needed to allow Palestine to support a larger population than at present.[38] This was a point he returned to the following year, writing for a symposium on 'Palestine regained' in a leading Jewish magazine in New York. He maintained that Palestine could accommodate a much larger population: around 300,000 more in its current state, but, with investment in the infrastructure (irrigation, reservoirs, and the like) the same number again. He looked to 'the liberality of those wealthy men who, both in Europe and America, have already shown their sympathy with the Zionist movement'.[39]

Race in Wartime

In February 1915 Bryce gave the Creighton lecture before the University of London. His subject was 'Race Sentiment as a Factor in History'. But this was no recapitulation of his Romanes lecture. This time he sounded a note of scepticism about racial determinism from the outset:

> Some writers have sought to represent certain political and social institutions as characteristic of certain linguistic families of mankind. When, however, it was found that the popular assembly—the Agora of Homeric Greece and the Folkmót of Saxon England—once supposed to be the peculiar glory of the Aryan peoples, could be paralleled by the Pitso of South African Basutos, this doctrine withered up and died. Neither has the attempt to determine racial affinities by the possession of a common stock of superstitions or religious rites and usages been more successful. Whoever looks into that vast treasury of folklore which the lifelong labours of Sir James Frazer have given us in the volumes called *The Golden Bough* will find that certain religious beliefs and ceremonial usages have prevailed over most of the world in forms practically identical. Traces survive in Western Europe of superstitions now alive among the aborigines of Queensland. Some day, no doubt, we may discover solid ground for a theory of race origins and race affinities, but at present we are only groping and guessing.[40]

He went on to puncture other staples of late nineteenth-century racial thought. All the races of modern Europe are the product of intermingling, he argued: Iceland alone was 'unaffected by immigration or conquest'.[41] National character was partly shaped by race, he agreed; but the importance of this determinant had been 'much exaggerated', and far more was 'due to the conditions physical and economic and social under which the nation has been developed'.

He thought that nations did have characters, or 'distinctive qualities'; but these were 'as much the consequences as the causes of its history'. A footnote added that the same argument could be made of the characters of prominent individuals: 'Environment and education, moulding ideas and implanting habits, how far do they not go?'[42]

The central focus of the lecture, however, was not on the extent to which race, as an objective fact, shaped history, but rather on the importance of racial consciousness in history. Bryce's argument was that the consciousness of race was largely a modern, indeed nineteenth-century, invention. He distinguished between national and racial consciousness: national sentiment he defined— much as he had done three decades earlier in his discussion of centripetal and centrifugal forces—in terms that call Renan to mind: it was 'the product of many things, such as a common language and literature, traditions and the memory of past exploits, a sense of collective interest, a belief in national institutions', even a belief in a 'national mission', but it might well have only 'a comparatively slender racial element'.[43] He invoked Switzerland (of course), and Belgium and Canada as instances of nationalities composed of different races and speaking different languages, and the republics of Spanish America as an instance of what was 'practically the same race' divided into several nations, sometimes hostile to one another.[44]

But Bryce was less interested, here, in race as a determinant of the cohesion of a nation, and more in race as a factor in a nation's external relations to other nations. A rapid survey of the ancient world led him to reiterate a point he had made in his comparison of Roman and British Empires, that antiquity knew little of the sentiment of race, and that the Romans, in particular 'showed little contempt for their provincial subjects and no racial aversion'.[45] The barbarian invasions may have been, objectively, 'a gigantic Race Movement'; but subjectively they were not. Contemporary sources gave little hint of opposition, let alone enmity, between 'Teutonic and Latin peoples', and the invaders—except the Huns—appear to have felt awe for Roman civilization. In the Middle Ages, meanwhile, it was religious distinctions that mattered: 'They were ages of incessant strife, but when men were not fighting for booty or conquest they were fighting to propagate their own creeds or worships.'[46]

It was in the early modern period—a term not used until much later—that Bryce traced the emergence of 'real nations', especially once the wars of religion were over. But they were 'real nations' in which the consciousness of race was weak: to illustrate this point, Bryce invoked the international prestige of French fashion and manners. Overall, 'down till the days of the French

Revolution there had been very little in any country, or at any time, of self-conscious racial feeling.'[47] By contrast, in Bryce's own time he found a world 'full of the rival pretensions and jarring claims of races'. Irredentism, separatist nationalisms in both parts of the Dual Monarchy, and Panslavism were all manifestations of the universal power of the sentiment of race in the modern world. National pride—harmless in itself—was degenerating into international hatred. It was something of a paradox, Bryce suggested, that this should be happening at a time of unprecedented global connections: peoples knew each other more than ever, traded with each other more than ever, yet also hated each other more than ever. There was little sign of the softening, pacific influence of what eighteenth-century economists and moralists called 'doux commerce'.[48] Why was this?

Part of the explanation lay in intellectual change: the intellectual tools, the scientific tools, were now available to classify languages and to classify peoples ethnologically.[49] But Bryce also adduced political explanations: the growing power of a racially tinged nationalism in international politics was the corollary of the rise of popular self-government in the wake of the American and French Revolutions. That was partly because the principle of popular sovereignty implicitly raised the issue of national self-determination; though Bryce was better here at explaining the rise of nationalism as a political force than he was at accounting for its racialization.[50]

This was indisputably a wartime text: not at all a piece of wartime propaganda, though clearly Bryce was quite capable of turning his hand to that; but certainly a lecture deeply imbued with a melancholia about where the liberal nationalist optimism of 1848 had led. In particular, since Bryce was by now president of the British Academy and wrestling with the challenges posed by the war to prospects of international intellectual cooperation, the lecture lamented the way in which history and literature had been distorted in being put to the service of political nationalism:

> Men's souls are raised by the recollection of great deeds done by their forefathers. But the study of the past has its dangers when it makes men transfer past claims and past hatreds to the present. A sage friend remarked to me lately while we were discussing the complications of South-eastern Europe: 'How much better if we could get rid of history altogether!' The learned men and the literary men, often themselves intoxicated by their own enthusiasms, never put their books to a worse use then when they filled each people with a conceit of its own super-eminent gifts and merits.[51]

Just as 'science has made war more hideous and terrible', so 'learning and literature have done something to prepare nations for war'. Yet 'a sounder learning and a deeper insight might have corrected this danger and taught the
peoples that they have at least as much to gain by co-operation as by competition, and more to gain from friendship than from hatred'.[52]

Drawing on Heinrich Heine, and perhaps also on Mazzini, Bryce reflected
on the tensions between duties to humanity and duties to nation:

> Those of us whose recollection extends over half a century sometimes think
> that there was then a stronger sense of the allegiance which the members
> of every nation owe to Humanity, and a more general sympathy with the
> efforts of backward peoples towards freedom and progress than the last few
> decades have shown. We are often told that the advance of democracy is
> tending to dispose nations to peace. It may be so, though longer experience
> is needed before this can be deemed certain. But democracy has not, so far,
> made nations less selfish or less vain of their own greatness.[53]

If democracy could not be expected to bring perpetual peace as a matter of
course, institutions would have to be devised to guard against the recurrence
of world war.

A League of Nations?

The role played by British intellectuals in the genesis of the League of Nations
has recently been reasserted in an important book by Sakiko Kaiga.[54] It is well
understood that the league was not simply a product of postwar peacemaking,
but was (as a project) an integral part of wartime diplomacy: in particular,
Britain's efforts to draw the United States, and other neutral nations, into the
war on the Allied side. But Kaiga amplifies this story by showing how this kind
of diplomatic effort only made sense in the context of previous efforts by pro-
league intellectuals to shape public opinion. Bryce is central to this story, first
as the figurehead (but by no means the leader) of the Bryce Group, which was
the first group to draw up clear plans for a postwar league of nations; and
second as one of the key intermediaries between British and American intellectual and political elites and the wider public.

One of the curious features of Bryce's wartime role was that at the very time
that he was actively collaborating with the British government's efforts to deploy evidence of German atrocities to generate popular backing for the war and
to win over the neutral nations, he was also working alongside near-pacifists

such as Arthur Ponsonby to devise schemes for the avoidance of future wars.[55] This was by no means a case of logical inconsistency: it was perfectly coherent to hold that the German invasion of Belgium had made war (on Britain's part) both just and necessary, and to believe that war is both bad and capable of being, if not abolished, at least rendered less likely. Moreover, both the demonstration of Germany's use of barbaric methods and the articulation of clear plans for the avoidance of future wars were practically useful in winning over the hearts and minds of neutral countries.[56] But psychologically it must have been something of a strain to be working to persuade the British and international public of the necessity of *this* war, and at the same time to be making the argument that the strongest long-term agency for the maintenance of peace must be a pacific international public opinion.[57]

It was within the Bryce Group that the idea of a league of nations for the prevention of future wars was nurtured: in fact the coinage of the term 'league of nations' is usually attributed to the group's founder, the Cambridge historian Goldsworthy Lowes Dickinson.[58] In particular, the group formulated the idea of collective security (not yet the term itself) as the key mechanism for the maintenance of peace; but there were disagreements over whether the threat of force, in addition to diplomatic and economic sanctions, would be needed to ensure that the will of the international community prevailed.[59] Those disagreements, important though they were, did not split the group, since its members were agreed that the ultimate objective was to create an international public opinion to uphold peace; institutional mechanisms were interim means to ensure the effectiveness of such public opinion as currently exists.

The precise nature of Bryce's role in the group remains somewhat opaque in the existing literature. Lowes Dickinson, who called it 'my group' in October 1914, recalled that Bryce 'attended several meetings during our later period', which is hardly brimming with a sense of his importance.[60] He repeatedly cited the heavy burden of war work as a reason to decline formal responsibilities: 'war correspondence takes nearly all my time', he told W. H. Dickinson early in 1917.[61] But the archival record—in particular, W. H. Dickinson's papers, and G. L. Dickinson's letters too—makes Bryce's contribution abundantly clear.[62] He contributed his name (of which copious use was made), his advice, especially on pragmatic considerations of timing, choice of allies, and reserve about distant objectives in the communication of proposals to influential individuals, to governments, and later to the wider public. He may not have attended many meetings, but the group's work in his absence was often structured around texts he had produced: in particular, a short memorandum he wrote in November 1914 which formed the basis for the group's work.[63] He advised on the drafting of texts and helped to ensure the circulation of the proposals to the right people. We know that he agreed to chair the group on condition that its deliberations remained private, and that until an end to the war was in sight its proposals should be limited to private circulation. As the elder statesman in the group—indeed, the only one of the core members with government experience—it was he who steered the group to avoid any suggestion of arguing for a world federation, and to limit itself to practical objectives that would not taint it with the suspicion of pacifism.[64] He told W. H. Dickinson in 1917 that, in issuing invitations to the inaugural meeting of the League of Nations Society in 1917, 'the great thing will be to avoid utopian cranks who talk about a "World State" & the immediate & final abolition of all War'.[65] He played an important role in setting up that meeting, which he chaired, and it was he who sent the 'big name' invitations: for instance, to the prime minister of Canada, Robert Borden.[66] It was certainly Bryce who ensured that the group's proposals gained traction in the United States, where it helped precipitate Theodore Marburg's creation of the League to Enforce Peace.[67] It was Bryce who facilitated Marburg's access to the British government, for example, by setting up a meeting between Marburg and Sir Edward Grey in March 1916.[68] He was chosen to chair the group for a reason—his name carried weight, in Britain and overseas—and that is why his name stuck to the group. Even though he was not the group's driving force, his role was clearly pivotal.

The dynamics within the group deserve further consideration. Bryce obviously belonged to a different generation from the other core members. He was seventy-six at the outbreak of war: Lowes Dickinson was fifty-two; Hobson and Wallas, fifty-six; Ponsonby, forty-one; Cross, fifty; Willoughby Dickinson, fifty-five. The others—Wallas being the notable exception—gravitated from Liberalism to the Labour Party in the wake of the war. It is difficult to imagine that Bryce would have done so, even had he lived to see Labour in power. Several of the other members exhibited (in other contexts) something of the post-Victorian generation's disdain for Bryce as an archetypal Victorian. Lowes Dickinson, an associate of the Bloomsbury Group, wrote that he admired Bryce's vitality, his wide-ranging knowledge, his moral courage ('which, in politics, appears to belong to the middle of the nineteenth century'), but he found his mind uninteresting, being too given over to practical purposes.[69]

Graham Wallas, a self-conscious (perhaps rather too self-conscious) modernist in his approach to social science, was dismissive of Bryce's notion of an 'ideal democracy', which (Wallas thought) meant 'the kind of democracy which might be possible if human nature were as he himself would like it to be, and as he was taught at Oxford to think that it was'.[70] One member of the group to whom Bryce was closer was Hobson, whom he had known since their days campaigning against the Boer War. It was Hobson who, at the very last moment, drew Bryce into a Neutrality Group in August 1914, and it may be this that was the genesis of the Bryce Group.[71]

The group's acceptance that the best long-term guarantee of peace would be an international public opinion opposed to war as a way of conducting international politics was very Brycean. It was the main theme of the 'prefatory note' that he prefixed to the 'Proposals for the Avoidance of War', which the group had printed and circulated privately in several drafts. 'The public opinion of the world', he wrote, 'would surely prove to possess a greater force than it has yet shewn if it could but find an effective organ through which to act.'[72] Advocates of international law as the remedy for the anarchic character of international relations had long faced this difficulty: without any *sanction* behind its decrees, how could international law even remotely resemble law properly so called, as defined by Bentham, Austin, and their followers?[73] Bryce, in fact, was a long-standing critic of Austinian jurisprudence, but he was conscious of the difficulty. International public opinion was the most promising solution he or anyone had been able to identify; and if it had 'an effective organ through which to act', that would constitute at least a rudimentary foundation for an incipient body of international law.[74]

This invocation of public opinion called to mind the optimistic faith in rationality that Wallas found, and critiqued, in Bryce and other Liberals of his generation. Bryce's lifelong interest in public opinion—in understanding it, and in acting on it—has been a recurrent theme in this book, and the following chapter will show in more detail how he thought it was formed. He certainly thought a rational and moral public opinion was not some kind of natural phenomenon but had to be shaped and led by the educated classes. The way in which the Bryce Group's proposal set up an enlightened public opinion not as the starting-point, but as the end to be achieved shows his influence. The institutions of international order had to be brought into being, at least in a rudimentary form, in order for any kind of developed international public opinion to take shape. Bryce put his faith both in ethics *and* in mechanism.[75]

The Humanities at War

Alongside his work in exposing German and then Turkish atrocities, and forming plans for an international organization to reduce the risk of future wars,
Bryce was also carving out for himself a new role as the foremost spokesman
for the humanities—newly labelled as such—at a time when they were perceived to be facing an existential threat from the newly self-confident science
community. Bryce was by nature no narrow partisan in this contest. He valued
educational breadth, and a breadth that encompassed the sciences, as his own
education certainly had. But he had long been concerned that, except in the
public schools, the sciences were increasingly regarded as the central, and the
humanities a peripheral, component of education. He worried that 'this
change would tend to produce a hard, dry unfertile type of mind as compared
with the type of mind which literary and human studies ought to produce'.[76]
Bryce's language—in private and to an extent in public too—was really quite
trenchant. 'It is high time that something was done to offer resistance to the
extravagant claims made for the teaching of science', he told the medieval historian Thomas Tout in 1916.[77]

The defence of the humanities has now become a genre in its own right: in
the Anglophone world alone, there are notable books by Martha Nussbaum,
Helen Small, and Stefan Collini.[78] It is instructive to analyse Bryce's contribution in this diachronic perspective, and to consider how far he foreshadowed
the kinds of argument made, or dissected, by these later writers; and also how
far he moved beyond the arguments made by high Victorian critics such as
Matthew Arnold and John Stuart Mill, who both wrote in a very different
cultural context in which the battle was still much more between the ancients
and the moderns than between the humanities and the sciences.

To understand why the humanities needed defending, however, we have
to attend to the wartime context. It is well established that the First World
War saw major efforts to mobilize science for military purposes: not immediately, but certainly from the middle of 1915 onwards, when a long war was
regarded as inevitable.[79] This gave the natural sciences a new prestige: 'the
word "science" is on everyone's lips', declared the *Cambridge Magazine* in
1916.[80] Lloyd George called the war an 'engineer's war'; more commonly it
was referred to as a chemists' war.[81] There was a concerted effort to use the
manifest military importance of the natural sciences to campaign for the
peacetime necessity of a radical rebalancing of the educational system
towards scientific education.

The British Science Guild, which had been founded in 1905, was vocal in making the case for greater investment in science—and priority for the sciences in secondary education—as an imperative for national and imperial efficiency. In 1916 it established an influential Committee on the Neglect of Science.[82] This maintained that ignorance of 'the ascertained facts and principles of science' ran through government, the civil service, Parliament, and indeed the general public, 'including a large proportion of those engaged in industrial and commercial enterprises'; and this had done material harm to the war effort.[83] The zoologist Ray Lankester and the novelist, social critic, and scientific popularizer H. G. Wells were protagonists in lambasting the British Establishment for its failure to embrace the imperative of investment in the natural sciences.[84] Lankester assembled a collection of essays on this subject in his *Natural Science and the Classical System in Education*, published on behalf of the Committee on the Neglect of Science 1918.[85] The Thomson Report on the Position of Natural Science in the Educational System of Great Britain (also 1918) was something of a landmark.[86]

Practitioners of the humanities were on the defensive—something that has subsequently become their habitual stance. For most of the nineteenth century they remained imbued with a self-confidence that a classical education conferred not only cultural capital but also material reward. But the experience of total war meant that the defenders of the humanities had to combat a sense of their lack of practical usefulness in comparison with the sciences.

In fact, humanities scholars were anything but useless in the world wars. In the Second World War, the disciplined skills of linguists, historians, philosophers, and others played a critical (though underappreciated) role in military intelligence at Bletchley Park and elsewhere.[87] There was no counterpart in the First World War, but historians, philosophers and others, Bryce among them, were very active in the war of information, and they brought specific skills and knowledge to these tasks.[88] Bryce argued that 'the German theory of the State' underpinned German aggression, and that thesis was widely shared by philosophers too—by Sir Henry Jones, J. H. Muirhead, and L. T. Hobhouse, who, after watching a Zeppelin raid on London, wrote that it was 'the visible and tangible outcome of a false and wicked doctrine', namely, 'the Hegelian theory of the god-state'.[89]

But the value of a few eminent historians and philosophers was one thing; it did not make the case for the importance of the humanities in the education of the many. Humanities scholars now sensed that they needed to organize to make their voice heard. Bryce was president of a Council of Humanistic

Studies founded in 1916 to coordinate the work of the Classical, English, Geo-graphical, Historical, and Modern Language Associations.[90] At the same time, several of the key figures in the Council of Humanistic Studies were active within the British Academy in leading a campaign for the expansion of the academy beyond its statutory limit of one hundred fellows. This split the acad-emy: there was strong resistance from those who felt that the most important function of the academy was to keep new members out in order to maintain standards. But those on the other side of the argument—notably the histori-ans Thomas Tout and George Prothero, with discreet support from Bryce as president—maintained that if the academy was to do anything beyond hold annual fellowship elections, it needed to be larger in order to sustain a critical mass of scholars in each of its disciplines and subdisciplines—and hence to make a stronger impression on the public. 'To my mind, the question of dis-tinction is secondary', Prothero told Tout; 'what we want is influence.' It was its numbers that gave the Royal Society its influence.[91]

It was in this context that the term 'the humanities' first came into common use. This is not a point that has hitherto been established in the literature. Helen Small, in one of the best contributions to the debate on the uses of the humani-ties, writes that it was in the 1940s that 'the humanities' came to designate a group of disciplines.[92] The 1940s did indeed see the start of a new phase in this conceptual history. But the new terminology was seeded earlier: in the First World War. When the British Academy was born in 1902—Bryce being one of the midwives—it did not use the term 'humanities' to define its remit. It was officially designated 'The British Academy for the Promotion of the Historical, Philosophical and Philological Studies.'[93] This definition was meant both to exclude the *belles lettres*, lest it be seen as a British version of the Académie Française, and to highlight the academy's scholarly and scientific character; but it was necessary to use an awkward circumlocution of this kind because neither 'the humanities' nor any alternative was a generally accepted way of referring to these disciplines. In the official deliberations on the establishment of the academy, no one invoked the term 'humanities' at all.[94] The preferred terms were 'exact literary studies' or 'philosophico-historical science', both used by the International Association of Academies, which met in Paris in 1901.[95] When 'moral sciences' (a rough counterpart of the German *Geisteswissenschaften*) was used, it tended to refer to sometimes to the social sciences, sometimes to phi-losophy and psychology, but not to the humanities as a whole.[96]

It was really in the period 1916–1917, towards the end of Bryce's stint as president of the academy, that the term 'humanities' came into common usage.

FIGURE 11.1. Sir Adophus Ward (1837–1924, left) with Bryce
on the drive at Hindleap. They had known each other since
both were professors at Owens College in the 1870s. Bryce
succeeded Ward as president of the British Academy in 1913.

It was then that, for the first time, we see it appearing (in more than an isolated
usage) in parliamentary debates, notably in a high-powered debate on 'the
training of the nation' initiated by Lord Haldane in the House of Lords in 1916,
when (in the context of pressure to strengthen the place of scientific education) a succession of speakers voiced concern over the future of the humanities
in the educational system. It was clear from that debate that 'the humanities'
was now starting to become an established way of referring to what had formerly been called 'the literary subjects'.[97]

Bryce himself made an intervention in this debate, warning against the cult of 'organization' that was taking hold. It was important, he argued, not to sacrifice the English spirit of independence and free individuality; important, in other words, that the focus on the means necessary for victory in war should not obscure the ends for which the war was being fought. Here Bryce took issue with Haldane, his former cabinet colleague but also long-standing opponent. Haldane had studied philosophy at Göttingen in the 1870s and was thereafter both a prominent advocate for philosophical idealism and also perhaps the leading Germanophile in British public life—and it was this enthusiasm for Germany that forced him out of the cabinet when the wartime coalition was formed in 1915.[98] He was a Liberal Imperialist—one of the trio who had unsuccessfully conspired to keep Campbell Bannerman out of the premiership in 1905—and a proponent of the collectivist turn of Liberalism in the name of national efficiency (one contemporary even thought, of course wrongly, that Haldane had invented the word 'efficiency').[99] He was one of the few Liberals who had backed the 1902 Education Act, which Bryce had taken the lead in opposing. He had little regard for Bryce, and the sentiment was reciprocated.[100] In private Bryce called him 'the incessantly active & flexible man from Auchterarder' (Haldane's Perthshire mansion, Cloan, was near Auchterarder). He continued (to his sisters): 'He has more flexibility than E. Grey, more restless ambition than Asquith, but less solid ability than the latter, less elevation of purpose than the former. You remember his S. African War record. His judgment is anything but sound.'[101] This Lords debate shone a light on the difference in mental outlook between these two leading Liberal statesmen-scholars.

In making the case for the humanities in this context, Bryce and his associates certainly made use of the old case for liberal as opposed to practical or vocational education and embraced a defence of pure as opposed to applied science as part of a rounded liberal education. The point was that education should be balanced and not subservient to instrumental objectives. This was the classic humanist defence: a university education should develop a taste for 'intellectual pleasures'—as Bryce told an audience at the University of Chicago in 1907.[102] In his presidential address to the Classical Association in January 1917, he took his stand not for the humanities *against* science, but for 'a large and philosophical conception of the aims of education, and that material, narrow, and even vulgar view which looks only to immediate practical results and confounds pecuniary with educational values'.[103]

A second line of argument focused on the fundamental place of the humanities in education for citizenship. This is the argument associated today in particular with the American philosopher Martha Nussbaum: the 'democracy needs us' argument.[104] As we saw in chapter 10, Bryce was a long-standing proponent of education for citizenship ('civics' in the United States). He did a lot to bring this argument to the fore. It was by no means entirely new, for it was certainly foreshadowed in J. S. Mill's *St Andrews Address* of 1867. But Mill wrote at a time when Britain was on the cusp of the transition to democracy and *before* it was widely accepted that Britain *was* a democracy, or was inevitably *becoming* a democracy, and certainly before it was widely accepted that democracy was something to be welcomed rather than to be mitigated. The context in which Bryce and others wrote in the early twentieth century was decisively different.

Finally, and most intriguingly, there was the appeal to a kind of 'international civics'. This kind of argument took advantage of the implicit connection between 'humanity' and 'the humanities' to suggest that education in the humanities, ancient and modern, could play a key role in the quest for international peace. We have seen that Bryce was a central figure in making the case for the creation of a League of Nations, and (crucially) acting as a bridge between British and American proponents of the league. Several leading proponents of the league in interwar Britain—notably Alfred Zimmern, Gilbert Murray, and Ernest Barker—were classicists who stressed the role of international civics in the creation of an international public opinion.[105] Others were modern historians such as G. P. Gooch and H. A. L. Fisher.[106] All five of these were well known to Bryce: Gooch was his parliamentary private secretary, Fisher his biographer, Barker a sort of research assistant for the new edition of *The Holy Roman Empire* in 1904. They all belonged, however, to the generation after him: all were born in the period 1865–1879. Most were Hellenists by inspiration, whereas Bryce was much more of a Romanist and a Latinist. There was a certain moral austerity in his conception of citizenship: much more so than in Murray or Zimmern.

The precise relationship between the concept of the humanities and the idea of an international civics is hard to demonstrate textually, because the play on the affinities between 'humanity' and 'the humanities' is oblique.[107] But Bryce was very clear that the projected league of nations could not rely on political machinery alone. It depended on the existence of a sentiment of belonging to a common humanity, and the league would have to take the initiative in fostering such a sentiment. He wrote that it 'relies upon and seeks to foster the sentiment of human brotherhood, making men recognize an allegiance to mankind, a sense of what they owe to its common welfare'.[108] That was in a wartime essay (dating, it seems, from 1918) expounding the vision of a league of nations. But it is even more revealing to turn to his presidential address to the British Academy in July 1916. There he made the same essential point, but fleshed it out by explicitly connecting it to the idea of an international public opinion:

> What is needed is the creation, not only of a feeling of allegiance to humanity and of an interest in the welfare of other nations as well as one's own—what in fact may be called an International or Supra-national Mind—but also of an International Public Opinion, a common opinion of many peoples which shall apply moral standards to the conduct of other nations with a judgment biased less than now by the consideration of the particular national interests which each nation conceives itself to have.[109]

He went on immediately to connect this point to a lament for the disruption to the practice of international academic relations in which he had been an important player before the war:

> The severance of friendly relations between the great peoples of Europe, the interruption of all personal intercourse, and of that co-operation in the extension of knowledge and the discovery of new truth from which every people has gained so much. The study of philosophy and history has done little for those of us who pursue it if it has not extended their vision beyond their own country and their own time, pointing out to them that human progress has been achieved by the united efforts of many races and many types of intellect and character, each profiting by the efforts of the others, and also reminding them that for further advance this co-operation is essential.'[110]

This was a prospectus for the project of 'intellectual co-operation' subsequently pursued by the League of Nations.[111]

Throughout the twentieth century and beyond the natural sciences far outpaced the humanities in terms of the practice of international cooperation. There is no reason to suppose that Bryce denied the potential of the natural sciences to contribute to the formation of an international public opinion. But he took it for granted that subjects like history, philosophy, law, and classics too, had a more direct bearing on the shaping of that public opinion, precisely because their subject was the study of humanity itself.

From the very outbreak of war in 1914, Bryce was on the one hand active in making the moral case for war, and at the same time in taking a leading role in thinking about schemes to avoid war in future: the schemes that resulted in the creation of the League of Nations. But a central theme in his thinking about war and peace from the beginning was that the restoration and preservation of peace would depend not primarily on machinery, which by itself would be ineffective, but on the formation of an international public opinion that would promote the peaceable resolution of conflicts: 'A Court or Council of persons representing the Great States might be created, but there is little chance that the Powers would grant it any executive authority or bind themselves to execute its decisions. It will have to rely on the public opinion of the world for support.'[112] He did not underestimate the difficulties involved in so shaping public opinion that it could work as a stable force for peace, not just nationally but internationally. 'Public opinion', he told Charles W. Eliot, 'is a real working force only in England, I should fear, and even here is amorphous, strong only when it has great leaders, of whom we see none. Hence I am not sanguine.'[113] Over time he came to appreciate that just as institutional machinery was useless without the backing of public opinion, so public opinion was ineffective without some kind of sanction.[114]

Peacemaking

Bryce was disappointed with the work of the peacemakers at Versailles. He thought the settlement a Carthaginian peace which would create lasting resentment in Germany and hamper both the prospects of the establishment of democratic government in Germany and the chances of securing peace. This was very much along the lines of the argument put forward by J. M. Keynes in *The Economic Consequences of the Peace* (1919), a work he much admired.[115] He also thought that the architects of the settlement had leant much too far in the direction of satisfying the territorial ambitions of the Allied powers at the expense of the defeated Central powers, irrespective of the principles involved (in particular, national self-determination) and the facts of the particular case. The two instances on which he was especially vocal were the territorial gains made by Greece at the expense of Bulgaria and Italy at the expense of Austria. He wrote a characteristic piece on the latter instance—the Tyrolese—in the *Manchester Guardian* in June 1919. The bone of contention was not the general question of Italy's claims to the Trentino, which Bryce recognized as legitimate. It was the fate of the German-speaking population of the northern Tyrol. In making his case, Bryce invoked his authority as an historian (the language barrier, starting about twenty miles south of Botzen, had existed at least since the eighth century) and as a traveller too, for the German-speaking Tyrolese were, he wrote, 'an honest, simple, industrious race of peasants, as those of us who have climbed among their peaks and glaciers know them to be'. He rebutted any suggestion of *parti pris*: he had shown a zealous enthusiasm for the Italian cause throughout his life and had 'been privileged to know such heroes of the Italian Risorgimento as Mazzini, Saffi, and Minghetti'. Unjust settlements of this kind would create a standing resentment which would hamper the new League of Nations from the start.[116] On this and other causes, he both wrote to the press and lobbied influential friends, such as the American diplomat Henry White, who was a leading member of his country's delegation at Versailles.[117]

A number of scholars working in the field of 'intellectual reconstruction' after the war have drawn attention to the importance of the imperative to defeat Bolshevism. In an anticipation of later critiques of totalitarianism, Bolshevism was seen as a resurgence of the kind of barbarism that had been defeated in the guise of the Kaiser's Germany.[118] Bryce certainly endorsed this understanding of Bolshevism, which loomed large in his postwar correspondence. He saw 'the Prussian militaristic mind' and 'the Bolshevik mind' alike as atavistic mental states, evidence, perhaps, that the human intellect was no longer advancing.[119] In February 1919 he took lunch with C. P. Scott. 'He was very strong on the Bolshevik barbarities', recorded Scott. 'Thought there was ample evidence for them and that they vastly exceeded those of the French Revolution. There was in truth "a sea of blood."'[120]

One of Bryce's most important interlocutors on Bolshevik Russia was the ancient historian Alfred Zimmern, who in 1919 was appointed by University College, Aberystwyth, to the world's first professorship of international relations. Zimmern shared Bryce's alarm at the actions of the Bolshevik regime and was keen to establish a society or committee of inquiry to gather information on what was happening in Russia, and to influence British and international public opinion.[121] Bryce was supportive. 'Anything that can be done to open men's eyes and make them realise the hideousness of what is now passing in Russia, ought to be done', he replied; but he declined Zimmern's invitation to take the chair, feeling that the amount of correspondence would be too much for him, given that he was 'already hopelessly overburdened with work'.[122]

———

What are we to make of this whirlwind of activities in Bryce's later years? Does it illustrate his inability to say no to an invitation? Or perhaps a reluctance, in defiance of his frequent professions of intent, to settle down and complete *Modern Democracies*, and thereafter to embark on his long-cherished ambition to write a life of Justinian? Psychologically neither of these accounts is totally wide of the mark, but they nevertheless fail to do justice to the significance of what he was doing. In making the case for the public importance of the humanities he was, at the same time, trying to lay the intellectual foundations for a lasting peace. Probably at no other point in his life were his scholarly and public personae so interlinked.

Equally, Bryce's wartime role consisted primarily in seeking to act on and shape public opinion: in Britain, but even more so in the neutral countries, including in particular the United States (neutral, of course, until 1917). He built on the experience of a lifetime devoted in large measure to opinion formation. Whereas for most of his career, at least until 1907, his attention had been primarily concerned with opinion in Britain, he now had to take the world as a whole as his audience. The work of shaping international public opinion was anticipated in his efforts on the Armenian Question, on which—at least from the 1890s onward—he had engaged his international networks to promote an international cause. It was because of this record of international opinion formation that it came naturally to him to conceptualize international public opinion as a key agency in his vision for a peaceful postwar world.

At the same time, Bryce was continuing to work on the book that would be the last to appear in his lifetime, his *Modern Democracies*. It was in this book that he articulated, more fully than anywhere else, the fundamental and pervasive role that he attributed to public opinion in modern politics. While the book exhibited, to a pronounced degree, Bryce's habitual preoccupation with 'the facts', it also revealed more about himself than he appreciated. This is the subject of the final chapter.

12

Democratic Travails

IT CANNOT BE SAID THAT Bryce enjoyed writing *Modern Democracies*. His correspondence depicts it as a burden he had to bear, but one that was preventing him from getting back to the books he really wanted to write: in particular, the life of Justinian, which he had conceived at least four decades before.[1] On its completion he wrote to Dicey, who had probably had to endure more of these complaints than anyone: 'It is indeed a relief to have done with a piece of work which had latterly become so tiresome that I was sorry that I had ever touched it—& tiresome chiefly in that it seemed and still seems to me that I have done little but supply fresh illustrations of antiquated truisms.'[2] This was hardly Gibbon taking his 'everlasting leave of an old and agreeable companion'. But it raises—more insistently than is the case with any of Bryce's other works—the questions of what caused him to embark on the project, why he found it so challenging, but also why he pressed ahead in the face of these challenges. Bryce left behind him several unfinished books, or projected books which never really became more than projects, but here was a book that was completed in spite of its author's lack of taste for it. No one, in truth, has ever claimed it as his best work: his obsession with 'the facts' and his reluctance to impose himself upon them were taken much too far; something that Dicey warned him about.[3] Even so, it is a book that tells us a good deal about its author: much more than he would ever have suspected, or wanted.

Genesis

The genesis of *Modern Democracies* goes back to the Godkin lectures, a series of five, that Bryce gave at Harvard in the autumn of 1904, in memory of his friend Edwin Godkin, who died in 1902. He toyed with different titles—perhaps 'The

Natural History of Democracy', perhaps 'Phases of Popular Government', or maybe (more American and less Brycean) 'Methods of Enquiry in Political Science', but he ended up with 'The Study of Popular Governments'. As he explained, the plural was deliberate: 'Governments not Government, as I propose to deal with the comparison of different forms or types of Popular Government.'[4] The lectures appear to have been well attended: announcing the second lecture, the *Harvard Crimson* promised that 'a larger force of ushers would be present' than at the first, and 'it is expected that members of the University will find no difficulty in obtaining seats': the clear implication being that some of them had experienced some difficulty at the first lecture.[5] In accordance with his preference, he lectured from notes rather than reading a prepared text. He seems to have taken up Harvard's offer of a stenographer, although he commented that he expected that the lectures would need to be rewritten for publication: 'My experience has however usually been that I can't say orally what I should print, but have to write de novo.'[6]

In fact he quickly arranged with George Prothero, editor of the *Quarterly Review*, to publish the revised lectures as a series of four articles, originally to have been completed by the end of 1905, while reserving his rights of publication in the United States.[7] He discussed publication in book form with John Murray, the publisher of the *Quarterly*, while corresponding with George P. Brett, head of Macmillan's New York office, about an American edition. The first two articles appeared—somewhat later than Bryce and Prothero at first envisaged—in July and October 1905, and shortly after the second was published, Bryce told Brett, 'I am working hard at my book on the Comparative Study of Democracy, or whatever that book is to be called with the wish to let you have it by April if possible'. 'I have just spent ten days in Switz[erland] getting up their politics for the purpose.' But the series then hit the buffers amid a flurry of political events: first the fall of the Balfour government, followed by Bryce's acceptance of office as chief secretary for Ireland, the general election campaign, the Liberal landslide victory, and the prospect of a long period in office. Prothero's first instinct was to skip an issue: 'How would it be if you deferred art. III of your series till April?' If there were to be a break after two articles, the remaining two articles would need to appear together, that is, in consecutive issues. Perhaps he was pessimistic about the Liberals' prospects. In the event, Bryce was sucked further into the business of politics and government ('laborious office' was how he put it), and his literary career had to pause:

What I feared has arrived: the Tory Government has fallen and my time may now be so otherwise occupied during the next months that it will be impossible for me to complete the book on Democracy which you had proposed to publish next spring. Half of it, or more, is written, but a great deal remains to be done to get even that part into it final shape and the part not yet written would require two or three months work. There is little prospect of such leisure at present, so I hope you have not announced the book.[8]

Bryce hoped this meant only a postponement, however. 'If life and health remain, I shall hope to send you the M.S. some day, enough to make a volume bigger than "S. Africa."'[9] He kept his promise: a six-year ambassadorship and numerous wartime commitments meant that the book did not appear until 1921, but whereas *Impressions of South Africa* was one fat volume, *Modern Democracies* was two even fatter ones.

Quite what a book on *Modern Democracies*, or whatever, would have looked like had Bryce fulfilled his hope of publishing it in 1906 is a matter of speculation. We do not have the notes from which he lectured at Harvard in 1904, but we have some indication of the scope of the lectures from the reports in the *Harvard Crimson*. The first dealt with the materials available for the study of democratic politics, and the second with methods: that is, they broadly correspond with the scope of the two articles he did publish in the *Quarterly Review*. We lack information about the third lecture, but it might well have been about the United States. The fourth evidently focused on Switzerland, Britain, and Britain's self-governing colonies. The fifth had more to say about Australia before turning to some general conclusions. That Switzerland would have featured in the planned book is certain: not just because Bryce repeatedly said it was the world's most successful democracy, but also because Marion's correspondence confirms that they spent 'an arctic week in Switzerland' in October 1905, when Bryce was 'collecting information about modern European democracy' in Zurich, Bern, and Geneva.[10] He was evidently proposing to include Australia, although he had not yet visited: after all, he thought it 'most nearly approaches a typical democracy'.[11] He was collecting information on New Zealand too.[12] Whether he was intending to include France is uncertain, although its absence would have constituted a big gap. French writers on democracy—Edmond Scherer, Emile Boutmy, Emile de Laveleye—were prominent among the literature to which Bryce referred in his opening article in the *Quarterly*.

The first of the two articles he published in the *Quarterly* focused to start with on the data for studying popular government. Alongside the framework documents—the written constitutions and laws—there were the records of 'the actual working of free governments': parliamentary debates, of course, but also press reports, the 'unofficial records of political struggles and discussions'. But over and above these two kinds of sources of data, there were 'a great mass of facts which scarcely find their way into print'. He stressed the importance of party proceedings, which were rarely published. And then—most strikingly of all—he pointed to the data that by their very nature are only accessible to the practitioner:

> Moreover, there are many phenomena of politics whose true nature and meaning could not be gathered from records of any kind, either official or unofficial, though familiar to those who bear a part in the working of any popular government. Take, for instance, the British House of Commons. Neither the rules and orders of the House, nor the reports of debates, nor the gossip and comments of the public press suffice to explain the real character of the proceedings of the House of Commons and of the way it is organised for work. It is hard for any one but a member of the House to know these thoroughly enough to be able to apprehend and set forth their significance.[13]

This tells us a lot about Bryce's motives, if not for entering the House of Commons, at least for staying there when he manifestly thought, much of the time, that he would be more productively occupied elsewhere.[14] For someone who wanted to make an academic study of political institutions and their *actual* working, there was no substitute for a working career in politics. On the whole that was not the view of his American counterparts, the men who launched the American Political Science Association in the year before Bryce delivered the Godkin lectures, and who elected Bryce as their fourth president in 1907: they were full-time academics. But Bryce was walking in the footsteps of Bagehot, and Bagehot—though principally a financial journalist and never a politician—believed that politics was an arcane pursuit that yielded up is secrets only to the first-hand observer of its actual practice.

Bryce then gave the reader what was, in effect, a prospectus for his study of *Modern Democracies*. Those who wanted to undertake a comparative study of the democratic political systems of the time could read the different constitutions, although they were not as readily accessible as they might be; they could read the legislative proceedings and press reports, not just of those proceedings but of extra-parliamentary speeches, the workings of the party apparatuses, and so on. But all that would enable them only to scratch the surface. To get deeper, more was needed:

> What is needed, and what unfortunately is not yet forthcoming, is a series of descriptions of the actual political phenomena of each free community based on close and penetrating personal study, and executed in a dispassionately scientific spirit. . . . Whoever sits down to try to think out the lines of a science of politics based on the observation of the modern world will find that the first difficulty which confronts him is the want of such books. Some time may elapse before they are produced; nor will it be easy to produce them, for the observer must have himself some practical experience of politics in order to know how and what to study. He must observe and write without fear, favour, or affection. He must have a magnetic quality which draws information, and yet a detachment of mind which enables him to receive statements from every quarter and every party with equal caution. He must be one who inspires more confidence than he gives.[15]

This was what Bryce wanted to attempt: a 'close and penetrating personal study' based on actual observation of democratic communities, and undertaken not in a partisan but in a 'dispassionately scientific spirit'. To do this the student must have first-hand experience of politics and must have the kind of 'magnetic quality'—he did not mean charisma—that would allow him to extract information from those who had it. This was precisely Bryce's gift: to travel, to meet the right people, and to ask the kind of questions that would enable them to open up and give an honest and direct impression of how things really worked. 'Talk is the best way of reaching the truth', he wrote, 'because in talk one gets directly at the facts.'[16]

Bryce did not say that practitioners necessarily had an intuitive understanding that would never be accessible to outsiders. That would effectively be a bar to any sort of comparative study. He never overvalued the importance of practitioner intuition. The practitioner unschooled in any kind of scientific method might know the arcana of the political world but would not understand their significance. What was needed was someone in command both of scientific method and of practical wisdom: someone, in fact, like Bryce. As he wrote: 'Whoever, having himself a considerable experience of politics, takes the trouble to investigate in this way will seldom go astray. There is a *flair* which long practice and "sympathetic touch" bestow. The trained observer learns how to profit by small indications, as an old seaman discerns, sooner than the landsman, the signs of coming storm.'[17]

If we can trace Bryce's *Modern Democracies* all the way back to his Godkin lectures on 'The Study of Popular Governments' in 1904, we then need to pause to ask why he chose this topic for those lectures. He was under some constraint, for the lecture series had been established with the remit of exploring the subjects of 'government and civic duty': subjects that were as close to Godkin's heart as they were to Bryce's. Godkin's widow may well have consulted Bryce about the nature of the Harvard lecture series she wished to establish: certainly Marion assured her that the Bryces thought it 'a most suitable & acceptable memorial of your husband's life & work & character'. She added: 'to have his name permanently associated with the work of stimulating the public spirit & responsible citizenship of the younger generations is just what he would have wished, & what his friends must warmly approve.'[18] All that said, Bryce might have lectured on a particular political system—the American or the British, for instance—or he might have chosen the duties of citizenship, a subject on which he would lecture at Yale four years later. Or he might have chosen one of the myriad other political and constitutional topics that interested him: race, on which he had spoken at Oxford two years before, or nationalism and internationalism, or war.

Democracy was certainly a fitting choice for a commemoration of Godkin, who wrote on *Problems of Modern Democracy* and *Unforeseen Tendencies of Democracy*.[19] The latter book was, indeed, one of the thirteen books in four languages around which Bryce professed to frame his *Quarterly Review* articles.[20] But there was a particular context against which Bryce chose to lecture, and then to write, about democratic politics in general. That context was the turn to imperialistic warfare, notably by the British in South Africa and the Americans in the Philippines. This was a tendency of which Bryce, as a prominent pro-Boer, wholeheartedly disapproved, and it led him to some gloomy thoughts about the future course of democracy. His correspondence of the time shows him to have been preoccupied with the figure of the demagogue (Joseph Chamberlain *par excellence*) in democratic politics. He was convinced that Chamberlain had undergone a process of 'moral deterioration'.[21] Bryce was equally obsessed with the role of the press in fomenting ignorant passions rather than in informing the public dispassionately.

Bryce's other pressing concern was that the flight from free trade was reducing politics from public service to haggling over material interests. The invitation from Charles W. Eliot to deliver the Godkin lectures came toward the end of the summer of 1903. In the spring of that year Joseph Chamberlain had launched his tariff reform campaign, which would dominate British politics

until the fall of the Balfour government in December 1905 and the Liberal landslide the following month.[22] Eliot fully shared Bryce's detestation of protectionism: 'a bad disease to get firmly seated in any government or nation ... a general
poison for the whole system.'[23] In 1902 Bryce's observations from Cuba led Eliot
to reflect further on the evils of protectionism and its connections with American imperial ambitions: 'We are just now seeing clearly how intolerably selfish
the doctrine of protection is when carried to an extreme. A small band of sugar-
beet people has thus far succeeded in preventing Congress from lowering the
excessive duties on Cuban sugar coming into this country.'[24]

Bryce, for his part, was vocal on the consequences of protectionism in the
United States, and in particular on its political and indeed moral consequences.
During his ambassadorship, this was a subject on which he often commented
in his correspondence with Dicey in particular: 'My horror of Protection
grows stronger every day I live here. Nothing has done more to demoralize
public life and check the forces making for good. Protection in England
couldn't fail to work similarly.'[25]

In short, Bryce conceived his study of modern democracies at a point when
he was acutely conscious of the damaging impact the twin perils of imperialism and protectionism threatened to have on public life and public opinion in
the United States, Britain, and elsewhere. 'Whether a man be in theory a Pro-
tectionist or a Free Trader, whether or not he desires to nationalize public
utilities, he must recognize the dangers incident to the passing of laws which
influential groups of wealthy men may have a personal interest in promoting
or resisting, because they offer a prospect of gain sufficiently large to make it
worthwhile to "get at" legislatures and officials.'[26]

Travels and Travails

Bryce seems to have set the book aside for some time following his appointment to Dublin in December 1905. Once he moved to Washington, he obviously had abundant opportunity to observe the operation of American democracy close at hand, but conventions surrounding the ambassadorial role
meant that his numerous public speeches and university addresses rarely even
touched on the subject. He told Dicey in 1911 that he had gone on accumulat-
ing material but did not expect ever to finish it: he was in his seventies, after
all, and had never expected to live so long. 'Australia & New Zealand seem to
be the places we must see before going further.'[27] The tour of Australia and
New Zealand which the Bryces made in the (northern) summer of 1912 was

certainly, among other things, intended as an opportunity to gather material, and well in advance he had started to ask for information from Australian officials.[28] We have a substantial body of his working notes, on loose sheets, and a good number of these can be dated, either from the contents or from the paper used: some were on headed notepaper from the House of Lords (hence from 1914 onwards), whereas others were on House of Commons Order Papers or sets of company accounts, or on dinner invitations or menus. Quite apart from helping us to date the notes, the material form gives us a nice glimpse into Bryce's working methods. We can imagine him sitting in the House of Commons—perhaps in the library, but maybe on occasion in the Chamber—and jotting some pencil notes about the referendum in the United States and in Switzerland; on other occasions, he might have taken advantage of a fortuitous seating plan at dinner to quiz a fellow guest on industrial relations in Australia and to jot some snippets down before leaving the table.

In some cases, there are notes on reading, with a source indicated. He made significant use of *The Round Table*, the 'Quarterly Review of the Politics of the British Empire' launched by Lord Milner and members of his imperial federationist 'Kindergarten' in 1910. Each issue would contain regular reports from the self-governing parts of the empire: Australia, New Zealand, Canada, South Africa, and the United Kingdom. This was just the kind of coverage Bryce would have appreciated. He read William Pember Reeves's *State Experiments in Australia and New Zealand*, H. G. Turner's *The First Decade of the Australian Commonwealth*. This same author's *History of the Colony of Victoria*, as well as two works by French diplomats, Louis Vossion and Georges Biard d'Aunet.[29] He certainly made use of the study of New Zealand by another Frenchman, the geographer and pioneer political scientist André Siegfried.[30] We have comments on Bryce's manuscript on Canada from Professor George Wrong, the Toronto historian, but we also have extended responses to a series of questions from Bryce: on Canada, from the Toronto economist James Mavor, who had been taught by Bryce's father at Glasgow High School, and on Australia, from the barrister and King's Counsel Sir Edward Fancourt Mitchell, the foremost authority on Australian constitutional law. We know that Bryce sent his questions to Mavor in April 1919, so it is clear that the chapter on Canada was written at quite a late stage, although Bryce could claim to be reasonably knowledgeable, since during his stint in Washington he had spent a good deal of time on Canadian business and had taken the trouble to visit several times.

The questions Bryce asked his contacts in Australia, New Zealand, and Canada tell us a lot about his preoccupations, even if in some cases we have to

FIGURE 12.1. The Bryces on the South Head at Sydney in 1912, in a wind.

infer the questions from the answers given. He asked his Colonial Office intermediary Arthur Berriedale Keith to get 'some expressions of opinion by
competent persons as to the influence brought to bear by public servants in
Australia on the Governments there'. What he meant by that—given the large
increase in public employment in Australia—was that he wanted to know
about the standing of public officials as employees who were capable of being
organized to promote their own sectional interests, just as other sections of
the workforce were.[31] This was a problem internationally when Bryce wrote:
in France, for instance, the legitimacy of strikes in the public services was
much debated at a level of some theoretical seriousness. Bryce's papers include
copies of the New South Wales Public Service Act of December 1895 and the
Government Railways and Tramways Act of 1901 as amended in 1906. His
hypothesis was that the growth of the public sector presented a new and pernicious source of corruption. The barrister and former premier of Victoria, William Irvine, was inclined to agree: 'I have come to the conclusion that the
greatest difficulty ahead of the movement towards State Collectivism is, not
the economic fallacies that underlie it, not the unstable equilibrium inherent
in it, but the constitutional (in the widest sense) or the politico-economical
difficulty. Are the servants of the State to be their own paymasters?'[32]

If Australia was the case where democratic politics had pushed the cause of socialism furthest, Bryce saw Canada as practically an opposite case: 'In thinking over the changes that are passing in the world I am struck by the fact that there seems to be less Socialism in Canada, less Labour unrest & less desire to enlarge the functions of the State and abandon Laissez Faire once for all than there is anywhere else in the world.' He therefore did not see any reason to push Mavor, or other Canadian interlocutors, on the constitutional implications of the collectivist state. Instead, he asked:

1) To what extent are the Provincial Legislatures tainted by corruption and jobbery?
2) Has the level and tone of politics generally risen or declined (in Provinces & in the Dominions[)] within the last twenty years?
3) Does the power of party organizations increase? I believe they are not very powerful, only much what we have in England.[33]

What is interesting about these questions is that they were not questions of fact so much as questions of informed opinion. They were a Royal Commissioner's questions, since witnesses before Royal Commissioners were commonly asked to make value-laden judgments of the kind that the first two of these questions certainly seemed to call for. It was almost as if Bryce were attempting a kind of one-man Royal Commission on Comparative Democracy.

That analogy might seem curious, but Bryce certainly wanted his book, above all things, to be *useful*; useful not because it recommended particular reforms or provided easy answers of any kind, but because it would help inform public debate. We return here to a recurrent theme in Bryce's political thinking: good policy-making required an understanding of the politics and political systems of other countries and yet was hampered by the lack of informed and reasonably objective sources of information about those systems. 'There is no use perhaps in trying to get the English to understand any country but their own', he complained to Godkin in 1882; but he made it a central part of his life's mission to make the attempt nonetheless.[34] It was absolutely not that he thought that easy lessons could be learnt from other countries: we have seen that he wrote *The American Commonwealth* in part to combat the simplistic efforts of conservative critics of democracy such as Sir Henry Maine to recommend borrowing American institutions such as the Supreme Court to shore up the barriers to democracy.[35] His point was not that lessons could not be learnt from other systems, but that those lessons could only be drawn from accurate and informed sources of information, not from the kind of superficial glance given in Maine's *Popular Government*. He told Dicey that Maine's argument that the referendum was a conservative institution relied too much on Switzerland, and that that example 'is not sufficient to bear the weight to be laid on it'. Circumstances in Switzerland were 'different altogether from those of the U.K.'[36]

We should take seriously, then, the account that Bryce gave in the preface to *Modern Democracies*:

> Many years ago, at a time when schemes of political reform were being copiously discussed in England, mostly on general principles, but also with references, usually vague and disconnected, to history and to events happening in other countries, it occurred to me that something might be done to provide a solid basis for argument and judgment by examining a certain number of popular governments in their actual working, comparing them with one another, and setting forth the various merits and defects which belonged to each.[37]

The book was written as an exercise in civics: it would provide 'a solid basis for argument and judgment'. That was the reason why, as he told Dicey, he as author had to be self-effacing, and his conclusions not be foregrounded as a priori theories but must appear as the logical conclusion from the largely descriptive accounts that had preceded them: 'My Democracy progresses very slowly, partly because I am trying hard to keep it short. Your remarks as to positive conclusions is [sic] a just one, but my plan obliges me to state the facts first, for the conclusions must be seen to grow out of them, that is the only justification for such a book at all on a theme so often treated.'[38]

He certainly did not succeed in keeping the book short; but probably it was precisely because he thought the need for such a book was greater than ever that he persisted. The Britain to which the Bryces returned in 1913 was in the throes of the famous trio of political conflicts to which George Dangerfield would later trace the 'strange death of Liberal England': industrial conflict, suffragette activism, and the spectre of civil war in Ulster. Bryce was appalled by all three. His embassy news cuttings from the early part of 1912 make it clear that he was avidly consuming news of the suffragette campaign, labour unrest, and the Home Rule crisis in Ulster. The American press favoured lurid headlines: 'Civil War in England' was the spectre that alarmed the Kansan *Wichita Eagle*, which focused on the threat of a coal strike.[39]

When he resumed serious work on the book in the aftermath of war, it was in the face of renewed labour unrest and a government—the Lloyd George coalition—for which he felt contempt.[40] The reluctance he felt was due to his

FIGURE 12.2. Charles William Eliot (1834–1926), president of Harvard 1869–1909, who invited Bryce to give the Godkin lectures at Harvard in 1904 and was a frequent correspondent on academic and international affairs.

sense that while the book was needed more than ever, it was less *wanted*, because the public had lost interest in constitutional questions, broadly conceived. 'The public is no longer interested in forms of government, but only in the work governments do.'[41] Or, as he wrote in *Modern Democracies*, absorption in 'ideas and schemes of social reconstruction' had diverted attention from 'those problems of free government which occupied men's minds when the flood-tide of democracy was rising seventy or eighty years ago', and hence he had the sense that he was addressing the last generation rather than the present one, which was interested less in institutions than in 'the purposes which institutions may be made to serve'.[42] Still, he insisted that the study of institutions had not lost its point at a moment when democracies were being established in the constituent parts of the defunct Russian and Austro-Hungarian empires, let alone when the prospect of popular government in India or China or Persia or the Philippines was contemplated.[43]

Bryce pressed upon the reader his own objectivity: 'The book is not meant to propound theories', but to describe 'the actual facts'; though he also stressed how difficult that was, for 'the facts are obscured to most people by the half-assimilated ideas and sonorous or seductive phrases that fill the air'. They were familiar enough to those who had been 'inside politics'; and those people—like Bryce himself—were better placed to 'get a fair impression of the facts in other countries'. They were largely hidden from the public, however, and that was the point of the book: 'What I desire is, not to impress upon my readers views of my own, but to supply them with facts, and (so far as I can) with explanations of facts on which they can reflect and from which they can draw their own conclusions.'[44] He explained to Charles Eliot that he had written for a practical purpose, as Eliot thought one always should, but he had taken the view that offering prescriptions (as opposed to identifying the problems) would not serve such a purpose: 'if the people do not find the remedies for themselves they will not be moved any more by my prescribing them.'[45]

Democracy and Opinion

Modern Democracies has never been claimed as Bryce's magnum opus, and in fact it has never been analysed at any length. But it deserves attention since it was in a sense his *summa*, the summation of his intellectual career. Harold Laski thought it 'a bad book', as did A. D. Lindsay, who wanted something more philosophical.[46] This judgment was unfair, but the book certainly suffered from being too long, overloaded with information, and so nuanced that he did not impress on his readers a decisive perspective on the subject. That said, for anyone who wants to understand the character of Bryce's mind and his understanding of the political transformations of his lifetime, it is invaluable. It is full of aperçus and *obiter dicta* that disclose far more about Bryce than he was, perhaps, aware. Like a number of pieces he wrote in his final decade—his preface to the *Encyclopaedia Britannica*, his final presidential address to the British Academy, and his Raleigh Lecture on *World History*—it shows Bryce demonstrating a mastery of a vast field of human knowledge. It was as if, aware that time was short, he was trying to set down something that would do justice to the huge range of his knowledge: 'one remembers also Ruskin's saying that the saddest thing in life is to have heaped knowledge or experience and lose the chance of using it just when it is most mature.'[47]

Bryce said in the preface to *Modern Democracies* that he would not 'propound theories' or propagate his own opinions but would aim to set forth 'the actual facts'.[48] This was a characteristically understated objective, comparable to that which Bryce set himself in a number of his works, especially the later ones. To today's reader, it obviously comes across as naïvely empiricist. Can anyone simply set forth 'the facts' about the merits and defects of political institutions of different countries and exclude any personal opinions? But in articulating his objective in this way, Bryce gave vent to his frustration at how difficult it was to gather accurate information about how different political systems worked. He was writing before the burgeoning of political science departments in universities: they existed in the United States, but the discipline barely existed in the United Kingdom, where it did not extend much beyond the LSE, where 'political science' was enshrined in the school's full name and was taught from its creation in 1895.

He fleshed out his objectives in some of his correspondence of the time. When Dicey offered some suggestions on the chapter on France in 1919, Bryce retorted that his purpose was

> not to trace French history, nor to analyse French Constitutions, but simply to show how Democracy works in France. I have taken Switzerland & France as two different types or forms of popular government, & tried to show how Democracy works itself out in them, all this for the sake of pointing out to other countries what things in Democracy to imitate or to avoid; & my only object is to fix the reader's mind on the working of popular sovereignty & universal suffrage. I hope you think that I have brought out these lessons. That is all I care for.[49]

He said much the same to Lowell, asking him in 1916 for suggestions of recent books on the United States, Canada, Australia, or New Zealand, or indeed on France or Switzerland, 'which deal with them <u>as democracies</u>, i.e., not with the constitutions or current political questions, but with those features of their politics which illustrate the tendencies of democracy'. He added that he was sure there were new books dealing with democracy in general, 'from a historical or philosophical, in fact an Aristotelian point of view. Few of those I have seen are of much value'.[50] In other words, he was aiming to write a book illuminating the general 'tendencies of democracy', but one firmly grounded in the empirical study of actual democratic politics. He was not here interested in constitutions per se. Nor was his subject simply the politics of the present. Indeed, in the preface he played down the objection that his empirical material had been collected before the war, and that the delay in completion as well as the transformations wrought by the war would make his findings dated even before they were published: 'it is not current politics but democracy as a form of government that I seek to describe. Events that happened ten years ago may be for this particular purpose just as instructive as if they were happening to-day.'[51] Still, his aim was to be practically useful, and the book's usefulness would clearly be maximized if it were up-to-date, and he was assiduous in trying to ensure his many correspondents and interlocutors checked the currency of his account.

By the nature of the work—its huge scope, and its inductive approach—*Modern Democracies* defies a straightforward summary. It is more productive to tease out what it tells us about Bryce's mature (even, by then, over-ripe) conception of democracy. 'People talk as if democracy was one thing politically everywhere', he complained to Dicey in 1909, and one of his central aims was to show that it was not, and why it was not.[52] What made it work better in some countries than others? Why, in particular, was it such a success in Switzerland? What were the peculiar dangers to which it was vulnerable?

The fundamental concept in Bryce's analysis of democracy was public opinion. This was a subject that had interested Bryce ever since the 1860s, when he wrote his report for the Schools Inquiry Commission in which he stressed that the good governance of endowed schools depended upon their accountability to public opinion. But it was in *The American Commonwealth* that he first developed his analysis of the political functions of public opinion, and specifically his conception of democracy as the rule of public opinion. There he presented the rule of public opinion as something of an American peculiarity, but in *Modern Democracies* he analysed all the political systems he considered in this way. Bryce wrestled with the same question that absorbed Dicey: if 'the people' were ultimately sovereign, how was that political sovereignty exercised? Was it confined to electing members of Parliament every four or five or seven years?[53] If so, that implied that a here-today-gone-tomorrow parliamentary majority might wreak fundamental constitutional change without explicit endorsement from the people. For Dicey, the popular will as expressed in a general election or a referendum was the *ultima ratio* in a democracy.[54] Bryce agreed that 'what purports to be the will of the people' might well be 'largely a factitious product, not really their will', since many electors voted not on the basis of the issues but of the personal qualities of the candidates; and indeed they might be swayed by intimidation or bribery or even simple party organization.[55] Still, he was loathe to place much trust in the confirmatory postlegislative referendum, Dicey's favourite nostrum: Bryce thought it would tend over time to legitimize the institution of the popular initiative, which had the potential to turn the referendum from a stabilizing into a destabilizing force. This was certainly not part of Dicey's plan, but as Bryce told him in December 1910: 'The recognition of popular sovereignty, once made, is likely to be pressed further and the[n] issue in the Initiative, whereby everything turns on a vote of the whole people when demanded by a certain proportion of the citizens, or perhaps authorized by the Legislature. What an engine for prompt & drastic change you have in that!'[56]

Bryce tried to use the concept of public opinion, which he acknowledged was a hazier concept, as an alternative way of thinking about the relationship between the practical authority of the legislature (the legal sovereignty of Parliament, in the British system) and the ultimate authority of the people. Between elections, did a majority in Parliament have the *moral* authority to do whatever it judged right? Dicey's answer was: this authority was limited by the proviso that fundamental change required a direct mandate either in a general election explicitly fought on the issue or in a referendum. For Bryce, that authority was limited by the ongoing consent of public opinion. The implication was that the health of a democratic political system depended upon the extent to which it had an informed and engaged public opinion. If the public were disengaged, it had no defence against the whims of a temporary majority. If the organs through which public opinion could be expressed were suborned or corrupted—if the press, for instance, served the interests of plutocratic owners—the people would likewise be unable to constrain their rulers.

It is clear that Bryce did not simply regard public opinion as something that might in principle be captured by an opinion poll; and neither was it simply an inferior proxy for a general election or a referendum. It was 'a better ruler, when its will can be ascertained, than the ballot'.[57] 'What democracy really needs to succeed is the rule of Opinion and not of Votes', he told Eliot, 'because that comes nearer to being the rule of the wiser and not mere numbers.'[58] Contrary to a commonsensical understanding, public opinion was not simply 'the aggregate of the views men hold regarding matters that affect or interest the community': so understood, public opinion was too confused to be effective.[59] Conceived as a sort of constituent power, it was preferable to a mere vote because it was more stable, rather than simply capturing a snapshot of what people think at a particular moment.[60] It was the outcome of a process of clarification, by which Bryce intended both that it needed to be made easier to understand, but also, and more importantly, that unwanted substances needed to be removed, as when butter is clarified.[61] Equally, it was not a value-neutral category. In some societies public opinion was robust, engaged, well-defined; in others it was fragmentary, indifferent, and incapable of speaking distinctly.[62] Bryce was centrally interested in whether, in the societies he studied, public opinion was effectively playing the role he sketched out for it in a healthy democratic order.

Bryce's understanding of the role of public opinion in a modern political system was undoubtedly influenced by Bagehot, whom he had known well and admired as 'the most acute of English political writers'—an opinion less widely shared at the start of Bryce's career than it later became.[63] In *The English Constitution* (1867), Bagehot had argued that one of the strengths of cabinet government was that it educated the people and shaped an active public opinion. It was a defect of the American system of presidential government that it did not engage the people in the same way, and the Americans, he thought, 'have not a public opinion finished and chastened as that of the English has been finished and chastened'.[64] Bryce disagreed with Bagehot about America: he thought Bagehot's account too focused on Washington, and insensitive to the importance of local politics in sustaining an active and engaged public opinion. He also disagreed with him about Britain, where Bagehot thought parliamentary debates engaged the public because they could determine the life or death of a government. Bagehot was essentially writing about the pre-1867 system in which prime ministers were commonly turned out as the result of parliamentary debates rather than by popular vote at a general election; from 1868 onwards that was rarely the case, and general elections assumed more of a plebiscitary character, determining who would form the government for the duration of the parliamentary term. But Bryce's framework of analysis was profoundly influenced by the celebrated editor of *The Economist*.

In this context it is illuminating to read what Bryce had to say in private correspondence about the impropriety of the Balfour government's clinging to power in 1905 when it had lost its effective working majority in the Commons and, more importantly still, lost the confidence of public opinion. Bryce regarded the Balfour ministry as 'practically dead' as far back as September 1903.[65] There was an uproar when Balfour declined to resign following defeat in the Commons in July 1905, on a motion to reduce the membership of the Irish Land Commission. Bryce's position was rather different: he told A. L. Lowell, the Harvard political scientist, that Balfour was within his rights not to regard that defeat as a resigning matter, but he had also told Lowell some months previously that 'Balfour's clinging to office' was 'unconstitutional' and 'incompatible with the spirit of our institutions', though of course perfectly legal.[66] What was unconstitutional, if (at that point) the government had suffered no parliamentary defeat? He elaborated his position in a letter in August: 'Balfour was within his rights in not resigning after the defeat of July 20th, but is violating the spirit of the Constitution in refusing to dissolve after so long and so unbroken a series of by-elections has proved that he has lost the confidence of the country.'[67] In other words, Bryce's point was that a series of by-elections had shown a decisive shift of public opinion away from the government, and in these circumstances it was against the spirit of the constitution to refuse a general election. That was quite a proposition from a trenchant defender of parliamentary government such as Bryce. The Unionists had won a decisive electoral mandate in 1900. Yet here was Bryce citing the obviously very partial evidence of by-election results to maintain that they had lost the confidence of the country. But Dicey maintained in his *Law of the Constitution* that it had been constitutionally proper, though unusual, for the monarch in 1784 and 1834 to dismiss a ministry that enjoyed a majority in the Commons and to dissolve Parliament, on the basis that there were prima facie reasons for thinking that the ministry no longer had the confidence of the country, or what Chatham called the 'great public'.[68] If that were correct—and it has to be said that no monarch since William IV has invoked that constitutional precedent—then Dicey's logic would support Bryce's position. Balfour's government was 'practically dead' because it had lost the support of the 'great public'.

What is particularly important here is that Bryce did not regard public opinion simply as a datum. He repeatedly dwelt on the process by which opinion on a given issue was constructed or, to use his term, clarified. Writing to Goldwin Smith in January 1905, he reflected that Balfour's long refusal to dissolve had been beneficial to the Liberals, for it had meant abundant time to bring Chamberlain's tariff reform scheme under the spotlight: 'the thorough and exhaustive discussion of his scheme has done much to fortify the nation in Free Trade principles.'[69] The outcome of this process of discussion was that the retention of free trade had won what Dicey in the *Law of the Constitution* termed 'the deliberate resolve of the nation', something that was decisively confirmed in the general election when it finally came in January 1906.[70] Government by public opinion was by no means the negation of what Bagehot had called 'government by discussion': when it worked well, it perfected government by discussion rather than cancelling it.[71]

As an instance of what happened when it did not work in this way, Bryce was disappointed by the US presidential election of 1904, but not because Theodore Roosevelt defeated Alton B. Parker, which is what he expected. Rather, he was disappointed because the campaign failed to educate: 'it did nothing to advance or bring to the minds of the people really important issues such as the control of the power of trusts and great corporations, and the mischievous effects of high tariffs.'[72] Bryce evidently had high expectations of elections. Their role, in his view, was not simply to decide, but to do so by first ensuring that the issues were sufficiently discussed that the people were in a position to make that deliberate resolution. In this respect Bryce's position was close to that of his friend Frederic Harrison, who back in the 1870s had criticized advocates of proportional representation for their conception of an election as an aggregation of the preferences of individuals. This was to neglect the collective dimension of an election campaign: it was the campaign, rather than the count, that formed a common national mind on the issues of the day.[73] Bryce, however, did not privilege the election campaign itself: in a healthy polity, opinion formation took place over a longer period, as in Britain, where the roots of the Liberal victory of January 1906 could be traced back to a movement of public opinion since Chamberlain launched his tariff reform campaign in 1903.

Bryce's correspondence with Dicey, Lowell, Goldwin Smith, and others on these themes is clustered around the period 1903–1905: this was the period of the demise of the Balfour government in the face of divisions over Chamberlain's tariff reform programme, but it was also precisely the period when he was starting to work on the book that eventually became *Modern Democracies*. It was in 1903 that Charles Eliot first approached him to give the Godkin lectures; it was in 1904 that he gave them; and it was in 1905 that he started to publish them, in the form of articles in the *Quarterly Review*.[74] While Bryce had long been absorbed by the problem of public opinion, the political conjuncture is important in explaining why he gave the concept such a prominent place in his study of *Modern Democracies*. The dominant political issue in Britain at the turn of the twentieth century was the conduct of the Second South African War ('Boer War'). Bryce was one of the foremost Liberal critics of the war, which he blamed primarily on 'the presumption, the ignorance and the temper of a single arrogant and vindictive minister', namely, his long-term antagonist, the Colonial Secretary Joseph Chamberlain.[75] For Bryce, Chamberlain was the archetypal demagogue: the best example of the demagogue England had produced, as he told Theodor Barth; and demagoguery was the principal vice by which democracies were liable to be seduced.[76] The ideological tools he used to seduce public opinion were jingoism and militarism. Bryce knew that Chamberlain was not the first demagogue to dominate British politics in his lifetime: we have seen that he frequently compared him with Disraeli in the 1870s and Lord Randolph Churchill in the 1880s. But a new factor was Chamberlain's ability to call on the subservient support of the press barons and through them the popular newspapers: 'Never has a press served a country worse, seldom so ill, as nearly the whole English press has done through these S. African troubles.'[77] There was, indeed, no 'pro-Boer' newspaper in London until 1901, when the Quaker George Cadbury bought the *Daily News*.[78] The Unionists' landslide victory in the Khaki election of 1900, at the height of Jingoistic fervour when British troops seemed (prematurely, as it turned out) to be on the verge of victory, demonstrated the liability of democratic public opinion to be led astray by a demagogue and his client press. Some months before the election, Bryce wrote to an American correspondent deploring 'the display which the last eight or ten months in England have given as of what may be effected by a partizan press distorting and colouring everything it states and a single audacious and unscrupulous will, prevailing, in spite of ignorance and blundering by sheer force of audacity, and carrying almost the whole of its party with it, though many secretly mourn, and feel the same distrust as we do'.[79]

It is hard not to call these passages to mind when reading the chapter on 'The Press in a Democracy' in volume 1 of *Modern Democracies*. This was centrally concerned with the tendency of the newspaper press to become less concerned with public discourse and more susceptible to distort news in the interests of partisanship or profit through sensationalism. The chapter was framed in general terms: no newspapers were mentioned by name, no proprietors, and no editors of the current generation. The only specific instances that Bryce cited of the role of the press in distorting news and suppressing truth were the American press on the eve of the Spanish-American War and the British press on the eve of the South African War: in the latter case the press suppressed the case for the Transvaal government, 'with the result that the British public never had the data necessary for forming a fair judgment'.[80]

There was a sociology underpinning Bryce's account of public opinion, although it has to be derived inductively from his analyses of the different political systems. Canada was one democratic system which he thought weakened by the defects of its public opinion. The main problem was the fissure between Francophone Catholics and Anglophone Protestants: 'where fundamental ideas and habits of thought are concerned, the French mind and the British mind do not move on the same lines, even when both may arrive at similar practical conclusions.' Hence 'one cannot talk of a general opinion of the whole people as one can for most purposes in Great Britain, and could in

Australia till the rise of the Labour party'.[81] So much is unsurprising: entrenched ethnic or religious or linguistic divisions within a nation hampered the formation of public opinion, and so frustrated the working of democracy. This was much the same as what Mill had said in *Representative Government* in 1861. But Bryce also emphasized the significance of geographical dispersal: there were only a small number of large urban centres, and they were separated by huge distances. 'Most of these cities are of recent growth, and in each of them the number of persons qualified to form and guide opinion is not large. The public opinion they create is fragmentary; it wants that cohesion which is produced by a constant interchange of ideas between those who dwell near one another; it is with difficulty organized to form an effective force.'[82]

There were two key propositions here. The first was that an effective public opinion was possible only in an urbanized society where physical closeness enabled 'constant interchange of ideas'. But the second was that very rapid urban growth could be a barrier to the formation of public opinion, since the latter required a degree of social or cultural hierarchy. Here Bryce seems to echo not so much Mill, but the French liberals whose thinking took an elitist direction in the wake of the Franco-Prussian war: thinkers such as Ernest Renan and Hippolyte Taine in particular. Certainly Bryce never wavered in his sense that a healthy public opinion required an educated class to lead it.

Civic Education and Public Opinion

The concept of public opinion was crucial because it was the conceptual bridge between Bryce's project of describing the actual operation of democratic political systems and his normative concerns with the core republican value of civic virtue and its inculcation through democratic education, understood in the largest sense. An engaged public opinion depended upon a politically educated public. How to ensure the political education of the citizenry was one of Bryce's central preoccupations in *Modern Democracies*. It was no surprise that he concluded that political education was at its most effective in Switzerland, the one country where democracy had been an unalloyed success.

A sense of Bryce's thinking can be had from this characteristic passage toward the end of his chapter on 'Democracy and Education':

> What have been the causes of the success of democracy in Switzerland? Not merely the high level of intelligence among the people and the attention paid to the teaching of civic duty, but the traditional sense of that duty in

all classes and, even more distinctly, the long practice in local self-government. Knowledge and practice have gone hand in hand. Swiss conditions cannot be reproduced elsewhere, but the example indicates the direction which the efforts of other democracies may take. The New England States of the North American Union, till they were half submerged by a flood of foreign immigrants, taught the same moral. Trained by local self-government to recognize their duty to their small communities, the citizens interested themselves in the business of the State and acquired familiarity with its needs by constant discussion among themselves, reading the speeches and watching the doings of their leaders. Not many were competent to judge the merits of the larger questions of policy debated in the National legislature. But they learnt to know and judge men. They saw that there are always two sides to a question. They knew what they were about when they went to the polls. Valuing honesty and courage, they were not the prey of demagogues. It is because such conditions as those of Switzerland and early Massachusetts cannot be secured in large modern cities that it becomes all the more necessary to try what systematic teaching can do to make up for the want of constant local practice.[83]

'Civic education' was an important concern for Bryce, over a long period. It was a concern that culminated in his series of four lectures on citizenship at Yale in 1908, published the following year as *Hindrances to Good Citizenship*. As chapter 10 showed, those lectures set out much of the agenda for *Modern Democracies*. But as we see here, Bryce did not regard civic education mechanically. Future citizens could not adequately be trained in the art of citizenship at school if the lessons of that training were not reinforced by the practice of citizenship. What was characteristic of Switzerland was that combination of the formal teaching of *civisme* with the practice of active self-government in the localities. Massachusetts and the other states of New England had historically possessed similar conditions, and in particular the institutions of local self-government in the townships that Tocqueville had famously admired. Bryce was unusually explicit about his conception of public spirit: it was a moral virtue, he acknowledged; but 'it is a virtue which intellectual training may help to form', and the role of history and philosophy, in particular, was 'so to enlarge our minds that we may see how each man's highest interest, conceived in its true moral aspect, is bound up with the public weal'.[84]

Bryce's explanation for the demise of the civic tradition in the New England states was equally telling: they had been 'half submerged by a flood of foreign immigrants.' This was not a racial argument per se so much as an argument about the tension between democracy and cultural heterogeneity. Bryce always deplored agitation against immigrants, the more so when it deployed dehumanizing rhetoric.[85] Elsewhere in *Modern Democracies* he specifically rebutted the argument that the effective operation of representative institutions in Britain could be attributed to a genius inherent in the Anglo-Saxon racial stock which was lacking in France. The difference in outcome was due to 'a set of geographical facts and a series of historical facts, for which neither country is to be praised or blamed'.[86] In the case of New England, the immigrants were predominantly white: from Ireland, from Germany, from Canada, and indeed from England and Scotland. It was the lack of cultural assimilation that acted as a barrier to the successful operation of self-government in countries that experienced high levels of immigration. Obviously this point highlighted the significance of the Swiss case, where a shared sense of nationhood transcended differences of language and religious confession. For Bryce the unity of the Swiss nation was 'a singular, perhaps a unique, phenomenon in history'. The Swiss were united but far from homogeneous.[87] But as Bryce reiterated in a number of different contexts, the circumstances of 'that little republic and its cantons' were peculiar, and lessons drawn from it could not readily be applied to large states such as France and Britain.

Implicit in Bryce's argument was a belief—a characteristically republican belief, of course—that small states were better suited than large ones to the practice of civic virtue and hence to the operation of free institutions. Sometimes he was explicit about this, as in an illuminating wartime letter to Dicey about the prospects of democracy in Russia, prompted by a pamphlet by the legal historian Paul Vinogradoff which Dicey had been reading:

> The trouble is that the country is so big. If it were like the Slavonic nations of nine centuries ago, scattered into small communities, the prospects would be far better. I am greatly struck by the evils of large states, and wish it were possible to go back to the small ones. Representative Government, which was supposed to have cured the dangers incident to great states, has not done so, and one doubts whether it can.[88]

The tension in Bryce's thought between the claims of large nations and those of small ones has already been noted, but his sympathy for small nations clearly grew stronger with time. Dicey's position was decidedly different. He seems not to have responded to Bryce's point here, but he broadly shared his cousin Fitzjames Stephen's somewhat Hobbesian belief in the strong state as an essential guardian against anarchy, the worst of all evils; and for him a large nation was better equipped than a small one to ward off the forces of social disintegration. Separatist nationalism always tended to put Dicey in mind of the separatist claims of the Confederacy in the American Civil War. He would surely have dissented from Bryce's rejection of the premises of large-nation liberalism.

Modern Democracies can be read in illuminating conjunction with Bryce's aspiration to write a history of the 'phases of opinion' of his own times. This is something he discussed extensively in his correspondence with Dicey in his final years; and these discussions are interlaced with discussions of his work on *Modern Democracies*. He first urged Dicey—who was the author, after all, of an influential study of law and public opinion in nineteenth-century England—to have a go at recording 'the accepted opinions and ways of looking at things' of their undergraduate days, and he regretted that Goldwin Smith's *Reminiscences* had failed to do this.[89] Bryce's point was that understanding the accepted commonplace beliefs of one time and place, and how they changed, is an extraordinarily important thing for the historian, but also an extraordinarily elusive one:

> Recollections of that kind, when written in the same philosophical spirit which was so much appreciated in your book on 'Law & Opinion', wd be a contribution to History. They are among the things that the newspapers do not give the historian and that he has to pick up disconnectedly from magazine articles & books. A connected view of the evolution of one type of opinion from another might be made highly illuminative. I had hope to find it in Morley's Recollections but have not so far succeeded.[90]

The influence of one of their Oxford mentors, Mark Pattison, was unmistakable here. His intellectual sensibility was profoundly shaped by the consciousness that ideas and, still more, commonplace opinions have a history, and that a central task for the historian was to trace how ideas that were unthinkable to one generation became the commonplaces of the next, and vice versa.[91]

A central theme in Bryce's correspondence with Dicey was how his own attitude toward democracy (and Dicey's too, no doubt) had changed in response to political change. So in August 1920 he looked back on the trip to the United States that he and Dicey made fifty years before. 'How pleasant it was to be young! It was a better world when it was still possible to believe in Democracy. These self-styled Labour Leaders are overturning not only the Constitution, but the principles of Democracy, trying to make a part of the community tyrant over the whole.'[92] The 'impact of labour', as Maurice Cowling

FIGURE 12.3. Bryce's last meeting with Goldwin Smith (1823–1910), at The Grange, Toronto, in 1907.

would later call it, was the central phenomenon that made Bryce more pessimistic about democracy:

> Don't you think that the whole problem of Democratic Government as we regarded it when we wrote those essays in 1866–7 has been fundamentally changed by the up-coming of the Labour movement into politics? This seems to have lowered the spirit & tone of public life. We used to complain of class legislation by landowners. Now we have it by working men; and it looks like presiding harder & longer.[93]

When he urged Dicey to write a supplement to *Law and Public Opinion* taking the story from 1890 to 1918, he no doubt hoped that Dicey would dwell on this point.[94]

The Uses of *Modern Democracies*

Bryce intended *Modern Democracies* to be useful, but we may wonder whether his readers found it so. It was certainly much used, which is presumably an important test of usefulness. It was widely prescribed on university courses, including PPE at Oxford, where it was well timed to go on the syllabus from the inception of the course.[95] It was quickly adopted on courses in political science (including political theory and political philosophy) and history across the British Empire, not least in India, and was still set for the honours course at Edinburgh in 1959–1960. The book's reach was all the greater as it was widely translated into European and some non-European languages.

It was in France, among continental European countries, that *Modern Democracies* received its earliest reception. That was partly because it was there that Bryce had the strongest name recognition, thanks to the influence of *The American Commonwealth* in particular. He was well-known in the circles associated with the Ecole Libres des Sciences Politiques, whose founding director, Emile Boutmy, was one of Bryce's closest French friends. Boutmy was himself an Americanist among other things, and his Ecole, which was liberal and Protestant in sympathies, was comparative and empirical in its approach and fostered a particular interest in 'Anglo-Saxon' societies. His *Eléments d'une psychologie politique du peuple américain* (1902) made substantial use of *The American Commonwealth*. Not long before his death in 1906, Boutmy spoke of his appreciation of *The American Commonwealth*: it was the work, he thought, of 'un politique' rather than 'un moraliste', the difference being that the former, while being shrewd and realistic, looks at events with a clear-sighted optimism. He must always belong to 'the party of life' as opposed to the party of death.[96]

The American Commonwealth was also a familiar reference point for French jurists, even before its translation into French, thanks in the first place to Adhémar Esmein, the foremost constitutional jurist of his time and author of the magisterial *Eléments de droit constitutionnel*. Already in its first edition (1896), it cited *The American Commonwealth* thirty-five times, and this increased still further in its second edition (1899, with the fuller title *français et comparé*), and further still in later editions, which, after the author's death in 1913, were revised by Joseph Barthélemy and then Henri Nézard. The other masters of French public law in Bryce's time, Maurice Hauriou and Léon Duguit, both cited *The American Commonwealth* frequently, once it had been translated into French (neither of them had Esmein's command of English). Duguit cited it frequently both in his *Manuel de droit constitutionnel* (1907) and in his *Traité de droit constitutionnel* (1911 and later editions), making use of, inter alia, Bryce's distinction between (in Duguit's words) ordinary laws and rigid constitutional laws.[97] Hauriou cited it just as much in his postwar *Précis de droit constitutionnel*, where he picked up on, among other things, the distinction between rigid and flexible constitutions (of which Hauriou was critical), the way Bryce traced the origins of state constitutions in the corporate charters of the colonial period (Hauriou found this fascinating and important), and his account of procedures for the amendment of state constitutions, especially in their connection with popular sovereignty.[98]

One of Bryce's keenest readers in France was the jurist-politician Joseph Barthélemy, whose biographer calls him 'a sort of French Bryce'.[99] Barthélemy was Esmein's successor as professor of constitutional law in Paris and revised his predecessor's *Eléments de droit constitutionnel* for its sixth edition in 1914. He also held a chair at Sciences Po. He valued Bryce's historical and inductive approach to the study of law, and his practitioner's approach to political science: the more so after he was himself elected deputy in 1919 and, as Bryce had done, combined a political career with his academic positions; something that was very much in line with the ethos of Sciences Po. He appears to have known Bryce well and was one of those Bryce consulted about the operation of the French Senate when he chaired the Conference on Second Chamber Reform in 1918. Barthélemy approved of the report: he watched Britain's rapid evolution in a democratic direction with keen interest and not a little anxiety, and in this context he commended Bryce's report for 'la hardiesse modérée par le sens des réalités et des possibilités pratiques'.[100] It was Barthélemy who wrote the preface to the French translation of *Modern Democracies*.[101] He was subsequently to figure prominently among those advocating a strengthening of the executive in the context of the movement for the 'reform of the state' in the 1930s; later (not alone among former 'moderate' republicans) he served Vichy, in his case in the prominent role of minister of justice.[102]

In general Bryce proved grist to the mill of the constitutional reformers of the 1930s, not least by those who looked to borrow from the American model. He was much cited by André Tardieu, a fellow Americanist, who thought *The American Commonwealth* 'admirable' and called Bryce 'my eminent friend'.[103] He was also much read by the jurists—many of them inductively minded comparativists—who were active in making the case for a reinforcement of the executive in the 1930s. If some of these, like Barthélemy, ended up at Vichy, this was only one of several trajectories. Some were firmly rooted in French republicanism, like the émigré Russian Boris Mirkine-Guetzévitch, perhaps the foremost pioneer of modern comparative law. Others played an active role in trying (in vain) to shape the constitution of the Fourth Republic along British parliamentary lines; and if they were in the end unsuccessful, it should be added that the constitution of the Fifth Republic (the text rather the practice) was closer to their vision. Michel Debré, the prime author of that constitution, had been a pupil of Barthélemy's at Sciences Po, and there were certainly intellectual convergences between the two, although (understandably) Debré did not much cite his Vichyite former teacher.[104]

On the whole, Bryce's French readers drew mostly on *The American Commonwealth*, and only secondarily on *Modern Democracies*. The position was rather different in Italy, where it was the latter work that counted most. One of its most important readers was Alcide de Gasperi, an erstwhile member of the Austrian Reichsrat and future leader of the Italian Christian Democrats and prime minister of Italy from 1945 to 1953.[105] Bryce would probably have been surprised to find himself celebrated by the leading figure in European Catholic politics, especially an Italian-speaker from the Trentino, but in a sense that unlikely intellectual influence demonstrated the success of his strategy of seeking to convey authority though a dispassionately inductive approach. Even more curious is the fact that it was Bryce's discussion of 'Democracy and Religion' that gave De Gasperi sustenance. Whereas the great Liberal and Idealist philosopher Benedetto Croce had seen Catholicism as essentially an antiliberal force, De Gasperi drew instead on Bryce's analysis both of the egalitarian heart of Christianity and of the church's role in disseminating the concept of spiritual liberty.[106]

It is, indeed, in Italy that *Modern Democracies*, and Bryce's other political-constitutional writings, have received most ongoing attention. The first Italian translation appeared in 1930–1931, published by Hoepli in Milan, shortly before De Gasperi encountered the book.[107] But a more significant landmark may have been the new edition brought out by Mondadori in 1949–1953, not least because Mondadori was Italy's largest publishing house and, in particular, the leading publisher of Italian translations of English-language books.[108] More than forty years after its publication, *Modern Democracies* was a fundamental reference point for Giovanni Sartori in *Democratic Theory*, the book that established Sartori as an internationally known authority on the subject.[109] Quite why Italian scholars in particular should have been so interested in Bryce's work is a puzzle. This was not the case in his lifetime, for although he had close friends in Italy, such as Pasquale Villari and especially Ugo Balzani, the pioneers of the elite theory of democracy, such as Pareto and Mosca, showed little familiarity with Bryce's writings.[110] Clearly, Italy was one of a number of European states that had a long struggle to establish a stable democracy, which is no doubt one reason why it had been fertile territory for theorizing democracy; and also why its theorists have drawn on empirical studies of working democracies.

In Britain, meanwhile, *Modern Democracies* was taken up by some of the proponents of the 'education for citizenship' movement that took off in the 1930s in response to the spectre of fascism in continental Europe. The architect of this movement was the industrialist and former Liberal MP Sir Ernest Simon (later Lord Simon of Wythenshawe), who founded the Association for Education in Citizenship in 1934.[111] Simon was long familiar with some of Bryce's other work: certainly *South America*, which he took with him on a tour of that continent in 1914, and of course *The American Commonwealth*.[112] But *Modern Democracies* evidently had a particular appeal, and Simon's practical cast of mind made him Bryce's ideal reader. Simon's own study of *The Smaller Democracies*, covering the four major Scandinavian countries and Switzerland, was explicitly Brycean in its approach. 'Lord Bryce's great book on *Modern Democracies*', which was cited several times, was almost the only authority Simon invoked.[113] He liked and tried to implement Bryce's distinctive method of learning principally from personal contacts.[114] His interpretation of and admiration for Swiss democratic culture were clearly indebted to Bryce, whom he cited on the role that tradition and institutions together played in forming Swiss citizens.[115] Simon's public addresses on the subject of training in citizenship made frequent reference to Bryce, 'one of the greatest democrats'.[116] He was particularly struck by Bryce's observation that after sixty years of general education it was unclear whether the people chose their rulers any better than they did before, from which Simon inferred that what was needed was an education that focused on the formation of citizens.[117] Bryce and Simon shared a conviction that the formation of intelligent and engaged public opinion was crucial for an effective democracy. 'Even in times of peace public opinion is not what it should be', wrote Simon, and since 'public opinion in this country is largely determined by a limited number of people' (a belief he shared with Bryce), he looked to the universities to take a lead in 'forming and guiding public opinion'.[118]

Most importantly, however, Bryce was a fundamental point of reference in the burgeoning international literature on public opinion in first three decades of the twentieth century. The key works in this literature are well-known: Lawrence Lowell's *Public Opinion and Popular Government* (1913), Walter Lippmann's *Public Opinion* (1922), Ferdinand Tönnies's *Kritik der öffentlichen Meinung* (1922), and Lowell's *Public Opinion in War and Peace* (1923). All invoked Bryce. Lowell's 1923 book was dedicated to Bryce's memory; both he and Lippmann cited Bryce a good deal; and so, perhaps more surprisingly, did Tönnies, who cited Bryce more than he cited any other author. Bryce was by no means always an unquestioned authority in this literature: Lippmann, for instance, followed his teacher Graham Wallas in depicting Bryce as a political scientist of the prescientific age, one not vouchsafed of a sense of what was new about what Wallas and Lippmann both called the 'great society'.[119] Bryce's analysis was institutional and constitutional, they claimed, and lacked the psychological insight to grasp the irrational character of public opinion.[120] A different view of Bryce came from Dr George Gallup, the American pioneer of opinion polling. From the 1930s onwards he frequently repeated his claim that Bryce had provided the theoretical case for opinion polling and foreseen the need for it. These particular claims are misleading and tell us less about Bryce's conception of public opinion than they do about the authority that his name still commanded in the United States in the mid-1930s, well over a decade after his death. But it was true that Bryce was a pioneer in placing the study of public opinion and its operation at the heart of the analysis of political systems. That is why it is seriously wrong to think of Bryce either as a formalist, focused on constitutions, or as a descriptive analyst of political institutions in the narrow sense. It would be truer to say that he foregrounded what we would now call *political culture*.

Epilogue

A Good Death

Bryce died, quite suddenly and in his sleep, while on a short holiday in Sidmouth, Dorset, in January 1922. Dr Alexander Fleming, the minister of St Columba's Church of Scotland in Pont Street, Belgravia, who took the funeral, wrote of Bryce's death: 'He lived to be eighty-three; he worked, and at his best, to his last hour; and he passed into the Light Perpetual in his sleep. "It was euthanasia".'[1] Numerous friends recalled the things Bryce had written to them about in the days before he died: with Sir Frederic Kenyon he discussed candidates for election to the British Academy; to President Lowell of Harvard he sent his lecture on American History and some reflections on the Anglo-Irish Treaty; with John Xavier Merriman, the former minister of Cape Colony, he discussed South African politics.[2] He wrote to Lord Lansdowne about Ireland and to the Spanish Embassy to acknowledge his election as a corresponding member of the Spanish Academy.[3]

That Bryce died a quintessential good death, in the fulness of time but still at the height of his powers, was a notion that rapidly gained traction. Marion gave a full account of his last hours to many friends in quite similar terms, and she evidently found some consolation in the narrative and wanted it to be known that he was actively working for the good of humanity up until the end. This is how she told the story to Bryce's physician, Sir Thomas Barlow:

> The blow fell with absolute suddenness, no illness & no warning. He had been very well & happy at Sidmouth, working part of each day & taking a walk in the afternoon as usual; & on that Saturday I had never seen him more like himself—talking eagerly about his work, & enjoying with all his keen zest the views & the striking sunset. At eleven o'clock he went out for

a few minutes to look at the night, as he always did, & when we went to bed there was nothing to show that he was not perfectly well, nor did he call me during the night. . . . When I awoke next morning I found that he had gone; there was no sign of any struggle or suffering, he seemed to have passed away peacefully in his sleep.

That death should come to him so gently, without pain & with all the strength of his mental and physical powers, I am deeply thankful. I had always dreaded suffering & decay for him, & he was spared that. He might perhaps have lived a little longer if he had not worked to the last; but a life that was no longer one of thought & service would have been impossible to that vital eager spirit, & I still think of him as living & serving elsewhere.

I have the wonderful memorial of all that we have had together through these many years to comfort me.[4]

She gave substantively the same account, and in very similar words, to others: to the former American secretary of state Elihu Root, for instance: 'I never saw him more eager & vital, more like himself, than on that last day of his life, & the end came as he would have wished.'[5] Other recipients certainly included Ilbert, Dicey, Sir George Trevelyan, the historian Adolphus Ward, the American diplomat Edward Mandell House, and the Archbishop of Canterbury, Randall Davidson. Davidson replied: 'Your account of the close of that wonderful life (so far as this world is concerned) shews it to have been entirely of a piece with all that went before—in its simplicity, its quiet and unhurried completion of all that he did. . . . But how glorious that it shd close thus painlessly and without struggle. And how it will have elsewhere than here, & in larger fields, a new opportunity & a new power.'[6] Lady Ilbert wrote: 'For him, beloved & wonderful soul, it was a most triumphant exit, closing his eyes for the last time after a happy day with you, spent just as he & you would have wished to spend it, watching the sun setting in its beauty & seeing the stars in their glory just the last thing, & so passing without one pang of pain, with no anguish of farewell, into whatever lies beyond, & one feels that "all the trumpets sounded on the other side."'[7]

There were innumerable letters of condolence—approaching a thousand—and very often they marvelled that Bryce should have been so vigorous and energetic and active to the end: 'that the last year should have been so full and so important seems a marvellous thing at the end of his long and busy life', wrote Charlotte Darwin.[8] Leonard Darwin, her husband, remarked (as others did) that 'one cannot but feel that in many ways it was what he would have asked for—entirely unimpaired vigour of mind and body till quite near the end, and then, as I hope, a peaceful departure'.[9] For Sir Edward Donner, one of Bryce's oldest friends, 'The end was, I fear, a great shock for you, but it is a very merciful one when one has passed the four-score years with undiminished powers. Our friendship was never for one moment clouded and it was to me a constant source of pride and happiness. And in all that he did to promote good feeling between England and the United States he has laid both nations and the whole world under a debt that cannot be repaid'.[10] C. P. Scott called it 'a beautiful end to the most strenuous of lives'; Eleanor Sidgwick, 'a blessed death—just going away when the work was done, without decay of the body, without trouble or much suffering'.[11]

The letters had plenty to say, as the obituaries would do, about his varied gifts and the distinction of his mind.[12] But the most important theme, apart from the energy and vitality that lasted into old age, was his nobility of *character*: his straightness, his steadfastness, his gift for friendship. 'I doubt if any other man of our generation had so many friends', observed Professor George Wrong of Toronto.[13] Laurence Lowell of Harvard thought that 'all Americans ... had an instinctive feeling that he was almost a personal friend'.[14] Lowell also pointed to 'his great simplicity that made him accept the company of ordinary folk & of young people'.[15] At least one correspondent wrote of his 'exquisite child-like simplicity—his eagerness to listen to quite ordinary people and get the most out of them & enter into their interests'.[16] There was a widespread sense of having lost someone unique: 'There has been no one in English history like your husband', wrote Gilbert Murray.[17] Scott, who shared the liberal internationalist outlook of Bryce and Murray, agreed: 'There is no one who can take his place either for us who cared for him or in the public life of the country'.[18] Almost all correspondents spoke of his kindness: many, like both Sir Herbert Samuel and Sir John Simon, of his generosity and encouragement to younger men in politics.[19]

Bryce died on the same day as Pope Benedict XV, but that barely detracted from press attention. His international renown ensured that his death was reported at length in the British and American newspapers and indeed across much of the world. Press reports highlighted his versatility but focused in particular on his work for Anglo-American friendship and for international peace. The moment of his death made these aspects of his career notably salient. The *Daily Sketch*'s headline was typical: 'Viscount Bryce. Scholar, Statesman, Mountaineer. Apostle of Anglo-American Friendship'. Nearly forty-six years after his ascent, it gave particular attention to Bryce's standing as 'one of the first Europeans to ascend Mount Ararat—that remote height on which the Ark is said to have grounded after the flood'.[20] *The Nation* (of London, not New York) entitled its tribute 'The Citizen of the World': the definite article was deliberate, for 'to no man could the name Citizen of the World, the highest title of humanity, be more perfectly ascribed than to Lord Bryce'.[21] King George V's tribute, in a message to Lady Bryce, was much quoted: 'I regarded Lord Bryce as an old friend and a trusted counsellor, to whom I could always turn, confident in the strength and wisdom of his advice.'[22] The American press carried tributes from President Harding, Vice-President Coolidge, Secretary of State Charles E. Hughes, Treasury Secretary Andrew Mellon, and Secretary of War John W. Weeks, as well as several former presidents and senior officials. Coolidge summed up the tenor: 'No one has done more to secure an understanding of the aims and ideals of the American Republic.'[23]

Marion opted for a private family funeral at Golders Green Crematorium, the oldest crematorium in Britain, so that his ashes could be laid to rest in Edinburgh, beside those of his parents and his sister Katharine. Dr Fleming's prayers gave thanks for 'a blessed and powerful peace-maker throughout the whole world, and especially between the nations of America and Great Britain; the champion of oppressed and persecuted peoples; the strong defender of liberty and right'. Bryce was, said Fleming, 'a city of high example which could not be hid'.[24] The following day there was a memorial service at Westminster Abbey, at which Bryce's friend Archbishop Davidson officiated, along with the dean, Herbert Ryle, and other members of the Abbey's Chapter. Bodies represented ranged from the Armenian Republic to the Norwegian Club, from Manchester University to Girton College. Learned societies represented included the British Academy, the Royal Society, the Royal Geographical Society, the Royal Historical Society, and the Classical Association.[25] The choice of Newman's 'Lead, Kindly Light' (a funeral favourite at the time), both for the funeral service and for the memorial service at the Abbey, may have reflected Bryce's piety toward Trinity College, where he and Newman had both been scholars and later honorary fellows.

Oriel College and Lincoln's Inn both held memorial services for Bryce; the former presided over by his good friend the provost, Lancelot Phelps. So, much more strikingly, did the Armenian community. This service, conducted according to the Armenian rite, was held at the Chapel Royal; the Armenian bishop in London, Dr Nazarian, presided. Charles Gore, the retired Bishop of Oxford, read the gospel in English, and a panegyric was delivered by James Aratoon Malcolm, president of the Armenian United Association and a member of the Armenian National Delegation that had led wartime and post-war negotiations on behalf of the Armenian people. It was a true panegyric:

> There is no Armenian, whether in our homelands or in our dispersion, who does not couple the name of Lord Bryce with that of Gladstone, whose mantle fell twenty-five years ago upon his shoulders. Whoever has failed us, those two great hearts never failed. . . .
>
> His death at such a time came as 'a swift and sudden disaster' to the Armenian people.[26]

A week later, the Armenian community in Constantinople celebrated a requiem for the repose of Bryce's soul. The Patriarch called him 'one of our own national benefactors and heroes'. He continued: 'While dowered with manifold qualities, Lord Bryce possessed the highest of all gifts, namely, the gift of love, which prompted him to consecrate himself to the good of an afflicted people in a distant land.'[27]

There was also a memorial service in the United States, at the Episcopalian Cathedral of St John the Divine, New York, in the first week of March.[28] There were three addresses. The Archbishop, William T. Manning, spoke not just of Bryce's varied achievements but in particular of his 'unqualified sincerity and integrity of character'. He also recalled that the last words Bryce had spoken to him the previous autumn were in support of the movement for Christian reunion.[29] John W. Davis, until recently American ambassador to the United Kingdom, stressed Bryce's polymathic thirst for knowledge and his 'democratic' approach to where it could be found: 'Every man whom he met, from cabinet officer to cab-driver, was made to yield something to his store of knowledge.' The final speaker was the geologist, palaeontologist, and eugenicist Professor Henry F. Osborn. He dwelt at some length on Bryce as a naturalist and especially as a traveller and a mountaineer, and he saw the ascent of Ararat as a formative event in Bryce's life: 'He seems to have found in that ascent and in the wonderful survey which that ascent gave him of the great tides of human history which have ebbed and flowed around the base of that mountain a new and fresh perspective for all his future historical works.' In this remark Osborn seems to have had in mind Bryce's particular fascination for parts of the world where very different racial groups were side by side:

> Himself retreading the paths worn by men for centuries, observing that wonderful variety of races of men where, in entering Transcaucasia, he came on the borders between Turkey and the Russian Dominions; again,

when in South Africa, he touched the life of the Kaffirs, of the Hottentots, and of that race of Bushmen which stands at the very bottom of the human scale; finally, in South America, at the age of seventy-four, he entered the intimate life of a people he had not touched before, of the Spanish, the Portuguese, the native Indians of the South American Continent.[30]

Obituary notices were numerous and lengthy. *The Times* carried a leading article entitled 'A Great Pacificator' and dwelt in particular on his work for Anglo-American friendship, as well as his passion for liberty. Its obituary the same day ran to two full columns and was comprehensive. One curious passage contained a note of criticism of a kind that was not often made. The obituarist thought that prior to his ambassadorship, Bryce's influence on American attitudes toward Britain had been negative, because his stance on British politics was, for the time, 'of an extremely advanced, almost Republican type': this coloured his writings, the obituarist thought, and 'his language and views undoubtedly encouraged hostility to British monarchical and aristocratic institutions.'[31] This remark, which was echoed by the *Spectator*, evidently annoyed Marion: Sir Courtenay Ilbert assured her 'That article in the Times was obviously made up hastily as these things are from materials supplied at different times & by different hands. There were bits that ought to have been struck out.'[32]

Probably the warmest of all newspaper tributes to him was that written by his long-standing friend and contemporary Frederic Harrison: 'one of the few survivors', he noted, 'of the Oxford men who knew James Bryce in his earliest days in the University'. Harrison's account drew attention to 'that most rare combination of amazing versatility with inexhaustible thoroughness in work', as well as to 'his inexhaustible interest in national and social betterment'. He concluded that 'in an age of meticulous specialism it is well to remember James Bryce's long life of incessant activity as a rare example that it is possible to have many varied interests and yet to attain to mastery in each.'[33]

The *Oxford Magazine* wrote that he 'remained unspoiled, loving Minerva still, though commandeered by Juno and Mercury'.[34] For Gilbert Murray, 'he used to seem an illustration of what the Ancients meant by "virtue" or "excellence". His was an all-round "excellence" after the classical model. Like an ancient philosopher, he held firmly all the "cardinal virtues" of wisdom, justice, temperance, and fortitude. He moved steadily with a *mens sana in corpore sano*.'[35]

If many quoted Woodrow Wilson's description of him as 'the greatest living Englishman', the *Scotsman* claimed him as 'A Scot of Dauntless Integrity', while for the *Northern Whig* he was 'A Great Belfastman'. His death was reported in

India, Canada, South Africa, France, Germany, Switzerland, Austria, the Netherlands, Denmark, Norway, Sweden, Bulgaria, Czechoslovakia, Turkey, and
Serbia, and no doubt in many other countries besides. The oppressed or subject peoples he championed were of course most vocal: not just the Armenians, but the Tyrolese, the Bulgarians, and the Greeks. As the Finnish *chargé
d'affaires* wrote to Marion, 'Finland has, like all small nations, particular reason
to mourn his death, for he was a great friend and a strong supporter of the
weak.'[36] The Czech minister in London told her that his country 'had the signal
honour of counting your dear husband among its sincerest friends'.[37] For the
Bulgarian minister in Washington, 'We Bulgarians have certainly lost in him a
good and sincere friend; but he was such a friend of all the Near Eastern nations and did all that he could to defend their interests and help them on to a
better future.'[38]

Distinction

Of all the tributes to Bryce, the one that was perhaps most pregnant with
significance for a book of this kind was that of Canon Barnes of Westminster
Abbey. Bryce, he said, was much more than a practical statesman. 'He was a
man of such distinction of mind and character that no apology was needed for
an attempt to describe the nature of his greatness.'[39] Bryce was widely recognized, not just on his death but for decades before, as a man of distinction, and
this quality was acknowledged in the award of numerous 'distinctions' that
were conventionally used as marks of 'distinction': honorary degrees, fellowships of national academies in Britain and overseas, and perhaps above all the
Order of Merit, conferred by Edward VII on the eve of Bryce's departure for
the United States in 1907.[40] Lord Melbourne is supposed to have said that what
he liked about the Order of the Garter was that there was 'no damned merit
about it'. The Order of Merit did not exist in Melbourne's time, but when it
was created in 1902 it was explicitly conceived as a recognition of distinction:
no damned heredity or patronage or corruption about it. Bryce's successor as
president of the British Academy, Sir Frederic Kenyon, thought him 'the very
type of man for whom the Order of Merit is suitable, because he had deserved
well of his country in so many ways'.[41]

Distinction is an elusive quality. Most of those who deployed the term
would have been hard pressed to define it, and yet they recognized it in Bryce
with little hesitation, even quite early in his career.[42] Bryce's career coincided
with the period of the formation of the academic profession in Britain, and

with the emergence of purely intra-academic conceptions of distinction, but Bryce's claim to distinction undoubtedly rested on the amphibious character of his career. When the British Academy was established, he was on everyone's list as one of the obvious first members, not just because of his scholarly eminence, but also because the new academy, to have public clout, needed to have some prominent public figures among its fellows. Bryce, indeed, played a key role in setting up the academy, because he was already a Fellow of the Royal Society: a distinction conferred not by virtue of any scientific work, but by dint of being a privy councillor and a man of learning.

Bryce's distinction in his own time greatly exceeded his posthumous fame. One reason for this was that whereas the amphibious character of his career and the polymathic quality of his mind undoubtedly strengthened his claim to distinction in his own day, they have not helped his subsequent reputation. There is no single intellectual innovation for which he was responsible, and no single field of activity in which he was dominant, in the way that, for instance, Dicey's name is forever connected with the concept of parliamentary sovereignty and the study of English constitutional law, or Sidgwick's with the defence of utilitarian ethics. His polymathic mind enhanced his stature in his own time but perhaps was been an obstacle to the durability of his reputation.

The point has been made, by his contemporaries and by later historians, that Bryce might have achieved more—something really enduring—had he spread himself less thinly. It is hard to disagree, and yet what was authentic and unique about him would have been lost had he devoted himself to being a specialist historian of late medieval Germany, or a legal historian, or, indeed, a government minister. He was a true polymath, and polymaths are driven by a quest for universal knowledge wherever it can be found.

Peter Burke's recent analysis of the phenomenon of the polymath is very suggestive for an appraisal of Bryce. Burke distinguishes several different kinds of polymath. Bryce could plausibly enough be called a 'clustered' polymath: one whose expertise spanned several neighbouring disciplines.[43] Most of his scholarly output was in history, law, political science, geography, sociology, and international relations: an impressive span, but different from the kind of polymathy exhibited by a Michael Polanyi or a Jonathan Miller, who both excelled in radically different disciplines. Still, this characterization fails to capture what was distinctive about Bryce, since when he wrote, these disciplines were by no means as clearly demarcated as they became in the second half of the twentieth century.

He had something of the 'passive' polymath about him: one who absorbed knowledge quasi-encyclopaedically and loved to synthesize it, like Aldous Huxley, whose conversation would betray the volume of the *Encyclopaedia Britannica* he was currently reading.[44] Indeed, Bryce commended the value of the encyclopaedia, a 'vast storehouse of knowledge' from which endless joy was to be derived.[45] Still, the epithet hardly does justice to Bryce's sheer *busy-ness*; and indeed an important dimension of Bryce's polymathy was that he moved so seamlessly between the active and the contemplative life. He probably suffered from something akin to the 'Leonardo syndrome': not completing projects due to a dispersal of activities.[46] But it was not boredom that led to dissipation: rather, he derived stimulus from the active life and hence committed himself to a relentlessly busy schedule that certainly frustrated the completion of long-term projects. The particular kind of expertise Bryce commanded stood at the intersection of the active life and the contemplative life, of public affairs and the academic world.

If 'distinction' entails, among other things, being distinctive, it is here that Bryce's particular claim to distinction is to be found. As a type of intellectual figure, his distinctiveness lay in the way in which he sought to synthesize the findings of academic scholarship with a wealth of insights derived from an active engagement in public affairs. If, as Burke suggests, polymaths succeed not just by virtue of their own abilities but also require a niche, Bryce's particular niche was at the intersection of the academy and the world of politics and government. If others had done that before him, they were much more common in Germany than in Britain, and in Britain he had the distinction of being the first professor to hold cabinet office. But the point is not so much about offices held as about the kind of intellectual contribution he made distinctively his own.

He did, in fact, complete a lot. The most illuminating insight into Bryce's psychological make-up comes from Arnold Toynbee, who, though fifty years Bryce's junior, got to knew him very well during the First World War. As Toynbee put it, Bryce knew that the life of Justinian—or, perhaps, the life of Justinian and Theodora—was the work which would bring him most pleasure. He therefore held that prospect out to himself as the project on which he would embark once he had finished his current book and the one after that. It was the prospect of immersing himself in Justinian and Theodora that drove him to complete *Modern Democracies*. But the Justinian book itself was destined to remain unfinished, and indeed unstarted; and Bryce probably knew as much.[47]

NOTES

Introduction

1. Studies that have appeared while work for this book has been in progress include Héctor Domínguez Benito, *James Bryce y los fundamentos intelectuales del internacionalismo liberal* (Madrid: Centro de Estudios Polítícos y Constitucionales, 2018); Jordan Rudinsky, 'James Bryce's Home Rule Constitutionalism and Victorian Historiography', in *Empire and Legal Thought: Ideas and Institutions from Antiquity to Modernity*, ed. Edward Cavanagh (Leiden: Brill, 2020), 492–519; Itzel Toledo García, 'América Latina en el pensamiento internacional británico: el caso de James Bryce', *Revista de historia de América*, no. 161 (2021): 115–39; Jordan Campos-Rudinsky, 'James Bryce and Parliamentary Sovereignty', *Modern Intellectual History* 19 (2022), 734–56; Cheryl B. Welch, 'An Immunity to Authoritarianism? Bagehot, Bryce, and Ostrogorski on the Risk of Caesarism in America', *Society* 60 (2023), 501–15.

2. H. S. Jones, *Intellect and Character in Victorian England: Mark Pattison and the Invention of the Don* (Cambridge: Cambridge University Press, 2007).

3. Quoted in Mark D. Walters, 'Dicey on Writing the Law of the Constitution', *Oxford Journal of Legal Studies* 32 (2012), 27, 48.

4. Dicey was not in the habit of preserving letters received. He did, however, keep Bryce's letters from the time he went to Washington as ambassador, and fortunately Bryce kept a great many of Dicey's: Bodleian Library, Bryce papers MS Bryce 473 f. 22, Dicey to Marion Bryce, 25 January 1922 (henceforth the Bryce papers are cited in the form MS Bryce [reference number], and Marion Bryce is EMB).

5. By contrast, Goldwin Smith, though an important intellectual influence, 'did his thinking alone': James Bryce, 'Goldwin Smith', *North American Review* 199 (April 1914), 522.

6. James Bryce, 'Special and General Education in Universities', in his *University and Historical Addresses Delivered During a Residence in the United States as Ambassador of Great Britain* (London: Macmillan, 1913) (henceforth UHA), 308–9.

7. Henry Morgenthau, *All in a Life-Time* (New York: Doubleday, Page, 1922), 227.

8. MS Bryce 509–1 f. 18, Margery Bryce to Roland Bryce, 26 March 1946.

9. Edmund Ions, *James Bryce and American Democracy 1870–1922* (London: Macmillan, 1968); Hugh Tulloch, *James Bryce's American Commonwealth: The Anglo-American Background* (Woodbridge: Boydell, 1988); Thomas Kleinknecht, *Imperiale und internationale Ordnung: eine Untersuchung zum anglo-amerikanischen Gelehrtenliberalismus am Beispiel von James Bryce (1838–1922)* (Göttingen: Vandenhoeck & Ruprecht, 1985); John T. Seaman, Jr., *A Citizen of the World: The Life of James Bryce* (London: Tauris, 2006).

10. The classic study by H.C.G. Matthew, *The Liberal Imperialists: The Ideas and Politics of a Post-Gladstonian Elite* (Oxford: Clarendon, 1973), seems to conflate him with his younger brother, John Annan Bryce. Both Bryces were starkly opposed to the Liberal Imperialists.

11. Caspar Sylvest, 'James Bryce and the Two Faces of Nationalism', in *British International Thinkers from Hobbes to Namer*, ed. Ian Hall and Lisa Hill (New York: Palgrave Macmillan, 2009), 161–79; Sakiko Kaiga, 'The Use of Force to Prevent War? The Bryce Group's "Proposals for the Avoidance of War"', 1914–15', *Journal of British Studies* 57 (2018), 308–32; Michelle Tusan, 'James Bryce's Blue Book as Evidence', *Journal of Levantine Studies* 5 (2015), 9–24; Oded Y. Steinberg, 'The Confirmation of the Worst Fears: James Bryce, British Diplomacy and the Armenian Massacres of 1894–1896', *Études arméniennes contemporaines* 11 (2018), 15–39; Paul Readman, 'Walking and Environmentalism in the Career of James Bryce: Mountaineer, Scholar, Statesman, 1838–1922', in *Walking Histories, 1800–1914*, ed. Chad Carl Bryant, Arthur Burns, and Paul Readman (London: Palgrave, 2016), 287–317.

12. Christopher Harvie, *The Lights of Liberalism: University Liberals and the Challenge of Democracy, 1860–86* (London: Allen Lane, 1976); Stefan Collini, Donald Winch, and J. W. Burrow, *That Noble Science of Politics: A Study in Nineteenth-Century Intellectual History* (Cambridge: Cambridge University Press, 1983). The importance of Bryce in Harvie's account was noted by Stefan Collini, 'Political Theory and the "Science of Society" in Victorian Britain', *Historical Journal* 23 (1980), 212 n. 17.

13. Alessandro Pace, *La Causa della rigidità costituzionale. Una rilettura di Bryce, dello Statuto albertino e di qualche altra costituzione* (Milan: CEDAM, 1996) (also translated into Spanish and Japanese); James Bryce, *Costituzioni flessibili e rigide*, ed. Alessandro Pace (Milan: Giuffrè, 1998); Francesca Lidia Viano, 'James Bryce e i modelli costituzionali', *Il pensiero politico* 32.3 (1999), 415–20; Francesca Lidia Viano, *Una democrazia imperiale: l'America di James Bryce* (Florence: Centro Editoriale Toscano, 2003); Valerio Marotta, 'Cittadinanza imperiale romana e britannica a confronto: le riflessioni di James Bryce', *Mélanges de l'Ecole française de Rome. Antiquité*, 118.1 (2006), 95–106. Pasquale Pasquino, another Italian scholar—but one who publishes in English—has also discovered Bryce's constitutional thought. See, e.g., Pasquale Pasquino, 'Flexible and Rigid Constitutions', in *Rationality, Democracy, and Justice: The Legacy of Jon Elster*, ed. Claudio López-Guerra and Julia Maskivker (Cambridge: Cambridge University Press, 2005), 85–96; and Pasquale Pasquino, 'Classifying Constitutions: Preliminary Conceptual Analysis', *Cardozo Law Review* 34.3 (February 2013), 999–1019.

14. Collini, Winch, and Burrow, *That Noble Science of Politics*, 243.

15. On which see in particular Sylvest, 'James Bryce and the Two Faces of Nationalism', 161–79. Sylvest notes that one underlying theme of *The Holy Roman Empire* was to try 'to breathe new life into its grand underlying idea of a universal brotherhood' (165).

16. Members of Parliament were unpaid throughout Bryce's career in the Commons, but of course he drew a salary from his ministerial positions, and as ambassador to the United States.

17. There is a chapter (useful but unreliable) on the Bryce family in June Marion Balshaw, 'Suffrage, Solidarity and Strife: Political Partnerships and the Women's Movement 1880–1930', PhD diss., University of Greenwich, 1998, 79–140.

18. This seems to have been the view of his Liberal colleague Augustine Birrell, who disliked Bryce intensely: Mark DeWolfe Howe, ed., *The Correspondence of Mr Justice Holmes and Harold J. Laski* (Cambridge, Mass: Harvard University Press, 1953), 2:1042, Laski to Holmes, 27 March 1928.

19. George Elder Davie, *The Democratic Intellect: Scotland and Her Universities in the Nineteenth Century* (Edinburgh: The University Press, 1961).

Chapter 1

1. Bryce, 'The Scoto-Irish Race in Ulster and America', in *UHA*, 217–18.

2. The strength of the Glasgow connection is best traced from Bryce's father, himself a Glasgow graduate. His father had studied there (though he did not graduate); two of his

brothers (Reuben John Bryce and Thomas Annan Bryce) were also Glasgow graduates, and two of his brothers-in-law, James Fitzpatrick and Robert Young, also studied there. So did his two sons. See W. Innes Addison, ed., *A Roll of the Graduates of the University of Glasgow from 31st December 1727 to 31st December 1897* (Glasgow: MacLehose, 1898), and W. Innes Addison, *The Matriculation Albums of the University of Glasgow from 1728 to 1858* (Glasgow: MacLehose, 1913).

3. For 'Scotchman', see, e.g., MS Bryce 11 ff. 155–57, Bryce to Gladstone 29 November 1886. The Conservative MP for East Down, James Rentoul, was critical of Bryce for supposedly hiding his Irishness: HC Deb 19 April 1893, vol. 11, c. 665, Government of Ireland Bill, 2nd Reading. On Scottish Teutonism, Colin Kidd, 'Teutonist Ethnology and Scottish Nationalist Inhibition, 1780–1880', *Scottish Historical Review* 74.1 (1995), 45–68.

4. When, in 1892, he was offered the Duchy of Lancaster rather than (as some expected) the Scottish Office, he did not regret missing out on the latter, 'save for the loss of opportunity of carrying out my uncle's and father's plans for Scotch Secondary Education': MS Bryce 450 ff. 28–29, Bryce to EMB, 21 August 1892.

5. 'Miss Mary Bryce', *The Times*, 27 April 1927.

6. A second son died in early childhood.

7. There are numerous examples, including MS Bryce 412, Bryce to mother, 26 March 1870; MS Bryce 437, Bryce to Mary and Katharine, 30 January 1908, and 14 January 1908.

8. MS Bryce 428 ff. 5–6, Bryce to Katharine, 2 December 1858. Katharine was eight at the time.

9. MS Bryce 428 ff. 7–8, Bryce to Mary, 16 November 1859.

10. MS Bryce 428 ff. 9–10, Bryce to Mary, 1 September 1860.

11. This was not as unusual as we might think: Stephen himself wrote the articles on his own father and grandfather. For Bryce's authorship, see MS Bryce 515 ff. 51–59 and 61–62, manuscripts of the two articles; MS Bryce 443 ff. 127–31, Bryce to Dr R. J. Bryce, 9 May 1884, and Dr R. J. Bryce to Bryce, 12 June 1884. Uncle John assisted with the articles but clearly thought he should have been asked to write them: 'I am afraid to trust you with the lives of your father & grandfather.'

12. This was partly because the DCL was acquired simultaneously with his professorial chair, and he was commonly known as 'Professor Bryce', even as an M.P. But, equally, members of the legal profession would rarely use the title 'Dr'.

13. The Anti-Burghers were Secessionists—they had seceded from the Kirk in the 1730s over the question of the threat that lay patronage posed to the right of a congregation to choose its own ministers—and had then, in 1747, split with the remainder of the Secession over whether to approve the religious clause in the burgess oaths.

14. The Covenanters were militant Presbyterians who, in the face of Charles I's attempts to bring the Kirk into line with the Church of England, upheld the right of resistance to an ungodly ruler.

15. Eleanor Alexander, ed., *Primate Alexander, Archbishop of Armagh: A Memoir* (London: Arnold, 1913), 37.

16. Robert Small, *History of the Congregations of the United Presbyterian Church from 1733 to 1900* (Edinburgh: Small, 1903), 2:476–77.

17. Anon. [James Bryce], 'Bryce, James, the Elder', *Dictionary of National Biography* archive ed., https://doi.org/10.1093/odnb/9780192683120.013.3798.

18. The United Secession Church was the product of the union, in 1820, of two secessionist groups, the New Light Burghers and the New Licht Anti-Burghers. The second article of the basis of union affirmed the Westminster Confession of Faith and the Larger and Shorter Catechisms as statements of their faith but added: 'it being always understood, however, that we do not approve or require an approbation of anything in those books, or in any other, which

teaches, or may be thought to teach, compulsory or persecuting and intolerant principles in matters of religion'. George C. Hutton, 'United Presbyterian principles and claims', in *Synod Hall Lectures on Church and State by Ministers of the United Presbyterian Church* (Edinburgh: United Presbyterian College Buildings, 1883), 141. The Relief Church, founded in 1761, stood for independence from lay patronage: Its founder, Thomas Gillespie, had been deposed by the General Assembly of the Church of Scotland in 1752 when he refused to take part in inducting a minister whom the parish did not want. On the merger, see 'Proceedings of the United Presbyterian Synod', in *United Presbyterian Magazine* N.S. 1 (1857), 322–25.

19. James Main Dixon, 'The Personality of James Bryce', *Methodist Review* 38 (1922), 705; Callum Brown, *Religion and Society in Scotland since 1707* (Edinburgh: Edinburgh University Press, 1997), 25.

20. Small, *History of the Congregations of the UPC* 2:478.

21. The submission of the church to the authority of the state: a heresy in the eyes of Scots Presbyterians, even those (the great majority) who accepted the principle of ecclesiastical establishment.

22. For 'cave-dwellers of Puritanism', William Law Mathieson, *The Awakening of Scotland: A History from 1747 to 1797* (Glasgow: Maclehose, 1910), 233

23. On Catherine Bryce as a teacher of Greek: Alexander, ed., *Primate Alexander*, 37.

24. In this book he will usually be referred to, depending on the context, either as Dr R. J. Bryce or as Uncle John. He is sometimes confused with his nephew Reuben John Bryce, the son of his brother William, who was the author of *A Short Study of State Socialism* (London: Baynes, 1903). This contended (p. 57) that 'Christians cannot approve of Socialism for it tends to materialism, and in effect denies the spiritual dependence of man upon God'.

25. 'Reminiscences of Robert Young', *Irish Booklore* 1 (1971), 10–11.

26. Thus Bryce's mother and grandmother both married their former teachers. A psycho-biographer might get to work on how this legacy shaped Bryce.

27. 'Reminiscences of Robert Young', 4–20, 235–42.

28. MS Bryce 515 f. 63, 'J. Bryce's Mother'.

29. 'Reminiscences of Robert Young', *Irish Booklore* 1 (1971), 18.

30. On Dr Hanna, Alexander Gordon, and Finlay Holmes, 'Hanna, Samuel (1771–1852), Minister of the Presbyterian Church in Ireland', *ODNB*, and Andrew R. Holmes, *The Shaping of Ulster Presbyterian Belief and Practice, 1770–1840* (Oxford: Oxford University Press, 2006), 1–51.

31. MS Bryce 515 f. 63, 'J. Bryce's Mother'.

32. MS Bryce 3 f. 18, Dicey to Bryce, 30 September 1902. See also, on similar lines, Dicey to Bryce, 14 August 1903.

33. MS Bryce USA 2 ff. 19–20, Bryce to Charles W. Eliot, 4 September 1903.

34. Phelps papers, Oriel College, Bryce to Phelps, 30 August 1903.

35. MS Bryce 438 ff. 18–19, Bryce to Mary and Katharine, 10 May 1910.

36. MS Bryce 14 ff. 169–70, Jessie Ilbert to Bryce, 4 September 1907.

37. MS Bryce 154 ff. 71–72, Emma Winkworth to Bryce, 23 August 1903.

38. James Bryce, *Transcaucasia and Ararat: Being Notes of a Vacation Tour in the autumn of 1876* (London: Macmillan, 1877), iv.

39. [R. J. Bryce and James Bryce], 'The Late Dr James Bryce', *United Presbyterian Magazine* N.S. 22 (1 January 1878), 6–7. The authorship is clear from Bryce's correspondence with his uncle: MS Bryce 442 ff. 194–99.

40. MS Bryce 515 f. 67.

41. *Christian Union. Report of Speeches on Union with the Free Church Delivered in the United Presbyterian Synod Friday, 15th May 1863*, rev. ed. (Edinburgh: Andrew Elliott, 1863), 34–35. For his continued doubts about union with the Free Church, see 'Reasons by Dr Bryce', *Proceedings of the United Presbyterian Synod* 4 (1870–1873), 277.

42. MS Bryce 419 ff. 11–13, Bryce to his mother, 13 April [no year given, but in fact 1864]: 'Uncle John has just sent me a Memoir of Grandpapa directed against the Donumites: & asks me to subscribe to giving a copy of it to every U.P. minister.'

43. MS Bryce 421 f. 13, Bryce to father, 6 June 1863.

44. MS Bryce 4 ff. 65–66, Bryce to Dicey, 9 June 1914; also James Bryce, *Studies in Contemporary Biography* (London: Macmillan, 1903), 315.

45. Oriel College Archives, Bryce to Lancelot Phelps, 18 April 1909.

46. MS Bryce 515 ff. 65–66.

47. The significance of walking and the observation of nature for Bryce is further explored by Readman, 'Walking and Environmentalism'.

48. On his eagerness to go to university as soon as possible, MS Bryce 458 f. 1, Bryce to the Revd James Bryce (grandfather), 7 November 1853.

49. The following narrative draws on Fisher, *James Bryce* 1:13–35.

50. MS Bryce 515 f. 66; certificate in MS Bryce 357; Fisher 1:20.

51. Bryce, 'The Mission of State Universities', *UHA*, 160.

52. Davie, *The Democratic Intellect*. English literature was added by the Universities (Scotland) Act of 1858: that is, after Bryce had left Glasgow for Oxford.

53. For an illuminating study of this educational tradition at work in forming the mind of a friend of Bryce's, sixteen years his junior, see Murdo Macdonald, *Patrick Geddes's Intellectual Origins* (Edinburgh: Edinburgh University Press, 2020), especially chap. 1.

54. MS Bryce 442 ff. 69–74, Bryce to Dr R. J. Bryce, 8 January 1868.

55. Gilbert Murray, *A Conversation with Bryce. The James Bryce Memorial Lecture, Somerville College, Oxford, Friday 12 November 1943* (London: Oxford University Press, 1944), 5–6.

56. Two notable examples are his 'Prefatory Note' to the *Encyclopaedia Britannica*, 11th ed. 'Handy volume' issue (Chicago: Hooper, 1915), 1:1–10; and 'The Next Thirty Years', his presidential address to the British Academy in July 1917. On the latter, Stefan Collini, 'Looking Back at "The Next Thirty Years,"' *British Academy Review*, Summer 2017, https://www.thebritishacademy.ac.uk/publishing/review/30/looking-back-at-next-thirty-years/.

57. Bryce of Killaig studied at Glasgow, though apparently he did not take a degree. Dr. James Bryce graduated BA, MA, and later LLD; Dr. R. J. Bryce graduated MA and LLD; and Thomas Annan Bryce, another of the sons of Bryce of Killaig, graduated MA.

58. Trinity required candidates for scholarship to be under age twenty at election, so Bryce would have been ineligible in 1858: MS Bryce 510 ff. 12–13, North Pinder to Revd Dr. R. J. Bryce, n.d. [20 May 1857].

59. MS Bryce 411 ff. 5–6, Bryce to mother, 12 June 1857. Campbell was a Scotsman who had gone up from Glasgow University to Balliol on a Snell Exhibition.

60. MS Bryce 420 ff. 9–10, Bryce to father, 27 May 1857. One mistake Luke made here was to assume that the rules would be more restrictive for scholars than for commoners. But commoners were admitted by the Head alone, and he was therefore free to impose such restrictions as he wished; whereas scholars, as members of the foundation, were elected by the whole Governing Body.

61. MS Bryce 420 ff. 15–16, Bryce to father, 1 June 1857.

62. Bryce to father, 1 June 1857

63. Bryce to father, 1 June 1857.

64. Bryce to father, 1 June 1857 ('U. John declared he had no objection to my going in if I cd get a Snell'); MS Bryce 420 ff. 19–20, Bryce to father, 3 June 1857 ('On this point U. John's views, from whom I had a letter this morning, seem to me over-strained').

65. Bryce to father, 1 June 1857.

66. James Bryce, 'Edward Augustus Freeman', in Bryce, *Studies in Contemporary Biography*, 264 n. 1. Bryce here draws the contrast between his time and Freeman's, fourteen years earlier, as well as a later generation around 1870.

67. MS Bryce 334, diary entry for 29 January 1858.

68. Blair Worden, 'The Victorians and Oliver Cromwell', in *History, Religion, and Culture: British Intellectual History 1750–1950*, ed. Stefan Collini, Richard Whatmore, and Brian Young (Cambridge: Cambridge University Press, 2000), 114–15.

69. Trinity College Archives Coll Govt XII A.4 (Minute Book).

70. MS Bryce 411 ff. 11–14, Bryce to mother, 17 November 1857.

71. MS Bryce 334, 20 March 1859; Henry Longueville Mansel, *The Limits of Religious Thought Examined* (Oxford: Murray, 1858).

72. MS Bryce 334, 6 February 1859 (Wayte), 27 February (Hook), 6 March (Meyrick).

73. MS Bryce 334, 13 February 1859 (Farrar).

74. Trinity College Archives, Register Camerarum (Room Register B 1826–65). This gives Bryce's room (Staircase X, Room E), but the rooms have been renumbered. I am most grateful to the college archivist, Clare Hopkins, for identifying the location of the rooms.

75. MS Bryce 334, 30 January to 5 February 1859. On Bryce's undergraduate walking practices, Readman, 'Walking and Environmentalism', 291.

76. MS Bryce 334: breakfast with Pinder, 6 February 1859

77. Churchill College, W.T. Stead papers, STED 1/11, Bryce to Stead, 17 March 1894: breakfast is 'the best time to see friends who live in town'.

78. 'The Rev. J. M. Marshall', *The Times*, 13 January 1926, p. 14. Marshall then became headmaster of Durham School.

79. Lampeter 17–20 May 1875; Newbold Verdon 2 November 1873; Rotherfield Greys 10–11 July 1875: MS Bryce 339 (1873) and 340 (1875).

80. On the founding of the Essay Society, see Harvie, *Lights of Liberalism*, 65. Old Mortality was Oxford's counterpart of the Cambridge Apostles; but, unlike the latter, Old Mortality proved very mortal indeed. It held its last meeting in 1866, and its last reunion in 1876: Gerald C. Monsman, 'Old Mortality at Oxford', *Studies in Philology* 67 (1970), 389. William C. Lubenow, *'Only Connect': Learned Societies in Nineteenth-Century Britain* (Woodbridge: Boydell, 2015), chap. 1, places Old Mortality in the wider context of the contribution of university clubs and societies to intellectual culture.

81. MS Bryce 334, diary 14 February 1859.

82. Conington's 'Miscellaneous Writings', *Pall Mall Gazette*, 6 January 1873, pp. 9–10. For the identification, see MSB 396, which records Bryce being paid £4-4-0 by PMG for the piece on Conington's writings.

83. Edward A. Freeman, 'Oxford After Forty Years', *Contemporary Review* 51 (May 1887), 611; Goldwin Smith in *Oxford Magazine*, 2 June 1886, quoted by Charles Edward Mallet, *History of the University of Oxford* (London: Methuen, 1927) 3:348 n. 9.

84. This moment—and the wider context—are evoked vividly by Linda Dowling, *Hellenism and Homosexuality in Victorian Oxford* (London: Cornell University Press, 1994), especially chapter 3.

85. Amber K. Regis, ed., *The Memoirs of John Addington Symonds: A Critical Edition* (London: Palgrave Macmillan, 2016), 170.

86. Emily Rutherford, 'Arthur Sidgwick's Greek Prose Composition: Gender, Affect, and Sociability in the Late-Victorian University', *Journal of British Studies* 56 (2017), 104.

87. He was, however, much closer to Henry Sidgwick, who certainly had some homosexual tendencies. See Bart Schultz, *Henry Sidgwick: Eye of the Universe* (Cambridge: Cambridge University Press, 2004), 17–18.

88. There was, however, a Roman contribution to modern homosexuality: Jennifer Ingleheart, ed., *Ancient Rome and the Construction of Modern Homosexual Identities* (Oxford: Oxford University Press, 2015).

89. H. S. Jones, 'University and College Sport', in *Nineteenth-Century Oxford*, part 2 (vol. 7 of *The History of the University of Oxford*), ed. M. G. Brock and M.C. Curthoys (Oxford: Clarendon, 2000), 517–43.

90. 'Mr James Bryce: Immoderate Devotion to Sport', *Manchester Guardian*, 28 November 1905, p. 8; also Churchill College, W. T. Stead papers, STED 1/11, Bryce to Stead, 14 January 1909. In particular, he followed Ostrogorski in regarding the passion for sport—especially watching it or (still worse) betting on it—as an essentially 'private' passion that detracted from civic virtue: James Bryce, *The Hindrances to Good Citizenship* (New Haven, CT: Yale University Press, 1909), 26; James Bryce, *Modern Democracies* (London: Macmillan, 1921) [henceforth MD], 2:582–83; on Ostogorski, Gregory Conti, 'Ostrogorski Before and After: Three moments in Antipartyism and "Elite Theory"', *Constellations* 27 (2020), 180 n. 13.

91. For example, MS Bryce 334, 18, 19, 21 March, for the 'Torpid' races.

92. MS Bryce 458 ff. 3–4, Bryce to Sarah Young (aunt), 7 February 1859.

93. Readman, 'Walking and environmentalism', 287–318. Accomplished women mountaineers in Bryce's circle included Emma Winkworth and Elizabeth Spence Watson.

Chapter 2

1. Stefan Collini, *Public Moralists: Political Thought and Intellectual Life in Britain* (Oxford: Clarendon, 1991), 35–36.

2. At Cambridge there were certainly a small number of instances of college fellows from a nonconformist background, but they had conformed in order to take the BA (prior to the reforms of the 1850s). I have not discovered a Cambridge case before 1862 of a non-Anglican who, like Bryce, contrived to be elected to a fellowship in spite of not conforming.

3. Harvie, *Lights of Liberalism*, 76.

4. These letters are all in MS Bryce 420.

5. For example, MS Bryce 412 ff. 155–56, Bryce to mother, 26 March [1870?]. In this confessedly somewhat priggish letter, Bryce warns that it would be best for his sisters to be brought up in Boweshill, away from the temptations and dissipations of town.

6. For his significant support to his parents following his father's retirement, MS Bryce 422 ff. 144–45, father to Bryce, 9 November 1875. 'It is something for you to know that in our few remaining years we are by your help so <u>extremely comfortable</u> & <u>nice</u> here.'

7. MS Bryce 404 ff. 88–89, Dr James Bryce to Dr R. J. Bryce, 16 August 1861.

8. This is probably Wayte of Trinity, with whom Dr Bryce corresponded on the question.

9. The statement referred to is in *The Patriot*, 25 July 1861, p. 13. This was a nonconformist weekly newspaper, dominated by Congregationalists: Philip March, 'The influence of Congregationalism on the New Journalism of W. T. Stead', PhD diss., Birkbeck, University of London, 2019, p. 105. It ceased to operate in 1866.

10. 'Political voluntaries' seems to mean something like the much more common term 'practical voluntaries': those who, though believing in the theory of Establishment, in practice advocated voluntaryism (because of the nature of real existing Establishment).

11. This is James Stirling, future judge, son of a UPC minister in Aberdeen, who went from King's College, Aberdeen, to Trinity College, Cambridge, where he was senior wrangler and first Smith's prizeman in 1860 but was ineligible for a fellowship. By the time this letter was written, there was a further case to be added: in January 1861 the Senior Wrangler was an English Baptist, William Steadman Aldis (he was also first Smith's prizeman). See James A. Aldis, 'Reminiscences of the Abolition of Religious Tests in the Universities of Oxford and Cambridge', *Baptist Quarterly* 4.6 (1929), 249–58.

12. Dr Bryce here seems to imply the automatic progression of a Senior Wrangler to a college fellowship. While this was not absolutely true, it was very nearly the case. Between 1800 and Stirling's case in 1860, I have identified only three Senior Wranglers who were not elected to fellowships.

13. MS Bryce 404 ff. 90–95, Dr James Bryce to Dr R. J. Bryce, 24 August 1861.

14. Ernest Nicholson, 'Hawkins, Monro, and University Reform', in *Oriel College: A History*, ed. Jeremy Catto (Oxford: Oxford University Press, 2013), 411–12, 418–19.

15. The best account of the Oriel election—in fact the only account (to my knowledge) that uses the material in the College Archive—is Nicholson, 'Hawkins, Monro, and University Reform', 426–29. Nicholson does not, however, use Bryce's own correspondence, especially with his family, on the Oriel election and thus does not give a rounded account.

16. MS Bryce 420 ff. 179–80, Bryce to father, 15 April 1862. Wayte was well placed to advise, since he had been secretary to the commissioners. Hawkins had been one of the heads who tried to refuse to cooperate with the commissioners.

17. MS Bryce 420 f. 183, Bryce to father, 21 April 1862.

18. Sir John Wither Awdry (1795–1878)—grandfather of the creator of *Thomas the Tank Engine*—had been fellow of Oriel 1819–1832. His legal career culminated in appointment as chief justice of Bombay.

19. Oriel College GOV 4 B1/1/7, 1861–1867: Notes on College Meetings and memoranda by Edward Hawkins. The 'last rubric but one' of the prayer book's order for Communion specifies that parishioners shall communicate at least three times a year, including on Easter.

20. *Ordinances framed by the Oxford University Commissioners, under the 17 & 18 Vict. C. 81, in relation to New, Worcester, Balliol, Oriel, Brasenose, Wadham, Trinity, All Souls, Jesus, Magdalen, and Merton College, respectively*, HC 1857 v. 138 XXXII.155, p. 58.

21. Paragraph 48 allowed for disputes over the construction of the College Statutes to be referred to the Lord Chancellor for a ruling.

22. Oriel College GOV 4 B1/1/7, 1861–1867, 25 April 1862.

23. 'Selwyn' was probably Charles [later Sir Charles] Selwyn, chancery barrister and future solicitor-general Lord Justice of Appeal. He was Conservative MP for Cambridge University.

24. Oriel College GOV 4 B1/1/7, 1861–1867, 6 April 1863.

25. *Spectator* no. 1765, 26 April 1862, p. 449.

26. Edward Hawkins, *Additional notes on subscription academical and clerical: with reference to the Clerical Subscription Act of 1865, the republication of tract XC, the Tests Abolition (Oxford) bills* (Oxford: Parker, 1866), 46.

27. MS Bryce 442 ff. 17–20, Bryce to R. J. Bryce, 10 February 1865.

28. [Bryce,] 'Tests in the English Universities', *North British Review* 42, no. 83 (March 1865): 107–36.

29. MS Bryce 442 f. 25, R. J. Bryce to Bryce, 10 April 1865.

30. [Bryce,] 'Tests in the English Universities', 115.

31. MS Bryce 442 f. 32, R. J. Bryce to Bryce, 26 June 1865.

32. [Bryce,] 'Tests in the English Universities', 111.

33. For instance, as summarized in MS Bryce 404 ff. 90–95, Dr James Bryce to Dr R. J. Bryce, 24 August 1861. But in fact Bryce told his Uncle John that he was quite willing to sign the Act of Uniformity (his words, for which his uncle pedantically reproached him): MS Bryce 442 ff. 35–36, Dr R. J. Bryce to Bryce, 26 July 1865. Incidentally, this constitutes evidence that he had not in fact been asked to make the statutory declaration of conformity.

34. [Bryce,] 'Tests in the English Universities', 112–13.

35. J. P. Parry, *Democracy and Religion: Gladstone and the Liberal Party, 1867–1875* (Cambridge: Cambridge University Press, 1986), 164.

36. Parry, 105.

37. Parry, especially 85–92 for the Whig-Liberal approach to these questions.

38. *State-aided Denominational Education and the "Voluntary Schools (England) Bill, 1897"* (Edinburgh: United Presbyterian College, 1897), 1. The differences between the United Presbyterians and the Free Church on the education question, including the question of religious education, are studied in Ryan Mallon, 'Scottish Presbyterianism and the National Education Debates, 1850–62', *Studies in Church History* 55 (2019): 363–80.

39. Data derived from the *Oxford University Calendar* for 1863.

40. M. G. Brock, 'The Oxford of Peel and Gladstone, 1800–1833', Richard Brent, 'Note: the Oriel Noetics', and K. C. Turpin, 'The Ascendancy of Oriel', in *Nineteenth-Century Oxford*, ed. M. G. Brock and M. C. Curthoys, part 1 (vol. 6 of *The History of the University of Oxford*) (Oxford: Clarendon, 1997), 7–71, 72–76, 183–92; Richard Brent, *Liberal Anglican Politics: Whiggery, Religion, and Reform 1830–1841* (Oxford: Clarendon, 1987), chap. 4. For a contemporary account, see Mark Pattison, *Memoirs* (London: Macmillan, 1885).

41. Rhodes went up to Oriel in 1873, aged twenty, but interrupted his undergraduate career after a term and returned in 1876. He did not take a degree. Whether Bryce knew him then is unclear, though he certainly knew him well by the 1890s.

42. This paragraph draws mostly on Nicholson, 'Hawkins, Monro, and University Reform', 408–43, and relevant entries in *ODNB*.

43. The college room rent ledger shows him as 'owner' of rooms from 1864: That meant that he derived rental income by letting them to other college members: Oriel College Archives TF 1 85/1. I am grateful to Rob Petre, college archivist, for locating this information for me.

44. MS Bryce 420 ff. 189–92, Bryce to father, 15 May 1862.

45. MS Bryce 421 ff. 178–79, Bryce to father, 19 November 1867.

46. These are the dates I have inferred from the Oriel ordinances and the university statutes. The Oriel ordinances stated at §17 that 'Every Fellow shall be required to take either the degree of Master of Arts, or the degrees of Bachelor and Doctor of Civil Law, or those of Bachelor and Doctor of Medicine, within one year after the time at which he shall be of sufficient standing to take those degrees respectively by the Statutes of the University, and in case of non-compliance shall vacate his Fellowship'. The University Statutes stipulated that the MA and BCL degrees could be taken in the twenty-seventh term from matriculation, and the DCL after five years from the BCL. Crucially, there were formally *four* terms in each year. Bryce matriculated on 8 June 1857: Joseph Foster, *Alumni Oxonienses: The Members of the University of Oxford, 1715–1886* (Oxford: Parker, 1888), 1:181. Foster indicates that Bryce's BCL was awarded by decree, but this is not so: we have the certificate from the examiners, dated 4 June 1864: this is MS Bryce 357 f. 33.

47. MS Bryce 11 ff. 1–2, Bryce to Gladstone, 11 April 1870. We appear not to have Gladstone's letter. The appointment was gazetted on 10 May 1870.

48. There was some (supportive) press comment, e.g., 'Oxford Gossip', *John Bull*, 23 April 1870, p. 5: this described Bryce as 'a Presbyterian, who is not thirty' (he was thirty-two), remarked that it was probably the first such appointment of one who was not a member of the Church of England, and concluded: 'It is curious, however, that Mr Bryce, not being an MA but BCL, will not have a vote in Congregation, and this may on some occasions cause some inconvenience.'

49. The ordinances did not exempt professor fellows from the requirement to proceed to a higher degree, and the time limits were defined in relation to matriculation and the date of the BCL, so that if Bryce as an ordinary fellow was out of time, so would be Bryce as a professor fellow.

50. *The Times*, 30 May 1870, p. 8; *Oxford University Gazette*, 31 May 1870, p. 1.

51. The act was signed into law in June 1871. By coincidence, this would have been just in time to save Bryce had he taken his BCL at the latest possible date.

52. Jonathan Parry, *The Rise and Fall of Liberal Government in Victorian Britain* (New Haven, CT: Yale University Press, 1993), 86–87.

53. The classic study is Harvie, *Lights of Liberalism*.

54. HC Deb, 14 June 1865, vol 180 cc. 200–201.

55. HC Deb, 14 June 1865, vol. 180 c. 245.

56. MS Bryce 421 ff. 85–86, Bryce to father, 15 June 1865.

57. MS Bryce 515 f. 67.

58. 'Lord Bryce's Religious Faith. Canon Barnes's Tribute', *Manchester Guardian* 30 January 1922, p. 10. Barnes was the son-in-law of Bryce's friend, the historian Sir Adolphus Ward. On Bryce's worshipping at Westminster Abbey, 'The Late Viscount Bryce, O.M., K.C.V.O.', *St Columba's Magazine*, n.d., MS Bryce 508 f. 26v. The abbey was only half a mile from Buckingham Gate, where the Bryces established their London home on their return from Washington in 1913.

59. James Bryce, 'The Late Dr Phillips Brooks', *Westminster Gazette*, 6 February 1893 [copy in MS Bryce 302 f. 97].

60. 'Lord Bryce's Religious Faith', p. 10.

61. Bryce, 'The Late Dr Phillips Brooks'.

62. MS Bryce 404 ff. 96–100, Dr James Bryce [father] to Dr R. J. Bryce, 22 November 1861.

63. MS Bryce 412 ff. 143–44, Bryce to mother, 11 May 1869.

64. MS Bryce 413 ff. 1–3, Bryce to mother, 12 January 1874.

65. MS Bryce 422 ff. 25–26, Bryce to father, 19 January [1874; misdated 1871 in pencil].

66. MS Bryce 411 ff. 11–14, Bryce to mother, 17 November 1857.

67. MS Bryce 428 ff. 20–21 Bryce to Mary Bryce, 30 April 1863.

68. MS Bryce 428 ff. 52–53, Bryce to Mary Bryce, 27 December 1864.

69. MS Bryce 428 ff. 52–53.

70. MS Bryce 421 ff. 47–50, Bryce to Dr James Bryce, 4 December 1864.

71. MS Bryce 4 ff. 52–54, Bryce to Dicey, 28 February 1913.

72. Daniel Pals, 'The Reception of "Ecce Homo"', *Historical Magazine of the Protestant Episcopal Church* 46 (1977), 77.

73. The fullest study is Ian Hesketh, *Victorian Jesus: J. R. Seeley, Religion, and the Cultural Significance of Anonymity* (Toronto: University of Toronto Press, 2017).

74. On the speculation about Goldwin Smith, see Ian Hesketh, 'Behold the (Anonymous) Man: J. R. Seeley and the Publishing of Ecce Homo', *Victorian Review* 38.1 (2012), 100–101. A. P. Stanley (who later gave the book an enthusiastic review) was one of those who was convinced of Smith's authorship. Bryce seems not to have been mentioned in the speculation.

75. British Library Add MS 55086 f. 13, Bryce to Alexander Macmillan, 22 January 1866.

76. MS Bryce 110 f. 27, Henry Nettleship to Bryce, 21 February 1866.

77. [J. R. Seeley], *Ecce Homo. A Survey of the Life and Work of Jesus Christ* (London: Macmillan, 1866), 186.

Chapter 3

1. Symonds published his famous seven-volume history of the Renaissance in Italy between 1875 and 1886.

2. The main exception was *Studies in History and Jurisprudence*, which consisted mostly of his Oxford public lectures and was published by the Clarendon Press.

3. The other changes in 1873 included the addition of a new section, 'Haughty demeanour of the Popes', at the end of chapter 13 on the fall of the Hohenstaufen, and in chapter 19, the section on Emperor Charles VII was retitled 'The Emperors Charles VII and Joseph II'. In the 1904 edition, the chapter on 'The New German Empire' was divided into two supplemental chapters (23 and 24), entitled 'The Progress of Germany Towards National Unity' and 'The New German Empire'.

4. Arnaldo Momigliano, 'Two Types of Universal History: The Cases of E. A. Freeman and Max Weber', *Journal of Modern History* 58 (1986), 239.

5. The main exception is now Oded Y. Steinberg, *Race, Nation, History: Anglo-German Thought in the Victorian Era* (Philadelphia: University of Pennsylvania Press, 2019), chap. 5. Of the various monographs on Bryce, the only one to give due weight to *The Holy Roman Empire* is Kleinknecht, *Imperiale und internationale Ordnung*, chaps. 2–3.

6. 'The Holy Roman Empire', *Spectator*, 29 October 1864, 1243.

7. James Bryce, *The Holy Roman Empire* (London: Macmillan, 1864) [henceforth HRE], 5. Cited in this edition unless otherwise indicated.

8. MS Bryce 9 f. 9, Bryce to Freeman, 3 February 1863.

9. H. S. Jones, 'Historical-mindedness and the World at Large: E. A. Freeman as Public Intellectual', in *Making History: Edward Augustus Freeman and Victorian Cultural Politics*, ed. G. A. Bremner and J. Conlin (Proceedings of the British Academy, vol. 202) (Oxford: Oxford University Press, 2015), 293–310.

10. W.R.W. Stephens, *The Life and Letters of Edward A. Freeman* (London: Macmillan, 1895), 2:464.

11. For the assertion that he was Bryce's teacher, see Kleinknecht, *Imperiale und internationale Ordnung*, 23 ('Sein Lehrer Freeman'); Marilyn Lake, 'The White Man Under Siege: New Histories of Race in the Nineteenth Century and the Advent of White Australia', *History Workshop Journal* 58 (2005), 46: 'Bryce . . . trained in the tradition of Freeman'; 'Bryce was one of Freeman's star pupils from Trinity College'; Gaetano Quagliariello, *Politics Without Parties: Moisei Ostrogorski and the Debate on Political Parties on the Eve of the Twentieth Century* (Aldershot: Avebury, 1996), 116: 'his principal teacher and one of the founding fathers of the comparative method'. Even Burrow casually accepts that 'Bryce had fallen, as an undergraduate at Trinity College, Oxford, under the influence of Edward Freeman': J. W. Burrow, 'Some British Views of the United States Constitution', in *The United Stated Constitution: The First 200 Years*, ed. R. C. Simmons (Manchester: Manchester University Press, 1989), 117.

12. MS Bryce 420 ff. 158–59, Bryce to father, 16 December 1861.

13. HRE, 26.

14. MS Bryce 9 ff. 1–2, Bryce to Freeman, 25 August 1862; HRE (1864), 26, 30 34, 35 (x2), 63 (x2), 72, 87, 88, 89 (x3), 95, 115.

15. MS Bryce 9 ff. 3–5, Bryce to Freeman, 25 November 1862.

16. MS Bryce 9 f. 17, Bryce to Freeman, 9 March 1863.

17. HRE, 19, 47. This is Ralph Colonna's *De translatione imperii Romani*.

18. This is Peter de Andlo's *De Imperi Romano*, referred to in HRE (1864) 47, 86, 88, 113.

19. HRE, 23. This is *De Formula imperii Romani*.

20. Liudprand, *Legatio Constantinopolitana*, cited in HRE, 60, 61, 84.

21. This is Ludwig Häusser, *Deutsche Geschichte seit dem Tode Friedrich's des Grossen*, cited in HRE, 142, 145, 148, 149. Cf. MS Bryce 9 ff. 24–25, Bryce to Freeman, 13 May 1863, from Heidelberg: 'The great historical light is Haüsser [sic], whose history you have got.'

22. MS Bryce 9 ff. 5–6, Bryce to Freeman, 25 November 1862.

23. MS Bryce 9 f. 5, Bryce to Freeman, 25 November 1862.

24. These were both included in the second (posthumous) edition of the first volume: Edward A. Freeman, *History of Federal Government in Greece and Italy*, 2nd ed., ed. J. B. Bury (London: Macmillan, 1893), 557–633.

25. See notably MS Bryce 9 ff. 28–31, Bryce to Freeman, 2 August 1863.

26. MS Bryce 5 ff. 19–21, Freeman to Bryce, 15 January 1865.

27. The fullest study of this subject is Ian Wood, *The Modern Origins of the Early Middle Ages* (Oxford: Oxford University Press, 2013).

28. MS Bryce 9 ff. 26–27, Bryce to Freeman, 2 July 1863.

29. In what follows, I cite the first edition in which the passage cited appeared. Bryce did not, on the whole, delete or amend text; he added. Hence, unless it is stated to the contrary, it can be assumed that passages referred to appeared in all editions starting from the one cited.

30. HRE, 6.

31. Robert S. Rait, ed., *Memorials of Albert Venn Dicey* (London: Macmillan, 1925), 29–30; MS Bryce 345 f. 31.

32. MS Bryce 4 ff. 236–37, Bryce to Dicey, 8 January 1920.

33. HRE [1866], 3. This section did not appear in the first edition. The lines about explaining a modern Act of Parliament or a conveyance of land are clearly those of one reading for the bar: he was called by Lincoln's Inn the following year, June 1867. Bryce did this for an act passed by Gladstone's first government just a few years later: James Bryce, 'The Judicature Act of 1873 in Its Relation to the History of the Judicial System in England', in *Essays and Addresses by Professors and Lecturers of the Owens College, Manchester* (London: Macmillan, 1874), 423–63. This traces the history of the English judicial system not just to Henry II's reign, but to the Saxon Witena-Gemot.

34. HRE, 55.

35. HRE, 24.

36. HRE, 29.

37. HRE [1866], 416. Steinberg appears to interpret 'little more successful' as if it read 'a little more successful', or even 'rather more successful'. Steinberg, *Race, Nation, History*, 145.

38. HRE [1866], 80–81. This passage is not in the first edition

39. This is a point that Oded Steinberg rightly makes, in the best—indeed, practically the only—modern study of *The Holy Roman Empire*: Steinberg, *Race, Nation, History*, 139, 156. Steinberg acknowledges the significant differences between Bryce and Freeman, but even he has a habit in falling back on meaningless quasi-explanatory propositions such as 'Together with Freeman, Bryce belonged to the Teutonic circle of scholars' (p. 139).

40. Montesquieu, *The Spirit of the Laws*, part 2, chap. 6.

41. One of the rare scholars to note this point is James Kirby, 'A. V. Dicey and English Constitutionalism', *History of European Ideas* 45 (2019), 44: 'He was always intellectually a civilian.'

42. HRE, 75.

43. James Bryce, *Studies in History and Jurisprudence* [henceforth SHJ] 1, essays 2–3, and SHJ 2, essays 14–16 (Oxford: Clarendon, 1901).

44. Even Steinberg, though he entitles his chapter on Bryce 'Teutonism and Romanism', passes over this important aspect of Bryce's career.

45. 'The action of centripetal and centrifugal forces on political constitutions', in SHJ 1:255–311.

46. Harvie, *Lights of Liberalism*, 100–105.

47. Viscount Bryce, *Race Sentiment as a Factor in History* (London: University of London Press, 1915), 4.

48. MS Bryce 421 ff. 66–68, father to Bryce, 23 February 1865; MS Bryce 412 ff. 1–3, Bryce to mother, 1 & 3 January 1865. He evidently borrowed Gregorovius's book from the library of Queen's College, Oxford: MS Bryce 148 ff. 21–22, E. M. Walker (librarian) to Bryce, 17 April 1891, asking for return of Gregorovius's volume 1 and Le Beau on Le Bas Empire volumes 8 and 9, 'borrowed by you some years ago'.

49. Bryce to mother, 1 & 3 January 1865.

50. Bryce to mother, 1 & 3 January 1865. The reference is to Arthur Hugh Clough's *Amours de Voyage* (1849), where the hero, Claude, says 'Rome disappoints me still; but I shrink and adapt myself to it'. 'Rossi' is Giovanni Battista de Rossi (1822–1894), a Roman archaeologist chiefly known for his work in rediscovering early Christian catacombs.

51. Letter dated 12 August 1866, recipient unknown, published in Evelyn Abbott and Lewis Campbell, *The Life and Letters of Benjamin Jowett* (London: Murray, 1897), 1:418.

52. HRE [1866], 2.

53. HRE, 37.

54. HRE, 37.

55. HRE, 37–38.

56. Numa Denis Fustel de Coulanges, *The Ancient City: A Study on the Religion, Laws, and Institutions of Greece and Rome* (Baltimore: Johns Hopkins University Press, 1980), 383. Bryce cited Fustel's book, in French, in MD 1:188.

57. HRE, 38.

58. Cowling notes that The Holy Roman Empire 'gave a subtle impetus to the internationalism to which he was to be committed later': Maurice Cowling, *Religion and Public Doctrine in Modern England, Volume 3: Accommodations* (Cambridge: Cambridge University Press, 2001), 170.

59. Parry, *Democracy and Religion*, 221, even suggests that this helps explain his later support for Irish Home Rule.

60. Heinz H. F. Eulau, 'Theories of Federalism Under the Holy Roman Empire', *American Political Science Review* 35, no. 4 (1941): 643–64; also Louis Le Fur and Paul Posener, *Bundesstaat und Staatenbund, Erster Band: Bundesstaat und Staatenbund in geschichtlicher Entwickelung* (Breslau: Kern, 1902), 75–89; and Joachim Whaley, 'Federal Habits: The Holy Roman Empire and the Continuity of German Federalism', in *German Federalism. New Perspectives in German Studies*, ed. Maiken Umbach (London: Palgrave Macmillan, 2002), 15–41.

61. Montesquieu, *De l'Esprit des Lois*, book 9, chap. 2.

62. Edward A. Freeman, *History of Federal Government: from the Foundation of the Achaian League to the Disruption of the United States* (London: Macmillan, 1863), 620–21.

63. It was by no means only those who sympathized with the Confederate cause who understood the Civil War in this way: Freeman and Dicey, both of them pro-Union, took the same line.

64. HRE, 123.

65. HRE, 141–42.

66. HRE, 142.

67. HRE, 142. For more on liberal preference for large-state nationalism over small-state particularism, see Hobsbawm, *Nations and Nationalism since 1789: Programme, Myth, Reality*, 2nd ed. (Cambridge: Cambridge Univeristy Press, 1992).

68. Compare with Ernest Gellner's argument in *Conditions of Liberty: Civil Society and Its Rivals* (Harmondsworth: Penguin, 1996), esp. 103–8.

69. HRE, 142–43.

70. HRE, 143.

71. HRE, 143.

72. 'Centripetal and Centrifugal Forces', 302–3.

73. 'Centripetal and Centrifugal Forces', 260.

74. *The Tablet*, 27 March 1869, pp. 709–10. This was apparently a review of the second edition, published in 1866.

75. *Pall Mall Gazette*, 23 September 1873, p. 1050.

76. [A. V. Dicey], 'The Influence of an Historical Idea', *Macmillan's Magazine* 11 (1 November 1864), 156. Attributed to Dicey by the Wellesley Index.

77. 'Influence of an Historical Idea', 156.

78. Jones, *Intellect and Character*, 232, for Pattison's influence on Dicey, and more generally on Pattison as the original Victorian pioneer of the history of ideas.

79. 'Influence of an Historical Idea', 158.

80. 'Influence of an Historical Idea', 160.

81. *Revue Critique*, 24 February 1890. My translation.

82. [W. R. Greg,] 'The Achievements and the Moral of 1867', *North British Review* 47 (1867), 205.

83. On the conception of 'diversity without democracy' the definitive study is Gregory Conti, *Parliament the Mirror of the Nation: Representation, Deliberation, and Democracy in Victorian Britain* (Cambridge: Cambridge University Press, 2019), esp. chaps. 1–2.

84. Robert Saunders, *Democracy and the Vote in British Politics, 1848–1867* (Farnham: Ashgate, 2011), 9–13; Parry, *Rise and Fall of Liberal Government*, 207–17; and, on radicalism, Eugenio F. Biagini, *Liberty, Retrenchment and Reform: Popular Liberalism in the Age of Gladstone, 1860–1880* (Cambridge: Cambridge University Press, 1992), chap. 5.

85. For Cranborne, see Paul Smith, ed., *Lord Salisbury on Politics: A Selection from His Articles in the Quarterly Review, 1860–1883* (Cambridge: Cambridge University Press, 1972); also Saunders, *Democracy and the Vote*, 205–8 on Lowe, and 236–39 on Cranborne.

86. The Hon. G. C. Brodrick, 'The Utilitarian Argument Against Reform, as Stated by Mr Lowe'; Albert Venn Dicey, 'The Balance of Classes'; C. H. Pearson, 'On the Working of Australian Institutions'; and Goldwin Smith, 'The Experience of the American Commonwealth', all in *Essays on Reform* (London: Macmillan, 1867), 1–25, 67–84, 191–216, 217–37.

87. James Bryce, 'The Historical Aspect of Democracy', *Essays on Reform*, 239–40.

88. For example, in his biographical notice on Freeman he pronounced that Freeman's conception of history as past politics was 'one which belonged to the eighteenth century rather than to our own time': Bryce, *Biographical Studies*, 267–68.

89. Bryce, 'Historical Aspect', 240.

90. Bryce, 243–44, 247–49, 273.

91. An argument that prefigures some aspects of Larry Siedentop, *Inventing the Individual: The Origins of Western Liberalism* (London: Allen Lane, 2014).

92. On Guizot as a pioneer, along with Niebuhr, of scientific history, see Bryce, 'The Writing and Teaching of History', *UHA*, 347.

93. Larry Siedentop, 'Two liberal traditions', in *The Idea of Freedom: Essays in Honour of Isaiah Berlin*, ed. Alan Ryan (Oxford: Oxford University Press, 1979), 153–74; Helena Rosenblatt, *The Lost History of Liberalism: From Ancient Rome to the Twenty-First Century* (Princeton, N.J.: Princeton University Press, 2018), chap. 1.

94. Bryce, 'Historical Aspect', 258–60.

95. Benjamin Constant, 'The Liberty of the Ancients Compared with That of the Moderns' [1819], in Benjamin Constant, *Political Writings*, ed. Biancamaria Fontana (Cambridge: Cambridge University Press, 1988), 309–28; Numa Denis Fustel de Coulanges, *La Cité Antique: Etude sur le culte, le droit, les institutions de la Grèce et de Rome* (Paris: Hachette, 1864).

96. There was more than a hint of it in Mill's 1853 review of Grote's history of Greece, but much less so in Grote himself: Peter Liddel, 'Liberty and Obligation in George Grote's Athens', *Polis* 23.1 (2006), 143.

97. Bryce, 'Historical Aspect', 266.

98. For example, Liverpool University Rathbone papers RP IX.7.41, Bryce to William Rathbone VI, 3 December 1891.

99. Bryce would not have found the label strange, least of all in the 1860s. , as is clear from his letter to his father from Switzerland in 1866, quoted on p. 185: MS Bryce 421 ff. 122–23, Bryce to father, 29 July 1866.

100. Bryce, 'Historical Aspect', 266–67.

101. Bryce, 268–71.

102. Bryce, 261.

103. Biagini, *Liberty, Retrenchment and Reform*, 67–69, and some morsels in Eugenio F. Biagini, *British Democracy and Irish Nationalism 1876–1906* (Cambridge: Cambridge University Press, 2007), 85, 107. But this subject deserves fuller investigation.

104. Cumbria Archive Centre, Carlisle, Papers of Sir Esme Howard, later Lord Howard of Penrith, DHR 5/30/4, Bryce to Esme Howard, 27 March 1914; MS Bryce 4 ff. 181–82, Bryce to Dicey, 7 and 13 June 1918.

105. MS Bryce 4 ff. 236–37, Bryce to Dicey, 8 January 1920.

106. MS Bryce 3 ff. 209–10, Dicey to Bryce, 9 February 1918. Morley is quoted by Kirby, 'Dicey and English Constitutionalism', 37.

107. MD 1:55.

108. MS Bryce 429 ff. 144–45, Bryce to Katharine, 14 January 1883. He was in fact twenty-five when he won the Arnold Prize and twenty-six when *The Holy Roman Empire* was first published.

109. James Bryce, *The Trade Marks Registration Acts 1875 & 1876* (London: Maxwell, 1877).

110. 'Prefatory Note', *English Historical Review* 1.1 (January 1886), 1–6; Doris S. Goldstein, 'The Origins and Early Years of the English Historical Review', *English Historical Review* 101 (1986), 6–19.

111. 'The Life of Justinian by Theophilus', *English Historical Review* 2 (1887), 657–86.

112. He was also attached to the Law and Economics section; but History was his primary location. Sectional membership is, however, curiously difficult to trace in the early records of the British Academy.

113. Bodl MS Fisher ff. 59–60, Bryce to H.A.L. Fisher, 20 November 1915.

Chapter 4

1. MS Bryce 159 f. 8, Lord Taunton to Bryce, 22 April 1865.

2. MS Bryce 144 f. 9, Frederick Temple to Bryce, 3 March 1865.

3. MS Bryce 159 f. 5, H. J. Roby to Bryce, 9 March 1865; MS Bryce 9 f. 70, Bryce to Freeman, 12 April [1865].

4. Bolton was one such borough: MS Bryce 68 ff. 171–72, Elizabeth Cleghorn Gaskell to Bryce, 17 May [1865]; MS Bryce 154 ff. 6–10, Emma Winkworth to Bryce, 6 January 1874.

5. In this chapter I make some use of material previously published in my essay 'James Bryce's Manchester: The Politics of the Remaking of Owens College, 1865–75', in *Manchester Minds: A University History of Ideas*, ed. Stuart Jones (Manchester: Manchester University Press, 2024), 60–76.

6. For the Victoria University: MS Bryce 358 f. 69, letter from the Lord President of the Council in April 1895 appointing him to the Court of the Victoria University for six years; confirmed by relevant volumes of the Victoria University Calendar; also 'The Victoria University: Meeting of the Court', *Manchester Guardian*, 13 November 1896. For the Victoria University of Manchester: UCT/3/1: Victoria University of Manchester Register of Members of the Court, vol. 1, and UCT/4/1 (Court of Governors Appointment Book). For Owens College, OCA/8/7/1: Owens Extension College Register of Governors.

7. He was awarded an honorary degree by the Victoria University in 1895: 'University Intelligence', *The Times*, 23 May 1895, p. 8. Understandably given his residence in London and Sussex, and his many competing commitments, Bryce hardly ever attended meetings of either Court of Governors: See University of Manchester Archive and Record Centre OCA/8/1 and OCA/8/7 (Owens College Court of Governors) and UCT/1/1, UCT/1/2, UCT/3/1, and UCT/3/2 (Victoria University of Manchester Court of Governors).

8. MS Bryce 460 ff. 6–9, Bryce to Elizabeth Ashton, 29 January 1898, on the death of her husband. Even for a letter of condolence, this letter is quite remarkable in conveying a sense of Bryce's esteem for his father-in-law.

9. New York Public Library, Macmillan Company Records VI b. 39, Bryce to O. W. Holmes, 19 September 1892 [copy].

10. Bryce certainly visited Manchester in May 1865, when he stayed with his Oxford friend, Edward Donner. He met Elizabeth Gaskell on that visit, probably the only time, for she died six months later: MS Bryce 428 ff 57–58, Katharine Bryce to Bryce, 15 May 1865. On the importance of this period in Manchester's history, see J. L. Hammond, *C.P. Scott of the Manchester Guardian* (London: Bell, 1934), chap. 5; and for an interpretation of the building projects in the city centre, Simon Gunn, *The Public Culture of the Victorian Middle Class: Ritual and Authority in the English Industrial City 1840–1914* (Manchester: Manchester University Press, 2000), 50–54.

11. There is an appraisal by Bryce in his *Studies in Contemporary Biography*, 196–210.

12. Arthur Burns, 'From "Th'Owd Church" to Manchester Cathedral, 1830–1914', in *Manchester Cathedral: A History of the Collegiate Church and Cathedral, 1421 to the Present*, ed. Jeremy Gregory (Manchester: Manchester University Press, 2021), 218; P. F. Clarke, *Lancashire and the New Liberalism* (Cambridge: Cambridge University Press, 1971), 59. Bryce's closeness to Bishop Fraser is apparent from the letters from Fraser's widow after his death: MS Bryce 67 ff. 21–29, A.E.F. Fraser to Bryce, 21 February and 9 March 1886. She offered (and Bryce accepted) some of Bishop Fraser's books.

13. Robert Dukinfield Darbishire (1826–1908): for biographical details, see obituary in *Manchester Guardian*, 9 November 1908.

14. William Gaskell—husband of Elizabeth—was minister of Cross Street Chapel. For the connections between the Darbishires and the Gaskells, see Jenny Uglow, *Elizabeth Gaskell: A Habit of Stories* (London: Faber & Faber, 1993), 110, 161. Robert Darbishire was trustee of Cross Street Chapel from 1864 to 1877: H. McLachlan, 'Cross Street Chapel in the Life of Manchester', *Manchester Memoirs* 84 (1939–41), 32.

15. Eight Darbishires were members at one time or another, starting with Robert's father, Samuel Dukinfield Darbishire, who was elected in 1822. Robert was elected in 1853, and served as a Council member 1869–85 and president in 1886.

16. P. O'Brien, *Warrington Academy 1757–86: Its Predecessors and Successors* (Wigan: Owl Books, 1989).

17. Barbara Smith, ed., *Truth, Liberty, Religion: Essays Celebrating Two Hundred Years of Manchester College* (Oxford: Manchester College Oxford, 1986), 314.

18. *Manchester College. Removal from London to Oxford. Revised Report of the Debate at the Annual Meeting of Trustees Held at University Hall, June 28, 1888* (Reprinted from the Inquirer Supplement of July 14, 1888) (London: Woodfall and Kinder, n.d.); R. D. Darbishire, ed., *Theology and Piety: Alike Free: From the Point of View of Manchester New College, Oxford. A Contribution to Its Effort Offered by an Old Student* (London: Kegan Paul, Trench & Trübner, 1890).

19. R. D. Darbishire, *Quare fremuerunt gentes? 'The Open Brotherhood.' The Christianity of Jesus. An Address Delivered in Manchester College, Oxford, on October 15th, 1900* (Manchester: Rawson, n.d.), 13 (on socialism) and 4 (on trade unionism).

20. Herbert McLachlan, 'Alexander Gordon and his Copy of the Dictionary of National Biography', in his *Essays and Addresses* (Manchester: Manchester University Press, 1950), 324.

21. Samuel J.M.M. Alberti, *Nature and Culture: Objects, Disciplines and the Manchester Museum* (Manchester: Manchester University Press, 2009), chap. 1. Darbishire was a Fellow of the Geological Society (elected 1861, and very active, giving papers and making donations to the Society's Library).

22. For the Hibbert Trust, see Alan R. Ruston, *The Hibbert Trust: A History* (London: The Hibbert Trust, 1984), the trustees being listed, 78–81. Darbishire was a trustee 1874–1902, and Thomas Ashton 1859–98.

23. MS Bryce 55 ff. 66–69, R. D. Darbishire to Bryce, 3 July 1865, and ff. 70–72, 11 July 1865. They clearly knew each other a little: On the one hand, Darbishire addressed his letters 'My dear Sir' (not 'Dear Sir', but not 'Dear Mr Bryce' nor 'My dear Bryce'); on the other hand, he invited Bryce to spend a Sunday with the family at his father's (Samuel Dukinfield Darbishire's) house near Conway (3 July).

24. MS Bryce 144 f. 9a, Frederick Temple to Bryce, 14 March 1866 [librarian has misdated this 1863]. On Temple and the Taunton Commission, Simon Green, 'Archbishop Frederick Temple on Meritocracy, Liberal Education and the Idea of a Clerisy', in *Public and Private Doctrine: Essays in British History Presented to Maurice Cowling*, ed. Michael Bentley (Cambridge: Cambridge University Press, 1993), 149–67; Peter Hinchliff, *Frederick Temple, Archbishop of Canterbury: A Life* (Oxford: Clarendon, 1998), chap. 4. Bryce regarded Temple as the commission's 'life and soul': E. G. Sandford, *Memoirs of Archbishop Temple* (London: Macmillan, 1906), 2:649.

25. MS Bryce 73 ff. 65–66, T. H. Green to Bryce, 23 March 1866. This has been misdated 1868, but the references to the Reform Bill and to a Commons debate on the University Tests Abolition Bill (21 March 1866) make it certain that the year was 1866. For Brodrick, MS Bryce 42 ff. 44–45, G C. Brodrick to Bryce, 5 April 1866.

26. 'University Tests Abolition: Public Meeting in Manchester', *Manchester Guardian* 9 April 1866, p. 3.

27. *Rugby School Register Volume 2 from 1850 to 1874 Inclusive* (Rugby: Lawrence, 1886). Cf. also University of Kentucky Special Collections Research Center, Darbishire Family Papers Box 1 folder 14, Harriet Darbishire to Godfrey Darbishire, 10 November 1869.

28. A man of principles, adhered to trenchantly, Darbishire (unlike his wife) severed his formal connection with the high school over the scheme of government drawn up by the Charity Commissioners in 1883 as the price for a substantial grant (£15,000 in capital and an annual grant of £1,000) from the Hulme Trust. Darbishire thought that the scheme gave insufficient weight to the principle of unsectarianism. See 'Mr R.D. Darbishire', MG 9 November 1908, p. 9, and Sara Burstall, *The Story of the Manchester High School for Girls, 1871–1911* (Manchester: University Press, 1911), 112.

29. Burstall, *Story of the Manchester High School*, 92.

30. A. B. Robertson, 'Manchester, Owens College and the Higher Education of Women: "a large hole for the cat and a small one for the kitten"', *Bulletin of the John Rylands Library* 77 (1995), 220.

31. Her brother, Henry Peyton Cobb, was MP for Banbury and a Hibbert Trustee alongside Darbishire; their father, Timothy Rhodes Cobb, was a trustee immediately before Darbishire joined.

32. MS Bryce 55 ff. 75–76, R. D. Darbishire to Bryce, 24 February [1889], and Harriet Darbishire to Bryce, also 24 February [1889].

33. Her resignation in 1899 was reported in *The Magazine of the Manchester High School* 1.3 (October 1899), 100, digitised archive of MHSG, https://www.mhsarchive.org/.

34. MS Bryce 428 ff. 57-58, Katharine Bryce to Bryce, 15 May 1865.

35. The eldest daughter, Marianne, married in 1866, and Florence (Flossy) in 1863.

36. Eleanor F. Rathbone, *William Rathbone: A Memoir* (London: Macmillan, 1905), 319–20 (Greece, 1885). For Alassio, MS Bryce 430 ff. 81–84; Bryce to Mary and Katharine, 13 and 21 October 1886.

37. Susan Pedersen, *Eleanor Rathbone and the Politics of Conscience* (London: Yale University Press, 2004), 68.

38. Marion Bryce was a governor of the high school prior to her marriage; subsequently her sisters Margaret and Charlotte (Lady Broadhurst) were governors, as her elder sister Harriet Gertrude (Mrs Arthur Lupton, d. 1888) had been before her: 'An Educational Jubilee: Fifty Years at the High School. Manchester Pioneers of 1874', *Manchester Guardian* 10 January 1924, p. 11. Thomas Ashton served on the provisional management committee and was a generous benefactor: William J. Smith, 'Manchester High School for Girls: The Pioneering Years, 1874–1924', PhD diss., University of Manchester, 2004, pp. 218, 474; MHSG Report for Year ending 31 August 1887, p. 50.

39. Viscount Bryce, O.M., 'The Function of the Modern University. Some Early Memories of Owens and Its Makers', *Manchester Guardian*, 7 May 1920, p. 18.

40. Bryce's diaries record that he stayed with the Winkworths in Bolton in October 1873, and in November and again in December 1875.

41. According to Mary Hamilton, Emma Winkworth's relationship with her husband was unhappy: he did not share her intellectual interests and resented that eminent guests wanted to talk to her rather than to him: Mary Agnes Hamilton, *Remembering My Good Friends* (London: Cape, 1944), 12–16. Mary Hamilton's mother had been brought up by the Winkworths.

42. On this connection, see Winifred Gérin, *Elizabeth Gaskell* (London: Oxford University Press, 1976), 92–93.

43. MS Bryce 68 ff. 171–72, Elizabeth C. Gaskell to Bryce, 17 May [1865]. This is published in J.A.V. Chapple and Arthur Pollard, eds., *The Letters of Mrs Gaskell* (Manchester: Mandolin, 1997), 785. The editors say: 'If to Bryce himself most likely 1864 or 1865.' It is certainly to Bryce, and certainly 1865.

44. Uglow, *Elizabeth Gaskell*, 88.

45. Manchester High School for Girls Archive, L 1875 1, John P. Thomasson to Robert Dukinfield Darbishire, 5 November 1875. This was repaid when the scheme was approved for support for the School from Hulme's Charity: Manchester High School for Girls Report 1884–1885, p. 40.

46. And Somerville too: see J. Percival, 'Higher Education of Women at Oxford' (letter), *Manchester Guardian*, 29 December 1880, p. 5.

47. Goldwin Smith, *Reminiscences*, ed. Arnold Haultain (New York: Macmillan, 1911), 364.

48. MS Bryce 428 ff. 168–69, Bryce to Katharine, 22 February 1871.

49. Caroline Dakers, *The Holland Park Circle: Artists and Victorian Society* (London: Yale University Press, 1999).

50. MS Bryce 4 ff. 15–16, Bryce to Dicey, 27 April 1909. He added, frustratingly: 'There was one sad episode in her life which I am not quite sure that you knew of which heightened my admiration for her, but it is too long to describe in a letter.' I have not been able to discover what this episode was.

51. MS Bryce 476 ff. 175–76, Stephen Winkworth to E. Marion Bryce (henceforth EMB in notes), n.d. [1922].

52. Ian J. Shaw, 'High Calvinists in Action, c. 1810–60: A Study of the Response of Some High Calvinist Ministers to Religious and Secular Problems in Manchester and London, Compared with the Work of Some Evangelical Calvinists', PhD diss., University of Manchester, 1996, chap. 6.

53. MS Bryce 428 f. 155, Bryce to Mary, 12 October 1870.

54. On Unitarians' support for the higher education of women, see Janet Howarth and Mark Curthoys, 'The Political Economy of Women's Higher Education in Late Nineteenth and Early Twentieth-Century Britain', *Historical Research* 60 (issue 142) (1987), 213.

55. Burstall, *The Story of the Manchester High School*, 5–6.

56. MS Bryce 119 ff. 66–67, North Pinder to Bryce, 12 April 1865. Pinder was under the mistaken impression that Bryce was secretary to the commission.

57. MS Bryce 421 ff. 72–75, father to Bryce, 2 March 1865. For the terms: MS Bryce 159 ff. 1–5, H. J. Roby to Bryce, 28 February, 7 March, 9 March 1865; f. 8, Lord Taunton to Bryce, 22 April 1865.

58. MS Bryce 428 ff. 168–69, Bryce to Katharine, 22 February 1871.

59. MS Bryce 429 ff. 1–2, Bryce to Mary, 24 January 1873.

60. MS Bryce 421 ff. 82–84, father to Bryce, 11 May 1865.

61. Schools Inquiry Commission PP 1867–8 [3966] V, 862–85: quotations at 862, 865 (henceforth cited in the form Schools Inquiry Commission 3966-V, 862).

62. On the concept of 'national education'—a term rich in connotations—see Joanna Innes, '"L'éducation nationale" dans les îles Britanniques, 1765–1815: variations britanniques et irlandaises sur un thème européen', *Annales. Histoire, Sciences Sociales* 65 (2010), 1087–1116; Jo Innes,

'National Education and Religion in the United Kingdom', blog post for the Opening Oxford 1871 project, https://openingoxford1871.web.ox.ac.uk/article/national-education, accessed 1 August 2023.

63. R. J. Bryce, *Sketch of a Plan for a System of National Education for Ireland Including Hints for the Improvement of Education in Scotland* (London: Cowie, 1828), v.

64. Bryce, 24, 40–41.

65. Bryce, 14, 50.

66. R. J. Bryce, *Practical Suggestions for Reforming the Educational Institutions of Scotland: Being an attempt to point out the necessity for desectarianising the schools and universities simultaneously; and the means whereby this may be accomplished* (Edinburgh: Oliphant, 1852).

67. R. J. Bryce, *Speech Against Sectarian Training Colleges* (Edinburgh: Morrison and Gibb, n.d. [1883]), 1. This was the substance of his speech at the United Presbyterian Synod. He died five years later, in his ninetieth year.

68. Bryce (nephew) also remained a consistent advocate of the organization, and professionalization, of the teaching profession, not least when he served as president of the Teachers' Guild: 'Mr Bryce on the Teaching Profession', *The Times*, 5 June 1899, p. 16.

69. The importance of Bryce's report in this regard can be gauged from the contents of D. Beale, ed., *Reports Issued by the Schools' Inquiry Commission, on the Education of Girls* (London: Nutt, n.d.). The extract from Bryce's report is at pp. 45–83. At thirty-nine pages it is by some distance the longest extract: the others range from 10 (Stanton) to 26 (Fearon). The chapter on girls' schooling in the general report (reprinted by Beale at pp. 1–20) makes significantly more of Bryce than of any other of the assistant commissioners' reports. Bryce is also the only one of the assistant commissioners cited by Elizabeth C. Wolstenholme, 'The Education of Girls, Its Present and Its Future', in *Woman's Work and Woman's Culture: A Series of Essays*, ed. Josephine E. Butler (London: Macmillan, 1869), 290–330, and indeed (in the same volume) in the Rev. G. Butler, 'Education Considered as a Profession for Women', 49–77.

70. On the significance of the desertion of the city by gentry families since the early eighteenth century, V.A.C. Gatrell, 'The Commercial Middle Class in Manchester, c. 1820–1857', PhD diss., University of Cambridge, 1971, pp. 140–42.

71. We lack a full study of the contests over the reform of these institutions. But there is a luminous study of Manchester Grammar School by R.F.I. Bunn, 'The History of the School', in *The Manchester Grammar School 1515–1965*, ed. J. A. Graham and B. A. Phythian, (Manchester: Manchester University Press, 1965), part 1, and a lively and detailed older history by Alfred A. Mumford, *The Manchester Grammar School 1515–1915: A Regional Study of the Advancement of Learning in Manchester since the Reformation* (London: Longmans, Green, 1919). On the Hulme Trust, the best study is I. B. Fallows, *William Hulme and His Trust* (Chichester: Pillimore, 2008).

72. Henry Enfield Roscoe, *The Life and Experiences of Henry Enfield Roscoe, D.C.L., LL.D., F.R.S.* (London: Macmillan, 1906), 111.

73. Schools Inquiry Commission 3966-IX, 531.

74. Schools Inquiry Commission 3966-IX, 764.

75. Schools Inquiry Commission 3966-IX, 165.

76. Schools Inquiry Commission 3966-IX, 120.

77. Schools Inquiry Commission 3966-IX, 170–76.

78. The school's historians are critical of Bryce's report for 'reproducing erroneous local gossip' about the Nowell endowments in particular: R. S. Paul and W. J. Smith, *A History of Middleton Grammar School 1412–1964* (Middleton: Queen Elizabeth's Grammar School, 1965), 23.

79. Schools Inquiry Commission 3966-XVII, 336–42. As in the case of Middleton, the historian of Bolton School thinks Bryce's report unduly harsh: W. E. Brown, *The History of Bolton School* (Bolton: Bolton School, 1976), 90.

80. Schools Inquiry Commission 3966-XVII, 182–8.

81. Schools Inquiry Commission 3966-XVII, 286.

82. The report, formally in the name of the commissioners themselves, can be treated as Bryce's, as it was in contemporary reports, e.g., 'School Inquiry Commission', *Manchester Guardian*, 5 March 1868, p. 3.

83. Marion Bryce's biographical notes on her father and her husband, MS Bryce 491 f. 101.

84. Schools Inquiry Commission 3966-XVII, 314.

85. 'Manchester Grammar School New Scheme', *Manchester Guardian*, 4 August 1875, p. 5; 'The Grammar School Scheme', *Manchester Times*, 27 May 1876, p. 7; 'Manchester Grammar School', *Manchester Guardian*, 14 May 1877, p. 5.

86. Schools Inquiry Commission 3966-IX, 719–20.

87. The interview with Greenwood (March 1866) is noted at MS Bryce 347 ff. 3v–5; these notes are followed by notes for a course of lectures on Jurisprudence at ff. 6–7;

88. For Bryce's salary, OCA/19/1; for the increase in 1871, see MS Bryce 357 f. 74, J. Holme Nicholson (Secretary of Owens College) to Bryce, 13 May 1872, re his income tax return; also David R. Jones, 'Governing the Civic University', *History of Education Quarterly* 25 (1985), 287. Bryce's own records appear to indicate that in 1871–1872 he received from Owens College £122-8-0, after deducting his payments to his assistant lecturers but before deduction of income tax. That was for two courses (fifteen lectures in total). The following year, when he gave eleven lectures, his earnings were £110: MS Bryce 357 f. 75, note headed 'Owens College'. The years in question can be established by comparing the names of the assistant lecturers with the syllabuses printed in the *Owens College Calendar* for the relevant year.

89. Thus in 1873–1874, when he just gave one course, on jurisprudence, he began on Monday, 13 October, staying in Manchester and Liverpool all week, lecturing at Owens on the Wednesday and the Friday as well. He then spent the weekend in Manchester, lectured again on the Monday, returned to Oxford on the Wednesday to attend the fiftieth anniversary dinner at the Union, returned to Manchester on the Friday to lecture at 4.30, spent the weekend with the Winkworths in Bolton, and the following week gave his three lectures at Owens on Monday, Wednesday, and Friday at 4.30, so completing the series of eight.

90. For the Regius stipend, see annual volumes of the *Oxford University Calendar*, e.g., that for 1881 at p. 23. This seems to indicate that the increased stipend was £440: i.e., the original £40 endowment, £100 from the Church Commissioners in lieu of the Canonry of Chichester that had once been attached to the chair, and an additional £300 from the Chest.

91. William Whyte, *Redbrick: A Social and Architectural History of Britain's Civic Universities* (Oxford: Oxford University Press, 2015), 96–100; W. H. Chaloner, *The Movement for the Extension of Owens College, Manchester, 1863–73* (Manchester: Manchester University Press, 1973).

92. Viscount Bryce, 'The Function of the Modern University', 18. On Roscoe's role, Peter J. T. Morris and Peter Reed, *Henry Enfield Roscoe: The Campaigning Chemist* (New York: Oxford University Press, 2024), chap. 6.

93. I develop my interpretation of the Owens College extension in H. S. Jones, 'The Owens College Extension of 1870–3: Rethinking the Origins of the Civic University Tradition in England', *Bulletin of the John Rylands Library* 100.2 (Autumn 2024), 53–74.

94. The bulk of the material is in the University of Manchester Archive and Record Centre OCA 7/2/48; but Bryce's manuscript draft is in Bodleian MS Bryce 162 ff. 160–67.

95. A. J. Scott, a Glasgow graduate, was a professor of English language and literature at University College prior to his appointment at Owens, while J. G. Greenwood was a graduate of University College.

96. University of Manchester Archive and Record Centre, 'Manchester and Owens College. Instructions to Mr Bryce', OCA/7/2/48.

97. Negley Harte, John North, and Georgina Brewis, *The World of UCL*, 4th ed. (London: UCL Press, 2018), 79.

98. 'Owens College Extension', *Manchester Guardian*, 4 December 1869.

99. 33 & 34 Victoria The Owens College, Manchester, [Ch. 2.] Act, 1870.

100. His general report on schools in Lancashire was published in volume 9 in March 1868 or thereabouts; his detailed reports toward the end of the following year.

101. Schools Inquiry Commission 3966-IX, 436.

102. Schools Inquiry Commission 3966-IX, 114.

103. Schools Inquiry Commission 3966-IX, 440–41.

104. 'Governing the Civic University', 302 n. 96; also David R. Jones, *The Origins of Civic Universities: Manchester, Leeds & Liverpool* (London: Routledge, 1988), 208 n. 92.

105. Schools Inquiry Commission 3966-IX, 721.

106. On this point, see H. S. Jones, 'Gladstonian Liberalism, Public Service and Private Interests: Reforming Endowments', in *The Many Lives of Corruption: The Reform of Public Life in Modern Britain*, ed. Ian Cawood and Tom Crook (Manchester: Manchester University Press, 2022), 200–219.

107. Intriguingly, in an address on Calvin's quatercentenary in 1909, he called Calvin 'more than anyone else the modern founder of a republican system in the Church', while also stressing that he was anything but a Liberal: 'James Bryce on John Calvin', *New York Observer and Chronicle*, 20 May 1909.

108. Schools Inquiry Commission 3966–1:659.

109. Lawrence Goldman, 'The Defection of the Middle Class: The Endowed Schools Act, the Liberal Party, and the 1874 Election", in *Politics and Culture in Victorian Britain: Essays in Memory of Colin Matthew*, ed. Peter Ghosh and Lawrence Goldman (Oxford: Oxford University Press, 2006), 118–35.

110. J. G. Fitch, 'Educational Endowments', *Fraser's Magazine* 79 (January 1869), 1–15; [James Bryce], 'The Worth of Educational Endowments', *Macmillan's Magazine* 19 (1868–1869), 517–24.

111. James Bryce, 'An Ideal University', *Contemporary Review* 45 (June 1884), 843.

112. For Bryce's comments on Lowe's economic fundamentalism, *Studies in Contemporary Biography*, 304.

113. [Bryce,] 'Worth of Educational Endowments', 521.

114. [Bryce,] 'Worth of Educational Endowments', 524.

115. Thomas Hare, *Usque ad Coelum. Thoughts on the Dwellings of the People, Charitable Estates, Improvement, and Local Government in the Metropolis* (London: Sampson, Law and Son, 1862), 14, estimated £50,000 a year.

116. [Bryce,] 'Worth of Educational Endowments', 524.

117. David Owen, 'The City Parochial Charities: The "Dead Hand" in Late Victorian London', *Journal of British Studies* 1.2 (1962), 116.

118. For Bryce's objections, and the commissioners' response, 'Return of Copies of Certain Objections and Suggestions', HC Paper 142 (1890) 60, 3–9.

119. HC Deb, 25 May 1881, vol. 261, cc. 1297, London City (Parochial Charities) Bill, Second Reading; also Bryce, 'An Ideal University', 844.

120. Jones, 'Gladstonian Liberalism', 215.

Chapter 5. A Liberal Ascent: Peaks and Troughs in the 1870s

1. MS Bryce 413 ff. 104–5, Bryce to mother, 20 March 1873.

2. MS Bryce 339, entries for 4 February, 14–15 May, 16 December 1873.

3. Henry James to William James, 4 March 1879, in *The Complete Letters of Henry James, 1878–1880* , ed. Pierre A. Walker and Greg W. Zacharias (Lincoln: University of Nebraska Press, 2014), 1:126.

4. Henry Adams to Sir Robert Cunliffe, 13 June 1879, in *The Letters of Henry Adams*, ed. Jacob C. Levenson (Cambridge, Mass.: Belknap Press, 1982), 2:365. At this time the Adamses were living in Half Moon Street, London, very near to Henry James, who was close to Mrs Adams in particular. So it is likely that Adams's assessment and James's were not wholly independent.

5. Since James wrote those lines shortly after a long conversation with Bryce, he may well have been reflecting Bryce's own sense of frustration.

6. Brodie was one of the friends Bryce would sometimes stay with when in Manchester: e.g., for a few days in October 1873: MS Bryce 422 ff. 80–81, Bryce to father, 7 October 1873.

7. MS Bryce 42 ff. 4–7, Erasmus Henry Brodie to Bryce, 12 March 1878. Brodie had graduated from Trinity in 1854, three years before Bryce's arrival. They got to know each other well when Brodie was a schools inspector in Manchester and Bryce was undertaking his Schools Inquiry work.

8. MS Bryce 413 ff. 104–5, Bryce to mother, 20 March 1873. He never found law as an intellectual discipline at all appealing, except in its historical dimensions. When studying in Heidelberg, he found that Vangerow's lectures made law 'charming' but added that 'English law wd no doubt be dull even under von Vangerow's hands'. Bryce to father, 8 August 1863, MS Bryce 421 ff. 25–26.

9. MS Bryce 428 ff. 170–71, Bryce to Mary, 6 March 1871,

10. Bryce to mother, 20 March 1873.

11. MS Bryce 59 ff. 65–66, Edward Donner to Bryce, 18 April 1873. Sale and Co. were a well-established firm of solicitors in Booth Street, Manchester. For examples of Bryce's stays with Donner, MS Bryce 422 f. 120, Bryce to father, 14 April [1875].

12. This was Arthur Hobhouse, later first Baron Hobhouse, the uncle of Leonard and Emily Hobhouse.

13. MS Bryce 413 ff. 60–63, Bryce to mother, 2 February [1872].

14. MS Bryce 13 ff. 27–28, C.P. Ilbert to Bryce, 15 December 1881. Ilbert was appointed after Bryce refused in 1881. The Celtic scholar Whitley Stokes served from 1877 to 1882: an internal appointment, for he had served in the Raj since 1862.

15. Collini, *Public Moralists*, chap. 1, is crucial here.

16. MS Bryce 422 f. 59, Bryce to father, 18 March 1873 [misdated 1872 by archivist]. This records the prospective increase in his professorial salary at Oxford, which is also confirmed by the Oxford University Calendar.

17. Data on Bryce's income comes from his Day Book at MS Bryce 396; some further details on his income from Owens College and Liverpool Law Society are in MS Bryce 357 ff. 74–76.

18. MS Bryce 413 ff. 72–3, Bryce to mother, 5 July 1872.

19. MS Bryce 429 ff. 68–69, Bryce to Mary, 21 August 1876. This was 43 Great Cumberland Place. Mrs Verney recalled those days in MS Bryce 476 ff. 137–38, Maude Verney to EMB, 23 January 1922.

20. Oscar Maurer, 'Leslie Stephen and the "Cornhill Magazine", 1871–82', *University of Texas Studies in English* 32 (1953), 67–95.

21. MS Bryce 4 ff. 245–46, Bryce to Dicey, 9 July 1920, for Bryce's recollection of the offer. Justin McCarthy was appointed instead, and he was replaced by John Morley in 1868.

22. MS Bryce 431 f. 14, Bryce to Mary, 16 January 1889.

23. MS Bryce 422 ff. 1–2, Bryce to father, 1 April 1869.

24. Cf. also MS Bryce 2 ff. 3–4, Dicey to Bryce, April 1870.

25. Edward Caird, the future Master of Balliol, and a contemporary of Bryce's at both Glasgow and Oxford, was at this time professor of moral philosophy at Glasgow. His brother John was principal of Glasgow University at this time, but it is probably Edward who is referred to here.

26. MS Bryce 422 ff. 122–23, Bryce to father, 7/10 June, probably 1875.

27. The first was in April 1866, with Leslie and Milly Stephen, Anne Thackeray, and Augusta Huth, as well as the Ritchie brothers, one of whom would marry Anne Thackeray a decade later.

28. 'It is a joy to see her so well again, and looking as charming as she did when I first knew her': Eton College Anne Thackeray Ritchie collection, Bryce to Anne Thackeray Ritchie, 12 January 1907; also 6 January 1914, after Augusta Freshfield's death, 'it is awfully sad to see that house without her who was its ornament and charm'.

29. There are two caches of material: Meta's letters to her intimate friend Euphemia (Effie) Wedgwood, held in the V&A Wedgwood Collection, and Meta's letters to Bryce. The latter are in MS Bryce 68, immediately after the one letter from Elizabeth Gaskell to Bryce: curiously, these letters (unlike Elizabeth's) are not listed in the catalogue to the Bryce papers.

30. Marianne, the eldest, married in 1866; Florence had married in 1863.

31. The main source for the story of the engagement to Captain Hill is Chapple and Pollard, eds., *Letters of Mrs Gaskell*, especially letter 395, to Charles Eliot Norton.

32. This correspondence has been published in Irene Wiltshire, ed., *Letters of Mrs Gaskell's Daughters* (Penrith: Humanities-Ebooks, 2012). But the editor does not comment on this sequence of letters concerning Bryce at all; nor does she so much as identify Bryce, whose name is at one point mistranscribed as 'Boyce'.

33. The eldest daughter of Wilbraham Spencer Tollemache, Julia later married Bryce's friend Charles Savile Roundell. There is an intriguing letter MS Bryce 449 ff. 86–8, EMB to Bryce, 28 January 1891: 'I have a note from Mrs Charles Roundell today asking us to dine there on the 4th February to meet Mr Albert Pell. Of course I have had to write & say that we are engaged— regretfully as to Mr Pell.' This seems to imply a degree of frostiness between them and Mrs Roundell.

34. 'V. L.' was probably Vernon Lushington.

35. V&A Wedgwood Collection, MS No. WE/WM/1/1/1/WM408, Meta Gaskell to Effie Wedgwood, 13 December [1871]. The letters from the Wedgwood Collection are cited with permission of the V&A. The collection was presented by the Artfund with major support from the Heritage Lottery Fund, private donations, and a public appeal.

36. For the financial aspect, V&A Wedgwood Collection, MS No. WE/WM/1/1/1/WM408, Meta Gaskell to Effie Wedgwood, 6 February 1872. This reported what she had heard (via Mrs Shuttleworth) from Harriet Darbishire, in whom Bryce had confided.

37. V&A Wedgwood Collection, MS No. WE/WM/1/1/1/WM408, Meta Gaskell to Effie Wedgwood, 21 January 1872.

38. Meta Gaskell to Effie Wedgwood, 6 February 1872.

39. MS Bryce 68 ff. 195–96, Meta Gaskell to Bryce, 'Wednesday night' [probably 14 May 1873]. Bryce's father did indeed have (temporary) mobility problems in 1872–1873.

40. MS Bryce 68 ff. 178–79, Meta Gaskell to Bryce, 23 December 1876. At first glance it looks as though Meta has written 1875, but the content of the letter makes it clear that it was 1876, after his ascent of Ararat. Closer examination shows that Meta has in fact written 1876.

41. MS Bryce 68 ff. 182–83, Meta Gaskell to Bryce, 8 October [1878].

42. 'The Armenians', *The Times*, 21 March 1878, p. 10.

43. J. Bryce, 'The Armenians. To the Editor of *The Times*', *The Times*, 6 July 1878, p. 13; Carnarvon, 'The Armenians. To the Editor of *The Times*', *The Times*, 8 July 1878, p. 10.

44. 'The Armenians', *The Times*, 2 July 1878, p. 5.

45. MS Bryce 68 ff. 185–90, Meta Gaskell to Bryce, 1 June [1878].

46. MS Bryce 68 f. 201. Undated draft headed '7 Norfolk Square, W'.

47. The importance of Unitarianism in girls' and women's education is emphasized by Ruth E. Watts, 'The Unitarian Contribution to the Development of Female Education, 1790–1850', *History of Education* 9.4 (1980), 273–86; while the specific contribution of *radical*

Unitarians in the early history of feminism is the focus of Kathryn Gleadle, *The Early Feminists: Radical Unitarians and the Emergence of the Women's Rights Movement, 1831–51* (Basingstoke: Macmillan, 1998).

48. MS Bryce 68 ff. 191–92, Meta Gaskell to Bryce, 4 June [1878].

49. MS Bryce 68 ff. 193–94, 9 July [1878].

50. MS Bryce 154 ff. 6–10, Emma Winkworth to Bryce, 6 January 1874.

51. [James Bryce,] 'Icelandic Travel', *Saturday Review* 24.894 (14 December 1872), 759–60; 'Iceland Politics', *Saturday Review* 36.931 (30 August 1873), 273–75; James Bryce, 'Impressions of Iceland', *Cornhill Magazine* 29 (May 1874), 553–70; 'Primitive Iceland', in James Bryce, SHJ 1:312–58. 'Impressions of Iceland' was reprinted as the first essay in the posthumous *Memories of Travel*.

52. *Vanity Fair* produced a cartoon portrait of Bryce as mountaineer in the spring of 1893, in the brief period when he was both a cabinet minister and a Regius Professor. The text records that he was 'the first man after Noah to climb Mount Ararat'. Yet Noah was presumably water-borne (fig 5.2).

53. John Warwick Montgomery, *The Quest for Noah's Ark* (Minneapolis: Bethany Fellowship, 1972).

54. MS Bryce 67 ff. 58–59, James Fraser to Bryce, 30 November 1876.

55. James Bryce, *Transcaucasia and Ararat: Being Notes of a Vacation Tour in the autumn of 1876* (London: Macmillan, 1877), iv.

56. C. P. Ilbert, 'Appendix to Chapter on Iceland', in Viscount Bryce, *Memories of Travel* (London: Macmillan, 1923), 297; National Library of Ireland, Papers of Alice Stopford Green MS 15070/1/1, Bryce to J. R. Green, 5 October 1872; James Bryce, 'Impressions of Iceland', 558. Of the three 'Englishmen', two were, of course, Scots.

57. Bryce, 'Impressions of Iceland', 556–57.

58. Bryce, 562–63.

59. MD 2:550–51.

60. James Bryce, *The American Commonwealth* (London: Macmillan, 1888) [henceforth AC], 1:12–14. Except when indicated otherwise, this is the edition that is cited. Later editions cited were also published in London by Macmillan. There were substantively distinct editions in Bryce's lifetime: iin 1888, 1889, 1893–1894, and 1910, and these are the ones cited in this book. There were some minor corrections and factual updates in interim reprints.

61. On Bryce's 'observational mindset', Readman, 'Walking and Environmentalism', 316.

62. Jo Laycock, *Imagining Armenia: Orientalism, Ambiguity and Intervention* (Manchester: Manchester University Press, 2009), 44.

63. *The Times*, 2 October 1876, p. 7; MS Bryce 429 ff. 73–74, Bryce to Mary, 15 September 1876. The ascent of Ararat took place on 13 September (Gregorian calendar).

64. MS Bryce 429 ff. 75–76, Bryce to Katharine, 9 September 1876.

65. James Bryce, 'Russia and Turkey', *Fortnightly Review* 20 (December 1876), 808.

66. Bryce, 'The Future of Asiatic Turkey', *Fortnightly Review* 23 (June 1878), 933–35.

67. Bryce, 936. For more on Armenian nationhood as a barrier against Russian expansion, Oded Steinberg, 'James Bryce and the Origins of the Armenian Question', *Journal of Levantine Studies* 5 (2015), 18.

68. MS Bryce 429 ff. 75–76, Bryce to Katharine, 9 September 1876.

69. Bryce, 'The Future of Asiatic Turkey', 935–36. I am grateful to Dr Giorgios Giannako-poulos for allowing me to see his draft chapter on Bryce and Armenia, which clarified my thinking on this and other points.

70. 'Mr Bryce MP on Asia Minor', *Illustrated London News*, 29 January 1881, p. 11.

71. *Aberdeen Journal*, 2 June 1917, p. 4, reporting a cable sent by Bryce to the *Jewish Morning Journal* (New York). This announced 'much sympathetic interest taken here in re-establishment

of Jews in Palestine' but also noted the large investment needed to develop Palestine so that it could support a larger population than at present.

72. MS Bryce 357 f. 107, R. W. Church to Bryce, 12 February 1878; Humphry Ward, *History of the Athenaeum 1824–1925* (London: Athenaeum Club, 1926), part 2 (for list of Rule II elections); Collini, *Public Moralists*, chap. 1, especially at 13.

73. Tower Hamlets, however, had afforded him little spare time: UCL CHADWICK/ 146-2181/391, Bryce to Edwin Chadwick, 24 March [1882].

74. MS Bryce 422 f. 87, Bryce to father, 8 February 1874.

75. *Manchester Times*, 3 April 1875, p. 5; *Sheffield Independent*, 15 September 1885, p. 3; *Edinburgh Evening News*, 12 January 1878, p. 2.

76. MS Bryce 423 ff. 48–49, Bryce to father, 27 October [1876].

77. *Northern Echo* (Darlington), 15 March 1879, p. 3.

78. MS Bryce 510 ff. 93–94, Emma Winkworth to Mary Bryce, 3 April 1880.

79. Newcastle University Special Collections, Spence Watson Collection SW 1/2/55, Bryce to Elizabeth Watson (Mrs Robert Spence Watson), 24 February 1880.

80. Houghton Library, Godkin papers MS Am 1083 (169), Bryce to Godkin, 29 March [1884].

81. New York Public Library, Macmillan Company Records, Bryce to Oliver Wendell Holmes Jr., 19 September 1892.

82. MS Bryce 9 ff. 201–2, Bryce to Freeman, 28 February 1877.

83. MS Bryce 450 ff. 36–37, Bryce to EMB, 23 August 1892.

84. MS Bryce 429 ff. 100–101, Bryce to Mary, 1 October 1880.

85. This paragraph is based on Lord Eversley, *Commons, Forests and Footpaths*, rev. ed. (London: Cassell, 1910), especially 194, 276.

86. See the stimulating book by Holly Case, *The Age of Questions* (Princeton, N.J.: Princeton University Press, 2018).

87. Tom Crewe, 'Lord Salisbury as Modern Political Man, c. 1880–1902', in *Culture, Thought and Belief in British Political Life since 1800*, ed. Paul Readman and Geraint Thomas (Woodbridge: Boydell, 2024), 254.

Chapter 6

1. He would have baulked at being reduced to 'an Irish Presbyterian and a contemporary of Lecky': Cowling, *Religion and Public Doctrine*, 169. Equally, it is at best a half-truth to say that he 'hailed from a prosperous [*sic*] family based in Belfast': N. C. Fleming, 'Gladstone and the Ulster Question', in *Gladstone and Ireland: Politics, Religion and Nationality in the Victorian Age*, ed. D. George Boyce and Alan O'Day (Basingstoke: Palgrave, 2010), 148.

2. James Bryce, *England and Ireland, an Introductory Statement* (London: Committee on Irish Affairs, 1884); 'Alternative Politics in Ireland', *The Nineteenth Century* 19 (February 1886), 312–28; 'The Past and Future of the Irish Question', *New Princeton Review* 3:1 (January 1887) 48–72; 'How We Became Home Rulers', *Contemporary Review* 51 (1887), 736–56; 'Introduction', in *Two Centuries of Irish History 1691–1870* (London: Kegan Paul, Trench., 1888), xi–xxxv; and 'England's Real Attitude on Ireland', *Current History* (New York) 12.6 (1920), 939–42. Well over twenty of his articles for *The Nation* (New York) focused on the Irish Question, mostly in the 1880s. He edited James Bryce, ed., *Handbook of Home Rule, Being Articles on the Irish Question* (London: Kegan Paul, Trench, 1887), which reprinted both 'The Past and Future of the Irish Question' and 'How We Became Home Rulers'.

3. HL Deb, 15 December 1921, vol. 48, cc. 103–13.

4. MS Bryce 443 ff. 240–41, R. J. Bryce to Bryce, 24 June 1886.

5. Quoted by Campos-Rudinsky, 'James Bryce and Parliamentary Sovereignty', 735.

6. Christopher Harvie, 'Ideology and Home Rule: James Bryce, A. V. Dicey and Ireland, 1880–1887', *English Historical Review* 91 (1976), 311–12. Harvie seems to be referring to [Bryce,] 'Conditions of the Irish Problem', *The Nation* [New York] 41 (15 September 1885), 296–97, but while the article gives due weight to the unionist argument, it is written from a position of authorial impartiality.

7. Campos-Rudinsky, 'James Bryce and Parliamentary Sovereignty', 734–56; also Rudinsky, 'James Bryce's Home Rule Constitutionalism', 492–519.

8. James Bryce, 'How We Became Home Rulers', 737–388.

9. Bryce, 737.

10. Bryce, 746.

11. HC Deb, 6 April 1893, vol. 10, c. 1605.

12. E. L. Godkin to Bryce, 7 June 1882, in *The Gilded Age Letters of E. L. Godkin*, ed. William M. Armstrong (Albany: State University of New York Press, 1974), 285.

13. Houghton Library, Godkin papers MS Am 1083 (77), Bryce to Godkin, 22 June 1882.

14. E. L. Godkin, 'An American View of Ireland', *Fortnightly Review* 12 (August 1882), 175–79.

15. Godkin, 179–85.

16. Godkin, 191.

17. Bryce, 'How We Became Home Rulers', 750–51.

18. Parry, *Rise and Fall of Liberal Government*, 297.

19. MS Bryce 458 ff. 78–79, A. H. Bryce to Bryce, 13 March 1887.

20. A. Hamilton Bryce, *The Irish Question: Its Rise, History, and Present Aspect* (Aberdeen: Wyllie, 1889).

21. The correspondence is at MS Bryce 459 ff. 62–74.

22. MS Bryce 459 ff. 70–72, Bryce to A. H. Bryce, 11 May 1893 (draft). He only wrote draft copies of letters that were especially sensitive or difficult.

23. R. J. Bryce, *Speech Against Sectarian Training Colleges*, 15.

24. MS Bryce 443, ff. 5–7, R. J. Bryce to Bryce, 16 February 1880.

25. MS Bryce 443, ff. 8–9, Bryce to R. J. Bryce, 9 March 1880.

26. Duke University Rubenstein Library Special Collections James Bryce papers, Bryce to unknown recipient, 25 May [1886], 'I quite admit that the existence of what some one calls "two nations" in Ireland is the chief difficulty in the way of an extended system of Home Rule. . . . The religious difficulties are, through four fifths of Ireland, much less dangerous than formerly—I do not think the Nationalist party would permit the priesthood to have its way.'

27. MS Bryce 443 ff. 110–13, Bryce to R. J. Bryce, 23 May 1883.

28. T. W. Moody, 'The Irish University Question of the Nineteenth Century', *History* 43 (1958), 102.

29. MS Bryce 443 ff. 127–278, Bryce to R. J. Bryce, 9 May 1884.

30. MS Bryce 442 ff. 146–51, R. J. Bryce to Bryce, 19 January 1875; MS Bryce 443, ff. 244–45, R. J. Bryce to Bryce, 17 July 1886.

31. MS Bryce 443 ff. 5–7, R. J. Bryce to Bryce, 16 February 1880.

32. 'Anent' is an archaic Scottish word meaning 'about'. It recurs frequently in Bryce's family correspondence.

33. MS Bryce 443 ff. 236–37, R. J. Bryce to Bryce, 18 May 1886.

34. MS Bryce 443 ff. 41–42, R. J. Bryce to Bryce, 15 December 1880.

35. MS Bryce 443 ff. 230–31, R. J. Bryce to Bryce, 30 April 1886.

36. MS Bryce 443 ff. 1–2, Bryce to R. J. Bryce, 9 January 1880.

37. MS Bryce 443 ff. 8–9, Bryce to R. J. Bryce, 9 March 1880.

38. MS Bryce 443 ff. 55–56, Bryce to R. J. Bryce, 18 February 1881.

39. MS Bryce 443 ff. 92–93, Bryce to R. J. Bryce, 27 June 1882.

40. MS Bryce 443, ff. 242–43, Bryce to R. J. Bryce, 5 July 1886.

41. MS Bryce 411 ff. 98–99, Bryce to mother, 19 March 1864 (misdated 1862 by cataloguers and hence out of order). Gladstone's speech was 16 March 1864.

42. On the importance of the Eastern Question in strengthening the bond between Gladstone the charismatic leader and popular Liberalism, Biagini, *Liberty, Retrenchment and Reform*, 385–95.

43. MS Bryce 10 ff. 64–65, Gladstone to Bryce, 8 July 1886.

44. MS Bryce 11 ff. 143–44, Bryce to Gladstone, 10 July 1886.

45. For the term 'literary campaign', MS Bryce 11 ff. 148–51, Bryce to Gladstone, 11 August 1886.

46. James Bryce, ed., *Handbook of Home Rule, Being Articles on the Irish Question* (London: Kegan Paul, Trench, 1887). This included Bryce's 'How We Became Home Rulers', 24–54, and 'The Past and Future of the Irish Question', 214–45. For Gladstone's piece, see MS Bryce 11 ff. 178–79, Bryce to Gladstone, 11 September 1887, where Bryce asks Gladstone for a contribution to a volume which the publisher would like to publish on 17 October (*sic*).

47. James Bryce, 'Introduction', in *Two Centuries of Irish History 1691–1870* (London: Kegan Paul, Trench, 1888), xi–xxxv. For Bryce's role in coordinating the preparation of this volume, see MS Bryce 11 ff. 158–61, Bryce to Gladstone, 22 December 1886, and ff. 162–63, Bryce to Gladstone, 28 December 1886. This was 'Lessons of Irish History in the Eighteenth Century', pp. 262–80.

48. Bryce, 'Introduction', in *Two Centuries of Irish History 1691–1870*, xi–xii.

49. Duncan Bell, *The Idea of Greater Britain: Empire and the Future of World Order, 1860–1900* (Princeton, N.J.: Princeton University Press, 2007), 93–98.

50. Quoted by Bell, *Idea of Greater Britain*, 96.

51. For the argument that while a federal version of Home Rule would entail an entrenched constitution enforced by a supreme court or similar, a version based on the model of Britain's self-governing colonies would not, see E. A. Freeman, 'Some Aspects of Home Rule', *Contemporary Review* 49 (February 1886), 159–60. On the wider issue, John Kendle, *Ireland and the Federal Solution: The Debate Over the United Kingdom Constitution, 1870–1921* (Kingston: McGill-Queen's University Press, 1989).

52. James Bryce, *Constitutions* (New York: Oxford University Press, 1905), vii.

53. *Oxford Magazine* 4 (17 February 1886), 58.

54. There is a very good treatment of Bryce's conception of nationality—the only such treatment that I know—by Sylvest, 'James Bryce and the Two Faces of Nationalism', 161–79. Sylvest makes little—to my mind too little—use of the essay on centripetal and centrifugal forces.

55. [W. E. Gladstone,] 'Germany, France, and England', *Edinburgh Review* 132 (October 1870), 557.

56. 'Political Causes of the American Revolution', *The Rambler*, 1861, in John Emerich Edward Dalberg-Acton (1st Baron Acton), *Essays on Freedom and Power*, ed. Gertrude Himmelfarb (Glencoe, Ill.: Free Press, 1948), 204. There are three other uses of 'centrifugal' in this volume, all significantly later.

57. HC Deb, 17 May 1870, vol. 201 c. 841 (M. E. Grant Duff) and 11 May 1876, vol. 229 c. 380 (Sir Henry James).

58. John Stuart Mill, *Considerations on Representative Government* (London: Parker, 1861), chap. 16.

59. It was noticed in the *Saturday Review*, where the reviewer compared Renan to Matthew Arnold and thought that the lecture was one which 'Mr Arnold could without any very great stretch of imagination be fancied as delivering in Albemarle Street'. He continued by observing that Renan's 'favourite political hobby' was 'the abolition of the theory which bases national integrity on distinctions of race and language': 'French literature', *Saturday Review* 53

(6 May 1882), 578. A later notice of Renan's *Discours et Conférences* opined that the lecture contained 'much dubious history': 'French literature', *Saturday Review* 63 (18 June 1887), 890.

60. Bryce, 'The Action of Centripetal and Centrifugal Forces', 268: 'that complex feeling, based upon affinities of race, of speech, of literature, of historic memories, of ideas, which we call the Sentiment of Nationality, a sentiment comparatively weak in the ancient world and in the Middle Ages, and which did not really become a factor of the first moment in politics till the religious passions of the sixteenth and seventeenth centuries had almost wholly subsided, and the gospel of political freedom preached in the American and French Revolutions had begun to fire men's minds'.

61. Bryce, 265.

62. James Bryce, *International Relations. Eight Lectures Delivered in the United States in August, 1921* (London: Macmillan, 1922), 116–17.

63. These letters are reprinted in *Mr Gladstone and the Nationalities of the United Kingdom* (London: Quaritsch, 1887).

64. *Mr Gladstone and the Nationalities of the United Kingdom*, 27.

65. Emily Jones, *Edmund Burke and the Invention of Modern Conservatism, 1830–1914: An Intellectual History* (Oxford: Oxford University Press, 2017), 127.

66. Bryce, 'The Action of Centripetal and Centrifugal Forces', 268–69.

67. HRE, 142.

68. It was also the appropriation of public powers and sovereign prerogatives by the descendants of feudal vassals.

69. Bryce, 'The Action of Centripetal and Centrifugal Forces', 270–71.

70. Bryce, *Constitutions*, vii.

71. Bryce to Gladstone, 6 June 1887, MS Bryce 11 ff. 174–75; Bryce to Gladstone, 15 October 1889, MS Bryce 12 ff. 16–19.

72. Bryce to Gladstone, 28 July 1892, MS Bryce 12 ff 42–43.

73. HC Deb, 8 April 1886, vol 304, cc 1046–48, and 13 April 1886, vol 304, c. 1541. Gladstone visited Norway in August 1885, when he was in the process of converting to the cause of Home Rule, and in Hammond's words 'he saw with delight a small people living under the forms and in the spirit of democracy, its manners unspoilt, its self-respect uncorrupted by the insolence of wealth. . . . To a man feeling his way to Home Rule these weeks in Norway were perhaps not less important than the weeks spent thirty years earlier in the capital of the Two Sicilies.' In his Letters to the Earl of Aberdeen (1851), Gladstone had described Naples as 'the negation of God erected into a system of government'. J. L. Hammond, *Gladstone and the Irish Nation* (London: Longmans, Green, 1938), 728.

74. HC Deb, 7 June 1886, vol 306, c. 1229.

75. HC Deb 6, April 1893, vol 10, c. 1610.

76. HC Deb, 6 April 1893, vol 10, c. 1608.

77. HC Deb, 17 May 1886, vol 305, cc. 1222–23.

78. HC Deb, 17 May 1886, cc. 1223–24.

79. MS Bryce 7 ff. 226–27, Freeman to Bryce, 9 May 1886.

80. MS Bryce 11 ff. 118–23, Bryce to Gladstone, 29 May 1886.

81. Disraeli HC Deb, 2 July 1874, c. 961. The two Irish members were McCarthy Downing and Sir Colman O'Loghlen.

82. G. O. Trevelyan, HC Deb, 25 May 1886, c. 97.

83. 'Neutral Nations and the War' [1914], in James Bryce, *Essays and Addresses in War Time* (London: Macmillan, 1918), 10–11.

84. Cumbria Record Office, papers of Sir Esme Howard (Lord Howard of Penrith), Bryce to Esme Howard, 26 November 1913. Howard had urged Bryce 'to do for Switzerland what you did for America': MS Bryce 82 f. 70, Howard to Bryce, 24 November 1913.

85. Bryce, *Memories of Travel*, 298.

86. Jocelyn Paul Betts, 'After the Freeholder: Republican and Liberal Themes in the Works of Samuel Laing', *Modern Intellectual History* 16 (2019), 57–86; Thomas Erskine May, *Democracy in Europe: A History* (London: Longmans, Green, 1877), 1:xlv–xlvi.

87. Bryce looms large in the admirable study of Victorian interest in Iceland by Sigrún Pàls-dóttir, 'Icelandic Culture in Victorian Thought: British Interpretations (c. 1850–1900) of the History, Politics and Society of Iceland', D.Phil diss., University of Oxford, 2001. Pàlsdóttir rightly observes that unlike other Victorian studies of the Icelandic Commonwealth, Bryce's essay on primitive Iceland 'is not grounded in a strong Teutonism and does not dilate on the supposed qualities of the Teutonic race' (pp. 98–99).

88. 'Icelandic Travel', *Saturday Review* 24.894 (14 December 1872), 759–60; 'Iceland Politics', *Saturday Review* 36.931 (30 August 1873), 273–75.

89. [James Bryce,] 'Cleasby and Vigfusson's Icelandic Dictionary', *The Nation* [New York] 18 (18 June 1874), 399–400.

90. The lecture can be dated precisely because Bryce's diary for 1873 survives: MS Bryce 339. It is rare for Bryce to give any detail of his scholarly writing in his diary, but this is an exception: he records 'Work at Iceland lecture' on 29th April and 'writing Iceland' on 17 May. This is surely an indication of the importance of the lecture to Bryce. That he invited Gudbrandur Vigfússon, editor of the Oxford Icelandic-English Dictionary, to dinner at Oriel on 12 March suggests that he was starting to work on the subject at the time and wanted to pick the brain of Oxford's leading (indeed, sole) Icelander.

91. The major scholarly authority on early Icelandic history was Konrad Maurer, whose work Bryce admired. But Maurer's major work on legal history, his *Island von seiner Entdeckung bis zum Untergange des Freistaats*, was published in 1874, i.e., after Bryce gave his lecture on primitive Iceland. Maurer's lectures on Old Norse legal history were published posthumously in 1907–1910. Bryce's main source when he gave his lecture was probably Maurer's *Die Entstehung des isländischen Staates und seiner Verfassung* (1852), the first volume of his *Beiträge zur Rechtsgeschichte des germanischen Norden*, which Bryce cited.

92. National Library of Ireland Papers of Alice Stopford Green, MS 15070/1/1, Bryce to J. R. Green, 5 October 1872.

93. Olaf Tryggvason was a tenth-century king of Norway, important in the conversion of the Norse to Christianity. Úlfljótr was Iceland's first lawspeaker—it was he who c. 927–930 was sent to Norway to investigate the legal system. Skapti Thoroddson was an eleventh-century law-speaker. Bryce refers here to volume 5 of the History of the Norman Conquest of England, which appeared in 1876. Volume 4 had appeared in 1871. Volume 5 (the final volume) treated the effects of the Conquest. Freeman evidently did not follow Bryce's advice on this point, for it contains nothing on Icelandic law.

94. MS Bryce 9 ff. 180–81, Bryce to Freeman, 10 November 1872.

95. James Bryce, 'Primitive Iceland', SHJ 1:316.

96. Bryce, 323.

97. Bryce, 332–33.

98. Bryce, 334.

99. Bryce, 335.

100. Bryce, 'Impressions of Iceland', *Cornhill Magazine* 29, no. 173 (May 1874), 565–66.

101. 'The Millennium of Iceland', *The Times*, 19 June 1874, p. 4.

102. James Bryce, 'The New Constitution of Iceland' (letter to the editor), *The Times*, 7 July 1874, p. 4.

103. James Bryce, 'The World and Its Story. A View Across the Ages. An Introduction to the History of the World', in *Harmsworth History of the World*, ed. Arthur Mee (London: Carmelite House, 1907), 1:12.

104. Royal Historical Society, Prothero papers PP/1/3/12, Bryce to Mary Frances Prothero (Mrs G. W. Prothero), 17 May 1910.

105. Viscount Bryce, 'Preface', to Jon Stefansson, *Denmark and Sweden with Iceland and Finland* (London: Fisher Unwin, 1916), xi–xii.

106. Viscount Bryce, *The Next Thirty Tears: Thoughts on the Work that Awaits Students of the Human Sciences. Presidential Address* (London: Milford for Oxford University Press, 1917), 15.

107. Bryce, *International Relations*, 162–63.

Chaper 7

1. It was already under way when he wrote two pieces on popular government—he projected four in total—for the *Quarterly Review* in 1905: 'The Study of Popular Governments I' and 'The Study of Popular Governments II', *Quarterly Review* 203 (1905), 170–91, 387–410. For the projected third and fourth articles, which fell victim to the Liberals' return to office, MS Bryce 283 ff. 115–16, G. W. Prothero to Bryce, 8 December 1905.

2. MS Bryce 4 ff. 55–56, Bryce to Dicey, 24 March 1913.

3. Houghton Library, Godkin papers MS Am 1083 (84), Bryce to Godkin, 29 March 1884.

4. Johns Hopkins University, D. C. Gilman papers, Bryce to Gilman, 24 September 1891.

5. MS Bryce 4 ff. 251–52, Bryce to Dicey 28, August 1920. Also MD 1:ix (for his aims); for Bryce's pessimism about democracy, see also, e.g., MS Bryce 4 f. 247, Bryce to Dicey, 22 July 1920 ('the root error of Democracy lies in the assumption that every citizen has an opinion'), and MS Bryce 4 ff. 257–58, Bryce to Dicey, 24 March 1921 ('please tell me whether I have made it clear that the general conclusion is that though Democracy is bad, there is no prospect of finding any better kind of government').

6. [Bryce,] 'The Troubles of England', *The Nation* [New York] 40 (26 February 1885), 175.

7. The classic work is Gareth Stedman Jones, *Outcast London: A Study in the Relationship between Classes in Victorian Society* (Oxford: Clarendon, 1971); also Jose Harris, *Private Lives, Public Spirit: A Social History of Britain 1870–1914* (Oxford: Oxford University Press, 1993).

8. For example, 'The Troubles of England', 175, and, especially, [Bryce,] 'England: The Progress of Democracy', *The Nation* [New York] 40 (12 February 1885), 134–36.

9. H. C. G. Matthew, R. I. McKibbin, and J. A. Kay, 'The Franchise Factor in the Rise of the Labour Party, *English Historical Review* 91 (1976), 724, though McKibbin takes a different position in Ross McKibbin, *Classes and Cultures: England 1918–1951* (Oxford: Oxford University Press, 1998). There is a very good overview in Angus Hawkins, *Victorian Political Culture: 'Habits of Heart and Mind'* (Oxford: Oxford University Press, 2015), chap. 8. Hawkins writes (p. 315): 'Prior to the 1890s the notion that parliament possessed only a delegated authority, thereby being morally restrained from dealing with questions not laid before voters at the preceding general election, was widely regarded as a dangerous political heresy. By the 1890s it was becoming orthodoxy.'

10. [Bryce,] 'The Franchise Bill campaign', *The Nation* [New York] 39 (13 November 1884), 415.

11. James Bryce, 'Do We Need a Second Chamber', *Contemporary Review* 46 (July 1884), 728.

12. [Bryce,] 'England: The Progress of Democracy', 134–36.

13. Gaetano Quagliariello, 'Moisei Yakovlevich Ostrogorski', *ODNB*, firmly asserts this; Quagliariello's earlier book is more tentative: Gaetano Quagliariello, *Politics Without Parties*, 27.

14. James Bryce, 'Preface', in M. Ostrogorski, *Democracy and the Organization of Political Parties* (London: Macmillan, 1902), 1: xlii–xliii; Quagliariello, *Politics Without Parties*, 28.

15. [Bryce,] 'England: The Progress of Democracy', 135.

16. [Bryce,] 'England: The Party Programmes', *The Nation* [New York] 41 (22 October 1885), 339.

17. On the platform speech as a central and largely new feature of political leadership in the 1880s, Crewe, 'Lord Salisbury as Modern Political Man', 252–71.

18. Bagehot, 'Mr Gladstone and the People', *The Economist* 4 November 1871, in *The Collected Works of Walter Bagehot*, ed. Norman St John-Stevas (London: The Economist, 1968), 3:461.

19. Max Weber, 'The Profession and Vocation of Politics', in Weber, *Political Writings*, ed. Peter Lassman and Ronald Speirs (Cambridge: Cambridge University Press, 1994), 342.

20. To that extent I see Bryce as closer to Weber than does Cheryl B. Welch, 'An Immunity to Authoritarianism?'.

21. [Bryce,] 'England: The Two Parties and Their troubles', *The Nation* [New York] 41 (20 August 1885), 151; [Bryce,] 'England: The Party Programmes', 339.

22. [Bryce,] 'England: The Two Parties and Their Troubles', 152. My emphasis.

23. On the importance of Bryce in the analysis of the plebiscitary character of democratic politics, William Selinger, *Parliamentarism from Burke to Weber* (Cambridge: Cambridge University Press, 2019), 194–95.

24. [Bryce,] 'The English Redistribution Bill', *The Nation* [New York] 40 (8 January 1885), 29.

25. AC 1:86.

26. MS Bryce 15 ff. 121–22, Bryce to Sidgwick, 12 April 1888.

27. [Bryce,] 'Surrender, or Compromise?', *The Nation* [New York] 39 (11 December 1884), 500.

28. Dicey, *Lectures Introductory*, 354: 'that power which in modern England is the true political sovereign of the state—the majority of the electors, or (to use popular though not quite accurate language) the nation'. See also p. 384, where there is a similar formulation.

29. [A. V. Dicey,] 'Democratic Assumptions. I—Vox Populi', *The Nation* [New York] 51 (20 November 1890), 398.

30. Ions, *James Bryce and American Democracy*; Tulloch, *James Bryce's American Commonwealth*.

31. AC 1:3–4

32. AC 1:5. More will be said later about Bryce's conception of 'race'. But like many of his contemporaries, he often (though not always) used the term to indicate a human population as shaped by history, culture, and environment, and this was evidently his primary meaning here.

33. AC 1:11–12.

34. [A. V. Dicey,] 'Bryce's American Commonwealth', *Edinburgh Review* 169 (April 1889), 505; quoted by James Thompson, *British Political Culture and the Idea of 'Public Opinion', 1867–1914* (Cambridge: Cambridge University Press, 2013), 158.

35. On Lecky, Quagliariello, *Politics Without Parties*, 112.

36. AC 1:8.

37. AC 1:8.

38. Henry Sumner Maine, *Popular Government: Four Essays* (London: Murray, 1885), 217–18.

39. AC 1:406, 345.

40. [Bryce,] 'English Opinion on the Presidential Contest', *The Nation* [New York] 39 (16 October 1884), 329. Here he takes issue with Lord Carnarvon on precisely this point.

41. HC Deb, 17 May 1886, vol. 305, cc. 1221–22.

42. Walter Bagehot, *The English Constitution*, ed. R.H.S. Crossman (London: Fontana, 1963), 66.

43. AC 1:395.

44. For example, Collini, Winch, and Burrow, *That Noble Science of Politics*, 244–45.

45. Curiously, Frank Prochaska—in a chapter on Bryce and American democracy which he entitled 'Anglo-Saxon Democracy'—and Duncan Bell both misquote *The American Commonwealth* thus: 'Whatever success it [the American Constitution] has attained must be in large measure ascribed to the political genius, ripened by long experience, of the Anglo-Saxon race.'

But Bryce wrote 'Anglo-American', not 'Anglo-Saxon'. See Frank Prochaska, *Eminent Victorians on American Democracy: The View from Albion* (Oxford: Oxford University Press, 2012), 96, and Duncan Bell, *Dreamworlds of Race: Empire and the Utopian Destiny of Anglo-America* (Princeton, N.J.: Princeton University Press, 2020), 59. The original is James Bryce, *The American Commonwealth* (London: Macmillan, 1888) 1:34. Freeman was also a trenchant critic of the nineteenth-century misuse (as he saw it) of the term 'Anglo-Saxon', notably in Edward A. Freeman, *Lectures to American Audiences* (Philadelphia: Porter & Coates, 1882), lecture on 'The English Name', 38–67.

46. Jonathan Conlin, 'The Consolations of Amero-Teutonism: E. A. Freeman's Tour of the United States, 1881–2', in Bremner and Conlin, *Making History*, 112.

47. My italics. For 'European traveller', 'European observers', and other variants, Bryce, *American Commonwealth* [1888] 1:1, 4, 12, 87, 98, 102, 144, 153, 159, 194, 200, 250, 254, 257, 264, 283, 323, 471; for 'European readers', 'European minds', and other variants, 1:xi, xii, xiii, 7, 122, 239, 276, 409, 449, 452, 467, 534.

48. 'Mugwumps' was the name originally given by their opponents to those independently minded Republicans who backed the successful Democratic candidate, Grover Cleveland, in the presidential election of 1884. They were repelled by the overt corruption of Cleveland's Republican opponent, James G. Blaine.

49. Wendy Donner, 'John Stuart Mill on Education and Democracy', in *J. S. Mill's Political Thought: A Bicentennial Reassessment*, ed. Nadia Urbinati (Cambridge: Cambridge University Press, 2007), 260; Stefan Collini, 'Introduction' to John Stuart Mill, *Essays on Equality, Law, and Education*, ed. John M. Robson, vol. 21 of *The Collected Works of John Stuart Mill* (London: Routledge & Kegan Paul, 1984), xlviii.

50. For instance, 'Historical Aspect', 266–67. But also see James Bryce, 'An Age of Discontent', *Contemporary Review* 59 (January 1891), 24: 'Men do not, as the followers of Mill have been apt to assume, become fit for their duties as citizens merely by being entrusted with those duties.' Also James Bryce, *The Hindrances to Good Citizenship* (New Haven, Conn.: Yale University Press, 1909), 12–13.

51. AC, 3rd ed. (1893–1894) 2:476–788.

52. AC, 3rd ed. (1893–1894) 2:481.

53. The standard modern study is Eric Foner, *Reconstruction: America's Unfinished Revolution 1863–1877*, updated ed. (New York: Harper & Row, 2014). On the Dunning School, John David Smith and J. Vincent Lowery, eds., *The Dunning School: Historians, Race, and the Meaning of Reconstruction* (Lexington: University Press of Kentucky, 2013).

54. MS Bryce 437 ff. 41–42, Bryce to Mary and Katharine Bryce, 24 April 1908.

55. HC Deb, 27 April 1892, vol 3, c. 1499.

56. MS Bryce 4 ff. 48–51, Bryce to Dicey, 22 January 1913.

57. HC Deb, 12 June 1884, vol 289, cc. 166, 170.

58. HC Deb, 27 April 1892, vol 3, cc. 1498–99.

59. HL Deb, 17 December 1917, vol 27, c. 178.

60. HC Deb, 12 June 1884 vol 289, c. 167, Amendment to Representation of the People Bill.

61. James Bryce, *The Relations of the Advanced and the Backward Races of Mankind. Romanes Lecture 1902* (Oxford: Clarendon, 1902), 38.

62. Bryce does not feature much in the literature on nineteenth-century republicanism. Christopher Harvie, however, has astutely noticed both the republican strain in the Bryce family heritage and Bryce's own 'essentially "civic republican" doctrine': Christopher Harvie, 'Bryce, James, Viscount Bryce (1838–1922)', *ODNB*, https://doi.org/10.1093/ref:odnb/32141.

63. On this alternative republican tradition, a key recent text is Bruno Leipold, Karma Nabulsi, and Stuart White, eds., *Radical Republicanism: Recovering the Tradition's Popular Heritage* (Oxford: Oxford University Press, 2020).

64. The fundamental work is J.G.A. Pocock, *The Machiavellian Moment: Florentine Political Thought and the Atlantic Republican Tradition* (Princeton, N.J.: Princeton University Press, 1975); but it was prefigured by work by Bernard Bailyn and Gordon Wood (both influenced by Pocock's earlier work) on the ideological character of the American Revolution: Bernard Bailyn, *The Ideological Origins of the American Revolution* (Cambridge, Mass.: Harvard University Press, 1967), and Gordon S. Wood, *The Creation of the American Republic 1776–1787* (Chapel Hill: University of North Carolina Press, 1969). For an important intellectual history of the republicanism-liberalism binary, David Craig, 'Republicanism Versus Liberalism: Towards a Pre-history', *Intellectual History Review* 33 (2023), 101–30.

65. For classic statements, Philip Pettit, *Republicanism: A Theory of Freedom and Government* (Oxford: Clarendon, 1997), notably 45–50; Quentin Skinner, *Liberty Before Liberalism* (Cambridge: Cambridge University Press, 1998), especially ix–x.

66. Jose Harris, 'Epilogue. French Revolution to Fin de Siècle: Political Thought in Retrospect and Prospect, 1800–1914', in *The Cambridge History of Nineteenth-Century Political Thought*, ed. Gareth Stedman Jones and Gregory Claeys (Cambridge: Cambridge University Press, 2011), 900; E. F. Biagini, 'Neo-Roman Liberalism: "Republican" Values and British Liberalism, ca. 1860–1875', *History of European Ideas* 29 (2003), 55–72.

67. For example, in Biagini, 'Neo-Roman Liberalism'; and, on the importance of the seventeenth-century Commonwealth tradition to T. H. Green, Duncan Kelly, *The Propriety of Liberty: Persons, Passions and Judgement in Modern Political Thought* (Princeton, N.J.: Princeton University Press, 2011), chap. 5.

68. James Bryce, 'Goldwin Smith', *North American Review* 199 (1914), 519.

69. Arthur Quiller-Couch, ed., *The Oxford Book of English Verse 1250–1900* (London: Oxford University Press, 1927), 601. Pym and Hampden were invoked again in James Bryce, *The Hindrances to Good Citizenship* (New Haven, Conn.: Yale University Press, 1909), 8. On Vane's importance to T. H. Green, Kelly, *Propriety of Liberty*, 233–35.

70. They disagreed, however, on Irish Home Rule (which Smith opposed) and empire (Smith favoured independence for the 'white' settler colonies, whereas Bryce favoured some kind of federation): Alexander Morrison, 'Oriel and the Wider World', in Catto, ed., *Oriel College*, 449–50. Goldwin Smith is neglected in the literature on Victorian intellectual history, but there is a good study by Tanja Bueltmann, 'Anglo-Saxonism and the Racialization of the English Diaspora', in *Locating the English Diaspora, 1500–2010*, ed. Tanja Bueltmann, David T. Gleeson, and Donald M. MacRaild (Liverpool: Liverpool University Press, 2012), 118–33.

71. The depth and seriousness of Bryce's early republicanism seems to me the strongest riposte to Roberto Romani's rather under-evidenced claim that 'to Bryce citizenship is in the end a question of how to cope with an emergency, namely a question of order and power, not of some "good life"': Roberto Romani, *National Character and Public Spirit in Britain and France, 1750–1914* (Cambridge: Cambridge University Press, 2002), 326.

72. Jonathan Parry, *The Politics of Patriotism: English Liberalism, National Identity and Europe, 1830–1886* (Cambridge: Cambridge University Press, 2006), 242–43.

73. Bryce, *International Relations*, 29; on Mazzini, see also James Bryce, 'The Secret of Influence', *Youth's Companion* [Boston], 28 September 1911, in MS Bryce 237 f. 268c.

74. MS Bryce 334 f. 1; biographical notes, MS Bryce 515, ff. 66–67; for the visit to Saffi in 1882, MS Bryce 338 ff. 157–59.

75. MS Bryce USA 23 ff. 162–63, Bryce to James F. Rhodes, 26 June 1919. Also *The Times*, 8 November 1919 (letter): 'I have been a devoted friend of Italy all my life, and was privileged to know Mazzini and Saffi.'

76. MS Bryce 421 ff. 122–23, Bryce to father, 29 July 1866. Freeman fully shared this enthusiasm for Swiss republicanism: Biagini, 'Neo-Roman Liberalism', 63.

77. MS Bryce 413 ff. 66–67, Bryce to mother, 24 February 1872.

78. There is a notably lucid discussion of virtue and corruption in the 'moral psychology' of republicanism in Alan Craig Houston, *Algernon Sidney and the Republican Heritage in England and America* (Princeton, N.J.: Princeton University Press, 1991), chap. 4.

79. For this purpose I have used the third edition of *The American Commonwealth* (1893–1894). The much later *Modern Democracies* has 104 uses.

80. AC, 3rd ed. (1893–1894) 2:391.

81. MD 1:53–54.

82. MD 1:503.

83. AC 3:327–29. On virtue and commerce, Istvan Hont and Michael Ignatieff, eds., *Wealth and Virtue: The Shaping of Political Economy in the Scottish Enlightenment* (Cambridge: Cambridge University Press, 1983). This has spawned a large literature.

84. MS Bryce 4 ff. 83–84, Bryce to Dicey, 6 April 1915 and 27 June 1916. For more on Disraeli as a demagogue, see MS Bryce 17 f. 184, Bryce to Goldwin Smith, 7 March 1900, f. 187, 25 September 1903, and f. 190, 29 March 1905 (typescripts of the originals). But cf, Bryce, *Studies in Contemporary Biography*, 68: 'he never becomes a demagogue.'

85. MS Bryce 26 ff. 150–51, Bryce to Theodor Barth n.d. [c. 1899]. This is a draft letter. Cf. MS Bryce USA 22 ff. 101–2, Bryce to Sarah Wyman Whitman, 17 October 1903: 'The restless demagogue who makes our history how has raised the banner of Protection, and obtains more following among the unthinking than we had deemed possible.'

86. Houghton Library, Godkin papers MS Am 1083 (96), Bryce to Godkin, 1 August 1886.

87. For Blaine as the exemplar of the demagogue, Houghton Library MS Am 1083 (96), Bryce to Godkin, 1 August 1886; for Godkin's comparison between Blaine and Chamberlain (each a 'charlatan'), MS Am 1083 (1053), Godkin to Bryce, 17 October 1887; for Blaine as the personification of corruption, Houghton Library MS Am 1083 (88), Bryce to Godkin, 12 November 1884. Goldwin Smith thought Gladstone an 'unscrupulous demagogue', an opinion Bryce certainly did not share; Smith also thought Asquith's conduct in the Boer War that of a demagogue: Goldwin Smith to Selborne, 3 May 1886, and to J. X. Merriman, 8 October 1908, Arnold Haultain, ed., *A Selection from Goldwin Smith's Correspondence* (New York: Duffield, 1913), 186, 504.

88. The best discussion of Whig and Liberal Unionist critiques of Gladstone is in Parry, *Rise and Fall of Liberal Government*, chap. 12 and epilogue.

89. MS Bryce 270 f. 182.

90. AC 2:320.

91. MD 2:607 and 1:361.

92. Biographical notes, MS Bryce 515 f. 67.

93. Bryce, 'The Scoto-Irish Race', 214–15. Witherspoon, the only member of the clergy to sign the declaration, was an early supporter of republicanism, even before leaving Scotland. He was also a slave-holder in New Jersey.

94. MS Bryce 443 ff. 23–24, Bryce to Dr R. J. Bryce, 28 August 1880.

95. MS Bryce 443 ff. 33–38, Dr R. J. Bryce to Bryce, 9 December 1880.

96. MS Bryce 443 ff. 25–26, Dr R. J. Bryce to Bryce, 3 September 1880: 'the state, which had formerly been shared, was torn to pieces' (Sallust, *The War with Jugurtha*, Loeb Classical Library translation).

97. MS Bryce 442 ff. 122–23, Dr R. J. Bryce to Bryce, 9 November 1871. The article was James Bryce, 'American Experience in the Relief of the Poor', *Macmillan's Magazine* 25 (1 November 1871), 54–65.

98. MS Bryce 443 ff. 122–25, Dr R. J. Bryce to Bryce, 29 February 1884, and insertion (a cutting at f. 125 from the Belfast News-Letter headed 'Crime, ignorance, and the franchise'. This letter to the editor (published 27 February) makes the parenthetical point that Dr Bryce was 'not a very ardent advocate for women's suffrage'. Dr Bryce took the issue of 'moral'

qualifications and disqualifications for the franchise very seriously, calling meetings of Belfast social reformers and temperance campaigners and republishing his letter, with accompanying documentation, as a pamphlet: R. J. Bryce, *Letters on Crime, Intemperance, & Ignorance, in Relation to the Franchise. Reprinted or Abridged from the Belfast Newspapers with Introductory and Explanatory Notices* (Belfast: Mullan & the Irish Temperance League, 1884).

99. MS Bryce 443 ff. 127–28, Bryce to Dr R. J. Bryce, 9 May 1884.

100. MS Bryce 443 ff. 129–31, Dr R. J. Bryce to Bryce, 12 June 1884, and ff. 148–49, Bryce to Dr R. J. Bryce, n.d. November 1884.

101. MS Bryce 443 ff. 148–49, Bryce to Dr R. J. Bryce, n.d. November 1884.

102. MS Bryce 442 ff. 39–40, Dr R. J. Bryce to Bryce, 30 September 1865.

103. MS Bryce 443 ff. 212–13, Dr R. J. Bryce to Bryce, 4 March 1886.

104. HL Deb, 17 December 1917 vol 27, c. 178.

105. Algernon Sidney is much discussed in the modern literature on classical republicanism and was invoked (as we have seen) by both Wordsworth and Goldwin Smith. But, as Mark Goldie notes, his *Discourses Concerning Government* was 'an eclectic book, also much preoccupied with the Gothic polity': Mark Goldie, 'Retrospect: The Ancient Constitution and the Languages of Political Thought', *Historical Journal* 62.1 (2019), 14.

106. Harris, *Private Lives, Public Spirit*, 13–17.

107. There is a larger literature on the continental thinkers than on the British, and curiously little that considers British critics of democracy in a wider context.

108. On which see Quagliariello, *Politics Without Parties*, 112: 'Lecky interpreted Bryce's analysis of the American "machine" as an irremediable contradiction between Bryce the Victorian moralist, outraged by the ghastly spectacle of the American parties, and Bryce the champion of popular government, trying to minimize the suspicion that this was the inevitable consequence of democracy.'

109. W.E.H. Lecky, *Democracy and Liberty* (London: Longmans, Green, 1896), 1:92.

110. Lecky, *Democracy and Liberty*, 1:69, 92.

111. Maine was Corpus Professor of Jurisprudence at Oxford from 1869 to 1877.

112. Bryce to Godkin, 9 March 1886. For further negative remarks on Maine on popular government, Bryce to Dicey, 30 October 1910 (on Maine's habit of using the South American republics as 'instances of the failure of "popular government" ').

113. MS Bryce 15 ff. 117–18, Bryce to Henry Sidgwick, 22 September 1887.

114. Johns Hopkins University Special Collections Gilman Papers, Bryce to D. C. Gilman, 24 March 1899. Bryce stressed to Gilman that he had the highest regard for Lecky's work on Irish history.

115. MS Bryce 4 ff. 31–35, Bryce to Dicey, 26 December 1910; also MS Bryce 4 ff. 83–84, Bryce to Dicey, 6 April 1915. Bryce certainly deployed Swiss comparisons himself, however: Switzerland was 'that most instructive patent museum of politics': AC 2:4.

116. James Bryce, *South America: Observations and Impressions* (London: Macmillan, 1912), 524–25.

117. AC 1:474.

Chapter 8

1. A pioneering work was Pat Jalland, *Women, Marriage and Politics 1860–1914* (Oxford: Oxford University Press, 1986). More recent examples include Susan Pedersen, 'The Women's Suffrage Movement in the Balfour Family' (Ben Pimlott Memorial Lecture 2018), *Twentieth Century British History* 30 (2019), 299–320; and Jennifer Davey, *Mary, Countess of Derby, and the Politics of Victorian Britain* (Oxford: Oxford University Press, 2019). On the broad question of the domestic foundations of intellectual production, Theodore Koditschek, '"Genius" and the

Household Mode of Intellectual Production: 1795–1885', *Journal of Social History* 39.2 (2005), 429–49.

2. See the correspondence in MS Bryce 422, where there are frequent requests to his father to make contacts of this kind: e.g., ff. 94–95, 12 July [1874?].

3. Henry James to Henry James Sr, 25 March [1878], in *The Complete Letters of Jenry James, 1876-1878*, ed. Pierre A. Walker and Greg W. Zacharias (Lincoln: University of Nebraska Press, 2013) 2:70. 'She is but a lass in her teens', wrote James: she was in fact almost thirty-one.

4. MS Bryce 429 ff. 68–70, Bryce to Mary, 21 August 1876.

5. MS Bryce 431 ff. 72–79, Mary to Bryce, 4 December 1889.

6. MS Bryce 431 ff. 104–11, Mary to Bryce, 9 August 1890.

7. MS Bryce 509–1 ff. 18–19, Margery Bryce to Roland Bryce, 26 March 1946.

8. MS Bryce 424 ff. 3–4, Jessie Ilbert [Lady Ilbert] to EMB, 24 January 1922.

9. The Gairs's ancestors were Highlanders, from Cromarty, and when staying with Andrew Carnegie at Skibo Castle in Sutherland in the summer of 1906, the Bryces tracked down the Gair family tombstone in the churchyard at Nigg: MS Bryce 461 ff. 23–24, Bryce to Elizabeth Ashton, 25 August 1906.

10. Elizabeth Ashton kept a genealogical notebook which traces the Gairs back to the middle of the eighteenth century and the Ashtons to the late seventeenth: Manchester Central Library, Papers of the Ashton Family of Hyde and Ford Bank, Didsbury, M107/2/9/1. Charles Eliot believed that Marion was visiting the United States for the first time in 1890, but this is incorrect: MS Bryce USA 1 ff. 19–20, Charles W. Eliot to William Eliot Furness, 23 September 1890.

11. 'Death of Lady Bryce: A Woman of Many Gifts and Wide Interests', *Manchester Guardian*, 29 December 1939, p. 8.

12. 'Lady Bryce', *The Times*, 29 December 1939.

13. The Bryces are, however, discussed in Jalland, *Women, Marriage and Politics*. This important study is, however, unreliable on details: Thomas Ashton was not a banker (231); Bryce was not Mary and Katharine's 'younger brother' (266), but some years their senior; Marion was thirty-five, not thirty-six, when she married.

14. Lady Simon of Wythenshawe, *Margaret Ashton and Her Times. The Margaret Ashton Memorial Lecture for 1948* (Manchester: Manchester University Press, 1949), 13. Marion's notes on her family at MS Bryce 491 f. 101 positively state that Bryce knew her father 'a good many years' before she met him.

15. University of Liverpool Special Collections RP XXV.1.170 Marion Ashton to Blanche Rathbone, 9 March 1889.

16. MS Bryce 449 ff. 12–13, Marion Ashton to Bryce, 21 July 1889.

17. MS Bryce 449 ff. 7–10, Marion Ashton to Bryce, 11 March 1889: 'Last summer when I looked at some of the old spots & thought of you I had no hope of what has since come into my life.'

18. MS Bryce 430 f. 141, Bryce to Katharine, 8 December 1888. Tom and Eva Ashton had married in December 1886, so the likelihood is that they were invited to dine at Bryanston Square soon after that, perhaps in the first half of 1887.

19. MS Bryce 127 ff. 5–6, Bryce to H. J. Roby, 18 March 1889.

20. These were the photographs taken by Elliott & Fry of Baker Street. Some were taken on 8 March; others, in evening dress, a few days later: MS Bryce 449 ff. 1–2, Marion Ashton to Bryce, 9 March 1889, and ff. 7–10, Marion Ashton to Bryce, 11 March 1889. They are to be found in MS Bryce 519, e.g. f. 12, f. 20, f. 21.

21. 'Marion is such a capable woman', wrote Harriet Darbishire (Robert's wife), who knew her well, not least from the governing body of Manchester High School for Girls: MS Bryce 55 f. 62, Harriet Darbishire to Bryce, 11 March 1889.

22. The colour of her eyes is helpfully confirmed by her 1927 passport in MS Bryce 483.

23. E. L. Godkin to Katherine Godkin, 19 June 1889, in Rollo Ogden, ed., *Life and Letters of Edwin Lawrence Godkin* (New York: Macmillan, 1907) 1:151.

24. 'Death of Lady Bryce', *Manchester Guardian*, 29 December 1939, p. 8.

25. MS Bryce 449 ff. 4–5, Marion Ashton to Bryce, 10 March 1889.

26. MS Bryce 449 ff. 7–10, EMB to Bryce, 11 March 1889.

27. MS Bryce 449 ff. 48–49, Bryce to EMB, 26 January [1890].

28. On the relative size of Ashton's fortune, W. D. Rubinstein, *Men of Property: The Very Wealthy in Britain since the Industrial Revolution* (London: Croom Helm, 1981), 114 n. 44.

29. He was re-elected to a professor fellowship, but this came without stipend.

30. MS Bryce 430 ff. 143–46, Mary to Bryce, 14 December 1888: 'I am sure you will feel the loss of the money seriously.'

31. For example, *Oxford Magazine*, 26 June 1890, p. 5: 'Professor Bryce—who represents his University more successfully outside its precincts than he does on his too rare appearances within its walls'. In the same spirit, *Oxford Magazine*, 27 May 1891, p. 365, and 23 June 1892, p. 4.

32. The accounts are in MS Bryce 491. For the gift from Thomas Ashton, MS Bryce 452 ff. 93–94, Bryce to EMB, 6 August 1895.

33. An obituary of Marion recorded that Hindleap was funded by the proceeds of *The American Commonwealth*: 'The Viscountess Bryce', *The English-Speaking World* 22.2 (February 1940), 38.

34. *Morning Post*, 5 May 1898, p. 9; *The Times*, 2 July 1914, p. 11.

35. There were three brothers: One died while an Oxford undergraduate; the eldest, Thomas Gair Ashton, was a former Liberal MP for Hyde and was married to Eva James, daughter of a Hertfordshire JP; the younger son, William Mark Ashton, married Letitia Kessler, sister of Grace Ashton's husband.

36. MS Bryce 458 ff. 93–94, Margaret Ashton to Bryce, 12 March 1889.

37. Notably Balshaw, 'Suffrage, Solidarity and Strife', 91.

38. Simon, *Margaret Ashton and Her Times*, 10.

39. Margaret Ashton to Bryce, 12 March 1889.

40. MS Bryce 459 ff. 31–32, Margaret Ashton to Bryce, 22 August 1892. Bryce described this to Marion as 'a very lively letter which I will shew you': MS Bryce 450 ff. 36–37, Bryce to EMB, 23 August 1892.

41. MS Bryce 443 ff. 92–3, Bryce to Mary, April 1898.

42. They stayed with Margaret in February 1903, when Bryce gave the Warburton Lecture at Owens College.

43. This was the meeting of the International Woman Suffrage Alliance.

44. MS Bryce 456 ff. 55–56, EMB to Bryce, 3 September 1906. 'The notorious Mrs Montefiore' was the prominent suffragette Dora Montefiore, who had featured in the popular press for her dispute with the tax authorities over her withholding of income tax payments as a protest against women's exclusion from the electorate. In July bailiffs seized goods to the value of the tax owed. Later that year she was imprisoned for her part in a WSPU lobby of Parliament.

45. MS Bryce 456 ff. 114–15, EMB to Bryce, 29 November 1906.

46. It is fair to add that that sense of humour was lost on some of his contemporaries and has certainly been lost to posterity: e.g., 'Chronicle', *Saturday Review* 80 (25 August 1895), 225.

47. MS Bryce 431 ff. 125–26, Mary and Katharine to Bryce, 12 September 1890.

48. MS Bryce 431 ff. 209–10, Mary to Bryce, 28 December 1895; MS Bryce 433, ff. 48–49, Mary to Bryce, 15 November 1896.

49. MS Bryce 433 ff. 1–4, Mary to Bryce, 6 January 1896.

50. MS Bryce 454 ff. 29–30, Bryce to EMB, 8 April 1897.

51. Bryce was actually rather critical if not of that speech, then of one he heard Gladstone give in the Sheldonian Theatre at Oxford in November 1861, when he advocated 'a scheme of

lower middle-class education on church (i.e. futile High Church) principles. The time is passed for such rubbish.' MS Bryce 420 ff. 156–57, Bryce to father, 28 November 1861.

52. MS Bryce 433 ff. 98–99, Bryce to Katharine, 22 May 1898. Ironically, Bryce was staying with Dicey, who certainly did not share this veneration for the former prime minister.

53. MS Bryce 431 ff. 192–3, Mary to Bryce, 4 October 1891; MS Bryce 432 ff. 149–50, Mary to Bryce, 19 December 1894.

54. MS Bryce 453 ff. 11–12, Bryce to EMB, 1 June 1896: 'What a Sacramentalist he is! Scarcely a molecule of Protestant spirit in his soul!' Also ff. 19–20, EMB's reply, 2 June 1896: 'I do wish he could keep quiet about these things'.

55. MS Bryce 433 ff. 1–4, Mary to Bryce, 6 January 1896.

56. MS Bryce 431 ff. 134–35, Bryce to Mary, 10 October 1890. The 'G.O.M.' (Grand Old Man) was Gladstone, of course.

57. Brian Harrison, *Separate Spheres: The Opposition to Women's Suffrage in Britain* (London: Croom Helm, 1978).

58. HC Deb, 12 June 1884, vol 289, cc. 166–71, Amendment to Representation of the People Bill, extending the franchise to women; HC Deb, 27 April 1892, vol 3, cc. 1493–1501: Parliamentary Franchise (Extension to Women) Bill; HL Deb, 17 December 1917, vol 27, cc. 176–90 (Representation of the People Bill).

59. On his correspondence with Ethel Harrison and Louise Creighton in 1889–1890, urging the creation of an antisuffrage organization, see notably Julia Bush, *Women Against the Vote: Female Anti-Suffragism in Britain* (Oxford: Oxford University Press, 2007), 158–59.

60. MD 1:55, 163.

61. Schools Inquiry Commission 3966-IX, 792.

62. Schools Inquiry Commission 3966-IX, 836.

63. Schools Inquiry Commission 3966-IX, 839.

64. Some of these activities are captured in the *Journal of the Women's Education Union*, e.g., no. 1 (January 1873) and no. 13 (January 1874) for his membership of the Union's Central Committee.

65. Women's Library LSE 3JBL/08/30, Josephine Butler to Mr Wilson, 6 December 1873.

66. For an example of his public advocacy on behalf of the college, see James Bryce, 'Girton College' [letter], *The Spectator* 49.2479 (1 January 1876), 14.

67. On which see Alice Gardner, *A Short History of Newnham College Cambridge* (Cambridge: Bowes & Bowes, 1921), 9; and Blanche Athena Clough, *A Memoir of Anne Jemima Clough* (London: Edward Arnold, 1897), 120, 131, 143.

68. Bryce's keen interest in women's higher education was recognized in Marion's will by legacies to Girton College and Somerville College. The latter, with which Bryce had no formal connection, was no doubt chosen because, of the four women's colleges in Oxford, it was the firmly nondenominational one. By a happy coincidence the principal at the time of Marion's death was Helen Darbishire, niece of Bryce's old friend and her father's collaborator Robert Darbishire. The college established a biennial lecture in Bryce's name.

69. MS Bryce 475 ff. 39–40, Emily Penrose to EMB, 26 February 1922.

70. On the Infant Custody Act and its origins, see Mary Lyndon Shanley, *Feminism, Marriage, and the Law in Victorian England, 1850–1895* (Princeton, N.J.: Princeton University Press, 1989), chap. 5, and Ben Griffin, *The Politics of Gender in Victorian Britain* (Cambridge: Cambridge University Press, 2012), chap. 5.

71. HC Deb, 12 June 1884, vol 289, c. 171, Amendment to Representation of the People Bill; HC Deb, 27 April 1892, vol 3, cc. 1493–1504: Parliamentary Franchise (Extension to Women) Bill; HL Deb, 17 December 1917, vol 27, c. 180 (Representation of the People Bill). The distinction between social and political equality was explicit here.

72. In 1891 he asked in the House whether the government had considered the possibility of appointing women as members of the Labour Commission: HC Deb, 16 March 1891, 1065–66.

This was something that Mary Bryce and others had campaigned for: MS Bryce 449 ff. 94–95, EMB to Bryce, 11 March 1891. See also 'Introduction', in *Office-Holders in Modern Britain: Volume 10, Officials of Royal Commissions of Inquiry 1870–1939*, ed. Elaine Harrison (London: University of London, 1995), xii–xxvii. *British History Online*, accessed April 6, 2021, http://www.british -history.ac.uk/office-holders/vol10/xii-xxvii. The editor speculates that Bryce may have been instrumental in appointing women to the Secondary Education Commission. He thought Mrs Sidgwick 'a charming person, whom I like more the more I know her. She has, as Mark Pattison wd say, a man's intellect in strength and quickness, with feminine fineness besides': MS Bryce 429 f. 141, Bryce to Mary, 6 January 1883; ff. 144–5, Bryce to Katharine, 14 January 1883.

73. For the Pankhursts—whom he knew when they had moved to London rather than in their Manchester years—see Christabel Pankhurst, *Unshackled* [1959], ed. Lord Pethick-Lawrence (London: Cresset, 1987), 29. This was probably not long before Bryce's marriage.

74. Emma Winkworth's letters are at MS Bryce 154 ff. 1–79. We do not have Bryce's letters to Mrs Winkworth, but hers are ample indeed.

75. MS Bryce 437 f. 131, Bryce to Mary and Katharine, 3 April 1909.

76. My understanding of the development of women's higher education has been greatly enhanced by advance sight of Samuel Rutherford, *Teaching Gender: the British University and the Rise of Heterosexuality, 1860–1939* (Oxford: Oxford University Press, 2025), esp. chap. 1.

77. Julia Bush, '"Special Strengths for Their Own Special Duties": Women, Higher Education and Gender Conservatism in Late Victorian Britain', *History of Education* 34 (2005), 387–405; Laura Schwartz, *A Serious Endeavour: Gender, Education and Community at St Hugh's, 1886–2011* (London: Profile, 2011), 35–42.

78. Girton College, GCPP Davies 15/1/2/4, Bryce to Emily Davies, 12 June? 1867. For Bryce's antipathy to the cult of examination: Bryce, 'An Ideal University', 838–42.

79. Jones, *Intellect and Character*, 90–92.

80. Elizabeth C. Wolstenholme Elmy, 'Mr Bryce and Women's Suffrage' (letter), *Manchester Guardian* 12 January 1898, p. 3. On Wolstenholme Elmy, Sandra Stanley Holton, *Suffrage Days: Stories from the Women's Suffrage Movement* (London: Routledge, 2016), chap. 1; Lucy Bland, *Banishing the Beast: Feminism, Sex and Morality* (London: Tauris, 1995), 135–39; and Laura Schwartz, *Infidel Feminism: Secularism, Religion and Women's Emancipation, England 1830–1914* (Manchester: Manchester University Press, 2013), 62–63, 154–72.

81. Ignota [pseud. for Elizabeth C. Wolstenholme Elmy], 'The Enfranchisement of Women', *Westminster Review* 164 (July 1905), 21; Ignota, 'The Case for the Immediate Enfranchisement of the Women of the United Kingdom', *Westminster Review* 166 (November 1906), 519; Ignota, 'Russia and the United Kingdom', *Westminster Review* 166 (September 1906), 288. In the last piece she remarks: 'The temporary services of Mr Asquith, Mr Bryce, Lord Crewe, and the other opponents of women's suffrage within the Cabinet, are less vital to the well-being of this nation than is the establishment of justice between the sexes, and the equality before the law of man and woman.'

82. *The Sun* [New York], 29 December 1909, cutting in MS Bryce 506 f. 52v.

83. MS Bryce 17 f. 175, Bryce to Goldwin Smith, 15 March 1884: 'I need not say that I am & have always been opposed to the Women's Suffrage and unable to understand the fascination it has for some politicians here who are usually judicious.' Also: MS Bryce 427 ff. 83–84, Bryce to Robert Young (uncle), 7 July 1897: 'I am and alw[ays] have been decidedly opposed to women's suffrage.' He added that Marion was 'even more opposed'. This is contrary to the impression given by Martin Pugh, *The March of the Women: A Revisionist Analysis of the Campaign for Women's Suffrage, 1866–1914* (Oxford: Oxford University Press, 2002), 57–58.

84. A. V. Dicey, *Letters to a Friend on Votes for Women* (London: Murray, 1909), 66.

85. Henry Sidgwick, *Elements of Politics*, 2nd ed. (London: Macmillan, 1897), 643–44.

86. For both points, HC Deb, 12 June 1884, vol 289, c. 166.

87. Harrison, *Separate Spheres*, 56 ff. But for a critique which deems the reduction of antisuf-fragism to the 'separate spheres' ideology to be 'too unidimensional', see Lucy Delap, 'Feminist

and Anti-feminist Encounters in Edwardian Britain', *Historical Research* 78 (2005), 377–99, esp. 379.

88. Fisher, *Bryce* 1:116

89. MS Bryce 492 f. 108, EMB, 'On being asked an opinion on Woman's Suffrage, June 24th 1910'.

90. Fisher married Lettice Ilbert, the daughter of Bryce's close friend and travelling companion, the jurist Sir Courtenay Ilbert. Mrs Fisher chaired the executive of the (suffragist, not suffragette) National Union of Women's Suffrage Societies from 1916 to 1918. For the invitation to become a godparent, MS Bryce 13, ff. 17–20, Courtenay Ilbert to Bryce, 27 June 1875, and Jessie Ilbert to Bryce, n.d. [but clearly shortly afterwards].

91. HC Deb, 12 June 1884, vol 289, c. 167, Amendment to Representation of the People Bill.

92. HC Deb, 27 April 1892, vol 3, cc. 1494, Parliamentary Franchise (Extension to Women) Bill.

93. HC Deb, 12 June 1884, vol 289, c. 167, Amendment to Representation of the People Bill.

94. '"Exile" of M.P.'s Wife', *Daily Mail*, 30 December 1909, p. 5.

95. It may well have been a relief to Bryce to be in Washington in the years of the fiercest clashes between the suffragettes and public order.

96. MS Bryce 437 ff. 41–42, Bryce to Mary and Katharine, 24 April 1908.

97. *Town Topics* [New York], 13 January 1910, cutting in MS Bryce 506 f. 53v and MS Bryce 236 f. 241: 'Naturally, the antics of Mrs Annan Bryce have not been pleasant for her austere brother-in-law and the scarcely less severe Mrs James Bryce. The suffragette question has always been a painful one at the British Embassy and few have been brave enough to broach it.'

98. For some American reports: 'Mrs Bryce Lunches with Suffragists', *World* [New York], 30 December 1909, MS Bryce 236 f. 207. This noted: 'Both Ambassador and Mrs Bryce [i.e., Marion] are strongly opposed to the ballot for women.' Also, 'Mrs Bryce Resents Suffrage Criticism. Sister-in-law of British Ambassador Takes issue with Strictures upon English Methods', *New York Times*, 31 December 1909, MS Bryce 236 f. 209.

99. The relevant cuttings are in MS Bryce 506 ff. 83–103.

100. *Daily Sketch*, 16 June 1911, and *Daily Graphic*, 16 June 1911, both in MS Bryce 506 ff. 83 and 84.

101. Daily *Telegraph*, 19 June 1911, MS Bryce 506 f. 91. For an example of a press report of Margery and her sister riding astride: 'Women Who Ride Astride', *Daily Graphic*, 23 October 1917.

102. MS Bryce 449 ff. 7–10, Marion Ashton to Bryce, 11 March 1889.

103. MS Bryce 449 ff. 4–5, Marion Ashton to Bryce, 10 March 1889.

104. MS Bryce 449 ff. 7–10, Marion Ashton to Bryce, 11 March 1889.

105. For example, MS Bryce 450 ff. 50–51, Bryce to EMB, 10 October [1892].

106. Houghton Library, Godkin papers MS Am 1083 (1246) EMB to Katherine Godkin, 27 October 1898.

107. 'Dr Angus Fraser', *British Medical Journal*, 13 April 1912, pp. 869–79; Houghton Library, Godkin papers MS Am 1083 (1244), EMB to Katherine Godkin, 18 December 1896: 'We spent a few days, too, up at Tillypronie with the Clarks at the end of September.'

108. 'Death of Lady Bryce', *Manchester Guardian*; also 'The Viscountess Bryce', 38.

109. These are in MS Bryce 492.

110. E.g., 'Norwich Women's Liberal Association: Address by Mrs Bryce', *Eastern Daily Press*, 6 April 1905, cutting at MS Bryce 492 f. 82, also notes for the same speech at ff. 75–81; also, speech at Aberdeen in December 1903, MS Bryce 492 ff. 3–40 (an address to the inaugural meeting of the Aberdeen Women's Liberal Association, of which she became honorary president).

111. Ilford, 15 December 1903, MS Bryce 492 f. 45.

112. 'Political Notes', *The Times*, 18 July 1903, p. 10; speeches at MS Bryce 492 ff. 83–86, 92–96; 'Some Results of Colonial Preference & Protection', draft at MS Bryce 492 ff. 87–91.

113. 'Mrs James Bryce on the War', *Manchester Courier*, 27 November 1900, p. 10; *Morning Post*, 17 January 1900, p. 2. On Marion Bryce as a pro-Boer, Eliza Riedi, 'The Women Pro-Boers: Gender, Peace and the Critique of Empire in the South African War', *Historical Research* 86 (2013), 92–115.

114. 'Mrs James Bryce on Liberalism', *Edinburgh Evening News*, 7 February 1903, p. 2.

115. 'Students' Careers Association. Viscountess Bryce at Bristol Meeting', *Western Daily Press*, 1 March 1934, p. 6.

116. Houghton Library, Godkin papers MS Am 1083 (1246), EMB to Katherine Godkin, 27 October 1898. The location may have suggested by their friends the Freshfields, who lived nearby: Hervey Fisher, *From a Tramp's Wallet: A Life of Douglas William Freshfield* (Banham, Norfolk: Erskine Press, 2001).

117. MS Bryce USA 22 ff. 82–83, Bryce to Sarah Wyman Whitman, 11 March 1900.

118. MS Bryce 453 f. 74, Bryce to EMB, 18 January 1897; ff. 80–81, Bryce to EMB, 19 January 1897; f. 83, Bryce to EMB, 20 January 1897; f. 85, Bryce to EMB, 21 January 1897.

119. He thought that the concept of nonconformity made sense in the English context but not in Scotland, where the Act of Uniformity did not apply. He also disliked the negative implications of 'nonconformity'. The term 'free churchman' was increasingly used in the late nineteenth century: Philip Williamson, 'What Happened to Political Nonconformity?', in Readman and Thomas, *Culture, Thought and Belief in British Political Life*, 194.

120. MS Bryce 419 ff. 11–13, Bryce to mother, 13 April [1864]: 'Did you not explain to Uncle John that I was not connected with any U.P. Church?'

121. MS Bryce 449 ff. 72–73, Bryce to EMB, 16 February [1890].

122. Mansfield College archive, minute book of the Oxford University Nonconformists' Union. Bryce addressed the Union on 25 February 1882 (ff. 14–15) and is recorded as asserting 'that Nonconformity was not a purely negative principle but embodied the truth of the need of having a free unconstrained spiritual life'. In all, the minute book shows that Bryce attended eleven times in the calendar years 1882–1886: a more than respectable record for a Member of Parliament.

123. W. B. Selbie, *The Life of Andrew Martin Fairbairn* (London: Hodder and Stoughton, 1914), 174, 198.

124. *The Times*, 16 November 1911, reported: 'A conference of members of the Church of Scotland and the United Free Church, held in Edinburgh yesterday, resolved to establish and maintain a permanent chaplaincy for Presbyterian students at Oxford, in view of the Anglican and other influences prevailing there.' It is clear from the full report that the English Presbyterians were present too—A. Dodds Fairbairn spoke on their behalf, as did Prof Anderson Scott.

125. *The Observer*, 7 June 1914, p. 15; *Daily Telegraph*, 8 June 1914, p. 5. Dedicated in 1915, the chapel became a full church, St Columba's, in 1931 and joined the United Reformed Church on the merger of the Presbyterians and Congregationalists in 1972.

126. Bryce was opposed to denominational colleges for women as for men: see Girton College, GCPP Davies 15/1/2/5, Bryce to Emily Davies, 20 November 1867.

127. On the significance of the *British Quarterly Review*: R. V. Osbourn, 'The British Quarterly Review', *Review of English Studies* 1.1 (1950), 147–52.

128. James Bryce, 'Nonconformity and the Universities. The Free Churches and a Theological Faculty', *British Quarterly Review* 158 (April 1884), 390–98, quotations at 394. On Anglican domination of the theology faculty, and Anglican monopoly of divinity degrees, Daniel Inman, *The Making of Modern English Theology: God and the Academy at Oxford, 1833–1945* (Minneapolis: Fortress, 2014), chaps. 2 and 3.

129. *The Nonconformist and Independent*, 19 April 1883, p. 354.

130. John Rylands Library, T. C. Horsfall papers TCH/1/1/2/6, Bryce to Horsfall, 7 March 1898.

131. Manchester Central Library, Letters to T. C. Horsfall, no. 99, Bryce to Horsfall, 18 May 1899.

132. Moody, 'The Irish University Question', 105–7.

133. 'Irish Education: Important Statement by Mr Bryce', *Manchester Guardian* 26 January 1907, p. 9.

134. Harris Manchester College, Oxford, MS Jacks 1 ff. 29–30: Bryce to L. P. Jacks, 14 April 1902, advising Jacks on people to recruit to the Hibbert Journal, which Jacks was just setting up.

135. A.G.B. Atkinson, ed., *Christian Conference Essays* (London: Black, 1900), vvii; also paper on the Christian Conference in MS Bryce 357 f. 122.

136. 'The Christian Conference', *The Times*, 23 June 1896, p. 4. Bryce's notes for his speech are at MS Bryce 284 ff. 30–31.

137. MS Bryce 284 ff. 68–70, 'Union of Xtendom', c. 1897. For the same point, MS Bryce 438 ff. 14–15, Bryce to Mary and Katharine, 6 April 1910: 'Reunion of the Christian Churches as respects fraternal spirit and putting aside of non-essentials is infinitely desirable: but I feel less clear as to whether much stress need be laid on formal and external Union. The vision of One Holy Catholic Church is beautiful, but it might have a weak side in practice.'

138. Wellcome Collection PP/BAR/C707, Bryce to Sir Thomas Barlow, 4 April 1911.

139. For more on Bryce's admiration of the Quakers, MS Bryce 438 ff. 14–15, Bryce to Mary and Katharine, 6 April 1910.

140. Viscount Bryce, 'Preface' to Arthur Tilney Bassett, *The Life of the Rt. Hon. John Edward Ellis M.P.* (London: Macmillan, 1914), vi–vii.

141. Bryce, 'Preface' to Bassett, *Life of Ellis*, viii.

142. Bryce, 'Dean Stanley', in his *Studies in Contemporary Biography*, 69–84. The twenty studies in this volume include five clergy of various denominations: Stanley, Archbishop Tait, Bishop Fraser, Cardinal Manning, and William Robertson Smith.

143. Bryce, *Studies in Contemporary Biography*, 312.

144. Robertson Smith was forced to take refuge, not indeed in the wilderness, but among the fellows of Christ's College, Cambridge.

145. Bryce, *Studies in Contemporary Biography*, 311.

146. Stopford Brooke to Bryce, 14 July 1909: Lawrence Pearsall Jacks, *Life and Letters of Stopford Brooke* (London: Murray, 1917), 2:645–66. An indication of the importance of the relationship is that this book devotes a whole chapter to Brooke's letters to Bryce.

147. In his last year at Oxford, Davidson attended Bryce's lectures on Roman law, in the first year of his professoriate: G.K.A. Bell, *Randall Davidson, Archbishop of Canterbury* (London: Oxford University Press, 1935), 1:24.

148. I am grateful to Julia Stapleton for drawing my attention to the friendship between Bryce and Henson.

149. Herbert Hensley Henson, *Christian Morality, Natural, Developing, Final. Being the Gifford Lectures 1935–1936* (Oxford: Clarendon, 1936), 3.

Chapter 9

1. G. J. Romanes, 'Founder's Preface', *Romanes Lectures Decennial Issue 1892–1900* (Oxford: Clarendon, 1900), n.p.

2. Louis Dyer, 'Mr Bryce's Romanes Lecture', *The Nation* [New York] 74 (26 June 1902), 503.

3. A. V. Dicey, 'Mr Bryce on the Relation Between Whites and Blacks', *The Nation* [New York] 75 (10 July 1902), 26–28.

4. James Bryce, *The Relations of the Advanced and the Backward Races of Mankind. Romanes Lecture 1902* (Oxford: Clarendon, 1902), 5–9. This was published in the same month as Bryce delivered the lecture.

5. Bryce, *Relations of the Advanced and the Backward Races*, 15.

6. Bryce, *Relations of the Advanced and the Backward Races*, 18.

7. Examples: AC, 3rd ed. (1893–1894), 2:503; 'The Roman Empire and the British Empire in India', SHJ 1:64; 'Centripetal and Centrifugal Forces', SHJ 1:292–93; Bryce, *Race Sentiment as a Factor in History*, 34.

8. Houghton Library, Norton family papers Box 35, MS Am 1088 (6693), Goldwin Smith to Charles Eliot Norton, 17 April 1865. This is quoted by Marilyn Lake and Henry Reynolds. *Drawing the Global Colour Line: White Men's Countries and the International Challenge of Racial Equality* (Cambridge: Cambridge University Press, 2008), 54. But they have 'essential principles' as 'splendid principles', and they capitalize 'negro'. See also 'Letters of Goldwin Smith to Charles Eliot Norton', *Proceedings of the Massachusetts Historical Society* series 3, 49 (1915–1916), 118.

9. Smith to Norton, 1 October 1865, quoted by Lake and Reynolds, *Drawing the Global Colour Line*, 54–55.

10. Bryce, *Relations of the Advanced and the Backward Races*, 29.

11. *Pace* Lake and Reynolds, *Drawing the Global Colour Line*, he did not say 'by many thousands of years', nor was he thinking of a time-scale of anything like that order of magnitude.

12. Bryce, *Relations of the Advanced and the Backward Races*, 39.

13. This is the tendency of Lake and Reynolds, *Drawing the Global Colour Line*, chap. 2. They suggest (p. 74) that 'His message was the impossibility of multi-racial democracy. His writing gave legitimacy to policies of segregation in the United States and South Africa and authority to Australian nation-builders.'

14. Dicey, 'Mr Bryce on the Relation Between Whites and Blacks', 27–28.

15. Dicey, 'The Balance of Classes', in *Essays on Reform*, 78.

16. Dicey, 'Mr Bryce on the Relation Between Whites and Blacks', 27.

17. Bryce, *Relations of the Advanced and the Backward Races*, 35.

18. This was Garrison's suggestion: MS Bryce USA 4 ff. 312–13, W. P. Garrison to Bryce, 29 July 1902.

19. Dyer, 'Mr Bryce's Romanes Lecture', 503–4.

20. MS Bryce USA 4 ff. 308–9, W. P. Garrison to Bryce, presumably 2 July 1902, though misdated 2 June.

21. Most recently by Sathnam Sanghera, *Empireworld: How British Imperialism Shaped the Globe* (London: Penguin, 2024), 194, who draws, inevitably (and exclusively), on Lake and Reynolds, *Drawing the Global Colour Line*, 68. Also Marilyn Lake, 'From Mississippi to Melbourne via Natal: The Invention of the Literacy Test as a Technique of Racial Exclusion', in *Connected Worlds: History in Transnational Perspective*, ed. Ann Curthoys and Marilyn Lake (Canberra: ANU Press, 2006), 214.

22. Garrison wrote at the end of the month: 'A little vacation has robbed me of the time needed to read your Romanes Lecture': MS Bryce USA 4 ff. 312–13, Garrison to Bryce, 29 July 1902. Those who cite Garrison's sharp rebuke to Bryce do not acknowledge the fact that at that time Garrison had not read the lecture: Tulloch, *James Bryce's American Commonwealth*, 198; Lake and Reynolds, *Drawing the Global Colour Line*, 68. Garrison had reviewed the new chapters of the third edition of *The American Commonwealth* in 'The South and the Black Man', *The Nation* [New York] 60 (31 January 1895), 86–87.

23. Garrison to Bryce, 2 July 1902.

24. MS Bryce USA 4 ff. 312–13, Garrison to Bryce, 29 July 1902. I am grateful to Eric Sheng for helping with a barely decipherable word ('praise').

25. Marilyn Lake implies that disagreements over the Romanes lecture led to a rupture in Bryce's relations with 'many erstwhile friends'. She mentions only Garrison and Dicey, but in neither case is there any evidence of a cooling of the friendship. Lake, 'White Man under Siege', 55.

26. He continued to deplore the absence of a systematic empirical investigation of the effect of intermarriage on the quality of the parent racial stocks when he gave the inaugural presidential address to the newly founded Sociological Society in 1904: James Bryce, 'Introductory Address on the Use and Purpose of a Sociological Society', *Sociological Papers* 1 (1904), xiv–xv.

27. James Bryce, *Impressions of South Africa* (London: Macmillan, 1897). A third edition appeared in November 1899, on the outbreak of war, with a new prefatory chapter.

28. An Ngram search of the Google Books database shows this pattern very clearly.

29. The suggestion that Bryce's Romanes lecture was much criticized is made, for instance, by Sanghera, *Empireworld*, 194. The account of Bryce in that book seems to come wholly from Lake and Reynolds and is a one-sided caricature.

30. Theophilus E. Samuel Scholes, *Glimpses of the Ages or the 'Superior' and 'Inferior' Races, So-Called, Discussed in the Light of Science and History* (London: Long, 1908), 308–11.

31. For a discussion of Scholes's argument in the context of projects of Anglo-American unity, Bell, *Dreamworlds of Race*, 385–94.

32. There were two index references (to a single page in each case) to the condition and future of negroes (Bryce's word, of course) and four to the negro vote.

33. MS Bryce 416 ff. 155–58, Bryce to mother from Richmond VA, 30 October 1890.

34. Lake and Reynolds, *Drawing the Global Colour Line*, 61, state that Bryce established 'a file for his research notes and thoughts in progress under the heading "The Negro Problem" in 1885'. In fact there are precisely thirteen words of notes under that heading, and these notes probably date from 1887–1888 rather than 1885: MS Bryce 341 f. 46.

35. Here I differ from Readman, 'Walking and Environmentalism', 315, who suggests that Bryce's racist stereotypes were absorbed when he was young, 'sitting at Freeman's feet', and were eroded by travel.

36. MS Bryce 416 f. 54, Bryce to mother, 26 October 1888.

37. MS Bryce 416 f. 70, Bryce to mother, 30 November 1888.

38. MS Bryce 416 f. 71, Bryce to mother, 30 November 1888.

39. MS Bryce 15, f. 139, Bryce to Sidgwick, 15 February 1889.

40. MS Bryce 416 f. 68, Bryce to mother, 30 November 1888.

41. The context makes it clear that he was talking about the Indian Civil Service proper, not his decision to turn down the position of legal member that Ilbert accepted instead.

42. MS Bryce 416 ff. 69–71, Bryce to mother, 30 November 1888.

43. MS Bryce 449 ff. 70–71, EMB to Bryce, 15 February 1890.

44. James Bryce, 'The Roman Empire and the British Empire in India' and 'The Extension of Roman and English Law Throughout the World', SHJ 1:1–84, 85–144; reprinted as James Bryce, *The Ancient Roman Empire and the British Empire in India. The Diffusion of Roman and English Law Throughout the World* (London: Oxford University Press, 1914).

45. 'Preface', SHJ 1:ix.

46. MS Bryce 339, diary entries for 29 April and 17 May 1873; *Oxford Magazine* 9 (6 May 1891), 320; 10 (27 April 1892), 301; 11 (23 November 1892), 100–101.

47. MS Bryce 285 ff. 67–84.

48. Pannonia: a province of the Roman Empire encompassing modern-day eastern Austria, western Hungary, and parts of Slovenia, Croatia, and Serbia.

49. MS Bryce 285 ff. 71–72.

50. MS Bryce 285, ff. 74–75. Kolarian: a term apparently coined by George Campbell in 1869. The more common modern term is Munda.

51. For instance, J. Deniker, *The Races of Man: An Outline of Anthropology and Ethnography* (London: Scott, 1900), 408.

52. MS Bryce 13 f. 30, quoted by Mary Bennett, *The Ilberts in India 1882–1886: An Imperial Miniature* (Putney: British Association for Cemeteries in South Asia, 1995), 56. Bennett's transcription is not quite accurate.

53. Bryce, *The Ancient Roman Empire and the British Empire in India*, 31–32.

54. James Bryce, 'Thoughts on the Negro Problem', *North American Review* 153 (December 1891), 641–80.

55. Bryce, 643. This quotation has been misused by Lake and Reynolds, and by others in their wake, by being juxtaposed with another quotation, assumed to be from Bryce but actually from Edward Eggleston, to the effect that many thousands of years must pass before the negro would reach 'the pinnacle of modern wisdom and knowledge upon which the Caucasian stands today'. See Lake and Reynolds, *Drawing the Global Colour Line*, 62; Mary Hawkesworth, *Embodied Power: Demystifying Disembodied Politics* (Abingdon: Routledge, 2016), 36–38; and Terri E. Givens, *The Roots of Racism: The Politics of White Supremacy in the U.S. and Europe* (Bristol: Bristol University Press, 2022), 40. It is demonstrable both that Bryce did not say that many thousands of years must pass, and also, more importantly, that he did not believe that the timescale involved was remotely of that magnitude.

56. Bryce, 'Thoughts on the Negro Problem', 643.

57. Bryce, 647.

58. Bryce, 648, 649.

59. Bryce, 649.

60. Bryce, 654–55.

61. For Bryce on Darwin, [Bryce,] 'The Death of Mr Darwin', *The Nation* [New York] 34 (4 May 1882), 377–78; and James Bryce, 'Personal Reminiscences of Charles Darwin and of the Reception of the "Origin of Species"', *Proceedings of the American Philosophical Society* 48, no. 193 (1909), iii–xiv. For Bryce's opinion of Spencer, MS Bryce 300 f. 11, typescript on Darwin's effect on the historical and political sciences, and MS Bryce 4 ff. 150–52, Bryce to Dicey, 27 September 1917.

62. AC, 3rd ed. (1893–1894), 2:469.

63. AC, 3rd ed. (1893–1894), 2:476–78.

64. Here I disagree with Mary Hawkesworth, *Embodied Power*, 37, who says that Bryce blamed African Americans for having exercised their rights of citizenship and that he thought they bore the responsibility for illegal action by whites to restore their dominance. That is the contrary of what Bryce believed and what he wrote. The blame (he thought) lay with Republican carpet-baggers and, ultimately, those who had passed the Fifteenth Amendment.

65. AC, 3rd ed. (1893–1894), 2:481.

66. HC Deb, 27 April 1892, vol 3, cc. 1499: Parliamentary Franchise (Extension to Women) Bill.

67. AC, 3rd ed. (1893–1894), 2:482.

68. J. X. Merriman to Bryce, 22 February 1892, in *Selections from the Correspondence of John X. Merriman 1890–1898*, ed. Phyllis Lewsen (Cape Town: Van Riebeeck Society, 1963), 93–94.

69. Merriman to Bryce, 25 February 1892, in Lewsen, *Selections 1890–1898*, 96.

70. Mark Mazower, *No Enchanted Palace: The End of Empire and the Ideological Origins of the United Nations* (Princeton, N.J.: Princeton University Press, 2009), chap. 1, esp. 32–34, 46–52.

71. James Bryce, *Impressions of South Africa*, 3rd ed. (London: Macmillan, 1899), 347.

72. Bryce, 358–59.

73. Bryce, 351–52.

74. Bryce, 360–61.

75. This was perhaps another instance of an implied appeal to a kind of Social Lamarckism.

76. Bryce, *Impressions of South Africa*, 364–65.

77. Bryce, 366.

78. Bryce, 367.

79. Bryce, 367.

80. Bryce, 368–69.

81. Alex Middleton, 'Latin America and British International Thought, 1880–1920', in Readman and Thomas, *Culture, Thought and Belief in British Political Life*, 326–27.

82. Bryce, *Relations of the Advanced and the Backward Races*, 18–19.

83. Bryce, *South America*, xix, xxi.

84. Bryce, 452–53.

85. Bryce, 479–80.

86. Bryce, 480.

87. Bryce, 481–82.

88. Bryce, 482. Alex Middleton, 'Latin America and British International Thought', 325, thinks that Bryce's racial conclusions must have been aimed at his American readers, since the British 'had never laid much stress on the racial dimension'. This suggestion seems to me to ignore Bryce's long-standing engagement with global questions of race.

89. Bryce, *South America*, 483.

90. This is quite explicitly the conclusion that Sanghera, *Empireworld*, 186–87, 194, draws from Lake and Reynolds.

91. Gunnar Myrdal, *An American Dilemma: The Negro Problem and Modern Democracy* (New York: Harper, 1944), 1316. On this point he quoted Bryce: 'Rights which the agricultural laborers [*sic*] of England did not obtain until 1885 were . . . thrust upon these children of nature'.

92. Walter A. Jackson, *Gunnar Myrdal and America's Conscience: Social Engineering & Racial Liberalism, 1938–1987* (Chapel Hill: University of North Carolina Press, 1990), xii, 293.

Chapter 10

1. MS Bryce USA 2 ff. 53–54, Bryce to Charles W. Eliot, 24 December 1906.

2. Ions, *James Bryce and American Democracy*, 199–201.

3. MS Bryce 109 ff. 11–12, Gilbert Murray to Bryce, 26 December 1914.

4. *New York Times*, 8 January 1907, cutting in MS Bryce 235 f. 1.

5. MS Bryce USA 2 ff. 53–56, Bryce to Charles W. Eliot, 24 December 1906, 4 January 1907.

6. James Bryce, *The American Commonwealth. Abridged Edition for the Use of Colleges and High Schools. Being an Introduction to the Government and Institutions of the United States* (New York: Macmillan, 1896). On the preparation of this edition, New York Public Library Macmillan Company Papers, Bryce to George Platt Brett snr, 15 July 1896.

7. According to the OED, it was coined in 1885 by H. R. Waite, who founded the American Institute of Civics in that year.

8. Frederick H. Clark, *Outlines of Civics. Being a Supplement to Bryce's "American Commonwealth", Abridged Edition* (New York: Macmillan, 1899), vi–vii.

9. A. G. Fradenburgh, *American Civics: A Text Book for High Schools, Normal Schools, and Academies* (New York: Hinds, Noble & Eldredge, 1906); C. W. Bardeen, *A Manual of Civics for New York Schools* (Syracuse, N.Y.: Bardeen, 1902); Frank David Boynton, *School Civics: An Outline Study of the Origin and Development of Government and the Development of Political Institutions in the United States* (Boston: Ginn, 1904).

10. James Bryce, 'The Teaching of Civic Duty', *Contemporary Review* 64 (July 1893), 14–28 ('civisme' is at 15), a slightly expanded version of an article that appeared under the same title in *The Forum* [New York] 15 (July 1893), 552–66. Both were based on an address given to the London Association of Head Masters of Public Elementary Schools in December 1892, a copy of which is in MS Bryce 302.

11. MS Bryce 465 ff. 51–52, Marion Bryce to Elizabeth Ashton, 12 March 1907.

12. MS Bryce USA 2 f. 62, Bryce to Charles W. Eliot, 3 May 1907.

13. Henry Adams to Charles Milnes Gaskell, 15 April 1907, in Jacob C. Levenson, ed., *The Letters of Henry Adams* (Cambridge, Mass.: Belknap, 1982), 6:62.

14. For an introduction to the historiographical significance of the cultural history of diplomacy and international relations, see Peter Jackson, 'Pierre Bourdieu, the "Cultural Turn", and the Practice of International History', *Review of International Studies* 34.1 (2008), 155–81; for a recent example of the cultural history of diplomacy at work, Charlotte Faucher, *Propaganda, Gender, and Cultural Power: Projections and Perceptions of France in Britain c. 1880–1944* (Oxford: Oxford University Press for the British Academy, 2022). Of course, states had always used soft power to promote their diplomatic objectives. But Bryce was exceptionally active in doing so, and the new kind of relationship with the American public was a distinctive aspect of his persona as ambassador. See Stephen Bowman, *The Pilgrims Society and Public Diplomacy, 1895–1945* (Edinburgh: Edinburgh University Press, 2018), which treats Bryce briefly in this context.

15. MS Bryce USA 2 f. 61, Bryce to Charles W. Eliot, 13 March 1907.

16. Parliamentary Archives Ilbert papers ILB/3/11, ff. 56–57, Bryce to Lady Ilbert 24 April 1908. This was from Memphis, where he had addressed a conference on education in the South.

17. Bowman, *Pilgrims Society*, 27.

18. MS Bryce 461 ff. 122–23, Bryce to Martha Young [a cousin in New York], 23 February 1907.

19. MS Bryce 465 ff. 51–52, Marion Bryce to Elizabeth Ashton, 12 March 1907.

20. MS Bryce 437 ff. 41–42, Bryce to Mary and Katharine, 24 April 1908.

21. Quoted by Ions, *James Bryce and American Democracy*, 210.

22. *Ottawa Citizen*, 25 September 1911, MS Bryce 237 f. 261.

23. MS Bryce 237 f. 221, 6 August 1911?, unidentified newspaper (the Romeike's press agency's label has been torn).

24. MS Bryce USA 2 f. 84, Bryce to Charles W. Elliot, 18 November 1912 (copy).

25. MS Bryce 436 ff. 72–73, Bryce to Mary and Katharine, 9 May 1907.

26. Bryce to Mary and Katharine, 9 May 1907.

27. Examples: *The Blade* [Toledo, Ohio], 18 May 1907, cutting MS Bryce 235 f. 18 ('democratic in his tastes' . . . but also 'a believer in the superiority of the Anglo-Saxon race').

28. *Milwaukee Journal* [Wisconsin], 10 February 1909, cutting MS Bryce 236 f. 87.

29. *Haverhill Gazette* [Mass.], 27 December 1909, MS Bryce 236 f. 197.

30. 'Various Topics', *Herald* [Decatur, Ill.] 24 May 1910, MS Bryce 236 f. 366.

31. For example, Gemma Allen, 'The Rise of the Ambassadress: English Ambassadorial Wives and Early Modern Diplomatic Culture', *Historical Journal* 62.3 (2019), 617–38; Corina Bastian, Eva Kathrin Dada, Hillard von Thiessen, and Christian Windler, eds., *Das Geschlecht der Diplomatie: Geschlechterrollen in den Aussenbeziehungen vom Spätmittelalter bis zum 20. Jahrhundert* (Cologne: Böhlau, 2014); Helen McCarthy, 'Petticoat Diplomacy: The Admission of Women to the British Foreign Service, c. 1919–1946', *Twentieth-Century British History* 20 (2009), 285–321.

32. Wellcome Collection, Sir Thomas Barlow papers, Bryce to Sir Thomas Barlow, 5 January 1907.

33. *Town Topics* [New York], 13 January 1910, MS Bryce 236 f. 241; for Lady Durant, *Pittsburg Sun*, 11 January 1907, MS Bryce 235 f. 12.

34. *Boston Post*, MS Bryce 235 f. 48.

35. *The Sun* [New York], MS Bryce 237 f. 173. Correctly, Sir Mortimer and Lady Durand.

36. 'Capital Society Women Endowed with Talent', *Washington Post*, 20 December 1909, p. 5.

37. 'Summer Vegetarian War', *Washington Post*, 9 August 1909, p. 7.

38. 'Fashions at the Capital', *Washington Post*, 25 February 1912, MS Bryce 238 f. 129.

39. Bodl. Morley papers MS Eng. d. 3563 ff. 77–78, Bryce to Morley, 22 January 1908. Also MS Bryce 461 ff. 136–37, Bryce to Robert M. Young, 23 January 1910.

40. MS Bryce USA 2 ff. 59–61, Bryce to Eliot, 3 March and 13 March 1907.

41. MS Bryce USA 1 ff. 85–86, Charles W. Eliot to Bryce, 4 January 1907.

42. At Wisconsin the topic was 'The Mission of State Universities'; at Union College, 'On the Writing and Teaching of History', both UHA. On the Union visit: 'The addresses of the Students at Schenectady were remarkably good. There is an active spirit of reform abroad in the U.S. & it finds expression through the young University men.' MS Bryce 438 ff. 86–87, Bryce to Mary and Katharine 16 June 1911.

43. 'The Character and Career of Abraham Lincoln', UHA.

44. 'Mr James Bryce Charms in Address on Gladstone', *New York Herald* 29 December 1909, MS Bryce 236 f. 194.

45. MS Bryce 436 ff. 74–75, Bryce to Mary and Katharine, 27 May 1907.

46. MS Bryce 436 ff. 101–2, Bryce to Mary and Katharine, 29 June 1907: 'One has to write out summaries for the press—so infamously bad is the reporting'; James Bryce, 'Allegiance to Humanity', *The Outlook*, 5 June 1909, 317–19, where the editor's note explains that 'in the actual delivery of the address its author amplified the text in some particulars.' This was the address Bryce gave at the Lake Mohonk Conference on International Arbitration in May 1909.

47. University of St Andrews, Wilfrid Ward papers MS38347-VII-51/2/1/13, Bryce to Ward 5, October 1913.

48. 'The American universities and colleges are in a state of transition': AC 3:460.

49. Bryce and Dicey dined with White on 26 September: Robert Morris Ogden, ed., *The Diaries of Andrew D. White* (Ithaca, N.Y.: Cornell University Library, 1959), 162. The following day White wrote Bryce a letter of introduction to Gilman (a Yale contemporary of White's), who was then professor of geography at Yale: 'Mr Bryce and his companion Mr Dicey . . . seek information regarding our System of Education and I have told them that I know no one better qualified than yourself to aid them': Cornell University Library, Andrew Dickson White papers, reel 10, 008801, White to Gilman, 27 September 1870. Bryce recalled his first meeting with Gilman in his memorial address in 1908: Rt Hon. James Bryce, 'Address', in *Daniel Coit Gilman. First President of the Johns Hopkins University 1876–1901* (Baltimore: Johns Hopkins University Press, 1908), 27–31.

50. E.g., *Diaries of Andrew D. White*, 254: 'Walked with Bryce . . . giving him information regarding Amer. Universities for his new book.'

51. AC 3:464.

52. AC 3:464.

53. AC 3:460–63.

54. Compare the response a century later from the historian Tony Judt, 'America, My Newfound Land', *New York Review of Books*, 27 May 2010.

55. *Des Moines Register and Leader* [Iowa], 5 January 1913, MS Bryce 238 f. 400.

56. 'National Parks—the Need of the Future', in Bryce, UHA, 392.

57. 'National Parks', 398–401.

58. 'National Parks', 406.

59. Ions, *James Bryce and American Democracy*, has a short chapter (chap. 18, 'Unorthodox Diplomacy') on Bryce's speech-making activities as ambassador, but apart from a mere reference to the address to the Laymen's Christian Missionary convention (misdated to 1907), religion is not mentioned.

60. James Bryce, 'Missions Past and Present: Address Delivered at the Laymen's Missionary Convention at Chattanooga, May 21, 1907', in UHA, 127–50. This is evidently misdated: There is no evidence (e.g., from press reports or his letters or Marion's letters) of Bryce being in Chattanooga in May 1907, and the text as published seems to correspond closely to reports of his speech he gave in April 1908: e.g. in *Raleigh Christian Advocate* 30 April 1908, p. 1, and James Bryce, 'The Duty of the Stronger to the Weaker Races', *Christian Advocate*, 19 June 1908, 6–9; copy in MS Bryce 302, ff. 156–58.

61. Cancellation of public functions following Edward VII's death forced Bryce to pull out of an engagement to address the Sunday School World Congress in Washington in May 1910. Likewise, two years later he agreed to address the Christian Conservation Congress in New York City but evidently had to withdraw: MS Bryce 238 f. 64, *New York Examiner*, 22 February 1912, advertises Bryce as one of the speakers at the forthcoming Congress.

62. MS Bryce 437 ff. 111–12, Bryce to Mary and Katharine Bryce, 12 February 1909.

63. 'Bryce Urges Fight to Uphold Religion', *Chicago Examiner*, 12 February 1909, cutting in MS Bryce 236 f. 89. Also *Evening Bulletin*, Providence, R.I., 12 February 1909, MS Bryce 236 f. 94.

64. MS Bryce 437 ff. 111–12, Bryce to Mary and Katharine Bryce, 12 February 1909.

65. James Bryce, 'Religion and Moral Education', *Religious Education* 4 (1909), 31. The article is not identified as the same as the Chicago address, but the correspondence between the text and the newspaper reports of the latter makes it clear that it was substantively the same.

66. Bryce, 'Religion and Moral Education', 31–32. The same warning about the threat posed to civic virtue by materialism and the pursuit of pleasure was to be found in Marion's speeches during the last years of Tory ascendancy under Balfour and Chamberlain: e.g., 'Aberdeen Women's Liberal Federation', *Aberdeen Journal*, 9 December 1903, p. 7.

67. MS Bryce 437 ff. 125–26, Bryce to Mary and Katharine, 2 April 1909.

68. MS Bryce 437 f. 131, Bryce to Mary and Katharine, 3 April 1909.

69. Bryce, 'Religion and Moral Education', 30.

70. Bryce, 'Missions Past and Present', 133, 134.

71. Bryce, 147.

72. Bryce, 149–50.

73. Bryce, 148.

74. Bryce, 149.

75. 'Even the nonconformists don't any longer care about Disestablishment', he wrote to Dicey in 1916: MS Bryce 4 ff. 100–103, Bryce to Dicey, 16 April 1916.

76. 'The Christian Conference', *The Times*, 23 June 1896, p. 4. Bryce's notes for his speech are at MS Bryce 284 ff. 30–31. Also MS Bryce 284 ff. 68–70, 'Union of Xtendom', c. 1897, and MS Bryce 438 ff. 14–15, Bryce to Mary and Katharine, 6 April 1910.

77. The Buddhist was Takahira Kogoro, 1854–1926, Japanese ambassador to the United States; the Jew was perhaps Oscar Straus, Roosevelt's secretary for commerce and labor, who was the first Jewish cabinet secretary in the United States.

78. This is the chapter in which St Paul sets out his understanding of the nature of Christ's presence in the sharing of bread and wine: it is the main scriptural foundation for the doctrine of the real presence in the Eucharist.

79. MS Bryce 437 ff. 82–3, Bryce to Mary and Katharine, 7 December 1908.

80. MS Bryce 439 ff. 84–85, n.d. but probably late May 1913, since the content of the letter makes it clear that he was en route for Korea and China following his three-day stop in Tokyo. He and Marion returned to Japan (including Tokyo) in July for a longer stay. Cf. also MS Bryce USA 2 f. 91, Bryce to Charles W. Eliot, 28 May 1913: 'Buddhist worship is not below the sort of R.C. worship one finds among the Indians in Peru and Bolivia, and not so very much below the R.C. worship of Spain or Sicily.'

81. MS Bryce 465 ff. 54–57, EMB to Elizabeth Ashton, 15 March 1907.

82. MS Bryce 436 ff. 46–47, Bryce to Mary and Katharine, 25 February 1907; f. 123, Bryce to Mary and Katharine, 19 October 1907.

83. James Bryce, *The Hindrances to Good Citizenship* (New Haven, Conn.: Yale University Press), 3–4. In *The American Commonwealth*, see especially the 'Introductory' for the *European* view of the United States.

84. Bryce, *Hindrances*, 9–10.

85. Bryce, 16.

86. Bryce, 45.

87. Bryce, 106.

88. University of Toronto, James Mavor papers, Bryce to Mavor, 3 April 1919.

89. For 'practical necessity', Bryce, *Hindrances*, 80; on the two-party system, MD 1: 134–38.

90. Bryce, *Hindrances*, 97.

91. The *locus classicus* of this historiography is Harris, *Private Lives, Public Spirit*, but Bryce makes no appearance. I have had the good fortune to have had access to the late Professor Harris's unpublished Ford Lectures of 1997 entitled 'A Land of Lost Content: Visions of Civic Virtue from Ruskin to Rawls', and Bryce is equally absent, although he would certainly belong well.

92. James Bryce, 'Allegiance to Humanity', *The Outlook*, 5 June 1909, 318.

93. *Daily Princetonian*, vol 42, no. 91, 29 September 1921.

94. 'Ambassador Bryce Stirs the Southern Farmers to Action', *Christian Science*, 5 November 1909, MS Bryce 236 f. 159.

95. AC, 4th ed. (1910) 2: 541–42. Incidentally, Bryce's preference for the lower case 'negro' was questioned by Booker T. Washington: Library of Congress, Booker T. Washington papers, Bryce to Washington, 7 September 1910.

96. Michael D. Biddiss, 'The Universal Races Congress of 1911', *Race* 13 (1971), 37.

97. M. E. Sadler, *Moral Instruction and Training in Schools: Report of an International Inquiry* (London: Longmans, Green, 1908), 2:xx. Bryce presided at the first meeting of the Advisory Council in February 1907, just before he left for the United States: 'Moral Training: Mr Bryce and the Teaching of Character', *Manchester Guardian*, 6 February 1907, p. 8.

98. Aldon D. Morris, *The Scholar Denied: W.E.B. Du Bois and the Birth of Modern Sociology* (Oakland: University of California Press, 2015), 104.

99. W. E. Burghardt Du Bois, *Dusk of Dawn: An Essay Toward an Autobiography of a Race Concept* [1940] (New York: Schocken, 1968), 49, 78–81; Morris, *The Scholar Denied*, 100. The slight referencing in Morris's work makes it hard to be precise about dates here.

100. W. E. Burghardt Du Bois, *The Souls of Black Folk* (Chicago: McClurg, 1903), 41, 43.

101. Du Bois, 46.

102. This is a point on which I am indebted to Gregory Conti's forthcoming work on Dicey.

103. This discussion is at AC 4th ed. (1910) 2:554–55.

104. MS Bryce USA 26 ff. 145–48, Bryce to Booker T. Washington, 9 July 1910 and 29 July 1910; Library of Congress, Booker T. Washington papers, Bryce to Washington, 7 September 1910.

105. Tulloch, *James Bryce's American Commonwealth*, 199–200.

106. W. E. Burghardt Du Bois, ed., *The Health and Physique of the Negro American* (Atlanta: Atlanta University Press, 1906), 28, 37–38.

107. University of Massachusetts at Amherst, W.E.B. Du Bois Papers Series 1A, Bryce to (probably) Benjamin Tucker Tanner, 23 November 1907, and Tanner to Singer Company, 22 November 1907.

108. University of Massachusetts at Amherst, W.E.B. Du Bois Papers Series 1A, Du Bois to Bryce, 22 January 1909 (the archive dates this 22 June 1909, which is clearly wrong, since the letter invites Bryce to speak in May 1909).

109. W.E.B. Du Bois, *The Negro* [1915] (Toronto: Dover, 2001), 72–74, 84, 99.

110. W. E. Burghardt Du Bois, 'Reconstruction and Its Benefits', *American Historical Review* 15.4 (1910), 781–99.

111. Micol Seigel, 'Beyond Compare: Comparative Method After the Transnational Turn', *Radical History Review* issue 91 (Winter 2005), 71.

112. AC, 4th ed. (1910) 2:556.

113. AC, 4th ed. (1910) 2:556–57.

114. AC, 4th ed. (1910) 2:564.

115. Library of Congress, Andrew Carnegie papers, Bryce to Carnegie, 13 November 1912.

116. 'Some Aspects of Travel—Discussion', *Geographical Journal* 43.4 (April 1914), 376.

117. MS Bryce USA 8, ff. 70–72, A. Lawrence Lowell to Bryce, 3 January 1917.

Chapter 11

1. Some of the range of this activity is captured in his mostly American correspondence that forms the basis for Keith G. Robbins, 'Lord Bryce and the First World War', *Historical Journal* 10 (1967), 255–78.

2. James Bryce, *Neutral Nations and the War* (London: Macmillan, 1914), and other pieces collected in *Essays and Addresses in War Time*. On the wider phenomenon of the involvement of humanities academics in the war effort, Stuart Wallace, *War and the Image of Germany: British Academics 1914–1918* (Edinburgh: Donald, 1988).

3. 'Lord Bryce on Retaliation', *Daily Telegraph*, 5 February 1916, p. 10.

4. For Hus, see UCL (SEESS) archives, Bryce to Seton-Watson 29 June, 1 July, and 10 July 1915; Viscount Bryce, 'Preface', in *Magna Carta Commemoration Essays*, ed. Henry Elliott Malden (London: Royal Historical Society, 1917), xi–xviii; 'Walter Raleigh Tercentenary. Observances in England and America', *The Observer*, 27 October 1918, 3; Viscount Bryce, 'Some Thoughts on Dante in His Relation to Our Own Time', in *Dante: Essays in Commemoration 1321–1921* (London: University of London Press, 1921), 1–15.

5. Bryce to Elizabeth Spence Watson, 8 July 1879, Newcastle University Special Collections SW 1/2/52

6. Bryce to W. T. Stead, 16 August 1901, Churchill College Archives.

7. Bryce to Goldwin Smith 29 March 1905; Bryce to A. L. Lowell, 12 November 1900; also Bryce, *Studies in Contemporary Biography*, 68.

8. MS Bryce USA 2 f. 102, Bryce to Charles W. Eliot, 17 September 1914 [copy].

9. MS Bryce 4 ff. 92–93, Bryce to Dicey, 28 October 1915.

10. Bryce, *Essays and Addresses in War Time*, 1.

11. James Bryce (Viscount Bryce), *Neutral Nations and the War* (London: Macmillan, 1914), 1. The pamphlet was translated into French, Italian, Spanish, Portuguese, Danish, Swedish, German, Dutch, and no doubt others too. It first appeared in the Daily Chronicle in October 1914.

12. 'Neutral Nations and the War', in *Essays and Addresses in War Time*, 13.

13. 'Neutral Nations and the War', 13.

14. MS Bryce USA 2 f. 117, Bryce to Charles W. Eliot, 25 June 1915.

15. 'Neutral Nations and the War', 14.

16. 'Neutral Nations and the War', 14.

17. Elie Halévy, *L'ère des tyrannies: études sur le socialisme et la guerre* (Paris: Gallimard, 1938), 214.

18. H. G. Wells, *The War That Will End War* (London: Palmer, 1914), 91. See also Pierre Purseigle, 'The First World War and the Transformations of the State', *International Affairs* 90 (2014), 249–64.

19. *Report of the Committee on Alleged German Outrages Appointed by His Majesty's Government* (London: HMSO, 1915).

20. The foregoing paragraph is principally based on Trevor Wilson, 'Lord Bryce's Investigation into Alleged German Atrocities in Belgium, 1914–15', *Journal of Contemporary History* 14 (1979), 369–83. This article is largely reproduced in Wilson's *The Myriad Faces of War: Britain and the Great War, 1914–1918* (Cambridge: Polity, 1986). For Bryce's initial scepticism about the allegations about German conduct, National Library of Ireland MS 42,222/35, Sir Horace Plunkett papers, diary, 1 June 1915.

21. Gary S. Messinger, *British Propaganda and the State in the First World War* (Manchester: Manchester University Press, 1992), 71. Messinger's account adds little of substance to Wilson's.

22. Notably John N. Horne and Alan Kramer, *German Atrocities, 1914: A History of Denial* (New Haven, Conn.: Yale, 2001); Horne and Kramer, 'War Between soldiers and Enemy Civilians, 1914–1915', in *Great War, Total War: Combat and Mobilization on the Western Front, 1914–1918*, ed. Roger Chickering and Stig Förster (Cambridge: Cambridge University Press, 2000), 153–68; and Isabel V. Hull, *Absolute Destruction: Military Culture and the Practices of War in Imperial Germany* (Ithaca, N.Y.: Cornell University Press, 2005), 207–15. Mark Mazower, 'Letters', *London Review of Books* 23.5 (8 March 2001), notes (both in connection with the Blue Book on Armenia and the report on German atrocities) that the fact that a report was published as part of a wartime propaganda campaign does not imply that its contents can be dismissed as fabrication.

23. Emily Robertson, 'Propaganda and "Manufactured Hatred": A Reappraisal of the Ethics of First World War British and Australian War Propaganda', *Public Relations Inquiry* 3 (2014), 253–54.

24. But the diaries, and other documentary evidence used by the Bryce Committee, do not survive.

25. John Horne and Alan Kramer, 'German "Atrocities" and Franco-German Opinion, 1914: The Evidence of German Soldiers' Diaries', *Journal of Modern History* 66 (1994), 1–33.

26. For instance, 'Lord Bryce on Reprisals', *The Times*, 5 February 1916, p. 3; MS Bryce 284 f. 95, Bryce to J. H. Morgan, 11 February 1916. Morgan's book, *German Atrocities: An Official Investigation* (London: Dutton, 1916), appeared without the preface that Bryce had been asked to write. The withdrawal was due to fundamental disagreement on the legitimacy of reprisals. One reason why Bryce was so strong on the question of reprisals was that American correspondents warned him that Britain's use of reprisals would weaken its cause in the United States: MS Bryce USA 8 ff. 216–199, Theodore Marburg to Bryce, 21 October 1915

27. Steinberg, 'James Bryce and the Origins of the Armenian Question', 27, stresses this continuity: that is, whether or not the 1915–16 genocide was 'objectively' anticipated in the atrocities of 1894–1896, in Bryce's eyes it certainly was; also Steinberg, 'The Confirmation of the Worst Fears', 15–39; Mark Mazower, 'The G-word', *London Review of Books* 23.3 (8 February 2001).

28. This is the account given by Arnold Toynbee, *Experiences* (Oxford: Oxford University Press, 1967), 149–51. Toynbee said that he did not appreciate this ulterior motive at the time and in retrospect regretted allowing himself to undertake work for a propagandistic purpose.

29. *The Treatment of Armenians in the Ottoman Empire 1915–16. Documents Presented to Viscount Grey of Fallodon, Secretary of State for Foreign Affairs, by Viscount Bryce* (London: Putnam's, 1916), xvii.

30. For this point, see especially Steinberg, 'The Confirmation of the Worst Fears', 15–39.

31. For example, Vincent Boland, 'Turkey Challenges Genocide "fraud"', *Financial Times*, 22 April 2005, p. 8. The word 'genocide' (coined in the 1940s) was not used by Bryce.

32. Bodleian MSS. Brit.Emp.s. 22/G506 (1), minute book of the British Armenia Committee (part of the Archive of the Anti-Slavery Society).

33. There is a useful discussion, focused on a somewhat earlier period, in Jean-Michel Johnston and Oded Y. Steinberg, 'Armenians, Jews and Humanitarianism in the "Age of Questions", 1830–1900', *Historical Journal* 66 (2023), 72–100.

34. James Bryce, 'Preface' to C. Russell and H. S. Lewis, *The Jew in London: A Study of Racial Character and Present-Day Conditions* (London: Fisher Unwin, 1900), ix–xviii.

35. Cumbria Archive Centre, Sir Esme Howard papers, Bryce to Howard, 27 March 1914. Bryce's 'Impressions of Palestine' were published in Bryce, *Memories of Travel*, 166–90.

36. Bryce, *Memories of Travel*, 182.

37. E.W.G. Masterman, 'Palestine: Its Resources and Suitability for Colonization', and Lord Bryce, Leonard King, Dr Gaster, and Canon Parfit, 'Palestine: Its Resources and Suitability for Colonization', both in *Geographical Journal* 50 (1917), 12–26, 26–32. Dr Gaster was the linguist and Zionist leader Moses Gaster, at whose house the Balfour Declaration had been first drafted the month before.

38. Reported in *Aberdeen Journal*, 2 June 1917, p. 4.

39. Viscount Bryce, 'The Future of Palestine and the Hopes of the Jews', *Menorah Journal* 4:3 (June 1918), 126–29; 'Room in Palestine. Lord Bryce's Estimate', *Manchester Guardian*, 3 July 1918, p. 3.

40. Bryce, *Race Sentiment*, 3–4.

41. Bryce, 4.

42. Bryce, 5–6, including 5 n. 2.

43. Bryce, 8.

44. Bryce, 8.

45. Bryce, *Race Sentiment*, 11.

46. Bryce, 13–14.

47. Bryce, 25. Bryce does not explain how he would reconcile the trade in African slaves with this argument.

48. On 'doux commerce', the *locus classicus* in modern scholarship is Albert O. Hirschman, *The Passions and the Interests: Political Arguments for Capitalism Before Its Triumph* (Princeton, N.J.: Princeton University Press, 1977), 58–63.

49. Bryce, *Race Sentiment*, 27–28.

50. Bryce, 30.

51. Bryce, 31.

52. Bryce, 33.

53. Bryce, 31–32. Bryce commended Heine (who was Jewish) as 'a great German writer, to whom the possession of a second and older nationality gave an unusual detachment and breadth of view'.

54. Sakiko Kaiga, *Britain and the Intellectual Origins of the League of Nations* (Cambridge: Cambridge University Press, 2021).

55. It is not clear that any of the Bryce Group's members were outright pacifists, but Ponsonby in particular is generally considered to have been close to pacifism: Martin Ceadel, *Pacifism in Britain, 1914–1945: The Defining of a Faith* (Oxford: Clarendon, 1980), 80. Several (Ponsonby, Wallas, Hobson) were members of the Union of Democratic Control, which was founded principally by opponents of the declaration of war in 1914.

56. On the importance of plans for peace in winning the sympathy of the neutral countries, especially the United States, MS Bryce USA 8 ff. 224–27, Marburg to Bryce, 11 April 1916.

57. 'The only effective and permanent remedy [to dispel the risks of future wars] would be to convince the several peoples of the world that they have far more to lose than to gain from strife, and to replace by a sentiment of mutual international goodwill the violent national antagonisms that now exist.' 'Proposals for reducing the number of future wars with a prefatory note by the Rt. Hon. Viscount Bryce, O.M.' (24 February 1915 draft), LSE Wallas 4/5.

58. MS Eng hist. c. 403, Theodore Marburg to W. H. Dickinson, n.d. c. 1931 [transcript]. Here Marburg attributes the coinage to the Bryce Group. C. P. Scott had used the term as long ago as 1870 (obviously a significant date), but this seems to have been an isolated usage. He wrote to his father, in connection with Russia's denunciation of the Black Sea Clauses of the Treaty of Paris of 1856: 'Some league of nations and code of international law must surely be evolved ere long to bring order into this chaos.' Hammond, *C. P. Scott*, 33.

59. Kaiga, *Britain and the Intellectual Origins*, 41, identifies collective security as the key original contribution from the Bryce Group.

60. MS Bryce 58 ff. 14–15, G. L. Dickinson to Bryce, 20 October 1914 (for 'my group'); G. Lowes Dickinson, *The Autobiography of G. Lowes Dickinson, and Other Unpublished Writings*, ed. Dennis Proctor (London: Duckworth, 1973), 190. E. M. Forster wrote: 'Two of the meetings of the committee were attended by Lord Bryce, and since he was the first person of public eminence to countenance the organisation, it is known as the "Bryce Group." It ought to be called the "Lowes Dickinson Group"': E. M. Forster, *Goldsworthy Lowes Dickinson* (London: Arnold, 1934), 164.

61. Bodl. Eng. hist c. 403, n. 176, Bryce to Dickinson, 18 January 1917.

62. These papers are MS Eng hist c. 403 part C, Correspondence with Lord Bryce, 1917–1919 (W. H. Dickinson), and MS Bryce 58 ff. 11–40 (letters to Bryce from G. L. Dickinson) and ff. 41–49 (letters to Bryce from W. H. Dickinson).

63. This memorandum, headed 'Lord Bryce's Notes. When the War Comes to an End', is at Bodl MS Eng hist c. 402 ff. 97–99. Several of the other texts in this box of W. H. Dickinson's papers are responses to this memorandum from other members of the group; see also MS Bryce 58 f. 19, G. L. Dickinson to Bryce, 2 December 1914.

64. Kaiga, *Britain and the Intellectual Origins*, 56.

65. Bryce to W. H. Dickinson, 21 April [1917], Bodl MS Eng hist c. 403, f. 177. He continued: 'They would only spoil the meeting, of course with the best possible intentions; for they are excellent people. "The Better is the enemy of the Good."'

66. MS Eng hist c. 403 f. 68, R. L. Borden to W. H. Dickinson, 28 April 1917.

67. Kaiga, *Britain and the Intellectual Origins*, 39; Bodl MS Eng hist. c. 403 f. 190, Bryce to W. H. Dickinson, 15 June 1917. The links are discussed by Theodore Marburg, *League of Nations: A Chapter in the History of the Movement* (New York: Macmillan, 1919), 57 and (for Bryce's role in particular) 99.

68. MS Bryce USA 8 ff. 233–35, Marburg to Taft, 13 May 1916.

69. G. L. Dickinson, *Autobiography*, 159.

70. Graham Wallas, *Human Nature in Politics* (London: Constable, 1908), 126–27.

71. J. A. Hobson, *Confessions of an Economic Heretic* (London: Allen & Unwin, 1938), 103–4. For Bryce's prior knowledge of Hobson, see James Bryce, 'Mr J.A. Hobson on the Causes and Effects of the Present War', *Manchester Guardian* 17 March 1900, p. 11; MS Bryce USA 2 ff. 17–18, Bryce to Charles W. Eliot, 27 May 1902.

72. Bryce, 'Prefatory note' to 'Proposals for Reducing the Number of Future Wars' (as revised up to 24 February 1915), Bodleian Library, Baron Dickinson papers, MS Eng hist. c. 402 f. 2.

73. On this subject, Georgios Varouxakis, *Liberty Abroad: J.S. Mill on International Relations* (Cambridge: Cambridge University Press, 2013), esp. chap. 2.

74. Bryce's insistence that the word sovereignty had 'in many ways clouded the domain of public law and jurisprudence' was certainly directed at Austin, and at the 'Benthamite school' named in the footnote: AC, 3rd ed. (1893–1894), 1:424. The footnote was present in the first edition, but the parenthetical reference to the Benthamite school was not. That Austin was the target is clear from MS Bryce 15 ff. 117–18, Bryce to Sidgwick, 22 September 1887: 'As to Sovereignty, it seems to me that all the Austinian discussions about it are in the air and quite without practical value.'

75. Martin J. Wiener, *Between Two Worlds: The Political Thought of Graham Wallas* (Oxford: Oxford University Press, 1971), 66.

76. 'Mr Bryce on the Teaching Profession', *The Times*, 5 June 1899, p. 16.

77. John Rylands Library, Tout papers, TFT/1/143/10, Bryce to Tout, 24 June 1916.

78. Martha C. Nussbaum, *Not for Profit: Why Democracy Needs the Humanities* (Princeton, N.J.: Princeton University Press, 2010); Helen Small, *The Value of the Humanities* (Oxford: Oxford University Press, 2013); Stefan Collini, *What Are Universities For?* (London: Penguin, 2012); Stefan Collini, *Speaking of Universities* (London: Verso, 2017).

79. Tomás Irish, *The University at War, 1914–25: Britain, France, and the United States* (Basingstoke: Palgrave, 2015), chap. 2; Roy MacLeod, 'Scientists', in *Cambridge History of the First World War*, vol. 2: *The State*, ed. Jay Winter (Cambridge: Cambridge University Press, 2014), 434–59; and Roy MacLeod, 'The Scientists Go to War: Revisiting Precept and Practice, 1914–1919', *Journal of War and Culture Studies* 2 (2009), 37–51.

80. MacLeod, 'The Scientists Go to War', 38.

81. Wilson, *The Myriad Faces of War*, 220; Roy MacLeod, 'The Chemists Go to War: The Mobilization of Civilian Chemists and the British War Effort, 1914–1918', *Annals of Science* 50 (1993), 458. The original formulations had 'engineer' in the singular and 'chemists' in the plural.

82. *The Neglect of Science: Report of Proceedings of a Conference Held in the Rooms of the Linnaean Society* (London: Harrison, 1916).

83. 'Neglect of Science: A Cause of Failures in War', *The Times*, 2 February 1916. On the debate on the 'neglect of science,' Anna-K. Mayer, 'Reluctant Technocrats: Science Promotion in the Neglect-of-Science Debate of 1916–1918', *History of Science* 43 (2005), 139–59.

84. 'The Mobilisation of Science', *Nature* 95, no. 2381 (17 June 1915), 419–20.

85. Sir Ray Lankester, ed., *Natural Science and the Classical System in Education: Essays New and Old* (London: Heinemann, 1918)

86. But note that it was paralleled by the Crewe Report on Classics (1921).

87. Nigel Vincent and Helen Wallace, 'Lost Without Translation: Why Codebreaking Is Not Just a Numbers Game', *British Academy Review*, no. 25 (February 2015), https://www.thebritishacademy.ac.uk/publishing/review/25/lost-without-translation-why-codebreaking-not-just-numbers-game/; and British Academy, 'Humanities Scholars Who Worked in Military Intelligence in the Second World War', https://www.thebritishacademy.ac.uk/publishing/memoirs/humanities-scholars-who-worked-military-intelligence-second-world-war/.

88. E.g., Viscount Bryce and others, *The International Crisis, the Theory of the State: Lectures delivered in February and March 1916* (London: Oxford University Press, 1916); also Wallace, War and the Image of Germany.

89. Wallace, *War and the Image of Germany*, 48–49.

90. 'Reorganising Education. "Humanistic" & "Scientific" Studies. A Basis for Common Action', *Manchester Guardian*, 5 September 1916, p. 3.

91. John Rylands Library, Tout papers, TFT/1/975/43, Prothero to Tout, 3 June [1917]. For Bryce's discreet support, Royal Historical Society Prothero papers PP/2/6/5/3, Tout to Prothero 1 June 1916 and PP/2/6/5/8, Bryce to Prothero 5 October 1916.

92. Small, *The Value of the Humanities*, 1. For the rich debates on the role of the humanities in the Second World War, see Claire Rydell Arcenas, 'On the Purpose of Humanities Education: A Historical Perspective from the Mid-Twentieth-Century United States', in *Writing the History of the Humanities: Questions, Themes and Approaches*, ed. Herman Paul (London: Bloomsbury, 2022), 345–64.

93. If this sounds convoluted—as it does to James Turner, *Philology: The Forgotten Origins of the Modern Humanities* (Princeton, N.J.: Princeton University Press, 2014), 384—it was positively snappy in comparison with the working title agreed by resolution of a meeting in July 1901: 'The British Academy of Historico-Philosophical Science, Including Philology and Archaeology, Political and Economic Science'.

94. See, for example, the documents reprinted in 'A Documentary Account of the Foundation of the British Academy', https://www.thebritishacademy.ac.uk/documents/2732/documentary-account-foundation-british-academy.pdf.

95. 'International Association of Academies', *The Times*, 11 April 1901.

96. E.g., Lord Reay's presidential address to the British Academy, 1903; also Prothero on BA sections, BA Archive BA 357 [A/90/2f-g], Papers and Correspondence 1910–1919. Curiously,

the German term *Geisteswissenschaft* was originally coined as a translation of the English 'moral science, as encountered in Book 6 of Mill's *System of Logic*.

97. Speeches by the Archbishop of York (Lang) and the Bishop of Ely (Chase), as well as Lords Parmoor, Crewe, Sheffield, Haldane, Curzon, Knutsford, and Cromer.

98. John Campbell in collaboration with Richard McLaughlan, *Haldane: The Forgotten Statesman Who Shaped Britain and Canada* (London: Hurst, 2020), 184–87.

99. G. R. Searle, *The Quest for National Efficiency: A Study in British Politics and Political Thought, 1899–1914* (Oxford: Blackwell, 1971), passim; p. 3 for the coinage of the term.

100. Richard Burdon Haldane, *An Autobiography* (London: Hodder & Stoughton, 1929), 133–34.

101. MS Bryce 437 ff. 34–35, Bryce to Mary and Katharine, 17 March 1908; and on similar lines, ff. 125–26, 2 April 1909.

102. Bryce, UHA, 17–31.

103. Lord Bryce, 'The President's Address: The Worth of Ancient Literature for the Modern World', *Proceedings of the Classical Association*, vol. 14 (1917), 13; 'Greek and Latin. Their Place in Teaching: Lord Bryce's Defence', *Manchester Guardian*, 6 January 1917, p. 5.

104. Nussbaum, *Not for Profit*; Small, *The Value of the Humanities*, chap. 4.

105. There is a very suggestive discussion of this subject in Liam Stowell, 'The Athens of Example: The Classical World in British International Thought, 1900–1939', PhD diss., University of Manchester, 2020; see also Mark Mazower, *No Enchanted Palace*, especially chap. 2 on Zimmern; and Julia Stapleton, 'The Classicist as Liberal Intellectual: Gilbert Murray and Alfred Eckhard Zimmern', in *Gilbert Murray Reassessed: Hellenism, Theatre, and International Politics*, ed. Christopher Stray (Oxford: Oxford University Press, 2007), 261–92.

106. On the historians, and more generally on internationalist education in interwar Britain, Helen McCarthy, *The British People and the League of Nations: Democracy, Citizenship and Internationalism* (Manchester: Manchester University Press, 2011), especially chap. 4. Gooch was an outlier: a Cambridge historian, he was the only one who had not been formed by Oxford Greats.

107. For an intriguing instance, see T. J. Cobden-Sanderson, 'An International Tongue' [letter], *The Times*, 23 May 1918. The author advanced the claims of Latin to be the international language. Universally taught, it would 'give all a training in the humanities, "in widest commonalty spread"'; and would give the promised League of Nations 'the essential common tongue of which no nation need be jealous, a tongue fashioned for use on a world-wide scale as it was fashioned for the use of an empire which first moulded Europe into Europe'.

108. Bryce, 'Concerning a League of Nations for Peace', *Essays and Addresses in War Time*, 176.

109. 'Presidential Address Delivered to the British Academy, July 14, 1916', *Essays and Addresses in War Time*, 123. The concept of the 'international mind' was coined by Bryce's friend, the president of Columbia University, Nicholas Murray Butler, and taken up notably by J. A. Hobson in Britain. It would underpin much liberal internationalist thought and practice in the 1920s: Jeanne Morefield, *Covenants Without Swords: Idealist Liberalism and the Spirit of Empire* (Princeton, N.J.: Princeton University Press, 2004), chap. 3.

110. 'Presidential Address 1916', 124.

111. The affinities between Bryce's thinking and the league's project of intellectual cooperation are noted by Tomás Irish, 'The "Moral Basis" of Reconstruction: Humanitarianism, Intellectual Relief and the League of Nations, 1918–1925', *Modern Intellectual History* 17 (2020), 769–800, esp. 782. On the league and history teaching, see Ken Osborne, 'Creating the "International Mind": The League of Nations Attempts to Reform History Teaching, 1920–1939', *History of Education Quarterly* 56 (2016), 213–40. Bryce's role in international intellectual cooperation included chairing the Allied Colonial Universities Conference in London in 1903 and

serving as vice-president (representing the British Academy) of the International Congress of Historical Sciences in Rome in 1903. When the next Congress was held in London in 1913, Bryce was appointed president, but the delay in extracting himself from his responsibilities in Washington meant that he was unable to attend.

112. MS Bryce USA 2 f. 106, Bryce to Charles W. Eliot, 13 November 1914.

113. MS Bryce USA 2 f. 124, Bryce to Charles W. Eliot, 23 September 1915.

114. MS Bryce USA 2 ff. 159–60, Bryce to Charles W. Eliot, 30 January 1917.

115. MS Bryce USA 23 f. 190, Bryce to J. F. Rhodes, 24 January 1920.

116. Lord Bryce, 'The Austrian Treaty: Italy's Claims in Tyrol', *Manchester Guardian*, 10 June 1919, p. 6.

117. Huntington Library, Henry White papers, Bryce to White 1 April 1919 (on Bulgaria), 19 May 1919 (on several boundary questions including these two), 30 May 1919 (stressing the impact on the League of Nations), and 12 June 1919 (enclosing a copy of the *Manchester Guardian* article).

118. Irish, 'The "Moral Basis" of Reconstruction', 780–81.

119. MS Bryce 4 ff. 215–16, Bryce to Dicey, 3 March 1919.

120. Trevor Wilson, ed., *The Political Diaries of C. P. Scott, 1911–1928* (London: Collins, 1970), 371.

121. Stowell, 'The Athens of Example', 15.

122. Zimmern papers, Bodleian Library, MS Zimmern 16 ff. 16, 22, Bryce to Alfred Zimmern, 13 February and 23 February 1919.

Chapter 12

1. MS Bryce 443 ff. 1–2, Bryce to Dr R. J. Bryce, 9 January 1880: 'Justinian, alas! is not likely to be out for years to come.'

2. MS Bryce 4 ff. 257–58, Bryce to Dicey, 24 March 1921.

3. MS Bryce 4 ff. 79–80, Bryce to Dicey, 2 January 1915. Bryce here responds to a letter from Dicey which seems not to survive.

4. MS Bryce USA 2 ff. 38–40, Bryce to Charles W. Eliot, 16 September 1904; also (for the earlier speculation about possible titles) ff. 23–24 and ff. 33–32, 29 April 1904 and 5 August 1904.

5. 'Study of Popular Governments', *Harvard Crimson*, 26 October 1904.

6. Bryce to Eliot, 16 September 1904.

7. New York Public Library Macmillan Company Records VI b. 39, Bryce to George P. Brett Sr, 7 December 1904; MS Bryce 283 ff. 115–16, Bryce to George W. Prothero, 8 December 1905.

8. NYPL Macmillan VI b. 39, Bryce to Brett, 8 December 1905 and 2 January 1906 (the latter miswritten as 1905).

9. Bryce to Brett, 8 December 1905.

10. Houghton Library, Godkin papers MS Am 1083 (1264), EMB to Katherine Godkin, 31 October 1905. On the 1905 visit and the people he saw, see Charles Borgeaud, 'Bryce et la Suisse', *Journal de Genève*, 5 February 1922, cutting in MS Bryce 508 f. 42v.

11. *Harvard Crimson*, 4 November 1904. See also his comments on Australia, in the context of a discussion of comparative democracy, in MS Bryce 17 f. 190, Bryce to Goldwin Smith, 29 March 1905: 'I have been reading a history of Victoria by a Mr Turner.'

12. MS Bryce 270 ff. 252–53 is a set of notes on New Zealand politics, and both internal evidence and the fact that the notes were written on a parliamentary order paper from 1905 allow us to date the notes to that year with some confidence.

13. 'The Study of Popular Governments', 1, *Quarterly Review* 203 (July 1905), 173–74.

14. However, having left the Commons, he told Morley (who had also just left) that 'away from it one realizes how much the most interesting of all assemblies it is, how full of a vivid and

varied life for the like of which one must go back to the ancient world': Bodl Morley MS. Eng. d. 3563 ff. 79–80, Bryce to Morley, 21 May 1908.

15. 'The Study of Popular Governments', 1:174–75.

16. MD 1:175.

17. MD 1:176.

18. Houghton Library, Godkin papers MS Am 1083 (1262), EMB to Katherine Godkin, 19 April 1903.

19. Edwin Lawrence Godkin, *Problems of Modern Democracy: Political and Economic Essays* (New York: Scribner, 1896); Edwin L. Godkin, *Unforeseen Tendencies of Democracy* (Boston: Houghton and Mifflin, 1898).

20. He did not, in fact, discuss any of them in any detail.

21. MS Bryce 56 ff. 86–87, H. Enfield Dowson to Bryce, 7 January 1901. It is clear from the context that the expression 'moral deterioration' was either Bryce's own or Dowson's paraphrase of what Bryce had written. Also Library of Congress, Andrew Carnegie papers, Bryce to Carnegie, 31 December 1903: 'The demagogue' (unnamed) is understood to be Chamberlain.

22. See Bryce's first reply to Charles W. Eliot on the subject, MS Bryce USA 2 ff. 19–20, Bryce to Eliot, 4 September 1903.

23. Eliot to Bryce 15 April 1904, MS Bryce USA 1 f. 55.

24. MS Bryce USA 1 f. 42, Eliot to Bryce, 14 March 1902. The Bryces visited Cuba, along with Mexico and Jamaica, toward the end of 1901, during the American occupation of the island following the Spanish American War of 1898. We do not have Bryce's letter to which Eliot was here responding, but he may well have sent Eliot, or alerted him to, the article he wrote on Cuba: James Bryce, 'Some reflections on the state of Cuba', *North American Review* no. 174 (1 January 1902), 445–56.

25. MS Bryce 4 ff. 23–24, Bryce to Dicey, 28 November 1909.

26. Bryce, *The Hindrances to Good Citizenship*, 117.

27. MS Bryce 4 ff. 38–43, Bryce to Dicey, 15 June 1911.

28. MS Bryce 270 ff. 1 2 and 7, letters from Arthur Berriedale Keith, Colonial Office official, 24 May 1911 and 4 April 1911.

29. William Pember Reeves, *State Experiments in Australia and New Zealand*, 2 vols. (London: Grant Richards, 1902); Henry Gyles Turner, *The First Decade of the Australian Commonwealth: A Chronicle of Contemporary Politics, 1901–1910* (Melbourne: Mason, Firth & M'Cutcheon, 1911); Henry Gyles Turner, *History of the Colony of Victoria*, 2 vols. (London: Longmans, Green, 1904); Louis Vossion, *La Nouvelle Australie et son avenir* (Paris: Guillaumin, 1902); Georges Biard d'Aunet *L'Aurore australe. La société australienne, le socialisme en Australie, la constitution australienne* (Paris: Pion-Nourrit, 1907). On Turner, see MS Fisher ff. 28–29, Bryce to Fisher, 11 October 1912: 'Not much doing in Australia in the historical way, but one Turner has written a good history of First Ten Years of Commonwealth.'

30. André Siegfried, *La Démocratie en Nouvelle Zélande* (Paris: Colin, 1904). Bryce evidently made notes on this in 1916: MS Bryce 270 f. 256.

31. See also Bryce, *The Hindrances to Good Citizenship*, 53–55.

32. MS Bryce 270 f. 3.

33. University of Toronto, James Mavor papers, Bryce to Mavor, 3 April 1919.

34. Houghton Library, Godkin papers MS Am 1083 (81), Bryce to Godkin, 7 November 1882.

35. Houghton Library, Godkin papers MS Am 1083 (79), Bryce to Godkin, 7 October 1882: 'I have been writing an article on some aspects of American politics intended to point out how misleading are the arguments drawn from the mischiefs there are to what will be the probably cause of democracy in England.'

36. MS Bryce 4 ff. 31–35, Bryce to Dicey, 26 December 1910.

37. MD 1:vii.

38. MS Bryce 4 ff. 79–80, Bryce to Dicey, 2 January 1915.

39. 'Civil War in England', *Wichita Eagle*, 29 February 1912, in MS Bryce 238 f. 228.

40. For his contempt for the Lloyd George coalition government, MS Bryce 4 ff. 266–67, Bryce to Dicey, 27 November 1921.

41. MS Bryce 4 ff. 234–35, Bryce to Dicey, 23/24 December 1919. Dicey saw the point: He thought the book 'as certain of success as any book can be, tho' I fully recognise the fact that the study of constitutions is as much underrated now as it was overrated 50 years ago'. MS Bryce 3 ff. 249–51, Dicey to Bryce, 23 August 1920.

42. MD 1:xi.

43. MD 1:xi–xii.

44. MD 1:ix.

45. MS Bryce USA 2 f. 226, Bryce to Charles W. Eliot, 24 January 1921.

46. Hull History Centre, Harold Laski collection, U DP217/12, Harold Laski to Maurice Firuski, 2 April 1921; Lindsay is quoted by Drusilla Scott, *A. D. Lindsay: A Biography* (Oxford: Blackwell, 1971), 268. Lindsay also thought Bryce wrong to think he could set to one side the problems created by the concentration of economic power: A. D. Lindsay, *The Modern Democratic State* (London: Oxford University Press, 1943), 1:107. But Lindsay's own conception of democracy—in particular, its emphasis on the importance of public opinion generated by the myriad of voluntary associations—was not unlike Bryce's.

47. Bodleian MS Facs d. 119 ff. 57–63, Bryce to Oliver Wendell Holmes Jr, 14 September 1916, finished 27 January 1917.

48. MD 1:vii–ix.

49. MS Bryce 4 ff. 211–14, Bryce to Dicey, 22 January 1919.

50. MS Bryce USA 23 f. 62, Bryce to Lowell, 22 November 1916.

51. MD 1:viii.

52. MS Bryce 4 ff. 15–16, Bryce to Dicey, 27 April 1909.

53. The British parliamentary term was seven years until the Parliament Act of 1911 reduced it to five.

54. His advocacy of the referendum was a development of the doctrine of the mandate formulated by Lord Salisbury in the years after 1885: the House of Lords would defer to a government proposals if they had been put to the electorate in the previous general election but otherwise would not concede the supremacy of the elected House. See House of Lords Library Note, https://www.parliament.uk/globalassets/documents/lords-library/hllsalisburydoctrine.pdf.

55. MD 1:171.

56. MS Bryce 4 f. 32, Bryce to Dicey, 26 December 1910.

57. MD 1:321.

58. MS Bryce USA 2 ff. 159–60, Bryce to Charles W. Eliot, 30 January 1917.

59. MD 1:173.

60. As James Thompson observes, it was common among political commentators of the time to distinguish between the electorate (whimsical, changeable) and public opinion (solid, stable): Thompson, *British Political Culture and the Idea of 'Public Opinion'*, 160.

61. MD 2:272: 'In Britain and France the legislatures do much to form, clarify, and formulate public opinion. In Australia, though there are seven of them, they do comparatively little.' Also MD 1:173.

62. On the sense in which public opinion may be an 'essentially contested concept', Thompson, *British Political Culture*, 14.

63. AC 1:382 n. 2. On the slow recognition of the importance of Bagehot's political writings, David M. Craig, 'Bagehot's Republicanism', in *The Monarchy and the British Nation 1780 to the Present*, ed. Andrzej Olechnowicz (Cambridge: Cambridge University Press, 2007), 140.

64. Bagehot, *English Constitution*, 72–73.

65. MS Bryce 17 f. 187, Bryce to Goldwin Smith, 25 September 1903.

66. MS Bryce USA 22 ff. 121–22, Bryce to Lowell, 28 March 1905; on similar lines, MS Bryce 17 f. 190, Bryce to Goldwin Smith, 29 March 1905.

67. MS Bryce USA 22 ff. 126–27, Bryce to Lowell, 15 August 1905.

68. A. V. Dicey, *Introduction to the Law of the Constitution*, 4th ed. (London: Macmillan, 1893), 360–64.

69. MS Bryce 17 f. 189, Bryce to Goldwin Smith, 26 January 1905.

70. Dicey, *Law of the Constitution*, 4th ed., 359.

71. [Walter Bagehot,] 'Why an English Liberal May Look Without Disapproval on the Progress of Imperialism in France', *Economist* 6 January 1874, p. 682, for the remark that 'a Parliamentary Government is essentially a Government by discussion; by constant speaking and writing a public opinion is formed which decides on all action and all policy'. But the phrase 'government by discussion' recurred in several of Bagehot's major works, including Walter Bagehot, *Physics and Politics: Or Thoughts on the Application of the Principles of "Natural Selection" and "Inheritance" to Political Society* [1873] (Cambridge: Cambridge University Press, 2010), 158, 161, 164, 166, 179, 192, 194, 196, 199, 204, 219, 221.

72. MS Bryce 17 f. 188, Bryce to Goldwin Smith, 19 November 1904.

73. Conti, *Parliament the Mirror of the Nation*, 339–40; Frederic Harrison, *Order and Progress* (London: Longmans, Green, 1875), 73–75.

74. For the original invitation: MS Bryce USA 1 f. 50, Charles W. Eliot to Bryce, 18 August 1903. This specified 'some subject connected with good government or good citizenship'.

75. MS Bryce 17 f. 183, Bryce to Goldwin Smith, 14 February 1900.

76. MS Bryce 26 f. 150, draft of letter from Bryce to Theodor Barth, n.d. [1899].

77. MS Bryce 17 f. 186, Bryce to Goldwin Smith, 27 December 1900.

78. Kenneth O. Morgan, 'The Boer War and the Media', *Twentieth Century British History* 13 (2002), 5, 8.

79. MS Bryce USA 22 ff. 80–83, Bryce to Sarah Wyman Whitman, 11 March 1900.

80. MD 1:114.

81. MD 1:545.

82. MD 1:548.

83. MD 1:87.

84. James Bryce, 'Thomas Jefferson: Third President of the United States and Founder of the University of Virginia', *UHA*, 142.

85. For an example, MS Bryce 352 f. 48, where he says that Australian democracy is discredited by 'hatred & fear of Coloured Races': he sympathized with 'White Australia', but not with its underpinning ideology.

86. MD 1:351.

87. MD 1:370–71.

88. MS Bryce 4 ff. 87–89, Bryce to Dicey, 19 May 1915. See also MS Bryce 3 f. 162, Dicey to Bryce, 21 May 1915, sending Vinogradoff's pamphlet. This was probably Paul Vinogradoff, *The Russian Problem* (London: Constable, 1914), later incorporated in his short book, *Self-Government in Russia* (London: Constable, 1915).

89. MS Bryce 4 ff. 36–37, Bryce to Dicey, 15 June 1911.

90. MS Bryce 4 ff. 179–80, Bryce to Dicey, 29 May 1918.

91. On Pattison's intellectual sensibility, Jones, *Intellect and Character*, chap. 6. I note there, at 232, that Dicey acknowledged that his interest in the history of public opinion was 'originally kindled' by Pattison's work.

92. MS Bryce 4 ff. 251–52, Bryce to Dicey, 28 August 1920.

93. MS Bryce 4 ff. 39–43, Bryce to Dicey, 15 June 1911.

94. MS Bryce 4 ff. 192–93, Bryce to Dicey, 28 August 1918. Dicey's second edition, in 1914, already contained a lengthy new introduction analysing changes in the early twentieth century:

Albert Venn Dicey, *Lectures on the Relation Between Law and Public Opinion During the Nineteenth Century* (London: Macmillan, 1914), xxiii–xciv.

95. MS Bryce 280 f. 118, W. D. Ross (fellow and future provost of Oriel) to Bryce, 30 April 1921: 'You may be interested to know that it is proposed to make it a prescribed work for the new Honour School of Philosophy Politics and Economics, so that it attains very quickly such immortality as the University can bestow.' At Queen's University, Kingston (Ontario), it was already prescribed in the calendar for 1922–1923.

96. 'Allocution de M. Alexandre Ribot', in *Le 50e Anniversaire de la Fondation de l'Ecole Libre des Sciences Politiques (1871–1921)* (Paris: 27 Rue Saint-Guillaume, 1921), 38. For a modern endorsement of the emphasis on Bryce's underlying optimism, Thompson, *British Political Culture*, 156.

97. Léon Duguit, *Manuel de droit constitutionnel: théorie générale de l'Etat, organisation* politique (Paris: A. Fontemoing, 1907), rigid constitutional laws at 1083; Léon Duguit, *Traité de droit constitutionnel* (Paris: A. Fontemoing, 1911).

98. Maurice Hauriou, *Précis de droit constitutionnel*, 2nd ed. (Paris: Sirey, 1929), 133, 216, 232, 243–44, 249–51. [1st ed.: 273–74 (rigid and flexible); 12–13, 278 (state constitutions and colonial origins); 288–89 (procedures for amending state constitutions).] Hauriou was critical of the notion that Britain had a 'flexible' constitution: he thought it had none at all (216) [1st ed.: 273].

99. Frédéric Saulnier, *Joseph-Barthélemy 1874–1945. La crise du constitutionnalisme libéral sous la IIIᵉ République* (Paris: LGDJ, 2004), 4: 'une sorte de Bryce français'. My understanding of the connection between Bryce and Barthélemy, and more generally of Bryce's place in French juristic thinking in the twentieth century, owes much to Emanuele Podda of the University of Warwick.

100. Saulnier, *Joseph-Barthélemy*, 4; MS Bryce 251 ff. 158–59, Joseph Barthélemy to Bryce, 20 May 1918 (the letter starts 'Monsieur et très honoré maître').

101. James Bryce, *Les Démocraties modernes*, 2 vols. (Paris: Payot, 1924).

102. On the logic underpinning this trajectory, Julian Jackson, *France: The Dark Years, 1940–1944* (Oxford: Oxford University Press, 2001), 50–51; Gilles Martinez, 'Joseph Barthélemy et la crise de la démocratie libérale', *Vingtième Siècle* 59 (1998), 28–47. Some of Barthélemy's solutions to the 'crisis of the state' of the 1930s were decidedly un-Brycean, including women's suffrage and proportional representation.

103. André Tardieu, *Notes sur les Etats-Unis* (Paris: Calmann-Lévy, 1908), 138 n. 1; André Tardieu, *La Révolution à refaire* t. 1, *Le Souverain captif* (Paris: Flammarion, 1936), 69.

104. Jérôme Perrier, 'Michel Debré et les avatars du libéralisme français (1936–1945)', *Vingtième Siècle. Revue d'histoire* 116.4 (2012), 94.

105. On De Gasperi's reading of Bryce, Giorgio Vecchio, 'Alcide de Gasperi negli anni del fascismo: esperienze, letture e riflessioni', *Annali dell'Istituto storico italo-germanico in Trento* 34 (2008), 283–92.

106. Barbara Taverni, 'For Italy in a Changing World: The Political Apogee of Alcide de Gasperi, 1948–1954', *Modern Italy* 14 (2009), 463. Federico Mazzei, 'Cattolici e liberali all'antifascismo alla seconda guerra mondiale (1925–1943)', PhD diss., University of Bologna, 2012–2013, pp. 220–21.

107. James Bryce, *Democrazie moderne*, ed. Luigi Degli Occhi, 2 vols. (Milan: Hoepli, 1930–1931).

108. James Bryce, *Democrazie moderne*, ed. Luigi Degli Occhi, 2 vols. (Milan: Mondadori, 1949–1953); Anna Lanfranchi, *Translation and Copyright in the Italian Book Trade: Publishers, Agents, and the State (1900–1947)*, chap. 4.

109. Giovanni Sartori, *Democratic Theory* (Detroit: Wayne State University Press, 1962).

110. Bryce met Pareto in April 1893, when Bryce was in Florence to accompany Queen Victoria: MS Bryce 451 ff. 14–15, Bryce to EMB, 4 April 1893. He described Pareto as 'an Italian Radical and pessimist Marchese'. But Pareto did not cite Bryce, and Mosca appears to have cited

The Holy Roman Empire but none of Bryce's writings on democracy: Gaetano Mosca, *Elementi di Scienza Politica* (Turin: Bocca, 1923), 372, 379–80.

111. Andrzej Olechnowicz, 'Civic Leadership and Education for Democracy: The Simons and the Wythenshawe Estate', *Contemporary British History* 14 (2000), 3–26; Hsiao-Yuh Ku, *Education for Democracy in England in World War II* (London: Routledge, 2020), chap. 8; Tom Hulme, 'Putting the City Back into Citizenship: Civics Education and Local Government in Britain, 1918–45', *Twentieth Century British History* 26 (2015), 26–51; Susanna Wright, *Morality and Citizenship in English Schools: Secular Approaches, 1897–1944* (London: Palgrave, 2016), chap. 7; John Ayshford et al., eds., *The Simons of Manchester: How One Family Shaped a City and a Nation* (Manchester: Manchester University Press, 2024), especially H. S. Jones and Chris Godden, 'Burghers and Citizens: The Simons and the University of Manchester', 251–73.

112. Mary Stocks, *Ernest Simon of Manchester* (Manchester: Manchester University Press, 1963), 45; E. D. Simon, '"City Manager". America's Municipal Experiment. What We Can Learn from It', *Manchester Guardian*, 21 December 1927, p. 9.

113. Sir E. D. Simon, *The Smaller Democracies* (London: Gollancz, 1939), 14; Stephen V. Ward, 'Searching for Effective and Democratic Town Planning: The International Travels of Sir Ernest Simon, 1936–1943', *Planning Perspectives* 32 (2017), 353–71.

114. Simon, *The Smaller Democracies*, 5.

115. Simon, 46. Bryce is also cited at 50.

116. 'North of England Education Conference', *Manchester Guardian*, 3 January 1936, p. 6. Also Sir E. D. Simon, 'Education for Democracy', *Political Quarterly* 5 (1934), 321–22.

117. 'Sir E. Simon Examines Democracy. Producing a Nation of Voters with Views of Their Own. The Effectiveness of Public Opinion', *Manchester Guardian*, 5 October 1935, p. 17.

118. E. D. Simon, 'A Citizen Challenges the Universities', *The Universities Review* 9 (1936), 7.

119. Tom Arnold-Forster, 'Walter Lippmann and Public Opinion', *American Journalism* 40 (2023), 55–57.

120. Among modern scholars, Roberto Romani largely echoes Wallas's view of Bryce as a scholar of the previous generation: specifically, he argues that Bryce tried to articulate a strong conception of citizenship and civic virtue without any substantive notion of community: 'One has the impression that the gospel of citizenship Bryce preaches addresses unrelated individuals': Romani, *National Character and Public Spirit*, 326.

Epilogue

1. 'The late Viscount Bryce, O.M., K.C.V.O.', *St Columba's Magazine*, MS Bryce 508 f. 26v.

2. MS Bryce 474 ff. 33–34, Sir Frederick Kenyon to EMB, 23 January 1922; MS Bryce 474 ff. 84–85, A. Laurence Lowell to EMB, 24 January 1922; MS Bryce 474 ff. 157–58, John X. Merriman to EMB, 24 January 1922.

3. MS Bryce 475 f. 51, Lord Lansdowne to EMB, 22 January 1922; MS Bryce 474 f. 163, Alfonso Merry del Val to EMB, 24 January 1922.

4. Wellcome Collection, Sir Thomas Barlow papers PP/BAR/C/1069, EMB to Sir Thomas Barlow, 1 February 1922.

5. Library of Congress, Elihu Root papers, box 139, EMB to Root, 3 February 1922.

6. MS Bryce 473, Randall T. Davidson to EMB, 24 January 1922. For Ilbert, MS Bryce 474 ff. 1–2, Ilbert to EMB, 24 January 1922: 'Old age did not touch him, could not touch him. I love to think of his having kept all his wonderful faculties unimpaired to the very last.'

7. MS Bryce 424 ff. 3–4, Jessie Ilbert [Lady Ilbert] to EMB, 24 January 1922.

8. MS Bryce 473 ff. 3–4, C. M. Darwin [Mrs Leonard Darwin] to EMB, 23 January 1922.

9. MS Bryce 473 ff. 5–6, Leonard Darwin to EMB, 24 January 1922.

10. MS Bryce 473 f. 33, Sir Edward Donner to EMB, 24 January 1922.

11. MS Bryce 476 f. 10, C. P. Scott to EMB, 25 January 1922; f. 31, Eleanor Sidgwick to EMB, 24 January 1922.

12. MS Bryce 475 ff. 74–75, John Dyneley Prince (American academic and diplomat) to EMB, 8 February 1922: 'His wonderful career of unceasing and marvellously versatile activity and his thorough treatment of every subject he undertook have made him a model for all scholars.'

13. MS Bryce 476 ff. 190–91, George Wrong to EMB, 5 February 1922.

14. MS Bryce 474 ff. 84–85, A. L. Lowell to EMB, 24 January 1922. See also MS Bryce 474 ff. 204–5, Sara Norton [daughter of Charles Eliot Norton] to EMB, 20 May 1922. She wrote of the 'real sense of personal loss' felt by many Americans, even if they had only a brief acquaintance with him.

15. MS Bryce 474 ff. 12–13, Godfrey James to EMB, 12 February 1922.

16. MS Bryce 474 ff. 39–40, Charlotte E. King to EMB, 28 January 1922. Mrs Godwin King was an antiquarian.

17. MS Bryce 474 f. 189, Gilbert Murray to EMB, 23 January 1922.

18. MS Bryce 476 f. 10, C. P. Scott to EMB, 25 January 1922.

19. MS Bryce 476 ff. 3–4, Sir Herbert Samuel to EMB, 27 January 1922; ff. 32–33, Sir John Simon to EMB, 1 February 1922.

20. *Daily Sketch*, 23 January 1922, cutting in MS Bryce 507 f. 97r.

21. 'The Citizen of the World', *The Nation* [London], 28 January 1922, cutting in MS Bryce 507 f. 100r. The same article pronounced: 'No man has so worthily represented to the world the best traditions of nineteenth-century British Liberalism, with its two guiding principles of free nationality and popular self-government.'

22. MS Bryce 477 ff. 63–66, telegram from the King and Queen; reported in, e.g., *Daily Telegraph*, 28 January 1922, p. 8.

23. 'The Late Viscount Bryce. American Tributes', *Daily Telegraph*, 24 January 1922, f. 31v.

24. 'The Late Lord Bryce', *Westminster Gazette*, 27 January 1922, cutting in MS Bryce 507 f. 97.

25. *The Times*, 28 January 1922, p. 13.

26. Typewritten text in MS Bryce 508 ff. 14–15

27. 'Armenian Tribute to Viscount Bryce', *Morning Post*, 31 January 1922, cutting in MS Bryce 508 f. 31r; also 'Armenian Tribute to Lord Bryce', *The Orient News*, 7 February 1922, MS Bryce 508 f. 60r.

28. In the capital, there was a commemorative service a year later at the (Presbyterian) Church of the Covenant: *Washington Post*, 29 January 1923, p. 2.

29. Writing to Marion, Manning declared that 'there has been no other influence at all equal to his on the common life of our two countries': MS Bryce 474 ff. 120–21, William T. Manning to EMB, 31 March 1922.

30. Printed addresses in MS Bryce 508 ff. 21–27.

31. 'Death of Lord Bryce', *The Times*, 23 January 1922, pp. 10–11.

32. MS Bryce 474 ff. 1–2, Ilbert to EMB, 24 January 1922; *Spectator*, 28 January 1922, cutting in MS Bryce 508 f. 34.

33. 'Lord Bryce. A Life of Incessant Activity. Mr Frederic Harrison's Appreciation', *The Times*, 6 February 1922, p. 6.

34. 'Notes and News', *Oxford Magazine*, 26 January 1922, cutting in MS Bryce 508 f. 35.

35. Gilbert Murray, 'Makers of History. Lord Bryce', *Headway* [n.d.], cutting in MS Bryce 508 f. 33.

36. MS Bryce 473 ff. 34–35, Ossian Donner to EMB, 27 January 1922.

37. MS Bryce 474 f. 137, Dr Adalbert Mastny to EMB, 23 January 1922. Both the Czech president, Masaryk, and the prime minister, Beneš, knew Bryce well. See also f. 134, Jan J. Masaryk (son) to EMB, 23 January 1922; also f. 138, Masty to EMB, 25 January 1922, where he transmits Beneš's sympathy for 'the loss of her husband and our unforgettable friend'.

38. MS Bryce 475 ff. 26–27, Stefan Panaretoff to EMB, 27 January 1922.

39. 'Viscount Bryce. Canon Barnes's Tribute to His Greatness', cutting in MS Bryce 508 f. 31, incorrectly labelled *The Times*, 31 January 1922. I think but have not been able to verify that it is from the *Morning Post* of the same date.

40. Curiously, when George Meredith died in 1909, Viscount Esher wrote a memorandum to the king recommending Bryce rather than Thomas Hardy as his successor in the Order of Merit, apparently not realising that Bryce had been appointed two years previously: Maurice V. Brett, ed., *Journals and Letters of Reginald Viscount Esher* (London: Nicholson & Watson, 1934), 2:389. I am grateful to Katharine Thomson of the Churchill Archives Centre for checking the original for me.

41. MS Bryce 424 ff. 33–34, F. G. Kenyon to EMB, 23 January 1922.

42. A point made long ago in by Collini, Winch, and Burrow in *That Noble Science of Politics*, 237.

43. Peter Burke, *The Polymath: A Cultural History from Leonardo da Vinci to Susan Sontag* (London: Yale University Press, 2021), 148–51.

44. Burke, *The Polymath*, 145–46.

45. 'Prefatory Note', *Encyclopaedia Britannica*, 10.

46. Burke, *The Polymath*, 188–90.

47. Arnold J. Toynbee, *Acquaintances* (London: Oxford University Press, 1967), 159.

BIBLIOGRAPHY

Primary Sourcces
Archival Collections

BODLEIAN LIBRARY, OXFORD

Papers of:

James Bryce (Viscount Bryce)
H. A. L. Fisher
John Morley (Viscount Morley)
Gilbert Murray
Arthur Ponsonby (1st Baron Ponsonby)
Sir Michael Sadler
Arnold Joseph Toynbee
Sir Alfred Zimmern

BRITISH ACADEMY

Archive of the Academy

BRITISH LIBRARY

Macmillan & Company Archive

CHURCHILL COLLEGE, CAMBRIDGE

Sir Cecil Arthur Spring Rice papers
William Thomas Stead papers

CUMBRIA ARCHIVE SERVICE

Sir Esme Howard (1st Baron Howard of Penrith) papers

DUKE UNIVERSITY (RUBENSTEIN LIBRARY)

James Bryce papers

ETON COLLEGE

Anne Thackeray Ritchie papers

GIRTON COLLEGE, CAMBRIDGE

Barbara Bodichon papers
Emily Davies papers

HARRIS MANCHESTER COLLEGE, OXFORD

L. P. Jacks papers

HARVARD UNIVERSITY (HOUGHTON LIBRARY)

Edwin Lawrence Godkin papers
Norton family papers

HULL HISTORY CENTRE

Harold Laski papers

JOHN RYLANDS LIBRARY, MANCHESTER

Edward Augustus Freeman papers
Guardian Archive
T. C. Horsfall papers
Thomas Frederick Tout papers

JOHNS HOPKINS UNIVERSITY, BALTIMORE

D. C. Gilman papers

KING'S COLLEGE, CAMBRIDGE

Oscar Browning papers

LIBRARY OF CONGRESS, WASHINGTON, DC

Andrew Carnegie papers
Theodore Roosevelt papers
Elihu Root papers
.Booker T. Washington papers

LONDON SCHOOL OF ECONOMICS AND POLITICAL SCIENCE

Josephine Butler papers
Frederic Harrison papers

MANCHESTER CENTRAL LIBRARY

Ashton family papers
Horsfall papers

MANCHESTER HIGH SCHOOL FOR GIRLS

School archive

MANSFIELD COLLEGE, OXFORD

Minute book of the Oxford University Nonconformists' Union

NATIONAL LIBRARY OF IRELAND

Alice Stopford Green papers
Sir Horace Plunkett papers

NEWCASTLE UNIVERSITY

Spence Watson collection

NEW YORK PUBLIC LIBRARY

Macmillan Company (NY) records

ORIEL COLLEGE, OXFORD

College archives
L. R. Phelps papers

PARLIAMENTARY ARCHIVES

Ilbert papers
Lloyd George papers

ROYAL HISTORICAL SOCIETY

George Prothero papers

ST ANDREWS UNIVERSITY

Wilfrid Ward papers

TRINITY COLLEGE, OXFORD

College archives

UNIVERSITY COLLEGE LONDON

Edwin Chadwick papers
Arthur Evans papers
Records of the Girls' Day School Trust and predecessors
Seton-Watson papers

UNIVERSITY OF LIVERPOOL LIBRARY

Rathbone family papers

UNIVERSITY OF MANCHESTER
ARCHIVE AND RECORD CENTRE

Owens College Archive
Victoria University Archive
Victoria University of Manchester Archive

UNIVERSITY OF TORONTO LIBRARY

James Mavor papers

WELLCOME COLLECTION

Sir Thomas Barlow papers

Printed Primary Sources

Bryce's works are listed in chronological order. This is not a comprehensive bibliography but is confined to works cited in the text and other substantial works. Bryce contributed almost three hundred articles to *The Nation* of New York over a period of more than four decades. Only those cited in the text are listed here. Articles in daily newspapers are not listed.

BRYCE'S BOOKS

The Holy Roman Empire (London: Macmillan, 1864; 2nd ed. 1866; 3rd ed. 1871). The 1904 edition has also been consulted.
The Trade Marks Registration Acts 1875 & 1876 (London: Maxwell, 1877).
Transcaucasia and Ararat: Being Notes of a Vacation Tour in the autumn of 1876 (London: Macmillan, 1877).
England and Ireland, an Introductory Statement (London: Committee on Irish Affairs, 1884).
The American Commonwealth (London: Macmillan, 1888, 3 vols.; 2nd ed., 2 vols., 1889; 3rd ed., 2 vols., 1893–1894; 4th ed., 2 vols., 1910).
Impressions of South Africa (London: Macmillan, 1897; 2nd ed. 1898, 3rd ed. 1899).
Studies in History and Jurisprudence (Oxford: Clarendon, 1901), 2 vols.
The Relations of the Advanced and the Backward Races of Mankind. Romanes Lecture 1902 (Oxford: Clarendon, 1902).
Studies in Contemporary Biography (London: Macmillan, 1903).
Constitutions (New York: Oxford University Press, 1905).
The Hindrances to Good Citizenship (New Haven, CT: Yale University Press, 1909).
South America: Observations and Impressions (London: Macmillan, 1912).
International Congress of Historical Studies, London, 1913: Presidential Address by the Right Hon. James Bryce, with Introductory and Supplementary Remarks by A. W. Ward (Oxford: Hart, 1913).
University and Historical Addresses Delivered During a Residence in the United States as Ambassador of Great Britain (London: Macmillan, 1913).

The Ancient Roman Empire and the British Empire in India. The Diffusion of Roman and English Law Throughout the World. Two Historical Studies (London: Oxford University Press, 1914).

Neutral Nations and the War (London: Macmillan, 1914).

Race Sentiment as a Factor in History (London: University of London Press, 1915).

Proposals for the Prevention of Future Wars (London: Allen & Unwin, 1917).

The Next Thirty Tears: Thoughts on the Work that Awaits Students of the Human Sciences. British Academy Presidential Address (London: Milford for Oxford University Press, 1917)

Essays and Addresses in War Time (London: Macmillan, 1918).

World History. The British Academy. The Annual Raleigh Lecture 1919 (London: Milford for Oxford University Press, 1919).

Modern Democracies (London: Macmillan, 1921), 2 vols.

The Study of American History: Being the Inaugural Lecture of the Sir George Watson Chair of American History, Literature and Institutions (Cambridge: Cambridge University Press, 1921).

International Relations: Eight Lectures Delivered in the United States in August, 1921 (London: Macmillan, 1922).

Memories of Travel (London: Macmillan, 1923).

BRYCE'S ARTICLES AND CONTRIBUTIONS TO BOOKS

'Tests in the English Universities', *North British Review* 42 (March 1865): 107–36.

'The Historical Aspect of Democracy', *Essays on Reform* (London: Macmillan, 1867), 239–78.

'The Worth of Educational Endowments', *Macmillan's Magazine* 19 (April 1869), 517–24.

'American Experience in the Relief of the Poor', *Macmillan's Magazine* 25 (November 1871), 54–65.

'The Legal Profession in America', *Macmillan's Magazine* 25 (January 1872), 206–17.

'American Judges', *Macmillan's Magazine* 25 (March 1872), 422–32.

'On Some Peculiarities of Society in America', *Cornhill Magazine* 26 (December 1872), 704–16.

'Icelandic Travel', *Saturday Review* 24.894 (14 December 1872), 759–60.

'The Organization of a Legal Department of Government', *Fortnightly Review* 13 (March 1873), 316–32.

'Iceland Politics', *Saturday Review* 36.931 (30 August 1873), 273–75.

'The Judicature Act of 1873 in Its Relation to the History of the Judicial System in England', in *Essays and Addresses by Professors and Lecturers of the Owens College, Manchester* (London: Macmillan, 1874), 423–63.

'Impressions of Iceland', *Cornhill Magazine* 29 (May 1874), 553–70.

'Cleasby and Vigfusson's Icelandic Dictionary', *The Nation* [New York] 18 (18 June 1874), 399–400.

'A Few Words on the Oxford University Bill', *Fortnightly Review* 19 (May 1876), 771–76.

'Russia and Turkey', *Fortnightly Review* 20 (December 1876), 793–808.

'Transcaucasia', *Cornhill Magazine* 35 (May 1877), 536–55.

'Constantinople', *Macmillan's Magazine* 37 (February 1878), 334–52.

'The Future of Asiatic Turkey', *Fortnightly Review* 23 (June 1878), 925–36.

'The Ascent of Ararat', *Alpine Journal* 8 (1878), 208–13.

'On Armenia and Mount Ararat', *Proceedings of the Royal Geographical Society* 22.3 (1878), 169–86.

'The Polish Alps', *Cornhill Magazine* 39 (February 1879), 213–30.

'Zips', *Cornhill Magazine* 39 (May 1879), 591–613.

'The Death of Mr Darwin', *The Nation* (New York) 34 (4 May 1882), 377–78.

'Professor T. H. Green', *Contemporary Review* 41 (May 1882), 857–81.

'Some Aspects of American Public Life', *Fortnightly Review* 32 (November 1882), 634–55.

'The Future of the English Universities', *Fortnightly Review* 33 (March 1883), 382–403.

'Green, John Richard. In Memoriam', *Macmillan's Magazine* 48 (May 1883), 59–74.

'Nonconformity and the Universities. The Free Churches and a Theological Faculty', *British Quarterly Review* 158 (April 1884), 390–98.

'An Ideal University', *Contemporary Review* 45 (June 1884), 836–56.

'Do We Need a Second Chamber?', *Contemporary Review* 46 (July 1884), 718–38.

'English Opinion on the Presidential Contest', *The Nation* (New York) 39 (16 October 1884), 328–29.

'The Franchise Bill Campaign', *The Nation* (New York) 39 (13 November 1884), 414–15.

'Surrender, or Compromise?', *The Nation* (New York) 39 (11 December 1884), 499–500.

'Suvarof in the Alps', *Saturday Review* 58.1520 (13 December 1884), 750–51.

'The English Redistribution Bill', *The Nation* (New York) 40 (8 January 1885), 27–29.

'M. Sardou's "Théodora"', *Contemporary Review* 47 (February 1885), 266–75.

'England: The Progress of Democracy', *The Nation* (New York) 40 (12 February 1885), 134–36.

'The Troubles of England', *The Nation* (New York) 40 (26 February 1885), 175–76.

'England: The Two Parties and Their troubles', *The Nation* (New York) 41 (20 August 1885), 151–52.

'Conditions of the Irish Problem', *The Nation* (New York) 41 (15 September 1885), 296–97.

'England: The Party Programmes', *The Nation* (New York) 41 (22 October 1885), 339–40.

'Prefatory Note', *English Historical Review* 1 (1886), 1–6.

'Alternative Policies in Ireland', *The Nineteenth Century* 19 (February 1886), 312–28.

'History and Geography', *Contemporary Review* 49 (March 1886), 426–43.

'The Relations of History and Geography', *Littell's Living Age* 169, no. 2181 (April 1886), 67–77.

'The Past and Future of the Irish Question', *New Princeton Review* 3.1 (January 1887), 48–72.

'The Life of Justinian by Theophilus', *English Historical Review* 2 (1887), 657–86.

'How We Became Home Rulers', *Contemporary Review* 51 (May 1887), 736–56.

'The Predictions of Hamilton and de Tocqueville', *Johns Hopkins University Studies in Historical and Political Science* Series 5 (September 1887), 5–57.

'Introduction', in *Two Centuries of Irish History 1691–1870* (London: Kegan Paul, Trench, 1888), xi–xxxv.

'A Word as to the Speakership', *North American Review* 151 (October 1890), 385–98.

'An Age of Discontent', *Contemporary Review* 59 (January 1891), 14–28.

'Thoughts on the Negro Problem', *North American Review* 153 (December 1891), 641–80.

'The Migrations of the Races of Men Considered Historically', *Contemporary Review* 62 (July 1892), 128–49.

'Edward Augustus Freeman', *English Historical Review* 7 (1892), 497–509.

'Political Organizations in the United States and England', *North American Review* 156 (January 1893), 105–18.

'Constitution and Political Institutions of the United States', in *The United States, with an Excursion in to Mexico: Handbook for Travellers*, ed. Karl Baedeker (Leipzig: Baedeker, 1893), xlvi–lxii.

'The Teaching of Civic Duty', *Contemporary Review* 64 (July 1893), 14–28.

'British Feeling on the Venezuelan Question', *North American Review* 162 (February 1896), 145–53.

'Two South African Constitutions', *The Forum* [New York] 21 (April 1896), 145–64.

'The Mayoralty Election in New York', *Contemporary Review* 72 (November 1897), 751–60.

'Equality', *The Century Illustrated Monthly Magazine* [New York] 56 (July 1898), 459–68.

'Some Thoughts on the Policy of the United States', *Harper's New Monthly Magazine* 97 (September 1898), 609–18.

'The Essential Unity of Britain and America', *Atlantic Monthly* 82 (1898), 22–29.

'Commercial Education', *North American Review* 168 (June 1899), 694–707.

'The Historical Causes of the Present War in South Africa', *North American Review* 169 (December 1899), 737–59.

'Introductory Essay', in *The World's History: A Survey of Man's Record*, ed. Dr H. F. Helmolt (London: Heinemann, 1901) 1: xvii–lx.

'Some Reflections on the State of Cuba', *North American Review* 174 (January 1902), 445–56.

'Some Traits of Mr Gladstone's Character', *Fortnightly Review* 71 (January 1902), 13–20.

'The Importance of Geography in Education', *The Geographical Teacher* 1 (February 1902), 49–61.

'A Few Words on the New Education Bill', *The Nineteenth Century and After* 51 (May 1902), 849–57.

'Introductory Address on the Use and Purpose of a Sociological Society', *Sociological Papers* 1 (1904), xiii–xviii.

'The Letters of Lord Acton', *North American Review* 178 (May 1904), 698–710.

'The Study of Popular Governments I', *Quarterly Review* 203 (1905), 170–91.

'The Study of Popular Governments II', *Quarterly Review* 203 (1905), 387–410.

'Some Difficulties in Colonial Government Encountered by Great Britain and How They Have Been Met', *Annals of the American Academy of Political and Social Science* 30.1 (1907), 16–23.

'The Influence of National Character and Historical Environment on the Development of the Common Law', *Journal of the Society of Comparative Legislation* 8.2 (1907), 203–216.

'What Is Progress?', *Atlantic Monthly* 100 (August 1907), 145–56.

'The World and Its Story. A View Across the Ages. An Introduction to the History of the World', in *Harmsworth History of the World*, ed. Arthur Mee (London: Carmelite House, 1907), 1:7–59.

'The Extension of Roman and English Law Throughout the World', in *Select Essays in Anglo-American Legal History* (Boston: Little, Brown, 1907), 1:574–621.

'The Methods and Conditions of Legislation in Our Time', *Columbia Law Review* 8.3 (March 1908), 157–71.

'The Duty of the Stronger to the Weaker Races', *Christian Advocate* 19 June 1908, 6–9.

'Religion and Moral Education', *Religious Education* 4 (1909), 30–33.

'Allegiance to Humanity', *The Outlook* 5 June 1909, 317–19.

'The Relations of Political Science to History and to Practice: Presidential Address, Fifth Annual Meeting of the American Political Science Association', *American Political Science Review* 3.1 (1909), 1–19.

'Personal Reminiscences of Charles Darwin and of the Reception of the "Origin of Species"', *Proceedings of the American Philosophical Society* 48, no. 193 (1909), iii–xiv.

'Impressions of a Traveller Among Non-Christian Races', *International Review of Mission* 1.1 (January 1912), 15–19.

'Goldwin Smith', *North American Review* 199 (April 1914), 513–27.

'Prefatory Note' to the *Encyclopaedia Britannica*, 11th ed. 'Handy volume' issue (Chicago: Hooper, 1915), 1:1–10.

'Stray Thoughts on American Literature', *North American Review* 201 (March 1915), 357–62.

'The Mental Training of a traveller', *Geographical Journal* 45.2 (1915), 110–22.

'Religion as a Factor in the History of Empires', *Journal of Roman Studies* 5 (1915), 1–22.

'The Defence of Right', in *For the Right: Essays and Addresses by Members of the 'Fight for Right' Movement*, by Francis Younghusband et al. (London: Unwin, 1916), 1–5.

'Preface', to Jon Stefansson, *Denmark and Sweden with Iceland and Finland* (London: Fisher Unwin, 1916), xi–xii.

'The President's Address: The Worth of Ancient Literature for the Modern World', *Proceedings of the Classical Association*, vol. 14 (1917), also published as 'Our Educational Future. The

Worth of Ancient Literature to the Modern World', *Fortnightly Review* 101 (April 1917), 552–66.

'The Future of Palestine and the Hopes of the Jews', *Menorah Journal* 4.3 (June 1918), 126–29.

'The Future of Armenia', *Contemporary Review* 114 (July 1918), 604–11.

'Some Thoughts on Dante in His Relation to Our Own Time', in *Dante: Essays in Commemoration 1321–1921* (London: University of London Press, 1921), 1–15.

Parliamentary Papers

Schools Inquiry Commission PP 1867–1868 [3966]

Other Contemporary Works

Atkinson, A.G.B., ed. *Christian Conference Essays* (London: Black, 1900).

Bagehot, Walter. *The English Constitution*, ed. R.H.S. Crossman (London: Fontana, 1963).

[Bagehot, Walter.] 'Mr Gladstone and the People', *The Economist* 4 November 1871, in *The Collected Works of Walter Bagehot*, ed. Norman St John-Stevas (London: The Economist, 1968), 3:461–64.

Bagehot, Walter. *Physics and Politics: Or Thoughts on the Application of the Principles of 'Natural Selection' and 'Inheritance' to Political Society* [1873] (Cambridge: Cambridge University Press, 2010).

Bardeen, C. W. *A Manual of Civics for New York Schools* (Syracuse: Bardeen, 1902).

Beale, D., ed. *Reports Issued by the Schools' Inquiry Commission, on the Education of Girls* (London: Nutt, n.d.).

Biard d'Aunet, Georges. *L'Aurore australe. La société australienne, le socialisme en Australie, la constitution australienne* (Paris: Pion-Nourrit, 1907).

Boynton, Frank David. *School Civics: An Outline Study of the Origin and Development of Government and the Development of Political Institutions in the United States* (Boston: Ginn, 1904).

Bryce, A. Hamilton. *The Irish Question: Its Rise, History, and Present Aspect* (Aberdeen: Wyllie, 1889).

Bryce, R. J. *Letters on Crime, Intemperance, & Ignorance, in Relation to the Franchise. Reprinted or Abridged from the Belfast Newspapers with Introductory and Explanatory Notices* (Belfast: Mullan & the Irish Temperance League, 1884).

Bryce, R. J. *Practical Suggestions for Reforming the Educational Institutions of Scotland: Being an Attempt to Point out the Necessity for Desectarianising the Schools and Universities Simultaneously; and the Means Whereby This May Be Accomplished* (Edinburgh: Oliphant, 1852).

Bryce, R. J. *Sketch of a Plan for a System of National Education for Ireland Including Hints for the Improvement of Education in Scotland* (London: Cowie, 1828).

Bryce, R. J. *Speech Against Sectarian Training Colleges* (Edinburgh: Morrison and Gibb, n.d. [1883]).

Bryce, Reuben John. *A Short Study of State Socialism* (London: Baynes, 1903).

Butler, Josephine E. *Woman's Work and Woman's Culture: A Series of Essays* (London: Macmillan, 1869).

Campbell, Lewis. *On the Nationalisation of the Old English Universities* (London: Chapman and Hall, 1901).

Christian Union. Report of Speeches on Union with the Free Church Delivered in the United Presbyterian Synod Friday, 15th May 1863, rev. ed. (Edinburgh: Andrew Elliott, 1863).

Clark, Frederick H. *Outlines of Civics. Being a Supplement to Bryce's 'American Commonwealth', Abridged Edition* (New York: Macmillan, 1899).

Dalberg-Acton, John Emerich Edward (1st Baron Acton). *Essays on Freedom and Power*, ed. Gertrude Himmelfarb (Glencoe, Ill.: Free Press, 1948).

Darbishire, R. D. *Quare fremuerunt gentes? 'The Open Brotherhood.' The Christianity of Jesus. An Address Delivered in Manchester College, Oxford, on October 15th, 1900* (Manchester: Rawson, n.d.).

Darbishire, R. D., ed. *Theology and Piety: Alike Free: From the Point of View of Manchester New College, Oxford* (London: Kegan Paul, Trench & Trübner, 1890).

Deniker, J. *The Races of Man: An Outline of Anthropology and Ethnography* (London: Scott, 1900).

[Dicey, A. V.] 'Democratic Assumptions. 1.—Vox populi', *The Nation* [New York] 51 (20 November 1890), 397–99; 'Democratic Assumptions. 2.—Progress and Popular Government', *The Nation* 52 (15 January 1891), 46–47; 'Democratic Assumptions. 3.—Liberty', *The Nation* 52 (18 June 1891), 497–98; 'Democratic Assumptions. 4.—Equality', *The Nation* 53 (16 July 1891), 46–47; 'Democratic Assumptions. 5.–Conclusion', *The Nation* 53 (30 July 1891), 83–84.

Dicey, A. V. *Introduction to the Law of the Constitution*, 4th ed. (London: Macmillan, 1893).

Dicey, Albert Venn. *Lectures on the Relations Between Law & Public Opinion in England During the Nineteenth Century* (London: Macmillan, 1905); 2nd ed. 1914.

Dicey, A. V. *Letters to a Friend on Votes for Women* (London: Murray, 1909).

Dicey, A. V. 'Mr Bryce on the Relation Between Whites and Blacks', *The Nation* [New York], 10 July 1902, 26–28.

Dixon, James Main. 'The Personality of James Bryce', *Methodist Review* 38.5 (1922), 701–13.

Du Bois, W. E. Burghardt. 'Reconstruction and Its Benefits', *American Historical Review* 15.4 (1910), 781–99.

Du Bois, W. E. Burghardt. *The Health and Physique of the Negro American* (Atlanta: Atlanta University Press, 1906).

Du Bois, W. E. Burghardt. *The Negro* [1915] (Toronto: Dover, 2001).

Du Bois, W. E. Burghardt. *The Souls of Black Folk* (Chicago: McClurg, 1903).

Duguit, Léon. *Manuel de droit constitutionnel: théorie générale de l'Etat, organisation* politique (Paris: A. Fontemoing, 1907).

Duguit, Léon. *Traité de droit constitutionnel* (Paris: A. Fontemoing, 1911).

Dyer, Louis. 'Mr Bryce's Romanes Lecture', *The Nation* 74 (26 June 1902), 503–4.

Essays on Reform (London: Macmillan, 1867).

Fradenburgh, A. G. *American Civics: A Text Book for High Schools, Normal Schools, and Academies* (New York: Hinds, Noble & Eldredge, 1906).

Freeman, Edward A. *History of Federal Government: from the Foundation of the Achaian League to the Disruption of the United States* (London: Macmillan, 1863).

Freeman, Edward A. 'Oxford After Forty Years', *Contemporary Review* 51 (May 1887), 609–23, and 51 (June 1887), 814–30.

Freeman, Edward A. 'Some Aspects of Home Rule', *Contemporary Review* 49 (February 1886), 153–68.

Fustel de Coulanges, Numa Denis, *La Cité Antique: Etude sur le culte, le droit, les institutions de la Grèce et de Rome* (Paris: Hachette, 1864); translated as *The Ancient City: A Study on the Religion, Laws, and Institutions of Greece and Rome* (Baltimore: Johns Hopkins University Press, 1980).

Garrison, Wendell Phillips. 'The South and the Black Man', *The Nation* [New York] 60 (31 January 1895), 86–87.

[Gladstone, William Ewart.] 'Germany, France, and England', *Edinburgh Review* 132 (October 1870), 554–93.

Godkin, Edwin Lawrence. *Problems of Modern Democracy: Political and Economic Essays* (New York: Scribner, 1896).

Godkin, Edwin L. *Unforeseen Tendencies of Democracy* (Boston: Houghton and Mifflin, 1898).

Harrison, Frederic. *Order and Progress* (London: Longmans, Green, 1875).

Hauriou, Maurice. *Précis de droit constitutionnel* (Paris: Sirey, 1923; 2nd ed. 1929).

Hawkins, Edward. *Additional Notes on Subscription Academical and Clerical: with Reference to the Clerical Subscription Act of 1865, the Republication of Tract XC, the Tests Abolition (Oxford) Bills* (Oxford: Parker, 1866).

Henson, Herbert Hensley. *Christian Morality, Natural, Developing, Final. Being the Gifford Lectures 1935–1936* (Oxford: Clarendon, 1936).

Hobhouse, L. T. *Democracy and Reaction* (London: Fisher Unwin, 1904).

Hobhouse, L. T. *Liberalism* (London: Thornton Butterworth, 1911).

Hobson, J. A. *The Crisis of Liberalism: New Issues of Democracy* (London: King, 1909).

'The Holy Roman Empire', *Spectator* 29 (October 1864).

Howe, Mark DeWolfe, ed. *The Correspondence of Mr Justice Holmes and Harold J. Laski*, 2 vols. (Cambridge, Mass: Harvard University Press, 1953).

Ignota (Elizabeth C. Wolstenholme Elmy). 'The Enfranchisement of Women', *Westminster Review* 164 (July and November 1905), 21–25 and 495–97.

Ignota (Elizabeth C. Wolstenholme Elmy). 'The Case for the Immediate Enfranchisement of the Women of the United Kingdom', *Westminster Review* 166 (November 1906), 508–21.

Ignota (Elizabeth C. Wolstenholme Elmy). 'Russia and the United Kingdom', *Westminster Review* 166 (August and September 1906), 164–68 and 284–93.

Lankester, Sir Ray, ed. *Natural Science and the Classical System in Education: Essays New and Old* (London: Heinemann, 1918).

Lecky, W.E.H. *Democracy and Liberty* (London: Longmans, Green, 1896).

Manchester College. Removal from London to Oxford. Revised Report of the Debate at the Annual Meeting of Trustees Held at University Hall, June 28, 1888 (Reprinted from the Inquirer Supplement of July 14, 1888) (London: Woodfall and Kinder, n.d.)

Mansel, Henry Longueville. *The Limits of Religious Thought Examined* (Oxford: Murray, 1858).

Marburg, Theodore. *League of Nations: A Chapter in the History of the Movement* (New York: Macmillan, 1919).

Mr Gladstone and the Nationalities of the United Kingdom (London: Quaritsch, 1887).

Masterman, C.F.G. *The New Liberalism* (London: Parsons, 1920).

Masterman, E.W.G. 'Palestine: Its Resources and Suitability for Colonization', *Geographical Journal* 50 (1917), 12–26.

May, Thomas Erskine. *Democracy in Europe: A History* (London: Longmans, Green, 1877).

Mill, John Stuart. *Considerations on Representative Government* (London: Parker, 1861).

Morgan, J. H. *German Atrocities: An Official Investigation* (London: Dutton, 1916).

Morgenthau, Henry. *All in a Life-Time* (New York: Doubleday, Page, 1922).

Mosca, Gaetano. *Elementi di Scienza Politica* (Turin: Bocca, 1923).

Muir, Ramsay. *The New Liberalism* (London: Daily News, 1923).

Murray, Gilbert. *A Conversation with Bryce. The James Bryce Memorial Lecture, Somerville College, Oxford, Friday 12 November 1943* (London: Oxford University Press, 1944).

The Neglect of Science: Report of Proceedings of a Conference Held in the Rooms of the Linnaean Society (London: Harrison, 1916).

Pattison, Mark. *Memoirs* (London: Macmillan, 1885).

'Proceedings of the United Presbyterian Synod', in *United Presbyterian Magazine* N.S. 1 (1857), 314–25.

'Reasons by Dr Bryce'. *Proceedings of the United Presbyterian Synod* 4 (1870–73), 54.

Reeves, William Pember. *State Experiments in Australia and New Zealand*, 2 vols. (London: Grant Richards, 1902).

Romanes Lectures Decennial Issue 1892–1900 (Oxford: Clarendon, 1900).

Roscoe, Henry Enfield. *The Life and Experiences of Henry Enfield Roscoe, D.C.L., LL.D., F.R.S.* (London: Macmillan, 1906).

Sadler, M. E. *Moral Instruction and Training in Schools: Report of an International Inquiry*, 2 vols. (London: Longmans, Green, 1908)

Scholes, Theophilus E. Samuel. *Glimpses of the Ages or the 'Superior' and 'Inferior' Races, So-Called, Discussed in the Light of Science and History* (London: Long, 1908).

[Seeley, John Robert.] *Ecce Homo. A Survey of the Life and Work of Jesus Christ* (London: Macmillan, 1866).

Sidgwick, Henry. *Elements of Politics* (London: Macmillan, 1891).

Siegfried, André. *La Démocratie en Nouvelle Zélande* (Paris: Colin, 1904).

Simon, Sir E. D. 'Education for Democracy', *Political Quarterly* 5 (1934), 307–22.

Simon, Sir E. D. *The Smaller Democracies* (London: Gollancz, 1939).

Smith, Goldwin. *Reminiscences*, ed. Arnold Haultain (New York: Macmillan, 1911).

Spencer, Herbert. *The Man Versus the State* (London: Williams & Norgate, 1884).

State-Aided Denominational Education and the 'Voluntary Schools (England) Bill, 1897' (Edinburgh: United Presbyterian College, 1897).

Synod Hall Lectures on Church and State by Ministers of the United Presbyterian Church (Edinburgh: United Presbyterian College Buildings, 1883).

Tardieu, André. *Notes sur les Etats-Unis* (Paris: Calmann-Lévy, 1908).

Tardieu, André. *La Révolution à refaire*, vol. 1, *Le Souverain captif* (Paris: Flammarion, 1936).

Turner, Henry Gyles. *The First Decade of the Australian Commonwealth: A Chronicle of Contemporary Politics, 1901–1910* (Melbourne: Mason, Firrth & M'Cutcheon, 1911).

Turner, Henry Gyles. *History of the Colony of Victoria*, 2 vols. (London: Longmans, Green, 1904).

Vossion, Louis. *La Nouvelle Australie et son avenir* (Paris: Guillaumin, 1902).

Wallas, Graham. *Human Nature in Politics* (London: Constable, 1908).

Wells, H. G. *The War that Will End War* (London: Palmer, 1914).

Secondary Sources

Unpublished Theses

Balshaw, June Marion. 'Suffrage, Solidarity and Strife: Political Partnerships and the Women's Movement 1880–1930', PhD diss., University of Greenwich, 1998.

Crewe, Thomas James. 'Political Leaders, Communication, and Celebrity in Britain, c. 1880–1900', PhD diss., University of Cambridge, 2016.

Gatrell, V.A.C. 'The Commercial Middle Class in Manchester, c. 1820–1857', PhD diss., University of Cambridge, 1971.

Lanfranchi, Anna. 'Negotiating Italian Translation Rights Across Anglo-American and Italian Publishing (1900–1947)', PhD diss., University of Manchester, 2021.

March, Philip. 'The Influence of Congregationalism on the New Journalism of W. T. Stead', PhD diss., Birkbeck, University of London, 2019.

Mazzei, Federico. 'Cattolici e liberali all'antifascismo alla seconda guerra mondiale (1925–1943)', PhD diss., University of Bologna, 2012–2013.

Pàlsdóttir, Sigrún. 'Icelandic Culture in Victorian Thought: British Interpretations (c. 1850–1900) of the history, politics and society of Iceland', D.Phil diss., University of Oxford, 2001.

Shaw, Ian J. 'High Calvinists in Action, c. 1810–60: A Study of the Response of Some High Calvinist Ministers to Religious and Secular Problems in Manchester and London, Compared with the Work of Some Evangelical Calvinists', PhD diss., University of Manchester, 1996.

Smith, William J. 'Manchester High School for Girls: The Pioneering Years, 1874–1924', PhD diss., University of Manchester, 2004.

Stowell, Liam. 'The Athens of Example: The Classical World in British International Thought, 1900–1939', PhD diss., University of Manchester, 2020.

Published works

Abbott, Evelyn, and Lewis Campbell. *The Life and Letters of Benjamin Jowett*, 2 vols. (London: Murray, 1897).

Addison, W. Innes. *The Matriculation Albums of the University of Glasgow from 1728 to 1858* (Glasgow: MacLehose, 1913).

Addison, W. Innes, ed. *A Roll of the Graduates of the University of Glasgow from 31st December 1727 to 31st December 1897* (Glasgow: MacLehose, 1898).

Alberti, Samuel J.M.M. *Nature and Culture: Objects, Disciplines and the Manchester Museum* (Manchester: Manchester University Press, 2009).

Aldis, James A. 'Reminiscences of the Abolition of Religious Tests in the Universities of Oxford and Cambridge', *Baptist Quarterly* 4.6 (1929), 249–58.

Alexander, Eleanor, ed. *Primate Alexander, Archbishop of Armagh: A Memoir* (London: Arnold, 1913).

Allen, Gemma. 'The Rise of the Ambassadress: English Ambassadorial Wives and Early Modern Diplomatic Culture', *Historical Journal* 62.3 (2019), 617–38.

Arcenas, Claire Rydell. 'On the Purpose of Humanities Education: A Historical Perspective from the Mid-Twentieth-Century United States', in *Writing the History of the Humanities: Questions, Themes and Approaches*, ed. Herman Paul (London: Bloomsbury, 2022), 345–64.

Armstrong, William M., ed. *The Gilded Age Letters of E. L. Godkin* (Albany: State University of New York Press, 1974).

Arnold-Forster, Tom. 'Walter Lippmann and Public Opinion', *American Journalism* 40.1 (2023), 51–79.

Ayshford, John, Martin Dodge, H. S. Jones, Diana Leitch, and Janet Wolff, eds., *The Simons of Manchester: How One Family Shaped a City and a Nation* (Manchester: Manchester University Press, 2024).

Bailyn, Bernard. *The Ideological Origins of the American Revolution* (Cambridge, Mass.: Harvard University Press, 1967).

Bassett, Arthur Tilney. *The Life of the Rt. Hon. John Edward Ellis M.P.* (London: Macmillan, 1914).

Bastian, Corina, Eva Kathrin Dada, Hillard von Thiessen, and Christian Windler, eds. *Das Geschlecht der Diplomatie: Geschlechterrollen in den Aussenbeziehungen vom Spätmittelalter bis zum 20. Jahrhundert* (Cologne: Böhlau, 2014).

Bebbington, D. W. *The Nonconformist Conscience: Chapel and Politics, 1870–1914* (London: Allen & Unwin, 1982).

Bell, Duncan. *Dreamworlds of Race: Empire and the Utopian Destiny of Anglo-America* (Princeton, N.J.: Princeton University Press, 2020).

Bell, Duncan. *The Idea of Greater Britain: Empire and the Future of World Order, 1860–1900* (Princeton, N.J.: Princeton University Press, 2007).

Bell, G.K.A. *Randall Davidson, Archbishop of Canterbury*, 2 vols. (London: Oxford University Press, 1935).

Benito, Héctor Domínguez. *James Bryce y los fundamentos intelectuales del internacionalismo liberal* (Madrid: Centro de Estudios Políticos y Constitucionales, 2018).

Bennett, Joshua. *God and Progress: Religion and History in British Intellectual Culture, 1845–1914* (Oxford: Oxford University Press, 2019).

Bennett, Mary. *The Ilberts in India 1882–1886: An Imperial Miniature* (Putney: British Association for Cemeteries in South Asia, 1995).

Betts, Jocelyn Paul. 'After the Freeholder: Republican and Liberal Themes in the Works of Samuel Laing', *Modern Intellectual History* 16.1 (2019), 57–86.

Biagini, Eugenio. *British Democracy and Irish Nationalism 1876–1906* (Cambridge: Cambridge University Press, 2007).

Biagini, Eugenio. *Liberty, Retrenchment and Reform: Popular Liberalism in the Age of Gladstone, 1860–1880* (Cambridge: Cambridge University Press, 1992).

Biagini, Eugenio F. 'Neo-Roman Liberalism: "Republican" Values and British Liberalism, ca. 1860–1875', *History of European Ideas* 29.1 (2003), 55–72.

Biddiss, Michael D. 'The Universal Races Congress of 1911', *Race* 13.1 (1971), 37–46.

Bland, Lucy. *Banishing the Beast: Feminism, Sex and Morality* (London: Tauris, 1995).

Bowman, Stephen. *The Pilgrims Society and Public Diplomacy, 1895–1945* (Edinburgh: Edinburgh University Press, 2018).

Boyce, D. George, and Alan O'Day. *Gladstone and Ireland: Politics, Religion and Nationality in the Victorian Age* (Basingstoke: Palgrave, 2010).

Bremner, G. A., and J. Conlin, eds. *Edward Augustus Freeman and Victorian Cultural Politics* (Proceedings of the British Academy, vol. 202) (Oxford: Oxford University Press, 2015).

Brent, Richard. *Liberal Anglican Politics: Whiggery, Religion, and Reform 1830–1841* (Oxford: Clarendon, 1987).

British Academy. 'Humanities Scholars Who Worked in Military Intelligence in the Second World War'. https://www.thebritishacademy.ac.uk/publishing/memoirs/humanities-scholars-who-worked-military-intelligence-second-world-war/.

Brock, M. G., and M. C. Curthoys, eds. *Nineteenth-Century Oxford*, Part 1 (Vol. 6 of The History of the University of Oxford) (Oxford: Clarendon, 1997) and Part 2 (Vol. 7) (Oxford: Clarendon, 2000).

Brown, Callum. *Religion and Society in Scotand since 1707* (Edinburgh: Edinburgh University Press, 1997).

Brown, W. E. *The History of Bolton School* (Bolton: Bolton School, 1976).

Bueltmann, Tanja. 'Anglo-Saxonism and the Racialization of the English Diaspora', in *Locating the English Diaspora, 1500–2010*, ed. Tanja Bueltmann, David T. Gleeson, and Donald M. MacRaild (Liverpool: Liverpool University Press, 2012), 118–33.

Burke, Peter. *The Polymath: A Cultural History from Leonardo da Vinci to Susan Sontag* (London: Yale University Press, 2021).

Burns, Arthur. 'From "Th'Owd Church" to Manchester Cathedral, 1830–1914', in *Manchester Cathedral: A History of the Collegiate Church and Cathedral, 1421 to the Present*, ed. Jeremy Gregory (Manchester: Manchester University Press, 2021), 186–240.

Burrow, J. W. 'Some British Views of the United States Constitution', in *The United Stated Constitution: The First 200 Years*, ed. R. C. Simmons (Manchester: Manchester University Press, 1989), 116–37.

Burstall, Sara. *The Story of the Manchester High School for Girls, 1871–1911* (Manchester: Manchester University Press, 1911).

Bush, Julia. '"Special Strengths for Their Own Special Duties": Women, Higher Education and Gender Conservatism in Late Victorian Britain', *History of Education* 34.4 (2005), 387–405.

Bush, Julia. *Women against the Vote: Female Anti-Suffragism in Britain* (Oxford: Oxford University Press, 2007).

Campbell, John, in collaboration with Richard McLaughlan. *Haldane: The Forgotten Statesman Who Shaped Britain and Canada* (London: Hurst, 2020).

Campos-Rudinsky, Jordan de. 'James Bryce and Parliamentary Sovereignty', *Modern Intellectual History* 19.3 (2022), 734–56.

Catto, Jeremy, ed. *Oriel College: A History* (Oxford: Oxford University Press, 2013).

Ceadel, Martin. *Pacifism in Britain, 1914–1945: The Defining of a Faith* (Oxford: Clarendon, 1980).

Chaloner, W. H. *The Movement for the Extension of Owens College, Manchester, 1863–73* (Manchester: Manchester University Press, 1973).

Chapple, J.A.V., and Arthur Pollard, eds. *The Letters of Mrs Gaskell* (Manchester: Mandolin, 1997).

Clarke, P. F. *Lancashire and the New Liberalism* (Cambridge: Cambridge University Press, 1971).

Clough, Blanche Athena. *A Memoir of Anne Jemima Clough* (London: Edward Arnold, 1897).

Collini, Stefan, Donald Winch, and J. W. Burrow. *That Noble Science of Politics: A Study in Nineteenth-Century Intellectual History* (Cambridge: Cambridge University Press, 1983).

Collini, Stefan. 'Introduction', in John Stuart Mill, *Essays on Equality, Law, and Education*, ed. John M. Robson (vol. 21 of *The Collected Works of John Stuart Mill* (London: Routledge & Kegan Paul, 1984), vii–lvi.

Collini, Stefan. 'Looking Back at "The Next Thirty Years"', *British Academy Review*, Summer 2017, https://www.thebritishacademy.ac.uk/publishing/review/30/looking-back-at-next-thirty-years/.

Collini, Stefan. 'Political Theory and the "Science of Society" in Victorian Britain', *Historical Journal* 23.1 (1980), 203–31.

Collini, Stefan. *Public Moralists: Political Thought and Intellectual Life in Britain* (Oxford: Clarendon, 1991).

Collini, Stefan. *Speaking of Universities* (London: Verso, 2017).

Collini, Stefan. *What Are Universities For?* (London: Penguin, 2012).

Constant, Benjamin. *Political Writings*, ed. Biancamaria Fontana (Cambridge: Cambridge University Press, 1988).

Conti, Gregory. 'Ostrogorski Before and After: Three Moments in Antipartyism and "Elite Theory"', *Constellations* 27 (2020), 169–84.

Conti, Gregory. *Parliament the Mirror of the Nation: Representation, Deliberation, and Democracy in Victorian Britain* (Cambridge: Cambridge University Press, 2019).

Cowling, Maurice. *Religion and Public Doctrine in Modern England, Volume 3: Accommodations* (Cambridge: Cambridge University Press, 2001).

Craig, David. 'Republicanism Versus Liberalism: Towards a Pre-history', *Intellectual History Review* 33.1 (2023), 101–30.

Dakers, Caroline. *The Holland Park Circle: Artists and Victorian Society* (London: Yale University Press, 1999).

Davey, Jennifer. *Mary, Countess of Derby, and the Politics of Victorian Britain* (Oxford, Oxford University Press, 2019).

Davie, George Elder. *The Democratic Intellect: Scotland and her Universities in the Nineteenth Century* (Edinburgh: Edinburgh University Press, 1961).

Delap, Lucy. 'Feminist and Anti-feminist Encounters in Edwardian Britain', *Historical Research* 78.201 (2005), 377–99.

Dickinson, G. Lowes. *The Autobiography of G. Lowes Dickinson, and Other Unpublished Writings*, ed. Dennis Proctor (London: Duckworth, 1973).

Dijn, Annelien de, *Freedom: An Unruly History* (Cambridge, Mass.: Harvard University Press, 2020).

Dowling, Linda. *Hellenism and Homosexuality in Victorian Oxford* (London: Cornell University Press, 1994).

Eulau, Heinz H. F. 'Theories of Federalism Under the Holy Roman Empire', *American Political Science Review* 35.4 (1941): 643–64.

Eversley, Lord. *Commons, Forests and Footpaths*, rev. ed. (London: Cassell, 1910).

Fallows, I. B. *William Hulme and his Trust* (Chichester: Pillimore, 2008).

Faucher, Charlotte. *Propaganda, Gender, and Cultural Power: Projections and Perceptions of France in Britain c. 1880–1944* (Oxford: Oxford University Press for the British Academy, 2022).

Fisher, Hervey. *From a Tramp's Wallet: A Life of Douglas William Freshfield* (Banham, Norfolk: Erskine Press, 2001).

Foner, Eric. *Reconstruction: America's Unfinished Revolution 1863–1877*, updated ed. (New York: Harper & Row, 2014).

Forster, E. M. *Goldsworthy Lowes Dickinson* (London: Arnold, 1934).

Foster, Joseph. *Alumni Oxoniensis: The Members of the University of Oxford, 1715–1886* (Oxford: Parker, 1888).

García, Itzel Toledo. 'América Latina en el pensamiento internacional británico: el caso de James Bryce', *Revista de historia de América*, no. 161 (2021), 115–39.

Gardner, Alice. *A Short History of Newnham College Cambridge* (Cambridge: Bowes & Bowes, 1921).

Gellner, Ernest. *Conditions of Liberty: Civil Society and Its Rivals* (Harmondsworth: Penguin, 1996).

Gérin, Winifred. *Elizabeth Gaskell* (London: Oxford University Press, 1976).

Ghosh, Peter. 'Mill Before Liberalism (parts I and II)', *History of European Ideas* 50.5 (2024), 785–836.

Givens, Terri E. *The Roots of Racism: The Politics of White Supremacy in the U.S. and Europe* (Bristol: Bristol University Press, 2022).

Gleadle, Kathryn. *The Early Feminists: Radical Unitarians and the Emergence of the Women's Rights Movement, 1831–51* (Basingstoke: Macmillan, 1998).

Goldie, Mark. 'The Ancient Constitution and the Languages of Political Thought', *Historical Journal* 62.1 (2019), 3–34.

Goldstein, Doris S. 'The Origins and Early Years of the English Historical Review', *English Historical Review* 101.1 (1986), 6–19.

Graham, J. A., and B. A. Phythian. *The Manchester Grammar School 1515–1965* (Manchester: Manchester University Press, 1965).

Green, Simon. 'Archbishop Frederick Temple on Meritocracy, Liberal Education and the Idea of a Clerisy', in *Public and Private Doctrine: Essays in British History Presented to Maurice Cowling*, ed. Michael Bentley (Cambridge: Cambridge University Press, 1993), 149–67.

Griffin, Ben. *The Politics of Gender in Victorian Britain* (Cambridge: Cambridge University Press, 2012).

Haldane, Richard Burdon. *An Autobiography* (London: Hodder & Stoughton, 1929).

Halévy, Elie. *L'Ère des tyrannies: études sur le socialisme et la guerre* (Paris: Gallimard, 1938).

Hamilton, Mary Agnes. *Remembering My Good Friends* (London: Cape, 1944).

Hammond, J. L. *C.P. Scott of the Manchester Guardian* (London: Bell, 1934).

Harris, Jose. *Private Lives, Public Spirit: A Social History of Britain 1870–1914* (Oxford: Oxford University Press, 1993).

Harrison, Brian. *Separate Spheres: The Opposition to Women's Suffrage in Britain* (New York: Holmes & Meier, 1978).

Harte, Negley, John North, and Georgina Brewis. *The World of UCL*, 4th ed. (London: UCL Press, 2018).

Harvie, Christopher. 'Ideology and Home Rule: James Bryce, A. V. Dicey and Ireland, 1880–1887', *English Historical Review* 91.2 (1976), 311–12.

Harvie, Christopher. *The Lights of Liberalism: University Liberals and the Challenge of Democracy, 1860–86* (London: Allen Lane, 1976).

Haultain, Arnold, ed. *A Selection from Goldwin Smith's Correspondence* (New York: Duffield, 1913).

Hawkesworth, Mary, *Embodied Power: Demystifying Disembodied Politics* (Abingdon: Routledge, 2016).

Hawkins, Angus. *Victorian Political Culture: 'Habits of Heart and Mind'* (Oxford: Oxford University Press, 2015).

Hesketh, Ian. 'Behold the (Anonymous) Man: J. R. Seeley and the Publishing of Ecce Homo', *Victorian Review* 38.1 (2012), 93–112.

Hesketh, Ian. *Victorian Jesus: J. R. Seeley, Religion, and the Cultural Significance of Anonymity* (Toronto: University of Toronto Press, 2017).

Hinchliff, Peter. *Frederick Temple, Archbishop of Canterbury: A Life* (Oxford: Clarendon, 1998).

Hobsbawm, Eric. *Nations and Nationalism since 1789: Programme, Myth, Reality*, 2nd ed. (Cambridge: Cambridge Univeristy Press, 1992).

Hobson, J. A. *Confessions of an Economic Heretic* (London: Allen & Unwin, 1938).

Holmes, Andrew R. *The Shaping of Ulster Presbyterian Belief and Practice, 1770–1840* (Oxford: Oxford University Press, 2006).

Holton, Sandra Stanley. *Suffrage Days: Stories from the Women's Suffrage Movement* (London: Routledge, 2016).

Hont, Istvan, and Michael Ignatieff, eds. *Wealth and Virtue: The Shaping of Political Economy in the Scottish Enlightenment* (Cambridge: Cambridge University Press, 1983).

Horne, John N., and Alan Kramer. 'German "Atrocities" and Franco-German Opinion, 1914: The Evidence of German Soldiers' Diaries', *Journal of Modern History* 66.1 (1994), 1–33.

Horne, John N., and Alan Kramer. *German Atrocities, 1914: A History of Denial* (New Haven, Conn.: Yale University Press, 2001).

Horne, John N., and Alan Kramer. 'War Between Soldiers and Enemy Civilians, 1914–1915', in *Great War, Total War: Combat and Mobilization on the Western Front, 1914–1918*, ed. Roger Chickering and Stig Förster (Cambridge: Cambridge University Press, 2000), 153–68.

Houston, Craig. *Algernon Sidney and the Republican Heritage in England and America* (Princeton, N.J.: Princeton University Press, 1991).

Howarth, Janet, and Mark Curthoys. 'The Political Economy of Women's Higher Education in Late Nineteenth and Early Twentieth-Century Britain', *Historical Research* 60. 142 (1987), 208–31.

Hull, Isabel V. *Absolute Destruction: Military Culture and the Practices of War in Imperial Germany* (Ithaca, N.Y.: Cornell University Press, 2005).

Hulme, Tom, 'Putting the City Back Into Citizenship: Civics Education and Local Government in Britain, 1918–45', *Twentieth Century British History* 26.1 (2015), 26–51.

Ingleheart, Jennifer, ed. *Ancient Rome and the Construction of Modern Homosexual Identities* (Oxford: Oxford University Press, 2015).

Inman, Daniel, *The Making of Modern English Theology: God and the Academy at Oxford, 1833–1945* (Minneapolis: Fortress, 2014).

Innes, Jo. 'National Education and Religion in the United Kingdom', blog post for the Opening Oxford 1871 project. https://openingoxford1871.web.ox.ac.uk/article/national-education, accessed 1 August 2023.

Innes, Joanna. '"L'éducation nationale" dans les îles Britanniques, 1765–1815: variations britanniques et irlandaises sur un thème européen', *Annales. Histoire, Sciences Sociales* 65.5 (2010), 1087–1116.

Ions, Edmund. *James Bryce and American Democracy 1870–1922* (London: Macmillan, 1968).

Irish, Tomás. 'The "Moral Basis" of Reconstruction: Humanitarianism, Intellectual Relief and the League of Nations, 1918–1925', *Modern Intellectual History* 17.3 (2020), 769–800.

Irish, Tomás. *The University at War, 1914–25: Britain, France, and the United States* (Basingstoke: Palgrave, 2015).

Jacks, Lawrence Pearsall. *Life and Letters of Stopford Brooke*, 2 vols. (London: Murray, 1917).

Jackson, Julian. *France: The Dark Years, 1940–1944* (Oxford: Oxford University Press, 2001).

Jackson, Peter. 'Pierre Bourdieu, the "Cultural Turn", and the Practice of International History', *Review of International Studies* 34.1 (2008), 155–81.

Jackson, Walter A. *Gunnar Myrdal and America's Conscience: Social Engineering & Racial Liberalism, 1938–1987* (Chapel Hill: University of North Carolina Press, 1990).

Jalland, Pat. *Women, Marriage and Politics 1860–1914* (Oxford: Oxford University Press, 1986).

Johnston, Jean-Michel, and Oded Y. Steinberg. 'Armenians, Jews and Humanitarianism in the "Age of Questions", 1830–1900', *Historical Journal* 66.1 (2023), 72–100.

Jones, David R. 'Governing the Civic Yniversity', *History of Education Quarterly* 25.3 (1985), 281–302.

Jones, David R. *The Origins of Civic Universities: Manchester, Leeds & Liverpool* (London: Routledge, 1988).

Jones, Emily. *Edmund Burke and the Invention of Modern Conservatism, 1830–1914: An Intellectual History* (Oxford: Oxford University Press, 2017).

Jones, H. S. 'Gladstonian Liberalism, Public Service and Private Interests: Reforming Endowments,' in *The Many Lives of Corruption: The Reform of Public Life in Modern Britain*, ed. Ian Cawood and Tom Crook (Manchester: Manchester University Press, 2022), 200–219.

Jones, H. S. *Intellect and Character in Victorian England: Mark Pattison and the Invention of the Don* (Cambridge: Cambridge University Press, 2007).

Jones, H. S. 'The Owens College Extension of 1870–3: Rethinking the Origins of the Civic University Tradition in England', *Bulletin of the John Rylands Library* 100.2 (2024).

Jones, H. S. 'University and College Sport', in *Nineteenth-Century Oxford*, part 2, vol. 7 of *The History of the University of Oxford*, ed. M. G. Brock and M.C. Curthoys (Oxford: Clarendon, 2000), 517–43.

Jones, Stuart. 'James Bryce's Manchester: The Politics of the Remaking of Owens College, 1865–75', in *Manchester Minds: A University History of Ideas*, ed. Stuart Jones (Manchester: Manchester University Press, 2024), 60–76.

Kaiga, Sakiko. *Britain and the Intellectual Origins of the League of Nations* (Cambridge: Cambridge University Press, 2021).

Kelly, Duncan. *The Propriety of Liberty: Persons, Passions and Judgement in Modern Political Thought* (Princeton, N.J.: Princeton University Press, 2011).

Kendle, John. *Ireland and the Federal Solution: The Debate over the United Kingdom Constitution, 1870–1921* (Kingston: McGill-Queen's University Press, 1989).

Kidd, Colin. 'Teutonist Ethnology and Scottish Nationalist Inhibition, 1780–1880', *Scottish Historical Review* 74.1 (1995), 45–68.

Kirby, James. 'A. V. Dicey and English Constitutionalism', *History of European Ideas* 45.1 (2019), 33–46.

Kleinknecht, Thomas. *Imperiale und internationale Ordnung: eine Untersuchung zum anglo-amerkanischen Gelehrtenliberalismus am Beipiel von James Bryce (1838–1922)* (Göttingen: Vandenhoeck & Ruprecht, 1985).

Koditschek, Theodore. '"Genius" and the Household Mode of Intellectual Production: 1795–1885', *Journal of Social History* 39.2 (2005), 429–49.

Ku, Hsiao-Yuh, *Education for Democracy in England in World War II* (London: Routledge, 2020).

'Letters of Goldwin Smith to Charles Eliot Norton', *Proceedings of the Massachusetts Historical Society* series 3, 49 (1915–16), 106–60.

Lake, Marilyn. 'From Mississippi to Melbourne via Natal: The Invention of the Literacy Test as a Technique of Racial Exclusion', in *Connected Worlds: History in Transnational Perspective*, ed. Ann Curthoys and Marilyn Lake (Canberra: ANU Press, 2006), 209–30.

Lake, Marilyn. 'The White Man Under Siege: New Histories of Race in the Nineteenth Century and the Advent of White Australia', *History Workshop Journal* 58.1 (2005), 41–62.

Lake, Marilyn, and Henry Reynolds. *Drawing the Global Colour Line: White Men's Countries and the International Challenge of Racial Equality* (Cambridge: Cambridge University Press, 2008).

Laycock, Jo. *Imagining Armenia: Orientalism, Ambiguity and Intervention* (Manchester: Manchester University Press, 2009).

Le Fur, Louis, and Paul Posener. *Bundesstaat und Staatenbund, Erster Band: Bundesstaat und Staatenbund in geschichtlicher Entwickelung* (Breslau: Kern, 1902).

Leipold, Bruno, Karma Nabulsi, and Stuart White, eds., *Radical Republicanism: Recovering the Tradition's Popular Heritage* (Oxford: Oxford University Press, 2020).

Levenson, Jacob C., ed. *The Letters of Henry Adams*. 6 vols. (Cambridge, Mass.: Belknap Press, 1982–1988).

Lewsen, Phyllis, ed. *Selections from the Correspondence of John X. Merriman 1890–1898* (Cape Town: The Van Riebeeck Society, 1963).

Liddel, Peter. 'Liberty and Obligation in George Grote's Athens', *Polis* 23.1 (2006), 139–61.

Lindsay, A. D. *The Modern Democratic State* (London: Oxford University Press, 1943).

Lubenow, William C. *'Only Connect': Learned Societies in Nineteenth-Century Britain* (Woodbridge: Boydell, 2015).

Macdonald, Murdo. *Patrick Geddes's Intellectual Origins* (Edinburgh: Edinburgh University Press, 2020).

MacLeod, Roy. 'The Chemists Go to War: The Mobilization of Civilian Chemists and the British War Effort, 1914–1918', *Annals of Science* 50.5 (1993), 455–81.

MacLeod, Roy. 'The Scientists Go to War: Revisiting Precept and Practice, 1914–1919', *Journal of War and Culture Studies* 2.1 (2009), 37–51.

MacLeod, Roy. 'Scientists', in *Cambridge History of the First World War*, vol. 2: *The State*, ed. Jay Winter (Cambridge: Cambridge University Press, 2014), 434–59.

Mallet, Charles Edward. *History of the University of Oxford*, vol. 3 (London: Methuen, 1927).

Mallon, Ryan. 'Scottish Presbyterianism and the National Education Debates, 1850–62', *Studies in Church History* 55 (2019), 363–80.

Marotta, Valerio. 'Cittadinanza imperiale romana e britannica a confronto: le riflessioni di James Bryce', *Mélanges de l'Ecole française de Rome. Antiquité* 118.1 (2006), 95–106.

Martinez, Gilles. 'Joseph Barthélemy et la crise de la démocratie libérale', *Vingtième Siècle* 59 (1998), 28–47.

Mathieson, William Law. *The Awakening of Scotland: A History from 1747 to 1797* (Glasgow: Maclehose, 1910).

Matthew, H.C.G. *The Liberal Imperialists: The Ideas and Politics of a Post-Gladstonian Elite* (Oxford: Clarendon, 1973).

Matthew, H.C.G., R. I. McKibbin, and J. A. Kay. 'The Franchise Factor in the Rise of the Labour Party', *English Historical Review* 91.4 (1976), 723–52.

Maurer, Oscar. 'Leslie Stephen and the "Cornhill Magazine", 1871–82', *University of Texas Studies in English* 32 (1953), 67–95.

Mayer, Anna-K. 'Reluctant Technocrats: Science Promotion in the Neglect-of-Science Debate of 1916–1918', *History of Science* 43.2 (2005), 139–59.

Mazower, Mark. *No Enchanted Palace: The End of Empire and the Ideological Origins of the United Nations* (Princeton, N.J.: Princeton University Press, 2009).

McCarthy, Helen. *The British People and the League of Nations: Democracy, Citizenship and Internationalism* (Manchester: Manchester University Press, 2011).

McCarthy, Helen. 'Petticoat Diplomacy: The Admission of Women to the British Foreign Service, c. 1919–1946', *Twentieth-Century British History* 20.3 (2009), 285–321.

McKibbin, Ross. *Classes and Cultures: England 1918–1951* (Oxford: Oxford University Press, 1998).

McLachlan, Herbert. 'Alexander Gordon and His Copy of the Dictionary of National Biography', in McLachlan, *Essays and Addresses* (Manchester: Manchester University Press, 1950), 290–310.

McLachlan, Herbert. 'Cross Street Chapel in the Life of Manchester', *Manchester Memoirs* 84 (1939–41), 29–41.

Messinger, Gary S. *British Propaganda and the State in the First World War* (Manchester: Manchester University Press, 1992).

Momigliano, Arnaldo. 'Two Types of Universal History: The Cases of E. A. Freeman and Max Weber', *Journal of Modern History* 58.1 (1986), 235–45.

Monsman, Gerald C. 'Old Mortality at Oxford', *Studies in Philology* 67.3 (1970), 359–89.

Montgomery, John Warwick. *The Quest for Noah's Ark* (Minneapolis: Bethany Fellowship, 1972).

Moody, T. W. 'The Irish University Question of the Nineteenth Century', *History* 43.148 (1958), 90–109.

Morefield, Jeanne. *Covenants Without Swords: Idealist Liberalism and the Spirit of Empire* (Princeton, N.J.: Princeton University Press, 2004).

Morgan, Kenneth O. 'The Boer War and the Media', *Twentieth Century British History* 13.1 (2002), 1–16.

Morris, Aldon D. *The Scholar Denied: W. E. B. Du Bois and the Birth of Modern Sociology* (Oakland: University of California Press, 2015).

Moyn, Samuel. *Liberalism Against Itself: Cold War Intellectuals and the Making of Our Times* (New Haven, Conn.: Yale University Press, 2023).

Mumford, Alfred A. *The Manchester Grammar School 1515–1915: A Regional Study of the Advancement of Learning in Manchester since the Reformation* (London: Longmans, Green, 1919).

Myrdal, Gunnar. *An American Dilemma: The Negro Problem and Modern Democracy* (New York: Harper, 1944).

Nussbaum, Martha C. *Not for Profit: Why Democracy Needs the Humanities* (Princeton, N.J.: Princeton University Press, 2010).

O'Brien, P. *Warrington Academy 1757–86: Its Predecessors and Successors* (Wigan: Owl Books, 1989).

Ogden, Robert Morris, ed. *The Diaries of Andrew D. White* (Ithaca, N.Y.: Cornell University Library, 1959).

Ogden, Rollo, ed. *Life and Letters of Edwin Lawrence Godkin.* 2 vols. (New York: Macmillan, 1907).

Olechnowicz, Andrzej. 'Civic Leadership and Education for Democracy: The Simons and the Wythenshawe Estate', *Contemporary British History* 14.1 (2000), 3–26.

Olechnowicz, Andrzej, ed., *The Monarchy and the British Nation 1780 to the Present* (Cambridge: Cambridge University Press, 2007).

Osborne, Ken. 'Creating the "International Mind": The League of Nations Attempts to Reform History Teaching, 1920–1939', *History of Education Quarterly* 56.2 (2016), 213–40.

Osbourn, R. V. 'The British Quarterly Review', *Review of English Studies* 1.1 (1950), 147–52.

Pace, Alessandro. *La Causa della rigidità costituzionale. Una rilettura di Bryce, dello statuto albertino e di qualche altra costituzione* (Milan: CEDAM, 1996)

Pals, Daniel. 'The Reception of "Ecce Homo"', *Historical Magazine of the Protestant Episcopal Church* 46 (1977), 63–84.

Pankhurst, Christabel. *Unshackled* [1959], ed. Lord Pethick-Lawrence (London: Cresset, 1987).

Parry, J. P. *Democracy and Religion: Gladstone and the Liberal Party, 1867–1875* (Cambridge: Cambridge University Press, 1986).

Parry, Jonathan. *The Politics of Patriotism: English Liberalism, National Identity and Europe, 1830–1886.*

Parry, Jonathan. *The Rise and Fall of Liberal Government in Victorian Britain* (New Haven, Conn.: Yale University Press, 1993).

Pasquino, Pasquale. 'Classifying Constitutions: Preliminary Conceptual Analysis', *Cardozo Law Review* 34.3 (2013), 999–1019.

Pasquino, Pasquale. 'Flexible and Rigid Constitutions', in *Rationality, Democracy, and Justice: The Legacy of Jon Elster*, ed. Claudio López-Guerra and Julia Maskivker (Cambridge: Cambridge University Press, 2005), 85–96.

Paul, R. S., and W. J. Smith. *A History of Middleton Grammar School 1412–1964* (Middleton: Queen Elizabeth's Grammar School, 1965).

Pedersen, Susan, *Eleanor Rathbone and the Politics of Conscience* (London: Yale University Press, 2004).

Pedersen, Susan. 'The Women's Suffrage Movement in the Balfour Family (Ben Pimlott Memorial Lecture 2018)', *Twentieth Century British History* 30 (2019), 299–320.

Perrier, Jérôme. 'Michel Debré et les avatars du libéralisme français (1936–1945)', *Vingtième Siècle* 116.4 (2012), 81–95.

Pettit, Philip. *Republicanism: A Theory of Freedom and Government* (Oxford: Clarendon, 1997).

Pocock, J.G.A. *The Machiavellian Moment: Florentine Political Thought and the Atlantic Republican Tradition* (Princeton, N.J.: Princeton University Press, 1975).

Prochaska, Frank. *Eminent Victorians on American Democracy: The View from Albion* (Oxford: Oxford University Press, 2012).

Pugh, Martin. *The Making of Modern British Politics 1867–1939* (Oxford: Blackwell, 1982).

Pugh, Martin. *The March of the Women: A Revisionist Analysis of the Campaign for Women's Suffrage, 1866–1914* (Oxford: Oxford University Press, 2002).

Purseigle, Pierre. 'The First World War and the Transformations of the State', *International Affairs* 90.2 (2014), 249–64.

Quagliariello, Gaetano. *Politics Without Parties: Moisei Ostrogorski and the Debate on Political Parties on the Eve of the Twentieth Century* (Aldershot: Avebury, 1996).

Rait, Robert S., ed. *Memorials of Albert Venn Dicey* (London: Macmillan, 1925).

Rathbone, Eleanor F. *William Rathbone: A Memoir* (London: Macmillan, 1905).

Readman, Paul. 'Walking and Environmentalism in the Career of James Bryce: Mountaineer, Scholar, Statesman, 1838–1922', in *Walking Histories, 1800–1914*, ed. Chad Carl Bryant, Arthur Burns, and Paul Readman (London: Palgrave, 2016), 287–317.

Regis, Amber K., ed. *The Memoirs of John Addington Symonds: A Critical Edition* (London: Palgrave Macmillan, 2016).

'Reminiscences of Robert Young', *Irish Booklore* 1 (1971), 4–20, 235–42.

Robbins, Keith G. 'Lord Bryce and the First World War', *Historical Journal* 10.2 (1967), 255–78.

Robertson, A. B. 'Manchester, Owens College and the Higher Education of Women: "A Large Hole for the Cat and a Small One for the Kitten"', *Bulletin of the John Rylands Library* 77.1 (1995), 201–20.

Robertson, Emily. 'Propaganda and "Manufactured Hatred": A Reappraisal of the Ethics of First World War British and Australian War Propaganda', *Public Relations Inquiry* 3.2 (2014), 245–66.

Romani, Roberto. *National Character and Public Spirit in Britain and France, 1750–1914* (Cambridge: Cambridge University Press, 2002).

Rosenblatt, Helena. *The Lost History of Liberalism: From Ancient Rome to the Twenty-First Century* (Princeton, N.J.: Princeton University Press, 2018).

Rubinstein, W. D. *Men of Property: The Very Wealthy in Britain since the Industrial Revolution* (London: Croom Helm, 1981).

Rudinsky, Jordan. 'James Bryce's Home Rule Constitutionalism and Victorian historiography', in *Empire and Legal Thought: Ideas and Institutions from Antiquity to Modernity*, ed. Edward Cavanagh (Leiden: Brill, 2020), 492–519.

Ruston, Alan R. *The Hibbert Trust: A History* (London: The Hibbert Trust, 1984).

Rutherford, Emily. 'Arthur Sidgwick's Greek Prose Composition: Gender, Affect, and Sociability in the Late-Victorian University', *Journal of British Studies* 56.1 (2017), 91–116.

Rutherford, Samuel. *Teaching Gender: The British University and the Rise of Heterosexuality, 1860–1939* (Oxford: Oxford University Press, 2025).

Sanghera, Sathnam. *Empireworld: How British Imperialism Shaped the Globe* (London: Penguin, 2024).

Sartori, Giovanni. *Democratic Theory* (Detroit: Wayne State University Press, 1962).

Saulnier, Frédéric. *Joseph-Barthélemy 1874–1945. La crise du constitutionnalisme libéral sous la IIIᵉ République* (Paris: LGDJ, 2004).

Saunders, Robert. *Democracy and the Vote in British Politics, 1848–1867* (Farnham: Ashgate, 2011).

Schultz, Bart. *Henry Sidgwick: Eye of the Universe* (Cambridge: Cambridge University Press, 2004).

Schwartz, Laura. *Infidel Feminism: Secularism, Religion and Women's Emancipation, England 1830–1914* (Manchester: Manchester University Press, 2013).

Schwartz, Laura. *A Serious Endeavour: Gender, Education and Community at St Hugh's, 1886–2011* (London: Profile, 2011).

Scott, Drusilla. *A. D. Lindsay: A Biography* (Oxford: Blackwell, 1971).

Seaman, John T., Jr. *A Citizen of the World: The Life of James Bryce* (London: Tauris, 2006).

Searby, Peter. *A History of the University of Cambridge volume 3 1750–1870* (Cambridge: Cambridge University Press, 1997).

Searle, G. R. *The Quest for National Efficiency: A Study in British Politics and Political Thought, 1899–1914* (Oxford: Blackwell, 1971).

Seigel, Micol. 'Beyond Compare: Comparative Method After the Transnational Turn', *Radical History Review* 91 (Winter 2005), 62–90.

Selbie, W. B. *The Life of Andrew Martin Fairbairn* (London: Hodder and Stoughton, 1914).

Selinger, William. *Parliamentarism from Burke to Weber* (Cambridge: Cambridge University Press, 2019).

Selinger, William, and Gregory Conti. 'The Lost History of Political Liberalism', *History of European Ideas* 46.3 (2020), 341–54.

Shanley, Mary Lyndon. *Feminism, Marriage, and the Law in Victorian England, 1850–1895* (Princeton, N.J.: Princeton University Press, 1989).

Siedentop, Larry. *Inventing the Individual: The Origins of Western Liberalism* (London: Allen Lane, 2014).

Siedentop, Larry. 'Two Liberal Traditions', in *The Idea of Freedom: Essays in Honour of Isaiah Berlin*, ed. Alan Ryan (Oxford: Oxford University Press, 1979), 153–74.

Simon of Wythenshawe, Lady (Shena Simon), *Margaret Ashton and Her Times. The Margaret Ashton Memorial Lecture for 1948* (Manchester: Manchester University Press, 1949).

Skinner, Quentin. *Liberty Before Liberalism* (Cambridge: Cambridge University Press, 1998).

Small, Helen. *The Value of the Humanities* (Oxford: Oxford University Press, 2013).

Small, Robert. *History of the Congregations of the United Presbyterian Church from 1733 to 1900* (Edinburgh: Small, 1903).

Smith, Barbara, ed., *Truth, Liberty, Religion: Essays Celebrating Two Hundred Years of Manchester College* (Oxford: Manchester College Oxford, 1986).

Smith, John David, and J. Vincent Lowery, eds. *The Dunning School: Historians, Race, and the Meaning of Reconstruction* (Lexington: University Press of Kentucky, 2013).

Smith, Paul, ed. *Lord Salisbury on Politics: A Selection from his Articles in the Quarterly Review, 1860–1883* (Cambridge: Cambridge University Press, 1972).

Stapleton, Julia. 'The Classicist as Liberal Intellectual: Gilbert Murray and Alfred Eckhard Zimmern', in *Gilbert Murray Reassessed: Hellenism, Theatre, and International Politics*, ed. Christopher Stray (Oxford: Oxford University Press, 2007), 261–92.

Stedman Jones, Gareth. *Outcast London: A Study in the Relationship Between Classes in Victorian Society* (Oxford: Clarendon, 1971).

Stedman Jones, Gareth, and Gregory Claeys, eds. *The Cambridge History of Nineteenth-Century Political Thought* (Cambridge: Cambridge University Press, 2011).

Steinberg, Oded Y. 'The Confirmation of the Worst Fears: James Bryce, British Diplomacy and the Armenian Massacres of 1894–1896', *Études arméniennes contemporaines* 11 (2018), 15–39.

Steinberg, Oded Y. 'James Bryce and the Origins of the Armenian Question', *Journal of Levantine Studies* 5.2 (2015), 13–33.

Steinberg, Oded Y. *Race, Nation, History: Anglo-German Thought in the Victorian Era* (Philadelphia: University of Pennsylvania Press, 2019).

Stephens, W. R. W. *The Life and Letters of Edward A. Freeman* (London: Macmillan, 1895), 2 vols.

Stocks, Mary. *Ernest Simon of Manchester* (Manchester: Manchester University Press, 1963).

Sylvest, Caspar. 'James Bryce and the Two Faces of Nationalism', in *British International Thinkers from Hobbes to Namier*, ed. Ian Hall and Lisa Hill (New York: Palgrave Macmillan, 2009), 161–79.

Taverni, Barbara. 'For Italy in a Changing World: The Political Apogee of Alcide de Gasperi, 1948–1954', *Modern Italy* 14.4 (2009), 459–71.

Thompson, James. *British Political Culture and the Idea of 'Public Opinion', 1867–1914* (Cambridge: Cambridge University Press, 2013).

Toynbee, Arnold J. *Acquaintances* (London: Oxford University Press, 1967).

Toynbee, Arnold. *Experiences* (Oxford: Oxford University Press, 1967)

Tulloch, Hugh. *James Bryce's American Commonwealth: The Anglo-American Background* (Woodbridge: Boydell, 1988).

Turner, James. *Philology: The Forgotten Origins of the Modern Humanities* (Princeton, N.J.: Princeton University Press, 2014).

Tusan, Michelle. 'James Bryce's Blue Book as Evidence', *Journal of Levantine Studies* 5.2 (2015), 9–24.

Uglow, Jenny. *Elizabeth Gaskell: A Habit of Stories* (London: Faber & Faber, 1993).

Urbinati, Nadia, ed. *J. S. Mill's Political Thought: A Bicentennial Reassessment* (Cambridge: Cambridge University Press, 2007).

Varouxakis, Georgios. *Liberty Abroad: J. S. Mill on International Relations* (Cambridge: Cambridge University Press, 2013).

Vecchio, Giorgio. 'Alcide de Gasperi negli anni del fascismo: esperienze, letture e riflessioni', *Annali dell'Istituto storico italo-germanico in Trento* 34 (2008), 283–92.

Viano, Francesca Lidia. 'James Bryce e i modelli costituzionali', *Il Pensiero Politico* 32.3 (1999), 415–20.

Viano, Francesca Lidia. *Una democrazia imperiale: l'America di James Bryce* (Florence: Centro Editoriale Toscano, 2003).

Vincent, Nigel, and Helen Wallace. 'Lost Without Translation: Why Codebreaking Is Not Just a Numbers Game', *British Academy Review* 25 (February 2015). https://www.thebritish academy.ac.uk/publishing/review/25/lost-without-translation-why-codebreaking-not-just -numbers-game/.

Walker, Pierre A., and Greg W. Zacharias, eds. *The Complete Letters of Henry James, 1876–1878*, 2 vols. (Lincoln: University of Nebraska Press, 2012–2013).

Walker, Pierre A., and Greg W. Zacharias, eds. *The Complete Letters of Henry James, 1878–1880*, 2 vols. (Lincoln: University of Nebraska Press, 2014–2015).

Wallace, Stuart. *War and the Image of Germany: British Academics 1914–1918* (Edinburgh, Donald, 1988).

Walters, Mark D. 'Dicey on Writing the Law of the Constitution', *Oxford Journal of Legal Studies* 32.1 (2012), 21–49.

Ward, Humphry. *History of the Athenaeum 1824–1925* (London: Athenaeum Club, 1926).

Ward, Stephen V. 'Searching for Effective and Democratic Town Planning: The International Travels of Sir Ernest Simon, 1936–1943', *Planning Perspectives* 32.3 (2017), 353–71.

Watts, Ruth E. 'The Unitarian Contribution to the Development of Female Education, 1790–1850', *History of Education* 9.4 (1980), 273–86.

Weber, Max, *Political Writings*, ed. Peter Lassman and Ronald Speirs (Cambridge: Cambridge University Press, 1994).

Welch, Cheryl B. 'An Immunity to Authoritarianism? Bagehot, Bryce, and Ostrogorski on the Risk of Caesarism in America', *Society* 60.4 (2023), 501–15.

Whaley, Joachim, 'Federal Habits: The Holy Roman Empire and the Continuity of German Federalism', in *German Federalism. New Perspectives in German Studies*, ed. Maiken Umbach (London: Palgrave Macmillan, 2002), 15–41.

Whyte, William. *Redbrick: A Social and Architectural History of Britain's Civic Universities* (Oxford: Oxford University Press, 2015).

Wiener, Martin J. *Between Two Worlds: The Political Thought of Graham Wallas* (Oxford: Oxford University Press, 1971).

Wilson, Trevor. 'Lord Bryce's Investigation into Alleged German Atrocities in Belgium, 1914–15', *Journal of Contemporary History* 14.3 (1979), 369–83.

Wilson, Trevor. *The Myriad Faces of War: Britain and the Great War, 1914–1918* (Cambridge: Polity, 1986).

Wilson, Trevor, ed. *The Political Diaries of C.P. Scott, 1911–1928* (London: Collins, 1970).

Wiltshire, Irene, ed. *Letters of Mrs Gaskell's Daughters* (Penrith: Humanities-Ebooks, 2012).

Wood, Gordon S. *The Creation of the American Republic 1776–1787* (Chapel Hill: University of North Carolina Press, 1969).

Wood, Ian. *The Modern Origins of the Early Middle Ages* (Oxford: Oxford University Press, 2013).

Wright, Susanna. *Morality and Citizenship in English Schools: Secular Approaches, 1897–1944* (London: Palgrave, 2016).

Zevin, Alexander. *Liberalism at Large: The World According to the Economist* (London: Verso, 2019).

ILLUSTRATION CREDITS

All images prefixed 'Bodleian' are reproduced courtesy of the Bodleian Libraries, University of Oxford.

1.1 Bodleian MS Bryce 521 fol. 2r.

1.2 Bodleian MS Bryce 521 fol. 59r.

1.3 Bodleian MS Bryce 522 fol. 2r.

1.4 Bodleian MS Bryce 520 fol. 82r.

1.5 Trinity College Archive, OM/8, photograph album of Henry E. Hulton. Courtesy of the President and Fellows of Trinity College, Oxford.

1.6 Bodleian MS Top. Oxon.b.255 fol. 5r.

1.1 Bodleian MS Bryce 516 fol. 8r.

3.1 Bodleian MS Bryce 525 fol. 8r.

4.1 Bodleian MS Bryce 520 fol. 22r.

4.2 Courtesy of Manchester Libraries, Information and Archives, m80249.

4.3 Courtesy of Manchester Libraries, Information and Archives, m64044.

5.1 Public domain via Wikimedia Commons.

5.2 Bodleian MS Bryce 501 fol. 6v.

6.1 Bodleian MS Bryce 525 fol. 7r.

7.1 Bodleian MS Bryce 525 fol. 5r.

8.1 Bodleian MS Bryce 519 fol. 20r.

8.2 Courtesy of Manchester Libraries, Information and Archives, m10012.

8.3 Bodleian MS Bryce 517 fol. 50r.

8.4 Bodleian MS Bryce 523 fol. 9v.

10.1 Library of Congress Prints and Photographs Division Washington, D.C. USA.

10.2 Bodleian MS Bryce 519 fol. 25r.

10.3 Public domain via Wikimedia Commons.

11.1 Bodleian MS Bryce 517 fol. 34r.

12.1 Library of Congress LC-DIG-ppmsca-46426, no known restrictions.

12.2 Bodleian MS Bryce 517 f. 20r.

12.3 Public domain via Wikimedia Commons.

INDEX

Page numbers in italics refer to figures.